MARKETING

MARKETING

THIRD CANADIAN EDITION

ERIC N. BERKOWITZ
University of Massachusetts

FREDERICK G. CRANE
QMA Consulting Group Limited

ROGER A. KERIN
Southern Methodist University

STEVEN W. HARTLEY
University of Denver

WILLIAM RUDELIUS
University of Minnesota

**McGraw-Hill
Ryerson**

Toronto • New York • Burr Ridge • Bangkok • Bogotá • Caracas
Lisbon • London • Madrid • Mexico City • Milan • New Delhi
Seoul • Singapore • Sydney • Taipei

McGraw-Hill
Ryerson Limited
A Subsidiary of The **McGraw·Hill** Companies

Marketing
Berkowitz, Crane, Kerin, Hartley, Rudelius
Third Canadian Edition

ISBN: 0-07-560315-7

1 2 3 4 5 6 7 8 9 10   GTC   7 6 5 4 3 2 1 0 9 8

Printed and bound in Canada

Senior Sponsoring Editor: Evelyn Veitch
Production Editor: Geraldine Kikuta
Associate Editor: Elke Price
Developmental Editor: Karina TenVeldhuis
Copy Editor: Shirley Corriveau
Production Co-ordinator: Nicla Dattolico
Cover Design: Dianna Little
Cover Illustration/Photo: Comstock Photofile
Compositor: Carlisle Communications, Ltd.
Typeface(s): Times Roman
Printer: Transcontinental Group

Canadian Cataloguing in Publication Data

Main entry under title:

Marketing

3rd Canadian ed.
Includes index.
ISBN 0-07-560315-2

1. Marketing. 2. Marketing—Canada. I. Berkowitz, Eric N.

HF5415.M293 1998   6588   C97-932707-5

PREFACE

As the twenty-first century approaches, the world of marketing is entering a new and exciting era that was unimaginable only a short time ago. Electronic shopping, virtual organizations, e-cash, interactive television, and the information superhighway are just a few indications of the many new changes marketing instructors, managers, and students are likely to face in the near future. We are eager to utilize the active learning approach of *Marketing,* Third Canadian Edition, to facilitate preparation for this extraordinary marketplace. In addition, we appreciate the opportunity to share our enthusiasm with you and we welcome you to your introduction to the field of marketing.

Marketing is the result of a product development process designed to focus on customer needs, and a commitment to provide exceptional customer value. We have retained the strengths of previous editions and added new dimensions to reflect changes in the business environment and in student and instructor interests. For example, users of previous editions frequently tell us that the text provides:

- An easy-to-read, high-involvement, interactive approach to the study of marketing.
- Comprehensive and integrated coverage of traditional and contemporary marketing and business topics.
- Up-to-date and relevant examples, cases, and exercises.
- Many extended examples involving people making marketing decisions that students can easily relate to text concepts.
- A rigorous pedagogical framework and a useful decision-making orientation.
- A package of support materials to accommodate a wide range of teaching styles and formats.

These attributes remain as the foundation of our product offering, while changes in topic emphasis, the order of chapters, the number of cases, and the overall length of the book are the result of our efforts at continuous quality and coverage improvement.

We are gratified by the continued success of the text. The innovative pedagogical approach we developed and introduced with the first edition in 1991, and improved in the subsequent edition, has helped thousands of students and hundreds of instructors study and teach one of the most dynamic and challenging areas of our global economic system. We have focused on creating customer value by providing exceptional knowledge, understanding, skills, decision-making tools, and support materials. This edition provides you with the best revision of what we believe is the best marketing textbook available today. We hope you agree!

NEW FEATURES IN THIS EDITION

The feedback we received through our formal marketing research efforts has led to several changes in the organization of this edition:

- Global marketing topics previously covered in two chapters have been consolidated into Chapter 5, Global Marketing and World Trade, and integrated throughout the text. This change reflects a truly global view of marketing and the extensive implications of world trade on all aspects of marketing practice.
- Chapter 13, Managing Services, has been moved from the end of the text to Part IV, Satisfying Marketing Opportunities. This change is consistent with the growing recognition of services as products, and the increasing importance of service components of product offerings.

- The strategic marketing process, previously covered in three chapters, is now covered in Chapter 2 and Chapter 22. This combination of chapters allows an early introduction to a framework that integrates topics covered in-depth later in the text—while acknowledging the time constraints faced by instructors today.
- A marketing plan now appears as Appendix A following Chapter 2. In the past, many instructors have used the framework presented in Chapter 2 as a guideline for a marketing plan assignment or lecture. This appendix provides an actual, up-to-date, and relevant marketing plan as a model for students to study and use as they write marketing plans as part of their class assignments.
- Additional cases are now included at the end of the book in Appendix D. These cases allow instructors the flexibility of additional case assignments if desired. The cases address marketing topics related to products, services, and companies that students will find interesting and familiar.
- A significant new addition to the text is *Marketing Math: An Interactive Tutorial* by R. David Nowell. Contained on a disk found in the back of each text, this interactive tutorial will guide students through the mathematics involved in marketing.

The content of *Marketing* has also been revised to provide complete and current coverage of emerging issues, new marketing terms, environmental trends, and changes in business practices. Examples include:

- The network organization
- Value propositions
- Total quality management
- Kaizen (continuous incremental improvement)
- Reengineering, streamlining, and restructuring
- Market orientation
- Emerging markets in South and East Asia and Eastern Europe
- Customer management teams
- Generational marketing
- Ethnic and regional marketing
- Recycling and precycling
- Intellectual property use (e.g., software piracy)
- Environmentally friendly new product development
- Global consumers and brand loyalty
- The North American Industrial Classification System (NAICS)
- Supply (channel) partnerships
- Electronic survey research
- Counterfeit brands and products
- Co-branding and co-marketing
- Emergence of "pay-for-use" services
- Cross-functional teams
- Strategic alliances
- Smart cards
- Salesforce automation
- Electronic markets (marketspace)

In addition, new sections have been added to several chapters. For example, the global marketing chapter now addresses global competition among global companies for global consumers, and the retailing chapter now includes a large section on nonstore retailing which covers direct mail, telemarketing, in-home shopping, direct selling, and automatic vending. The personal selling and sales management chapter provides an up-to-date treatment of salesforce automation with a focus on information and communication technologies.

Marketplace examples have been updated to reflect the most recent activities of large and small organizations, and to provide relevant, logical illustrations of the concepts discussed in the text. Some of these include:

- Rogers Cantel Inc. and AT&T Canada Inc.'s long-term strategic alliance and co-branding agreement in the wireless communications industry.
- Clearly Canadian Beverage Corporation's successful launch of their new alternative beverage called Orbitz.
- Gulf Canada Resources Limited's quest to become a major international force in the petroleum industry.
- TSN's innovative use of web site advertising.
- The use of upfront marketing research by The Co-operators Co. of Ontario in order to help refine their entry into the "insurance by phone" market.

Several topics continue to have such an important impact on the field of marketing that they receive unique coverage in separate chapters of *Marketing,* Third Canadian Edition. These include Ethics and Social Responsibility (Chapter 4) and Information Technology (Chapter 10). Topics which are integrated through every chapter of the text include:

- Customer value
- The impact of technology
- Ethics and social responsibility
- Global perspectives
- Cross-functional issues

Finally, the package of support materials has been expanded to provide a wide variety of value-added opportunities for students and instructors. In addition, we have completely revised and updated every other component of the supplement package.

HELPFUL PEDAGOGICAL FEATURES

As in previous editions, we want to involve you in the study of marketing by encouraging you to think about your personal experiences as a consumer and by asking you to take the role of a marketing decision maker. Examples of contemporary people and organizations, and their marketing decisions appear in the chapter opening vignettes, the Marketing NewsNet boxes, extended examples that are included in the text, and in the end-of-chapter and end-of-text cases. To help you understand potential explanations for the success or failure of marketing programs, each chapter also integrates research related to specific marketing decisions.

The book alerts the reader to special topics with corresponding icons. These include: general topics, customer value, global topics, technology, cross-functional topics, and ethics and social responsibility issues.

In addition, the book reinforces major concepts as they are introduced in each chapter to stimulate your understanding of them and foster your ability to apply them appropriately. At the end of every major section, Concept Checks pose two or three questions to test your recall. The Learning Objectives at the beginning of each chapter and the Summary and Key Terms and Concepts at the close provide further reinforcement.

We believe that the use of these unique learning aids lets you learn about, understand, and integrate the many marketing topics covered in our textbook, and allows you to apply them in the constantly changing marketing environment you will encounter as a consumer and a marketing manager.

THE ORGANIZATION OF *MARKETING*

Marketing is divided into five parts. *Part I, Initiating the Marketing Process,* looks first at what marketing is and how it identifies and satisfies consumer needs (Chapter 1). Then Chapter 2 provides an overview of the strategic marketing process that occurs in an organization—which provides a structure for the text. Appendix A provides a sample marketing plan as a reference for students. Chapter 3 analyzes the five major environmental factors in our changing marketing environment, while Chapter 4 discusses the significance of ethics and social responsibility in marketing decisions.

Part II, Understanding Buyers and Markets, first describes, in Chapter 5, the nature and scope of world trade and the influence of cultural differences on global marketing practices. Next, Chapter 6 describes how ultimate consumers reach buying decisions. Finally, because of their important differences from ultimate consumers, industrial and organizational buyers and how they make purchase decisions are covered in Chapter 7.

In *Part III, Targeting Marketing Opportunities,* the marketing research function is discussed in Chapter 8. The process of segmenting and targeting markets and positioning products appears in Chapter 9. The increasing importance of relationship marketing, how today's marketing managers use strategic information systems, and sales forecasting are described in Chapter 10.

Part IV, Satisfying Marketing Opportunities, covers the four Ps—the marketing mix elements. Unlike most competitive textbooks, the product element is divided into the natural chronological sequence of first developing new products (Chapter 11) and then managing the existing products (Chapter 12). Services are discussed as separate product offerings and as components of product offerings (Chapter 13). Pricing is covered in terms of underlying pricing analysis (Chapter 14), followed by actual price setting (Chapter 15), and the related Appendix B, Financial Aspects of Marketing. Three chapters address the place (distribution) aspects of marketing: Marketing Channels and Wholesaling (Chapter 16), Physical Distribution and Logistics Management (Chapter 17), and Retailing (Chapter 18). Retailing is a separate chapter because of its importance and interest as a career for many of today's students. Promotion is also covered in three chapters. Chapter 19 discusses integrated marketing communications and presents an in-depth treatment of sales promotion, an activity that often exceeds advertising in the promotional budgets of many firms but receives minimal coverage in many textbooks. Chapter 19 also covers public relations. Advertising (Chapter 20) and Personal Selling and Sales Management (Chapter 21) complete the coverage of promotional activities.

Part V, Managing the Marketing Process, expands on Chapter 2 to describe specific techniques and issues related to blending the four marketing mix elements to plan, implement, and control (Chapter 22) marketing programs. The part closes with Appendix C, Career Planning in Marketing, which discusses marketing jobs themselves and how to get them, and Appendix D, Alternate Cases.

A detailed glossary, and three indexes (author; company and product; and subject) complete the book.

As we observe in Chapter 1, we genuinely hope that somewhere in *Marketing* the reader will discover not only the challenge and excitement of marketing, but possibly a career as well.

EXTENSIVE SUPPLEMENTAL RESOURCES

Providing a comprehensive and integrated package of high-quality innovative instructional supplements continues to be a priority for us. We have been involved, as authors or supervisors, in the production of all of the supplements that now accompany our text. Much attention has been given to providing elements and features in these supplements that were requested by both inexperienced and experienced instructors. As a result, each supplement contains several features not offered with any other marketing text.

Instructor's Manual   The Instructor's Manual includes lecture notes, transparency masters, discussions of the Marketing NewsNet boxes and the Ethics and Social Responsibility Alerts, and answers to the end-of-chapter Problems and Applications questions. Supplemental Lecture Notes and In-Class Activities are also provided. The Instructor's Manual also includes teaching suggestions and detailed information about integrating the other supplements.

Transparency Acetates   A set of 200 four-colour overhead transparency acetates is available free to adopters. More than 50 percent of these have been developed from information outside the text. In addition, the acetates now include a greater ratio of print advertisements that demonstrate key marketing theories. Several of the ads correspond with the companies that are featured in the video cases, making it possible to teach a more integrated lecture. Each of the transparency acetates from outside of the text is accompanied by lecture notes to assist instructors in integrating the material into their lectures.

Electronic Slides   New to this edition, this software includes a PowerPoint® viewer and a set of over 200 PowerPoint® slides. The slides include topics not covered in the acetate package and other key concepts covered in the text. Those instructors who have PowerPoint® can customize and add to this valuable presentation tool.

Computerized Test Bank   Our Computerized Test Bank has been developed and class tested to provide an accurate and exhaustive source of test items for a wide variety of examination styles. It contains more than 3000 questions, categorized by topic and level of learning (definitional, conceptual, or application). The test questions are more application-oriented and include questions for each end-of-chapter case. A Test Item Table allows instructors to select questions from any section of a chapter at any of the three levels of learning. The Test Bank includes approximately 10 essay questions, over 100 multiple-choice questions per chapter as well as questions for Appendices A, B, and D, making it one of the most comprehensive test packages on the market. This Test Bank, which is available free to adopters, allows the instructor to select from any of the questions, change if desired, or add new questions—and quickly print out a finished set customized to the instructor's course.

Video Case Studies   A unique series of contemporary marketing cases is available on videotape cassettes. Each video case corresponds with chapter specific topics or cases in the text. The video cases feature a variety of organizations and provide balanced coverage of services, consumer products, small businesses, global corporations, and business-to-business examples.

Study Guide   The Study Guide enables the students to learn and apply marketing principles instead of simply memorizing facts for an examination. The Study Guide includes chapter outlines for student note-taking, sample tests, critical thinking questions, and flash cards. The new format is based on the results of student focus groups.

Computer-Problem Software   This software features short cases and problems that allow students to learn about and apply marketing concepts and see the results of marketing decisions on a personal computer.

Marketing Planning Software   Revised for Windows,® the marketing plan software is designed to help students use the strategic marketing process introduced in Chapter 2 and Appendix A and discussed in detail in Chapter 22. The software provides a personal and computer-based tool for involving students in the planning process.

Presentation CD-ROM   The new Instructor CD-ROM for *Marketing* will contain video clips, slides, and acetates for the text. Great for enhancing class presentations, CD-ROM enables the instructor to show video segments as they pertain to lectures or access the software or electronic slides instantly. The CD-ROM will also include the print supplements and electronic supplements so that the instructor has access to all of the supplements on one disc.

Virtual Marketing Careers CD-ROM   More than just a careers application, this innovative, interactive software puts the students in the role of several marketing professions: sales manager, brand manager, marketing research manager, advertising manager, and retail manager. This virtual reality environment gives students the opportunity to make decisions within a realistic environment and have fun while learning to apply concepts.

Case Teaching Notes   This supplement includes teaching notes for all cases found in the text.

Marketing Home Page   Our new home page is a source of information for students and instructors alike. The home page includes additional teaching ideas and hot links to home pages that are relevant to anyone interested in learning more about marketing.

DEVELOPMENT OF THIS BOOK

Through each of the editions of this text, we have been fortunate to utilize the extensive development resources of our publisher. Building on that history, the third edition development process included several phases of evaluation and a variety of stakeholder (e.g., student, instructor, etc.) audiences. The first phase of the review process asked adopters to focus on recommendations for the organization of the text and improvements that could be made to the supplements package. The second phase encompassed a more detailed review of each chapter as the text was used by adopters in the classroom. We also listened to students to find out what they liked about the book and what changes they would suggest. Finally, a key group of instructors who do not use the text gave us feedback on the previous editions.

ACKNOWLEDGMENTS

Reviewing a book or supplement takes an incredible amount of energy and attention, and we are glad that so many of our colleagues took the time to do it. Their comments have inspired us to do our best.

Reviewers and case authors who contributed to this edition of the text include:

James Boyes
Durham College

Suzanne Kavanagh
George Brown College

Peter Burgess
George Brown College

Megan Mills
Okanagan University College

Baiba Butkus
Lambton College

Art Pierce
Ryerson Polytechnic University

Wayne Carlson
Southern Alberta Institute of Technology

Lynne Ricker
University of Calgary

Bill Inglis
Capilano College

Reviewers and case authors who have contributed to the previous editions of the text include:

D. Wesley Balderson

Karen Blotnicky

Robert G. Blunden

Mary Brooks

Gerry Byars

Jan Charbonneau

Malika Das

Gerald Edwards

Ian B. Fenwick

Scott B. Fellows

Dan Gardiner

F. Stephen Grant

Shannon Goodspeed

Cathy Goodwin

Clifford Hurt

Steve Janisse

Ted Kahl

Michelle McCann

Peter Sianchuk

David Stewart

Chris Vaughan

Anne Walker

Ken Wong

The business community also provided great help in making available information that appears in the test and supplements—much of it for the first time in a college or university text. Thanks are due to Alberta Health, Rogers Cantel Inc., Goldfarb Consultants, McDonald's Restaurants of Canada, Molson Breweries, National Hockey League, Polaroid Canada, Pulse Marketing, Second Harvest, Television Bureau of Canada, Clearly Canadian Beverage Corporation, Chrysler Canada, BBDO, Canadian Pacific Hotels, Canadian Advertising Foundation, Volkswagen of America, Gulf Canada Resources Limited, Milltronics Ltd., Oxfam Canada, The Galileo Group Inc., Harrod & Mirlin, Dairy Farmers of Canada, TSN, W. K. Buckley Ltd., Federation des producteurs d'oeufs de consommation du Quebec, Compusearch, Sobeys, Cadbury.

Finally, we acknowledge the professional efforts of the McGraw-Hill Higher Education Group staff. Completion of our book and its many supplements required the attention and commitment of many editorial, production, marketing, and research personnel. Thanks to Elke Price, associate editor for her gracious and kind assistance, and to Shirley Corriveau, Geraldine Kikuta, and Lenore Gray Spence. Also, we would like to specifically acknowledge Evelyn Veitch, senior sponsoring editor, for her care and support throughout the project and her role as product champion.

I am responsible for the Canadianization of this text, so any questions or concerns about the book should be directed to me. I would like to thank my co-authors for their continued support. I would also like to thank my sister Jeanne for her help on this project.

I am dedicating this book to my beautiful wife, Doreen, who is my sunshine on my darkest days; to Erinn, Jacquelyn, and Brenna (my special girls); to my parents for their unending support; and to God, for all his blessings.

Frederick G. Crane

CONTENTS IN BRIEF

CONTENTS

PART III TARGETING MARKETING OPPORTUNITIES 189

MARKETING

PART ONE

INITIATING THE MARKETING PROCESS

Chapter 1
Marketing: A Focus on the Consumer

Chapter 2
Linking Marketing and Corporate Strategies
Appendix A: A Sample Marketing Plan

Chapter 3
The Changing Marketing Environment

Chapter 4
Ethics and Social Responsibility in Marketing

Satisfying consumers in local, national, and global markets is the essence of the marketing process described in Part I. Chapter 1 introduces the marketing process by describing the marketing actions of Rollerblade, Inc., and their plan for international growth. Chapter 2 describes how organizations like Coca-Cola utilize the strategic marketing process to serve their customers. Following Chapter 2 is a sample marketing plan (Appendix A) which illustrates the outcome of the strategic marketing process and provides a reference for students to study and use. In Chapter 3 the dimensions of the marketing environment and how it has and will change are presented. These changes are described in terms of social, economic, technological, competitive, and regulatory forces. Finally, Chapter 4 provides a framework for including ethical and social responsibility considerations in marketing decisions.

CHAPTER 1

Marketing: A Focus on the Consumer

AFTER READING THIS CHAPTER YOU SHOULD BE ABLE TO:

• Define marketing and explain the importance of (1) discovering and (2) satisfying consumer needs and wants.

• Distinguish between marketing mix elements and environmental factors.

• Describe how today's market orientation era differs from prior eras oriented to production and selling.

• Understand the meaning of ethics and social responsibility and how they relate to the individual, organizations, and society.

• Know what is required for marketing to occur and how it creates customer value and utilities for consumers.

ROLLERBLADES SKATE TO THE EXTREMES!

Did you get a ticket to the Extreme Games? Did you watch the games on TV? If not, you may not be on the cutting edge of sports! A week-long event broadcast on all-sports cable channels ESPN and ESPN2, the Extreme Games consist of 27 olympic-style competitive events including vertical ramp, street, and downhill in-line skating. Coverage of the Games was broadcast to more than 150 countries and attracted 11.1 million viewers in 8.3 million homes! If you missed the games you can check out what happened by surfing the Net and connecting to ESPN's web site-Sportszone (Espnet.sportszone.com).

How is it possible that a sport that did not exist 10 years ago is so popular today? The answer is a marketing success story—Rollerblades![1] (www.rollerblade.com)

In the early 1700s a Dutch inventor trying to simulate ice skating in the summer created the first roller skates by attaching spools to his shoes. His in-line arrangement was the standard design until 1863 when the first skates with rollers set as two pairs appeared. This design became the standard, and in-line skates virtually disappeared from the market.

In 1980, two hockey-playing brothers found an old pair of in-line skates while browsing through a sporting goods store. Working in their garage, they modified the design to add polyurethane wheels, a molded boot shell, and a toe brake. They sold their product, which they dubbed "Rollerblade skates," out of the back of their truck to hockey players and skiers as a means of staying in shape during the summer. In the mid-1980s an entrepreneur bought the company from the brothers and then hired a marketing expert—Mary Horwath—to figure out how to market Rollerblade skates.[2]

On understanding the consumer "When I came here," remembers Horwath, "I knew there had to be a change." By focusing only on serious athletes who used in-line skates to train for other sports, Rollerblades had developed an image as a training product. Conversations with in-line skaters, however, convinced Horwath that using Rollerblade skates:

- Was incredible fun.
- Was a great aerobic workout and made the skater stronger and healthier.
- Was quite different from traditional roller skating, which was practised alone, mostly inside, and by young girls.
- Would have great appeal to people other than just off-season ice skaters and skiers.

A fresh approach to the firm's marketing, advertising, and public relations was needed. Horwath explains the change:

> We decided that if we wanted to sell more skates, we had to create new reasons for people to skate. We had to create and market a new sport—the sport of in-line skating. By creating a new sport, we could stop marketing the product to only a small audience of serious athletes and begin marketing to everyone. We were the only company making in-line skates, so we knew that we would get all the publicity surrounding a new sport. If we could build a sport, Rollerblade, Inc. would grow. But our challenge was huge, because we had to build an entire sport from nothing.[3]

Horwath saw her task as changing the image in people's minds—or "repositioning"—Rollerblade skates to highlight the benefits people saw in in-line skating. "I also wanted to change the 'male-skewed' image of in-line skates," she laughs. But her task still remained: how could she gain the marketing exposure and publicity to grow an in-line skate industry on a tiny annual marketing budget of $200 000? She felt she needed what she calls "guerilla marketing"—gaining national exposure for Rollerblade skates using relatively inexpensive, creative ways to show the product to potential buyers.

Here are some of the key questions to which she and her team sought answers as they developed a marketing strategy for Rollerblade:

- What age group of potential buyers should they target?
- What benefits or points of difference should they stress to potential buyers to reposition Rollerblade skates in the minds of potential buyers?
- How should they spend their $200 000 budget to gain awareness for Rollerblade skates and get people to try them, in hopes of growing a new industry?

Looking back, it's clear that the future of the industry—and the company—hinged on finding good answers to these questions.

Rollerblade skates, marketing, and you   What marketing strategy did Mary Horwath and her marketing team initiate to achieve the skyrocketing growth of in-line skating shown in Figure 1-1? By the time you reach the end of this chapter, you will know the answer to this question.

One key to how well Horwath succeeded lies in the subject of this book: marketing. In this chapter and in the rest of the book we'll introduce you to many of the people, organizations, ideas, activities, and jobs in marketing that have spawned the products and services that have been towering successes, shattering failures, or something in between.

Marketing affects all individuals, all organizations, all industries, and all countries. This text seeks not only to teach you marketing concepts, but also to demonstrate its many applications and how it affects our lives. This knowledge should make you a better consumer, help you in your career, and enable you to be a more informed citizen.

In this chapter and those that follow, you will feel the excitement of marketing. You will be introduced to the dynamic changes that will affect all of us in the future. You

FIGURE 1-1

NUMBER OF IN-LINE SKATERS IN NORTH AMERICA. WHAT LED TO THIS SKYROCKETING GROWTH? FOR SOME ANSWERS, SEE THE TEXT.

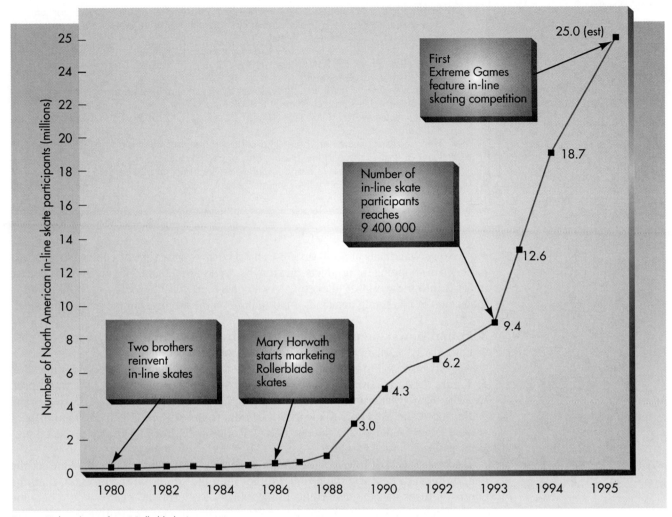

Source: "In-line skating facts," Rollerblade, Inc. report.

will also meet many men and women—like Mary Horwath—whose marketing creativity sometimes achieved brilliant, extraordinary results. And who knows? Somewhere in these pages you may find a career.

WHAT IS MARKETING?

Being a Marketing Expert: Good News—Bad News

In many respects you are a marketing expert already. But just to test your expertise, try the "marketing expert" questions in Figure 1-2. These questions—some of them easy, others mind boggling—show the diverse problems marketing executives grapple with every day. You'll find the answers in the next few pages.

The good news: you already have marketing experience   You are somewhat of an expert because you do many marketing activities every day. You already know many marketing terms, concepts, and principles. For example, would you sell

**ANSWER THE QUESTIONS BELOW. THE CORRECT ANSWERS
ARE GIVEN LATER IN THE CHAPTER.**

1. In a magazine article, a well-known actress said she often "Rollerbladed" for fun and exercise. What was Rollerblade, Inc.'s reaction? (a) delighted, (b) upset, or (c) somewhere in between. Why?
2. What is "Polavision"? (a) a new breathable contact lens, (b) a TV network that competes with Home Box Office, (c) special bifocal glasses, (d) instant movies, or (e) a political newspaper.
3. Right after World War II, International Business Machines Corporation (IBM) commissioned a study to estimate the *total* market for electronic computers. The study's results were (a) less than 10, (b) 1000 (c) 10 000, (d) 100 000, or (e) 1 million or more.
4. True of false: "Customer value" is a critical marketing issue today, and the new view of it goes beyond just quality and price.
5. How could Mary Horwath and Rollerblade, Inc. find an inexpensive way to get prospective buyers to try their in-line skates?

more Sony Walkmans at $500 or $50 each? The answer is $50, of course, so your experience in shopping for products, and maybe even selling them, already gives you great insights into the world of marketing. As a consumer, you've already been involved in thousands of marketing decisions—but mainly on the buying, not the marketing, side.

The bad news: surprises about the obvious   Unfortunately, common sense doesn't always explain some marketing decisions and actions.

An actress's saying in a national magazine that she "often Rollerbladed" (question 1, Figure 1-2) sounds like great publicity, right? But Rollerblade, Inc. was upset. Legally, Rollerblade is a registered trademark of Rollerblade, Inc. and, as a brand name, should be used only to identify its products and services. With letters to offenders and advertisements like the one below, Rollerblade, Inc. is trying to protect a precious asset: its brand identity.

Under trademark law, if consumers generally start using a brand name as the generic term to describe the product rather than the source of the product, then the company loses its exclusive rights to the name. "Rollerblade" skates would become "rollerblade," just another English word to describe all kinds of in-line skating. That

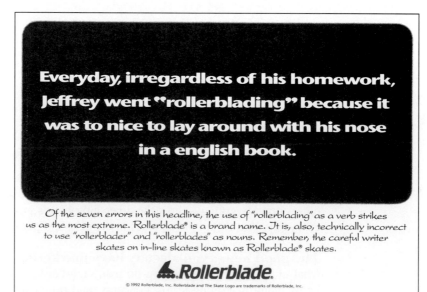

fate has already befallen some famous products such as linoleum, aspirin, cellophane, escalator, yo-yo, corn flakes, and trampoline. In fact, Random House Webster's College Dictionary says it's "almost 100 percent sure" that the word *Rollerblade* will appear in its next edition—but with a capital "R" to recognize it as a trademark.[4]

Today firms are spending millions of dollars in both advertising and court cases to protect their important brand names. Examples are Kimberly-Clark's Kleenex tissues and towels and 3M's Scotch tape. Coca-Cola takes dozens of restaurants to court every year for serving another cola drink when the patron asks for a Coca-Cola or even a Coke. Because legal and ethical issues such as the Rollerblade skates trademark problem are so central to many marketing decisions, they are addressed throughout the book.

The point here is that although your common sense usually helps you in analyzing marketing problems, sometimes it can mislead you. This book's in-depth study of marketing augments your common sense with an understanding of marketing concepts to help you assess and make marketing decisions more effectively.

Marketing: Using Exchanges to Satisfy Needs

The American Marketing Association, representing marketing professionals in the United States and Canada, states that "**marketing** is the process of planning and executing the conception, pricing, promotion, and distribution of ideas, goods, and services to create exchanges that satisfy individual and organizational objectives."[5] Many people incorrectly believe that marketing is the same thing as advertising or personal selling; this definition shows marketing to be a far broader activity. Further, this definition stresses the importance of beneficial exchanges that satisfy the objectives of both those who buy and those who sell ideas, goods, and services—whether they be individuals or organizations.

To serve both buyers and sellers, marketing seeks (1) to discover the needs and wants of prospective customers and (2) to satisfy them. These prospective customers include both individuals buying for themselves and their households and organizations that buy for their own use (such as manufacturers) or for resale (such as wholesalers and retailers). The key to achieving these two objectives is the idea of **exchange,** which is the trade of things of value between buyer and seller so that each is better off after the trade. This vital concept of exchange in marketing is covered below in more detail.

The Diverse Factors Influencing Marketing Activities

Although an organization's marketing activity focuses on assessing and satisfying consumer needs, countless other people, groups, and forces interact to shape the nature of its activities (Figure 1-3). Foremost is the organization itself, whose mission and objectives determine what business it is in and what goals it seeks. Within the organization, management is responsible for establishing these goals. The marketing department works closely with a network of other departments and employees to help provide the customer-satisfying products required for the organization to survive and prosper.[6]

Figure 1-3 also shows the key people, groups, and forces outside the organization that influence marketing activities. The marketing department is responsible for facilitating relationships, partnerships, and alliances with the organization's customers, its shareholders (or often representatives of groups served by a nonprofit organization), its suppliers, and other organizations. Environmental forces such as social, technological, economic, competitive, and regulatory factors also shape an organization's marketing activities. Finally, an organization's marketing decisions are affected by and in turn often have an important impact on society as a whole.

AN ORGANIZATION'S MARKETING DEPARTMENT RELATES TO MANY PEOPLE, GROUPS, AND FORCES

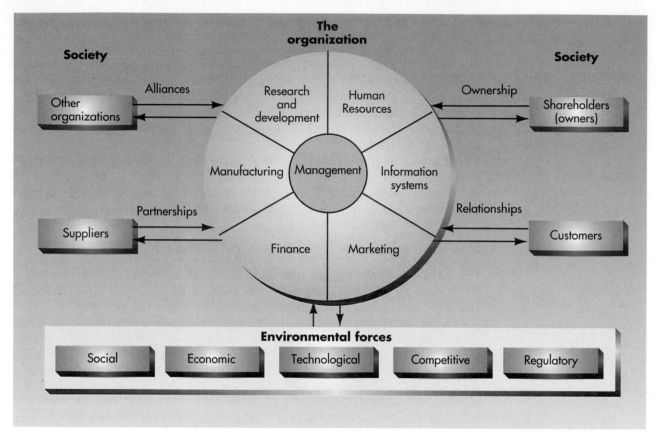

The organization must strike a continual balance among the sometimes differing interests of these individuals and groups. For example, it is not possible to simultaneously provide the lowest-priced and highest-quality products to customers and pay the highest prices to suppliers, highest wages to employees, and maximum dividends to shareholders.

Requirements for Marketing to Occur

For marketing to occur, at least four factors are required: (1) two or more parties (individuals or organizations) with unsatisfied needs, (2) a desire and ability on their part to be satisfied, (3) a way for the parties to communicate, and (4) something to exchange.

Two or more parties with unsatisfied needs   Suppose you've developed an unmet need—a desire for information about how technology is reshaping the workplace and the personal lives of consumers—but you didn't yet know that *Time Digital* magazine existed. Also unknown to you was that several copies of *Time Digital* were sitting on the magazine rack at your nearest supermarket, waiting to be purchased. This is an example of two parties with unmet needs: you, with a need for technology-related information, and your supermarket owner, needing someone to buy a copy of *Time Digital*.

Desire and ability to satisfy these needs   Both you and the supermarket owner want to satisfy these unmet needs. Furthermore, you have the money to buy the item and the time to get to the supermarket. The store's owner has not only the desire to sell *Time Digital* but also the ability to do so since it's stocked on the shelves.

A way for the parties to communicate   The marketing transaction of buying a copy of *Time Digital* will never occur unless you know the product exists and its location. Similarly, the store owner won't stock the magazine unless there's a market of potential consumers near the supermarket who are likely to buy. When you receive a free sample in the mail or see the magazine on display at the checkout lane, this communications barrier between you (the buyer) and your supermarket (the seller) is overcome.

Something to exchange   Marketing occurs when the transaction takes place and both the buyer and seller exchange something of value. In this case, you exchange your money for the supermarket's *Time Digital*. Both of you have gained something and also given up something, but you are both better off because you have each satisfied your unmet needs. You have the opportunity to read *Time Digital*, but you gave up some money; the store gave up the *Time Digital* but received money, which enables it to remain in business. This exchange process and, of course, the ethical and legal foundations of exchange are central to marketing.[7]

CONCEPT CHECK

1. What is marketing?

2. Marketing focuses on _____ and _____ consumer needs.

3. What four factors are needed for marketing to occur?

How Marketing Discovers and Satisfies Consumer Needs

The importance of discovering and satisfying consumer needs is so critical to understanding marketing that we look at each of these two steps in detail next.

Discovering Consumer Needs

The first objective in marketing is discovering the needs of prospective consumers. Sound simple? Well, it's not. In the abstract, discovering needs looks easy, but when you get down to the specifics of marketing, problems crop up.

Some product disasters   With much fanfare, a decade ago, Coca-Cola replaced its 98-year-old Coke with a better-tasting cola called New Coke. Polaroid, flushed with the success of its instant still-photography business, introduced Polavision (question 2, Figure 1-2) as the first instant home movie camera. Similarly, after investing $40 million, IBM introduced a personal computer called the PCjr.

While Coca-Cola reintroduced its original formula only 79 days after New Coke's launch, Polaroid withdrew its product, and IBM redirected its efforts to a replacement product only a short time after the products were introduced. All three firms lost millions in their failed attempts to introduce new products.

These are three of the best-known product disasters in recent history, but thousands of lesser-known products fail in the marketplace every year. One major reason is that, in each case, the firm miscalculated consumers' wants and needs for these products. In the case of New Coke, Coca-Cola provoked a nationwide uproar from old formula loyalists by failing to understand their bond with the existing product. Polaroid did not anticipate that consumers would prefer the convenience of videotape technology over Polavision. Finally, the PCjr failed because consumers did not like the keyboard, and competitors' computers were lower priced.[8]

The solution to preventing such product failures seems embarrassingly obvious. First, find out what consumers need and want. Second, produce what they do need and want and don't produce what they don't need and want. This is much more difficult than it sounds.

It's frequently very difficult to get a precise reading on what consumers want and need when they are confronted with revolutionary ideas for new products. Right after World War II, IBM asked one of the most prestigious management consulting firms in the world to estimate the total future market for *all* electronic computers for *all* business, scientific, engineering, and government uses (question 3, Figure 1-2). The answer was less than 10! Fortunately, key IBM executives disagreed, so IBM started building electronic computers anyway. Where would IBM be today if it had assumed the market estimate was correct? Most of the firms that bought computers five years after the market study had not actually recognized they were prospective buyers because they had no understanding of what computers could do for them—they didn't recognize their own need for faster information processing.

Consumer needs and consumer wants   Should marketing try to satisfy consumer needs or consumer wants? The answer is both! Heated debates rage over this question, and a person's position in the debate usually depends on the definitions of needs and wants and the amount of freedom given to prospective customers to make their own buying decisions.

A *need* occurs when a person feels physiologically deprived of basic necessities such as food, clothing, and shelter. A *want* is a felt need that is shaped by a person's knowledge, culture, and personality. So if you feel hungry, you have developed a basic need and desire to eat something. Let's say you then want to eat an apple or a candy bar because, based on your past experience and personality, you know these will satisfy your hunger need. Effective marketing, in the form of creating an awareness of good products at convenient locations, clearly can shape a person's wants. Rollerblade in-line skates are an example.

At issue is whether marketing persuades prospective customers to buy the "wrong" things—say, a candy bar rather than an apple to satisfy hunger pangs. Certainly, marketing tries to influence what we buy. A question then arises—at what point do we want government and society to step in to protect consumers? Most consumers would say they want government to protect us from harmful drugs and unsafe cars but not from candy bars and soft drinks. The issue is not clear-cut, which is why legal and social issues are central to marketing. Because even psychologists and economists still debate the exact meanings of *need* and *want,* we will avoid the semantic arguments and use the terms interchangeably in the rest of the book.

As shown in Figure 1-4, discovering needs involves looking carefully at prospective customers, whether they are children buying M&M's candy, college students buying Rollerblade in-line skates, or firms buying Xerox photocopying machines. A principal activity of a firm's marketing department is to scrutinize its consumers carefully in order to understand what they need, to study industry trends, to examine competitors' products, and even to analyze the needs of a customer's customer.

What a market is   Potential consumers make up a **market,** which is (1) people (2) with the desire and (3) with the ability to buy a specific product. All markets ultimately are people. Even when we say a firm bought a Xerox copier, we mean one or several people in the firm decided to buy it. People who are aware of their unmet needs may have the desire to buy the product, but that alone isn't sufficient. People must also have the ability to buy, such as the authority, time, and money. As we saw earlier in the definition of marketing, people may buy, or accept, more than

FIGURE 1-4

MARKETING'S FIRST TASK:
DISCOVERING CONSUMER NEEDS

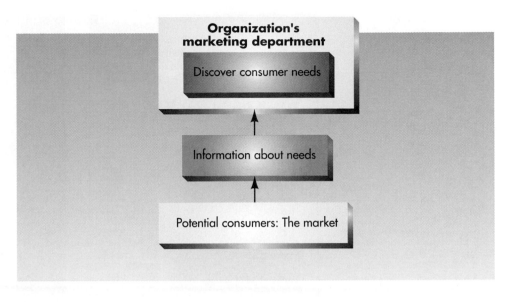

just goods or services. For example, they may buy an idea that results in an action, such as having their blood pressure checked annually or turning down their thermostat to save energy.

Satisfying Consumer Needs

Marketing doesn't stop with the discovery of consumer needs. Since the organization obviously can't satisfy all consumer needs, it must concentrate its efforts on certain needs of a specific group of potential consumers. This is the **target market,** one or more specific groups of potential consumers toward which an organization directs its marketing program.

The four Ps: controllable marketing mix factors   Having selected the target market consumers, the firm must take steps to satisfy their needs. Someone in the organization's marketing department, often the marketing manager, must take action and develop a complete marketing program to reach consumers by using a combination of four tools, often called the *four Ps*—a useful shorthand reference to them first published by Professor E. Jerome McCarthy:[9]

- *Product.* A good, service, or idea to satisfy the consumer's needs.
- *Price.* What is exchanged for the product.
- *Promotion.* A means of communication between the seller and buyer.
- *Place.* A means of getting the product into the consumer's hands.

We'll define each of the four Ps more carefully later in the book, but for now it's important to remember that they are the elements of the marketing mix, or simply the **marketing mix.** These are the marketing manager's controllable factors, the marketing actions of product, price, promotion, and place that he or she can take to solve a marketing problem. The marketing mix elements are called *controllable factors* because they are under the control of the marketing department in an organization.

The uncontrollable, environmental factors   There are a host of factors largely beyond the control of the marketing department and its organization. These factors can be placed into five groups (as shown in Figure 1-3): social, technological, economic, competitive, and regulatory forces. Examples are what consumers themselves want and need, changing technology, the state of the economy in terms of whether it is expanding or contracting, actions that competitors take, and government restrictions. These are the **environmental factors** in a marketing decision, the uncontrollable factors involving social, economic, technological, competitive, and regulatory forces. These five forces may serve as accelerators or brakes on marketing, sometimes expanding an organization's marketing opportunities and other times restricting them. These five environmental factors are covered in Chapter 3.

Traditionally, many marketing executives have treated these environmental factors as rigid, absolute constraints that are entirely outside their influence.[10] However, recent studies and marketing successes have shown that a forward-looking, action-oriented firm can often affect some environmental factors. IBM's technical breakthroughs gave birth to the entire digital electronic computer industry, even though initial estimates of demand were low. Cable TV companies have redefined their competition to include telephone compa-

MARKETING NEWSNET

CUSTOMER VALUE IS WHATEVER CUSTOMERS VALUE

Until quite recently it was assumed that customer value was how prospective buyers judged a good or service on some combination of quality and price. Today, value is a much broader concept that also includes dimensions such as convenience, on-time delivery, and service. Customers now want more of the dimensions they value: if they value convenience, they want their purchase to be easy; if they value low price, they want the lowest possible price; if they value speed, they want the purchase to be extremely fast.

Curiously, to provide customer value a manufacturer, retailer, or service provider does not have to compete on all these dimensions. Research by management experts Michael Treacy and Fred Wiersema suggests that firms cannot succeed by being all things to all people. Instead they must find the unique value that they alone can deliver to a selected market. Many successful firms have chosen to deliver outstanding customer value with one of three value strategies—best price, best product, or best service.

Companies such as Wal-Mart, Price/Costco, and Dell Computer have all been successful offering consumers the best price. Other companies such as Nike, Starbucks, Microsoft, and Johnson & Johnson claim to provide the best products on the market. Finally, companies such as Lands' End and Home Depot deliver value by building long-term relationships with customers and providing exceptional service.

How should a firm choose a value proposition? By assessing its customers, competitors, and itself, say Treacy and Wiersema.

VALUE PROPOSITIONS

BEST PRICE	BEST PRODUCT	BEST SERVICE
Guaranteed low price	The best product, period	We take care of you

nics. After more than a decade of negotiations with Soviet bureaucrats, McDonald's opened a 700-seat restaurant in Moscow and served more than 10 million customers its first year. These technological, competitive, and regulatory factors might have forestalled productive marketing actions had they been seen as completely uncontrollable.

New standards in customer value   The intensity of competition in both domestic and global markets has caused massive restructuring of many Canadian industries and businesses, and the trend continues. Canadian managers are seeking ways to compete more effectively in this new, more intense level of global competition. For ideas, these managers often study firms that have been successful, try to understand the reasons for their success, and then duplicate them.

One reason for the success of many firms is their focus on providing customer value. Consequently, "customer value" has become *the* critical marketing issue for both sellers and buyers (question 4, Figure 1-2). That firms gain loyal customers by providing unique value is the essence of successful marketing. What is new, however, is a more careful attempt at understanding how a firm's customers perceive value. For our purposes, **customer value** is the unique combination of benefits received by targeted buyers that includes quality, price, convenience, on-time delivery, and both before-sale and after-sale service. The Marketing NewsNet explains how companies such as Dell Computer, Lands' End, and Nike have followed very successful—but different—marketing strategies to provide value to their targeted customers.[11] We will expand on these ideas throughout the book.

FIGURE 1-5

MARKETING'S SECOND TASK:
SATISFYING CONSUMER NEEDS

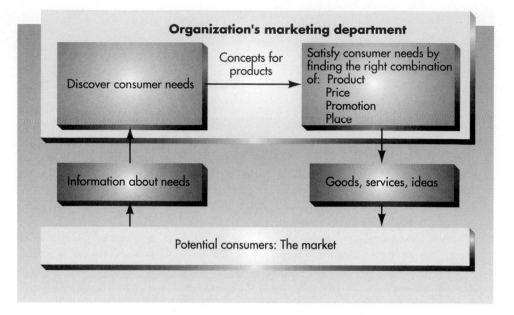

Providing customer value over a long period of time can be a challenge because firms face continually changing environmental factors. Changes in technology, competition, and regulation, in addition to issues such as globalism, diversity, ethics, and the environment, can influence consumers' perceptions of value. As a result, several important business principles are helping firms respond to changes with new or improved value offerings. *Total quality management* (TQM) programs, for example, help firms focus on the needs of the customer. Efforts at what the Japanese call *kaizen,* or continuous incremental improvement, encourage firms to do what they already do only better. Finally, *reengineering* programs involve rejecting existing assumptions, traditions, and processes and inventing new approaches to providing value. All of these approaches are likely to be part of the blueprints for success from today into the twenty-first century.[12]

The marketing program   To discover what prospective customers need, the marketing manager must translate the information from consumers into some concepts for products the firm might develop (Figure 1-5). These concepts must then be converted into a tangible **marketing program**—a plan that integrates the marketing mix to provide a good, service, or idea to prospective buyers. These prospects then react to the offering favourably (by buying) or unfavourably (by not buying), and the process is repeated. As shown in Figure 1-5, in an effective organization this process is continuous: consumer needs trigger product concepts that are translated into actual products that stimulate further discovery of consumer needs.

A marketing program for Rollerblade, Inc.   To see some specifics of an actual marketing program, let's return to the earlier example of Mary Horwath, Rollerblade, Inc., and their in-line skates.

With Rollerblade, Inc.'s small size and the limited marketing budget, Mary Horwath knew that she faced big problems in gaining awareness and consumer "trial"—actually having potential buyers put on her brand of skates and use them. Enter Guerilla Marketing 101.

Horwath started by:

- *Finding the right demographic group to target with in-line skates.* Horwath focused Rollerblade, Inc.'s marketing efforts on 18- to 35-year-old men and women. They were active, health and sports conscious, and had money to spend.

- *Changing the image of—or repositioning—skating.* As Horwath observes, "We had to build a new image for in-line roller skating. People already knew about traditional roller skating, which was done inside and attracted mostly young girls. But we didn't want to be associated with that image. Our sport happened outside in the sunshine, and we built our image around freedom and excitement. This proved to be a key element of our new marketing strategy."[13]
- *Finding the right benefits—or competitive "points of difference" (discussed in Chapter 11)—to stress in marketing the Rollerblade brand of skates.* She chose three benefits and points of difference that set the tone for all subsequent marketing efforts: (1) fun, (2) fitness and health, and (3) excitement.

Now Horwath set about finding a way to use her meagre budget to get exposure for Rollerblade skates and to make people aware of them and put them on. She explains, "We knew that if people could try the skates, they would fall in love with the sport."

So Horwath's strategy—both simple and brilliant—was to give hundreds of free skates away where they would make people most aware of the new product and also enable key "opinion leaders" to try them.[14] Examples of recipients of the free skates and why Horwath chose them include:

- *Entertainment celebrities like Michael J. Fox, Janet Jackson, and Arnold Schwarzenegger.* These stars then turned up wearing the skates in magazine photos or on television, giving Rollerblade, Inc. lots of free publicity.
- *Cheerleaders for the professional sports teams.* When the cheerleaders wore Rollerblade skates on the sidelines during games, millions of TV viewers saw the skates, many for the first time.
- *Professional athletes* to use in off-season training.

These "freebies" led to tens of thousands of converts to in-line skating (see Figure 1-1), and sales of Rollerblade skates started to take off. This enabled Horwath's marketing budget to expand, and so did her ideas for promoting Rollerblade skates. She created a series of 10-kilometre in-line races involving thousands of competitors—most of whom skated with the Rollerblade brand. Horwath got product endorsements from sports teams such as the Boston Bruins hockey team. She also started Team Rollerblade, a group of 10 top male and female

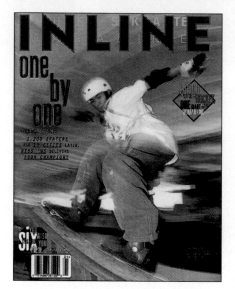

skaters who dance and perform acrobatic stunts on skates, everywhere from the local shopping mall to major sporting events such as the Olympics.[15]

Because Horwath was convinced that if people tried the skates once they would love them, she filled up "demo vans" with skates so people across the United States and Canada could try the skates for free (question 5, Figure 1-2). Action-packed skating videos that retailers could show on VCRs, Club Rollerblade for skaters, and the how-to book *Wheel Excitement* appeared later. She even got Rollerblade skates displayed on six million Golden Grahams cereal boxes in a joint promotion with General Mills that gave away 1000 pairs of skates. In research studies, sports medicine doctors found that in-line skating could be as healthful as running or bicycling. All of these activities were part of a complete marketing program for Rollerblade, Inc. that included the following features:

MARKETING MIX ELEMENT	MARKETING PROGRAM ACTIVITY	RATIONALE FOR MARKETING PROGRAM ACTIVITY
Product	Continuously improved products, such as the *heel* brake, the 2-lb.-lighter Lightning skate, and the Macroblade with buckles like ski boots	Desire to make the highest-quality product necessitates continuing new product research and extensive testing to maintain and improve quality
Price	$79 to $399 a pair	Attempt to have prices that appeal to various market segments
Promotion	Free skates to key opinion leaders, 10-K races, Team Rollerblade, "demo vans," skating videos, Club Rollerblade, and book	Attempt to increase awareness of in-line skating and its benefits and to facilitate prospects' actual trial of skates
Place	Distribution and sales of Rollerblade skates at major sporting goods stores	Desire to make it easy for prospective buyers to buy skates

So what happened? How did Horwath and Rollerblade, Inc.'s strategy turn out? Fantastically! Rollerblade's sales doubled each year during the late 1980s. In 1990, sales of in-line skates exploded and *Time* magazine called in-line skating "the sport of the 90s." *Business Week* magazine selected Rollerblade's Bravoblades with automatic braking technology (ABT) as one of the best new products on the market.[16] Today, Rollerblade, Inc. production lines often turn out more than 20 000 pairs of skates a day.

The popularity of Rollerblades also spawned the fastest growing youth team sport—roller hockey—and the Roller Hockey International league with 19 teams in Canada and the United States. In addition, in-line skating enthusiasts can now read *Inline* magazine for reviews of new products, coverage of skating events, and information about new skating techniques.[17]

So Rollerblade, Inc. and Mary Horwath's marketing strategy had succeeded in creating a new sport and a new industry. This meant they had no problems, right? Not at all. In a free-market system, success encourages competition and imitations. Rollerblade, Inc. created the in-line skate industry, but it now must shift its efforts from marketing the sport to marketing its Rollerblade brand against new competitors. This is the marketing issue discussed in the Rollerblade case at the end of the chapter.

CONCEPT CHECK
  1. An organization can't satisfy the needs of all consumers, so it must focus on one or more subgroups, which are its _____.

  2. What are the four marketing mix elements that make up the organization's marketing program?

  3. What are uncontrollable variables?

HOW MARKETING BECAME SO IMPORTANT

Marketing is a driving force in the modern global economy. To understand why this is so and some related ethical aspects, let us look at (1) the evolution of the market orientation, (2) ethics and social responsibility in marketing, and (3) the breadth and depth of marketing activities.

Evolution of the Market Orientation

Many market-oriented manufacturing organizations have experienced four distinct stages in the life of their firms. We can use the Pillsbury Company as an example.

Production era   Goods were scarce in the early years of North America, so buyers were willing to accept virtually any goods that were produced and make do with them as best they could. French economist J. B. Say described the prevailing business theory of the period: "Production creates its own demand." The central notion was that products would sell themselves, so the major concern of business firms was production, not marketing.[18]

In 1869, Charles Pillsbury founded his company on the basis of high-quality wheat and the accessibility of cheap water power. Robert Keith, a Pillsbury president, described his company at this stage: "We are professional flour millers. Blessed with a supply of the finest North American wheat, plenty of water power, and excellent milling machinery, we produce flour of the highest quality. Our basic function is to mill quality flour."[19] As shown in Figure 1-6, this production era generally continued in North America through the 1920s.

Sales era   About that time, many firms discovered that they could produce more goods than their regular buyers could consume. Competition became more significant, and the problems of reaching the market became more complex. The usual solution was to hire more salespeople to find new markets and consumers. Pillsbury's philosophy at this stage was summed up simply by Keith: "We must hire salespersons to sell it [the flour] just as we hire accountants to keep our books." The role of the Pillsbury salesforce, in simplified terms, was to find consumers for the goods that the firm found it could produce best, given its existing resources. This sales era continued into the 1950s for Pillsbury and into the 1960s for many other firms (see Figure 1-6).

The marketing concept era   In the 1960s, marketing became the motivating force in Pillsbury. Since then its policy can be stated as, "We are in the business of satisfying needs and wants of consumers." This is really a brief statement of what has come to be known as the **marketing concept;** the idea is that an organization should (1) strive to satisfy the needs of consumers (2) while also trying to achieve the organization's goals.

The statement of a firm's commitment to satisfying consumer wants and needs that probably launched the marketing concept appeared in a 1952 annual report of General Electric Company:[20] "The concept introduces . . . marketing . . . at the beginning rather than the end of the production cycle and integrates marketing into each phase of the business." This statement had two important points. First, it recognized that sales is just one element of marketing, or in other words, that marketing includes a much broader range of activities. Second, it changed the point at which marketing ideas are fed into the production cycle from *after* an item is produced to *before* it is designed. Clearly the marketing concept is a focus on the consumer. Unfortunately, although many companies endorsed the marketing concept and defined the purpose of their business as the creation and retention of satisfied customers, implementation of the concept proved to be very difficult.

The market orientation era   Many of the implementation issues are now being addressed by the total quality management movement. Firms such as Sony, McDonald's and Toyota have achieved great success in the marketplace by putting huge effort into implementing the marketing concept, giving their firms what has been called a *market orientation*. An organization that has a **market orientation** focuses its efforts on (1) continuously collecting information about customers' needs and competitors' capabilities, (2) sharing this information across departments, and (3) using the information to create customer value.

A key aspect of this market orientation is that understanding consumers and competitors requires involvement of managers and employees throughout the firm. DuPont, for example, encourages employees to learn about customers' needs by participating in their "Adopt a Customer" program. Similarly, Marriott sends employees to stay in competitors' hotels and assess their facilities and services. To encourage information sharing, many firms such as Procter & Gamble, Ralston Purina, and General Mills allocate personnel and resources from many functional areas to *customer management teams.* These teams are also responsible for understanding value assessments of their suppliers and their customers' customers. Research shows that firms having a demonstrated market orientation are more profitable than those lacking it.[21]

Ethics and Social Responsibility: Balancing the Interests of Different Groups

As organizations have changed their orientation, society's expectations of marketers have also changed. Today, the standards of marketing practice have shifted from an emphasis on producers' interests to consumers' interests. In addition, organizations are increasingly encouraged to consider the social and environmental consequences of their actions. Because the interests of consumers, organizations, and society may differ, marketing managers must often find solutions acceptable to all parties. Guidelines for ethical and socially responsible behaviour can help managers with the complex decisions involved in balancing consumer, organizational, and societal interests.

Ethics   Many marketing issues are not specifically addressed by existing laws and regulations. Should information about a firm's customers be sold to other organizations? Should advertising by professional service providers, such as accountants and lawyers, be restricted? Should consumers be responsible for assessing the safety of a product in "normal-use" situations? These, and many other questions, relate to **ethics,** which are the moral principles and values that govern the actions and decisions of an individual or group. Many companies, industries, and professional associations have developed codes of ethics to assist managers. Levi Strauss, for example, has developed a set of corporate statements to guide all major decisions. The company believes it "must provide clarity about our expectations and must enforce these standards throughout the corporation."[22]

Social responsibility   While many difficult ethical issues involve only the buyer and seller, others involve society as a whole. For example, suppose you buy batteries for your portable CD player, and, when their charge runs low, you throw them away. Is this just a transaction between you and the battery manufacturer? Not quite! Thrown in a trash dump, the batteries may contaminate the soil, so society will bear a portion of the cost of your battery purchase. This example illustrates the issue of **social responsibility,** the idea that organizations are part of a larger society and are accountable to society for their actions. The well-being of society at large should also be recognized in an organization's marketing decisions.[23] In fact, some marketing experts stress the **societal marketing concept,** the view that an organization should discover and satisfy the needs of its consumers in a way that also provides for society's well-being. The difficulty firms face as they attempt to be socially responsible and competitive is discussed in the Ethics and Social Responsibility Alert.[24]

The societal marketing concept is directly related to **macromarketing,** which looks at the aggregate flow of a nation's goods and services to benefit society.[25] Macromarketing addresses broad issues such as whether marketing costs too much, whether advertising is wasteful, and what resource scarcities and pollution side effects result from the marketing system. While macromarketing issues are addressed briefly in this book, the book's main focus is on how an individual organization directs its

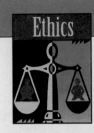
SOCIALLY RESPONSIBLE, ENVIRONMENTALLY FRIENDLY, *AND* COMPETITIVE?

Many organizations today are trying to incorporate social responsibility into their marketing activities. One reason is that socially responsible decisions are likely to have a significant positive impact on society by improving the marketplace and the environment. Another reason is that most of an organization's constituents are taking interest in the issue. Investors now evaluate environmental track records, consumers express interest in environmental issues, and employees often encourage socially responsible behaviour.

Unfortunately, many environmentally friendly products have been costly to produce, and consumers have not been willing to pay a premium for them. As a result, companies often question if they can be socially responsible and competitive.

In the past, policy makers protected the environment through strict environmental regulations even if it eroded competitiveness, while companies tried to appeal to consumers with the often intangible environmental benefits of their products. More recently, some experts have suggested that the solution is innovation that either offsets the cost of improving environmental impact or increases customer value. For example, Scotchbrite Never Rust Wool Soap Pads from 3M—which are made from recycled plastic bottles—are more expensive than competitors (S.O.S. and Brillo) but superior because they don't rust or scratch.

Should companies consider social responsibility in their decisions? Must environmentally friendly products be competitively priced?

marketing activities and allocates its resources to benefit its customers, or **micromarketing.** An overview of this approach appears in Chapter 2. Because of the importance of ethical and social responsibility issues in marketing today, they—and related legal and regulatory actions—are discussed throughout this book. In addition, Chapter 4 focuses specifically on issues of ethics and social responsibility.

The Breadth and Depth of Marketing

Marketing today affects every person and organization. To understand this, let's analyze (1) who markets, (2) what they market, (3) who buys and uses what is marketed, (4) who benefits from these marketing activities, and (5) how they benefit.

Who markets?   Every organization markets! It's obvious that business firms involved in manufacturing (Xerox, Heinz, Nike), retailing (Kmart, Toys "Я" Us, The Bay), and providing services (Merrill Lynch, Canadian Broadcasting Corporation, Air Canada) market their offerings. Today many other types of marketing are also popular. Nonprofit organizations (Winnipeg Ballet, Canadian Red Cross, Canadian Museum of Civilization, your local church) also engage in marketing.[26] Your college or university, for example, probably has a marketing program to attract students, faculty members, and donations. Places (cities, provinces, countries) often use marketing efforts to attract tourists, conventions, or businesses. Chile's "Make the Move" campaign is designed to attract businesses interested in a South American location. Organizations associated with special events or causes use marketing to inform and influence a target audience. These marketing activities range from announcements regarding the Olympics to government agencies encouraging AIDS prevention. Finally, individuals often use marketing to gain attention and preference. Celebrities such as Jay Leno, for example, may use marketing activities to increase the size of their "audience," while political candidates such as Jean Chrétien and Paul Martin seek financial support and votes.

MARKETING IS USED BY NONPROFIT
ORGANIZATIONS, CAUSES, AND
PLACES.

What is marketed?   Goods, services, and ideas are marketed. Goods are physical objects, such as toothpaste, cameras, or computers, that satisfy consumer needs. Services are intangible items such as airline trips, financial advice, or telephone calls. Ideas are intangibles such as thoughts about actions or causes. Some of these, such as lawn mowers, dry cleaning, and annual physical examinations, may be bought or accepted by individuals for their own use. Others, such as high-volume office copiers and vending-machine repair services, are bought by organizations. Finally, the products marketed in today's global marketplace are increasingly likely to cross a nation's boundaries and involve exports, imports, and global marketing (covered in Chapter 5).

Who buys and uses what is marketed?   Both individuals and organizations buy and use goods and services that are marketed. **Ultimate consumers** are the people—whether 80 years or 8 months old—who use the goods and services purchased for a household. A household may consist of 1 person or 10. (The way one or more of the people in the household buys for it is the topic of consumer behaviour in Chapter 6.) In contrast, **organizational buyers** are units such as manufacturers, retailers, or government agencies that buy goods and services for their own use or for resale. (Organizational buyer behaviour is covered in Chapter 7.) Although the terms *consumers, buyers,* and *customers* are sometimes used for both ultimate consumers and organizations, there is no consistency on this. In this book you will be able to tell from the example whether the buyers are ultimate consumers, organizations, or both.

Who benefits?   In our free-enterprise society there are three specific groups that benefit from effective marketing: consumers who buy, organizations that sell, and society as a whole. True competition between products and services in the marketplace ensures that we consumers can find value from the best products, the lowest prices, or exceptional service. Providing choices leads to the consumer satisfaction and quality of life that we have come to expect from our economic system.

Organizations that provide need-satisfying products with effective marketing programs—for example, McDonald's, IBM, Avon, and Merrill Lynch—have blossomed, but competition creates problems for ineffective competitors. For example, Osborne Computers, and DeLorean cars were well-known names years ago but may now be unknown to you. Effective marketing actions result in rewards for organizations that serve consumers and in millions of marketing jobs such as those described in Appendix C.

Finally, effective marketing benefits society. It enhances competition, which, in turn, improves both the quality of products and services and lowers their prices. This makes the countries more competitive in world markets and provides jobs and a higher standard of living for their citizens.

How do consumers benefit?   Marketing creates **utility,** the benefits or customer value received by users of the product. This utility is the result of the marketing exchange process. There are four different utilities: form, place, time, and possession. The production of the good or service constitutes *form utility. Place utility* means having the offering available where consumers need it, whereas *time utility* means having it available when needed. *Possession utility* is getting the product to consumers so they can use it.

Thus, marketing provides consumers with place, time, and possession utilities by making the good or service available at the right place and right time for the right consumer. Although form utility usually arises in manufacturing activity and could be seen as outside the scope of marketing, an organization's marketing activities influence the product features and packaging. Marketing creates its utilities by bridging space (place utility) and hours (time utility) to provide products (form utility) for consumers to own and use (possession utility).

CONCEPT CHECK

1. Like Pillsbury, many firms have gone through four distinct orientations for their business: starting with the _____ era and ending with today's _____ era.

2. What are the two key characteristics of the marketing concept?

3. In this book the term *product* refers to what three things?

SUMMARY

1. Combining personal experience with more formal marketing knowledge will enable us to identify and solve important marketing problems.

2. Marketing is the process of planning and executing the conception, pricing, promotion, and distribution of ideas, goods, and services to create exchanges that satisfy individual and organizational objectives. This definition relates to two primary goals of marketing: (*a*) assessing the needs of consumers and (*b*) satisfying them.

3. For marketing to occur, it is necessary to have (*a*) two or more parties with unmet needs, (*b*) a desire and ability to satisfy them, (*c*) communication between the parties, and (*d*) something to exchange.

4. Because an organization doesn't have the resources to satisfy the needs of all consumers, it selects a target market of potential customers—a subset of the entire market—on which to focus its marketing program.

5. Four elements in a marketing program designed to satisfy customer needs are product, price, promotion, and place. These elements are called the *marketing mix,* the *four Ps,* or the *controllable variables* because they are under the general control of the marketing department.

6. Environmental factors, also called *uncontrollable variables,* are largely beyond the organization's control. These include social, technological, economic, competitive, and regulatory forces.

7. Customer value, perhaps *the* critical marketing issue for buyers and sellers, is the unique combination of benefits received by targeted buyers that includes quality, price, convenience, on-time delivery, and both before-sale and after-sale service.

8. In marketing terms, North American business history is divided into four periods: the production era, the sales era, the marketing concept era, and the current market orientation era.

9. Marketing managers must balance consumer, organizational, and societal interests. This involves issues of ethics and social responsibility.

10. Both profit-making and nonprofit organizations perform marketing activities. They market products, services, and ideas that benefit consumers, organizations, and countries. Marketing creates utilities that give benefits, or customer value, to users.

KEY TERMS AND CONCEPTS

marketing p. 9
exchange p. 9
market p. 12
target market p. 13
marketing mix p. 13
environmental factors p. 14
customer value p. 15
marketing program p. 16
marketing concept p. 20

market orientation p. 20
ethics p. 21
social responsibility p. 21
societal marketing concept p. 21
macromarketing p. 21
micromarketing p. 22
ultimate consumers p. 23
organizational buyers p. 23
utility p. 24

CHAPTER PROBLEMS AND APPLICATIONS

1. What consumer wants (or benefits) are met by the following products or services? (*a*) Carnation Instant Breakfast, (*b*) Adidas running shoes, (*c*) Hertz Rent-A-Car, and (*d*) television shopping programs.

2. Each of the four products or stores in question 1 has substitutes. Respective examples are (*a*) a ham and egg breakfast, (*b*) regular tennis shoes, (*c*) taking a bus, and (*d*) a department store. What consumer benefits might these substitutes have in each case that some consumers might value more highly than those products mentioned in question 1?

3. What are the characteristics (e.g., age, income, education) of the target market customers for the following products or services? (*a*) *National Geographic* magazine, (*b*) *Wired* magazine, (*c*) Toronto Blue Jays baseball team, and (*d*) the Canadian Open tennis tournament.

4. A college in a metropolitan area wishes to increase its evening-school offerings of business-related courses such as marketing, accounting, finance, and management. Who are the target market customers (students) for these courses?

5. What actions involving the four marketing mix elements might be used to reach the target market in question 4?

6. What environmental factors (uncontrollable variables) must the college in question 4 consider in designing its marketing program?

7. Polaroid introduced instant still photography, which proved to be a tremendous success. Yet Polavision, its instant movie system, was a total disaster. (*a*) What benefits does each provide to users? (*b*) Which of these do you think contributed to Polavision's failure? (*c*) What research could have been undertaken that might have revealed Polavision's drawbacks?

8. Mary Horwath and Rollerblade, Inc. are now trying to grow in-line skating—and the company—globally, just as they succeeded in doing in North America. What are the advantages and disadvantages of trying to reach new global markets?

9. Does a firm have the right to "create" wants and try to persuade consumers to buy goods and services they didn't know about earlier? What are examples of "good" and "bad" want creation? Who should decide what is good and bad?

CASE 1-1   Rollerblade, Inc.

Rollerblade, Inc. (www.rollerblade.com) is an incredible marketing success story. In just over a decade the company has created a sport that is now more popular than amateur baseball or football. How did it happen? "Achieving success wasn't easy," reflects Mary Horwath. "It took months and years of hard work . . . and perhaps most of all, it took lots of imagination!"

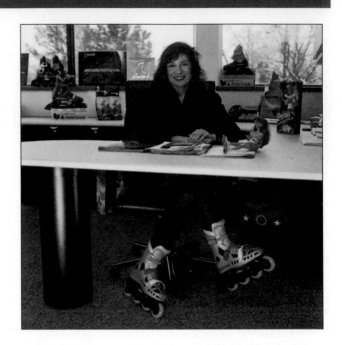

THE SITUATION

But Horwath, now vice president of Marketing Services and International at Rollerblade, Inc., hears footsteps. She summarizes Rollerblade's success:

> We had introduced a product and created a sport. We had arrived. Rollerblade was rapidly becoming a part of the American way of life. But now we were faced with another challenge. It may have been a marketer's dream that people thought that in-line skating was "Rollerblading." But we knew that every skate wasn't a Rollerblade skate. And, for the first time, we had competition from other companies. We had always built brand identity during our years of building the sport. But now it was time to focus especially on marketing the Rollerblade brand. Of course we continued to build the sport because we knew that as the sport grew, so would Rollerblade, Inc.[27]

The future of the in-line skating industry looks good. In-line skating is the fastest growing sport in North America. With more than 25 million skaters, in-line skating has now surpassed football, baseball, and soccer in total number of participants. Industry sales are expected to exceed $1 billion in 1998. Optimists see the possibility of the international in-line skate market to be even greater.

THE COMPETITION

Horwath's concern about competitors is genuine. When Rollerblade, Inc. was founded, it was the only manufacturer of in-line skates in the world. Today it has more than 30 direct competitors, most that sell lower-priced skates than Rollerblade skates through mass merchandising chains such as Wal-Mart and Kmart—outlets that Rollerblade, Inc. has historically avoided in favour of sporting goods stores.

MARKETS AND PRODUCTS

Horwath sees Rollerblade's primary target market as active adults. But from skating with skaters on Rollerblade skates, Horwath has concluded that potential skaters are far more diverse than the 18- to 35-year-old target and that skaters use Rollerblade skates for many different reasons: racing, fun, exercise, street hockey, transportation to and from work or school, and even for complex acrobatics.

With these diverse markets, Rollerblade, Inc. develops a variety of in-line designs targeted at different market segments. Some examples:

- *Metroblade*®. A lightweight nylon/leather walking shoe that fits into a molded skate shell designed for transportation that requires going into buildings.
- *Problade*®. Designed for serious racing for speed skaters with a low-cut leather boot and five oversize (80-mm) wheels.
- *Macroblade Equipe*®. Vented, molded plastic shell that makes a lightweight, breathable skate.
- *Mondoblade*®. Skates for starting out in in-line skating.
- *Microblade*®. Skates with wild colours, for kids.

In addition, Rollerblade offers a complete line of skating accessories that includes knee pads, wrist guards, gloves, jerseys, shorts, T-shirts, and helmets.

Designing a high-quality in-line skate is a lot more complex than it may appear. In fact, Rollerblade, Inc. holds more than 185 patents for its in-line skating products. Its industry "firsts" include polyurethane boots and wheels, metal frames, dual bearings, heel brakes, buckle closures, ventilated shells, and breathable liners. One of Rollerblade's latest innovations, Active Brake Technology (ABT), offers skaters greater speed control and stopping power.

Because of the speeds involved in in-line skating, Rollerblade, Inc. has been an industry leader in promoting safety and the use of proper equipment. Its "Asphalt Bites^{SM}" safety awareness campaign is designed to educate consumers about the benefits of wearing full protective gear and skating safety. The campaign includes videos featuring Olympic gold-medal speed skater Bonnie Blair giving safety tips, a pocket-size in-line safety guide, and a 30-second public service announcement (for use by television stations).

GLOBAL ALLIANCES

To obtain financial strength for the future, Rollerblade, Inc. developed an alliance with Italy's Nordica Sportsystem, a leading ski boot manufacturer. Nordica, owned by a Benetton family holding company, bought 50 percent ownership in Rollerblade, Inc. Besides capital, Nordica provides Rollerblade, Inc. with increased research, development, and manufacturing capabilities and access to global distribution networks. Today, Nordica's ski boot technology is used in many models of Rollerblade skates. Another Benetton company, Benetton Sportsystem Canada Inc., is the distributor for all Rollerblade products in Canada.

Questions

1. What trends in the environmental forces (social, economic, technological, competitive, and regulatory) identified in Figure 1-3 in the chapter (*a*) work for and (*b*) work against Rollerblade, Inc.'s growth?

2. What are the differences in marketing goals for Rollerblade, Inc., in (*a*) growing a new industry, and (*b*) marketing its Rollerblade brand of in-line skates against competition?

3. How should Mary Horwath translate the broad goals identified in question 2 into a specific marketing program—a plan that integrates product, price, promotion, and place actions?

4. Horwath believes significant opportunities exist for Rollerblade skates in global markets. To which countries or regions should she initially try to market Rollerblade skates? Why?

gulf canada

resources limited

mission
2006:

Linking Marketing and Corporate Strategies

AFTER READING THIS CHAPTER YOU SHOULD BE ABLE TO:

• Describe the three organizational levels of strategy and their components.

• Describe how the three organizational levels of strategy relate to each other and how they influence the marketing function.

• Describe the strategic marketing process and its three key phases: planning, implementation, and control.

• Understand how organizations search for new marketing opportunities and select target markets.

• Explain how the marketing mix elements are blended into a cohesive marketing program.

• Describe how marketing control compares actual results with planned objectives and acts on deviations from the plan.

GULF CANADA PLANS TO CELEBRATE 100TH ANNIVERSARY IN 2006

and expects to be one of the world's preeminent oil and gas companies.

Gulf Canada Resources Limited (www.gulf.ca) Canada's eighth-largest oil and gas producer intends not only to survive to celebrate its 100th anniversary in 2006, but to have become a major international force in the petroleum industry by that time. What the company will look like at that time is uncertain, but it is alive and kicking despite predictions by experts that it wouldn't survive the nineties.

The turnaround began when James Perry ("J. P.") Bryan took over as Gulf's CEO in January 1995, bringing with him a group of investors and a much-needed $300 million equity investment to the company's treasury. Bryan acted quickly and decisively, working both sides of the street, to cut costs and increase production and revenue. He streamlined the organization, reducing the employee base by 40 percent; he paid off or rescheduled Gulf's debt; and he dramatically increased capital investment and drilling in Canada and Indonesia. In short, Bryan provided the type of action-oriented leadership that many experts believed was lacking at Gulf.

"I do not think there was a clear vision as to where this company was going. Clearly Gulf was a company in liquidation: they were cutting capital investment and selling assets," he says. Still, he was excited at the prospect of turning the company around, suggesting that the company's weaknesses were "pretty simple things to correct. You don't grow a company by cutting costs. You become efficient and then you've got to have clear growth strategy and a bias for action."[1]

Bryan believes that Gulf has specific strengths and assets that provide it with true growth potential: undeveloped oil and gas reserves in the Canadian arctic and offshore east coast, huge gas and oil exploration potential in Indonesia, and a diversified worldwide production portfolio.

In particular, Bryan is a great believer in the largely untapped potential of Canada's oil sands. Gulf holds a 9.03 percent interest in the Syncrude project, and administers the affairs of the Athabasca Oil Sands Trust. Bryan created the Trust in late 1995 to purchase the Government of Alberta's 11.4 percent of Syncrude stake. The Trust has more than doubled from its $10 issue price, and has outperformed even Bryan's projections of a 10 percent tax-free annual distribution.

"Where else in the world can you find almost perpetual reserves, with no finding and development costs, decreasing operating costs, and increasing production?" asks Bryan. "This is an investment vehicle you can buy for your grandchildren" (which he did.)[2] J. P. Bryan sees himself as an entrepreneur leading a major company: an entrepreneur who looks for an opportunity and finds a way to make it work. The ultimate goal remains—to make Gulf a preeminent international oil and gas producer by 2006. It won't be easy, but Bryan suggests the company has taken the right steps: costs are going down and production is going up; all employees now receive a competitive base salary, stock options, and a bonus paid under the same targets and guidelines for everyone; and lastly, the company is adding value both via the drill bit and acquisitions at home and abroad.

Chapter 2 describes how organizations set their overall direction and link these activities to marketing strategies—the very tasks J. P. Bryan is facing at Gulf Canada. In essence, this chapter describes how organizations try to implement the marketing concept to provide genuine value to their customers and shareholders.

LEVELS OF STRATEGY IN ORGANIZATIONS

This chapter first distinguishes among different kinds of organizations and the various levels within them. It then compares strategies at three different levels in an organization.

Today's Organizations: Kinds and Levels

Large organizations in existence today are often extremely complex. While this is not true for your corner deli or for some of the small businesses highlighted in our textbook cases, all of us deal in some way with huge organizations every day, so it is useful to understand both (1) the two basic kinds of organizations and (2) the levels that exist in them.

Kinds of organizations   Today's organizations can be broadly divided into business firms and nonprofit organizations. A *business firm* is a privately owned organization that serves its customers in order to earn a profit. Business firms must earn profits to survive. **Profit** is the reward to a business firm for the risk it undertakes in offering a product for sale; the money left over after a firm's total expenses are subtracted from its total revenues. In contrast to business firms, a *nonprofit organization* is a nongovernmental organization that serves its customers but does not have profit as an organizational goal. For simplicity in the rest of the book, however, the terms *firm, company, corporation,* and *organization* are used to cover both business and nonprofit operations.

Levels in organizations and how marketing links to them   Whether explicit or implicit, organizations have a strategic direction. Marketing not only helps shape this direction but must also help implement it. Figure 2-1 summarizes the focus of this direction at each of the three levels in an organization.

The **corporate level** is where top management directs overall strategy for the entire organization. Multimarket, multiproduct firms such as Hewlett-Packard or Johnson & Johnson really manage a portfolio of businesses, variously termed strategic business units (SBUs), strategic business segments, and product-market units (PMUs).[3]

FIGURE 2-1

THE THREE LEVELS OF STRATEGY IN ORGANIZATIONS

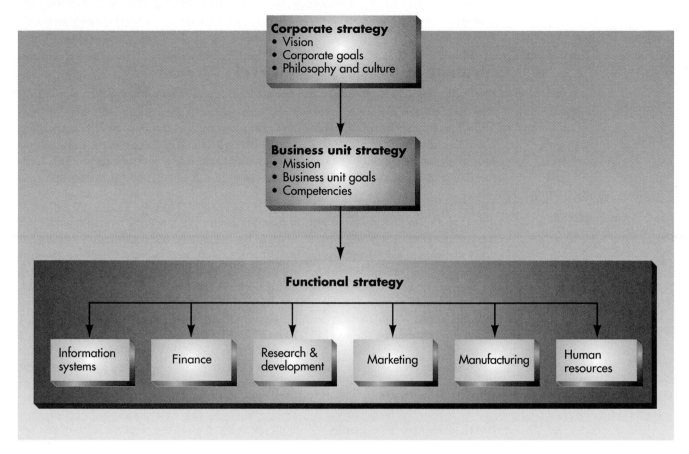

The term **business unit** refers to an organization that markets a set of related products to a clearly defined group of customers. The **business unit level** is the level at which business unit managers set the direction for their products and markets. The strategic direction is more specific at the business level of an organization. For less complex firms with a single business focus, such as Pennisula Farms, a Canadian yogourt producer, the corporate and business unit levels may merge.

Each business unit has marketing and other specialized activities (e.g., finance, research and development, or human resource management) at the **functional level,** which is where groups of specialists create value for the organization. The term *department* generally refers to these specialized functions, such as the marketing department or information systems department. At the functional level, the strategic direction becomes more specific and focused. So, just as there is a hierarchy of levels within organizations, there is also a hierarchy of strategic direction set by management at that level.

Marketing has a role at each of these organizational levels. In a larger corporation with multiple business units, the marketing department may be called upon to build a broad corporate image. It may also be called upon to provide comparative analyses of business unit market strengths and opportunities as part of a business portfolio analysis, which is covered later in the chapter. At the business level, the marketing department provides leadership for the other functional activities when applying the marketing concept. But it also must serve as part of a team of functional specialists that develops and implements actual programs at the functional level, which is why cross-functional teams are so vital in today's competitive world. To help develop these programs, the marketing department conducts marketing research and competitive evaluations to identify strategic marketing issues. Armed with an understanding of the marketplace, the marketing department then identifies key target markets and develops specific programs to serve them.

Strategy at the Corporate Level

Complex organizations such as Coca-Cola, Kraft General Foods, and Alcan Aluminium must ask themselves not just what *business* they are in but what *portfolio of businesses* they are in. As shown in Figure 2-1, this portfolio of businesses is often coordinated with a corporate strategy consisting of a common corporate vision, common goals, and a common philosophy that unites them. We will define these terms carefully, but, in actual practice, the terms are not used rigorously and often overlap.

Developing the corporate vision   A **corporate vision** is a clear word picture of the organization's future, often with an inspirational theme. It sets the overall direction for the organization, describing what it strives to be—stretching the organization, but not beyond the imagination. Even though the terms are often used interchangeably, a vision is something to be pursued, while a mission (discussed later) is something to be accomplished. Ideally, this vision is a short statement that can inspire employees, investors, and customers.

   Gulf Canada's vision is to be "one of the world's preeminent oil and gas companies." Similarly, Coca-Cola's vision is simple but effective: "to put a Coke within arm's reach of every consumer in the world."[4] For Coca-Cola this vision really does include the entire world. In fact, in order to make this vision a reality, Coca-Cola actually eliminated the very concept of "domestic" and "international" operating units. With less than 25 percent of its revenues from North American sales, Coca-Cola seems to be actively pursuing its Coke within-an-arm's-reach-of-every-consumer's vision.[5]

Setting corporate goals   Broadly speaking, a **goal** is a targeted level of performance set in advance of work.[6] Therefore, corporate goals provide strategic performance targets that the entire organization must reach to pursue its vision. Several different types of goals have been identified that business firms can pursue, each of which has some strengths and limitations:

- *Profit.* Classic economic theory assumes a firm seeks to maximize long-run profit, achieving as high a financial return on its investment as possible. One difficulty with this is what is meant by *long run.* A year? Five years? Twenty years? Barbara Thomas, president of Pillsbury Canada, for example, set a five-year goal for the company, referred to as Vision 2000, which calls for the company to triple profits by the end of this decade.[7]
- *Sales revenue.* If profits are acceptable, a firm may elect to maintain or increase its sales level even though profitability may not be maximized. Increased sales revenue may gain promotions for key executives.
- *Market share.* A firm may choose to maintain or increase its market share, sometimes at the expense of greater profits if industry status or prestige is at stake. **Market share** is the ratio of sales revenue of the firm to the total sales revenue of all firms in the industry, including the firm itself.
- *Unit sales.* Sales revenue may be deceiving because of the effects of inflation, so a firm may choose to maintain or increase the number of units it sells, such as cars, cases of breakfast cereal, or TV sets.
- *Quality.* A firm may emphasize the need to maintain or improve the quality of its products and services, especially if quality has been poor in the past.
- *Employee welfare.* A firm may recognize the critical importance of its employees by having an explicit goal stating its commitment to good employment opportunities and working conditions for them.

ETHICS AND SOCIAL RESPONSIBILITY ALERT

THE GLOBAL DILEMMA: HOW TO ACHIEVE SUSTAINABLE DEVELOPMENT

Corporate executives and world leaders are increasingly asked to address the issue of "sustainable development," a term that involves having each country find an ideal balance between protecting its environment and providing its citizens with the additional goods and services necessary to maintain and improve their standard of living.

Eastern Europe and the nations of the former Soviet Union provide an example. Tragically, poisoned air and dead rivers are the legacies of seven decades of communist rule. With more than half of the households of many of these nations below the poverty level, should the immediate goal be a cleaner environment or more food, clothing, housing, and consumer goods? What should the heads of these governments do? What should Western nations do to help? What should Western firms trying to enter these new, growing markets do?

Should the environment or economic growth come first? What are the societal trade-offs?

- *Social responsibility.* A firm may respond to advocates of corporate responsibility and seek to balance conflicting goals of consumers, employees, and shareholders to promote overall welfare of all these groups, even at the expense of profits.

Many private organizations that do not seek profits also exist in Canada. Examples are museums, symphony orchestras, operas, and research institutes. These organizations strive to provide goods or services to consumers with the greatest efficiency and the least cost. The nonprofit organization's survival depends on its meeting the needs of the consumers it serves. Although technically not falling under the definition of "nonprofit organization," government agencies also perform marketing activities in trying to achieve their goal of serving the public good. Such organizations include all levels of federal, provincial, and local government as well as special groups such as city schools, public universities, and public hospitals. As discussed later, marketing is an important activity for nonprofit firms and government agencies, just as it is for profit-making businesses.

Developing a corporate philosophy and culture   An organization may also have a **corporate philosophy** that establishes the values and "rules of conduct" for running it.[8] Statements such as "respecting the dignity of all employees" or "being a good citizen of the local community" are examples of corporate philosophies. The Ethics and Social Responsibility Alert describes a critical corporate citizenship issue. An organization's **corporate culture** refers to a system of shared attitudes and behaviours held by the employees that distinguish it from other organizations. Firms around the world are frantically trying to change their corporate cultures in response to increased global competition. Hewlett-Packard, 3M, Sony and Motorola are well known for corporate cultures that stimulate innovation and new product development. As described later in the chapter, George Fisher, Kodak's chief operating officer, who came from Motorola, is working diligently to try to change Kodak's corporate philosophy and culture from one of red-tape review of every decision to one of risk taking and innovation. Similarly, when Khalil Barsoum took over the helm of IBM Canada one of his top priorities was to continue the process of transforming the old bureaucratic IBM into a more responsive entrepreneurial culture. And, Bobbi Gaunt is not only the first woman to run Ford of Canada, she is also a savvy marketer who is reaffirming Ford's customer-oriented philosophy.[9]

CONCEPT CHECK

1. What are the three levels in today's large organizations?

2. What is the difference between corporate vision and corporate goals?

Strategy at the Business Unit Level

The strategic direction for each business unit spells out how it will help the organization accomplish its vision. This business unit strategy has three major components: mission, business unit goals, and competencies. Each component is critical and must be understood if marketing activities are to be relevant.

Defining the business unit's mission   This is probably the best-known mission statement anywhere:

> To explore strange new worlds, to seek out new life and new civilizations, to boldly go where no one has gone before.

This is the five-year mission for the Starship Enterprise, as Gene Roddenberry wrote in the "Star Trek" adventure series. The "business unit goals" of the Starship Enterprise vary with each trip, but the competencies centre on advanced technology, strong leadership, and a skilled crew. All these contribute to pursuing the vision of the Starship Enterprise's larger organization, the Federation.

The **business mission** (or **business unit mission**) is a statement that specifies the markets and product lines in which a business will compete. It affects the range of a firm's marketing activities by narrowing or broadening the competitive playing field. In other words, the mission determines the arena in which the business will compete. In many cases, the mission statement is often accompanied by a set of guiding principles that provide meaning and direction for both employees and customers. An example of a mission statement and guiding principles is shown in Figure 2-2. By clearly defining the business mission, marketing activities can be more focused and effective. Moreover, for a business to remain focused and effective, missions must often be redefined as the business itself and/or market conditions change over time.

Specifying the business unit's goals   A **business unit goal** is a performance target the business unit seeks to reach in an effort to achieve its mission. Goals measure how well the mission is being accomplished. These goals must be balanced to form a consistent, achievable pattern and should address fundamental issues such as customer satisfaction, innovation, internal processes, and, of course, financial performance.[10] At IBM Canada, customer satisfaction goals are set and tracked the same as financial revenue figures. In fact, customer satisfaction goals are taken so seriously that a percentage of every employee's salary is based on achievement of the customer satisfaction goals set by the business units.[11]

FIGURE 2-2

MISSION AND GUIDING PRINCIPLES
OF THE HOLIDAY INN BURLINGTON

> The Holiday Inn Burlington is dedicated to providing quality hospitality product and service. Although we try to anticipate guest concerns before they arise, we understand that every customer is an individual who requires special attention. Therefore,
>
> If a customer has a need or want, we fill it.
>
> If a customer has a question, we find the answer.
>
> If a customer has a concern, we resolve it.
>
> If a customer is lost, we show them the way.

In many cases, business unit goals are called **objectives,** which are specific, measurable performance targets and deadlines. Because there is no consistency in the use of the terms *goals* and *objectives,* the terms are used interchangeably throughout this book.

The use of quantified performance measures and targets can be illustrated by an approach developed by the Boston Consulting Group (BCG), *business portfolio analysis,* that analyzes a firm's business units (called strategic business units, or SBUs, in the BCG analysis) as though they were a collection of separate investments.[12] While used at the business unit level here, this BCG analysis has also been applied at the product line or individual product or brand level. The popularity of this kind of portfolio analysis is shown by the fact that more than 75 percent of the largest firms in North America have used it in some form.

BCG, an internationally known management consulting firm, advises its clients to locate the position of its SBUs on a growth-share matrix (Figure 2-3). The vertical axis is the *market growth rate,* which is the annual rate of growth of the specific market or industry in which a given SBU is competing. This axis in the figure runs from 0 to 20 percent, although in practice it might run even higher. The axis has arbitrarily been divided at 10 percent into high-growth and low-growth areas.

The horizontal axis is the *relative market share,* defined as the sales of the SBU divided by the sales of the largest firm in the industry. A relative market share of 10x (at the left end of the scale) means that the SBU has 10 times the share of its largest competitor, whereas a share 0.1 × (at the right end of the scale) means it has only 10 percent of the sales of its largest competitor. The scale is logarithmic and is arbitrarily divided into high and low relative market shares at a value of 1x.

BCG has given specific names and descriptions to the four resulting quadrants in its growth-share matrix based on the amount of cash they generate for or require from the firm:

- Cash cows (lower-left quadrant) are SBUs that typically generate large amounts of cash, far more than they can invest profitably in their own product line. They have a dominant share of a slow-growth market and provide cash to pay large amounts of company overhead and to invest in other SBUs.

FIGURE 2-3

BOSTON CONSULTING GROUP GROWTH-SHARE MATRIX FOR A STRONG, DIVERSIFIED FIRM SHOWING SOME STRATEGIC PLANS

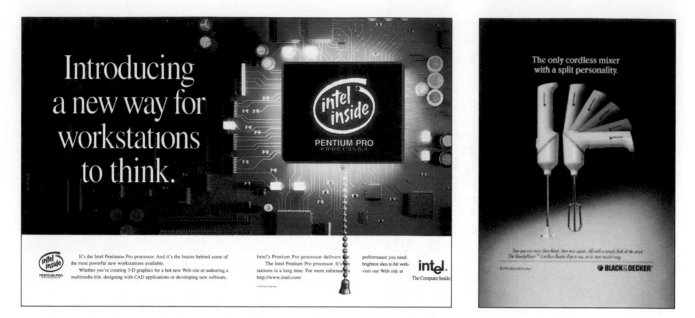

- Stars (upper-left quadrant) are SBUs with a high share of high-growth markets that may not generate enough cash to support their own demanding needs for future growth. When their growth slows, they are likely to become cash cows.
- Question marks or problem children (upper-right quadrant) are SBUs with a low share of high-growth markets. They require large injections of cash just to maintain their market share, much less increase it. Their name implies management's dilemma for these SBUs: choosing the right ones to invest in and phasing out the rest.
- Dogs (lower-right quadrant) are SBUs with a low share of low-growth markets. Although they may generate enough cash to sustain themselves, they do not hold the promise of ever becoming real winners for the firm. Dropping SBUs in this quadrant from a business portfolio is generally advocated except when relationships with other SBUs, competitive considerations, or potential strategic alliances exist.[13]

The 14 circles in Figure 2-3 show the current SBUs in a strong, diversified firm. The area of each circle is proportional to the corresponding SBU's annual sales revenue.

The portfolio in Figure 2-3 is a mixed one. On the favourable side, one-half of its SBUs are large and have high market shares, but, unfortunately, the other half are small with low market shares. Because most firms have limited influence on the market growth rate (the factor shown on the vertical axis), their main alternative in a growth-share matrix framework is to try to change the relative market share (the factor on the horizontal axis).

To accomplish this, management makes conscious decisions on what role each SBU should have in the future and either injects or removes cash from it. Four alternative strategies are available for each SBU. The firm can invest more in the SBU to *build* its share (SBU A in Figure 2-3). Or it can invest just enough to *hold* the SBU's share at about its current level (SBU B in the figure). Or it can *harvest* the SBU (SBU C in the figure), trying to milk its short-term cash flow even though it may lose share and become a dog in the longer run. Finally, the firm can *divest* the SBU (SBU D) by phasing it out or actually selling it to gain cash to invest in the remaining SBUs.

A COMPETITIVE ADVANTAGE FROM INNOVATION AND FAST CYCLE TIME. HEWLETT-PACKARD'S COMBINATION COLOUR PRINTER-COPIER.

The primary strengths of business portfolio analysis include (1) forcing a firm to assess each of its SBUs in terms of its relative market share and industry market growth rate, which, in turn, (2) requires the firm to forecast which SBUs will be cash producers and cash users in the future. Weaknesses are that (1) it is often difficult to get the information needed to locate each SBU on the growth-share matrix, (2) there are other important factors missing from the analysis such as possible synergies among the SBUs when they use the same salesforce or research and development facilities, and (3) there are problems in motivating people in an SBU that has been labelled a dog or even a cash cow and is unlikely to get new resources from the firm to grow and provide opportunities for promotion.[14] In addition, planners have had difficulty incorporating competitive information into portfolio analysis,[15] and formal experiments show the technique may not provide as effective an allocation of resources as more traditional methods of financial analysis.[16]

Specifying the business unit's competencies   Whereas the mission defines the scope of the business or business unit and the goals define its strategic performance dimensions, its **business unit competencies**—special capabilities resulting from its personnel, resources, or functional units—determine the means for achieving success.[17] These competencies should be distinctive enough to provide a **competitive advantage,** a unique strength relative to competitors, often based on quality, time, cost, innovation, or customer intimacy; knowing customers better than the competition and building a rock-solid relationship with those customers that the competition *cannot* break (see relationship marketing in Chapter 10).[18]

For example, if a firm such as 3M or Hewlett-Packard has a goal of generating a specific portion of its sales from new products, it must have a supporting competency

MARKETING NEWSNET

QUALITY AS A COMPETITIVE ADVANTAGE

Quality consultants see a quality strategy as the one solution for all organizations that want to become more competitive; some claim that quality is just as important as financial results or that it will lead to improved financial performance. A focus on quality has helped make Ford Motor Company ("Quality is Job One") more profitable and has helped propel the Ford Taurus to a best-seller. But a focus on quality has not had the same effect for General Motors' Saturn business unit. Why?

A study of 150 successful organizational turnarounds found that total quality management is not a cure-all and that typical TQM approaches have limited impact. It also noted that poor quality is only the fifth most important cause of business downturn or failure, following high costs, high debt, strategic errors, and bad investments.

Nonetheless, poor product and service quality can be competitive disadvantages, especially since customers to-

day often demand quality on a par with competition. This is a lesson the North American automobile industry has learned the hard way, and it explains why many organizations with past quality problems are inclined to pursue a quality strategy with an increased focus on their customers. However, a high cost structure or a bad strategy will not be saved by devotion to quality.

The experience with General Motors' Saturn business illustrates this. Saturn has focused on providing top value to the customers through low defects and excellent, low-pressure service. Unfortunately, Saturn has yet to make a profit after several years of operation, at least in part because of a high cost structure and a product that offers few benefits beyond the competitors' offerings. Successful organizations must emphasize quality—but not as a way to solve more fundamental strategic problems.

in research and development. It must also have a supportive competency to manufacture and market its new products in a timely and effective way. Hewlett-Packard has a truly competitive advantage with its fast cycle time, which allows it to bring innovative products to markets in large volume rapidly.[19] In fact, in the mid-1990s Hewlett-Packard reported that more than half its orders were for products introduced within the previous two years.[20] These topics are covered again in Chapters 11 and 22.

Another currently popular strategy is to develop a competency in total quality management (TQM). **Quality** here means those features and characteristics of a product that influence its ability to satisfy customer needs. Firms often try to improve quality or reduce new product cycles through **benchmarking**—discovering how others do something better than your own firm so you can imitate or leapfrog competition. Benchmarking often involves studying operations in completely different businesses. When General Mills sought ideas on how to reduce the time to convert its production lines from one cereal to another, it sent a team to observe the pit crews at the Indianapolis 500 race. The result: General Mills cut its plant change-over time by more than half.

If properly done, TQM—and the resulting high quality—can often serve as a competitive advantage because most firms have not yet adopted TQM. Also, there is evidence that the price of stocks of firms implementing a quality initiative perform slightly better than the stocks of firms that do not.[21] A note of caution, however, is that specific TQM practices of quality training, process improvement, and benchmarking may not produce a competitive advantage by themselves. Rather, more basic management competencies such as developing an open culture, empowering employees, and sustaining executive commitment must be present first. Such practices can produce an advantage, with or without a formal TQM effort, as explained in the Marketing NewsNet box.[22] Formal TQM activities can then complement these management factors to provide a further competitive advantage. This is the secret behind companies such as Ford, Motorola, and Xerox, who have gone beyond matching competitors' quality and are now using quality as a weapon themselves.

Strategy at the Functional Level

The functional departments, such as marketing, respond to the corporate and business strategic directions by creating functional goals, which are simply extensions of the corporate and business goals. At Sears, an example of a functional marketing goal is "to create a new image that emphasizes the soft side of merchandising." To accomplish functional goals requires program plans that spell out very specific marketing objectives with associated actions, responsibilities, and dates. An objective of the new Sears promotional program was to increase customer awareness about its new marketing efforts. Not only have most Canadians heard about the "Softer Side of Sears," many actually sing the new jingle!

However, marketing does not operate by itself in an organization. When Sears launched its "Soft Side" promotional program, financial specialists had to develop a funding program. Operation specialists were needed to remodel stores, and human resource specialists had to train sales associates to provide better service consistent with the new market position.

Successful marketing efforts today are really cross-functional team efforts involving specialists from all the functional units to analyze, implement, and control programs to accomplish the corporate and business strategic directions. The strategic marketing process described in the next section provides the framework for making this happen.

CONCEPT CHECK

    1. What is business portfolio analysis?

    2. What is a competitive advantage, and why is it important?

THE STRATEGIC MARKETING PROCESS

All approaches to planning try to find answers to these key questions:

    1. Where are we now?
    2. Where do we want to go?
    3. How do we allocate our resources to get to where we want to go?
    4. How do we convert our plans into actions?
    5. How do our results compare with our plans, and do deviations require new plans and actions?

This same approach is used in the **strategic marketing process,** whereby an organization allocates its marketing mix resources to reach its target markets. This process is divided into three phases: planning, implementation, and control (Figure 2-4).

The strategic marketing process is so central to the activities of most organizations that they formalize it as a **marketing plan,** which is a road map for the marketing activities of an organization for a specified future period of time, such as one year or five years. Appendix A at the end of this chapter provides guidelines for writing a marketing plan and also presents a sample marketing plan for Paradise Kitchens,® Inc., a firm that produces and distributes a line of spicy chilies under the Howlin' Coyote® brand name. The sequence of activities that follows parallels the elements of the marketing plan that appears in Appendix A.

FIGURE 2-4

THE STRATEGIC MARKETING PROCESS

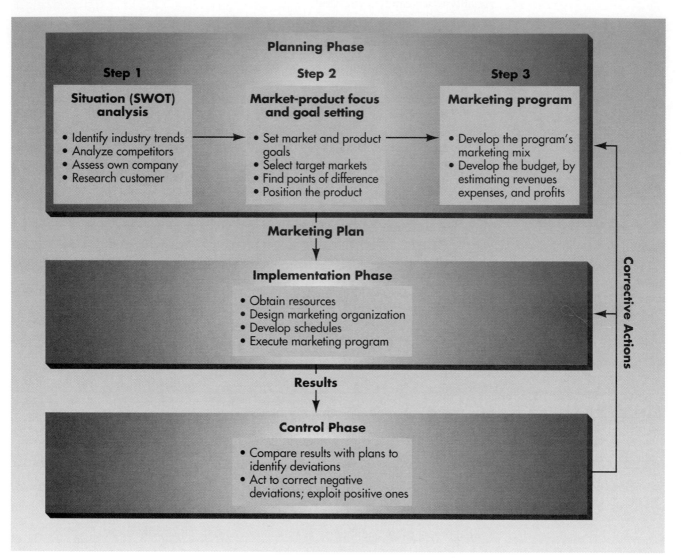

The following section gives an overview of the strategic marketing process that places Chapters 3 through 21 in perspective. In Chapter 22 we examine the strategic marketing process again in more depth.

Strategic Marketing Process: The Planning Phase

As shown in Figure 2-4, the planning phase of the strategic marketing process consists of the three steps shown at the top of the figure: (1) situation analysis, (2) market-product focus and goal setting, and (3) the marketing program. Let's use the recent marketing planning experiences of several companies to look at each of these steps.

Step 1: situation (SWOT) analysis   The essence of the **situation analysis** is taking stock of where the firm or product has been recently, where it is now, and where it is headed in light of the organization's plans and the external factors and trends affecting it. The situation analysis box in Figure 2-4 is the first of the three steps in the planning phase.

LOCATION OF FACTOR	TYPE OF FACTOR	
	FAVOURABLE	**UNFAVOURABLE**
Internal	**Strengths**	**Weaknesses**
	• Industry leader • Innovative, in products and design • Strong brand awareness • Strong position in sporting goods and specialty outlets	• Premium-priced position puts off the "value-conscious" consumer • Limited distribution in mass merchandising outlets.
External	**Opportunities**	**Threats**
	• Identify new market segments to serve • Develop a brand for the "value-conscious" consumer • Expand distribution globally • Expand accessories line	• Fierce competition at both the premium and low-end of market. • Brand name may become a generic term for in-line skates.

An effective short-hand summary of the situation analysis is a **SWOT analysis,** an acronym describing an organization's appraisal of its internal *s*trengths and *w*eaknesses and its external *o*pportunities and *t*hreats. Both the situation and SWOT analyses can be done at the level of the entire organization, the business unit, the product line, or the specific product. As an analysis moves from the level of the entire organization to the specific product, it, of course, gets far more detailed. For small firms or those with basically a single product line, an analysis at the firm or product level is really the same thing.

Remember Rollerblade, Inc. from Chapter 1? Figure 2-5 shows what a SWOT analysis might look like for that firm. Note that the SWOT table shown has four cells formed by the combination of internal and external factors (the rows) and favourable versus unfavourable factors (the columns) that summarize Rollerblade, Inc.'s strengths, weaknesses, opportunities, and threats.

A more in-depth SWOT analysis might use more detailed checklists of internal and external factors in the table. For example, internal factors might be broken down to include key elements such as products offered and the effectiveness of the functional areas such as sales or research and development (R&D) that affect marketing activities. Similarly, external factors are often formalized in the SWOT analysis by using the external or environmental factors affecting marketing activities, such as competition, consumer, or technological trends. An example of using these detailed breakdowns of internal and external factors appears in the Paradise Kitchens SWOT in Appendix A. For simplicity, the Rollerblade, Inc.'s SWOT does not contain this level of detail.

A SWOT analysis helps a firm identify the strategy-related factors in these four cells that can have a major effect on the firm. However, all factors in such an analysis are not of equal value, so the ultimate goal is to identify the *critical* factors affecting the firm and then build on vital strengths, correct glaring weaknesses, exploit significant opportunities, and avoid disaster-laden threats. That is a big order. This ultimate goal is not simply to develop the SWOT analysis but to translate the results of the analysis into specific actions to help the firm grow and succeed.

Although the SWOT analysis is a shorthand look at the situation analysis, it is based on an exhaustive study of the four areas shown in Figure 2-4 that are the foundation on which the firm builds its marketing program:

• Identifying trends in the firm's industry.
• Analyzing the firm's competitors.
• Assessing the firm itself.
• Researching the firm's present and prospective customers.

MARKETS	PRODUCTS	
	CURRENT	NEW
Current	**Market Penetration** Selling more in-line skates to Canadians	**Product Development** Selling a new product like its Bladerunner brand to the "value-conscious" consumer
New	**Market Development** Selling in-line skates in Australia	**Diversification** Selling in-line skating accessories like helmets and clothing, or entering into the bicycle business

Examples of more in-depth analysis in these four areas appear in the marketing plan in Appendix A and the chapters in this text cited in that plan.

One way for firms to utilize the SWOT results and exhaustive study of their industry, competitors, own firm, and customers is to assess market-product strategies. Four such strategies representing the four combinations of (1) current and new markets and (2) current and new products appear in Figure 2-6.

As Rollerblade, Inc. attempts to increase sales revenue, it must consider all four of the alternative market-product strategies shown in Figure 2-6. For example, it can try to use a strategy of *market penetration*—increasing sales of present products in existing markets, in this case by increasing sales of its present in-line skates to Canadian consumers. There is no change in either the product line or the market served, but increased sales are possible through actions such as better advertising, lower prices, or expanded distribution in retail outlets.

Market development, which for Rollerblade, Inc. means selling existing Rollerblade Inc.'s products to new markets, is a reasonable alternative. Australia and Western European consumers are good candidates as possible new markets.

An expansion strategy using *product development* involves selling a new product to existing markets. Figure 2-6 shows that Rollerblade, Inc. could sell a new product like its Bladerunner in-line skate for the "value-conscious" consumer. One problem with this strategy is the possibility of *product cannibalism*—a firm's new product gaining sales by stealing them from its other products. For example, Rollerblade, Inc.'s new Bladerunner in-line skate was added to the product line to increase overall sales, not to take away from sales of existing products.

Diversification involves developing new products and selling them in new markets. This is potentially a high-risk strategy for most firms because the company has neither previous production experience nor marketing experience on which to draw. However, there are varying degrees of diversification. *Related diversification* occurs when new products and markets have something in common with existing operations. For example, Rollerblade, Inc. sells in-line skating accessories including helmets and clothing. *Unrelated diversification* means that the new products and markets have nothing in common with existing operations. In this case, Rollerblade, Inc. might diversify into a completely new area such as the bicycle business.

Step 2: market-product focus and goal setting   Finding a focus on what product offerings will be directed toward which customers (step 2 of the planning phase in Figure 2-4) is essential for developing an effective marketing program (step 3). This focus often comes from the firm's using **market segmentation,** which involves aggregating prospective buyers into groups, or segments, that (1) have common needs and (2) will respond similarly to a marketing action. Ideally a firm can use market segmentation to identify the segments on which it will focus its efforts—its target market segments—and develop one or more marketing programs to reach them.

Goal setting here involves setting measurable marketing objectives to be achieved, possibly for a specific market, a specific product or brand, or an entire marketing program. As mentioned earlier, there is a hierarchy of goals and objectives flowing from the corporate strategy set by top management on down to the levels of the marketing managers.

We can illustrate steps 2 and 3 in the planning phase of the strategic marketing process by using the Paradise Kitchens® marketing plan from Appendix A. This firm is trying to expand its line of Howlin' Coyote® spicy chilies from 3 to 20 metropolitan markets during the last half of the 1990s. Stated simply, the five-year marketing plan for Paradise Kitchens specifies these step 2 activities:

- *Set marketing and product goals.* As mentioned later in Chapter 11, the chances of new product success are increased by specifying both market and product goals. Paradise Kitchens® will grow its present markets by expanding brands and flavours, add 17 new metropolitan markets in the next five years, enter the food-service market, and add new products.
- *Select target markets.* Howlin' Coyote® chilies will be targeted at one- to three-person households with annual incomes above $30 000 in which both adults are likely to work outside the home—adventurous consumers wanting premium-quality Mexican food products.
- *Find points of difference.* **Points of difference** are those characteristics of a product that make it superior to competitive substitutes. (Chapter 11 points out that this is the single-most important factor in the success or failure of a new product.) For Howlin' Coyote® chilies these are unique spicy taste; quality, convenience, and a range of flavours; and premium packaging.

FIGURE 2-7

ELEMENTS OF THE MARKETING MIX
THAT COMPOSE A COHESIVE
MARKETING PROGRAM

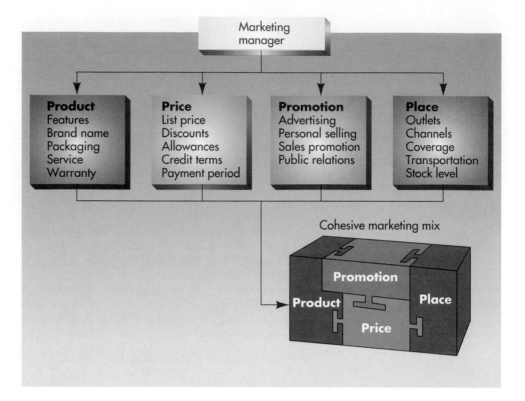

• *Position the product.* Howlin' Coyote® chilies will be "positioned" in consumers' minds as "very high-quality, authentic Mexican tasting chilies that can be prepared easily and quickly."

Details in these four elements of step 2 provide a solid foundation to use in developing the marketing program—the next step in the planning phase of the strategic marketing process.

Step 3: marketing program Activities in step 2 tell the marketing manager which customers to target and which customer needs the firm's product offerings can satisfy—the *who* and *what* aspects of the strategic marketing process. The *how* aspect, step 3 in the planning phase, involves developing the program's marketing mix and its budget.

Figure 2-7 shows components of each marketing mix element that are combined to provide a cohesive marketing program. For the five-year marketing plan of Paradise Kitchens, these marketing mix activities include the following:

• *Product strategy.* Offer a current line of five Howlin' Coyote® chilies with proprietary flavouring, high-quality ingredients without preservatives, and distinctive packaging that communicates the brand's uniqueness.
• *Price strategy.* Price Howlin' Coyote® chili at $2.89 for a 300 g package, comparable to other frozen offerings and higher than the canned and dried chili varieties.
• *Promotion strategy.* Feature in-store demonstrations to highlight the product's unique qualities, recipes using the brand to stimulate use, and various kinds of cents-off coupons to generate trial and repeat-purchase of the brand.
• *Place (distribution) strategy.* Use food distributors with current sales volumes, shifting to brokers as increased sales volumes justify them.

Putting this marketing program into effect requires that the firm commit time and money to it in the form of a budget. The budgeting process starts with a sales forecast based on estimates of units expected to be sold—probably by month, quarter, and year.

Estimated expenses for the marketing mix activities comprising the marketing program are estimated and balanced against expected revenues to estimate the program's profitability. This budget is really the "sales" document presented to top management to gain approval for the budgeted resources to implement the marketing program.

CONCEPT CHECK

1. What is the difference between a strength and an opportunity in a SWOT analysis?
2. If Rollerblade, Inc. attempts to enter Australia with its in-line skates, which market-product strategy would it be using?
3. What is market segmentation?

Strategic Marketing Process: The Implementation Phase

As shown in Figure 2-4, the result of the tens or hundreds of hours spent in the planning phase of the strategic marketing process is the firm's marketing plan. Implementation, the second phase of the strategic marketing process, involves carrying out the marketing plan that emerges from the planning phase. If the firm cannot put the marketing plan into effect—in the implementation phase—the planning phase was a waste of time. Figure 2-4 also shows the four components of the implementation phase: (1) obtaining resources, (2) designing the marketing organization, (3) developing schedules, and (4) actually executing the marketing program designed in the planning phase. Eastman Kodak provides a case example of a firm facing both the implementation and control phases of the strategic marketing process.

Kodak has been known as a rather bureaucratic, paternalistic, slow-moving, and isolated company. But changes have occurred and continue to occur at Kodak. The agent of change is George Fisher, its chief executive officer, who gave up a similar job at spectacularly successful Motorola to try to move Kodak's little yellow boxes and new technologies into the twenty-first century. His early decisions are classic management and marketing lessons in implementing and controlling the activities of a corporate giant.

Obtaining resources   When George Fisher arrived at Kodak, he observed, "There are textbook types of things that are wrong with this company. Decisions are too slow. People don't take risks."[23] So he pushed some revolutionary and, to him, obvious decisions:

- Focus on Kodak's core business: imaging.
- Serve customer needs better and stress quality.
- Shorten product-development cycles.
- Encourage a more dynamic, risk-taking, fast-decision culture.

Fisher needed financial resources to implement these ideas, however, so he sold or spun off Kodak's health, household-products, and chemicals businesses. The $6 billion he got for these sales provided the resources to enable Kodak to try to implement its strategy to grow its core imaging business.

Designing the marketing organization   A marketing program needs a marketing organization to implement it. This is especially true for firms such as Kodak which face constantly changing global markets. Figure 2-8 shows the organization chart of a typical manufacturing firm, giving some details of the marketing department's structure. Four managers of marketing activities are shown to report to the vice president of marketing: product planning, marketing research, sales, and adver-

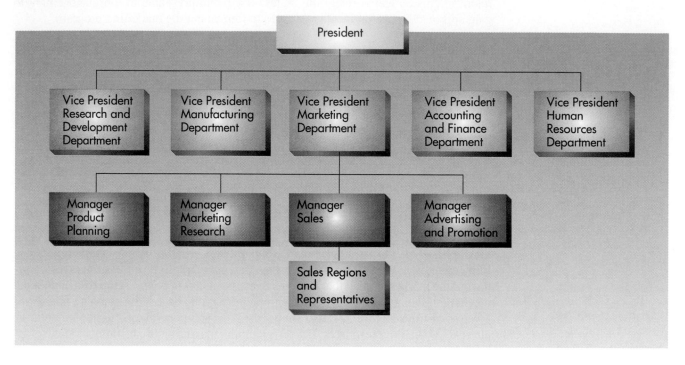

tising and promotion. Depending on the size of the organization, there may be several product planning managers, each responsible for a separate product line. Also, several regional sales managers and an international sales manager may report to the manager of sales. This marketing organization is responsible for converting marketing plans to reality.

Developing schedules   One key to effective implementation is setting deadlines, which are supported by schedules of important milestones that make the deadlines achievable. "Half the people in the world have yet to take their first picture," says Fisher. So he sees huge opportunities for Kodak in global developing markets and in digital imaging technologies that may replace film in many applications. In 1994 he set these deadlines:

- Introduce Kodak CopyPrint Stations in July 1995. Benefiting from Kodak's digital imaging technology, you can blow up your tiny 20-year-old snapshot (*not* the negative, which you've lost!) into a surprisingly clear 4 × 6 or 8 × 10 enlargement.[24]
- Introduce sleek, improved, single-use camera by spring 1995.
- Relaunch Photo CD (for compact disc) System in March 1995, this time targeting desktop computer users.
- Introduce the Advanced Photographic System (APS), a "smart" film and camera, by the end of 1996 that will store information such as shutter speed as each picture is taken, thereby improving print quality.
- Set up improved distribution networks in emerging countries such as China, Russia, India, and Brazil.

To make sure his managers meet the targets in these schedules, Fisher devised a new management compensation structure to tie salary more closely to performance.

Executing the marketing program   Without effective execution, marketing plans are meaningless pieces of paper. Effective execution requires attention to detail for both marketing strategies and marketing tactics. A **marketing strategy** is the means by which a marketing goal is achieved, usually characterized by a specified target market and a marketing program to reach it. Although the term *strategy* is often used loosely, it implies both the end sought (target market) and the means to achieve it (marketing program).

To implement a marketing program successfully, hundreds of detailed decisions are required, about matters such as advertising copy or the amount for temporary price reductions. These decisions, called **marketing tactics,** are detailed day-to-day operational decisions essential to the overall success of marketing strategies. Compared with marketing strategies, marketing tactics generally involve actions that must be taken right away. We cannot cover many aspects of marketing tactics in detail in a book of this size, and the emphasis here is on marketing strategy—the strategic marketing process. Here are examples of both kinds of decisions Fisher made at Kodak:[25]

- Marketing strategy decision: develop a strategic partnership with five Japanese companies (including Fuji, Canon, and Nikon) to develop its smart film and camera—the Advanced Photographic System.
- Marketing tactics decision: assign 10 newly formed teams the responsibility of studying issues such as cycle-time improvement to squeeze excessive time and costs out of Kodak's bloated, slow-moving, new product development process.

Issues that surface at the marketing tactics level can become marketing strategy or corporate strategy issues. There are no precise lines between marketing strategies and marketing tactics because one shades into the other. Clearly, however, effective marketing program implementation requires excruciating concern for details in both marketing strategies and marketing tactics.

Strategic Marketing Process: The Control Phase

The control phase of the strategic marketing process seeks to keep the marketing program moving in the direction set for it (see Figure 2-4). Accomplishing this requires the marketing manager (1) to compare the results of the marketing program with the goals in the written plans to identify deviations and (2) to act on these deviations, correcting negative deviations and exploiting positive ones.

FIGURE 2-9

EVALUATION AND CONTROL OF
KODAK'S MARKETING PROGRAM

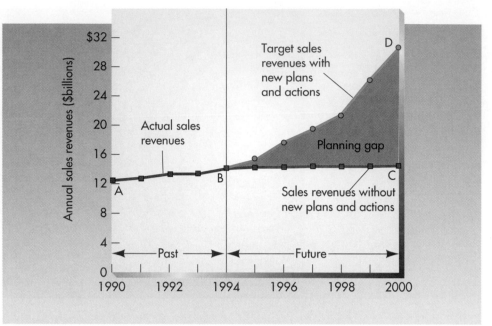

Comparing results with plans to identify deviations   In early 1995, shortly after George Fisher took over at Kodak, he wanted to set sales targets for the company through the end of the decade. As Fisher looked at the company's sales revenues (from continuing operations) from 1990 through 1994, he didn't like what he saw: the very flat trend, or AB in Figure 2-9. Technological innovations such as digital cameras were redefining the entire amateur photographic market. Also, Fuji was giving far greater competition in Kodak's traditional film and photographic markets than expected. These and other factors were inhibiting Kodak's growth opportunities.

Extending the 1990–1994 trend to the end of the century (BC in Figure 2-9) showed flat sales revenues, a totally unacceptable, no-growth strategy. Fisher announced that, in the five years following 1995, his goal for Kodak was to double its return on assets. Applying this same annual growth rate to sales revenue gives the target sales revenue line through the year 2000, shown as BD in Figure 2-9. This reveals a huge wedge-shaped shaded gap in the figure. Planners call this the *planning gap,* the difference between the projection of the path to reach a new goal (line BD) and the projection of the path of the results of a plan already in place (line BC).

This target goal is actually set earlier in the strategic marketing process, in the planning phase. The ultimate purpose of the firm's marketing program is to "fill in" this planning gap, in Kodak's case, to move its future sales revenue line from the essentially no-growth line BC up to the challenging high-growth target of line BD.

Having a challenging series of quantified annual sales revenue targets is not enough. Poor performance of Kodak or intense competition could result in actual sales revenues being far less than the targeted levels. This is the essence of evaluation—comparing actual results with planned objectives.

Acting on deviations   When the evaluation shows that actual performance is not up to expectations, a corrective action is usually needed to adjust and improve the program and help it achieve the planned objective. In contrast, comparing results with plans may sometimes reveal that actual performance is far better than the plan called for. In this case the marketing manager wants to uncover the reason for the good performance and act to exploit it.

After only a few months on the job, Fisher recognized the vital importance of fast action and moving new, high-quality Kodak products into the marketplace. This is the

KODAK IS BETTING ON ITS DIGITAL
IMAGING TECHNOLOGIES TO HELP
FILL ITS PLANNING GAP.

reason for the flurry of new and upgraded products released by Kodak in 1995 and
1996. Effective control at Kodak, and all organizations, requires that deviations not
only be identified but that positive deviations be exploited and negative ones be corrected. Two recent Kodak "mid-course corrections" to act on deviations from targets
illustrate these principles:

- *Exploiting a positive deviation.* The Kodak CopyPrint Stations found spectacular consumer acceptance in enlarging small prints quickly and easily. Kodak
  exploited this success by not only installing several thousand of these machines
  around the world but by quickly designing and introducing even more sophisticated do-it-yourself machines for use by consumers in their local photo
  shops.[26]
- *Correcting a negative deviation.* The Photo CD System utilizing Kodak's digital imaging technologies did not gain the consumer acceptance expected, so
  Kodak upgraded its design and relaunched the product, this time targeting
  desktop computer users.[27]

The strategic marketing process is discussed in greater detail again in Chapter 22.

CONCEPT CHECK

1. What is the control phase of the strategic marketing process?
2. How do the objectives set for a marketing program in the planning phase
   relate to the control phase of the strategic marketing process?

SUMMARY

1. Today's large organizations, both business firms and nonprofit organizations, are often divided into three levels. These
levels are, from highest to lowest, the corporate, business unit,
and functional levels.

2. At the highest level, corporate strategy involves setting the
strategic direction for the entire organization, using statements
of corporate vision, corporate goals, and corporate philosophy
and culture.

3. At the business unit level, direction comes from the business unit's mission, goals, and competencies. Concepts such as portfolio analysis, competitive advantage, total quality management, and benchmarking help the business unit achieve its mission and goals.

4. Strategy and direction at the functional level come from having the marketing department work closely with other functional units, such as manufacturing and finance, to achieve the vision, mission, and goals coming from all three organizational levels.

5. The strategic marketing process involves an organization allocating its marketing mix resources to reach its target markets. It has three phases: planning, implementation, and control.

6. The planning phase of the strategic marketing process has three steps, each with more specific elements: situation (SWOT) analysis, market-product focus and goal setting, and marketing program.

7. The implementation phase of the strategic marketing process has four key elements: obtaining resources, designing the marketing organization, developing schedules, and executing the marketing program.

8. The control phase of the strategic marketing process involves comparing results with the planned targets to identify deviations and taking actions to correct negative deviations and exploit positive ones.

KEY TERMS

profit p. 30
corporate level p. 30
business unit p. 31
business unit level p. 31
functional level p. 31
corporate vision p. 32
goal p. 32
market share p. 32
corporate philosophy p. 33
corporate culture p. 33
business (unit) mission p. 34
business unit goal p. 34
objectives p. 35

business unit competencies p. 37
competitive advantage p. 37
quality p. 38
benchmarking p. 38
strategic marketing process p. 39
marketing plan p. 39
situation analysis p. 40
SWOT analysis p. 41
market segmentation p. 42
points of difference p. 43
marketing strategy p. 47
marketing tactics p. 47

CHAPTER PROBLEMS AND APPLICATIONS

1. (*a*) Explain what a vision statement is. (*b*) Using Coca-Cola as an example from the chapter, explain how it gives a strategic direction to its organization. (*c*) Create a vision statement for your own career.

2. (*a*) How might top management try to change the "corporate culture" of its organization? (*b*) What has George Fisher done at Kodak to change its corporate culture?

3. Using the mission statement shown in Figure 2-2 as a guide, write a plausible mission statement for: (*a*) your college or university's business school and (*b*) Air Canada.

4. Why does a product often start as a question mark and then move counterclockwise around BCG's growth-share matrix shown in Figure 2-3?

5. What organizational or business unit competencies best describe (*a*) your college or university, (*b*) your favourite restaurant, and (*c*) the company that manufactures the computer you own or use most often?

6. What is the main result of each of the three phases of the strategic marketing process? (*a*) planning, (*b*) implementation, and (*c*) control.

7. Select one strength, one weakness, one opportunity, and one threat from the SWOT analysis for Rollerblade, Inc. shown in Figure 2-5, and suggest a specific possible action that might result.

8. Many Canadian liberal arts universities have traditionally offered an undergraduate degree in liberal arts (the product) to full-time 18- to 22-year-old students (the market). How might such a university use the four market-product expansion strategies shown in Figure 2-6 to compete in the year 2000?

9. The goal-setting step in the planning phase of the strategic marketing process sets quantified objectives for use in the control phase. What actions are suggested for a marketing manager if measured results are below objectives? Above objectives?

10. Read Appendix A, "A Sample Marketing Plan." Then develop a table of contents for the Paradise Kitchens marketing plan to the level of (*a*) A-level headings and (*b*) B-level headings. (*c*) Write a 600-word executive summary for the marketing plan using the numbered headings shown in the plan.

CASE 2-1   Specialized Bicycle Components, Inc.

The speaker leans forward with both intensity and pride in his voice. "We're in the business of creating a bike that delivers to customers the best possible ride," he explains. "When the customer sees our red 'S,' they say this is the company that understands the cyclist. It's a company of riders. The products they make are the rider's products." The speaker is Chris Murphy, Director of Marketing for Specialized Bicycle Components, Inc.—or just "Specialized" to serious riders.

THE COMPANY

Specialized was founded in 1974 by Mike Sinyard, a cycling enthusiast who sold his VW van for the $1500 startup capital. Mike started out importing hard-to-find "specialized" bike components, but the company began to produce its own bike parts by 1976. Specialized introduced the first major production mountain bike to the world in 1980, revolutionizing the bike industry, and since then has maintained a reputation as the technological leader in the bike and bike accessory market. In fact, since the company's founding, its formal mission statement has remained unchanged: "To give everyone the best ride of their life!"

You probably recognize the Stumpjumper and the Rockhopper, both made by Specialized, as two of the most popular mountain bikes today. The company continues to innovate, with its introduction of a European-style city bike, the Globe. It also sells road bikes and an extensive line of bike accessories, including helmets, water bottles, jerseys, and shoes. As Chris says, "The customer is buying the ride from us, not just the bike."

The first professional mountain bike racing team was created by Specialized in 1983, and Ned Overland, the Team Specialized captain, became the first-ever world champion. Specialized also counts Ned as one of its design consultants. The company banks on the perception, and reality, that this race-proven technology trickles down to the entire line of Specialized bikes and products.

THE ENVIRONMENT

The bike market is driven by innovation and technology, and with the market becoming more crowded and competitive, the fight for the consumer is intense. Specialized divides the bike market into two categories: (1) the independent retailer, and (2) the end-user consumer. While its focus in designing the product is on the end-user consumer, it only sells directly to the retailer, and realizes a strong relationship with the dealers is a key factor for success.

The end-user consumer is broken down into two target age groups: the 18–25 year old college or university students and the 30–40 year old professional "techies." To differentiate itself from the rest of the market, Specialized positions itself as the innovator in mountain bikes—its models are what the rest of the industry imitates.

Mountain bikes account for approximately two-thirds of total industry bike sales, with road bikes accounting for the other third. The sport of mountain biking experienced a huge surge from 1989 to 1993, but in 1994 sales began to flatten. Does Chris believe this trend will hurt Specialized? "We believe we will see growth in the next six or seven years as the entry level participants trade up—trade their lower end bikes for higher end bikes," he explains.

Specialized began cultivating what was to become an extensive global distribution network as early as 1982. It now boasts subsidiaries in twenty-five countries in Asia, North America, South America, Europe, and Australia, enabling the red "S" to become a symbol of performance-driven products around the world.

THE ISSUES

How can Specialized stay at the forefront of an industry that now includes more than twenty manufacturers? Strategic placement in the marketplace is one way.

Specialized recently designed its own server, the World Ride Web, on the Internet (www.specialized.com/bikes/). The web site offers international mountain bike trail and road bike trail directories, e-mail access to Specialized engineers, a trail preservation network, and a dealer directory that connects users directly to dealer homepages, in addition to the standard product information. Specialized's new bike, the Globe, appeared on *Seinfeld* and was on display in Gap clothing stores. Specialized believes these nontraditional promotional strategies are helping to keep the Specialized name on the cutting edge and in front of the end-user consumer.

Targeting its other market segment, the dealers, Specialized launched a "Best Ride Tour." It loaded up trailers full of the new models and visited over 30 cities enabling retailers and shop employees to test ride the bikes they will be ordering for the coming year—"Ride Before You Buy."

Specialized is also eager to become involved in joint ventures to keep its technological edge. In 1989 it released the Composite wheel, which was a joint venture between Specialized and Du Pont. The wheel is so aerodynamic it actually saves a rider more than ten minutes over a 160-kilometre ride. Specialized also entered into a distribution relationship with GripShift in 1994, allowing the high-end gear manufacturer access to its extensive dealer network. Why is this beneficial to Specialized? It's another way to support the dealers by providing a top-notch product for its customers that Specialized can support in its marketing efforts.

Specialized sponsors races, provides racer support teams, initiates mountain biking safety programs, and is involved in trail-access advocacy groups all over the world. But, as it was in Specialized's early years, Mike sees a commitment to top quality and design as the most important factor for future success: "Even though we've been around for 20 years, this company still feels like it has something to prove. I expect it will always be that way."

Questions

These questions focus on the three steps of the planning phase of the strategic marketing process.

1. Do a SWOT analysis for Specialized. Use Figure 2-5 in Chapter 2 and Figure 1 in Appendix A as guides. In assessing internal factors (strengths and weaknesses), use the material provided in the case. In assessing external factors (opportunities and threats) augment the case material with what you see happening in the bicycle industry.

2. As part of Step 2 of the planning phase, and using your SWOT analysis, select target markets on which you might focus for present and potential bikers.

3. As part of Step 3 of the planning phase and using your answers in questions 1 and 2 above, outline Specialized's marketing programs for the target market segments you chose.

A Sample Marketing Plan

"New ideas are a dime a dozen," observes Arthur R. Kydd, "and so are new products and new technologies." Kydd should know. As chief executive officer of St. Croix Venture Partners, he and his firm have provided the seed money and venture capital to launch more than 60 startup firms in the last 25 years. Today those firms have more than 5000 employees.

Kydd elaborates:

> I get 200 to 300 marketing and business plans a year to look at, and St. Croix provides startup financing for only two or three. What sets a potentially successful idea, product, or technology apart from all the rest is markets and marketing. If you have a real product with a distinctive point of difference that satisfies the needs of customers, you may have a winner. And you get a real feel for this in a well-written marketing or business plan.[1]

This appendix (1) describes what marketing and business plans are, including their purposes and guidelines in writing effective plans, and (2) provides a sample marketing plan.

MARKETING PLANS AND BUSINESS PLANS

After explaining the meanings, purposes, and audiences of marketing plans and business plans, this section describes some writing guidelines for them and what external funders often look for in successful plans.

Marketing and Business Plans: Meanings, Purposes, and Audiences

A *marketing plan* is a road map for the marketing activities of an organization for a specified future period of time, such as one year or five years.[2] It is important to note that no single "generic" marketing plan applies to all organizations and all situations. Rather, the specific format for a marketing plan for an organization depends on the following:

- *The target audience and purpose.* Elements included in a particular marketing plan depend heavily on (1) who the audience is and (2) what its purpose is. A marketing plan for an internal audience seeks to point the direction for future marketing activities and is sent to all individuals in the organization who must implement the plan or who will be affected by it. If the plan is directed to an external audience, such as friends, banks, venture capitalists, or potential investors, for the purpose of raising capital, it has the additional function of being an important sales document. In this case it contains elements such as the strategic plan/focus, organization, and biographies of key personnel that would rarely appear in an internal marketing plan. Also, the financial information is far more detailed when the plan is used to raise capital.
- *The kind and complexity of the organization.* A small restaurant serving a local market has a somewhat different marketing plan than Nestlé, which serves international markets. The restaurant's plan would be relatively simple and directed at serving customers in a local market. In Nestlé's case, because there is a hierarchy of marketing plans, various levels of detail would be used, such as the entire organization, the business unit, or the product line.
- *The industry.* Both the restaurant serving a local market and Medtronic, selling heart pacemakers globally, analyze competition. Not only are their geographic thrusts far different, but the complexities of their offerings and, hence, the time periods likely to be covered by their plans also differ. A one-year marketing plan may be adequate for the restaurant, but Medtronic may need a five-year planning horizon because product-development cycles for complex, new medical devices may be three or four years.

In contrast to a marketing plan, a *business plan* is a road map for the entire organization for a specified future period of time, such as one year or five years.[3] A key difference between a marketing plan and a business plan is that the business plan contains details on the research and development (R&D)/operations/manufacturing activities of the organization. Even for a manufacturing business, the marketing plan is probably 60 or 70 percent of the entire business plan. For businesses like a small restaurant or auto repair shop, their marketing and business plans are virtually identical.

The Most-Asked Questions by Outside Audiences

Lenders and prospective investors reading a business or marketing plan that is used to seek new capital are probably the toughest audiences to satisfy. Their most-asked questions include the following:

1. Is the business or marketing idea valid?
2. Is there something unique or distinctive about the product or service that separates it from substitutes and competitors?
3. Is there a clear market for the product or service?
4. Are the financial projections realistic and healthy?
5. Are the key management and technical personnel capable, and do they have a track record in the industry in which they must compete?
6. Does the plan clearly describe how those providing capital will get their money back and make a profit?

Rhonda M. Abrahms, author of *The Successful Business Plan,* observes that "within the first five minutes of reading your . . . plan, readers, must perceive that the answers to these questions are favourable."[4] While her comments apply to plans seeking to raise capital, the first five questions just listed apply equally well to plans for internal audiences.

Writing and Style Suggestions

There are no magic one-size-fits-all guidelines for writing successful marketing and business plans. Still, the following writing and style guidelines generally apply:[5]

- Use a direct, professional writing style. Use appropriate business terms without jargon. Present and future tenses with active voice are generally better than past tense and passive voice.
- Be positive and specific to convey potential success. At the same time, avoid superlatives ("terrific," "wonderful,"). Specifics are better than glittering generalities. Use numbers for impact, justifying projections with reasonable quantitative assumptions, where possible.
- Use bullet points for succinctness and emphasis. As with the list you are reading, bullets enable key points to be highlighted effectively and with great efficiency.
- Use "A-level" (the first level) and "B-level" (the second level) headings under the numbered section headings to help readers make easy transitions from one topic to another. This also forces the writer to organize the plan more carefully. Use these headings liberally, at least one every 200 to 300 words.
- Use visuals where appropriate. Photos, illustrations, graphs, and charts enable massive amounts of information to be presented succinctly.
- Shoot for a plan 15 to 35 pages in length, not including financial projections and appendixes. But an uncomplicated small business may require only 15 pages, while a high-technology startup may require more than 35 pages.
- Use care in layout, design, and presentation. Laser or ink-jet printers give a more professional look than do dot matrix printers or typewriters. Use 10 or 11 point type (you are now reading 10.5 point type) in the text. Use a serif type (with "feet," like that you are reading now) in the text because it is easier to read, and sans serif (without "feet") in graphs and charts. A bound report with a nice cover and clear title page adds professionalism.

These guidelines are used, where possible, in the sample marketing plan that follows.

SAMPLE FIVE-YEAR MARKETING PLAN FOR PARADISE KITCHENS,® INC.

To help interpret the marketing plan for Paradise Kitchens,® Inc. that follows, we will describe the background on the company and suggest some guidelines in interpreting the plan.

Background on Paradise Kitchens,® Inc.

With a degree in chemical engineering, Randall F. Peters spent 15 years working for General Foods and Pillsbury with a number of diverse responsibilities: plant operations, R&D, restaurant operations, and new business development. His wife Leah, with degrees in both molecular cellular biology and food science, held various Pillsbury executive positions in new category development and packaged goods and restaurants R&D. Both hobby chefs, Randy and Leah developed and perfected several spicy chili recipes in their own kitchen over a 10-year period. While driving late one night in 1989 they got the inspiration for their registered Howlin' Coyote® brand of chilies and decided to start their own business, Paradise Kitchens, Inc. In its startup years, the company survived on the savings of its cofounders, Randy and Leah. Today Randy serves as president and CEO of Paradise Kitchens, and Leah focuses on R&D and corporate strategy. The first products entered distribution in 1990.

Interpreting the Marketing Plan

The marketing plan for Paradise Kitchens, Inc. which follows is based on an actual plan developed by the company.[6] To protect proprietary information about the company, a number of details and data have been altered, but the basic logic of the plan has been preserved. For example, to keep the plan simpler, it does not include details on a line of spicy salsas developed and marketed.

This sample marketing plan is intended as an *internal* road map to guide marketing activities for the coming five years, during which time the company plans to enter 17 new metropolitan markets.

Notes in the margins of the marketing plan fall into two categories:

1. *Substantive notes* are shaded blue and elaborate on the rationale or significance of an element in the marketing plan and are often keyed to chapter references in this text.
2. *Writing style, format, and layout notes* are shaded red and explain the editorial or visual rationale for the element.

A closing word of encouragement! Writing an effective marketing plan is hard—but challenging and satisfying—work. However, dozens of the authors' students have used effective marketing plans which they wrote for class as an important part of their interviewing portfolio to show prospective employers what they could do and to help them get their first job.

The Table of Contents provides quick access to the topics in the plan, usually organized by section and subsection headings. See questions 10a and 10b at end of Chapter 2.

Seen by many exerts as the single-most important element in the plan, the Executive Summary, with a maximum of two pages, "sells" the document to readers through its clarity and brevity. See question 10c at the end of Chapter 2.

The Company Description highlights the recent history and recent successes of the organization.

The Strategic Focus and Plan sets the strategic direction for the entire organization, a direction with which proposed actions of the marketing plan must be consistent. This section is not included in all marketing plans. See Chapter 2.

The qualitative Mission/Vision statement focuses the activities of Paradise Kitchens for the stakeholder groups to be served. See Chapter 2.

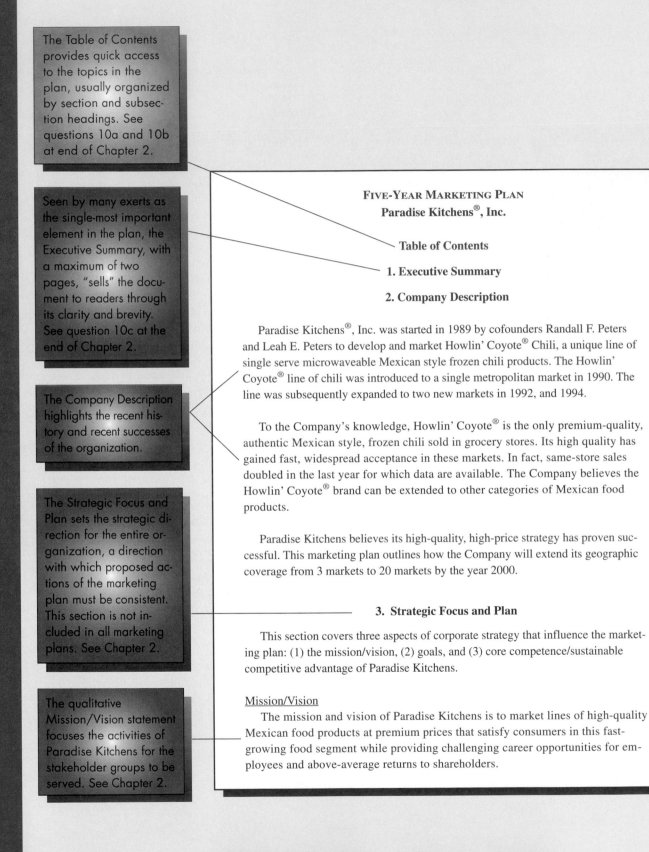

FIVE-YEAR MARKETING PLAN
Paradise Kitchens®, Inc.

Table of Contents

1. Executive Summary

2. Company Description

Paradise Kitchens®, Inc. was started in 1989 by cofounders Randall F. Peters and Leah E. Peters to develop and market Howlin' Coyote® Chili, a unique line of single serve microwaveable Mexican style frozen chili products. The Howlin' Coyote® line of chili was introduced to a single metropolitan market in 1990. The line was subsequently expanded to two new markets in 1992, and 1994.

To the Company's knowledge, Howlin' Coyote® is the only premium-quality, authentic Mexican style, frozen chili sold in grocery stores. Its high quality has gained fast, widespread acceptance in these markets. In fact, same-store sales doubled in the last year for which data are available. The Company believes the Howlin' Coyote® brand can be extended to other categories of Mexican food products.

Paradise Kitchens believes its high-quality, high-price strategy has proven successful. This marketing plan outlines how the Company will extend its geographic coverage from 3 markets to 20 markets by the year 2000.

3. Strategic Focus and Plan

This section covers three aspects of corporate strategy that influence the marketing plan: (1) the mission/vision, (2) goals, and (3) core competence/sustainable competitive advantage of Paradise Kitchens.

Mission/Vision
The mission and vision of Paradise Kitchens is to market lines of high-quality Mexican food products at premium prices that satisfy consumers in this fast-growing food segment while providing challenging career opportunities for employees and above-average returns to shareholders.

Box explains significance of Marketing Plan element

Box gives writing style, format, and layout guidelines

The Goals section sets both the financial and nonfinancial targets—where possible in quantitative terms—against which the company's performance will be measured. See Chapter 2.

Lists use parallel construction to improve readability—in this case a series of infinitives starting with "To . . .".

Goals

For the coming five years Paradise Kitchens seeks to achieve the following goals:

- Nonfinancial goals
  1. To retain its present image as the highest-quality line of Mexican products in the food categories in which it competes.
  2. To enter 17 new metropolitan markets.
  3. To increase the production and distribution capacity to satisfy future sales while maintaining present quality.
  4. To add a new product line every third year.
  5. To be among the top three chili lines—regardless of packaging (frozen, canned) in one-third of the metro markets in which it competes by 1998 and two-thirds by 2000.

- Financial goals
  1. To obtain a real (inflation-adjusted) growth in earnings per share of 8 percent per year over time.
  2. To obtain a return on equity of at least 20 percent.
  3. To have a public stock offering by the year 2000.

IN KEEPING WITH THE GOAL OF ADDING A NEW PRODUCT LINE EVERY THIRD YEAR, PARADISE KITCHENS IS INTRODUCING A NEW LINE OF SALSAS.

Core Competency and Sustainable Competitive Advantage

In terms of core competency, Paradise Kitchens seeks to achieve a unique ability (1) to provide distinctive, high-quality chilies and related products using Mexican recipes that appeal to and excite contemporary tastes for these products and (2) to deliver these products to the customer's table using effective manufacturing and distribution systems that maintain the Company's quality standards.

To translate these core competencies into a sustainable competitive advantage, the Company will work closely with key suppliers and distributors to build the relationships and alliances necessary to satisfy the high taste standards of our customers.

To improve readability, each numbered section usually starts on a new page. (This is not done in this plan to save space.)

The Situation Analysis is a snapshot to answer the question, "Where are we now?" See Chapter 2.

The SWOT Analysis identifies strengths, weaknesses, opportunities, and threats to provide a solid foundation as a springboard to identify subsequent *actions* in the marketing plan. See Chapter 2.

Each long table, graph, or photo is given a figure number and title. It then appears as soon as possible after the first reference in the text, accommodating necessary page breaks. This also avoids breaking long tables like this one in the middle. Short tables or graphs that are less than $1\frac{1}{2}$ inches are often inserted in the text without figure numbers because they don't cause serious problems with page breaks.

Effective tables seek to summarize a large amount of information in a short amount of space.

4. Situation Analysis

This situation analysis starts with a snap shot of the current environment in which Paradise Kitchens finds itself by providing a brief SWOT (strengths, weaknesses, opportunities, threats) analysis. After this overview, the analysis probes ever finer levels of detail: industry, competitors, company, and consumers.

SWOT Analysis

Figure 1 shows the internal and external factors affecting the market opportunities for Paradise Kitchens. Stated briefly, this SWOT analysis highlights the great strides taken by the company in the five years since its products first appeared on grocers' shelves. In the Company's favour internally are its strengths of an experi-

FIGURE 1   SWOT ANALYSIS FOR PARADISE KITCHENS

INTERNAL FACTORS	STRENGTHS	WEAKNESSES
Management	Experienced and entrepreneurial management and board	Small size can restrict options
Offerings	Unique, high-quality, high-price products	Many lower-quality, lower-price competitors
Marketing	Distribution in 3 markets with excellent acceptance	No national awareness or distribution
Personnel	Good work force, though small; little turnover	Big gap if key employee leaves
Finance	Excellent growth in sales revenues	Limited resources may restrict growth opportunities when compared to giant competitors
Manufacturing	Sole supplier ensures high quality	Lack economies of scale of huge competitors
R&D	Continuing efforts to ensure quality in delivered products	
EXTERNAL FACTORS	**OPPORTUNITIES**	**THREATS**
Consumer/Social	Upscale market, likely to be stable; Mexican food category is fast-growing segment	Premium price may limit access to mass markets
Competitive	Distinctive name and packaging in its markets	Not patentable; competitors can attempt to duplicate product
Technological	Technical breakthroughs enable smaller food producers to achieve many economies available to large competitors	
Economic	Consumer income is high; convenience important to households	More households "eating out," and bringing prepared take-out into home
Legal/Regulatory	High government regulatory standards eliminate fly-by-night competitors	

This text discussion of Figure 1 (the SWOT Analysis table) elaborates on its more important elements. This "walks" the reader through the information from the vantage of the plan's writer. (in terse plans this accompanying discussion is sometimes omitted, but is generally desirable to give the reader an understanding of what the company sees as the critical SWOT elements.)

The industry Analysis section provides the backdrop for the subsequent, more detailed analysis of competition, the company, and the company's customers. Without an in-depth understanding of the industry, the remaining analysis may be misdirected. See Chapter 2.

Even though relatively brief, this in-depth treatment of the Spicy Mexican food industry demonstrates to the plan's readers the company's understanding of the industry in which it competes. It gives both external and internal readers confidence that the company thoroughly understands its own industry.

This summary of sales in the Mexican product category shows it is significant and provides a variety of future opportunities for Paradise Kitchens.

enced management team and board of directors, excellent acceptance of its lines in the three metropolitan markets in which it competes, and a strong manufacturing and distribution system to serve these limited markets. Favourable external factors (opportunities) include the increasing appeal of Mexican foods, the strength of the upscale market for the Company's products, and food-processing technological breakthroughs that make it easier for smaller food producers to compete.

These favourable factors must be balanced against unfavourable ones, the main weakness being the limited size of Paradise Kitchens relative to its competitors in terms of the depth of the management team, available financial resources, and national awareness and distribution of product lines. Threats include the potential danger that the Company's premium prices may limit access to mass markets, no legal patent protection for its foods (although it has registered its Howlin' Coyote® brand), and competition from the "eating-out" and "take-out" markets.

Industry Analysis: Trends in Spicy and Mexican Foods

In the past 10 years, hot-spice consumption has doubled. Currently, Mexican food and ingredients are used in 46 percent of households. Burritos, enchiladas, and taco dinner kits, which had insignificant numbers in 1981, reached 7 percent to 16 percent of households in 1992. By 1997, volume of Mexican dinner kits in Canada grew by 41 percent over 1996. Experts predict rapid growth in the Mexican food category and huge market potential.[7]

These trends reflect a generally more favourable attitude toward spicy foods. Total spice consumption increased 50 percent from 1983 to 1993, according to the Spice Trade Association. The retail grocery market for Mexican foods (excluding tortilla chips) was more than $4 billion in annual sales in 1994. The Mexican market includes the foods shown in Figure 2.

FIGURE 2   FOODS INCLUDED IN THE MEXICAN PRODUCT CATEGORY

Food	1994 Sales ($1 000 000)	% Change from 1993 to 1994
Dry chili mix	$121	6.0%
Canned chili	578	2.3
Salsa and sauces	1438	10.3
Mexican frozen	602	4.5
Mexican foods canned	353	4.4
Peppers	242	2.5
Chilies	90	0.3
Mexican foods dry	1259	5.3
Total	$4681	6.0%

As with the Industry Analysis, the Competitors Analysis demonstrates that the company has a realistic understanding of who its major competitors are and what their marketing strategies are. Again, a realistic assessment gives confidence to both internal and external readers that subsequent marketing actions in the plan rest on a solid foundation. See Chapters 2, 3, and 8.

This page uses a "block" style and does *not* indent each paragraph, although an extra space separates each paragraph. Compare this page with page 61, which has indented paragraphs. Most readers find indented paragraphs in marketing plans and long reports are easier to follow.

Paradise Kitchens addresses the issue of the difficulty and unlikelihood of competitors jumping easily into this niche market.

The Company Analysis provides details of the company's strengths and marketing strategies that will enable it to achieve the mission, vision, and goals identified earlier. See Chapter 2, 8, and 22.

Competitors in Mexican Market

The chili market represents $699 million in annual sales. The products fall primarily into two groups: canned chili (81 percent of sales) and dry chili (17 percent of sales). The remaining 2 percent of sales go to frozen chili products. Besides Howlin' Coyote®, Stouffers and Marie Callender's offer frozen chilies as part of their broad line of frozen dinners and entrees. Major canned chili brands include Hormel, Wolf, Dennison, Stagg, Chili Man, and Castleberry's. Their retail prices range from $1.09 to $1.49.

Bluntly put, the major disadvantage of the segment's dominant product, canned chili, is that it does not taste very good. A taste test described in the October 1990 issue of *Consumer Reports* magazine ranked 26 canned chili products "poor" to "fair" in overall sensory quality. The study concluded, "Chili doesn't have to be hot to be good. But really good chili, hot or mild, doesn't come out of a can."

Dry mix brands include such familiar spice brands as Lawry's, McCormick, French's, and Durkee, along with smaller offerings such as Wick Fowler's and Carroll Shelby's. Their retail prices range from $1.79 to $1.99. The *Consumer Reports* study was more favourable about dry chili mixes, ranking them from "fair" to "very good." The magazine recommended, "If you want good chili, make it with fresh ingredients and one of the seasoning mixes we tested." A major drawback of dry mixes is that they require the preparers to add their own meat, beans, and tomatoes and take more preparation time than canned or frozen chilies.

The *Consumer Reports* study did not include the frozen chili entrees from Stouffer's or Marie Callender's (Howlin' Coyote® was not yet on the market at the time of the test). However, it is fair to say that these products—consisting of ground beef, chili beans, and tomato sauce—are of average quality. Furthermore, they are not singled out for special marketing or promotional programs by their manufacturers. Marie Callender's retails for $2.97, and Stouffer's retails for under $2.00.

While it is feasible for another food company to match Howlin' Coyote® and create a similar product, no known current companies are in a position to quickly match the offerings. Small companies face technical capacity issues. Large companies view the products as too much outside the mainstream of frozen-food retailing to be attracted to the market, at least initially.

Company Analysis

The husband-and-wife team that cofounded Paradise Kitchens, Inc. in 1989 has 38 years of experience between them in the food-processing business. Both have played key roles in the management of the Pillsbury Company. They are being advised by a highly seasoned group of business professionals, who have extensive understanding of the requirements for new product development.

This "introductory overview" sentence tells the reader the topics covered in the section—in this case customer characteristics and health and nutrition concerns. While this sentence may be omitted in short memos or plans, it helps readers see where the text is leading. These sentences are used throughout this plan. This text also generally utilizes these introductory overview sentences to aid your comprehension.

The higher-level "A heading" of Customer Analysis has a more dominant typeface and position than the lower-level "B heading" of Customer Characteristics. These headings introduce the reader to the sequence and level of topics covered. The organization of this text uses this kind of structure and headings.

Satisfying customers and providing genuine value to them is why organizations exist in a market economy. This section addresses the question of "Who are the customers for Paradise Kitchens's products?" See Chapters 5, 6, 7, and 8.

Currently, Howlin' Coyote® products compete in the chili and Mexican frozen entree segments of the Mexican food market. While the chili obviously competes as a stand-alone product, its exceptional quality means it can complement such dishes as burritos, nachos, and enchiladas and can be readily used as a smothering sauce for pasta, rice, or potatoes. This flexibility of use is relatively rare in the prepared food marketplace.

In its growth strategy, Howlin' Coyote® is retracing a path taken by such enterprising food companies as Snapple Beverages, Celestial Seasonings, and Tombstone Pizza. These companies all broke from the pack of their respective categories and established a new approach. Snapple showed that iced tea and fruit drinks can be fun and highly variable. Celestial Seasonings make tea into a "lifestyle" drink. Tombstone Pizza moved frozen pizza upscale in taste and price, creating the first alternative to "cardboard" home pizzas. Likewise, with Howlin' Coyote® Paradise Kitchens is broadening the position of frozen chili in a way that can lead to impressive market share for the new product category.

The Company now uses a single outside producer with which it works closely to maintain the consistently high quality required in its products. The greater volume has increased production efficiencies, resulting in a steady decrease in the cost of goods sold.

Customer Analysis

In terms of customer analysis, this section describes (1) the characteristics of customers expected to buy Howlin' Coyote® products and (2) health and nutrition concerns of consumers today.

Customer Characteristics. Demographically, chili products in general are purchased by consumers representing a broad range of socioeconomic backgrounds. Howlin' Coyote® chili is purchased chiefly by consumers who have achieved higher levels of education and whose income is $30 000 and higher. These consumers represent 57 percent of canned and dry mix chili users.

THE FIVE HOWLIN' COYOTE®
ENTREES OFFER A QUICK, TASTY
MEAL WITH HIGH-QUALITY
INGREDIENTS.

The household buying Howlin' Coyote® has one to three people in it. Among married couples, Howlin' Coyote® is predominantly bought by households in which both spouses work. While women are a majority of the buyers, single men represent a significant segment. Anecdotally, Howlin' Coyote® has heard from fathers of teenaged boys who say they keep a freezer stocked with the chili because the boys devour it.

Because the chili offers a quick way to make a tasty meal, the product's biggest users tend to be those most pressed for time. Howlin' Coyote®'s premium pricing also means that its purchasers are skewed toward the higher end of the income range. Buyers range in age from 25 to 55.

Health and Nutrition Concerns. Coverage of food issues in the media is often erratic and occasionally alarmist. Because consumers are concerned about their diets, studies from organizations of widely varying credibility frequently receive significant attention from the major news organizations. For instance, a study of fat levels of movie popcorn was reported in all the major media. Similarly, studies on the healthfulness of Mexican food have received prominent "play" in print and broadcast reports. The high caloric levels of most Mexican food has been widely reported and often exaggerated.

Less certain is the link between these reports and consumer buying behaviour. Most indications are that while consumers are well-versed in dietary matters, they are not significantly changing their eating patterns. The experience of other food manufacturers is that consumers expect certain foods to be high in calories and are not drawn to those that claim to be low-calorie versions. Low-fat frozen pizza was a flop. Therefore, while Howlin' Coyote® is already lower in calories, fat, and sodium than its competitors, those qualities are not being stressed in its promotions. Instead, in the space and time available for promotions, Howlin' Coyote®'s taste, convenience, and flexibility are stressed.

5. Market-Product Focus

This section describes the five-year marketing and product objectives for Paradise Kitchens and the target markets, points of difference, and positioning of its lines of Howlin' Coyote® chilies.

Marketing and Product Objectives

Howlin' Coyote®'s marketing intent is to take full advantage of its brand potential while building a base from which other revenues sources can be

---

This section demonstrates the company's insights into a major trend that has a potentially large impact.

Size of headings should give a professional look to the report and not overwhelm the reader. These two headings are too large.

An noted in Chapter 11, the chances of success for a new product are significantly increased if objectives are set for the product itself and if target market segments are identified for it. This section makes these explicit for Paradise Kitchens. The objectives also serve as the planned targets against which marketing activities are measured in program implementation and control.

A heading should be spaced closer to the text that follows (and that it describes) than the preceding section to avoid confusion for the reader. This rule is *not* followed for the "Target Markets" heading, which now unfortunately appears to "float" between the preceding and following paragraphs.

This section identifies the specific niches or target markets toward which the company's products are directed. When appropriate and when space permits, this section often includes a market-product grid. See Chapter 9.

---

mined—both in and out of the retail grocery business. These are detailed in four areas below:

- Current markets. Current markets will be grown by expanding brand and flavour distribution at the retail level. In addition, same-store sales will be grown by increasing consumer awareness and repeat purchases. With this increase in same-store sales, the more desirable broker/warehouse distribution channel will become available, increasing efficiency and saving costs.

- New markets. By the end of Year 5, the chili and salsa business will be expanded to a total of 20 metropolitan areas. This will represent 55 percent of food store sales.

- Foods service. Food service sales will include chili products and smothering sauces. Sales are expected to reach $580 000 by the end of Year 3 and $1.2 million by the end of Year 5.

- New products. Howlin' Coyote®'s brand presence will be expanded at the retail level through the addition of new products in the frozen-foods section. This will be accomplished through new product concept screening in Year 1 to identify new potential products. These products will be brought to market in Years 2 and 3. Additionally, the brand may be licensed in select categories.

Target Markets

The primary target market for Howlin' Coyote® products is households with one to three people, where often both adults work, with individual income typically above $30 000 per year. These households contain more experienced, adventurous consumers of Mexican food and want premium quality products.

TO HELP BUYERS SEE THE MANY DIFFERENT USES FOR HOWLIN' COYOTE® CHILI, RECIPES ARE EVEN PRINTED ON THE *INSIDE* OF THE PACKAGES.

An organization cannot grow by offering only "me-too products." The greatest single factor in a new product's failure is the lack of significant "points of difference" that sets it apart from competitors' substitutes. This section makes these points of difference explicit. See Chapter 11.

A positioning strategy helps communicate the company's unique points of difference of its products to prospective customers in a simple, clear way. This section describes this positioning. See Chapters 9 and 11.

Everything that has gone before in the marketing plan sets the stage for the marketing mix actions—the 4 Ps—covered in the marketing program. See Chapters 11 through 21.

This section describes in detail three key elements of the company's product strategy: the product line, its quality and how this is achieved, and its "cutting edge" packaging. See Chapters 11, 12, and 13.

Points of Difference

The "points of difference"—characteristics that make Howlin' Coyote® chilies unique relative to competitors—fall into three important areas:

- Unique taste and convenience. No known competitor offers a high-quality, "authentic" frozen chili in a range of flavours. And no existing chili has the same combination of quick preparation and home-style taste.

- Taste trends. The consumer's palate is increasingly intrigued by hot spices, and Howlin' Coyote® brands offer more "kick" than most other prepared chilies.

- Premium packaging. Howlin' Coyote®'s high-value packaging graphics convey the unique, high-quality product contained inside and the product's non-traditional positioning.

Positioning

In the past chili products have been either convenient or tasty, but not both. Howlin' Coyote® pairs these two desirable characteristics to obtain a positioning in consumers' minds as very high-quality "authentic Mexican tasting" chilies that can be prepared easily and quickly.

6. Marketing Program

The four marketing mix elements of the Howlin' Coyote® chili marketing program are detailed below. Note that "chile" is the vegetable and "chili" is the dish.

Product Strategy

After first summarizing the product line, the approach to product quality and packaging are covered.

Product Line. Howlin' Coyote® chili, retailing for $2.89 for a 300 g serving, is available in five flavours. The five are:

- Green Chile Chili: braised extra-lean pork with fire-roasted green chilies, onions, tomato chunks, bold spices, and jalapeno peppers.

- Red Chile Chili: extra-lean cubed pork, deep-red acho chilies, and sweet onions.

- Beef and Black Bean Chili: lean braised beef with black beans, tomato chunks, and Howlin' Coyote®'s own blend of red chilies and authentic spicing.

Using parallel structure this bulleted list presents the product line efficiently and crisply.

- Chicken Chunk Chili: hearty chunks of tender chicken, fire-roasted green chilies, black beans, pinto beans, diced onions, and zesty spices.
- Mean Bean Chili: vegetarian, with nine distinctive bean varieties and fire-roasted green chilies, tomato chunks, onion, and a robust blend of spices and rich red chilies.

Unique Product Quality. The flavouring systems of the Howlin' Coyote® chilies are proprietary. The products' tastiness is due to extra care lavished upon the ingredients during production. The ingredients used are of unusually high quality. Meats are low-fat cuts and fresh, not frozen, to preserve cell structure and moistness. Chilies are fire-roasted for fresher taste, not the canned variety used by more mainstream products. Tomatoes and vegetables are select quality. No preservatives or artificial flavours are used.

Packaging. Reflecting the "cutting edge" marketing strategy of its producers, Howlin' Coyote® bucks conventional wisdom in packaging. It avoids placing predictable photographs of the product on its containers. (Head to any grocer's freezer and you will be hardpressed to find a product that does not feature a heavily stylized photograph of the contents.) Instead, Howlin' Coyote®'s package communicates the product's out-of-the-ordinary positioning. This approach signals the product's nontraditional qualities: "adventurous" eating with minimal fuss—a frozen meal for people who do not normally enjoy frozen meals.

A brief caption on photos and sample ads ties them to the text and highlights the reason for being included.

HOWLIN' COYOTE®'S PACKAGES STAND OUT IN A SUPERMARKET'S FREEZER CASE.

This Price Strategy section makes the company's price point very clear, along with its price position relative to potential substitutes. When appropriate and when space permits, this section might contain a break-even analysis. See Chapters 14 and 15.

Price Strategy

Howlin' Coyote® Chili is, at $2.89 for a 300 g package, priced comparably to the other frozen offerings and higher that the canned and dried chili varieties. However, the significant taste advantages it has over canned chilies and the convenience advantages over dried chilies justify this pricing strategy.

Elements of the Promotion Strategy are highlighted here with B-headings in terms of the three key promotional activities the company is emphasizing for its product line: in-store demonstrations, recipes featuring its Howlin' Coyote® chilies, and cents-off coupons. See Chapters 19, 20, and 21.

Photos or sample ads can illustrate key points effectively, even if they are not in colour as they appear here.

Promotion Strategy

Key promotion programs feature in-store demonstrations, recipes, and cents-off coupons.

In-Store Demonstrations. In-store demonstrations will be conducted to give consumers a chance to try Howlin' Coyote® products and learn about their unique qualities. Demos will be conducted regularly in all markets to increase awareness and trial purchases.

Recipes. Because the products' flexibility of use is a key selling point, recipes will be offered to consumers to stimulate use. The recipes will be given at all in-store demonstrations, on the back of packages, and through a mail-in recipe book offer. In addition, recipes will be included in coupons sent by direct-mail or free-standing inserts. For new markets, recipes will be included on in-pack coupon inserts.

Cents-Off Coupons. To generate trial and repeat-purchase of Howlin' Coyote® products, coupons will be distributed in four ways:

- In Sunday newspaper inserts. Inserts are highly read and will help generate awareness. Coupled with in-store demonstrations, this has been a very successful technique so far.

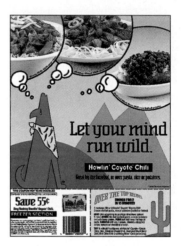

SUNDAY NEWSPAPER INSERTS ENCOURAGE CONSUMER TRIAL AND PROVIDE RECIPES TO SHOW HOW HOWLIN' COYOTE® CHILI CAN BE USED IN SUMMER MEALS.

Another bulleted list adds many details for the reader, including methods of gaining customer awareness, trial, and repeat purchases as Howlin' Coyote® enters new metropolitan areas. The lack of a space between bulleted items makes it more difficult reading for some readers compared to, say, the bulleted list on page 64.

The Place Strategy is described here in terms of both (1) the present method and (2) the new one to be used when the increased sales volume makes it feasible. See Chapters 16, 17, and 18.

All the marketing mix decisions covered in the just-described marketing program have both revenue and expense effects. These are summarized in this section of the marketing plan. See Appendix B.

Note that this section contains no introductory overview sentence. While the sentence is not essential, many readers prefer to see it to avoid the abrupt start with Post Sales Revenues.

The graph shows more clearly the dramatic growth of sales revenue than data in a table would do.

- In-pack coupons. Inside each box of Howlin' Coyote® chili will be coupons for $1 off two more packages of the chili. These coupons will be included for the first three months the product is shipped to a new market. Doing so encourages repeat purchases by new users.
- Direct-mail chili coupons. Those households that fit the Howlin' Coyote® demographics described above will be mailed coupons. This is likely to be an efficient promotion due to its greater audience selectivity.
- In-store demonstrations. Coupons will be passed out at in-store demonstrations to give an additional incentive to purchase.

Place (Distribution) Strategy

Howlin' Coyote® is distributed in its present markets through a food distributor. The distributor buys the product, warehouses it, and then resells and delivers it to grocery retailers on a store-by-store basis. This is typical for products that have moderate sales—compared with, say, staples like milk or bread. As sales grow, we will shift to a more efficient system using a broker who sells the products to retail chains and grocery wholesalers.

7. Financial Data and Projections

Past Sales Revenues

Historically, Howlin' Coyote® has had a steady increase in sales revenues since its introduction in 1990. In 1994, sales jumped spectacularly, due largely to new promotion strategies and the opportunities represented by the products' expansion to Western markets. The trend in sales revenues appears in Figure 3.

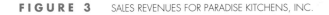

FIGURE 3   SALES REVENUES FOR PARADISE KITCHENS, INC.

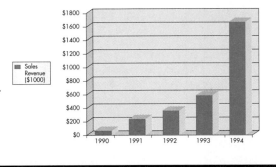

One key indicator of what future sales will be is to look at what past sales have been. Paradise Kitchens is justifiably proud of the dramatic growth in its past sales revenues and highlights this information.

Because this table is very short, it is woven into the text, rather than given a figure number and title.

Because the plan proposes to enter 17 new metropolitan markets in the coming five years (for a total of 20), it is not possible to simply extrapolate the trend in Figure 3. Instead, management's judgment must be used. Methods of making sales forecasts—including the "lost horse" technique used here—are discussed in Chapter 10.

The Five-Year Financial Projections section starts with the judgment forecast of cases sold and the resulting net sales. Gross profit and then operating profit—critical for the company's survival—are projected and show the company passes break-even and becomes profitable in Year 2. An actual plan often contains many pages of computer-generated spreadsheet projections, usually shown in a appendix to the plan.

During the five years since their introduction, Howlin' Coyote® chilies have achieved sales growth of 80 percent annually. New sales-promotion techniques have been so effective that 1994 sales have more than tripled those of 1993.

Five-Year Projections

Five-year financial projections for Paradise Kitchens appear below:

Financial Element	Units	Year 1 1996	Year 2 1997	Year 3 1998	Year 4 1999	Year 5 2000
Cases sold	1 000	195	353	684	889	1 249
Net sales	$1 000	2 832	5 123	9 913	12 884	18 111
Gross profit	$1 000	936	2 545	4 820	6 257	8 831
Operating profit (loss)	$1 000	(423)	339	985	2 096	2 805

These projections reflect the continuing growth in number of cases sold (with 8 packages of Howlin' Coyote® chili per case) and increasing production and distribution economies of scale as sales volume increases.

8. Organization

Paradise Kitchens' present organization appears in Figure 4. It shows the four people reporting to the President. Below this level are both the full-time and part-time employees of the Company.

At present Paradise Kitchens operates with full-time employees in only essential positions. It now augments its full-time staff with key advisers, consultants, and subcontractors. As the firm grows, people with special expertise will be added to the staff.

FIGURE 4   THE PARADISE KITCHENS ORGANIZATION

The Organization of Paradise Kitchens appears here. It reflects the bare-bones organizational structure of successful small businesses. Often a more elaborate marketing plan will show the new positions expected to be added as the firm grows. See Chapter 22.

9. Implementation Plan

Introducing Howlin' Coyote® chilies to new metropolitan areas is a complex task and requires that creative promotional activities gain consumer awareness and initial trial among the target market households identified earlier. The anticipated rollout schedule to enter these metropolitan markets appears in Figure 5.

FIGURE 5   ROLLOUT SCHEDULE TO ENTER NEW MARKETS

YEAR	NEW MARKETS ADDED	CUMULATIVE MARKETS	CUMULATIVE PERCENTAGE OF MARKET
Today (1995)	0	3	7
Year 1 (1996)	1	4	10
Year 2 (1997)	2	6	18
Year 3 (1998)	3	9	28
Year 4 (1999)	4	13	39
Year 5 (2000)	7	20+	55

10. Evaluation and Control

Monthly sales targets in cases have been set for Howlin' Coyote® chili for each metropolitan area. Actual case sales will be compared with these targets and tactical marketing programs modified to reflect the unique sets of factors in each metropolitan area. The speed of the roll-out program may increase or decrease, depending on Paradise Kitchens's performance in the successive metropolitan markets it enters.

CHAPTER 3

The Changing Marketing Environment

AFTER READING THIS CHAPTER YOU SHOULD BE ABLE TO:

• Understand how environmental scanning provides information about social, economic, technological, competitive, and regulatory forces.

• Explain how social forces such as demographics and culture and economic forces such as macroeconomic conditions and consumer income affect marketing.

• Describe how technological changes and their ecological impacts can affect marketing.

• Understand the competitive structures that exist in a market, the role of marketing within each, and key components of competition.

• Explain the major legislation that ensures competition and regulates the elements of the marketing mix.

NEXT UP . . . GENERATION X-CELLENT

Most students currently enrolled in Canadian colleges and universities were born between 1965 and 1976. If you were born during this period you are considered to be a member of Generation X. This group of consumers have plenty in common. Xers spend billions of dollars each year on computers, entertainment, economical and functional clothing, and leisure activities. They use pagers, fax machines, answering machines, and e-mail as necessities; and as a group, are perhaps the most educated and entrepreneurially oriented generation in history. Generation X is positioned to displace older generations, such as baby boomers, as the primary influence on popular culture.

Generation X is shaping the future in many ways. They are increasingly interested in visual images rather than written words. They are closer to their parents than any previous generation, and they are delaying marriage until their education is complete and a career has been established. In addition, they readily accept racial and sexual diversity. All of these characteristics are likely to translate into a future with different lifestyles, new purchase decision approaches, and new product and service preferences.

Recognition of these changes is altering the marketplace. Because Generation X dislikes any form of hype, for example, advertisers are developing campaigns with less overstatement. Other changes include new products and services designed for practical use rather than image or status. Small, sporty, economical automobiles such as the Geo Metro, the Chrysler Neon, and the Ford Escort ZX2 are very popular with Generation X.[1]

Generation X is clearly changing the marketing environment. It represents a demographic shift, an economic influence, and a force likely to increase the use of technology. Anticipating changes such as these and responding to them often means the difference between marketing success and failure. This chapter describes how the marketing environment has changed in the past and is likely to change in the future.

ENVIRONMENTAL SCANNING IN THE 1990S

Changes in the business and marketing environment are a source of opportunities and threats to be managed. The process of continually acquiring information on events occurring outside the organization in order to identify and interpret potential trends is called **environmental scanning.**

Tracking Environmental Trends

Environmental trends typically arise from five sources: social, economic, technological, competitive, and regulatory forces. As shown in Figure 3-1 and described later in this chapter, these forces affect the marketing activities of a firm in numerous ways.

To illustrate how environmental scanning is used, consider the following trend:[2] Coffee industry experts have observed that the percentage of adults who drink coffee at home has been on the decline. While 83 percent of adults drank coffee at home in 1985, the number of drinkers is forecasted to fall to under 75 percent by 1998. Age-specific analysis indicates that coffee consumption is declining among all age groups, including 18 to 24 year olds, despite the perception that young adults are leading a revival in coffee drinking.

What types of businesses are likely to be influenced by this trend? What future would you predict for coffee?

You may have concluded that this trend is likely to influence coffee manufacturers and supermarkets. If so, you are absolutely correct—manufacturers have responded by offering new flavours, and supermarkets have added coffee boutiques to try to reverse the trend. Predicting the future of coffee requires assumptions about the number of years the declining trend will continue and the rate of decline in various age groups. Did you consider these issues in your analysis? Since experts make different assumptions, their forecasts range from a 30 percent decline to a 13 percent increase by 2005—a range that probably includes your forecast!

Environmental scanning also involves explaining trends. Why has coffee consumption been declining? One explanation is that consumers are switching from coffee to other beverages such as soft drinks, juices, or water. Another explanation is that pref-

FIGURE 3-1

ENVIRONMENTAL FORCES AFFECTING THE ORGANIZATION, AS WELL AS ITS SUPPLIERS AND CUSTOMERS erences have shifted to better tasting but more expensive types of coffee, and consumers have reduced their use to maintain the same level of expenditure. Identifying and interpreting trends, such as the decline in coffee consumption, and developing explanations, such as those offered in this paragraph, are essential to successful environmental scanning.

An Environmental Scan of the 1990s

What other trends might affect marketing in the 1990s? A firm conducting an environmental scan of Canada might uncover key trends such as those listed in Figure 3-2 for each of the five environmental factors. Although the list of trends is far from complete, it reveals the breadth of an environmental scan—from identifying consumers' new "do-it-yourself" attitudes and their growing desire for improved product quality and customer service to breakthroughs in information technology and competitive changes due to the restructuring of Canadian corporations. These trends affect consumers and the businesses and nonprofit organizations that serve them. Trends such as these are covered as the five environmental forces and are described in the following pages.

SOCIAL FORCES

The **social forces** of the environment include the characteristics of the population, its values, and its behaviour. Changes in these forces can have a dramatic impact on marketing strategy.

Demographics

Demographics is the study of the characteristics of a human population. These characteristics include size, growth rate, age, gender, marital status, education, ethnicity, income, and so forth.

F I G U R E 3 - 2   AN ENVIRONMENTAL SCAN OF CANADA

ENVIRONMENTAL FORCE	TREND IDENTIFIED BY AN ENVIRONMENTAL SCAN
Social	• Movement toward self-reliance and a "do-it-yourself" philosophy • Growing number and importance of older Canadians • Continuing population shifts to urban areas • Greater desire for product quality and customer service
Economic	• Growing concern over the Canadian budget deficit • More Canadian firms will look to foreign markets for growth • Stagnation of real per capita income of Canadians • Increasing consumer debt
Technological	• Increased use of information and communication technology • Major breakthrough in biotechnology • More problems with pollution and solid and nuclear wastes • Growing use of electronic money or "e-cash"
Competitive	• More employment in small, innovative firms • Downsizing and restructuring of many corporations • Mergers will reduce costs through economies of scale • More international competition from Europe and Asia
Regulatory	• Less regulation of Canadian firms competing in international markets • New requirements for electric cars and alternative forms of transportation • Greater concern for ethics and social responsibility in business • Renewed emphasis on self-regulation

FIGURE 3-3

THE FORECASTED AGE DISTRIBUTION
OF THE CANADIAN POPULATION FOR
THE YEAR 2011

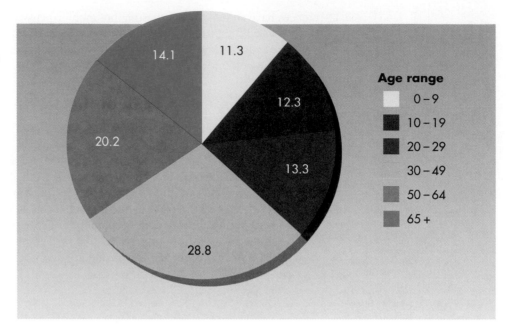

Population size and growth   The current population of Canada is almost 30 million, with the population growth rate averaging slightly over 1 percent per year.[3] The population is expected to be almost 32 million by 2001, and over 35 million by 2011.[4]

Age waves   Because age affects the needs, values, and purchasing habits of consumers, tracking consumers by age groupings is also part of an environmental scan. The size, habits, and relative purchasing power of various age groups is closely examined in an environmental scan.

Canadians are getting older. In 1996 the median age of the population was 33 years, which means 50 percent of the population was below that age but 50 percent was also above 33 years of age. The median age in Canada is projected to be over 40 years by the year 2011. The forecasted age distribution of Canada's population for the year 2011 is shown in Figure 3-3.[5] As you can see, over 34 percent of the population will be over the age of 50 by that time. This is a significant demographic trend which indicates the greying of Canada.

The over-50 age group—sometimes called the **mature market**—is a fast-growing age segment in Canada. In recent years, greater marketing attention has been focused on this market because people over 50 years of age control much of the *accumulated wealth* in this country—the value of net assets accumulated by households in the form of real property, financial securities, deposits, and pension assets. Many Canadian companies have responded aggressively to this important market including developing products and services specific to the mature market such as retirement communities, using older celebrities in ads, and placing larger type on product labels.

A major reason for the greying of Canada is that the **baby boomers**—the generation of children born between 1946 and 1964—are growing older. As millions of boomers have aged, their participation in the workforce and their earnings have increased, making them an important consumer market. It has been estimated that this group accounts for the majority of the purchases in most consumer product and service categories. As the older boomers become part of the mature market, their buying behaviour is changing to reflect greater concern for their children's future and their own retirement. Even the younger boomers are showing greater concern about saving and financial planning.

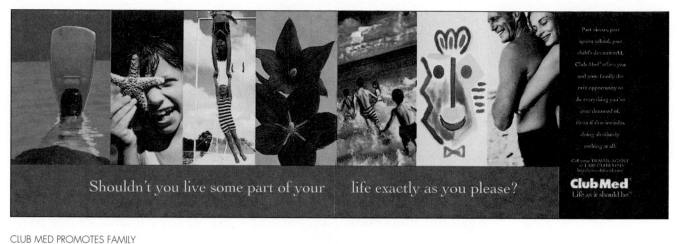

Shouldn't you live some part of your   life exactly as you please?

Club Med
Life as it should be

CLUB MED PROMOTES FAMILY
VACATIONS TO AGING BABY
BOOMERS.

As a group, boomers are shifting their focus from indulgence and luxury to quality and value.[6] Companies such as Club Med and Lee jeans are refocusing their strategies to a more mature boomer market. Club Med is trying to augment its singles image by promoting family vacations and facilities with child care in addition to vacations that cater to singles and couples, and Lee is responding to an aging baby boomer with loose-fitting jeans and advertising, "You're not a kid anymore."[7]

Generation X, as you know, is the group of Canadians born between 1965 and 1976. Members of Generation X (Xers), represent under 15 percent of the Canadian population. It is a generation of consumers who are not prone to extravagance and are likely to pursue lifestyles and prefer products and services that are very different from baby boomers. They are also likely to be more demanding consumers. Marketers are very much aware of this group of consumers and are interested in tracking this generation to identify the dominant consumption values of the twenty-first century.[8]

The **baby boomlet** refers to Canadians born in 1977 and later. As children, the boomlet generation already exerts influence in music, sports, computers, and video game purchases. Later in the twenty-first century, this group will influence markets, attitudes, and society—much like the baby boomers do now and Generation X will do soon.[9]

The Canadian family   The types of families in Canada are changing in both size and structure. The average family size in Canada is about three persons, and this figure is expected to decline further by the year 2000. In 1971 one in three Canadian families consisted of the once-typical scenario of a husband working outside the home, with a wife inside the home with their children. Today, only one in seven families fall into this category. The dual-income family is the norm in Canada, representing over 60 percent of all husband-wife families.

About 50 percent of all first marriages in Canada end in divorce. Thus, the single-parent family is becoming more typical in Canadian society. But the majority of divorced people eventually remarry, giving rise to the **blended family,** one formed by the merging into a single household of two previously separated units. Today, many Canadians are finding themselves as a stepparent, stepchild, stepsibling, or some other member of a blended family. Hallmark Cards specially designs cards and verses for such blended families. Still, many people do not remarry, and single-parent families represent close to 15 percent of all family units in Canada.

Population shifts   Since the mid-1970s there has been a major shift in the Canadian population from rural to urban areas. In fact, over 80 percent of Canadians are urban dwellers.[10] Most Canadians live in **census metropolitan areas** (CMAs), geographic labour market areas having a population of 100 000 persons or more. The top 25 CMAs in Canada include cities such as Toronto, Montreal, Vancouver, Ottawa, and Edmonton and account for more than 60 percent of the Canadian population. With the concentration of the population in or near CMAs, marketers can reach large segments of the market efficiently and effectively. Some experts have predicted that by the year 2010, most Canadians will be located in seven or eight city-states and be within easy reach of most marketers.[11]

There has not been much of a shift in how the population is distributed across the country. More than 60 percent of Canadians live in two provinces, Ontario and Quebec. Over the next 10 years, population growth is expected to increase in all provinces, but Ontario, Quebec, Alberta, and British Columbia are expected to enjoy the largest increases.

Regional marketing　　A recent trend within marketing focuses not only on the shifting of consumers geographically, such as the move from rural to urban areas, but also on the differences in their product preferences based on where they live. This concept has been referred to as **regional marketing,** which is developing marketing plans designed to reflect the specific area differences in taste preferences, perceived needs, or interests. Given the vastness of Canada, many marketers view the country as being composed of regions such as Atlantic Canada, Quebec, Ontario, Western Canada, and British Columbia. In Chapter 9, you will learn more about this approach to the market referred to as *geographic segmentation.*

Because of differences in economics, topography, and natural resources, consumption patterns in the regions of Canada tend to differ. Some products and brands that sell successfully in one region do not do well in another. Strategies and tactics to sell them may also differ. Colgate-Palmolive found that marketing their Arctic Power "cold water" clothes detergent on an "energy savings" dimension worked well in Quebec but not in the West where simply saving money on the product itself was more important. The company adjusted its marketing strategy accordingly.

Technology has aided marketers in understanding the variations in regional preferences. Computerized cash registers, for example, have allowed companies to coordinate and analyze sales data for geographic regions, determining what does and does not sell well in various regions. Pepsi-Cola can be a market leader in one region while Coca-Cola can be the leader in another. And, with advances in database technology (Chapter 10), this focus on regional marketing allows for better targeting of ads and products. Still, the ability to market on a regional basis not only depends on the variance in regional preferences, but also on the sufficiency of size of the region and the cost of localized efforts. Often, regional or localized efforts can be more costly than one simple national effort. But, a better understanding of the geographic regions of Canada and any resultant differences in consumer preferences can lead to more successful marketing. For example, while Harvey's Restaurants sells the same products across Canada, it uses original French-language advertising for Quebec featuring Bernard Fortin, a high-profile and well-liked actor in Quebec. The uniqueness of the campaign has paid off for Harvey's. Sears Canada, for the first time, features celebrities on the covers of its catalogues. For the English catalogue, Michelle Wright graces the front, while Quebec pop singer Julie Masse appears on the French version. And, finally, Pizza Hut Canada runs a Quebec-specific TV spot for a Quebec-specific product: a medium-size stuffed crust pizza.

Ethnic diversity　　While we often think of Canada as consisting of French and English Canadians, close to 3 out of 10 Canadians are of neither French nor British descent. While the majority of the non-British, non-French population are of European descent, there has been growth in other ethnic groups and visible minorities. In fact, close to 70 percent of all immigrants to Canada today are classified as visible minorities, primarily people from China, Southeast Asia, Africa, and India. Hong Kong

Chinese and Southeast Asians are the fastest-growing ethnic groups in Canada, representing close to 3 percent of the Canadian population. Visible minorities are projected to represent close to 18 percent of the Canadian population by the year 2001, or over 5.5 million Canadians.[12]

Much of the ethnic population can be found in major metropolitan areas such as Toronto, Vancouver, Montreal, Calgary, and Edmonton. Close to 20 percent of the populations in those areas register their native language as something other than English or French. Marketers have recognized the growing ethnic diversity in Canada. Many companies such as the Royal Bank, Benetton, Ultramar, and Bell Canada are putting "ethnic faces" in mainstream advertising. Many other companies such as Cantel and American Express devote marketing efforts to cater specifically to these ethnic groups which includes advertising in their language and providing personnel who speak their language. Recently, the Vancouver Grizzlies basketball team has begun targeting Asian-Canadians as part of the marketing effort, capitalizing on Asian fan interest in the NBA.[13]

Culture

A second social force, **culture,** incorporates the set of values, ideas, and attitudes of a homogeneous group of people that are transmitted from one generation to the next. Culture includes both material and abstract elements, so monitoring cultural trends in Canada is difficult but important for effective marketing. We will deal with noteworthy cultural trends in Canada in this section. Cross-cultural analysis needed for successful global marketing is discussed in Chapter 5.

The changing roles of women and men   One of the most notable changes in Canada over the past three decades has been the change in the roles of women and men in society. These changes have had a significant impact on marketing practices. Distinctions between the traditional gender roles assigned to females and males have become blurred. One of the major trends has been the emergence of women as an integral part of the workforce. Nationally more than 65 percent of women work outside the home. This figure is expected to rise to close to 75 percent by the year 2000. With more women working outside the home, the number of tasks to do is expanding while the time available to do them is shrinking. This phenomenon is often referred to as *time poverty*. As a result, the male spouse has had to assume certain tasks. More men are shopping for groceries and assuming greater roles in child care and housekeeping duties. As consumers' lives become more hectic, supermarkets are finding one of their hottest-selling categories is frozen, prepared entrees. Stouffer's, whose parent company is Nestlé Canada, says entrees are the fastest growing segment of the frozen food category in Canada because people are time poor and need quick, convenient meal solutions.

Marketers are becoming more aware of the necessity not to stereotype female or male behaviour and preferences. *Parents* magazine, for example, has revised its coverage to reflect a growing male readership.[14] Moreover, in an effort to assist consumers in overcoming their time poverty, many marketers offer greater convenience such as express lanes at checkouts, longer store hours, drive-through windows, and delivery services.

Changing attitudes and values   Culture also includes attitudes and values. In recent years, Canadians have experienced some major attitudinal changes toward work, lifestyles, and consumption. There is a growing sense that the Puritan work ethic of "I live to work" may be redefined as "I work to live." Work is now more likely seen as a means to an end—recreation, leisure, and entertainment. Canadian consumers are placing more emphasis on quality of life as opposed to work, which has contributed to a growth in sales of products such as sports equipment, vacations, electronic entertainment equipment, and easily prepared foods.

There is greater concern for health and well-being, as evidenced by the level of fitness activity and sports participation in Canada. Firms like Nike and Reebok are profiting from this trend. Canadians are also more concerned about their diets, especially because of the linkage between diet and health. Growth in sales of no-fat, or low-fat, and cholesterol-free foods is evidence of this concern. The beverage industry has also seen major changes. Consumers are drinking healthier products including more bottled water and juices as opposed to traditional soft drinks. Canadians buy over 100 million litres of spring water from the grocery stores annually as well as healthful beverages of all kinds. Northpole Beverages Co. of Montreal, for example, sells a fruit-flavoured beverage with ginseng called $E = MC^2$.

Health-conscious Canadians are also buying medical self-diagnostic kits. Lifescan Canada Ltd. of Burnaby, BC, markets a variety of self-testing kits that can monitor cholesterol levels or test for colorectal cancer. The company suggests well-educated and aging consumers are taking greater responsibility for their health care and are now into self-diagnosis. Planta Dei Plant Medicines Inc. of Nackawic, NB, is also capitalizing on the health-consciousness trend in Canada. The company markets phytopharmaceuticals—medicines made from medicinal plants—via 2000 retail pharmacies across Canada.

A change in consumption orientation is also apparent. Conspicuous consumption marked much of the past 20 years. Today, and for the foreseeable future, **value consciousness**—or the concern for obtaining the best quality, features, and performance of a product or service for a given price—will drive consumption behaviour. Innovative marketers have responded to this new orientation in numerous ways. Holiday Inn Worldwide has opened Holiday Express Hotels designed to offer comfortable accommodations with room rates lower than Holiday Inns. Sobeys, Inc., one of Canada's top food retailers, now offers consumers its *Signal* brand of products which is a private-label, value-based line that comes with a low-price guarantee.[15] Even Canada's major banks are recognizing the value-consciousness trend and are offering consumers credit cards with lower interest rates and value-added enhancements such as frequent flyer programs and cashback offers.[16]

RESPONDING TO CONSUMER
DEMAND FOR VALUE, SOBEYS OFFERS
A VALUE-BASED LINE OF PRODUCTS
THAT COME WITH A LOW-PRICE
GUARANTEE.

CONCEPT CHECK

1. What is environmental scanning?
2. What is a census metropolitan area?
3. What are the marketing implications of blended families?

ECONOMIC FORCES

Another component of the environmental scan, the **economy,** pertains to the income, expenditures, and resources that affect the cost of running an organization or a household. We'll consider two aspects of these economic forces: a macroeconomic view of the marketplace and a microeconomic perspective of consumer income.

Macroeconomic Conditions

Of particular concern at the macroeconomic level is the inflationary or recessionary state of the nation's economy, whether actual or perceived, by consumers or businesses. In an inflationary economy, the cost to produce and buy products and services escalates as prices increase. From a marketing standpoint, if prices rise faster than consumer incomes, the number of items consumers can buy decreases.

Whereas inflation is a period of price increases, recession is a time of slow economic activity. Businesses decrease production, unemployment rises, and many consumers have less money to spend. The Canadian economy experienced recessions in the early 1970s, early 1980s, and early 1990s.

Assessing consumer expectations of an inflationary and recessionary economy is an important element of environmental scanning. Consumer spending, which accounts for two-thirds of Canadian economic activity, is affected by expectations of the future.

Surveys of consumer expectations are tracked over time by researchers, who ask questions such as "Do you expect to be better or worse off financially a year from now?" Surveyors record the share of positive and negative responses to this question and related ones to develop an index, sometimes called a consumer confidence or consumer sentiment index. The higher the index, the more favourable are consumer expectations. Many firms evaluate such indexes in order to plan production levels. Chrysler, for example, uses such indexes to plan its automobile production levels in order to avoid overproducing cars during a recessionary economy.

Consumer Income

The microeconomic trends in terms of consumer income are important issues for marketers. Having a product that meets the needs of consumers may be of little value if they are unable to purchase it. A consumer's ability to buy is related to income, which consists of gross, disposable, and discretionary components.

Gross income   The total amount of money made in one year by a person, household, or family unit is referred to as **gross income.** Figure 3-4 shows the distribution of annual income among Canadian families.[17] Average gross family income in Canada is slightly over $55 000. But family income in Canada varies by province as well as by the education level and profession of the head(s) of the family. For example, the majority of families earning $75 000 or more are headed by college graduates.

Disposable income   The second income component, **disposable income,** is money a consumer has left after paying taxes to use for necessities such as food, shelter, and clothing. Thus, if taxes rise at a faster rate than does disposable income, consumers must economize. In recent years consumers' allocation of income has shifted. For example, the proportion of disposable income devoted to eating in the home has increased, while the proportion devoted to eating out has decreased. Two environmental factors account for this: the recession of the early 1990s caused people to cut back on expenses such as eating out, and many baby boom households are in the midst of their child-raising years, causing increased spending on food at home.[18]

FIGURE 3-4

INCOME DISTRIBUTION OF
CANADIAN FAMILIES

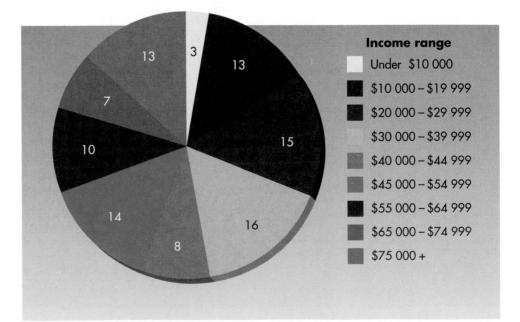

Income range
- Under $10 000
- $10 000 – $19 999
- $20 000 – $29 999
- $30 000 – $39 999
- $40 000 – $44 999
- $45 000 – $54 999
- $55 000 – $64 999
- $65 000 – $74 999
- $75 000 +

AS CONSUMERS' DISCRETIONARY
INCOME INCREASES, SO DOES THE
ENJOYMENT OF PLEASURE TRAVEL.

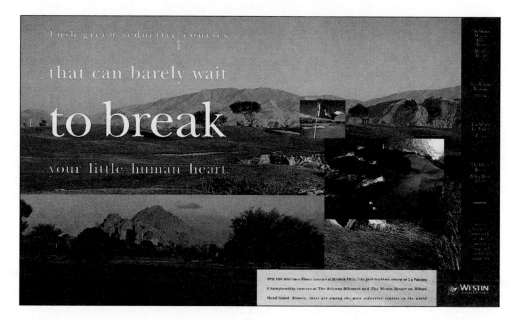

Discretionary income   The third component of income is **discretionary income,** the money that remains after paying taxes and necessities. Discretionary income could be used for luxury items such as vacations at a Westin resort. An obvious problem in defining discretionary versus disposable income is determining what is a luxury and what is a necessity. Observation can be a way to make this determination—if a family has Royal Doulton china, Rolex watches, and Lexus automobiles, one could assume that they have, or had, discretionary income. Still, it is important to note that a product defined as a necessity by one individual may be viewed as a luxury by another. For example some Canadians view an automatic dishwasher as a necessity while others see it as a luxury item.

TECHNOLOGICAL FORCES

Our society is in a period of technological change. **Technology,** a major environmental force, refers to inventions or innovations from applied science or engineering research. Each new wave of technological innovation can replace existing products and companies. Do you recognize the item pictured on page 82 and what it may replace?

Technology of Tomorrow

Technological change is the result of research, so it is difficult to predict. Some of the most dramatic technological changes occurring now, however, include the following:

1. Continued improvement in the power of microprocessors.
2. The convergence of television, personal computer, and telephone technologies, including digital personal communications services (PCS) that provide paging and e-mail on a digital cellphone with a display screen.
3. The emergence of the Internet or "cyberspace."
4. Greater use of electric cars and alternative forms of transportation.

These trends in technology are seen in today's marketplace. The power of microprocessors has doubled every 18 months for the past 25 years—suggesting that Intel's Pentium processor with 3.2 million transistors will be replaced by the Micro 2000 processor with more than 30 million transistors. The Internet already offers electronic magazines, shopping, and advertising, and more businesses and subscribers are becoming involved every day. Other technologies such as satellite disks, CDs and CD-ROMs, and electric cars are likely to replace or substitute for existing technologies such as cable TV, records and floppy disks, and even gas-powered cars![19]

Technology's Impact on Customer Value

Advances in technology are having important effects on marketing. First, the cost of technology is plummeting, causing the customer value assessment of technology-based products to focus on other dimensions such as quality, service, and relationships. When Microsoft introduced Windows 95, for example, it gave away 500 000 copies of the software program so customers could try it and later buy upgrades. A similar approach is used by many cellular telephone companies, who charge little or nothing for the telephone if the purchase leads to a cellular service contract.[20]

Technology also provides value through the development of new products. Oldsmobile now offers customers an auto-navigation system that uses satellite signals to help the driver reach any destination, while Lincoln Continental's vehicles automatically adjust 24 features—including seat and steering wheel positions, temperature, choice of CDs, and suspension and steering effort settings—to the preferences of the driver. Under development are radarlike collision-avoidance systems that disengage cruise control, reduce engine speed, and even apply the brakes. Finally, research and testing are under way to make auto glass that will dim, to deter theft, when the ignition is off and the car is unoccupied.[21]

Ultimately, the benefit of technology for marketers will be in allowing them to better understand and serve the customer. Technology is vital in assisting marketers to get existing products to the right consumers with greater speed and at lower costs. Using everything from desktop personal computers to satellites in space, entire industries are using technology to improve research, to reduce costs of production and distribution, to control inventory, and to stay in closer contact with customers and suppliers.

In many cases, consumers see and enjoy the benefits of technology used by marketers. Technology can often provide the customer with improved convenience, speed, accessibility and efficiency. For example, some Canadian banks offer automated telephone banking (ATB) where a customer can receive cash over the phone by transferring funds to a "smart card," like a debit card.[22] Still, some customers prefer individual and personal attention when dealing with organizations, and to them technology is not seen as beneficial. Automated technologies such as automated call centres (ACDs) or technologically based customer service programs, for example, can lead to dissatisfaction for some customers.[23] Smart marketers will

TECHNOLOGICAL CHANGES LEADS TO NEW PRODUCTS. WHAT PRODUCT MIGHT BE REPLACED BY THIS INNOVATION?

use technology wisely. They will assess the impact of technology on their customers and use it where appropriate. A particular challenge for marketers in this decade and the next will be to keep pace with the possibilities of rapid advances in technologies, specifically advances in computer-based technology, as is discussed in Chapter 10.

Ecological Impact of Technology

Technology has affected society in the development of products and in the ecological balance of the world's resources. **Ecology** refers to the relationship of physical resources in the environment. There is growing recognition that decisions today on the use of Earth's resources have long-term consequences to society. Such products as mercury-laden batteries, fertilizers, paints, and combustion engines have an effect on our land, air, and water. Companies are turning to technology to develop more environmentally sound alternatives—gasoline producers, for example, are developing reformulated gasoline products in an effort to reduce air pollution.[24]

Products that do not have obvious negative effects on the environment may also be a concern because of the growing problem of waste disposal. With landfill space growing short, there is increasing pressure from consumer and regulatory groups to reduce the amount of waste associated with a product.

Many companies have responded with recycling programs designed to send products through the manufacturing cycle several times. In Germany, Ford emphasizes that its cars are assembled with parts that can be recycled. The ad below shows a child's toy and exclaims "I was a car" in the headline.

Another approach is *precycling*, a term which describes efforts by manufacturers to reduce waste by decreasing the amount of packaging they use. DuPont, for example, developed a "minisip" collapsible pouch as an alternative to milk cartons in school lunch programs. In many cases, companies respond to environmental requests made by retailers. Wal-Mart, for example, requests that its suppliers provide environmentally safe products. This topic is discussed further in Chapter 4 as a matter of social responsibility. Future ecological concerns are discussed in the Marketing Newsnet box.[25]

EXAMPLES OF A RECYCLING PROGRAM BY FORD AND A PRECYCLING PROGRAM BY LEVER.

COMPETITIVE FORCES

Another component of the environmental scan is competition. **Competition** refers to the alternative firms that could provide a product to satisfy a specific market's needs. There are various forms of competition, and each company must consider its present and potential competitors in designing its marketing strategy.

Alternative Forms of Competition

There are four basic forms of competition that form a continuum: pure competition, monopolistic competition, oligopoly, and monopoly. Chapter 14 contains further discussions on pricing practices under these four forms of competition.

At one end of the continuum is *pure competition,* in which every company has a similar product. Companies that deal in commodities common to agribusiness (for example, wheat, rice, and other grains) are often in a pure competition position in which distribution (in the sense of shipping products) is important but other elements of the marketing mix have little impact.

In the second point on the continuum, *monopolistic competition,* the many sellers compete with their products on a substitutable basis. For example, if the price of coffee rises too much, consumers may switch to tea. Coupons or frequent sales are marketing tactics often used in monopolistic competition.

Oligopoly, a common industry structure, occurs when a few companies control the majority of industry sales. Because there are few sellers in an oligopolistic situation, price competition among firms is not desirable because it would lead to reduced revenue for all producers. Instead, nonprice competition is common, which means competing on other dimensions of the marketing mix such as product quality, distribution, and/or promotion. Canada is sometimes referred to by some economists as the "land of oligopoly," because it has several major industries that can be considered oligopolistic including the airline industry and the banking industry.

The final point on the continuum, *monopoly,* occurs when only one firm sells the product or service. It has been common for producers of goods and services considered essential to a community: water, electricity, or telephone service. Typically, marketing plays a small role in a monopolistic setting because it is regulated by a provincial or the federal government. Government control usually seeks to ensure price protection for the buyer. Historically, there was no competition in the long-distance telephone business in Canada, but deregulation has given rise to new entrants such as MCI, AT&T Canada, and Sprint. Bell Canada, and the various provincial telephone companies across Canada now must compete in a different marketing environment, a monopolistic-competitive one. Marketing has now assumed a more important role at the traditional telephone companies. More recent deregulation of the communications industry has now opened the local telephone services market in Canada. For a century, the telephone companies providing local service had a monopoly. This has now ended and local providers, long-distance carriers, and cable TV firms now compete in each other's markets.[26]

Components of Competition

In developing a marketing strategy, companies must consider the components that drive competition: entry, bargaining power of buyers and suppliers, existing rivalries (domestic and foreign) and substitution possibilities.[27] Scanning the environment requires a look at all of them. These relate to a firm's marketing mix decisions and may be used to create a barrier to entry, to increase brand awareness, or to intensify a fight for market share.

Entry   In considering competition, a firm must assess the likelihood of new entrants. Additional producers increase industry capacity and tend to lower prices. A company scanning its environment must consider the possible **barriers to entry** for other firms, which are business practices or conditions that make it difficult for new firms to enter the market. Barriers to entry can be in the form of capital requirements, promotional expenditures, product identity, distribution access, or switching costs. The higher the expense of the barrier, the more likely it will deter new entrants. For example, IBM once created a switching cost barrier for organizations that considered Apple Computer equipment because IBM had a different programming language for its machines.

Power of buyers and suppliers   A competitive analysis must consider the power of buyers and sellers. Powerful buyers exist when they are few in number, there are low switching costs, or the product represents a significant share of the buyer's total costs. This last factor leads the buyer to exert significant pressure for price competition. A supplier gains power when the product is critical to the buyer and when it has built up the switching costs.

Existing competition and substitutes   Competitive pressures among existing firms depend on the rate of industry growth. In slow-growth settings, competition is more heated for any possible gains in market share. High fixed costs also create competitive pressure for firms to fill production capacity. For example, many Canadian universities are increasing their advertising and public relations activities to fill classrooms, which represent a high fixed cost.

The New Look in Canadian Corporations

Increased domestic and global competition has had two other important effects on Canadian corporations: (1) the restructuring of corporations, and (2) the birth and growth of many small businesses.

Restructuring corporations Although the process is known by various names—reengineering, streamlining, or **restructuring**—the objective is the same: increase corporate efficiency in order to compete. For many firms, restructuring means reducing duplicate efforts in multiple company locations, closing or changing unprofitable plants and offices, and often laying off hundreds or thousands of employees. For example, Ford Motor Company merged some of its product development operations, refurbished seven plants, and reduced the number of managers by 20 percent. IBM moved sales representatives from multiple offices to one location—a "virtual office" consisting primarily of temporary work spaces assigned by computer on the three or four days each month that an employee may not be with customers. Many other companies from General Electric to Sunbeam have also restructured their organizations.

The result has been an improvement in efficiency. Ford has reduced the amount of time needed to get an engine from design to testing from 24 months to 100 days. Another result, however, has been a huge reduction in the number of employees at many corporations. Sunbeam, for example, recently cut its work force in half. This trend means there may be fewer opportunities for those entering the work force. It also suggests that employers are shifting from a philosophy of unconditional lifetime employment to one of "lifelong employability." This view is based on the idea that employers have an obligation to provide an opportunity of self-improvement and employees have an obligation to take charge of their own careers.[28]

Another approach to restructuring has been through mergers, acquisitions, and takeovers. Upjohn merged with Sweden's Pharmacia, and Kimberly-Clark acquired Scott Paper. McCain Foods Ltd. of New Brunswick acquired the food-service frozen French fry and potato specialties Ore-Ida Foods Inc.[29] What is the explanation? In general, firms are striving for market dominance by ensuring control of distribution channels, access to markets, and cost reduction through economies of scale. Businesses are also discovering that information technology will allow effective management of large and complex organizations. Experts debate whether these mergers are good for the economy. While firms that dominate a market might command higher prices, they may also be vulnerable to faster, customer-focused entrepreneurs.[30]

Regardless of the size of the organization, most firms are also changing the way employees work. Managers and employees are now empowered to make fast decisions about issues related to their job or the customers they serve. Cross-functional teams, which bring together employees from multiple functions, are used to ensure that all aspects of a product meet customer needs. Finally, continuous training is a necessity to maintain a smaller but better educated work force and to take advantage of improvements in technology and processes.

Startup and growth of small businesses Firms that have restructured their organization often increase their reliance on **outsourcing**—contracting work that formerly was done in-house by employees in marketing research, advertising, public relations, data processing, and training departments to small, outside firms. This has been one factor triggering the major growth in new business startups and in employment in small businesses. While many large Canadian companies continue to downsize, the bulk of the new employment in this country will be created as a result of business startups and expansion of existing small businesses.

CONCEPT CHECK

1. What is the difference between a consumer's disposable and discretionary income?

2. In pure competition there are _____ number of sellers.

3. What does restructuring a firm mean?

REGULATORY FORCES

For any organization, marketing and broader business decisions are constrained, directed, and influenced by regulatory forces. **Regulation** consists of restrictions the provincial and federal laws place on business with regard to the conduct of its activities. Regulation exists to protect companies as well as consumers. Much of the regulation from the federal and provincial levels has been passed to ensure competition and fair business practices. For consumers, the focus of legislation is to protect them from unfair trade practices and ensure their safety.

Protecting Competition and Consumers

Legislation and regulations exist in Canada at all three levels of government—federal, provincial, and municipal—to protect and encourage a competitive environment, which is deemed desirable because it permits the consumer to determine which competitor will succeed and which will fail.

The Competition Act   The key legislation designed to protect competition and consumers in Canada is the **Competition Act,** which replaced the Combines Investigation Act. The Combines legislation, in effect since 1923, has been found to be rather ineffectual. The Competition Act was introduced in two stages, in 1975 and 1986. The purpose of the Competition Act is:

> to maintain and encourage competition in Canada in order to promote the efficiency and adaptability of the Canadian economy, in order to expand opportunities for Canadian participation in world markets while at the same time recognizing the role of foreign competition in Canada, in order to ensure that small- and medium-sized enterprises have an equitable opportunity to participate in the Canadian economy and in order to provide consumers with competitive prices and product choices.[31]

In essence, the act is designed to protect and to balance the interests of competitors and consumers. The Bureau of Competition Policy, which is part of the federal department of Consumer and Corporate Affairs, is responsible for administering and enforcing the provisions of the act. The act contains both criminal and noncriminal provisions.

Criminal offences under Part VI of the act include conspiracy (e.g., price-fixing), bid-rigging, discriminatory and predatory pricing, price maintenance, and misleading or deceptive marketing practices such as double-ticketing or bait-and-switch selling.

Noncriminal reviewable matters under Part VIII of the act include mergers, abuse of dominant position, refusal to deal, consignment selling, exclusive dealing, tied selling, market restriction and delivered pricing. The Director of the Bureau of Competition Policy refers these matters to the Competition Tribunal under noncriminal law standards. The tribunal was established when the act took effect and is governed by the Competition Tribunal Act. The tribunal adjudicates all reviewable matters under the act.

Consumer and Corporate Affairs Canada is responsible for most of the legislation affecting business practices in Canada. Figure 3-5 lists the more significant federal legislation that protects competition and consumers in Canada. Marketers must also be cognizant of the fact that, in addition to federal laws and regulations, there are many more at the provincial level. Many provinces have their own departments of consumer affairs in order to administer any such legislation and regulations enacted on the provincial government level.

Unfortunately, the laws and regulations at the provincial level vary from province to province. A marketer may find it necessary to adapt some aspect of the marketing mix or some broader business practice depending on the province. For example, in Quebec there are specific laws dealing with store signage, packaging, and labelling. Additionally, advertising directed toward children is prohibited in Quebec. Many

Bank Cost Borrowing Act	Fish Inspection Act
Bankruptcy Act	Food and Drugs Act
Bills of Exchange Act	Hazardous Products Act
Board of Trade Act	Income Tax Act
Broadcasting Act	Industrial Design Act
Canada Agricultural Products	Maple Products Industry Act
Standards Act	Motor Vehicle Safety Act
Canada Cooperative Association Act	Offical Languages Act
Canada Corporations Act	Patent Act
Canada Dairy Products Act	Precious Metals Marketing Act
Canadian Human Rights Act	Small Loans Act
Competition Act	Standards Council of Canada Act
Consumer Packaging and Labelling Act	Textile Labelling Act
Copyright Act	The Interest Act
Criminal Code	Timber Marketing Act
Department of Consumer and	Trade Marks Act
Corporate Affairs Act	True Labelling Act
Electricity Inspection Act and Gas	Weights and Measures Act
Inspection Act	Winding-up Act

provinces, including Quebec, also have consumer protection acts and/or business or trade practices acts.

Self-Regulation

The government has provided much legislation to create a competitive business climate and protect the consumer. An alternative to government control is **self-regulation,** where an industry attempts to police itself. The Canadian Broadcasting Association, whose members include major television networks and radio stations across the country, has a code of ethics which helps govern the conduct of its members in terms of protecting the consumer against deceptive trade practices such as misleading advertising. Similarly, the Advertising Standards Council, the self-regulatory arm of the Canadian Advertising Foundation, has established the Canadian Code of Advertising Standards for its members to follow. The members of this organization consist of major advertising agencies who are responsible for allocating the bulk of advertising dollars in Canada. The Canadian Radio-Television Commission, the federal agency responsible for licensing and regulating broadcasting in Canada, is in favour of greater industry self-regulation.

The Canadian Direct Marketing Association, whose members represent 80 percent of direct-marketing sales in Canada, has mandated that its members comply with the consumers' right to privacy and honour consumers who request not to be contacted by telephone or mail for selling purposes. Critics argue that telemarketers in Canada demonstrate what is wrong with self-regulation efforts: noncompliance by members and enforcement (see the accompanying Ethics and Social Responsibility Alert).

Another well-known self-regulatory group is the Better Business Bureau (BBB). This organization is a voluntary alliance of companies whose goal is to help maintain fair business practices. Although the BBB has no legal power, it does try to use "moral suasion" to get members to comply with its regulations.

Consumerism

Regulation by government and self-regulation by industry help in protecting the consumer in the marketplace. But the consumer can also play a direct and active role. **Consumerism** is a movement to increase the influence, power, and the rights of con-

ETHICS AND SOCIAL RESPONSIBILITY ALERT

ALL IS NOT RIGHT WITH TELEMARKETING

Telemarketing does not have a good image with most consumers. In fact, survey after survey shows that the majority of consumers asked feel telemarketing is an invasion of privacy, is an offensive way to market, and a waste of the consumer's time. Why are many Canadians turned off by telemarketers? In some cases, there are telemarketers who engage in illegal and deceptive practices as well unethical behaviour. For example, take the case of a telemarketing company who phones consumers and tells them they have won prizes. The consumers are then asked to pay the shipping and handling costs for the prizes, the cost of which greatly exceeds the real costs of shipping and handling as well as the value of the prize.

In another case, consider telemarketing company representatives who lead consumers to believe they are volunteers requesting donations for a charity. In fact, that are paid fundraisers who are working on commission. What about a telemarketer who uses a telemail program where a consumer receives a direct-mail piece and is asked to phone an 800-number for further information? Unknown to the consumer, the telemarketer uses an automatic number identification or caller ID intrusion system that identifies the incoming caller's number without their knowledge or consent. If the consumer does not buy the product or service initially, the company now has the consumer's telephone number and begins recalling the consumer in an attempt to sell them. The telemarketer also has an opportunity to capture and sell consumers' unlisted telephone numbers.

In many cases, they are telemarketers who are simply guilty of deception, legally, and in other cases, engaging in unethical, but perhaps not illegal practices. This has not only tarnished the image of reputable telemarketers but all other professional marketers. Do you have any personal experiences with a telemarketer who has engaged in an illegal or unethical practice? What can be done about these unethical telemarketers?

---

sumers in dealing with institutions. Modern consumerism in Canada and the United States really began in the 1960s. US president John F. Kennedy, in a speech entitled "Consumer Bill of Rights," outlined four basic consumer rights: (1) the right to safety, (2) the right to be informed, (3) the right to choose, and (4) the right to be heard. Although not passed as laws, these proclaimed rights serve as the basis for modern consumerism. Shortly after President Kennedy's Consumer Bill of Rights was unveiled in the United States, the Canadian government formed the Department of Consumer and Corporate Affairs, making it the agency responsible for protecting consumers and regulating corporate activities.

Canada also has many independent consumer organizations who advance the cause of consumerism. The Consumer's Association of Canada (CAC), is the largest consumer group working on behalf of the Canadian consumer. The CAC serves as a channel for supplying consumers' views to government and industry, providing consumer information, and studying consumer problems and presenting recommended solutions to those problems. In addition to ensuring the four original consumer rights are protected, the consumer movement of the 1990s also includes consumer demands for environmentally safe products and ethical and socially responsible business practices.

CONCEPT CHECK

1. The _____ Act is the most important legislation designed to protect competition and consumers in Canada.

2. An alternative to legislation protecting competition and consumers is self-_____.

3. What is consumerism?

SUMMARY

1. The population in Canada is estimated at 30 million. The population is aging, and the number of traditional families as seen in the 1950s is diminishing. The dual-income family is now the norm in Canada and a blended family structure is becoming more common.

2. It is estimated that close to 80 percent of Canadians are urban dwellers, with most living in census metropolitan areas (CMAs). Regional marketing, developing marketing mixes designed to reflect the specific geographic area differences in taste preferences, perceived needs, or interests is something Canadian marketers must consider.

3. Canada is becoming more ethnically diverse, including recent growth in the population of visible minorities.

4. Culture represents abstract values and material possessions. Values are changing toward work, quality of life, the roles of women and men, and consumption.

5. Disposable income is the number of dollars left after taxes. Discretionary income is the money consumers have after purchasing their necessities.

6. Technological advances are changing the ways companies do business. Growing environmental concern is also leading companies to be more ecologically responsible in the development and marketing of products.

7. There are various forms of competition, and each company must consider its present and potential competitors in designing its marketing strategy. Many are restructuring in an effort to improve efficiency in order to compete in a more competitive arena.

8. For any organization, marketing and broader business decisions are constrained, directed, and influenced by regulatory forces. The most important legislation in Canada designed to protect competition and consumers is the Competition Act.

9. An alternative to government control is self-regulation, where an industry attempts to police itself. The effectiveness of self-regulation is coming under greater scrutiny.

10. The consumer can also play a direct and active role in influencing what happens in the marketplace. Consumerism is a movement to increase the influence, power, and the rights of consumers in dealing with institutions. Modern consumers are demanding more environmentally safe products and ethical and socially responsible business practices.

KEY TERMS AND CONCEPTS

environmental scanning p. 72
social forces p. 73
demographics p. 73
mature market p. 74
baby boomers p. 74
generation X p. 75
baby boomlet p. 75
blended family p. 75
census metropolitan areas p. 75
regional marketing p. 76
culture p. 77
value consciousness p. 78
economy p. 79

gross income p. 80
disposable income p. 80
discretionary income p. 81
technology p. 81
ecology p. 83
competition p. 84
barriers to entry p. 85
restructuring p. 86
outsourcing p. 86
regulation p. 87
Competition Act p. 87
self-regulation p. 88
consumerism p. 88

CHAPTER PROBLEMS AND APPLICATIONS

1. For many years Gerber has manufactured baby food in small, single-sized containers. In conducting an environmental scan, identify three trends or factors that might significantly affect this company's future prospects, and then propose how Gerber might respond to these changes.

2. Describe the target market for a luxury item such as the Mercedes Benz 190 (the lowest-priced Mercedes). List three or four magazines in which you would advertise to appeal to this target market.

3. The growing concern with the environment was discussed in this chapter. Marketing in an ecologically or environmentally

sensitive manner is more important to firms. Suggest how the following companies and products might respond to environmental concerns: (*a*) Gillette safety razor division, (*b*) Kentucky Fried Chicken restaurants, (*c*) Hallmark greeting cards.

4. In the Canadian brewing industry, two large firms control most of the beer sales in Canada (Labatt's and Molson). But they are now facing competition from many smaller regional brands. In terms of the continuum of competition, how would you explain this change?

5. With the deregulation of the Canadian long-distance telephone industry, how do you think the role of marketing in the industry will change? What elements of the marketing mix are more or less important since deregulation?

6. With time poverty being a concern for many dual-income families, how can marketers help these families better balance work and family?

7. Today's consumer is more value-conscious. How could a retail home improvement centre sell the exact same products but still offer the consumer greater perceived value? What specific things could the retailer do?

CASE 3-1: Imagination Pilots Entertainment

What develops critical thinking, problem solving, and math skills, has an original musical score and sound effects, utilizes full-colour graphics, and involves an adventure with the circus? The answer is one of the newest forms of edutainment—a CD-ROM game developed for children called "Where's Waldo?" The game is part of a growing number of offerings from an industry that is rapidly adapting to a wide variety of changes in the business environment. According to the *Hollywood Reporter,* which follows the new developments, "interactive start-ups face new challenges as they stake a claim in a rapidly changing market."

THE COMPANY

The developer of the "Where's Waldo?" game is a fast-growing, entrepreneurial company called Imagination Pilots Entertainment. The founder of the company, Howard Tullman, has focused on developing multimedia entertainment, educational software, and interactive "cinematic" adventures with strong game content. One of the company's first products was the interactive CD-ROM game called *Blown Away,* which was developed as part of a joint venture with MGM/United Artists and released after the movie by the same name. Imagination Pilot's *Blown Away* won the "Game of the Year" award from *Computer Life* magazine, the Gold Medal Invision Award for Best Graphic Design from *New Media* magazine, and the Innovators Software Showcase Award. Other Imagination Pilots products include *Panic in the Park* starring Erika Eleniak; *Virtual Erector Set,* which allows children to build 3-D, real-time models of vehicles; and an adventure game sequel to Arnold Schwarzenegger's movie, *Eraser.*

THE CHANGING ENVIRONMENT

Managers at Imagination Pilots are constantly monitoring social, economic, technological, competitive, and regulatory trends that may influence their business or the CD-ROM game industry. The most obvious trend, for ex-

ample, is the rapid growth of the software market. Revenues for the packaged software market are expected to grow at an annual rate of 13 percent reaching $153 billion by 2000. In addition, while many industries are laying off employees, the software industry is a net creator of jobs. A niche within the overall software market is the multimedia software market. Multimedia products combine video, animation, still pictures, voice, music, graphics, and text into a single system, usually on CD-ROM and very often for education or entertainment applications. Sales of CD-ROM titles have doubled each year for the past several years and now exceed $1.2 billion.

Related trends are the increasing penetration of computers into homes due to declining PC prices, and the increasing number of installed CD-ROM drives. According to Tullman, "There are only now becoming enough PC CD-ROM computers in the marketplace, in terms of total units, to permit a number of products to be successful." Although the number has been increasing at an annual rate of 25 percent, the number of worldwide CD-ROM computers was still just 21 million in 1996. The price of software is also declining while consumer expectations are increasing. Tullman observes that "the price of children's software is decreasing, and continues to decrease even while there is a greater demand for quality . . . the consumer and parents want to pay less for individual games, but they want them to be of high quality."

Increasing competition also represents a challenge for Imagination Pilots. In the children's entertainment category software developers include Electronic Arts, Acclaim Entertainment, Sierra On-Line, Broderbund, Xiphias, and a very large number of relatively small firms. In addition, as growth of computer sales slows in the corporate market, many large firms, including Microsoft, IBM, Compaq, and Apple Computer are expected to try to develop children's software as a way into the home market. Many new titles are being introduced by both past developers and new entrants—creating a very competitive market.

A final factor Imagination Pilots and other developers must consider is the possibility of regulation. Concern about the content of some games had led to a discussion about the potential need for a rating system, much like the system used for movies.

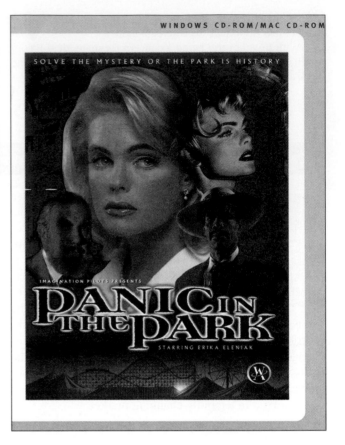

THE ISSUES

Imagination Pilots is faced with several key challenges. First, it must attempt to ensure the success of new titles planned for development. Second, it must obtain distribution for existing and future products. Although the two are related, they require attention to very different issues.

Establishing a new title in a cluttered marketplace is likely to be difficult for any software developer. Estimates suggest that from $800 000 to $1.5 million is required to develop a competitive CD-ROM product. As a result, many firms seek partnerships or alliances to spread costs and reduce risk. Recovering the investment may be difficult, however, if sales volume is low or the profit margin of each unit sold is low. Part of Imagination Pilot's strategy is to license rights to existing stories, such as "Where's Waldo?," or movies, such as *Blown Away* and *Eraser*. Tullman believes that the name recognition of licensed titles is important to ensure adequate consumer interest. Some developers of children's software have used product line extensions to extend the life of existing titles. Sierra On-line's *Quest,* for example, is now in its sixth release. New titles will need much more, though, to gain a foothold in the market.

Daniel P. Di Caro, Chief Operating Officer at Imagination Pilots, argues that "distribution is increasingly becoming the most important factor in the success of a product, assuming you have a good product to start with." In the past the traditional channel of distribution was through software specialty stores such as Egghead Software, Babbages, and Software Etc. More recently, sales have increased in computer superstores, department stores such as Sears and Wal-Mart, consumer electronic stores, and warehouse stores. Their relationship with Warner Music Group provides Imagination Pilots with a strong distribution partner with access to many of these channels. In the future additional channels such as catalogues, interactive television channels, and kiosks may offer the company new distribution opportunities. Imagination Pilots is already testing an on-line service which makes its games available to the Internet and World Wide Web community!

Questions

1. Conduct an environmental scan for Imagination Pilots Entertainment. How are each of the five environmental forces (social, economic, technological, competitive, and regulatory) likely to influence their multimedia game business?

2. What are the key challenges facing Imagination Pilots? Describe the actions taken by Imagination Pilots to (*a*) ensure the success of, and (*b*) obtain distribution for its games.

3. What are the advantages of making Imagination Pilot's games available on-line?

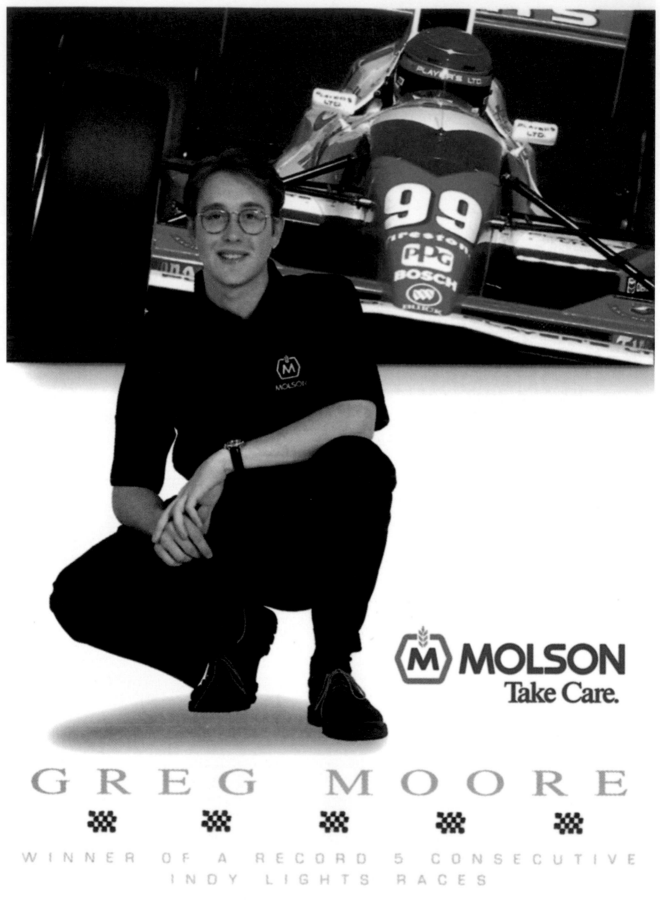

CHAPTER 4

Ethics and Social Responsibility in Marketing

AFTER READING THIS CHAPTER YOU SHOULD BE ABLE TO:

• Appreciate the nature and significance of ethics in marketing.

• Understand the differences between legal and ethical behaviour in marketing.

• Identify factors that influence ethical and unethical marketing decisions.

• Distinguish among the different concepts of ethics and social responsibility.

• Recognize the importance of ethical and socially responsible consumer behaviour.

AT MOLSON BREWERIES, THERE IS MORE BREWING THAN BEER

Why would a company spend millions of dollars trying to convince people not to abuse its products? Ask Molson Breweries (www.molson.com), one of Canada's largest brewers and a leader in the campaign for the responsible use of alcohol. As one of Canada's leading corporate citizens, Molson recognizes the need to support meaningful public dialogue and programs to raise community awareness about this issue. Molson's "Take Care" program is a multimillion dollar national communications program that goes beyond conventional "drinking and driving" campaigns. It puts responsible use of alcohol in a broader context—of work, health, and quality of life.

The program includes broadcast, print, and outdoor advertising, promotions tied to Molson sports and entertainment properties across the country, educational initiatives in schools and colleges, and support to community and interest groups.

Molson acts on what it views as an ethical obligation to its customers with its "Take Care" campaign. At the same time, the company is also involved in multifaceted efforts to support the communities in which it operates and to protect our natural environment. Molson has a long history of supporting countless charities and has founded some of the country's major health, educational, and cultural institutions. In the spirit of this commitment to social responsibility, the Molson Companies Donations Fund was incorporated in the 1970s to focus the corporation's philanthropic activities. Molson has also made the protection of the environment a high priority. For example, over 98 percent of its bottles and 75 percent of its cans are returned to points of sale to be retrieved for reuse or recycling. Molson ensures that its breweries are environmentally efficient throughout all stages of the brewing process, and all its offices have recycling programs. The company also supports a variety of environmental initiatives across Canada including Pollution Probe Foundation and the Young Naturalist Foundation.[1]

This chapter focuses on ethics and social responsibility in marketing. You will see how some companies recognize that while ethically and socially responsible behaviour often comes with a price tag, the price for unethical and socially irresponsible behaviour is often much higher. In essence, in this marketplace, companies can "do well by doing good."

NATURE AND SIGNIFICANCE OF MARKETING ETHICS

Ethics are the moral principles and values that govern the actions and decisions of an individual or group.[2] Simply put, ethics serve as guidelines on how to act rightly and justly when faced with moral dilemmas. For marketing managers, ethics concern the application of moral principles and values to marketing decision making.

Ethical/Legal Framework in Marketing

A good starting point for understanding the nature and significance of ethics is the distinction between legality and ethicality of marketing decisions. Figure 4-1 helps you to visualize the relationship between laws and ethics.[3] While ethics deal with personal and moral principles and values, **laws** are society's values and standards that are enforceable in the courts.[4]

In general, what is illegal is also unethical. For example, deceptive advertising is illegal. It is also unethical, because it conflicts with the moral principles of honesty and fairness. But not all unethical conduct is illegal. For instance, price gouging is usually not illegal, but is often viewed as unethical. Marketing managers often find themselves

FIGURE 4-1

CLASSIFYING MARKETING DECISIONS ACCORDING TO ETHICAL AND LEGAL RELATIONSHIPS

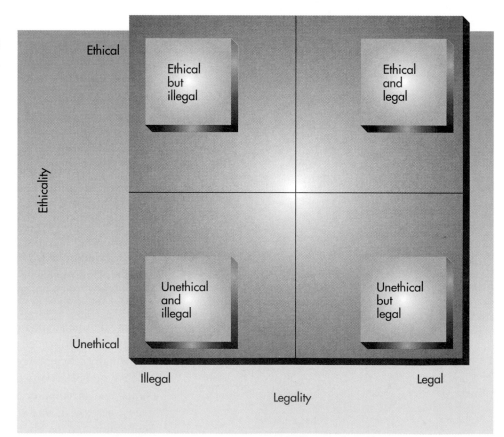

in many situations where they must make judgments in defining ethical and legal boundaries. For some, the distinction between ethics and laws can sometimes lead to the rationalization that if a behaviour is within legal limits, then it is not really unethical. For example, recently, a group of Canadian business students were surveyed and asked: "Is it okay to charge a higher price than normal when you know the customer really needs the product and will pay the higher price?" Almost 35 percent of the business students who took part in the survey responded "Yes."[5] How would you have answered this question?

Now consider the following situations. After reading each, assign it to the cell in Figure 4-1 that you think best fits the situation along the ethical-legal continuum.

1. Several companies meet and agree to bid-rigging for sealed tendered government contract work. Bid-rigging is illegal under the Competition Act since it eliminates free and open competition.

2. A company uses a technique called "slugging" or selling under the guise of research. Once prospective customers agree to take part in the research, the salespeople switch to their sales pitch.

3. A real estate agent sells a high-rise condo unit to a customer, primarily because the customer loves the city view looking out the condo windows. The agent knows that in one year another high-rise will be built, effectively blocking the view so important to the customer. The agent decides not to tell that customer.

4. A company interviews a very qualified female for an industrial sales position. She is more qualified than any males who were interviewed. However, the company knows that some male purchasing agents prefer to deal with a male salesperson, so they hire a less qualified male applicant.

Do these situations fit neatly into Figure 4-1 as clearly defined ethical and legal or unethical and illegal? Some probably do not. As you read further in this chapter, you will be asked again to consider other ethical dilemmas.

Current Perceptions of Ethical Behaviour

There has been much discussion over the possible deterioration of personal morality and ethical standards on a global scale. The news media offers well-publicized examples of personal dishonesty, hypocrisy, cheating, and greed. There also has been a public outcry about the ethical practices of businesspeople. In particular, there is widespread concern over unethical marketing practices such as price-fixing, bribery, deceptive advertising, and unsafe products. Public opinion surveys as well as other research shows that most adults believe the ethical standards of business have declined over the years.[6] One study found that consumers believed advertising practitioners and car salespeople were among the least ethical professions.[7]

There are at least four possible reasons why the state of perceived ethical business conduct is at its present level. First, there is increased pressure on businesspeople to make decisions in a society characterized by diverse value systems.[8] Second, there is a growing tendency for business decisions to be judged publicly by groups with different values and interests. Third, the public's expectations regarding ethical business behaviour has increased. Finally, and most disturbing, ethical business conduct may have declined.

CONCEPT CHECK

1. What are ethics?

2. What are laws?

UNDERSTANDING ETHICAL MARKETING BEHAVIOUR

Researchers have identified numerous factors that influence ethical marketing behaviour.[9] Figure 4-2 presents a framework that shows these factors and their relationships.

Societal Culture and Norms

As described in Chapter 3, *culture* refers to the set of values, ideas, and attitudes of a homogeneous group of people that are transmitted from one generation to the next. Culture also affects ethical relationships between individuals, groups, and the institutions and organizations they create. In this way, culture serves as a socializing force that dictates what is morally right and just. This means that moral standards are relative to particular societies. These standards often reflect the laws and regulations that affect social and economic behaviour, including business practices, which can create moral dilemmas. For example, Levi Strauss decided to end much of its business dealings in China because of what the company called "pervasive human rights abuses." According to its vice president for corporate marketing: "There are wonderful commercial opportunities in China. But when ethical issues collide with commercial appeal, we try to ensure ethics as the trump card. For us, ethical issues precede all others."[10]

Actions that restrain trade, fix prices, deceive buyers, and result in unsafe products are considered morally wrong in Canada and other countries. However, different cultures view marketing practices differently. Consider the use of another's ideas, copyright, trademark, or patent. These are viewed as intellectual property and unauthorized use is illegal and unethical in Canada. Hallmark Cards, Inc., was charged with copying ideas of a smaller card company without its consent. The courts ruled that Hallmark must stop publishing the cards, buy back existing cards from Hallmark stores, and pay damages to the owners of the company.[11]

Outside Canada, however, is another story.[12] Unauthorized use of copyrights, trademarks, and patents is routine in countries such as China, Mexico, and Korea and cost the authorized owners billions of dollars annually. In Korea, for instance, copying is partly rooted in its society's culture. According to international trade officials, many Koreans have the idea that the thoughts of one man should benefit all, and the Korean government rarely prosecutes infringements. Read the accompanying Marketing Newsnet,[13] keeping in mind the ethical-legal framework in Figure 4-1. Would the unauthorized use of copyrighted computer software be considered unethical despite its prevalence?

FIGURE 4-2

A FRAMEWORK FOR
UNDERSTANDING ETHICAL
BEHAVIOUR

MARKETING NEWSNET

SOFTWARE PIRACY IN CYBERSPACE: THE DARK SIDE OF GLOBAL ELECTRONIC NETWORKING

The Internet links some 100 countries and an estimated 25 million computer users. The many benefits of electronic networking often overshadow its dark side: software piracy. Anyone with a computer and modem can distribute software silently, instantaneously, and illegally. Indeed, a 20-year-old college student was recently attributed with distributing an estimated $1 million worth of copyrighted programs through the Internet.

The Software Publishers Association (SPA) estimates that the unauthorized copying of computer software costs their producers the equivalent of $13 billion in worldwide sales annually. Software piracy has become pandemic in many developing countries. According to the SPA, 98 percent of the software in China is pirated, 95 percent in Russia, 92 percent in Thailand, 87 percent in India and Pakistan, 84 percent in the Czech and Slovak Republics, and 82 percent in Mexico.

Software programs are intellectual property, and their unauthorized use is illegal in many countries. But, for some, their reproduction and distribution is not considered unethical.

Business Culture and Industry Practices

Societal culture provides a foundation for understanding moral and ethical behaviour in business activities. *Business cultures* "comprise the effective rules of the game, the boundaries between competitive and unethical behaviour, [and] the codes of conduct in business dealings."[14] Consumers have witnessed numerous instances where business cultures in the brokerage (inside trading), insurance (deceptive sales practices), and defence (bribery) industries went awry. Business culture affects ethical conduct both in the exchange relationship between sellers and buyers and in the competitive behaviour among sellers.

Ethics of exchange   The exchange process is central to the marketing concept. Ethical exchanges between sellers and buyers should result in both parties being better off after a transaction.[15]

Prior to the 1960s, the legal concept of **caveat emptor**—let the buyer beware—was pervasive in Canadian business culture. The growth and strength of the consumer movement resulted in this concept becoming an unacceptable marketplace philosophy. A codification of ethics between buyers and sellers was established, with consumers recognizing their rights to safety, to be informed, to choose, and to be heard. Consumers expect and often demand that these rights be protected. Most businesses comply but exceptions exist. In terms of not ensuring consumer safety, A. H. Robbins sold the Dalkon Shield, an intrauterine device, that was known to be potentially harmful to women. The company has since established a $2.5 billion fund to compensate women harmed by the device.[16]

The consumer's right to be informed means that marketers have an obligation to give consumers complete and accurate information about products and services, but this is not always the case. In 1997, Canadian investors lost millions of dollars after

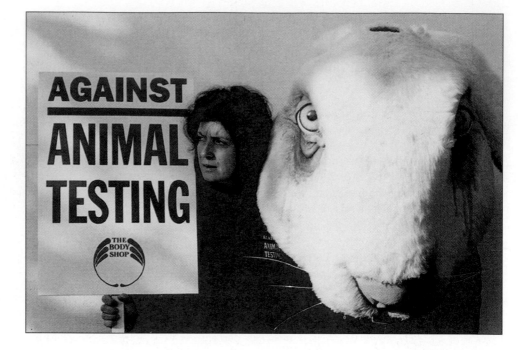

buying shares in Bre-X Minerals, a Canadian exploration company. The company had led investors to believe that it had found the world's largest ore body at its Indonesian gold mine. The information was false and investors sued the company for fraud.

Relating to the right to choose, today many supermarket chains demand "slotting allowances" from manufacturers, in the form of cash rebates or free goods, to stock new products. This practice could limit the number of new products available to consumers and interfere with their right to choose. One critic of this practice remarked: "If we had had slotting allowances a few years ago, we might not have had granola, herbal tea, or yogourt."[17]

Finally, the right to be heard means consumers should have access to company and/or public-policy makers regarding comments or complaints about products and services. Many Canadian companies have set up customer service departments to deal with customer comments or complaints. Consumer complaints against the use of animals for product testing have led to curbs against this practice, particularly among cosmetic manufacturers.

Ethics of competition   Business culture also affects ethical behaviour in competition. Two kinds of unethical behaviour are most common: (1) industrial espionage and (2) bribery.

Industrial espionage is the clandestine collection of trade secrets or proprietary information about a company's competitors. Many Canadian and American firms have uncovered espionage in some form, costing them billions of dollars a year.[18] This practice is most prevalent in high-technology industries such as electronics, specialty chemicals, industrial equipment, aerospace, and pharmaceuticals, where technical know-how and secrets separate industry leaders from followers.

But espionage can occur anywhere—the toy industry and even the ready-to-eat cookie industry! Procter & Gamble charged that competitors photographed its plants and production lines, stole a sample of its cookie dough, and infiltrated a confidential sales presentation to learn about its technology, recipe, and marketing plan. The competitors paid Procter & Gamble $120 million in damages after a lengthy dispute.[19]

The second form of unethical competitive behaviour is giving and receiving bribes and kickbacks. Bribes and kickbacks are often disguised as gifts, consultant fees, and favours. This practice is more common in business-to-business and government marketing than consumer marketing. There is also a prevalence of bribery in international marketing where it is looked upon differently in many business cultures. In Denmark, bribes paid to foreign companies are actually considered a tax-deductible expense![20]

In general, ethical standards are more likely to be compromised in industries experiencing intense competition and in countries in earlier stages of economic development. For example, bribery of government officials or political parties in developing countries by international companies is very common. These bribes are paid to obtain or retain business in that country, or to receive special exemptions from regulations or taxes.

Corporate Culture and Expectations

A third influence on ethical practices is corporate culture. As defined in Chapter 2, *corporate culture* refers to a system of shared attitudes and behaviours held by employees that distinguish it from other organizations. The culture of a corporation demonstrates itself in the dress ("We don't wear ties"), sayings ("The IBM Way"), and the manner of work (team efforts) of employees. Corporate culture is also apparent in the expectations for ethical behaviour present in formal codes of ethics and the ethical actions of top management and co-workers.

Codes of ethics   A **code of ethics** is a formal statement of ethical principles and rules of conduct. Ethics codes and committees typically address contributions to government officials and political parties, relations with customers and suppliers, conflicts of interest, and accurate recordkeeping. For example, General Mills provides guidelines for dealing with suppliers, competitors, and customers, and recruits new employees who share these views. However, an ethics code is rarely enough to ensure ethical behaviour. Johnson & Johnson has an ethics code and emphasizes that its employees be just and ethical in their behaviour. But neither prevented some of its employees from shredding papers to hinder a government probe into the firm's marketing of an acne cream, Retin-A.[21]

The lack of specificity is one of the major reasons for the violation of ethics codes. Employees must often judge whether a specific behaviour is really unethical. The American Marketing Association, representing Canadian and American marketing professionals, has addressed this issue by providing a detailed code of ethics, which all members agree to follow. This code is shown in Figure 4-3.

Ethical behaviour of management and co-workers   A second reason for violating ethics codes rests in the perceived behaviour of top management and co-workers.[22] Observing peers and top management and gauging responses to unethical behaviour plays an important role in individual actions. For example, what message do employees receive when they see personnel being rewarded for engaging in ethically troubling behaviour and seeing others punished for refusing to engage in unethical behaviour? Clearly, ethical dilemmas often bring personal and professional conflict. In many cases, **whistleblowers**, employees who report unethical or illegal actions of their employers, often face recrimination. Some firms like General Dynamics and Dun & Bradstreet, have appointed ethics officers responsible for safeguarding such individuals.[23]

Personal Moral Philosophy and Ethical Behaviour

Ultimately, ethical choices are based on the personal moral philosophy of the decision maker. Moral philosophy is learned through the process of socialization with friends and family, and by formal education. It is also influenced by the societal, business, and corporate culture in which a person finds him- or herself. Moral philosophies are of two types: (1) moral idealism and (2) utilitarianism.[24]

Moral idealism   **Moral idealism** is a personal philosophy that considers certain individual rights or duties as universal (e.g., right to freedom) regardless of the outcome. This philosophy is favoured by moral philosophers and consumer interest

FIGURE 4-3

AMERICAN MARKETING ASSOCIATION CODE OF ETHICS

CODE OF ETHICS

Members of the American Marketing Association (AMA) are committed to ethical professional conduct. They have joined together in subscribing to this Code of Ethics embracing the following topics:

Responsibilities of the Marketer

Marketers must accept responsibility for the consequence of their activities and make every effort to ensure that their decisions, recommendations, and actions function to identify, serve, and satisfy all relevant publics: customers, organizations, and society.

Marketers' professional conduct must be guided by:

1. The basic rule of professional ethics: not knowingly to do harm.
2. The adherence to all applicable laws and regulations.
3. The accurate representation of their education, training and experience.
4. The active support, practice, and promotion of this Code of Ethics.

Honesty and Fairness

Marketers shall uphold and advance the integrity, honor, and dignity of the marketing profession by:

1. Being honest in serving consumers, clients, employees, suppliers, distributors, and the public.
2. Not knowingly participating in conflict of interest without prior notice to all parties involved.
3. Establishing equitable fee schedules including the payment or receipt of usual, customary, and/or legal compensation or marketing exchanges.

Rights and Duties of Parties in the Marketing Exchange Process

Participants in the marketing exchange process should be able to expect that:

1. Products and services offered are safe and fit for their intended uses.
2. Communications about offered products and services are not deceptive.
3. All parties intend to discharge their obligations, financial and otherwise, in good faith.
4. Appropriate internal methods exist for equitable adjustment and/or redress of grievances concerning purchases.

It is understood that the above would include, *but is not limited to,* the following responsibilities of the marketer:

In the area of product development and management

- Disclosure of all substantial risks associated with product or service usage.

- Identification of any product component substitution that might materially change the product or impact on the buyer's purchase decision.
- Identification of extra-cost added features.

In the area of promotions

- Avoidance of false and misleading advertising.
- Rejection of high-pressure manipulation, or misleading sales tactics.
- Avoidance of sales promotions that use deception or manipulation.

In the area of distribution

- Not manipulating the availability of a product for purpose of exploitation.
- Not using coercion in the marketing channel.
- Not exerting undue influence over the reseller's choice to handle the product.

In the area of pricing

- Not engaging in price fixing.
- Not practicing predatory pricing.
- Disclosing the full price associated with any purchase.

In the area of marketing research

- Prohibiting selling or fund raising under the guise of conducting research.
- Maintaining research integrity by avoiding misrepresentation and omission of pertinent research data.
- Treating outside clients and suppliers fairly.

Organizational Relationships

Marketers should be aware of how their behavior may influence or impact on the behavior of others in organizational relationships. They should not demand, encourage, or apply coercion to obtain unethical behavior in their relationships with others, such as employees, suppliers, or customers.

1. Apply confidentiality and anonymity in professional relationships with regard to privileged information.
2. Meet their obligations and responsibilities in contracts and mutual agreements in a timely manner.
3. Avoid taking the work of others, in whole or in part, and represent this work as their own or directly benefit from it without compensation or consent of the originator or owner.
4. Avoid manipulation to take advantage of situations to maximize personal welfare in a way that unfairly deprives or damages the organization or others.

Any AMA members found to be in violation of any provision of this Code of Ethics may have his or her Association membership suspended or revoked.

Source: Reprinted by permission of the American Marketing Association.

groups. This philosophy also applies to ethical duties such as informing the consumer about the safety hazards of a particular product; even conducting a large-scale recall of a deceptive product, regardless of cost, in order to uphold that consumer right to safety.

Utilitarianism   An alternative perspective on moral philosophy is **utilitarianism,** which is a personal moral philosophy that focuses on "the greatest good for the greatest number," by assessing the costs and benefits of the consequences of ethical behaviour. If the benefits exceed the costs, then the behaviour is ethical. If not, then the behaviour is unethical. This philosophy underlies the economic tenets of capitalism[25] and, not surprisingly, is embraced by many business executives and students.[26]

SOME INFANTS HAD ALLERGIC REACTIONS TO NESTLÉ'S GOOD START FORMULA. READ THE TEXT TO FIND OUT WHAT THE COMPANY DID.

Utilitarian reasoning was apparent in Nestlé Food Corporation's marketing of Good Start infant formula, sold by Nestlé's Carnation Company. The formula, promoted as hypoallergenic, was designed to prevent or reduce colic caused by an infant's allergic reaction to cow's milk—a condition suffered by 2 percent of babies. However, some severely milk-allergic infants experienced serious side effects after using Good Start, including convulsive vomiting. Physicians and parents charged that the hypoallergenic claim was misleading, and the government investigated the matter. A Nestlé vice president defended the claim and product, saying, "I don't understand why our product should work in 100 percent of cases. If we wanted to say it was foolproof, we would have called it allergy-free. We call it hypo-, or less, allergenic."[27] Nestlé officials seemingly believed that most allergic infants would benefit from Good Start—"the greatest good for the greatest number." However, other views prevailed, and the claim was dropped from the product label.

An appreciation for the nature of ethics, coupled with a basic understanding of why unethical behaviour arises, alerts a person to when and how ethical issues exist in marketing decisions. Ultimately, ethical behaviour rests with the individual, but the consequences affect many.

CONCEPT CHECK

1. What is caveat emptor?
2. What is a code of ethics?
3. What is meant by moral idealism?

UNDERSTANDING SOCIAL RESPONSIBILITY IN MARKETING

As we saw in Chapter 1, the societal marketing concept stresses marketing's social responsibility by not only satisfying the needs of consumers but also providing for society's welfare. **Social responsibility** means that organizations are part of a larger society and are accountable to that society for their actions. Like ethics, agreement on the nature and scope of social responsibility is often difficult to come by, given the diversity of values present in different societal, business, and organizational cultures.

Concepts of Social Responsibility

Figure 4-4 shows three concepts of social responsibility: (1) profit responsibility, (2) stakeholder responsibility, and (3) societal responsibility.

FIGURE 4-4

THREE CONCEPTS OF SOCIAL
RESPONSIBILITY

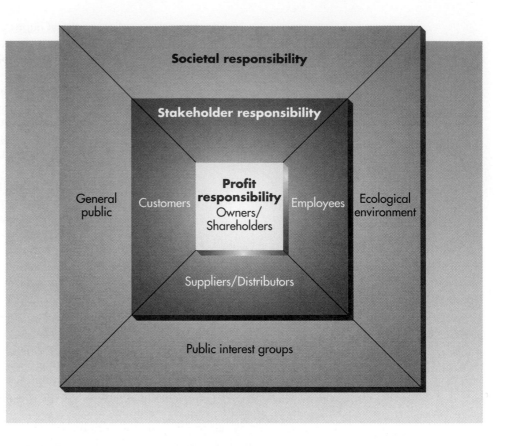

Profit responsibility   *Profit responsibility* holds that companies have a simple duty—to maximize profits for their owners or shareholders. This view is expressed by Nobel Laureate Milton Friedman, who said, "There is one and only one social responsibility of business—to use its resources and engage in activities designed to increase its profits so long as it stays within the rules of the game, which is to say, engages in open and free competition without deception or fraud."[28] Genzyme, the maker of Ceredase, a drug that treats a genetic illness called Gaucher's disease that affects 20 000 people worldwide,

WHICH OF THE THREE CONCEPTS OF
SOCIAL RESPONSIBILITY DO YOU
THINK PERRIER APPLIED WHEN IT
LEARNED OF QUALITY PROBLEMS
WITH ITS POPULAR WATER? READ THE
TEXT TO LEARN HOW THEY
RESPONDED TO THIS PROBLEM AND
THEIR REASONING.

has been criticized for apparently adopting this view in its pricing practices. Genzyme charges up to $200 000 for a year's worth of Ceredese. A Genzyme spokesperson responded by saying that Ceredase profits are below industry standards and that the company freely gives the drug to patients without insurance.[29]

Stakeholder responsibility   Frequent criticism of the profit view has led to a broader concept of social responsibility. *Stakeholder responsibility* focuses on the obligations an organization has to those who can affect achievement of its objectives. These constituencies include customers, employees, suppliers, and distributors. Source Perrier S. A., the supplier of Perrier bottled water, exercised this responsibility when it recalled 160 million bottles of water in 120 countries after traces of a toxic chemical were found in 13 bottles. The recall cost the company $35 million, and $40 million more was lost in sales. Even though the chemical level was not harmful to humans, Source Perrier's president believed he acted in the best interests of the firm's consumers, distributors, and employees by removing "the least doubt, as minimal as it might be, to weigh on the image of the quality and purity of our product."[30]

Societal responsibility   An even broader concept of social responsibility has emerged in recent years. *Societal responsibility* refers to obligations that organizations have to the (1) preservation of the ecological environment and (2) general public. Concerns about the environment and public welfare are represented by interest and advocacy groups such as Greenpeace, an international environmental organization.

Chapter 3 detailed the growing importance of ecological issues in marketing. Companies have responded to this concern through what is termed **green marketing**— marketing efforts to produce, promote, and reclaim environmentally sensitive products. Green marketing takes many forms.[31] The Canadian aluminum industry recycles nearly two-thirds of all aluminum cans for reuse. The Grocery Products Manufacturers of Canada has a program known as the *Canadian Industry Packaging Stewardship Initiative,* designed to promote responsible waste and product recycling. Procter & Gamble introduced Downy Refill liquid fabric softener, which reduces solid waste pollution. The product's plastic bottle is reuseable, and the refill carton uses 75 percent less packaging material. Levi Strauss and Esprit have clothing lines using cotton that is naturally coloured, thus reducing

PROCTER & GAMBLE MINIMIZED SOLID WASTE BY INTRODUCING DOWNY REFILL, WHICH USES 75 PERCENT LESS PACKAGING MATERIAL.

the need for dyes, a source of pollution. Black Photo of Markham, Ontario, is a leader in chemical waste management in the photofinishing industry. The environment is factored into everything from product conception to manufacturing, distribution, and sales. And even small businesses and entrepreneurs are engaged in green marketing. James Floyd, a Canadian landscape architect, is helping to preserve heavily used green spaces from Toronto to Tokyo. His Urban Turf, a mixture of sand, compost, and used-tire chips overlaid with grass, bounces back under the heels and wheels of urbanites. You can see his Urban Turf at Toronto Harbourfront's Ann Tindal Park, a park that stays green despite close to 3 million visitors a year.

Socially responsible efforts on behalf of the general public are becoming more common. A formal practice is **cause-related marketing** (CRM), which occurs when the charitable contributions of a firm are tied directly to the customer revenues produced through the promotion of one of its products.[32] This definition distinguishes CRM from a firm's standard charitable contributions, which are outright donations. For example, Procter & Gamble raises funds for the Special Olympics when consumers purchase selected company products, and MasterCard International linked usage of its card with fund raising for institutions that combat cancer, heart disease, child abuse, drug abuse, and muscular dystrophy. Avon Products, Inc. focuses on different issues in different countries: breast cancer in the United States, Canada, Philippines, Mexico, Venezuela, Malaysia, and Spain; programs for women who care for senior citizens in Japan; emotional and financial support for mothers in Germany; and AIDS in Thailand. CRM programs incorporate all three concepts of social responsibility by addressing public concerns, satisfying customer needs, and enhancing corporate sales and profits.

The Social Audit

Converting socially responsible ideas into actions involves careful planning and monitoring of programs. Many companies develop, implement, and evaluate their social responsibility efforts by means of a **social audit,** which is a systematic assessment of a firm's objectives, strategies, and performance in the domain of social responsibility. Frequently, marketing and social responsibility programs are integrated, as is the case with McDonald's. The company's concern for the needs of families with children who are chronically or terminally ill was converted into some 130 Ronald McDonald Houses. These facilities, located near treatment centres, enable families to stay together during the child's care. In this case, McDonald's is contributing to the welfare of a portion of its target market.

A social audit consists of five steps:[33]

1. Recognition of a firm's social expectations and the rationale for engaging in social responsibility endeavors.
2. Identification of social responsibility causes or programs consistent with the company's mission.
3. Determination of organizational objectives and priorities for programs and activities it will undertake.
4. Specification of the type and amount of resources necessary to achieve social responsibility objectives.
5. Evaluation of social responsibility programs and activities undertaken and assessment of future involvement.

MARKETING NEWSNET

AT 3M, THE CHALLENGE IS CLEAR: CREATE ENVIRONMENTALLY FRIENDLY PRODUCTS THAT PROVIDE VALUE FOR CONSUMERS

"People didn't like getting stuck by steel wool," observed Moe S. Nozari, vice president of 3M's consumer products division, after seeing the results from consumer interviews. Consumers also said they would pay a little extra for a scouring pad that didn't rust or fray. Here was an opportunity for 3M in the $300 million scouring pad market dominated by Clorox and its S.O.S. brand—provided company researchers could develop an environmentally friendly product.

At 3M, product development opportunities emanate both from consumer research and its "Pollution Prevention Pays" program. Begun in 1975, this program solicits employee suggestions on how to cut waste and recycle materials. This program has generated 4100 ideas that have eliminated 1.3 billion pounds of pollutants from the environment and saved 3M more than $170 million.

The challenge to 3M researchers was clear: develop a scouring pad that appealed to consumers and was environmentally friendly. The result: 3M's Scotch-Brite™ Never Rust™ Wool Soap Pad. Scotch-Brite Never Rust pad was made from recycled plastic, used a nonphosphorous soap that does not pollute rivers and streams, and was packaged in a 100 percent recycled paper box. Scotch-Brite

pads were priced 12 percent higher than competitive brands, but they still captured 16 percent of the scouring pad market and have become a tidy $20-plus million business. For good measure, the reduced waste from manufacturing cut pollution and decreased 3M's costs.

Attention to the social audit on environmental matters has increased since 1989, when the Exxon *Valdez* oil tanker spilled 11 million gallons of crude oil off the Canadian and American west coast. This spill killed tens of thousands of birds and mammals and fouled a thousand miles of coastline. Soon after, the Coalition for Environmentally Responsible Economics drafted guidelines designed to focus attention on environmental concerns and corporate responsibility. These guidelines, called the **Valdez Principles,** encourage companies to (1) eliminate pollutants, minimize hazardous wastes, and conserve nonrenewable resources; (2) market environmentally safe products and services; (3) prepare for accidents and restore damaged environments; (4) provide protection for employees who report environmental hazards; and (5) appoint an environmentalist to their boards of directors, name an executive for environmental affairs, and develop an environmental audit of their global operations to be made available for public inspection.[34] Numerous companies now embrace these guidelines and have environmental policy officers. Nevertheless, environmental mishaps still occur.

Development and use of a social audit will depend on the extent to which a company's culture embraces social and environmental responsibility as part of its overall mission. 3M is considered an innovator in this regard. Read the accompanying Marketing NewsNet to see how 3M is responding to the need for environmentally safe products that also create customer value.[35]

Turning the Table: Consumer Ethics and Social Responsibility

Consumers also have an obligation to act ethically and responsibly in the exchange process and in the use and disposition of products. Unfortunately, consumer behaviour is spotty on both counts.

Unethical practices of consumers are a serious concern to marketers.[36] These practices include filing warranty claims after the claim period, misredeeming coupons, making fraudulent returns of merchandise, providing inaccurate information on credit applications, tampering with utility meters, tapping cable TV lines, recording copyrighted music and videocassettes, and submitting phony insurance claims. The cost to marketers in lost sales revenue and prevention expenses is huge.[37] For example, consumers who redeem coupons for unpurchased products or use coupons destined for other products cost manufacturers millions of dollars each year. The record industry alone loses millions of dollars annually due to illegal recording, and many VCR owners make illegal copies of videotapes, costing producers millions of dollars in lost revenue. Electrical utilities lose between 1 and 3 percent of yearly revenues due to meter tampering.

Consumer purchase, use, and disposition of environmentally sensitive products relate to consumer social responsibility.[38] Research indicates that consumers are generally sensitive to ecological issues. However, research also shows that consumers (1) may be unwilling to sacrifice convenience and pay potentially higher prices to protect the environment and (2) lack the knowledge to make informed decisions dealing with the purchase, use, and disposition of products.[39]

Many marketers suggest consumers must become aware of and increase their demand for environmentally sensitive products. For example, producers of environmentally certified lumber, say the market for "green wood" is very small in Canada. Certified lumber comes from forest companies that use sustainable harvesting practices and produce wood products with the least environmental impact. J. D. Irving Co., a Canadian timber and energy conglomerate, has been pursuing certification of its forest lands. The company suggests that consumers should look for and demand wood products from certified forests. In doing so, consumers could end widespread clear-cutting, chemical spraying, and other destructive forestry practices. "Green wood" products can be easily identified by a trademark product label: a green cross superimposed on a globe.[40]

Ultimately, marketers and consumers are accountable for ethical and socially responsible behaviour. The twenty-first century will prove to be a testing period for both.

CONCEPT CHECK

1. What is meant by social responsibility?

2. Marketing efforts to produce, promote, and reclaim environmentally sensitive products are called _____ .

3. What is a social audit?

SUMMARY

1. Ethics are the moral principles and values that govern the actions and decisions of an individual or group. Laws are society's values and standards that are enforceable in the courts. Operating according to the law does not necessarily mean that a practice is ethical.

2. Ethical behaviour of businesspeople has come under severe criticism by the public. There are four possible reasons for this criticism: (a) increased pressure on businesspeople to make decisions in a society characterized by diverse value systems, (b) a growing tendency to have business decisions judged

publicly by groups with different values and interests, (c) an increase in the public's expectations for ethical behaviour, and (d) a possible decline in business ethics.

3. Numerous external factors influence ethical behaviour of businesspeople. These include the following: (a) societal culture and norms, (b) business culture and industry practices, and (c) corporate culture and expectations. Each factor influences the opportunity to engage in ethical or unethical behaviour.

4. Ultimately, ethical choices are based on the personal moral philosophy of the decision maker. Two moral philosophies are most prominent: (a) moral idealism and (b) utilitarianism.

5. Social responsibility means that organizations are part of a larger society and are accountable to that society for their actions.

6. There are three concepts of social responsibility: (a) profit responsibility, (b) stakeholder responsibility, and (c) societal responsibility.

7. Growing interest in societal responsibility has resulted in systematic efforts to assess a firm's objectives, strategies, and performance in the domain of social responsibility. This practice is called a *social audit*.

8. Consumer ethics and social responsibility are as important as business ethics and social responsibility.

KEY TERMS AND CONCEPTS

ethics p. 96
laws p. 96
caveat emptor p. 99
code of ethics p. 101
whistleblowers p. 101
moral idealism p. 101

utilitarianism p. 103
social responsibility p. 103
green marketing p. 105
cause-related marketing p. 105
social audit p. 106
Valdez Principles p. 107

CHAPTER PROBLEMS AND APPLICATIONS

1. What concepts of moral philosophy and social responsibility are applicable to the practices of Molson Breweries described in the introduction to this chapter? Why?

2. Where would the following situations fit in Figure 4-1? (a) exaggerating the performance of a product to get a sale and (b) selling a used automobile knowing it had a major mechanical problem and not telling the buyer.

3. A recent survey of Canadian business students asked "Is calling your office pretending to be sick in order to take the day off ethical or unethical behaviour? How would you respond to this question?

4. Compare and contrast moral idealism and utilitarianism as alternative personal moral philosophies.

5. How would you evaluate Milton Friedman's view of the social responsibility of a firm?

6. The text lists several unethical practices of consumers. Can you name others? Why do you think consumers engage in unethical conduct?

7. Cause-related marketing programs have become popular. Describe two such programs that you are familiar with.

CASE 4-1   Pricing in the Pharmaceutical Industry

Canadians spend billions of dollars annually for prescription drugs to treat acute and chronic ailments. The pharmaceutical industry in Canada has often been criticized for its pricing practices. Many public health officials, government departments or agencies, and consumer advocacy groups argue that, in many cases, the industry is simply charging too much money for its products. Pharmaceutical company executives have responded to such criticism by citing large research and development costs, extensive testing requirements to obtain government approval to market the products, and mar-

ketplace uncertainties as valid reasons for the prices they charge for their drugs.

FAIR AND REASONABLE PRICING

A central issue in the debate concerning prescription drug pricing relates to what is a "fair and reasonable price." Critics of drug pricing spotlight instances where they believe the prices charged are excessive. For instance, Ceredase, a drug for victims of rare metabolic disorder, sells for $200 000 annually per patient. Clozapine, designed to treat schizophrenia, cost patients almost $9000 per year. A drug to prevent an AIDS-related blindness, called Foscavir, costs $21 000 per patient annually. Pharmaceutical firms counter critics' charges of excessive pricing using a variety of arguments. For example, the maker of Foscavir claimed the high price was necessary to recoup its financial investment in the drug. When Johnson & Johnson introduced a drug to treat colon cancer, the company cited some 1400 studies involving 40 000 patients conducted over 25 years as the reason for the $1250 price for a one-year supply. The price for Retrovir, an antiviral drug to treat AIDS, was justified with a variety of considerations, including its maker's "responsibility to patients and shareholders, the very real remaining uncertainties in the marketplace, and the vital need to fund our continuing research and development programs."

Debate over what is a "fair and reasonable" price for drugs typically focuses on economic versus societal factors, and the relative importance of a firm's stakeholders in setting prices. Often the final pricing decision depends on the individual judgment and moral sensitivity of the managers making the decision.

PROLIFE: PRICING ADL

Issues in the pricing of ADL, a treatment for Alzheimer's disease which affects the elderly, were recently faced by Prolife, a small pharmaceutical company. A task force of company executives was considering the pricing strategy for ADL. Two points of view were expressed: (1) pursuing a high-price strategy designed to recoup the costs of the drug quickly and getting a jump on the competition, and (2) pursuing a lower-price strategy to increase the drug's availability to victims of the disease.

Steve Vaughn, an Assistant Product Manager at Prolife, was the principal proponent of a lower-price strategy. He argued that a less aggressive price strategy made sense even though it would take slightly longer to recoup the initial investment in ADL. Having a family member afflicted with Alzheimer's disease, Mr. Vaughn felt that the ability of victims and their families to pay for the drug should be considered when setting the price for ADL. He was overruled, however, by the task force members. Believing that his views deserved attention and action, and that "bottom line" considerations did not negate his position, he lobbied other task force members and has thought about expressing his opinion to senior executives at Prolife. He was cautioned by Bill Compton, a Prolife Senior Product Manager and his mentor, to reconsider his position noting that Prolife is a business and that "rocking the boat" might not be an advantage to his career at Prolife.

Questions

1. Who are the primary stakeholders that must be considered when setting prices for prescription drugs?
2. How might the personal moral philosophies of moral idealism and utilitarianism be applied to prescription drug pricing in general and in the specific case of ADL?
3. How might the three concepts of social responsibility described in Chapter 4 be applied to prescription pricing in general and in the specific case of ADL?
4. If you were Steve Vaughn, what would you do in this situation?

PART TWO

UNDERSTANDING BUYERS AND MARKETS

Chapter 5
Global Marketing and World Trade

Chapter 6
Consumer Behaviour

Chapter 7
Organizational Markets and Buyer Behaviour

Using local and global perspectives to understand people as individual consumers and as members of companies that become organizational buyers is the focus of Part II. Chapter 5 describes the nature and scope of world trade and examines the global marketing activities of such companies as W. K. Buckley Ltd., McDonald's, Milltronics Ltd., Clearly Canadian Beverages, Ganong Brothers, Nestlé, Caterpillar, Ford, Coca-Cola, and Procter & Gamble. Chapter 6 examines the actions buyers take in purchasing and using products, and explains how and why one product or brand is chosen over another. Chapter 7 explains how manufacturers, retailers, and government agencies also buy goods and services for their own use or resale. Together these chapters help marketing students understand individual, family, and organizational purchases in a variety of cultural environments.

Het is even slikken...

...maar dan ben je wel mooi van je hoest af.

Speciaal voor kinderen is er een zoete, zachte hoestsiroop.

Buckley's
HOESTSIROOP

BUCKLEY'S REKENT AF MET HEESHEID EN HOEST.

CHAPTER 5

Global Marketing and World Trade

AFTER READING THIS CHAPTER YOU SHOULD BE ABLE TO:

• Describe the nature and scope of world trade from a global perspective and its implications for Canada.

• Explain the effects of economic protectionism and the implications of economic integration for global marketing practices.

• Understand the importance of environmental factors (cultural, economic, and political) in shaping global marketing efforts.

• Describe alternative approaches firms use to enter and compete in global markets.

• Identify specific challenges marketers face when crafting worldwide marketing programs.

COMPETING IN THE GLOBAL MARKETPLACE

Canadian marketers cannot ignore the vast potential of global markets. Over 99 percent of the world's population lives outside of Canada and collectively these potential customers possess tremendous purchasing power. Not only are global markets substantial, but many are growing faster than comparable markets in Canada—a fact not lost on both large and small global-minded Canadian companies.

Successful Canadian marketers have responded to three challenges in the global marketplace. First, they have satisfied the needs of a discriminating global consumer who increasingly purchases goods and services on the basis of value. Ontario-based W. K. Buckley Ltd. is a small Canadian company that competes effectively in foreign markets with a quality product, a cough-remedy known as Buckley's Mixture. Buckley's famous "tastes bad and it works" positioning theme has struck a resonant chord with global consumers from the United States to Australia, and from Holland to China.[1]

Second, Canadian marketers have capitalized on trends favouring free trade among industrialized nations throughout the world. For example, the North American Free Trade Agreement (NAFTA) has opened up the Mexican market for Canadian companies and many have found opportunities there in a variety of sectors including telecommunications and engineering services. Finally, Canadian marketers have pursued opportunities in the newly emerging democracies in Eastern Europe and the former Soviet Union, including McDonald's Restaurants of Canada Ltd.

Pursuit of global markets by Canadian and foreign marketers ultimately results in world trade. The purpose of this chapter is to describe the nature and scope of world trade and to highlight challenges involved in global marketing.

DYNAMICS OF WORLD TRADE

The dollar value of world trade has grown an average of 12 percent per year since 1970 and will approach $8 trillion in 2005. Manufactured goods and commodities account for 80 percent of world trade. Service industries, including telecommunications, transportation, insurance, education, banking, and tourism, represent the other 20 percent of world trade.

World Trade Flows

All nations and regions of the world do not participate equally in world trade. World trade flows reflect interdependencies among industries, countries, and regions and manifest themselves in country, company, industry, and regional exports and imports.

Global perspective   Figure 5-1 shows the estimated dollar value of exports and imports among North American countries, Western Europe, Asian/Pacific Rim countries, and the rest of the world, including intraregional trade flows.[2] The United States, Western Europe, Canada, and Japan together account for two-thirds of world trade.[3]

Not all trade involves the exchange of money for goods or services.[4] In a world where 70 percent of all countries do not have convertible currencies or where government-owned enterprises lack sufficient cash or credit for imports, other means of payment are used. An estimated 20 percent of world trade involves **countertrade,** the practice of using barter rather than money for making global sales. As an example, PepsiCo trades its soft drink syrup concentrate in Russia in exchange for Stolichnaya vodka, which the

FIGURE 5-1

ILLUSTRATIVE WORLD TRADE FLOWS
(BILLIONS OF DOLLARS)

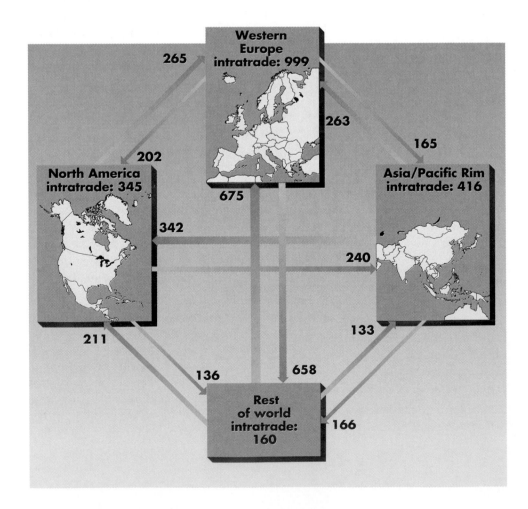

company sells through Monsieur Henri Wines Ltd. in North America. Initial shipments of vodka in 1973 totalled 20 000 cases; in 25 years, this countertrade has expanded to more than a million cases plus two oil tankers! Countertrade is popular with many Eastern European nations and developing countries.

A global perspective on world trade views exports and imports as complementary economic flows: a country's imports affect its exports and exports affect its imports. Every nation's imports arise from the exports of other nations. As the exports of one country increase, its national output and income rise, which, in turn, leads to an increase in the demand for imports. This nation's greater demand for imports stimulates the exports of other countries. Increased demand for exports of other nations energizes their economic activity, resulting in higher national income, which stimulates their demand for imports. In short, imports affect exports and vice versa. This phenomenon is called the **trade feedback effect** and is one argument for free trade among nations.

Continually rising consumer income in Japan, Taiwan, India, China, South Korea, Hong Kong, and other Asian/Pacific Rim countries, fuelled by their growth in exports, has prompted demand for imported goods and services. Many North American companies are benefiting from rising consumer incomes in the Asian/Pacific Rim including General Motors, which exports cars to Taiwan, Johnson & Johnson, with a robust business for lotions and shampoos in South Korea, and Kodak, which dominates the $1 billion film market for professional photography in Japan. Even small Canadian companies are benefiting such as New Brunswick-based Ganong Brothers which exports its chocolates and candy to Asia.

Canadian perspective   Canada's **gross domestic product** (GDP), the monetary value of all goods and services produced in a country during one year, is valued at almost $800 billion. Canada exports a significant percentage of the goods and services it produces. In fact, it exports over 30 percent of GDP making it an important trading nation.[5]

The difference between the monetary value of a nation's exports and imports is called the **balance of trade.** When a country's exports exceed its imports, it incurs a surplus in its balance of trade. When imports exceed exports, a deficit has occurred. Canada maintains an overall surplus in its balance of trade at this time. Figure 5-2 shows the trends in the Canadian balance of trade.

Almost every Canadian is affected by Canada's trading activity. The effects vary from the products we buy (Samsung computers from Korea, Waterford crystal from

FIGURE 5-2

TRENDS IN THE CANADIAN
BALANCE OF TRADE.

	1993	1994	1995	1996
Imports				
Value ($ millions)	171 927.9	203 000.4	225 431.2	233 025.5
% change	15.2	18.1	11.0	3.4
Exports				
Value ($ millions)	181 251.3	217 935.9	253 820.8	268 203.2
% change	16.6	20.2	16.5	5.7
Trade balance				
Value ($ millions)	9 323.4	14 935.5	28 389.6	35 177.7
Ratio of exports to imports	1.05	1.07	1.13	1.15

Source: Statistics Canada, Catalogue No. 65-001.

Ireland, Lindemans wine from Australia) to those we sell (Moosehead beer to Sweden, Milltronics Ltd.'s measurement devices to New Zealand, Sullivan Entertainment Inc.'s *Anne of Green Gables* videos and merchandise to Japan) and the additional jobs and improved standard of living that can result from world trade.

World trade flows to and from Canada reflect demand and supply interdependencies for goods and services among nations and industries. While Canada trades with dozens of other countries, the three largest importers of Canadian goods and services are the United States (accounting for over 80 percent), Japan, and the European Union (EU). These countries are also the top three exporters to Canada. The EU enjoys a trade surplus with our country while the United States and Japan incur a trade deficit.

Competitive Advantage of Nations

As companies in many industries find themselves competing against foreign competitors at home and abroad, government policy makers around the world are increasingly asking why some companies and industries in a country succeed globally while others lose ground or fail. Michael Porter suggests a "diamond" to explain a nation's competitive advantage and why some industries and firms become world leaders.[6] He identified four key elements, which appear in Figure 5-3:

1. *Factor conditions.* These reflect a nation's ability to turn its natural resources, education, and infrastructure into a competitive advantage. The Dutch lead the world in the cut-flower industry because of their research in flower cultivation, packaging, and shipping—not because of their weather.

FIGURE 5-3

PORTER'S "DIAMOND" OF NATIONAL COMPETITIVE ADVANTAGE

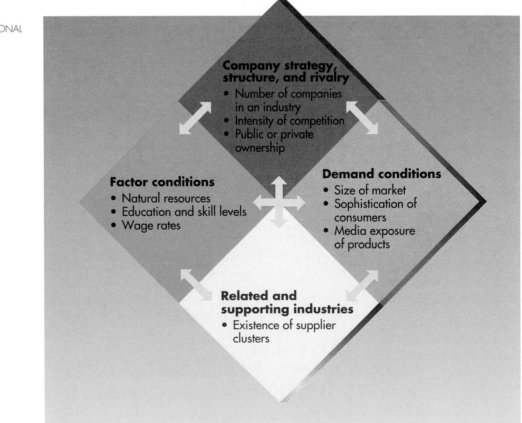

2. *Demand conditions.* These include both the number and sophistication of domestic customers for an industry's product. Japan's sophisticated consumers demand quality in their TVs and radios, thereby making Japan's producers the world leaders in the electronics industry.
3. *Related and supporting industries.* Firms and industries seeking leadership in global markets need clusters of world-class suppliers that accelerate innovation. The German leadership in printing relates directly to the cluster of supporting German suppliers.
4. *Company strategy, structure, and rivalry.* These factors include the conditions governing the way a nation's businesses are organized and managed, along with the intensity of domestic competition. The Italian shoe industry has become the world leader because of intense domestic competition that enhances quality and innovation.

In Porter's study, case histories of firms in more than 100 industries were analyzed. While the strategies employed by the most successful global competitors were different in many respects, a common theme emerged—a firm that succeeds in global markets has first succeeded in intense domestic competition. Hence competitive advantage for global firms grows out of relentless, continuing improvement, innovation, and change.

It is important to note, however, that it is not essential to be a gigantic company to gain benefits in global markets. Numerous small firms succeed in foreign niche markets by offering unique products or by leveraging advanced technology. Ontario-based

ONTARIO-BASED MILLTRONICS LTD. COMPETES SUCCESSFULLY IN GLOBAL MARKETS WITH ITS PRODUCT, THE PROBE.

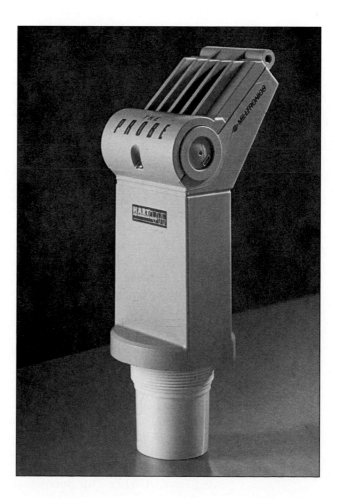

Milltronics Ltd. developed a noncontacting ultrasonic device for measuring levels of liquids, slurries and sludges called THE PROBE (see accompanying photo). It measures levels of liquids as diverse as corn syrup and phenol acids in open or closed vessels by emitting pulses of high-frequency sound that bounce back to the device. The product has been used in dozens of ways including measuring the amount of milk produced by cows in New Zealand to detecting the depth of snow in Japan. THE PROBE currently accounts for 12 percent of Milltronics worldwide revenue. Another example is Winsire Enterprises Corporation of BC which has been successful in having its multihead screwdriver added to the Tim Allen Signature Line of Tools.

CONCEPT CHECK

1. What is the trade feedback effect?

2. What variables influence why some companies and industries in a country succeed globally while others lose ground or fail?

EMERGENCE OF A BORDERLESS ECONOMIC WORLD

Three trends in the late twentieth century have significantly affected world trade. One trend has been a gradual decline of economic protectionism exercised by individual countries. The second trend is apparent in the formal economic integration and free trade among nations. A third trend is evident in global competition among global companies for global consumers.

Decline of Economic Protectionism

Protectionism is the practice of shielding one or more sectors of a country's economy from foreign competition through the use of tariffs or quotas. The principal economic argument for protectionism is that it preserves jobs, protects a nation's political security, discourages economic dependency on other countries, and encourages the development of domestic industries. Read the accompanying Ethics and Social Responsibility Alert and ask yourself if protectionism has an ethical and social responsibility dimension.[7]

Tariffs and quotas discourage world trade and often result in higher domestic prices on the goods and services produced by protected industries. **Tariffs,** which are a government tax on goods or services entering a country, primarily serve to raise prices on imports. Import tariffs on manufactured goods to Japan average 5 percent and those to Western European countries average 5.9 percent. Mexico's tariffs average 8 percent.[8]

The effect of tariffs on world trade and consumer prices is substantial. Consider rice imports to Japan. Experts believe that if the Japanese rice market were opened to imports by lowering tariffs, lower prices would save Japanese consumers billions of dollars annually.

A **quota** is a restriction placed on the amount of a product allowed to enter or leave a country. Quotas can be mandatory or voluntary, and may be legislated or negotiated by governments. Import quotas seek to guarantee domestic industries access to a certain percentage of their domestic market. The best-known quota concerns the mandatory or voluntary limits on foreign automobile sales in many countries. Quotas imposed by European countries make European cars 25 percent more expensive than similar models in Japan, costing European customers billions of dollars per year. Less visible quotas apply to the importation of many other products such as electronics and produce.

Every country engages in some form of protectionism. However, protectionism has declined over the past 50 years due in large part to the *General Agreement on Tariffs and Trade (GATT)*. This international treaty was intended to limit trade barriers and

ETHICS AND SOCIAL RESPONSIBILITY ALERT

GLOBAL ETHICS AND GLOBAL ECONOMICS: THE CASE OF PROTECTIONISM

World trade benefits from free and fair trade among nations. Nevertheless, governments of many countries continue to use tariffs and quotas to protect their various domestic industries. Why? Protectionism earns profits for domestic producers and tariff revenue for the government. There is a cost, however. For example, protectionist policies cost Japanese consumers billions of dollars annually. Canadian consumers also pay higher prices for imported goods and services that are subject to tariffs and other protective restrictions.

Sugar import quotas in the United States, automobile import quotas in many European countries, beer import tar- iffs in Canada, and rice import tariffs in Japan protect domestic industries but also interfere with world trade for these products. Regional trade agreements, such as those found in the provisions of the European Union and the North American Free Trade Agreement, may also pose a situation whereby member nations can obtain preferential treatment in quotas and tariffs whereas nonmember nations do not.

Protectionism, in its many forms, raises an interesting global ethical question. Is protectionism, no matter how applied, an ethical practice?

promote world trade through the reduction of tariffs, which it did. However, GATT did not explicitly address nontariff trade barriers, such as quotas and world trade in services, which often sparked heated trade disputes between nations. As a consequence, the major industrialized nations of the world formed a permanent forum to address a broad array of world trade issues, called the **World Trade Organization (WTO)**, which came into being January 1, 1995. The WTO is an institution that sets rules governing trade between its members through a panel of trade experts who (1) decide on trade disputes between members and (2) issue binding decisions. There are more than 100 countries that belong to the WTO, including Canada. These countries are expected to account for more than 80 percent of world trade in 1998.[9]

Rise of Economic Integration

In recent years a number of countries with similar economic goals have formed transnational trade groups or signed trade agreements for the purpose of promoting free trade among member nations and enhancing their individual economies. Three of the best-known examples are the European Union (or simply EU), the North American Free Trade Agreement, and Asian Free Trade Areas.

European Union   On January 1, 1993, 12 European countries effectively eliminated most of the barriers to the free flow of goods, services, capital, and labour across their borders. This event, after decades of negotiation, formed a single market composed of 350 million consumers. Original members of the European Union were Great Britain, Ireland, Denmark, Belgium, the Netherlands, Luxembourg, Germany, France, Italy, Greece, Portugal, and Spain. Austria, Finland, and Sweden joined the European Union in 1995, bringing its membership to 15 countries (see Figure 5-4). The Swiss have elected not to join the European Union.[10]

Numerous marketing opportunities were made possible with creation of the European Union. Most visibly, firms no longer find it necessary to exclusively market their products and services on a nation-by-nation basis. Rather, Pan-European marketing strategies are possible due to greater uniformity in product and packaging

FIGURE 5-4

THE COUNTRIES OF THE
EUROPEAN UNION

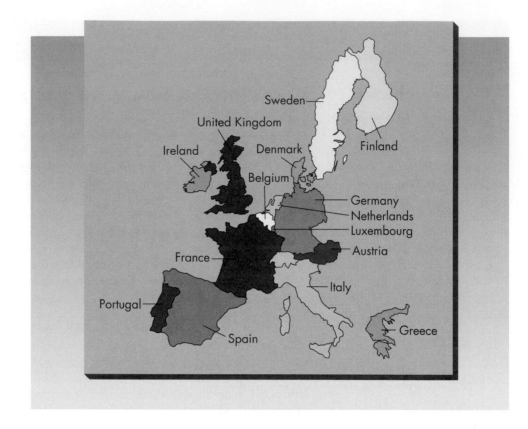

standards, fewer regulatory differences on advertising and promotion imposed by countries, and removal of most tariffs that affect pricing practices. For example, Colgate-Palmolive Company now markets its Colgate toothpaste with one formula and package across EU countries at one price. This practice was previously impossible because of different government regulations and tariffs. Europeanwide distribution from a single location in one of the 15 EU nations also became feasible given open borders.[11] Pan-European marketing opportunities will benefit further from the adoption of a common currency called the "euro" scheduled for issuance in 2002.

North American Free Trade Agreement   The North American Free Trade Agreement (NAFTA) became effective January 1, 1994, and lifted many trade barriers between Canada, the United States, and Mexico. This agreement, when coupled with the 1988 Canada–US Free Trade Agreement (FTA), established a North American trade arrangement similar to that of the European Union. The reduction of tariffs and other provisions of NAFTA promoted relatively free trade among Canada, the United States, and Mexico and created a marketplace with about 380 million consumers. Negotiations are in progress to expand NAFTA to create a Free Trade Area of the Americas by 2005. This agreement would include Canada, the United States, Mexico, and Latin American and Caribbean countries.

NAFTA has stimulated trade flows among member nations as well as cross-border manufacturing and investment. For example, Whirlpool Corporation's Canadian subsidiary stopped making washing machines in Canada and moved that operation to Ohio. Whirlpool then shifted the production of household trash compactors, kitchen ranges, and compact dryers to Canada.

While NAFTA has created an opportunity for freer trade between Canada, the United States, and Mexico, many interprovincial trade barriers still exist within Canada that restrict the free movement of goods and services between the provinces. The federal government and most of the provincial governments continue to work on agreements to remove or lessen the trade barriers between the provinces.

Asian free trade agreements   Efforts to liberalize trade in East Asia—from Japan and the four "Little Dragons" (Hong Kong, Singapore, South Korea, and Taiwan) through Thailand, Malaysia, and Indonesia—are also growing. While the trade agreements are less formal than those underlying the European Union and NAFTA, they have reduced tariffs among countries and promoted trade.[12]

A New Reality: Global Competition among Global Companies for Global Consumers

The emergence of a largely borderless economic world has created a new reality for marketers of all shapes and sizes. Today, world trade is driven by global competition among global companies for global consumers.

Global competition   **Global competition** exists when firms originate, produce, and market their products and services worldwide. The automobile, pharmaceutical, apparel, electronics, aerospace, and telecommunications fields represent well-known industries with sellers and buyers on every continent. Other industries that are increasingly global in scope include soft drinks, cosmetics, ready-to-eat cereals, snack chips, and retailing.

Global competition broadens the competitive landscape for marketers. The familiar "Pepsi Challenge" taste comparison waged by Pepsi-Cola against Coca-Cola in Canada has been repeated around the world, most recently in India and Argentina. Procter & Gamble's Pampers and Kimberly-Clark's Huggies have taken their disposable diaper rivalry from Canada to Western Europe. Boeing, McDonnell-Douglas, and Europe's Airbus Industries can be found vying for lucrative commercial aircraft contracts on virtually every continent.[13]

Collaborative relationships also are becoming a common way to meet the demands of global competition. Global **strategic alliances** are agreements among two or more independent firms to cooperate for the purpose of achieving common goals such as a competitive advantage or customer value creation. For instance, a strategic alliance involving Duracell (North America), Toshiba (Japan), and Varta Batterie AG (Germany) has been formed to research and develop rechargeable batteries for high-power electronic

AVON SUCCESSFULLY EMPLOYS ITS DIRECT-SELLING APPROACH AROUND THE WORLD.

products such as cellular telephones produced by Nokia (Finland) and notebook computers made by Acer (Taiwan). General Mills and Nestlé of Switzerland created Cereal Partners Worldwide for the purpose of fine-tuning Nestlé's European cereal marketing and distributing General Mills cereals worldwide. This global alliance is expected to produce worldwide sales of $1 billion by 2000.[14]

Global companies   Three types of companies populate and compete in the global marketplace: (1) international firms, (2) multinational firms, and (3) transnational firms.[15] All three employ people in different countries, and many have administrative, marketing, and manufacturing operations (often called divisions or subsidiaries) around the world. However, a firm's orientation toward and strategy for global markets and marketing defines the type of company it is or attempts to be.

An *international firm* engages in trade and marketing in different countries as an extension of the marketing strategy in its home country. Generally speaking, these firms market their existing products and services in other countries the same way they do in their home country. Avon, for example, successfully distributes its product line through direct selling in Asia, Europe, and South America, employing virtually the same marketing strategy used in Canada and the United States.[16]

A *multinational firm* views the world as consisting of unique parts and markets to each part differently. Multinationals use a **multidomestic marketing strategy,** which means that they have as many different product variations, brand names, and advertising programs as countries in which they do business. For example, Lever Europe—a division of Unilever—markets its fabric softener known as Snuggle in Canada in 10 different European countries under seven brand names, including Kuschelweich in Germany, Coccolino in Italy, and Mimosin in France. These products have different packages, different advertising programs, and occasionally different formulas.[17]

A *transnational firm* views the world as one market and emphasizes cultural similarities across countries or universal consumer needs and wants more than differences. Transnational marketers employ a **global marketing strategy**—the practice of standardizing marketing activities when there are cultural similarities and adapting them

MARKETING NEWSNET

THE GLOBAL TEENAGER: A MARKET OF 230 MILLION CONSUMERS

The "global teenager" market consists of 230 million 13- to 19-year-olds in Europe, North and South America, and industrialized nations of Asia who have experienced intense exposure to television (MTV broadcasts in more than 25 countries), movies, travel, and global advertising by companies such as Bennetton, Sony, Nike, and Coca-Cola. More and more marketers are recognizing that these teenagers have many things in common including an appreciation for fashion and music and a desire for novelty and trendier designs and images. In fact, many suggest that the similarities among these teens are greater than their differences. A global study of teenagers' rooms in 25 countries indicated it was difficult, if not impossible, to tell whether the rooms were in Vancouver, Mexico City, Tokyo, or Paris. Why? Teens buy a common gallery of products: Nintendo and Sega video games, Levi's blue jeans, Nike athletic shoes, Procter & Gamble Cover Girl makeup, and Clearasil facial medicine. Not surprisingly, Reebok launched its Insta-Pump line of sneakers simultaneously in North America, Germany, Japan, and 137 other countries through a global advertising campaign aimed at teens.

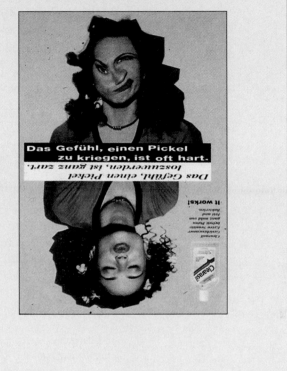

when cultures differ. This approach benefits marketers by allowing them to realize economies of scale from their production and marketing activities.

Global marketing strategies are popular among many business-to-business marketers such as Caterpillar and Komatsu (heavy construction equipment) and Texas Instruments, Intel, Hitachi, and Motorola (semiconductors). Consumer goods marketers such as Timex, Seiko, and Citizen (watches), Coca-Cola and Pepsi-Cola (cola soft drinks), and McDonald's (fast foods) successfully execute this strategy. Recently Ford, through its Ford 2000 initiative, embarked on a global strategy for marketing a "world car." Called the Mondeo in Europe and the Ford Contour and Mercury Mystique in Canada, this car is engineered to meet the differing needs of consumers around the world. The Ford 2000 initiative also includes significant organizational changes designed to transform Ford from a multinational company to a transnational company.[18]

Global consumers   Global competition among global companies often focuses on the identification and pursuit of global consumers. **Global consumers** consist of customer groups living in many countries or regions of the world who have similar needs or seek similar features and benefits from products or services.[19] Evidence suggests the emergence of a global middle-income class, a youth market, and an elite segment, each consuming or using a common assortment of products and services regardless of geographic location.[20] A variety of companies have capitalized on the global consumer. Whirlpool, Sony, and IKEA have benefited from the growing global middle-income class desire for kitchen appliances, consumer electronics, and home furnishings respectively. Levi's, Nike, and Sega have tapped the global youth market as described in the Marketing NewsNet on the next page.[21] Debeers, Chanel, Gucci, and Rolls Royce successfully cater to the elite segment for luxury goods worldwide.

CONCEPT CHECK
1. What is protectionism?
2. The North American Free Trade Agreement was designed to promote free trade among which countries?
3. What is the difference between a multidomestic marketing strategy and a global marketing strategy?

A GLOBAL ENVIRONMENTAL SCAN

Global companies conduct continuing environmental scans of the five sets of environmental factors described earlier in Chapter 3 (Figure 3-1)—social, economic, technological, competitive, and regulatory forces. This section focuses on three kinds of uncontrollable environmental variables—cultural, economic, and political-regulatory variables—that affect global marketing practices in strikingly different ways than those in domestic markets.

Cultural Diversity

Marketers must be sensitive to the cultural underpinnings of different societies if they are to initiate and consummate mutually beneficial exchange relationships with global consumers. A necessary step in this process is **cross-cultural analysis,** which involves the study of similarities and differences among consumers in two or more nations or societies.[22] A thorough cross-cultural analysis involves an understanding and an appreciation for the values, customs, symbols, and language of other societies.

Values   A society's **values** represent personally or socially preferable modes of conduct or states of existence that are enduring. Understanding and working with these aspects of a society are important factors in successful global marketing. For example:[23]

- A door-to-door salesperson would find selling in Italy impossible because it is improper for a man to call on a woman if she is home alone. Similarly, a popular Procter & Gamble commercial for Camay soap in Western Europe flopped when it aired in Japan. The ad, which showed a husband interrupting his wife's bath, was thought to be in poor taste since it is considered improper for a Japanese man to intrude on his wife.
- McDonald's does not sell hamburgers in its restaurants in India because the cow is considered sacred by almost 85 percent of the population.
- Germans have not been overly receptive to the use of credit cards such as Visa or MasterCard and installment debt to purchase goods and services. Indeed, the German word for debt, *schuld,* is the same as the German word for guilt.

These examples illustrate how cultural values can influence behaviour in different societies. Cultural values become apparent in the personal values of individuals that affect their attitudes and beliefs and the importance assigned to specific behaviours and attributes of goods and services. These personal values affect consumption-specific values, such as the use of installment debt by Germans, and product-specific values, such as the importance assigned to credit card interest rates.

Customs   **Customs** are the norms and expectations about the way people do things in a specific country. Clearly customs can vary significantly from country to country. For example, General Mills designed a cake mix especially for preparation in the rice cookers used by Japanese consumers. It failed because of a lack of understanding of Japanese consumers and customs: Japanese take pride in the purity of their rice, which they thought would be contaminated if the cooker were used to prepare another food. The 3M Company's Scotch-Brite floor-cleaning product got lukewarm sales in the Philippines. When a Filipino employee explained that consumers there often clean floors by pushing coconut shells around with their feet, 3M changed the shape of the pad to a foot and sales soared![24] Some other customs are unusual to Canadians. Consider, for example, that in France, men wear more than twice the number of cosmetics that women do and that Japanese women give Japanese men chocolates on Valentine's Day.[25]

Customs also relate to nonverbal behaviour of individuals in different cultural settings.[26] For example, in many European countries it is considered impolite not to have both hands on the table in business meetings. A simple gesture in a commercial such as pointing a finger is perfectly acceptable in Western culture, but is perceived as an insult in Middle and Far Eastern countries. Direct eye contact is viewed positively in North and Latin America but negatively in Japan. Casual touching is also inappropriate in Japan while men often hold hands in Middle Eastern countries as a sign of friendship. Business executives in Japan like to hold their opinions, listen longer, and pause before responding in meetings. Sometimes the silence is misread by North American executives as being nonresponsive.

Cultural symbols   **Cultural symbols** are things that represent ideas and concepts. Symbols or symbolism play an important role in cross-cultural analysis because different cultures ascribe different meanings to things. So important is the role of symbols that a field of study, called **semiotics,** has emerged that examines the correspondence between symbols and their role in the assignment of meaning for people. By adroitly using cultural symbols, global marketers can tie positive symbolism to their products and services to enhance their attractiveness to consumers.

For example, North Americans are superstitious about the number 13, and Japanese feel the same way about the number four. *Shi,* the Japanese word for four, is also the word for death. Knowing this, golf ball manufacturers do not sell golf balls in packages of four in Japan.

Global marketers often discover that cultural symbols evoke deep feeling. Just ask executives at Coca-Cola Company's Italian office.

In a series of advertisements directed at Italian vacationers, the Eiffel Tower, and the tower of Pisa were turned into the familiar Coca-Cola bottle. However, when the white marble columns in the Parthenon that crowns Athens's Acropolis were turned into Coca-Cola bottles, the Greeks were outraged. Greeks refer to the Acropolis as the "holy rock," and a government official said the Parthenon is an "international symbol of excellence" and that "whoever insults the Parthenon insults international culture." Coca-Cola apologized for the ad.[27]

Global marketers are also sensitive to the fact that the "country of origin or manufacture" of products and services can symbolize superior or poor quality in some countries. For example, Russian consumers believe products made in Japan and Germany are superior in quality to products from North America and the United Kingdom. Japanese consumers believe Japanese products are superior to those made in Europe and North America.[28]

COUNTRY OF ORIGIN OR
MANUFACTURE OF PRODUCTS OR
SERVICES CAN SYMBOLIZE QUALITY
IN SOME COUNTRIES. FOR EXAMPLE,
ITALIAN-MADE SHOES SYMBOLIZE
QUALITY AROUND THE WORLD.

"THEY'RE MADE IN ITALY."

Language   Global marketers should not only know the native tongues of countries in which they market their products and services but also the nuances and idioms of a language. Even though about 100 official languages exist in the world, anthropologists estimate that at least 3000 different languages are spoken. There are 11 official languages spoken in the European Union, and Canada has two official languages (English and French). Fifteen major languages are spoken in India alone, although English is the official language.

English, French, and Spanish are the principal languages used in global diplomacy and commerce. However, the best language to communicate with consumers is their own, as any seasoned global marketer will attest. Unintended meanings of brand names and messages have ranged from the absurd to the obscene:[29]

- When the advertising agency responsible for launching Procter & Gamble's successful Pert shampoo in Canada realized that the name means "lost" in French, it substituted the brand name Pret, which means "ready."
- In Italy, Cadbury Schweppes, the world's third-largest soft drink manufacturer, realized that its Schweppes Tonic Water brand had to be renamed Schweppes Tonica because "il water" turned out to be the idiom for a bathroom.
- The Vicks brand name common in Canada is German slang for sexual intimacy; therefore, Vicks is called Wicks in Germany.

Experienced global marketers use **back translation,** where a translated word or phrase is retranslated into the original language by a different interpreter to catch errors. For example, IBM's first Japanese translation of its "Solutions for a small planet" advertising message yielded "Answers that make people smaller." The error was caught and corrected.[30] Nevertheless, unintended meanings still occur in the most unlikely situations. Recently, a Japanese tire manufacturer found it necessary to publicly apologize in Brunei (a British-protected sultanate on the coast of Borneo) for the tread grooves on one of its tire brands. Some critics claimed the tread resembled a verse from the Koran, the sacred book of the Muslims written in Arabic.

Cultural ethnocentricity   The tendency for people to view their own values, customs, symbols, and language favourably is well-known. However, the belief that aspects of one's culture are superior to another's is called *cultural ethnocentricity* and is a sure impediment to successful global marketing.

An outgrowth of cultural ethnocentricity exists in the purchase and use of goods and services produced outside of a country. Global marketers are acutely aware that certain groups within countries disfavour imported products, not on the basis of price, features, or performance, but purely because of their foreign origin. **Consumer ethnocentrism** is the tendency to believe that it is inappropriate, indeed immoral, to purchase foreign-made products.[31] Ethnocentric consumers believe that buying imported products is wrong because such purchases are unpatriotic, harm domestic industries, and cause domestic unemployment. The prevalence of consumer ethnocentrism in the global marketplace is unknown. However, a recent study indicated that 5 percent of consumers in the United Kingdom and France and 6 percent of consumers in Germany said that knowing a product was made in their country was the single-most important factor when considering the purchase of a product.[32]

Cultural change   Cultures change slowly. Nevertheless, fewer impediments to world trade are likely to accelerate the rate of cultural change in societies around the world. A challenge facing global marketers is to anticipate how cultures are changing, particularly with respect to the purchase and use of goods and services.

An acknowledged master of anticipating cultural change and responding quickly is Nestlé, the world's largest packaged food manufacturer, coffee roaster, and chocolate maker. Nestlé derives 98 percent of its sales outside of its home country, Switzerland, because the company is always among the first to identify changing consumption patterns in diverse cultures. Consider Great Britain and Japan, with two very different cultures but a common passion—tea. Nestlé pioneered coffee marketing in both countries with its Nescafé instant coffee. The cultural preference for tea was changing, and Nestlé capitalized on this change. Today, Britons consume one cup of coffee for every two cups of tea. Thirty years ago, the ratio was one cup of coffee for every six cups of tea. The Japanese are now among the world's heaviest consumers of instant coffee on a per capita basis. Nestlé is a dominant coffee marketer in both countries.[33]

Economic Considerations

Global marketing also is affected by economic considerations. Therefore, a scan of the global marketplace should include (1) a comparative analysis of the economic development in different countries, (2) an assessment of the economic infrastructure in these countries, (3) measurement of consumer income in different countries, and (4) recognition of a country's currency exchange rates.

Stage of economic development   There are more than 200 countries in the world today, each of which is at a slightly different point in terms of its stage of economic development. However, they can be classified into two major groupings that will help the global marketer better understand their needs:

- *Developed* countries have somewhat mixed economics. Private enterprise dominates, although they have substantial public sectors as well. Canada, the United States, Japan, and most of Western Europe can be considered developed.
- *Developing* countries are in the process of moving from an agricultural to an industrial economy. There are two subgroups within the developing category: (1) those that have already made the move and (2) those that remain locked in a preindustrial economy. Countries such as Poland, Hungary, Israel, Venezuela, and South Africa fall into the first group. In the second group are Pakistan, Sri Lanka, Tanzania, and Chad, where living standards are low and improvement will be slow. The economies of developing countries are expected to average 5 percent annual growth compared with 2 percent annual growth for developed countries through 2000.[34]

A country's stage of economic development affects and is affected by other economic factors, as described next.

Economic infrastructure   The **economic infrastructure**—a country's communications, transportation, financial, and distribution systems—is a critical consideration in determining whether to try to market to a country's consumers and organizations. Parts of the infrastructure that North Americans or Western Europeans take for granted can be huge problems elsewhere—not only in developing nations but even in countries of Eastern Europe and the former Soviet Union where such an infrastructure is assumed to be in place. Consider, for instance, transportation and distribution systems in these countries. Two-lane roads with horse-drawn carts that limit average speeds to 55 or 65 kilometres per hour are commonplace—and a nightmare for firms requiring prompt truck delivery. Wholesale and retail institutions tend to be small, and 95 percent are operated by new owner-managers still learning the ways of a free market system. These conditions have prompted firms such as Danone, a French food company, to establish their own wholesale, retail, and delivery systems. Danone delivers its products to 700 shops in Russia and has set up 60 shops-in-shops, where it has its own retail sales associates and cash registers.[35]

The communication infrastructure in these countries, including telecommunications and postal systems, also differ. About one-in-ten people have a telephone. As for postal systems, *Reader's Digest* learned to send its magazine by registered mail in brown envelopes—or by private delivery services—because attractive packages tend to get "lost" frequently.[36] These problems have led to several billion dollar investments to upgrade telecommunication and postal systems in these countries.

Even the financial and legal system can cause problems. Common operating procedures among financial institutions and private properties did not exist under communism. The legal red tape involved in obtaining title to buildings and land for manufacturing, wholesaling, and retailing operations has been a huge problem. Nevertheless, Coca-Cola has invested $85 million to build two bottling and distribution facilities in Russia, and Allied Lyons has spent $30 million to build a plant to make Baskin-Robbins ice cream.[37]

Consumer income and purchasing power   A global marketer selling consumer goods must also consider what the average per capita or household income is among a country's consumers and how the income is distributed to determine a nation's purchasing power.[38] Per capita income varies greatly between nations. Average yearly per capita income in EU countries is $20 000 and is less than $200 in some developing countries such as Vietnam. A country's income distribution is important because it may give a more reliable picture of a country's purchasing power. Generally speaking, as the proportion of middle-income class households in a country increases, the greater a nation's purchasing power tends to be. Figure 5-5 shows the worldwide disparity in the

FIGURE 5-5

HOW PURCHASING POWER DIFFERS
AROUND THE WORLD

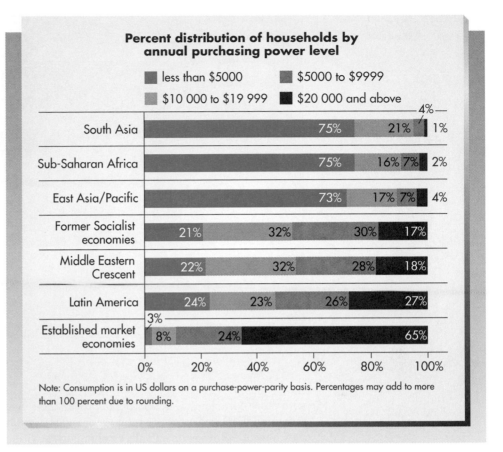

Percent distribution of households by
annual purchasing power level

Note: Consumption is in US dollars on a purchase-power-parity basis. Percentages may add to more than 100 percent due to rounding.

percentage distribution of households by level of purchasing power. In established market economies such as those in North America and Western Europe, 65 percent of households have an annual purchasing capability of $20 000 or more. In comparison, 75 percent of households in the developing countries of South Asia have an annual purchasing power of less than $5000.

Seasoned global marketers recognize that people in developing countries often have government subsidies for food, housing, and health care that supplement their income. Accordingly, people with seemingly low incomes are actually promising customers for a variety of products. For example, a consumer in South Asia earning the equivalent of $250 per year can afford Gillette razors. When that consumer's income rises to $1000, a Sony television becomes affordable, and a new Volkswagen or Nissan can be bought with an annual income of $10 000. In developing countries of Eastern Europe, a $1000 annual income makes a refrigerator affordable, and $2000 brings an automatic washer within reach. These facts have not gone unnoticed by Whirlpool, which now aggressively markets these products in Eastern Europe.

Currency exchange rates   Fluctuations in exchange rates among the world's currencies are of critical importance in global marketing. Such fluctuations affect everyone from international tourists to global companies.

Exchange rate fluctuations have a direct impact on the prices charged and the profits made by global companies. When foreign currencies can buy more Canadian dollars, for example, Canadian products are less expensive for the foreign customer. Short-term fluctuations, however, can have a significant effect on the profits of global companies. Hewlett-Packard gained nearly a half million dollars in additional profit through exchange-rate fluctuations in one year. On the other hand, Nestlé has lost as much as a million dollars in six months due to fluctuations in the Swiss franc compared

CURRENCY EXCHANGE RATES AFFECT
INTERNATIONAL TRAVEL AND
TOURISM.

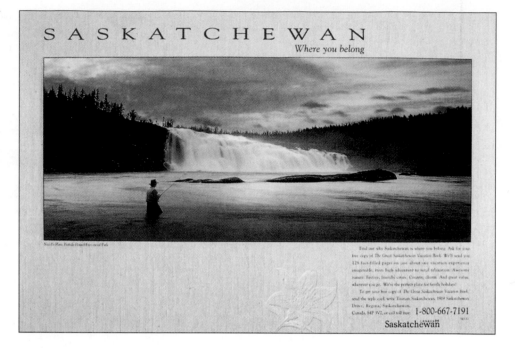

with other currencies.[39] In seeking to protect their investments, global companies must remain vigilant and carefully monitor changes in exchange rates. Many global companies have employees or outside foreign currency traders who work around the clock carefully watching fluctuations in exchange rates in order to make decisions on when to buy or sell foreign currencies.

Political-Regulatory Climate

The political and regulatory climate for marketing in a country or region of the world lies not only in identifying the current climate but in determining how long a favourable or unfavourable climate will last. An assessment of a country or regional political-regulatory climate includes an analysis of its political stability, trade regulations, and trade incentives.

Political stability   Trade among nations or regions depends on political stability. Billions of dollars have been lost in the Middle East and the former Federal Republic of Yugoslavia as a result of internal political strife and war. Losses such as these encourage careful selection of politically stable countries and regions of the world for trade.

When instability is suspected, companies do everything they can to protect their interests. Companies may limit their trade to exporting products into the country, thereby minimizing investments in new plants in the foreign economy. Currency is converted as soon as possible. Many global companies are keeping a close watch on how China manages Hong Kong and whether the political and economic stability of the former British crown colony will be maintained. Similarly, global companies carefully monitor the political situations in Eastern Europe and Latin America.

Trade regulations   Countries have a variety of rules that govern business practices within their borders. These rules can often serve as trade barriers.[40] For example, Japan has some 11 000 trade regulations. Japanese car safety rules effectively require all automobile replacement parts to be Japanese and not North American or European; public health rules make it illegal to sell aspirin or cold medicine without a pharmacist present. The Malaysian government recently adopted advertising regulations warning that "advertisements must not project or promote an excessively aspirational lifestyle," and Sweden outlaws all advertisements to children.

Trade regulations also appear in free trade agreements among countries. European Union nations abide by some 10 000 rules that specify how goods are to be made and marketed. For instance, the rules for a washing machine's electrical system are detailed on more than 100 typed pages. Regulations related to contacting consumers via telephone, fax, and e-mail without their prior consent and toy advertising to children also exist. The European Union's ISO 9000 quality standards, though not a trade regulation, have the same effect on business practice. **ISO 9000** standards, developed by the International Standards Organization (ISO) in Geneva, Switzerland, refer to standards for registration and certification of a manufacturer's quality management and quality assurance system. Many European companies require suppliers to be ISO 9000 certified as a condition of doing business with them. Certified companies have undergone an on-site audit that includes an inspection of its facilities to ensure that documented quality control procedures are in place and that all employees understand and follow them. More than 100 countries have adopted ISO 9000 standards, and 40 000 certificates have been issued worldwide.[41]

Trade incentives   Just as countries and regions can discourage international trade through trade barriers, they can also encourage it by offering investment incentives, helping in site location, and providing other services. Hungary is currently offering a five-year "tax holiday"—a period during which no corporate taxes will be assessed— to encourage foreign firms to develop manufacturing facilities there. The Republic of Indonesia actively promotes its modern economic infrastructure, pro-investment posture, and quality of life through a worldwide advertising and promotional campaign. In addition, a country or group of countries can establish equitable standards to enable foreign producers and products to compete fairly in their domestic markets. Free trade agreements are viewed as a trade incentive in this respect.

CONCEPT CHECK

1. Semiotics involves the study of _____.

2. When foreign currencies can buy more Canadian dollars, are Canadian products more or less expensive for a foreign consumer?

GLOBAL MARKET-ENTRY STRATEGIES

Once a company has decided to enter the global marketplace, it must select a means of market entry. Four general options exist: (1) exporting, (2) licensing, (3) joint venture, and (4) direct investment.[42] As Figure 5-6 demonstrates, the amount of financial commitment, risk, marketing control, and profit potential increases as the firm moves from exporting to direct investment.

Exporting

Exporting is producing goods in one country and selling them in another country. This entry option allows a company to make the least number of changes in terms of its product, its organization, and even its corporate goals. Host countries usually do not like this practice because it provides less local employment than under alternative means of entry.

FIGURE 5-6

ALTERNATIVE GLOBAL MARKET-ENTRY
STRATEGIES

Indirect exporting is when a firm sells its domestically produced goods in a foreign country through an intermediary. It involves the least amount of commitment and risk but will probably return the least profit. This kind of exporting is ideal for the company that has no overseas contacts but wants to market abroad. The intermediary is often a broker or agent that has the marketing know-how and the resources necessary for the effort to succeed.

Direct exporting is when a firm sells its domestically produced goods in a foreign country without intermediaries. Most companies become involved in direct exporting when they believe their volume of sales will be sufficiently large and easy to obtain that they do not require intermediaries. For example, the exporter may be approached by foreign buyers that are willing to contract for a large volume of purchases. Direct exporting involves more risk than indirect exporting for the company but also opens the door to increased profits.

Remember W. K. Buckley Ltd. and its cough-remedy product (Buckley's Mixture) from the chapter opener? This company uses an indirect exporting strategy for the Australian market, and a direct exporting strategy for the United States market. Sullivan Entertainment Inc. of Toronto, creators of the *Road to Avonlea* television series, also uses an exporting strategy to market the show (a season of 13 episodes is sold as a unit) in over 100 countries including Bolivia, the Czech Republic, and South Korea.[43]

Licensing

Under licensing, a company offers the right to a trademark, patent, trade secret, or other similarly valued items of intellectual property in return for a royalty or a fee. In global marketing the advantages to the company granting the license are low risk and capital-free entry into a foreign country. The licensee gains information that allows it to start with a competitive advantage, and the foreign country gains employment by having the product manufactured locally. W. K. Buckley Ltd. used licensing for entering Holland. Similarly, Clearly Canadian Beverages of Vancouver used licensing to enter several markets including the United States and Japan.

There are some serious drawbacks to this mode of entry, however. The licensor forgoes control of its product and reduces the potential profits gained from it. In addition, while the relationship lasts, the licensor may be creating its own competition. Some licensees are able to modify the product somehow and enter the market with product and marketing knowledge gained at the expense of the company that got them started. To offset this disadvantage, many companies strive to stay innovative so that the licensee remains dependent on them for improvements and successful operation. Finally, should the licensee prove to be a poor choice, the name or reputation of the company may be harmed.

Two variations of licensing, local manufacturing and local assembly, represent alternative ways to produce a product within a foreign country. With local manufacturing, a Canadian company may contract with a foreign firm to manufacture products according to stated specifications. The product is then sold in the foreign country or exported back to Canada. With local assembly, the Canadian company may contract with a foreign firm to assemble (not manufacture) parts and components that have been shipped to that country. In both cases, advantage to the foreign country is the employment of its people, and the Canadian firm benefits from lower wage rates in the foreign country.

A third variation of licensing is franchising. Franchising is one of the fastest-growing market-entry strategies. Franchises include soft-drink, motel, retailing, fast-food, and car rental operations and a variety of business services. McDonald's is a premier global franchiser: 70 percent of the company's stores are franchised, and 45 percent of the company's operating income comes from foreign operations.[44]

Joint Venture

When a foreign company and a local firm invest together to create a local business, it is called a **joint venture.** These two companies share ownership, control, and profits of the new company. Investment may be made by having either of the companies buy shares in the other or by creating a third and separate entity. This was done by Caterpillar, Inc., the world's largest manufacturer of earth-moving and construction equipment. It recently created NEVAMASH with its joint venture partner, Kirovsky Zvod, a large Russian manufacturer of heavy equipment.

The advantages of this option are twofold. First, one company may not have the necessary financial, physical, or managerial resources to enter a foreign market alone. Through a joint venture, Ford and Volkswagen combined resources to make four-wheel-drive vehicles in Portugal. Second, a government may require or strongly encourage a joint venture before it allows a foreign company to enter its market. This is the case in China where foreign corporations are discouraged from establishing solely owned subsidiaries. Recently, W. K. Buckley Ltd. used a joint venture arrangement to enter the Chinese market.

The disadvantages arise when the two companies disagree about policies or courses of action for their joint venture or when governmental bureaucracy bogs down the effort. For example, Canadian firms often prefer to reinvest earnings gained, whereas foreign companies may want to spend those earnings. Or a Canadian firm may want to return profits earned to Canada, while the local firm or its government may oppose this—the problem now faced by many joint ventures in Eastern Europe and South Asia.

Direct Investment

The biggest commitment a company can make when entering the global market is **direct investment,** which entails a domestic firm actually investing in and owning a foreign subsidiary or division. Examples of direct investment are Toyota's automobile plant in Ontario and Hyundai's plant in Quebec. Many Canadian-based companies are also switching to this mode of entry. Alcan Aluminium built a recycling plant in Worrington, England, and Ganong Brothers opened a plant to manufacture chocolates in Thailand.

For many firms, direct investment often follows one of the other three market-entry strategies.[45] For example, Ernst & Young, an international accounting and management consulting firm, entered Hungary first by establishing a joint venture with a local company. Ernst & Young later acquired the company, making it a subsidiary with headquarters in Budapest.

The advantages of direct investment include cost savings, better understanding of local market conditions, and fewer local restrictions. Firms entering foreign markets using direct investment believe that these advantages outweigh the financial commitments and risks involved.

CONCEPT CHECK

1. What mode of entry could a company follow if it has no previous experience in global marketing?

2. How does licensing differ from a joint venture?

CRAFTING A WORLDWIDE MARKETING EFFORT

The choice of a market-entry strategy is a necessary first step for a marketer when joining the community of global companies. The next step involves the challenging task of designing, implementing, and controlling marketing programs worldwide.

Product and Promotion Strategies

Global companies have five strategies for matching products and their promotion efforts to global markets. As Figure 5-7 shows, the strategies focus on whether a company extends or adapts its product and promotion message for consumers in different countries.

A product may be sold globally in one of three ways: (1) in the same form as in its home market, (2) with some adaptations, or (3) as a totally new product.

1. *Product extension.* Selling virtually the same product in other countries is a product extension strategy. It works well for products such as Coca-Cola, Gillette razors, Wrigley's gum, and Levi's jeans. However, it didn't work for Jell-O (a more solid gelatin was preferred to the powder in England) or Duncan Hines cakes (which were seen as too moist and crumbly to eat with tea in England).
2. *Product adaptation.* Changing a product in some way to make it more appropriate for a country's climate or preferences is a product adaptation strategy. Heinz baby food offers strained lamb brains for Australians and strained brown beans in the Netherlands.

FIGURE 5-7

FIVE PRODUCT AND PROMOTION
STRATEGIES FOR GLOBAL MARKETING

3. *Product invention.* Designing a product to serve the unmet needs of a foreign nation is a product invention strategy. This is probably the strategy with the most potential since there are so many unmet needs, yet it is actually the least used. National Cash Register has followed a reverse invention strategy by introducing crank-operated cash registers in some developing nations that have unreliable or inaccessible electric power.

An identical promotion message is used for the product extension and product adaptation strategies around the world. Gillette, for example, uses the same global message for its men's toiletries: "Gillette, the Best a Man Can Get."

Global companies may also elect to adapt their promotion message. For instance, the same product may be sold in many countries but advertised differently. As an example, L'Oreal, a French health and beauty products marketer, recently introduced its Golden Beauty brand of sun care products through its Helena Rubenstein subsidiary in Western Europe with a communication adaptation strategy.[46] Recognizing that cultural and buying motive differences related to skin care and tanning exist, Golden Beauty advertising features dark tanning for Northern Europeans, skin protection to avoid wrinkles among Latin Europeans, and beautiful skin for Europeans living along the Mediterranean Sea, even though the products are the same. Other companies use a dual adaptation strategy by modifying both their products and promotion messages. Nestlé does this with Nescafe coffee. Nescafe is marketed using different coffee blends and promotional campaigns to match consumer preferences in different countries.

Distribution Strategy

Distribution is of critical importance in global marketing. The availability and quality of retailers and wholesalers as well as transportation, communication, and warehousing facilities are often determined by a country's stage of economic development. Figure 5-8 outlines the channel through which a product manufactured in one country must travel to reach its destination in another country. The first step involves the seller; its headquarters is the starting point and is responsible for the successful distribution to the ultimate consumer.

The next step is the channel between two nations, moving the product from one country to another. Intermediaries that can handle this responsibility include resident buyers in a foreign country, independent merchant wholesalers who buy and sell the product, or agents who bring buyers and sellers together.

FIGURE 5-8   CHANNELS OF DISTRIBUTION IN GLOBAL MARKETING

Once the product is in the foreign nation, that country's distribution channels take over.[47] These channels can be very long or surprisingly short, depending on the product line. In Japan fresh fish go through three intermediaries before getting to a retail outlet. Conversely, shoes only go through one intermediary. In other cases, the channel does not even involve the host country. Procter & Gamble sells its soap door to door in the Philippines because there are no other alternatives in many parts of that country. The sophistication of a country's distribution channels increases as its economic infrastructure develops. Supermarkets facilitate selling products in many nations, but they are not popular or available in many others where culture and lack of refrigeration dictate shopping on a daily rather than a weekly basis. For example, when Coke and Pepsi entered China, both had to create direct-distribution channels, investing in trucks and refrigerator units for small retailers.

Pricing Strategy

Global companies also face many challenges in determining a pricing strategy as part of their worldwide marketing effort.[48] Individual countries, even those with free trade agreements, may impose considerable competitive, political, and legal constraints on the pricing latitude of global companies. Of course, economic factors such as the costs of production, selling, and tariffs, plus transportation and storage costs, also affect global pricing decisions.

Pricing too low or too high can have dire consequences. When prices appear too low in one country, companies can be charged with dumping, a practice subject to severe penalties and fines. **Dumping** is when a firm sells a product in a foreign country below its domestic price or below its actual cost. This is often done to build a company's share of the market by pricing at a competitive level. Another reason is that the products being sold may be surplus or cannot be sold domestically and, therefore, are already a burden to the company. The firm may be glad to sell them at almost any price. Recently, potato farmers from Maine claimed that New Brunswick and Prince Edward Island producers were dumping potatoes into the New England market at well below the actual cost of production. They petitioned the Maine state government to take action against the Canadian potato growers and block the entry of these potatoes at the border. Maine farmers argued that the cheaper Canadian potatoes were depressing the prices that New England wholesalers and retailers were paying for Maine-grown potatoes and driving them out of business.

When companies price their products very high in some countries but competitively in others, they face a grey market problem.[49] A **grey market**, also called parallel importing, is a situation where products are sold through unauthorized channels of distribution. A grey market comes about when individuals buy products in a lower-priced country from a manufacturer's authorized retailer, ship them to higher-priced countries, and then sell them below the manufacturer's suggested retail price through unauthorized retailers. Many well-known products have been sold through grey markets, including Olympus cameras, Seiko watches, IBM personal computers, and Mercedes-Benz cars.

CONCEPT CHECK

1. Products may be sold globally in three ways. What are they?

2. What is dumping?

SUMMARY

1. The dollar value of world trade has grown an average of 12 percent per year since 1970 and will likely approach $8 trillion in 2005. Manufactured goods and commodities account for 80 percent of world trade, while services account for 20 percent.

2. Not all world trade involves the exchange of money for goods or services. About 20 percent of world trade involves countertrade, the practice of using barter rather than money for making global sales.

3. A global perspective on world trade views exports and imports as complementary economic flows. A country's exports affect its imports and vice versa. This phenomenon is called the *trade feedback effect.*

4. Canada is a trading nation, exporting over 30 percent of its gross domestic product on an annual basis.

5. The reason some companies and some industries in a country succeed globally while others do not lies in their nation's competitive advantage. A nation's competitive advantage arises from specific conditions in a nation that foster success.

6. Three trends in the late twentieth century have significantly affected world trade: (1) a gradual decline of economic protectionism, (2) an increase in formal economic integration and free trade among nations, and (3) global competition among global companies for global consumers.

7. Although global and domestic marketing are based on the same marketing principles, many underlying assumptions must be reevaluated when a firm pursues global opportunities. A global environmental scan typically considers three kinds of uncontrollable environmental variables. These include cultural diversity, economic conditions, and political-regulatory climate.

8. Four global market-entry strategies are exporting, licensing, joint venture, and direct investment. The relative difficulty of global marketing, as well as the amount of financial commitment, risk, marketing control, and profit potential, increase in moving from exporting to direct investment.

9. Crafting a worldwide marketing effort involves designing, implementing, and controlling a marketing program that standardizes marketing mix elements when there are cultural similarities and adapting them when cultures differ.

KEY TERMS

countertrade p. 116
trade feedback effect p. 117
gross domestic product p. 117
balance of trade p. 117
protectionism p. 120
tariffs p. 120
quota p. 120
World Trade Organization p. 121
global competition p. 123
strategic alliances p. 123
multidomestic marketing strategy p. 124
global marketing strategy p. 124
global consumers p. 125
cross-cultural analysis p. 126

values p. 126
customs p. 127
cultural symbols p. 127
semiotics p. 127
back translation p. 128
consumer ethnocentrism p. 129
economic infrastructure p. 130
ISO 9000 p. 133
exporting p. 133
joint venture p. 135
direct investment p. 136
dumping p. 138
grey market p. 138

CHAPTER PROBLEMS AND APPLICATIONS

1. What is meant by this statement: "Quotas are a hidden tax on consumers, whereas tariffs are a more obvious one"?

2. Is the trade feedback effect described in the text a long-run or short-run view on world trade flows? Explain your answer.

3. Since English is the official language in Australia, some Canadian global companies might select it as an easy market to enter. Others believe that this similarity in language could make it harder to successfully enter that market. Who's right? Why?

4. How successful would a television commercial in Japan be if it featured a husband surprising his wife in her dressing area on Valentine's Day with a small box of chocolates containing four candies? Why?

5. As a novice in global marketing, which alternative for global market-entry strategy would you be likely to start with? Why? What other alternatives do you have for a global market entry?

6. Coca-Cola is sold worldwide. In some countries, Coca-Cola owns the bottling facilities; in others, it has signed contracts with licensees or relies on joint ventures. When selecting a licensee in each country, what factors should Coca-Cola consider?

7. Now that China has taken back control of Hong Kong, what advice would you give to Canadian companies currently doing, or planning to do business in Hong Kong?

CASE 5-1   The Coca-Cola Company: Japan

Video

The Coca-Cola Company (www.coca-cola.com) is the world's largest carbonated soft-drink producer. In 1994, the company sold the equivalent of 11.8 billion cases of soft drinks worldwide. Approximately 75 percent of the company's soft-drink revenues and 80 percent of soft-drink operating income arise from sales outside North America. These statistics are not surprising since Coke and Coca-Cola are among the world's best-known trademarks.

THE COCA-COLA COMPANY: A GLOBAL ENTERPRISE

The global presence of The Coca-Cola Company is evident in numerous ways. Four of the world's top five carbonated soft drinks are sold by the company. These brands include Coca-Cola/Coca-Cola Classic, diet Coke,

Coca-Cola Light, Fanta, and Sprite. The company captured 46 percent of the worldwide market for carbonated soft-drink flavour segments: cola, orange, and lemon-lime. Exhibit 1 illustrates the worldwide leadership position of Coca-Cola.

One of the reasons for Coca-Cola's worldwide presence is its extensive, efficient, and effective bottling network. This bottling network, which includes company-owned bottlers, joint ventures with established bottlers in various countries, and franchised bottlers, allows for Coca-Cola/Coca-Cola Classic to be distributed in more than 195 countries, Fanta and Sprite in 164 countries, and diet Coke/Coca-Cola Light in 117 countries.

COCA-COLA MARKETING IN JAPAN

The Coca-Cola Company sold its products in Japan as early as the 1920s. However, it did not establish a formal Japanese subsidiary until 1957. Since that time, the com-

EXHIBIT 1

COCA-COLA'S MARKET POSITION IN 15 COUNTRIES (SHARE OF FLAVOURED, CARBONATED SOFT-DRINK SALES)

COUNTRY	MARKET LEADER	LEADERSHIP MARGIN	SECOND PLACE
Australia	Coca-Cola	3.9–1	diet Coke
Belgium	Coca-Cola	9.0–1	Fanta
Brazil	Coca-Cola	3.7–1	Brazilian brand
Chile	Coca-Cola	4.5–1	Fanta
France	Coca-Cola	4.2–1	French brand
Germany	Coca-Cola	3.5–1	Fanta
Great Britain	Coca-Cola	1.8–1	diet Coke
Greece	Coca-Cola	3.7–1	Fanta
Italy	Coca-Cola	2.8–1	Fanta
Japan	Coca-Cola	2.2–1	Fanta
Korea	Coca-Cola	1.6–1	Korean brand
Norway	Coca-Cola	2.7–1	Coca-Cola light
South Africa	Coca-Cola	3.8–1	Sparletta
Spain	Coca-Cola	2.4–1	Spanish brand
Sweden	Coca-Cola	3.6–1	Fanta

Source: *The Coca-Cola Company 1994 Annual Report*, p. 29.

pany has built a dominant position in the Japanese soft-drink market. For example, Coca-Cola is sold in 1 million stores and some 700 000 vending machines in Japan. The Coca-Cola Company captures more than 33 percent of all carbonated and noncarbonated soft drinks sold in Japan. It is estimated that the Coca-Cola brand captures 70 percent of the Japanese cola market; Coca-Cola Light captures 20 percent. Pepsi-Cola captures less than 10 percent of this market. Industry analysts estimate that advertising spending for the Coca-Cola brand is about five times higher than the amount spent by Pepsi-Cola.

The successful entry into Japan by the Coca-Cola Company and subsequent performance provide valuable insights into global marketing in general and the need to consider cultural issues. For instance, company executives emphasize that adaptation to the local culture manifests itself in numerous ways. Its management practices focus on consensus and group-building consistent with Japanese values. Customs such as lifetime employment for Japanese employees are adopted. Efforts to localize consumer communications is also evident in the language used in advertising and the group settings featuring the consumption of the product.

Questions

1. Which of the four global market-entry strategies does Coca-Cola use most often when expanding its worldwide presence? Which strategy does it appear that Coca-Cola uses the least?

2. After watching the video tape featuring television commercials for Coca-Cola in Japan, what similarities do you see with Coca-Cola commercials in Canada?

CHAPTER 6

Consumer Behaviour

AFTER READING THIS CHAPTER YOU SHOULD BE ABLE TO:

• Outline the stages in the consumer decision process.

• Distinguish between three variations of the consumer decision process: routine, limited, and extended problem solving.

• Explain how psychological influences affect consumer behaviour, particularly purchase decision processes.

• Identify major sociocultural influences on consumer behaviour and their effects on purchase decisions.

• Recognize how marketers can use knowledge of consumer behaviour to better understand and influence individual and family purchases.

VOLKSWAGEN IS HOPING THAT WOMEN WILL LIKE THE NEW BUG.

Who will buy at least half of all cars in 2000? Who already spends millions on new cars and trucks for their personal use and influences 80 percent of all new-car sales? Women—yes, women. And, Volkswagen (www.volkswagen.com) hopes that women will like the reintroduction of the Beetle in 1998.

Until recently, automakers viewed women chiefly as passengers not purchasers. Today, most have marketing-to-women task forces, and have hired women design engineers and marketing executives to help them understand this "new" consumer. What have they learned? First, women prefer "sporty" cars that are relatively inexpensive and fun to drive rather than "sports cars" with better engines and higher price tags. Second, a car's "feel" is important to women. Sleek exteriors and interior designs that fit proportions of smaller drivers as well as opening ease of doors, trunks, and hoods are equally important.

Third, women approach car buying in a deliberate manner, including reading automotive publications that deal with car buying. Fourth, while men and women look for the same car features, their priorities differ. Both sexes value dependability most, but more women consider it a higher priority. Women also rank low price and safety higher than men. Finally, automakers have learned that, when shopping for cars, both sexes dislike high-pressure tactics.

Since women prefer sporty, relatively inexpensive, safe, and fun-to-drive cars, Volkswagen appears to have a winner with the new bug. Women purchasers, specifically, single women under 30 years of age, who are looking for something avant garde will likely be attracted to the new Beetle. While VW will probably do well with both young male and female car purchasers, many experts agree that females, in particular, will be visiting VW dealerships to take a look at the new bug.[1]

This chapter examines **consumer behaviour,** the actions a person takes in purchasing and using products and services, including the mental and social processes that precede and follow these actions. This chapter shows how the behavioural sciences help answer questions such as why people choose one product or brand over another, how they make these choices, and how companies use this knowledge to provide value to consumers.

CONSUMER PURCHASE DECISION PROCESS

Behind the visible act of making a purchase lies an important decision process that must be investigated. The stages a buyer passes through in making choices about which products and services to buy is the **purchase decision process.** This process has the five stages shown in Figure 6-1: (1) problem recognition, (2) information search, (3) alternative evaluation, (4) purchase decision, and (5) postpurchase behaviour.

Problem Recognition: Perceiving a Need

Problem recognition, the initial step in the purchase decision, is perceiving a difference between a person's ideal and actual situations big enough to trigger a decision.[2] This can be as simple as finding an empty milk carton in the refrigerator; noting, as a first-year college student, that your high school clothes are not in the style that other students are wearing; or realizing that your laptop computer may not be working properly.

In marketing, advertisements or salespeople can activate a consumer's decision process by showing the shortcomings of competing (or currently owned) products. For instance, an advertisement for a compact disc (CD) player could stimulate problem recognition because it emphasizes the sound quality of CD players over that of the conventional stereo system you may now own.

Information Search: Seeking Value

After recognizing a problem, a consumer begins to search for information, the next stage in the purchase decision process. First, you may scan your memory for previous experiences with products or brands.[3] This action is called *internal search.* For frequently purchased products such as shampoo, this may be enough. Or a consumer may undertake an *external search* for information.[4] This is especially needed when past experience or knowledge is insufficient, the risk of making a wrong purchase decision is high, and the cost of gathering information is low. The primary sources of external information are: (1) *personal sources,* such as relatives and friends whom the consumer trusts; (2) *public sources,* including various product-rating organizations such as *Consumer Reports,* government agencies, and TV "consumer programs"; and

FIGURE 6-1   PURCHASE DECISION PROCESS

Problem recognition: Perceiving a need → Information search: Seeking value → Evaluation of alternatives: Assessing value → Purchase decision: Buying value → Postpurchase behaviour: Value in consumption or use

(3) *marketer-dominated sources,* such as information from sellers that include advertising, salespeople, and point-of-purchase displays in stores.

Suppose you consider buying an expensive or complex product, such as a CD player. You will probably tap several of these information sources: friends and relatives, CD-player advertisements, and several stores carrying CD players (for demonstrations). You might study the comparative evaluation of carousel changer CD players that appeared in *Consumer Reports,* published by a product-testing organization, a portion of which appears in Figure 6-2.[5]

Alternative Evaluation: Assessing Value

The information search stage clarifies the problem for the consumer by (1) suggesting criteria to use for the purchase, (2) yielding brand names that might meet the criteria, and (3) developing consumer value perceptions. Based only on the information shown in Figure 6-2, what selection criteria would you use in buying a CD player? Would you use price, bump resistance, taping ease, or some combination of these and other criteria?

For some of you, the information provided may be inadequate because it does not contain all the factors you might consider when evaluating CD players. These factors are a consumer's **evaluative criteria,** which represent both the objective attributes of a brand (such as track-locate speed) and the subjective ones (such as prestige) you use to compare different products and brands. Firms try to identify and capitalize on both types of criteria to create the best value for the money sought by you and other consumers.

FIGURE 6-2   *CONSUMER REPORTS'* EVALUATION OF CAROUSEL CHANGER COMPACT DISC PLAYERS (ABRIDGED)

Brand	Model	Price	Disc-error correction	Track-locate speed	Bump resistance	Overall convenience	Taping ease
Onkyo	DX-C211	$270	Better	Very good	Fair	Good	Very good
Sony	CDP-C445	230	Good	Very good	Good	Better	Better
Denon	DCM-340	260	Better	Very good	Fair	Good	Very good
Technics	SL-PD1000	260	Fair	Better	Very good	Very good	Good
Philips	CDC 935	240	Fair	Very good	Better	Very good	Fair
Kenwood	DP-R6060	250	Good	Very good	Fair	Very good	Very good
Marantz	CC-45	300	Good	Very good	Better	Good	Fair
Yamaha	CDC-645	270	Good	Very good	Fair	Very good	Good
Teac	PD-D900	155	Good	Good	Good	Very good	Fair
Fisher	DAC-2403	265	Good	Good	Very good	Good	Very good

Rating: ● Better   ◒ Very good   ○ Good   ◓ Fair   ⬤ Poor

Consumers often have several criteria for evaluating brands. (Didn't you in the preceding exercise?) Knowing this, companies seek to identify the most important evaluative criteria that consumers use when judging brands. For example, among the evaluative criteria shown in the columns of Figure 6-2, suppose that you use three in considering brands of CD players: (1) a list price under $250 (column 3), (2) overall convenience (column 7), and (3) taping ease (column 8). These criteria establish the brands in your **evoked set**—the group of brands that a consumer would consider acceptable from among all the brands in the product class of which he or she is aware.[6] Your three evaluative criteria result in only two models, Sony and Philips, in your evoked set. If these brands don't satisfy you, you can change your evaluative criteria to create a different evoked set of models.

Purchase Decision: Buying Value

Having examined the alternatives in the evoked set, you are almost ready to make a purchase decision. Two choices remain: (1) from whom to buy and (2) when to buy. For a product like a CD player, the information search process probably involved visiting retail stores, seeing different brands in catalogues, or viewing CD player promotions on a home shopping television channel. The choice of which seller to buy from will depend on such considerations as the terms of sale, your past experience buying from the seller, and the return policy. Often a purchase decision involves a simultaneous evaluation of both product attributes and seller characteristics. For example, you might choose the second-most preferred CD player brand at a store with a liberal refund and return policy versus the most preferred brand at a store with more conservative policies.

Deciding when to buy is frequently determined by a number of factors. For instance, you might buy sooner if one of your preferred brands is on sale or its manufacturer offers a rebate. Other factors such as the store atmosphere, pleasantness of the shopping experience, salesperson persuasiveness, time pressure, and financial circumstances could also affect whether a purchase decision is made or postponed.[7]

Postpurchase Behaviour: Value in Consumption or Use

After buying a product, the consumer compares it with his or her expectations and is either satisfied or dissatisfied. If the consumer is dissatisfied, marketers must decide whether the product was deficient or consumer expectations too high. Product deficiency may require a design change; if expectations are too high, perhaps the company's advertising or the salesperson oversold the product's features.

Sensitivity to a customer's consumption or use experience is extremely important in a consumer's value perception. For example, research on long-distance telephone services provided by MCI, Sprint, and AT&T indicates that satisfaction or dissatisfaction affects consumer value perceptions.[8] Studies show that satisfaction or dissatisfaction affects consumer communications and repeat-purchase behaviour. Satisfied buyers tell eight other people about their experience. Dissatisfied buyers complain to 22 people![9] Satisfied buyers also tend to buy from the same seller each time a purchase occasion arises. As described in the accompanying Marketing NewsNet, the financial impact of repeat-purchase behaviour is significant.[10] Accordingly, firms such as Nissan Canada, Johnson & Johnson, Coca-Cola, and British Airways focus attention on postpurchase behaviour to maximize customer satisfaction and retention.[11] These firms, among many others, now provide toll-free telephone numbers, offer liberalized return and refund policies, and engage in staff training to handle complaints, answer questions, and record suggestions. For example, Nissan Canada, increased its market share by offering 24-hour roadside assistance and a 100 percent satisfaction commitment. The use of customer satisfaction and product and service guarantee programs are central to Nissan's customer-retention initiatives.[12]

MARKETING NEWSNET

THE VALUE OF A SATISFIED CUSTOMER

Customer satisfaction is an important focus of the marketing concept. But, how much is a satisfied customer worth? This question has prompted firms to calculate the financial value of a satisfied customer over time. Frito-Lay, for example, estimates that the average loyal consumer eats 21 pounds of salty snack chips a year. At a price of $2.50 a pound, this customer spends $52.50 annually on the company's salty snacks such as Lays and Ruffles potato chips and Doritos and Tostitos tortilla chips. Esso estimates that a loyal customer will spend $500 annually for its branded gasoline, not including candy, snacks, oil, or repair services purchased at its gasoline stations. Kimberly-Clark reports that a loyal customer will buy 6.7 boxes of its Kleenex tissues each year and will spend $994 on facial tissue over 60 years, in today's dollars.

These calculations have focused marketer attention on customer retention. Ford Motor Company has set a target of increasing customer retention—the percentage of Ford owners whose next car is also a Ford—from 60 percent to 80 percent. Why? Ford executives say that each additional percentage point is worth a staggering $100 million in profits!

Often a consumer is faced with two or more highly attractive alternatives, such as a Sony or a Philips CD player. If you choose the Philips, you may think, "Should I have purchased the Sony?" This feeling of postpurchase psychological tension or anxiety is called **cognitive dissonance.** To alleviate it, consumers often attempt to applaud themselves for making the right choice. So after your purchase, you may seek information to confirm your choice by asking friends questions like, "Don't you like my CD player?" or by reading ads of the brand you chose. You might even look for negative information about the brand you didn't buy and decide that the taping ease of the Philips which was rated "fair" in Figure 6-2, was actually a serious deficiency. Firms often use ads or follow-up calls from salespeople in this postpurchase stage to try to convince buyers that they made the right decision. For many years, Buick ran an advertising campaign with the message, "Aren't you really glad you bought a Buick?"

Involvement and Problem-Solving Variations

Sometimes consumers don't engage in the five-step purchase decision process. Instead, they skip or minimize one or more steps depending on the level of **involvement,** the personal, social, and economic significance of the purchase to the consumer.[13] High-involvement purchase occasions typically have at least one of three characteristics—the item to be purchased (1) is expensive, (2) can have serious personal consequences, or (3) could reflect on one's social image. For these occasions, consumers engage in extensive information search, consider many product attributes and brands, form attitudes, and participate in word-of-mouth communication. Low-involvement purchases, such as toothpaste and soap, barely involve most of us, whereas stereo systems and automobiles are very involving. Researchers have identified three general variations in the consumer purchase process based on consumer involvement and product knowledge. Figure 6-3 summarizes some of the important differences between the three problem-solving variations.[14]

Routine problem solving   For products such as toothpaste and milk, consumers recognize a problem, make a decision, and spend little effort seeking external information and evaluating alternatives. The purchase process for such items is virtually a

CHARACTERISTICS OF PURCHASE DECISION PROCESS	EXTENDED PROBLEM SOLVING	LIMITED PROBLEM SOLVING	ROUTINE PROBLEM SOLVING
Number of brands examined	Many	Several	One
Number of sellers considered	Many	Several	Few
Number of product attributes evaluated	Many	Moderate	One
Number of external information sources used	Many	Few	None
Time spent searching	Considerable	Little	Minimal

FIGURE 6-3   COMPARISON OF PROBLEM-SOLVING VARIATIONS

habit and typifies low-involvement decision making. Routine problem solving is typically the case for low-priced, frequently purchased products. It is estimated that about 50 percent of all purchase occasions are of this kind.

Limited problem solving   In limited problem solving, consumers typically seek some information or rely on a friend to help them evaluate alternatives. In general, several brands might be evaluated using a moderate number of different attributes. You might use limited problem solving in choosing a toaster, a restaurant for dinner, and other purchase situations in which you have little time or effort to spend. Limited problem solving accounts for about 38 percent of purchase occasions.

Extended problem solving   In extended problem solving, each of the five stages of the consumer purchase decision process is used in the purchase, including considerable time and effort on external information search and in identifying and evaluating alternatives. Several brands usually are in the evoked set, and these are evaluated on many attributes. Extended problem solving exists in high-involvement purchase situations for items such as CD players, VCRs, and investments in stocks and bonds. Firms marketing these products put significant effort into informing and educating these consumers. About 12 percent of purchase occasions fall into this category.

Situational Influences

Often the purchase situation will affect the purchase decision process. Five **situational influences** have an impact on your purchase decision process: (1) the purchase task, (2) social surroundings, (3) physical surroundings, (4) temporal effects, and (5) antecedent states.[15] The purchase task is the reason for engaging in the decision in the first place. Information searching and evaluating alternatives may differ depending on whether the purchase is a gift, which often involves the social visibility, or for the buyer's own use. Social surroundings, including the other people present when a purchase decision is made, may also affect what is purchased. Physical surroundings such as decor, music, and crowding in retail stores may alter how purchase decisions are made. Temporal effects such as time of day or the amount of time available will influence where consumers have breakfast and lunch and what is ordered. Finally, antecedent states, which include the consumer's mood or the amount of cash on hand, can influence purchase behaviour and choice.

Figure 6-4 shows the many influences that affect the consumer purchase decision process. The decision to buy a product also involves important psychological and sociocultural influences, the two important topics discussed during the remainder of this chapter. Marketing mix influences are described in Chapters 11 through 21.

FIGURE 6-4

INFLUENCES ON THE CONSUMER
PURCHASE DECISION PROCESS

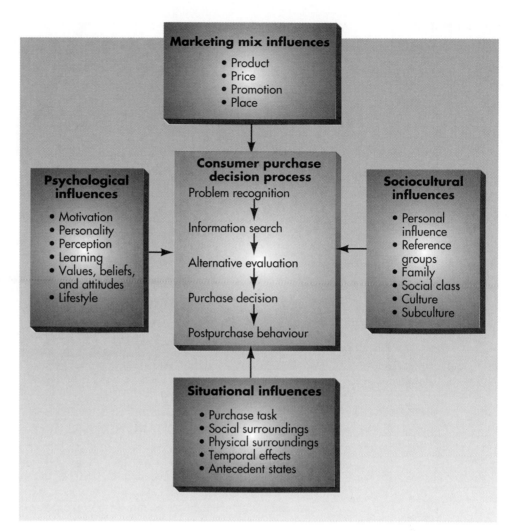

FIGURE 6-4

INFLUENCES ON THE CONSUMER PURCHASE DECISION PROCESS

CONCEPT CHECK

1. What is the first step in the consumer purchase decision process?

2. The brands a consumer considers buying out of the set of brands in a product class of which the consumer is aware is called the _____ .

3. What is the term for postpurchase anxiety?

PSYCHOLOGICAL INFLUENCES ON CONSUMER BEHAVIOUR

Psychology helps marketers understand why and how consumers behave as they do. In particular, concepts such as motivation and personality; perception; learning; values, beliefs, and attitudes; and lifestyle are useful for interpreting buying processes and directing marketing efforts.

Motivation and Personality

Motivation and personality are two familiar psychological concepts that have specific meanings and marketing implications. They are both used frequently to describe why people do some things and not others.

FIGURE 6-5

HIERARCHY OF NEEDS

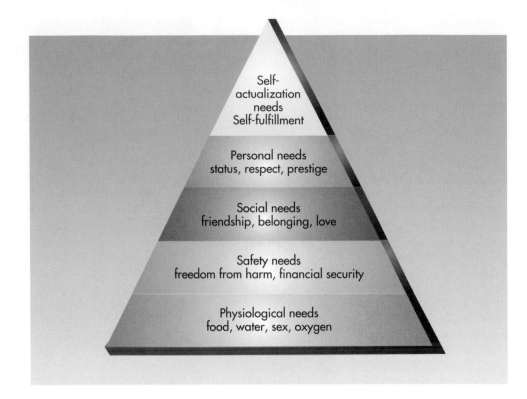

Motivation   **Motivation** is the energizing force that causes behaviour that satisfies a need. Because consumer needs are the focus of the marketing concept, marketers try to arouse these needs.

An individual's needs are boundless. People possess physiological needs for basics such as water, sex, and food. They also have learned needs, including esteem, achievement, and affection. Psychologists point out that these needs are hierarchical; that is, once physiological needs are met, people seek to satisfy their learned needs. Figure 6-5 shows one need hierarchy and classification scheme that contains five need classes.[16] *Physiological needs* are basic to survival and must be satisfied first. A Burger King advertisement featuring a juicy hamburger attempts to activate the need for food. *Safety needs* involve self-preservation and physical well-being. Smoke detector and burglar alarm manufacturers focus on these needs. *Social needs* are concerned with love and friendship. Dating services and fragrance companies try to arouse these needs. *Personal needs* are represented by the need for achievement, status, prestige, and self-respect. The American Express Gold Card and Brooks Brothers Clothiers appeal to these needs. Sometimes firms try to arouse multiple needs to stimulate problem recognition. Michelin combined security with parental love to promote tire replacement as shown in the accompanying advertisement. *Self-actualization needs* involve personal fulfillment such as completing your degree.

Personality   **Personality** refers to a person's consistent behaviours or responses to recurring situations. Although numerous personality theories exist, most identify key traits—enduring characteristics within a person or in his or her relationship with others. Such traits include assertiveness, extroversion, compliance, dominance, and aggression, among others. For example, cigarette smokers have been identified as having traits such as aggression and dominance, but not compliance.[17] Research suggests that compliant people prefer known brand names and use more mouthwash and toilet soaps. In contrast, aggressive types use razors, not electric shavers, apply more cologne and

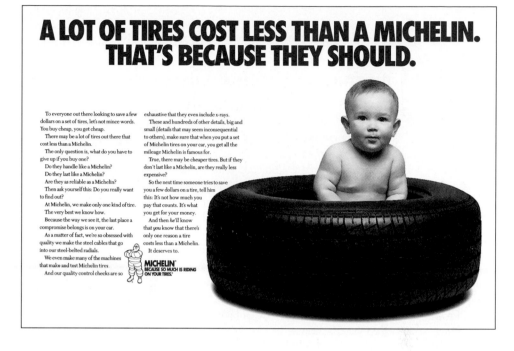

after-shave lotions, and purchase signature goods such as Gucci, Yves St. Laurent, and Donna Karan as an indicator of status.

Cross-cultural analysis also suggests that residents of different countries have a **national character,** or a distinct set of personality characteristics common among people of a country or society.[18] For example, Americans and Germans are relatively more assertive than Canadians.

Perception

One person sees a Cadillac as a mark of achievement; another sees it as ostentatious. This is the result of **perception**—the process by which an individual selects, organizes, and interprets information to create a meaningful picture of the world.

Selective perception   Because the average consumer operates in a complex environment, the human brain attempts to organize and interpret information through a filtering process called *selective perception.* The four stages of selective perception are selective exposure, selective attention, selective comprehension, and selective retention. First, consumers are not exposed to all information or messages in the marketplace. In other words, there is *selective exposure.* For example, you may watch CTV, but not CBC television. In doing so, you do not expose yourself to any information broadcast on the CBC network. Because of selective exposure, marketers must work to determine where consumers are most likely to be exposed to information.

But even if a consumer is exposed to a message, either by accident or design, the consumer may not attend to that message. In general, with *selective attention,* the consumer will only pay attention to messages that are consistent with their attitudes and beliefs and will ignore those that are inconsistent. Consumers are also more likely to attend to messages when they are relevant or of interest to them. For example, a consumer is likely to pay attention to an ad about a product they just bought, or to an ad for a product they are interested in buying.

Selective comprehension involves interpreting information so that it is consistent with your attitudes and beliefs. A marketer's failure to understand this can have

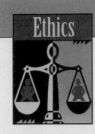

ETHICS AND SOCIAL RESPONSIBILITY ALERT

THE ETHICS OF SUBLIMINAL MESSAGES

For almost 50 years, the topic of subliminal perception and the presence of subliminal messages embedded in commercial communications has sparked debate. To some, the concept of subliminal messages is a hoax. To others, the possibility of a person being influenced without their knowledge is either an exciting or frightening concept. Many experts suggest that the use of subliminal messages by marketers, effective or not, is deceptive and unethical. The Entertainment Leisure Software Publishers Association of Great Britain is presently considering banning these messages altogether.

But there are marketers who pursue opportunities to create these messages. For example, Time Warner Interactive's Endorfun, a CD-ROM puzzle game, has a music soundtrack with more than 100 subliminal messages meant to make players feel good about themselves, even if they can't solve the puzzle. One message says, "I am a winner." Puzzle players are informed that subliminal messages exist and instructions on how to turn off the soundtrack are provided.

Do you believe that attempts to implant subliminal messages are a deceptive practice and unethical, regardless of their intent?

disastrous results. For example, Toro introduced a small, lightweight snowblower called the Snow Pup. Even though the product worked, sales failed to meet expectations. Why? Toro later found out that consumers perceived the name to mean that Snow Pup was a toy or too light to do any serious snow removal.[19]

Selective retention means that consumers do not remember all the information they see, read, or hear, even minutes after exposure to it. This affects the internal and external information search stage of the purchase decision process. This is why furniture and automobile retailers often give consumers product brochures to take home after they leave the showroom.

Since perception plays such an important role in consumer behaviour, it is not surprising that the topic of subliminal perception is a popular item for discussion. **Subliminal perception** means that you see or hear messages without being aware of them. The presence and effect of subliminal perception on behaviour is a hotly debated issue, with more popular appeal than scientific support. Indeed, evidence suggests that such messages have limited effects on behaviour.[20] If these messages did influence behaviour, would their use be an ethical practice? (See the accompanying Ethics and Social Responsibility Alert.[21])

Perceived risk   Perception plays a major role in the perceived risk in purchasing a product or service. **Perceived risk** represents the anxieties felt because the consumer cannot anticipate the outcomes of a purchase but believes that there may be negative

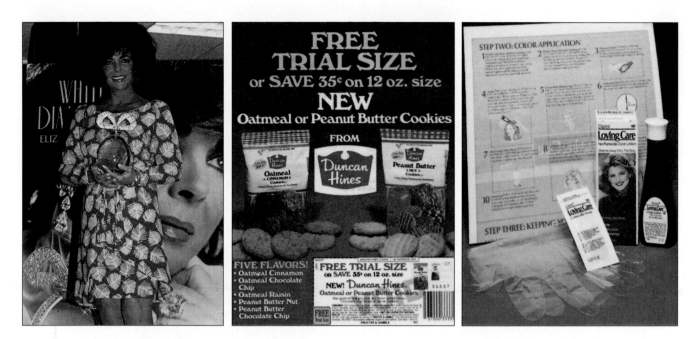

COMPANIES USE A VARIETY OF STRATEGIES TO REDUCE CONSUMER-PERCEIVED RISK.

consequences. Examples of possible negative consequences are the size of the financial outlay required to buy the product (Can I afford $200 for those skis?), the risk of physical harm (Is bungee jumping safe?), and the performance of the product (Will the hair colouring work?). A more abstract form is psychosocial (What will my friends say if I wear that sweater?). Perceived risk affects information search because the greater the perceived risk, the more extensive the external search phase is likely to be.

Recognizing the importance of perceived risk, companies develop strategies to reduce the consumer's risk and encourage purchases. These strategies and examples of firms using them include the following:

- Obtaining seals of approval: the Good Housekeeping seal or Canadian Standards Association (CSA) seal.
- Securing endorsements from influential people: Elizabeth Taylor's White Diamonds fragrance.
- Providing free trials of the product: sample packages of Duncan Hines Peanut Butter Cookies mailed by P&G.
- Giving extensive usage instructions: Clairol haircolouring.
- Providing warranties and guarantees: Cadillac's four-year, 80 000-km, Gold Key Bumper-to-Bumper warranty.

Learning

Much consumer behaviour is learned. Consumers learn which information sources to use for information about products and services, which evaluative criteria to use when assessing alternatives, and, more generally, how to make purchase decisions. **Learning** refers to those behaviours that result from (1) repeated experience and (2) thinking.

Behavioural learning   *Behavioural learning* is the process of developing automatic responses to a situation built up through repeated exposure to it. Four variables are central to how consumers learn from repeated experience: drive, cue, response, and reinforcement. A *drive* is a need that moves an individual to action.

Drives, such as hunger, might be represented by motives. A *cue* is a stimulus or symbol perceived by consumers. A *response* is the action taken by a consumer to satisfy the drive, and a *reinforcement* is the reward. Being hungry (drive), a consumer sees a cue (a billboard), takes action (buys a hamburger), and receives a reward (it tastes great!).

Marketers use two concepts from behavioural learning theory. *Stimulus generalization* occurs when a response elicited by one stimulus (cue) is generalized to another stimulus. Using the same brand name for different products is an application of this concept, such as Tylenol Cold & Flu and Tylenol P.M. *Stimulus discrimination* refers to a person's ability to perceive differences in stimuli. Consumers' tendency to perceive all light beers as being alike led to Budweiser Light commercials that distinguished between many types of "lights" and Bud Light.

Cognitive learning   Consumers also learn through thinking, reasoning, and mental problem solving without direct experience. This type of learning, called *cognitive learning,* involves making connections between two or more ideas or simply observing the outcomes of others' behaviours and adjusting your own accordingly. Firms also influence this type of learning. Through repetition in advertising, messages such as "Advil is a headache remedy" attempt to link a brand (Advil) and an idea (headache remedy) by showing someone using the brand and finding relief.

Brand loyalty   Learning is also important because it relates to habit formation—the basis of routine problem solving. Furthermore, there is a close link between habits and **brand loyalty,** which is a favourable attitude toward and consistent purchase of a single brand over time. Brand loyalty results from the positive reinforcement of previous actions. So a consumer reduces risk and saves time by consistently purchasing the same brand of shampoo and has favourable results—healthy, shining hair. There is evidence of brand loyalty in many commonly purchased products in Canada and the global marketplace. However, the incidence of brand loyalty appears to be declining in North America, Mexico, European Union nations, and Japan. In fact, a Canadian grocery shopper survey found that loyalty to a single store for major grocery shopping dropped to 15 percent in 1996 from 20 percent in 1993.[22]

Values, Beliefs, and Attitudes

Values, beliefs, and attitudes play a central role in consumer decision making and related marketing actions.

Attitude formation   An **attitude** is a "learned predisposition to respond to an object or class of objects in a consistently favourable or unfavourable way."[23] Attitudes are shaped by our values and beliefs, which are learned. Values vary by level of specificity. We speak of Canadian core values, including material well-being and humanitarianism. We also have personal values, such as thriftiness and ambition. Marketers are concerned with both, but focus mostly on personal values. Personal values affect attitudes by influencing the importance assigned to specific product attributes. Suppose thriftiness is one of your personal values. When you evaluate cars, fuel economy (a product attribute) becomes important. If you believe a specific car has this attribute, you are likely to have a favourable attitude toward it.

Beliefs also play a part in attitude formation. **Beliefs** are a consumer's subjective perception of *how well* a product or brand performs on different attributes. Beliefs are based on personal experience, advertising, and discussions with other people. Beliefs about product attributes are important because, along with personal values, they create the favourable or unfavourable attitude the consumer has toward certain products and services.

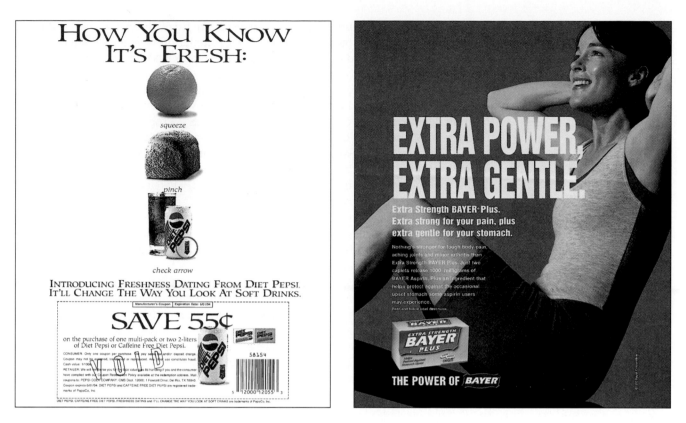

ATTITUDES TOWARD PEPSI-COLA AND EXTRA STRENGTH BAYER ASPIRIN WERE SUCCESSFULLY CHANGED BY THESE ADS. HOW? READ THE TEXT TO FIND OUT HOW MARKETERS CAN CHANGE CONSUMER ATTITUDES TOWARD PRODUCTS AND BRANDS.

Attitude change   Marketers use three approaches to try to change consumer attitudes toward products and brands, as shown in the following examples.[24]

1. *Changing beliefs about the extent to which a brand has certain attributes.* To allay consumer concern that aspirin use causes an upset stomach, The Bayer Company successfully promoted the gentleness of its Extra Strength Bayer Plus aspirin.

2. *Changing the perceived importance of attributes.* Pepsi-Cola made freshness an important product attribute when it stamped freshness dates on its cans. Prior to doing so, few consumers considered cola freshness an issue. After Pepsi spent about $25 million on advertising and promotion, a consumer survey found that 61 percent of cola drinkers believed freshness dating was an important attribute![25]

3. *Adding new attributes to the product.* Chevron's Techron additive was put into its gasoline, hoping consumers would perceive this new attribute favourably, which they did.

Lifestyle

Lifestyle is a mode of living that is identified by how people spend their time and resources (activities), what they consider important in their environment (interests), and what they think of themselves and the world around them (opinions). Moreover, lifestyle reflects consumers' **self-concept,** which is the way people see themselves and the way they believe others see them.[26]

The analysis of consumer lifestyles (also called *psychographics*) has produced many insights into consumers' behaviour. For example, lifestyle analysis has proven useful in segmenting and targeting consumers for new and existing products (see Chapter 9).

Lifestyle analysis typically focuses on identifying consumer profiles. Perhaps the best-known example of this type of analysis is the Values and Lifestyles (VALS 2) Program developed by SRI International.[27] The VALS 2 Program has identified eight interconnected categories of adult lifestyles based on a person's self-orientation and resources. Three patterns have been uncovered; they are oriented toward principles, status, and action. A person's resources encompass income, education, self-confidence, health, eagerness to buy, intelligence, and energy level. This dimension is a continuum ranging from minimal to abundant.

While the VALS Program is the most widely known lifestyles or psychographics system in North America, it has only been a few times in Canada for commercial applications. Canada has a few home-grown systems, with the most comprehensive being the Goldfarb Segments.

The Goldfarb Segments   Many experts believe that Canadian and Americans are different in terms of values and buying behaviour, and that, therefore, an indigeneous psychographic system would be more useful for the Canadian marketplace. The Goldfarb Segments were produced as a result of sampling 1400 adult Canadians and examining their responses to approximately 200 questions concerning their activities, interests, and opinions. After analyzing the data, six lifestyle or psychographic segments were identified and labelled the Goldfarb Segments.[28] The six segments were classified according to two broad categories: more traditional and less traditional.

As you can see from Figure 6-6, the more traditional segments, representing 52 percent of the adult population, include day-to-day watchers, the old-fashioned puritans,

FIGURE 6-6   THE GOLDFARB SEGMENTS

SEGMENT	PERCENT OF POPULATION	CHARACTERISTICS
More Traditional		
Day-to-day-watchers (Conformistes)	24%	Traditional value structure; prefer the tried and true; research their purchases; satisfied with life as it is.
Old-fashioned puritans (Prudes démodés)	16%	Conservative; afraid of change; home and family-oriented; least likely to try new brands; least likely to own credit cards; heavily insured.
Responsible survivors (Casaniers diligents)	12%	Respect the status quo; usually want and seek advice; enjoy self-rewards; very brand loyal; heavy TV viewers.
	52%	
Less Traditional		
Joiner-activists (Réformistes)	21%	Non-conformists; dynamic and leading-edge thinkers; quality and convenience-oriented; like new technology; willing to spend; eat out frequently; heavy pleasure trip takers.
Disinterested self-indulgents (Hèdonistes non-engagés)	17%	Insular and self-oriented; interested in self-gratification, risk-oriented; impulse purchasers; borrow heavily; heavy lottery ticket buyers; like product innovation.
Aggressive achievers (Conquérants aggressifs)	10%	Success-oriented; want to be leaders; need to have psyches stroked; love status-signalling products; flaunt material possessions.
	48%	

and the responsible survivors. The less traditional segments, representing 48 percent of the adult population, include the joiner-activists, the disinterested self-indulgents, and the aggressive achievers. Figure 6-6 also highlights selected lifestyle and behavioural characteristics of each segment.

CONCEPT CHECK

1. The problem with the Toro Snow Pup was an example of selective _____ .

2. What three attitude-change approaches are most common?

3. What does *lifestyle* mean?

SOCIOCULTURAL INFLUENCES ON CONSUMER BEHAVIOUR

Sociocultural influences, which evolve from a consumer's formal and informal relationships with other people, also exert a significant impact on consumer behaviour. These involve personal influence, reference groups, the family, social class, culture, and subculture.

Personal Influence

A consumer's purchases are often influenced by the views, opinions, or behaviours of others. Two aspects of personal influence are important to marketing: opinion leadership and word-of-mouth activity.

Opinion leadership   Individuals who exert direct or indirect social influence over others are called **opinion leaders.** Opinion leaders are more likely to be important for products that provide a form of self-expression. Automobiles, clothing, club membership, home video equipment, and PCs are products affected by opinion leaders, but appliances are not.[29]

Only a small percentage of adults are considered opinion leaders.[30] Identifying, reaching, and influencing opinion leaders is a major challenge for companies. Some firms use sports figures or celebrities as spokespersons to represent their products, such as Wayne Gretzky for Sharp and Coca-Cola, or Donovan Bailey for Maple Leaf and Cindy Crawford for Revlon, in the hope that they are opinion leaders. Others promote their products in media believed to reach opinion leaders. Still others use more direct approaches. For example, Chrysler Corporation invited influential community leaders and business executives to test drive its Dodge Intrepid, Chrysler Concorde, and Eagle Vision models. Some 6000 accepted the offer, and 98 percent said they would recommend their tested car. Chrysler estimated that the number of favourable recommendations totalled 32 000.[31]

Word of mouth   People influencing each other during their face-to-face conversations is called **word of mouth.** Word of mouth is perhaps the most powerful information source for consumers because it typically involves friends viewed as trustworthy. A Canadian study found that 70 percent of those surveyed relied on word of mouth when selecting a bank; and 95 percent said they used advice from friends when choosing a physician.[32]

The power of personal influence has prompted firms to promote positive and retard negative word of mouth.[33] For instance, "teaser" advertising campaigns are run in advance of new product introductions to stimulate conversations. Other techniques such as advertising slogans, music, and humour also heighten positive word of mouth. On the other hand, rumours about Kmart (snake eggs in clothing), McDonald's (worms in

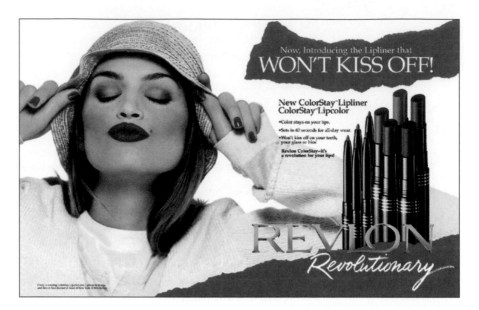

hamburgers), and Corona Extra beer (contaminated beer) have resulted in negative word of mouth, none of which was based on fact. Overcoming or neutralizing negative word of mouth is difficult and costly. Several food products in Indonesia, including some sold by Nestlé, were rumoured to contain pork, which is prohibited to the 160 million Muslim consumers in that country. Nestlé had to spend $250 000 in advertising to counteract the rumour.[34] Firms have found that supplying factual information, providing toll-free numbers for consumers to call the company, and giving appropriate product demonstrations also have been helpful.

Reference Groups

Reference groups are people to whom an individual looks as a basis for self-appraisal or as a source of personal standards. Reference groups affect consumer purchases because they influence the information, attitudes, and aspiration levels that help set a consumer's standards.[35] For example, one of the first questions one asks others when planning to attend a social occasion is, "What are you going to wear?" Reference groups have an important influence on the purchase of luxury products but not of necessities—reference groups exert a strong influence on the brand chosen when its use or consumption is highly visible to others.[36]

Consumers have many reference groups, but three groups have clear marketing implications. A *membership group* is one to which a person actually belongs, including fraternities, social clubs, and the family. Such groups are easily identifiable and are targeted by firms selling insurance, insignia products, and charter vacations. An *aspiration group* is one that a person wishes to be a member of or wishes to be identified with, such as a professional society. Firms frequently rely on spokespeople or settings associated with their target market's aspiration group in their advertising. A *dissociative group* is one that a person wishes to maintain a distance from because of differences in values or behaviours. Believing that motorcycle ownership and usage has a "black leather-jacketed biker" stigma, Honda Motor Company has focused its promotional efforts on disassociating its motorcycles from this group.[37]

Family Influence

Family influences on consumer behaviour result from three sources: consumer socialization, passage through the family life cycle, and decision making within the family.

Consumer socialization The process by which people acquire the skills, knowledge, and attitudes necessary to function as consumers is **consumer socialization.**[38] Children learn how to purchase (1) by interacting with adults in purchase situations and (2) through their own purchasing and product usage experiences. Research shows that children evidence brand preferences at age two, and these preferences often last a lifetime.[39] This knowledge has prompted Sony to introduce "My First Sony," a line of portable audio equipment for children; Time, Inc. to launch *Sports Illustrated for Kids;* Polaroid to develop the Cool Cam camcorder for children between ages 9 and 14; and Prodigy to create special areas where young audiences can view their children's menu—Just for Kids and Kids Only, respectively.

Family life cycle Consumers act and purchase differently as they go through life. The **family life cycle** concept describes the distinct phases that a family progresses through from formation to retirement, each phase bringing with it identifiable purchasing behaviours.[40] Figure 6-7 illustrates the traditional progression as well as

FIGURE 6-7   MODERN FAMILY LIFE CYCLE

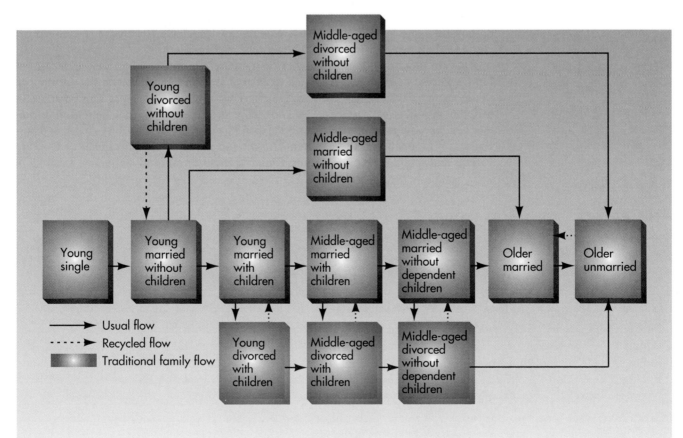

contemporary variations of the family life cycle, including the prevalence of single-person households with and without children.

Young singles' buying preferences are for nondurable items, including prepared foods, clothing, personal care products, and entertainment. They represent a target market for recreational travel, automobile, and consumer electronics firms. Young married couples without children are typically more affluent than young singles because usually both spouses are employed. These couples exhibit preferences for furniture, housewares, and gift items for each other. Young marrieds with children are driven by the needs of their children. They make up a sizeable market for life insurance, various children's products, and home furnishings. Single parents with children are the least financially secure of households with children. Their buying preferences are affected by a limited economic status and tend toward convenience foods, child care services, and personal care items.

Middle-aged married couples with children are typically better off financially than their younger counterparts. They are a significant market for leisure products and home improvement items and represent a fast-growing family life cycle stage. Middle-aged couples without children typically have a large amount of discretionary income. These couples buy better home furnishings, status automobiles, and financial services.

Persons in the last two phases—older married and older unmarried—are a sizeable market for prescription drugs, medical services, vacation trips, and gifts for younger relatives. These consumers also represent a fast-growing family life cycle stage.

Family decision making   A third influence in the decision-making process occurs within the family. Two decision-making styles exist: spouse-dominant and joint decision making. With a joint decision-making style, most decisions are made by both husband and wife. Spouse-dominant decisions are those for which either the husband or the wife is responsible. The types of products and services typically associated with the decision-making styles are shown in Figure 6-8.[41] However, these tendencies are changing with the rise in dual-income families. Today, 40 percent of all food-shopping dollars are spent by male customers. Women now purchase 70 percent of men's dress shirts, and almost 50 percent of all condoms purchased.

Roles of individual family members in the purchase process are another element of family decision making. Five roles exist: (1) information gatherer, (2) influencer, (3) decision maker, (4) purchaser, and (5) user. Family members assume different roles for different products and services. This knowledge is important to firms. Increasingly, preteens and teenagers are the information gatherers, influencers, decision makers, and purchasers of products and services items for the family, given the prevalence of working parents and single-parent households. Children under 18 currently influence a variety of

FIGURE 6-8   INFLUENCE CONTINUUM OF SPOUSE IN FAMILY DECISION MAKING

Husband dominant   Joint influence   Wife dominant

- Life insurance
- Garden tools

- Husband's suits
- Forms of investments

- Family vacation
- Movies
- Schools

- Living room furniture
- Children's clothing
- Food products

- Wife's clothing
- Household cleaning products

family purchase decisions. General Mills, Nabisco, Kraft-General Foods Canada, Pizza Hut and others advertise on music and children stations to reach this young and influential consumer.

Social Class

A more subtle influence on consumer behaviour than direct contact with others is the social class to which people belong. **Social class** may be defined as the relatively permanent, homogeneous divisions in a society into which people sharing similar values, interests, and behaviour can be grouped. A person's occupation, source of income (not level of income), and education determine his or her social class. Generally speaking, three major social class categories exist—upper, middle, and lower—with subcategories within each. This structure has been observed in Canada, the United States, Great Britain, Western Europe, and Latin America.[42]

To some degree, persons within social classes exhibit common attitudes, lifestyles, and buying behaviours. Compared with the middle classes, people in the lower classes have a more short-term time orientation, are more emotional than rational in their reasoning, think in concrete rather than abstract terms, and see fewer personal opportunities. Members of the upper classes focus on achievements and the future and think in abstract or symbolic terms.

Companies use social class as a basis for identifying and reaching particularly good prospects for their products and services.

Culture and Subculture

As described in Chapter 3, culture refers to the set of values, ideas, and attitudes that are accepted by a homogeneous group of people and are transmitted to the next generation. This we often refer to as Canadian culture, American culture, British culture, or the Japanese culture, etc. (Cultural underpinnings of Canadian buying patterns are described in Chapter 3, whereas Chapter 5 explores the role of culture in global marketing.)

Subgroups within the larger, or national culture, who share unique values, ideas, and attitudes are referred to as **subcultures.** Subcultures can be identified by age (e.g., baby boomers vs. Generation X), geography (e.g., Western Canadian vs. Atlantic Canadian), and ethnicity. Here, we focus on ethnic subcultures.

An *ethnic subculture* is a segment of a larger society whose members are thought, by themselves and/or by others, to have a common origin and to participate in shared activities felt to be culturally significant.[43] Common traits such as customs, language, religious, and values hold ethnic subcultures together. Because of Canada's pluralistic tradition, ethnic groups do not necessarily join the cultural mainstream. Some people have referred to this concept as a *salad bowl* phenomenon, where a potpourri of people mix but do not blend. This allows for the maintenance of subcultural traditions and values.

French Canadian Subculture   There are approximately 7 million French-speaking Canadians in this country, about 25 percent of the population. The overwhelming majority of French Canadians live in Quebec. Research shows that French-speaking Quebecers do exhibit different consumption behaviour from the rest of Canadians.[44] French Quebecers link price to perceived value but will pass on a buy rather than buy on credit. They are more willing to pay higher prices for convenience and premium brands, and they give more credence to advertising than the average Canadian. Metro-Richelieu Inc., a Quebec grocery store chain says their research shows that 56 percent of Quebecers consult the grocery chain's weekly circulars.

But French Quebecers are cautious of new products and often postpone trial until after the product has proven itself. They do exhibit brand loyalty but will switch for specials. They also prefer convenience and health food stores over food warehouses and

SAME BUTTER, DIFFERENT STRATEGY IN QUEBEC

Hugh MacLennan's classic 1945 novel *Two Solitudes* captured the idea of Canada's two peoples living side by side, but functioning as two nations within one. And his theory is proving no less true in the marketing business. Marketers have three choices when marketing in Quebec: use the same strategy and the same creative execution as the rest of Canada; use the same strategy but a different execution that reflects the distinctiveness of the market; or use a different strategy and a different execution. The Dairy Farmers of Canada switched from the same strategy/same creative to the same strategy/different creative in its butter advertising. It made the move because it discovered differences between English and French Canada when it comes to eating. A campaign using children on camera talking about butter was not as well-received in English Canada as in Quebec. This forced the organization to re-think its same strategy and same execution option.

The Dairy Farmers of Canada have the same basic strategy—demonstrating that butter has superior taste over competitive products. But the view that butter is a cholesterol demon is more prevalent in English Canada than French Canada. So, in English Canada, new TV spots will focus on butter as a good food choice in moderation. But the ones in Quebec will be unchanged. The health preoccupation is there in French Canada but it is not as acute as it is in the anglophone market. Using the same strategy and the same creative may be a frugal choice, but the Dairy Farmers of Canada realized that to be effective two different creative executions were required—one for English Canada, and one for French Canada.

local grocery stores. French Quebecers are less likely to buy grocery items on impulse and are increasingly calculating in their food purchases. Metro-Richelieu Inc. has responded by offering more discount coupons, weekly specials, and money-saving tips under one plan called EconoMetro. Also, French Quebecers are more concerned with personal grooming and fashion, and more likely to shop in specialized clothing boutiques. Eaton's has shifted its advertising approach in Quebec in an attempt to appeal to Quebecers' heightened fashion sense while recognizing that department stores are not the most popular option for fashion in La Belle Province.

French Quebec has a higher percentage of wine and beer drinkers and more smokers. And, while Quebecers enjoy their beer, Molson says its research indicates that French Quebecers prefer a stronger beer. Accordingly, Molson launched O'Keefe 6.2. Brand (which contains 6.2 percent alcohol) exclusively for the Quebec market. There are fewer golfers, joggers, and gardeners, and the proportion of people who go to movies or entertain at home is also lower. There are, however, more cyclists, skiers, and live theatre fans.

French Quebecers are big buyers of lottery tickets and more likely to subscribe to book clubs, but they make fewer long-distance phone calls. They travel less, whether for business or pleasure. More French Quebec adults hold life insurance policies but they are less likely to have a credit card. They also tend to use credit unions (caisses populaires) more than banks.

Some argue that French Quebec can be characterized by a set of values that are traditional, consistent, and relatively static. But changes are evident. While values are still strong about family life, about having children in a marriage, and about giving them religious training, the use of birth control is on the rise and the marriage rate is below the national average.

Marketers must realize that certain products and other elements of the marketing mix may have to be modified in order to be successful in French Quebec. In addition to cultural differences, there are other issues marketers must address. Commercial advertising to children is prohibited and greater restrictions exist for alcohol advertising. Provincial regulations also require that labels and packages must be both in French and English, while storefront signage must be in French, not English. Good investigation and analysis of this market is a requirement for all companies wishing to do business there. As the Marketing NewsNet points out, the Dairy Farmers of Canada made a switch in strategy when marketing in Quebec after research showed cultural differences between French and English Canadians.[45]

Acadian subculture   Many Canadians assume that French Canadians are basically the same. Even though the majority of French-speaking Canadians do reside in Quebec, there is another special group of French-speaking Canadians who live outside of Quebec. These people are the Acadians, most of whom live in New Brunswick and are proud of their distinctive heritage. The Acadians are often referred to as the "forgotten French market."

Acadians are different from French Quebecers in many ways. In terms of consumption, Acadians are very fashion-oriented and tend to dine out more often than their French counterparts in Quebec. Acadians are also very price-conscious. They also prefer companies who speak to them in their language, which is slightly different than French Quebecois.

Chinese Canadian subculture   The Chinese Canadian market currently represents over 3 percent of Canada's population, but it is one of the fastest-growing subcultures in Canada. This ethnic group is made up predominantly of immigrants from Hong Kong and Taiwan and is concentrated largely in Toronto and Vancouver.

Chinese Canadians have unique values. While most Canadians value straight-line thinking (logic), the Chinese value circular thinking (what goes around comes around). They value work, family and education. They have different purchasing patterns and often perceive products differently than other Canadians. This group also appreciates companies who speak to them in their language. For example, many firms produce ads in Mandarin or Cantonese and run them in specialty publications such as the *Sing Tao,* a Toronto newspaper for Chinese readers.

The average Chinese-Canadian has a higher income, is better educated, less likely to be unemployed, and is significantly younger than the general Canadian population. Because of these characteristics, many firms see Chinese Canadians as a viable target market for a variety of products. For example, the Royal Bank sees them as good prospects for RSP and mutual fund products, while Cantel markets its cellular phones to this group.

Other ethnic subcultures   Many other ethnic Canadians can be found in large metropolitan centres or clustered in certain geographic areas. Kitchener-Waterloo has a large German Canadian population: Winnipeg is home to many Ukrainian Canadians, and Toronto has a large number of Italian Canadians. The emerging trend in Canada today is that 70 percent of all immigrants to this country are visible minorities. In addition to Asia, many new Canadians are coming from Africa, and India. Marketers must appreciate the fact that these new ethnic Canadians may carry with them distinctive social and cultural behaviour that will affect their buying patterns. Subcultural research and sensitivity can aid organizations in developing effective marketing strategies designed to appeal to these groups. For example, a common misconception is that ethnic Canadians have less spending power than Canadian-born people. However, studies show that arriving immigrants are bringing in large amounts of capital. This is particularly true of immigrants from Hong Kong who have and continue to migrate here due to mainland China's takeover of Hong Kong. Moreover, it has been found that foreign-born Canadians earn more money, comparatively, than native-born Canadians.[46]

CONCEPT CHECK
1. What are the two primary forms of personal influence?
2. Marketers are concerned with which types of reference groups?
3. What is an ethnic subculture?

SUMMARY

1. When a consumer buys a product, it is not an act but a process. There are five steps in the purchase decision process: problem recognition, information search, alternative evaluation, purchase decision, and postpurchase behaviour.

2. Consumers evaluate alternatives on the basis of attributes. Identifying which attributes are most important to consumers, along with understanding consumer beliefs about how a brand performs on those attributes, can make the difference between successful and unsuccessful products.

3. Consumer involvement with what is bought affects whether the purchase decision process involves routine, limited, or extended problem solving. Situational influences also affect the process.

4. Perception is important to marketers because of the selectivity of what a consumer sees or hears, comprehends, and retains.

5. Much of the behaviour that consumers exhibit is learned. Consumers learn from repeated experience and reasoning. Brand loyalty is a result of learning.

6. Attitudes are learned predispositions to respond to an object or class of objects in a consistently favourable or unfavourable way. Attitudes are based on a person's values and beliefs concerning the attributes of objects.

7. Lifestyle is a mode of living reflected in a person's activities, interests, and opinions of himself or herself and the world. Lifestyle is a manifestation of a person's self-concept.

8. Personal influence takes two forms: opinion leadership and word-of-mouth activity. A specific type of personal influence exists in the form of reference groups.

9. Family influences on consumer behaviour result from three sources: consumer socialization, family life cycle, and decision making within the household.

10. Within Canada there are social classes and subcultures that affect a consumer's values and behaviour. Marketers must be sensitive to these sociocultural influences when developing a marketing mix.

KEY TERMS AND CONCEPTS

consumer behaviour p. 144
purchase decision process p. 144
evaluative criteria p. 145
evoked set p. 146
cognitive dissonance p. 147
involvement p. 147
situational influences p. 148
motivation p. 150
personality p. 150
national character p. 151
perception p. 151
subliminal perception p. 152
perceived risk p. 152

learning p. 153
brand loyalty p. 154
attitude p. 154
beliefs p. 154
lifestyle p. 155
self-concept p. 155
opinion leaders p. 157
word of mouth p. 157
reference groups p. 158
consumer socialization p. 159
family life cycle p. 159
social class p. 161
subcultures p. 161

CHAPTER PROBLEMS AND APPLICATIONS

1. Demonstrate your understanding of the five-stage consumer purchase decision process by using your experience in selecting your college or university.

2. Review Figure 6-2 in the text, which shows the CD-player attributes identified by *Consumer Reports*. Which attributes are important to you? What other attributes might you consider? Which brand would you prefer?

3. Suppose Apple Computer discovers that some prospective buyers still are anxious about buying a personal computer. What strategies might you recommend to the company to reduce the buyers' perceived risk?

4. A Porsche salesperson was taking orders on new cars because he was unable to satisfy demand with the limited number of cars in the showroom and lot. Several persons had backed out of the contract within two weeks of signing the order. What explanation can you give for this behaviour, and what remedies would you recommend?

5. Which social class would you associate with each of the following items or actions? (*a*) Tennis club membership, (*b*) an arrangement of plastic flowers in the kitchen, (*c*) *True Romance* magazine, (*d*) MacLean's magazine, (*e*) formally dressing for dinner frequently, and (*f*) being a member of a bowling team.

6. Assign one or more levels of the hierarchy of needs and motives described in Figure 6-5 to the following products: (*a*) life insurance, (*b*) cosmetics, (*c*) *The Financial Post Magazine,* and (*d*) hamburgers.

7. With which stage of the family life cycle would the purchase of the following products and services be most closely identified? (*a*) bedroom furniture, (*b*) life insurance, (*c*) a Caribbean cruise, (*d*) a house mortgage, and (*e*) children's toys.

8. "The greater the perceived risk in a purchase situation, the more likely that cognitive dissonance will result." Does this statement have any basis given the discussion in the text? Why?

CASE 6-1 Three Sisters Cafe

Three Sisters Cafe is a medium-sized (120 seats), upscale restaurant that had been in business for five years. The owners, three sisters, are happy with the restaurant's performance but would like to do better. They believe their customers like the restaurant and repeat business is very good. In a highly competitive market, however, the sisters feel they must find ways to attract more business. After much discussion and debate, the three sisters decided to hire a local consulting firm to conduct some consumer research. Basically, the three sisters wanted to know (1) the attributes that a licensed sit-down restaurant must possess in order for consumers to patronize an establishment; (2) how well Three Sisters Cafe measured up on those attributes; and (3) consumers' satisfaction and dissatisfaction with Three Sisters Cafe. A telephone survey of restaurant goers was conducted. A person had to have dined out in the last four weeks to be part of the survey. A total of 320 respondents participated. Of this total, 140 had dined at Three Sisters Cafe at least once in the previous four weeks.

CONSUMER RESEARCH FINDINGS

First, consumer awareness levels were obtained for the licensed sit-down restaurants in the area. It was particularly important to examine consumer awareness of a business or brand since awareness is a necessary prerequisite to purchase. A restaurant with low awareness levels may mean consumers will not think of that particular restaurant when they consider dining out. Three Sisters Cafe had an overall awareness score of 60 percent. In other words, 60 percent of consumers surveyed were aware of Three Sisters Cafe. Many of its competitors had lower awareness scores, ranging from 25 percent to 55 percent. One nearby competitor, however, had the highest awareness score at 85 percent.

The consulting firm uncovered the attributes required by consumers in order to patronize a licensed sit-down restaurant. Exhibit 1 depicts what respondents believed to be the "ideal" attributes making up such an establishment. It was derived by examining the percentage of those who, on the dimension under consideration, rated the attributes as "Very Important or Must Have It." The element was considered to be an ideal element if 70 percent or more respondents indicated it to be very important or a must have. There were no differences between users of Three Sisters Cafe and nonusers in terms of the ideal attributes that a restaurant must have in order to patronize. Exhibit 1 also shows how Three Sisters Cafe was rated by users on those ideal attributes.

The consulting firm also examined customer satisfaction with Three Sisters Cafe. The analysis revealed that 87 percent of users were satisfied with their experience while 13 percent were dissatisfied. Of those who were dissatisfied, 70 percent stated food quality to be the reason for their dissatisfaction, while 30 percent stated high prices was their reason for dissatisfaction. All three sisters reviewed the findings and wondered about the ratings their restaurant received, as well as the awareness scores and the satisfaction data. They realized the key issue now is what to do with the information?

Questions

1. Which attributes (evaluative criteria) do you think are most critical in the consumers' assessment of value when selecting a restaurant?
2. What is the relationship between a consumer's awareness of given restaurants and his or her evoked set of choice?
3. What do you think about the consumers' satisfaction levels with Three Sisters Cafe? Do you think this is a problem area they need to address? Why or why not?

EXHIBIT 1   ATTRIBUTES A RESTAURANT MUST POSSESS AND HOW USERS RATE THREE SISTERS CAFE ON THOSE ATTRIBUTES

	IDEAL ATTRIBUTES (% MENTIONING AS VERY IMPORTANT OR MUST HAVE IT, ALL RESPONDENTS)	USERS' RATINGS OF THREE SISTERS (% RATING IT AS VERY GOOD/EXCELLENT ON THAT ATTRIBUTE)
Good food	95.0%	66.0%
Atmosphere	90.0	84.0
Efficient service	83.0	82.0
Friendly service	80.0	77.0
Comfortable seating	78.0	87.0
Decor	77.0	92.0
Good prices	76.0	26.0
Table presentation	75.0	85.0
Good wine list	73.0	76.0
	N = 320	N = 140

CHAPTER 7

Organizational Markets and Buyer Behaviour

AFTER READING THIS CHAPTER YOU SHOULD BE ABLE TO:

• Distinguish among industrial, reseller, and government markets.

• Recognize key characteristics of organizational buying that make it different from consumer buying.

• Understand how types of buying situations influence organizational purchasing.

• Recognize similarities and differences in industrial and reseller purchase behaviour.

FIBER OPTICS: COMMUNICATING IN A FLASH OF LIGHT

Steve Whitacer views light very differently from most people.

As marketing manager for Fiber-Optic Products at Honeywell (www.honeywell.ca), MICRO SWITCH Division, Whitacer is responsible for fiber-optic products (like those pictured on the opposite page) that sense, modulate, and transmit infrared light for the data communications industry. Converting technology into products and bringing these products to market are part and parcel of his typical day.

Marketing fiber-optic technology and products is a challenging assignment. Buyer experience with the technology is often limited, even though potential applications are numerous in data communications, computer networks, and industrial automation. Honeywell, MICRO SWITCH Division, and other suppliers such as Hewlett-Packard, Toshiba, Mitsubishi, and ABB HAFO (Sweden) must often convey the value of fiber-optic technology and specific products through advertising, trade shows, personal selling, and demonstrations. This task often involves communicating with a diverse set of organizational buyers ranging from industrial firms to governmental agencies throughout the world and in different languages. It also requires knowing which people influence the purchasing decision; what factors they consider important when choosing suppliers and products; and when, where, and how the buying decision is made.

Whitacer believes Honeywell, MICRO SWITCH Division, is poised to capture a significant share of the multibillion dollar global fiber-optics market. Ultimate success will depend on continued product development that creates customer value and effective marketing to an ever-growing number of prospective buyers for fiber-optic technology in a worldwide marketplace.[1]

The challenge facing Whitacer of marketing to organizations is often encountered by both small, startup corporations and large, well-established companies such as Honeywell. Important issues in marketing to organizations are examined in this chapter which analyzes types of organizational buyers, key characteristics of organizational buying, and some typical buying decisions.

THE NATURE AND SIZE OF ORGANIZATIONAL MARKETS

Steve Whitacer and Honeywell's MICRO SWITCH Division engage in business marketing. **Business marketing** is the marketing of goods and services to commercial enterprises, government, and other profit and nonprofit organizations for use in the creation of goods and services that they then produce and market to other business customers, as well as individuals and ultimate consumers.[2] Because many Canadian business school graduates take jobs in firms that engage in business marketing, it is important to understand the fundamental characteristics of organizational buyers and their buying behaviour.[3]

Organizational buyers are those manufacturers, retailers, and government agencies that buy goods and services for their own use or for resale. For example, all these organizations buy computers and telephone services for their own use. However, manufacturers buy raw materials and parts that they reprocess into the finished goods they sell, whereas retailers resell goods they buy without reprocessing them. Organizational buyers include all the buyers in a nation except the ultimate consumers. These organizational buyers purchase and lease tremendous volumes of capital equipment, raw materials, manufactured parts, supplies, and business services. In fact, because they often buy raw materials and parts, process them, and sell the upgraded product several times before it is purchased by the final organizational buyer or ultimate consumer, the aggregate purchases of organizational buyers in a year are far greater than those of ultimate consumers.

Organizational buyers are divided into three different markets: (1) industrial, (2) resellers, and (3) government markets.

Industrial Markets

There are thousands of firms in the industrial, or business, market in Canada. **Industrial firms** in some way reprocess a good or service they buy before selling it again to the next buyer. This is certainly true of a steel mill that converts iron ore into steel. It is also true (if you stretch your imagination) of a firm selling services, such as a bank that takes money from its depositors, reprocesses it, and "sells" it as loans to its commercial borrowers.

There has been a marked shift in the scope and nature of the industrial marketplace. Service industries are growing and currently make the greatest contribution to Canada's gross domestic product (GDP). Because of the importance of service firms, service marketing is discussed in detail in Chapter 13. Industrial firms and primary industries currently contribute less than 25 percent to Canada's GDP. Nevertheless, primary industries (e.g., farming, mining, fishing, and forestry) and the manufacturing sector are important components of Canada's economy. There are about 40 000 manufacturers in Canada whose estimated value of shipments are over $300 billion.

Reseller Markets

Wholesalers and retailers who buy physical products and resell them again without any reprocessing are **resellers.** There are over 200 000 retailers and over 65 000 wholesalers operating in Canada. In Chapters 16 through 18 we see how manufacturers use wholesalers and retailers in their distribution ("place") strategies as channels through which their products reach ultimate consumers. In this chapter we look at resellers mainly as organizational buyers in terms of (1) how they make their own buying decisions and (2) which products they choose to carry.

Government Markets

Government units are the federal, provincial, and local agencies that buy goods and services for the constituents they serve. Their annual purchases vary in size from the billions of dollars for a federal department such as National Defence to millions or thousands of dollars for a local university or school. The bulk of the buying at the federal government level is done by the Department of Supply and Services Canada. Most provincial governments have a government services department that does the buying on the provincial level. Hundreds of government departments, including agencies and Crown corporations such as CN, and the Royal Canadian Mint, must purchase goods and services to operate. The federal government is a large organizational consumer making total purchases of goods and services in excess of $100 billion annually.[4]

Global Organizational Markets

Industrial, reseller, and government markets also exist on a global scale. In fact, many of Canada's top exporters including Nortel, Noranda, Abitibi-Price and Pratt & Whitney, focus on organizational customers, not ultimate consumers.

The majority of world trade involves manufacturers, resellers, and government agencies buying goods and services for their own use or for resale to others. The exchange relationships often involve numerous transactions spanning the globe. For example, Honeywell, MICRO SWITCH Division sells its fiber-optic technology and products to manufacturers of data communication systems worldwide, through electronic component resellers in more than 20 countries, and directly to national governments in Europe and elsewhere. Europe's Airbus Industrie, the world's largest aircraft manufacturer, sells its passenger airplanes to Air Canada which flies Canadian businesspeople to the Orient. A North American firm solicits advertising for and a publisher in Germany prints the Moscow Yellow Pages on behalf of the Moscow city government and telephone system for resale to businesses through Moscow stores, hotels, and international trade centres.

MEASURING DOMESTIC AND GLOBAL INDUSTRIAL, RESELLER, AND GOVERNMENT MARKETS

The measurement of industrial, reseller, and government markets is an important first step for a firm interested in gauging the size of one, two, or all three of these markets in Canada and around the world. This task has been made easier with the publication of the **North American Industry Classification System (NAICS).**[5] NAICS provides common industry definitions for Canada, Mexico, and the United States, which will help facilitate the measurement of economic activity in the three member countries of the North American Free Trade Agreement (NAFTA). NAICS replaced the Standard Industrial Classification (SIC) system, a version of which has been in place for more than 50 years in the three NAFTA member countries. The SIC neither permitted comparability across countries nor accurately measured new or emerging industries. Furthermore, NAICS will be consistent with the International Standard Industrial Classification of All Economic Activities, published by the United Nations, to facilitate measurement of global economic activity.

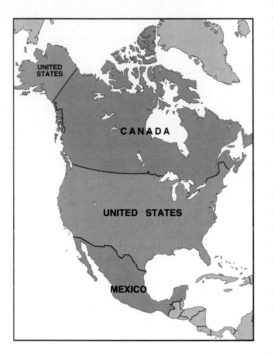

The NAICS will group economic activity to permit studies of market share, demand for goods and services, import competition in domestic markets, and similar studies. Like the earlier SIC system, NAICS will designate industries with a numerical code in a defined structure. The first digit of the NAICS code will designate a sector of the economy and will be followed by a two-digit code signifying a subsector. Subsectors will be further divided into three-digit industry groups, four-digit industries, and five-digit country-specific industries. Figure 7-1 presents an abbreviated breakdown within the broadcasting and telecommunications industry to illustrate the classification scheme.

The NAICS will permit a firm to find the NAICS codes of its present customers and then obtain NAICS-coded lists for similar firms. Also, it will be possible to monitor NAICS categories to determine the growth in various sectors and industries to identify promising marketing opportunities. However, NAICS codes, like the earlier SIC codes, will have important limitations. The NAICS will assign one code to each organization based on its major economic activity, so large firms that engage in many different activities will still be given only one NAICS code. A second limitation is that five-digit National industry codes will not be available for all three countries because the respective governments will not reveal data when too few organizations exist in a category. Despite these limitations, development of NAICS represents yet another effort toward economic integration in North America and the world.

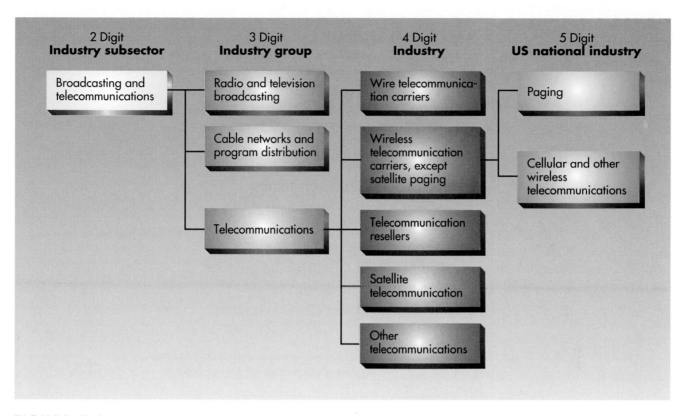

| 2 Digit
Industry subsector | 3 Digit
Industry group | 4 Digit
Industry | 5 Digit
US national industry |

Broadcasting and telecommunications

Radio and television broadcasting

Cable networks and program distribution

Telecommunications

Wire telecommunication carriers

Wireless telecommunication carriers, except satellite paging

Telecommunication resellers

Satellite telecommunication

Other telecommunications

Paging

Cellular and other wireless telecommunications

FIGURE 7-1   NAICS BREAKDOWN FOR BROADCASTING AND TELECOMMUNICATIONS INDUSTRIES (ABBREVIATED)

CONCEPT CHECK

1. What are the three main types of organizational buyers?
2. What is the North American Industry Classification System (NAICS)?

CHARACTERISTICS OF ORGANIZATIONAL BUYING

Organizations are different from individuals, so buying for an organization is different from buying for yourself or your family.[6] True, in both cases the objective in making the purchase is to solve the buyer's problem—to satisfy a need or want. But unique objectives and policies of an organization put special constraints on how it makes buying decisions. Understanding the characteristics of organizational buying is essential in designing effective marketing programs to reach these buyers.

Organizational buying behaviour is the decision-making process that organizations use to establish the need for products and services and identify, evaluate, and choose among alternative brands and suppliers. Some key characteristics of organizational buying behaviour are listed in Figure 7-2 and discussed in the following pages.[7]

Demand Characteristics

Consumer demand for products and services is affected by their price and availability and by consumers' personal tastes and discretionary income. By comparison, industrial demand is derived. **Derived demand** means that the demand for industrial products and services is driven by, or derived from, demand for consumer products and services.

FIGURE 7-2

KEY CHARACTERISTICS OF
ORGANIZATIONAL BUYING
BEHAVIOUR

MARKET CHARACTERISTICS
- Demand for industrial products and services is derived.
- Few customers typically exist, and their purchase orders are large.

PRODUCT OR SERVICE CHARACTERISTICS
- Products or services are technical in nature and purchased on the basis of specifications.
- There is a predominance of raw and semifinished goods purchased.
- Heavy emphasis is placed on delivery time, technical assistance, postsale service, and financing assistance.

BUYING PROCESS CHARACTERISTICS
- Technically qualified and professional buyers exist and follow established purchasing policies and procedures.
- Buying objectives and criteria are typically spelled out, as are procedures for evaluating sellers and products (services).
- Multiple buying influences exist, and multiple parties participate in purchase decisions.
- Reciprocal arrangements exist, and negotiation between buyers and sellers is commonplace.

OTHER MARKETING MIX CHARACTERISTICS
- Direct selling to organizational buyers is the rule, and physical distribution is very important.
- Advertising and other forms of promotion are technical in nature.
- Price is often negotiated, evaluated as part of broader seller and product (service) qualities, typically inelastic owing to derived demand, and frequently affected by trade and quantity discounts.

For example, the demand for MacMillan Bloedal's pulp and paper products is based on consumer demand for newspapers, Domino's "keep warm" pizza-to-go boxes, Federal Express packages, and disposable diapers. Derived demand is often based on expectations of future consumer demand. For instance, Whirlpool purchases parts for its washers and dryers in anticipation of consumer demand, which is affected by the replacement cycle for these products and by consumer income.

As demand for the products that comprise the Information Superhighway grows, so too will the demand for the technology that makes them possible. Read the accompanying Marketing NewsNet to see how companies that produce microchips and microprocessors will benefit from the merging of telecommunications, information, and data networks on the Information Superhighway.[8]

Number of Potential Buyers

Firms selling consumer products or services often try to reach thousands or millions of individuals or households. For example, your local supermarket or bank probably serves thousands of people, and Quaker Oats tries to reach millions of Canadian households with its breakfast cereals and probably succeeds in selling to a third or half of these in any given year. In contrast, firms selling to organizations are often restricted to far fewer buyers. Gulfstream Aerospace Corporation can sell its business jets to fewer than 1000 organizations throughout the world, and B. F. Goodrich sells its original equipment tires to fewer than 10 car manufacturers.

Organizational Buying Objectives

Organizations buy products and services for one main reason: to help them achieve their objectives. For business firms the buying objective is usually to increase profits

MARKETING NEWSNET

THE GLOBAL INFORMATION SUPERHIGHWAY IS PAVED WITH SILICON CHIPS

The twenty-first century will witness the merging of telecommunications, information, and data networks into what has been labelled the "Information Superhighway." As new products and applications emerge for use by business and consumers alike, demand for microchips (the small piece of silicon that holds a complex electronic circuit) and demand for microprocessors (a miniature computer consisting of one or more microchips) will expand dramatically.

Companies that produce microchips and microprocessors will benefit from the demand derived from the sale of a multitude of products and technologies that comprise the Information Superhighway. Powerful microprocessors and multimedia graphics software will boost demand for DRAMS (dynamic random-access memory chips), a business dominated by Korean and Japanese firms. Demand for digital-signal-processing chips that speed up video and graphics will boost the fortunes of Texas Instruments and Europe's SGS-Thomson. Demand for multimedia chips will grow as telephone and cable TV companies begin buying video services and set-top boxes to deliver movies and interactive games to homes.

"The Information Highway will be paved with silicon," says William P. "Pat" Weber, vice chairman of Texas Instruments, and microchip demand will be driven by the telecommunication, information, and data networks that travel the highway.

through reducing costs or increasing revenues. Southland Corporation buys automated inventory systems to increase the number of products that can be sold through its 7-Eleven outlets and to keep them fresh. Nissan Motor Company switched its advertising agency because it expects the new agency to devise a more effective ad campaign to help it sell more cars and increase revenues. To improve executive decision making, many firms buy advanced computer systems to process data. The objectives of nonprofit firms and government agencies are usually to meet the needs of the groups they serve. Thus, a hospital buys a high-technology diagnostic device to serve its patients better. Understanding buying objectives is a necessary first step in marketing to organizations. Recognizing the high costs of energy, Sylvania promotes to prospective buyers cost savings and increased profits made possible by its fluorescent lights.

Organizational Buying Criteria

In making a purchase the buying organization must weigh key buying criteria that apply to the potential supplier and what it wants to sell. **Organizational buying criteria** are the objective attributes of the supplier's products and services and the capabilities of the supplier itself. These criteria serve the same purpose as the evaluative criteria used by consumers and described in Chapter 6. Seven of the most commonly used criteria are (1) price, (2) ability to meet the quality specifications required for the item, (3) ability to meet required delivery schedules, (4) technical capability, (5) warranties and claim policies in the event of poor performance, (6) past performance on previous contracts, and (7) production facilities and capacity.[9] Suppliers that meet or exceed these criteria create customer value.

Many organizational buyers today are transforming their buying criteria into specific requirements that are communicated to prospective suppliers. This practice, called **reverse marketing,** involves the deliberate effort by organizational buyers to build relationships that shape suppliers' products, services, and capabilities to fit a buyer's needs and those of its customers.[10] For example, consider the case of Johnson Controls, Inc., the supplier of seats for Chrysler's small car, the Plymouth Neon.[11] Johnson was able to meet Chrysler's cost target but not its safety, weight, and comfort requirements. After five 11-hour days, Johnson and Chrysler engineering and marketing staffs jointly worked out the technical details to satisfy Chrysler's performance requirements at a price acceptable to both parties. Ongoing reverse marketing efforts also exist. Harley-Davidson expects even its long-term suppliers to provide written plans of their efforts to improve quality, and it monitors the progress of these suppliers toward achieving these goals.[12]

With many Canadian manufacturers adopting a "just-in-time" (JIT) inventory system that reduces the inventory of production parts to those to be used within hours or days, on-time delivery is becoming an even more important buying criterion and, in some instances, a requirement.[13] Caterpillar trains its key suppliers at its Quality Institute in JIT inventory systems and conducts supplier seminars on how to diagnose, correct, and implement continuous quality improvement programs.[14] The just-in-time inventory system is discussed further in Chapter 17.

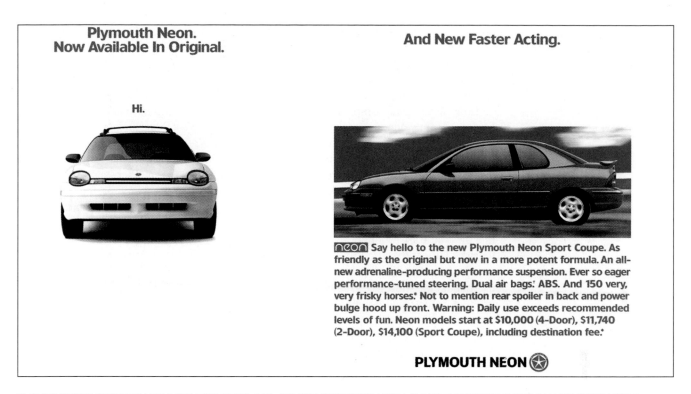

READ THE TEXT TO LEARN HOW JOHNSON CONTROLS, INC., THE SEAT SUPPLIER FOR NEON, PLAYED AN IMPORTANT ROLE IN MAKING THE NEON A SUCCESS.

Size of the Order or Purchase

The size of the purchase involved in organizational buying is typically much larger than that in consumer buying. The dollar value of a single purchase made by an organization often runs into the thousands or millions of dollars. For example, SAP Canada and OmmiLogic were awarded a major contract by Imperial Tobacco to provide client-server applications software to streamline their financial accounting, sales, manufacturing and human resources functions.[15] With so much money at stake, most organizations place constraints on their buyers in the form of purchasing policies or procedures. Buyers must often get competitive bids from at least three prospective suppliers when the order is above a specific amount, such as $5000. When the order is above an even higher amount, such as $50 000, it may require the review and approval of a vice president or even the president. Knowing how the size of the order affects buying practices is important in determining who participates in the purchase decision and makes the final decision, and also the length of time required to arrive at a purchase agreement.[16]

Buyer–Seller Relationships and Supply Partnerships

Another distinction between organizational and consumer buying behaviour lies in the nature of the relationship between organizational buyers and suppliers. Specifically, organizational buying is more likely to involve complex and lengthy negotiations concerning delivery schedules, price, technical specifications, warranties, and claim policies. These negotiations can last for more than a year. This was the case when a customer recently purchased a $35 million Cray Research T90 supercomputer that performs up to 60 million calculations per second.[17]

Reciprocal arrangements also exist in organizational buying. **Reciprocity** is an industrial buying practice in which two organizations agree to purchase each other's products and services. For example, GM purchases Borg-Warner transmissions, and Borg-Warner buys trucks and cars from GM.[18] Consumer and Corporate Affairs Canada frowns on reciprocal buying because it restricts the normal operation of the free market. However, the practice exists and can limit the flexibility of organizational buyers in choosing alternative suppliers. Regardless of the legality of reciprocal buying, do you believe this practice is ethical? (See the accompanying Ethics and Social Responsibility Alert.)[19]

Long-term relationships are also prevalent.[20] As an example, Scandinavian Airlines System recently announced the purchase of 35 Boeing 737–600 airliners with an option to buy another 35 in the future for a total expenditure of $2.4 billion. With aircraft deliveries beginning in late 1998 and continuing into the next century, Scandinavian Airlines cited its desire for a long-term relationship with "a professional and solid supplier" such as Boeing.[21]

In some cases, buyer-seller relationships develop into supply partnerships.[22] A **supply partnership** exists when a buyer and its supplier adopt mutually beneficial objectives, policies, and procedures for the purpose of lowering the cost and/or increasing the value of products and services delivered to the ultimate consumer. Intel, the world's largest manufacturer of microprocessors and the "computer inside" most personal computers, is a case in point. Intel supports its suppliers by offering them quality management programs and by investing in supplier equipment that produces fewer product defects and boosts supplier productivity. Suppliers, in turn, provide Intel with consistent high-quality products at a lower cost for its customers, the makers of personal computers, and finally you, the ultimate customer. Retailers, too, are forging partnerships with their suppliers. Wal-Mart and Kmart have such a relationship with Procter & Gamble for ordering and replenishing P&G's products in their stores. By using computerized cash register scanning equipment and direct electronic linkages to P&G, these retailers can tell P&G what merchandise is needed, along with how much, when, and to which store to deliver it on a daily basis. Since supply partnerships also involve the physical distribution of goods, they are again discussed in Chapter 17.

INTEL USES A UNIQUE SUPPLY PARTNERSHIP AGREEMENT.

ETHICS AND SOCIAL RESPONSIBILITY ALERT

SCRATCHING EACH OTHER'S BACK: THE ETHICS OF RECIPROCITY IN ORGANIZATIONAL BUYING

Reciprocity, the buying practice in which two organizations agree to purchase each other's products and services, is frowned upon in many countries because it restricts the normal operation of the free market. Reciprocal buying practices do exist, however, in a variety of forms, including certain types of countertrade arrangements in international marketing. Furthermore, the extent to which reciprocity is viewed as an ethical issue varies across cultures. In many Asian countries, for instance, reciprocity is often a positive and widespread practice.

Reciprocity is occasionally addressed in the ethics code of companies. For instance, the Quaker Oats Company's code of ethics states:

In many instances, Quaker may purchase goods and/or services from a supplier who buys products or services from us. This practice is normal and acceptable, but suppliers may not be asked to buy our products and services in order to become or continue to be a supplier.

Do you think reciprocal buying is unethical?

The Buying Centre: A Cross-Functional Group

For routine purchases with a small dollar value, a single buyer or purchasing manager often makes the purchase decision alone. In many instances, however, several people in the organization participate in the buying process. The individuals in this group, called a **buying centre,** share common goals, risks, and knowledge important to a purchase decision. For most large multistore chain resellers, such as Sears Canada, 7-Eleven convenience stores, Zellers, or Safeway, the buying centre is highly formalized and is called a *buying committee.* However, most industrial firms or government units use informal groups of people or call meetings to arrive at buying decisions.

The importance of the buying centre requires that a firm marketing to many industrial firms and government units understand the structure, technical and business functions represented, and behaviour of these groups. One researcher has suggested four questions to provide guidance in understanding the buying centre in these organizations:[23] Which individuals are in the buying centre for the product or service? What is the relative influence of each member of the group? What are the buying criteria of each member? How does each member of the group perceive our firm, our products and services, and our salespeople?

Answers to these questions are difficult to come by, particularly when dealing with industrial firms, resellers, and governments outside Canada.[24] For example, Canadian firms are often frustrated by the fact that Japanese buyers "ask a thousand questions" but give few answers, sometimes rely on third-party individuals to convey views on proposals, are prone to not "talk business," and often say yes to be courteous when they mean no. Firms in the global chemical industry recognize that production engineering personnel have a great deal of influence in Hungarian buying groups, while purchasing agents in the Canadian chemical industry have relatively more influence in buying decisions.

People in the buying centre   The composition of the buying centre in a given organization depends on the specific item being bought. Although a buyer or purchasing manager is almost always a member of the buying centre, individuals from other functional areas are included depending on what is to be purchased. In buying a million-dollar machine tool, the president (because of the size of the purchase) and the production vice president or manager would probably be members. For key components to be incorporated in a final manufactured product, a cross-functional group of individuals from research and development (R&D), engineering, and quality control are likely to be added. For new word-processing equipment, experienced secretaries who will use the

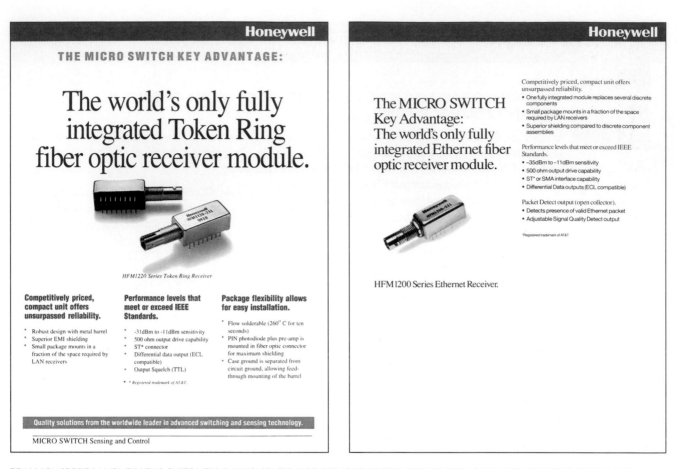

equipment would be members. Still, a major question in penetrating the buying centre is finding and reaching the people who will initiate, influence, and actually make the buying decision.[25] The accompanying Marketing NewsNet shows how Honeywell, MICRO SWITCH Division, tailors its advertisements like those above to reach different members of the buying centres in its customer organizations.[26]

Roles in the buying centre   Researchers have identified five specific roles that an individual in a buying centre can play.[27] In some purchases the same person may perform two or more of these roles.

- *Users* are the people in the organization who actually use the product or service, such as a secretary who will use a new word processor.
- *Influencers* affect the buying decision, usually by helping define the specifications for what is bought. The information systems manager would be a key influencer in the purchase of a network computer system.
- *Buyers* have formal authority and responsibility to select the supplier and negotiate the terms of the contract. The purchasing manager probably would perform this role in the purchase of a network computer system.
- *Deciders* have the formal or informal power to select or approve the supplier that receives the contract. Whereas in routine orders the decider is usually the buyer or purchasing manager, in important technical purchases it is more likely to be someone from R&D, engineering, or quality control. The decider for a key component being incorporated in a final manufactured product might be any of these three people.

COMMUNICATING VALUE TO DIFFERENT MEMBERS OF A BUYING CENTRE WITH CUSTOMIZED ADVERTISEMENTS

Different members of a buying centre value different things when choosing suppliers and products. At Honeywell, MICRO SWITCH Division, the marketing staff responsible for fiber optics products develop customized advertisements for each person in a customer's buying centre—design engineers, production engineers, engineering management, and purchasing agents. Design and production engineers see value in new technologies and products that are easy to design, install, and use. Engineering management is concerned with supplier capabilities, including a proven track record and service. Purchasing agents see value in low cost and reliable delivery.

Recognizing that different business and technical functions value different things, Steve Whitacer, marketing manager for Fiber Optic Products, carefully chooses different messages and media to communicate to each buying centre member. For instance, the ad on the left is directed toward design and production engineers and focuses on what they value. The ad on the right is designed for engineering management and deals with information they value.

Does the added effort and expense of customized advertisements pay off? Yes, it does! Inquiries about the company's line of fiber optics products increased 50 percent after this practice was implemented.

- *Gatekeepers* control the flow of information in the buying centre. Purchasing personnel, technical experts, and secretaries can all keep salespeople or information from reaching people performing the other four roles.

Stages in an Organizational Buying Decision

As shown in Figure 7-3 (and covered in Chapter 6), the five stages a student might use in buying a compact disc (CD) player also apply to organizational purchases.[28] However, comparing the two right-hand columns in Figure 7-3 reveals some key differences. For example, when a CD player manufacturer buys headphones for its units from a supplier, more individuals are involved, supplier capability becomes more important, and the postpurchase evaluation behaviour is more formalized. The headphone-buying decision illustrated is typical of the steps in a purchase made by an organization.[29] Later in the chapter we will analyze a more complex purchase made by an industrial organization.

Types of Buying Situations

The number of people in the buying centre and the length and complexity of the steps in the buying process largely depend on the specific buying situation. Researchers who have studied organizational buying identify three types of buying situations, which they have termed **buy classes.**[30] These buy classes vary from the routine reorder, or **straight rebuy,** to the completely new purchase, termed **new buy.** In between these extremes is the **modified rebuy.** Some examples will clarify the differences:

- *Straight rebuy.* Here the buyer or purchasing manager reorders an existing product or service from the list of acceptable suppliers, probably without even checking with users or influencers from the engineering, production, or quality control departments. Office supplies and maintenance services are usually obtained as straight rebuys.
- *Modified rebuy.* In this buying situation the users, influencers, or deciders in the buying centre want to change the product specifications, price, delivery schedule,

STAGE IN THE BUYING DECISION PROCESS	CONSUMER PURCHASE: CD PLAYER FOR A STUDENT	ORGANIZATIONAL PURCHASE: HEADPHONES FOR A CD PLAYER
Problem recognition	Student doesn't like the sound of the stereo system now owned and desires a CD player.	Marketing research and sales departments observe that competitors are including headphones on their models. The firm decides to include headphones on their own new models, which will be purchased from an outside supplier.
Information search	Student uses past experience, that of friends, ads, and *Consumer Reports* to collect information and uncover alternatives.	Design and production engineers draft specifications for headphones. The purchasing department identifies suppliers of CD player headphones.
Alternative evaluation	Alternative CD players are evaluated on the basis of important attributes desired in a CD player.	Purchasing and engineering personnel visit with suppliers and assess (1) facilities, (2) capacity, (3) quality control, and (4) financial status. They drop any suppliers not satisfactory on these factors.
Purchase decision	A specific brand of CD player is selected, the price is paid, and it is installed in the student's room.	They use (1) quality, (2) price, (3) delivery, and (4) technical capability as key buying criteria to select a supplier. Then they negotiate terms and award a contract.
Postpurchase behaviour	Student reevaluates the purchase decision, may return the CD player to the store if it is unsatisfactory, and looks for supportive information to justify the purchase.	They evaluate suppliers using a formal vendor rating system and notify supplier if phones do not meet its quality standard. If problem is not corrected, they drop the firm as a future supplier.

F I G U R E   7 - 3   COMPARING THE STAGES IN CONSUMER AND ORGANIZATIONAL PURCHASES

or supplier. Although the item purchased is largely the same as with the straight rebuy, the changes usually necessitate enlarging the buying centre to include people outside the purchasing department.

- *New buy.* Here the organization is a first-time buyer of the product or service. This involves greater potential risks in the purchase, so the buying centre is enlarged to include all those who have a stake in the new buy. The purchase of CD player headphones was a new buy.

Figure 7-4 summarizes how buy classes affect buying centre tendencies in different ways.[31]

The marketing strategies of sellers facing each of these three buying situations can vary greatly because the importance of personnel from functional areas such as purchasing, engineering, production, and R&D often varies with (1) the type of buying situation and (2) the stage of the purchasing process.[32] If it is a new buy for the manufacturer, you should be prepared to act as a consultant to the buyer, work with technical personnel, and expect a long time for a buying decision to be reached. However, if the manufacturer has bought the component part from you before (a straight or modified rebuy), you might emphasize a competitive price and a reliable supply in meetings with the purchasing agent.

CONCEPT CHECK

1. What one department is almost always represented by a person in the buying centre?

2. What are the three types of buying situations or buy classes?

	BUY-CLASS SITUATION	
BUYING CENTRE DIMENSION	**NEW BUY**	**STRAIGHT/MODIFIED REBUY**
People involved	Many	Few
Decision time	Long	Short
Problem definition	Uncertain	Well-defined
Buying objective	Good solution	Low-price supplier
Suppliers considered	New/present	Present
Buying influence	Technical/operating personnel	Purchasing agent

FIGURE 7-4   HOW THE BUYING SITUATION AFFECTS BUYING CENTRE BEHAVIOUR

AN ORGANIZATIONAL NEW BUY DECISION

New buy purchase decisions are ones where the most purchasing expertise is needed and where both the benefits of good decisions and penalties of bad ones are likely to be greatest. This means that effective communication among people in the buying centre is especially important. Tracing the stages in the buying decisions made by a manufacturer highlights some of the important aspects of organizational buying. It also illustrates the challenges involved in marketing to organizations.

An Industrial Purchase: Machine Vision Systems

Machine vision is becoming widely regarded as one of the keys to the factory of the future. The chief elements of a machine vision system are its optics, light source, camera, video processor, and computer software. Vision systems are mainly used for product inspection. They are also becoming important as one of the chief elements in the information feedback loop of systems that control manufacturing processes. Vision systems, selling in the price range of $5000, are mostly sold to original equipment manufacturers (OEMs) who incorporate them in still larger industrial automation systems, which sell for $50 000 to $100 000.

Finding productive applications for machine vision involves the constant search for technology and designs that satisfy user needs. The buying process for machine vision

THE PURCHASE OF MACHINE VISION SYSTEMS INVOLVES A LENGTHY ORGANIZATIONAL BUYING PROCESS.

components and assemblies is frequently a new buy since many machine vision systems contain elements that require some custom design. Let's track five purchasing stages that a company such as the Industrial Automation Division of Siemens, a large German industrial firm, would follow when purchasing components and assemblies for the machine vision systems it produces and installs.

Problem recognition   Sales engineers constantly canvass industrial automation equipment users and manufacturers such as Ford Motor Company, Grumman Aircraft, and many Asian and European firms for leads on upcoming industrial automation projects. They also keep these firms current on Siemens' technology, products, and services. When a firm needing a machine vision capability identifies a project that would benefit from Siemens' expertise, company engineers typically work with the firm to determine the kind of system required to meet the customer's need.

After a contract is won, project personnel must often make a **make-buy decision**—an evaluation of whether components and assemblies will be purchased from outside suppliers or built by the company itself. (Siemens' produces many components and assemblies.) When these items are to be purchased from outside suppliers, the company engages in a thorough supplier search and evaluation process.

Information search   Companies such as Siemens employ a sophisticated process for identifying outside suppliers of components and assemblies. For standard items like connectors, printed circuit boards, and components such as resistors and capacitors, the purchasing agent consults the company's purchasing databank, which contains information on hundreds of suppliers and thousands of products. All products in the databank have been prenegotiated as to price, quality, and delivery time, and many have been assessed using **value analysis**—a systematic appraisal of the design, quality, and performance of a product to reduce purchasing costs.

For one-of-a-kind components or assemblies such as new optics, cameras, and light sources, the company relies on its engineers to keep current on new developments in product technology. This information is often found in technical journals and industry magazines or at international trade shows where suppliers display their most recent innovations. In some instances, supplier representatives might be asked to make presentations to the buying centre at Siemens. Such a group often consists of a project engineer; several design, system, and manufacturing engineers; and a purchasing agent.

Alternative evaluation   Three main buying criteria are used to select suppliers: price, performance, and delivery. Other important criteria include assurance that a supplier will not go out of business during the contractual period, assurance that the supplier will meet product quality and performance specifications, and service during the contractual period. Typically, two or three suppliers for each standard component and assembly are identified from a **bidders list**—a list of firms believed to be qualified to supply a given item. This list is generated from the company's purchasing databank as well as from engineering inputs. Specific items that are unique or one-of-a-kind may be obtained from a single supplier after careful evaluation by the buying centre.

Firms selected from the bidders list are sent a quotation request from the purchasing agent, describing the desired quantity, delivery date(s), and specifications of the components or assemblies. Suppliers are expected to respond to bid requests within 30 days.

Purchase decision   Unlike the short purchase stage in a consumer purchase, the period from supplier selection to order placement to product delivery can take several weeks or even months. Even after bids for components and assemblies are submitted, further negotiation concerning price, performance, and delivery terms is likely. Sometimes conditions related to warranties, indemnities, and payment schedules have to be agreed on.

The purchase decision is further complicated by the fact that two or more suppliers of the same item might be awarded contracts. This practice can occur when large orders are requested. Furthermore, suppliers who are not chosen are informed why their bids were not selected.

Postpurchase behaviour   As in the consumer purchase decision process, post-purchase evaluation occurs in the industrial purchase decision process, but it is formalized and often more sophisticated. All items purchased are examined in a formal product acceptance process. The performance of the supplier is also monitored and recorded. Performance on past contracts determines a supplier's chances of being asked to bid on future purchases, and poor performance may result in a supplier's name being dropped from the bidders list.

The preceding example of an organizational purchase suggests four lessons for marketers to increase their chances of selling products and services to organizations. Firms selling to organizations must (1) understand the organization's needs, (2) get on the bidders list, (3) find the right people in the buying centre, and (4) provide value to the organizational buyer.

CONCEPT CHECK

1. What is a make-buy decision?
2. What is a bidders list?

SUMMARY

1. Organizational buyers are divided into three different markets: industrial, reseller, and government.

2. Measuring industrial, reseller, and government markets is an important first step for firms interested in gauging the size of one, two, or all three markets. The newly created North American Industry Classification System (NAICS) is a convenient starting point to begin this process.

3. Many aspects of organizational buying behaviour are different from consumer buying behaviour. Some key differences between the two include demand characteristics, number of potential buyers, buying objectives, buying criteria, size of the order or purchase, buyer–seller relationships and partnerships, and multiple buying influences within companies.

4. The buying centre concept is central to understanding organizational buying behaviour. Knowing who composes the buying centre and the roles they play in making purchase decisions is important in marketing to organizations. The buying centre usually includes a person from the purchasing department and possibly representatives from R&D, engineering, and production, depending on what is being purchased. These people can play one or more of five roles in a purchase decision: user, influencer, buyer, decider, or gatekeeper.

5. The three types of buying situations, or buy classes, are the straight rebuy, the modified rebuy, and the new buy. These form a scale ranging from a routine reorder to a totally new purchase.

6. The stages in an organizational buying decision are the same as those for consumer buying decisions: problem recognition, information search, alternative evaluation, purchase decision, and postpurchase behaviour. An example of an organizational purchase described is the purchase of machine vision technology components by an electronics manufacturer.

7. To market more effectively to organizations, a firm must try to understand the organization's needs, get on the right bidders list, reach the right people in the buying centre, and provide value to organizational buyers.

KEY TERMS AND CONCEPTS

business marketing p. 168
organizational buyers p. 168
industrial firms p. 168
resellers p. 168
government units p. 169
North American Industry Classification System (NAICS) p. 170
organizational buying behaviour p. 171
derived demand p. 171
organizational buying criteria p. 173
reverse marketing p. 174

reciprocity p. 175
supply partnership p. 176
buying centre p. 177
buy classes p. 179
straight rebuy p. 179
new buy p. 179
modified rebuy p. 179
make-buy decision p. 182
value analysis p. 182
bidders list p. 182

CHAPTER PROBLEMS AND APPLICATIONS

1. Describe the major differences among industrial firms, resellers, and government units in Canada.

2. Explain how the North American Industry Classification System (NAICS) might be helpful in understanding industrial, reseller, and government markets, and discuss the limitations inherent in this system.

3. List and discuss the key characteristics of organizational buying that make it different from consumer buying.

4. What is a buying centre? Describe the roles assumed by people in a buying centre and what useful questions should be raised to guide any analysis of the structure and behaviour of a buying centre.

5. Effective marketing is of increasing importance in today's competitive environment. How can firms more effectively market to organizations?

6. If many of the federal government's purchases are classified as straight rebuys, how can a new firm wanting to do business with the government break into this market?

7. A firm that is trying to market multimillion-dollar wastewater treatment systems to cities has been unable to sell a new type of system. To date, the firm's marketing efforts have been directed to city purchasing departments to get on approved bidder's lists. Talks with city-employed personnel have indicated that the new system is very different from current systems and therefore city sanitary and sewer department engineers, directors of these two departments, and city council members are unfamiliar with the workings of the system. Consulting engineers, hired by cities to work in the engineering and design features of these systems and paid on a percentage of system cost, are also reluctant to favour the new system. (*a*) What role do the various individuals play in the purchase process for a wastewater treatment system? (*b*) How could the firm improve the marketing effort behind the new system?

CASE 7-1 Energy Performance Systems, Inc.

"What we need," says David Ostlie matter-of-factly, "is just one electric utility to say 'yes'—to try our technology. Then the Whole-Tree Energy™ technology will speak for itself." David Ostlie is president of Energy Performance Systems, Inc. (EPS), a firm he founded in 1988 to produce environmentally clean, cheap electricity by growing, harvesting, transporting, drying, and burning *whole* hardwood trees (trunks, branches, and all) in either (1) old retrofitted coal and oil (fossil fuel) power plants or (2) new power plants.

THE IDEA

Dave Ostlie points to three key features that make the EPS-owned and patented Whole-Tree Energy™ (WTE) technology unique:

1. Using *whole* hardwood trees. The use of whole trees saves a tremendous amount of time and energy over using wood chips—a common form for wood burned to produce electricity. "Hardwood trees" here means all broadleaf trees—mainly species such as cottonwood, aspen, birch, maple, and poplar (essentially all trees but conifers).
2. Drying the whole trees. Moisture is the culprit that leads to incomplete wood combustion and reduced energy output, resulting in emissions that lead to air pollution and acid rain. So the WTE process dries the trees to remove about 70 percent of the moisture prior

to combustion, using waste heat from the combustion process itself.
3. Three-stage combustion. The whole trees burn at three levels in the furnace: (*a*) as trees in a 3.6-m deep, mid-level pile, (*b*) as wood char that falls and is burned on a grate below the pile, and (*c*) as volatile gases (gasified wood) above the pile that burns cleanly like natural gas. The result is an incredibly *environmentally clean,* efficient combustion process.

The simplicity of the technology is a big plus compared to many of the current alternative energy technologies being studied around the world.

THE COMPANY

EPS is based on the Whole-Tree Energy™ technology and owns US, Canadian, European, and Japanese patents. The WTE™ technology has been scaled up in four successive tests that have demonstrated the feasibility of large-scale power production from sustained burning of whole trees. The mission of EPS: To commercialize the Whole-Tree Energy™ technology.

THE ISSUES

In assessing the Whole-Tree Energy™ technology, three critical issues soon emerge: (1) the environment and pollution, (2) jobs and economic development, and (3) buying interest of utilities.

The Environment and Pollution

Conventional coal-fired power plants, the staple for utilities, produce large volumes of SO_2, NO_x, ash, and extra CO_2 that contribute to air pollution, acid rain, and global warming. Based on test results, a WTE™ plant produces far less pollution than comparable fossil-fuel plants. Compared to a coal plant, the following levels of pollution have been demonstrated for a WTE™ plant:

- SO_2—less than $\frac{1}{400}$ of that for coal (on a fuel comparison basis) because wood contains virtually no sulfur.
- NO_x—approximately $\frac{1}{10}$ of that for coal due to the naturally low nitrogen content of wood fuel and the multistage WTE™ combustion process.
- Ash—less than $\frac{1}{10}$ of that for coal. The ash produced can be returned to the forest or sold as a fertilizer. Coal ash is considered a hazardous waste and must be stored indefinitely in specially designed storage ponds.
- Extra CO_2—Coal plants release enormous amounts of CO_2 to the atmosphere by burning the remnants of prehistoric plant life—coal—in large quantities. The rapidly increasing level of atmospheric CO_2 due to the burning of fossil fuels is a significant cause of global climate change. In contrast, using biomass—including trees—as a fuel results in no net addition of CO_2 to the atmosphere because the amount of CO_2 removed over the life of the tree is equal to that released by the tree, regardless of the tree's end use.

The net effect of burning a renewable biomass—trees—instead of fossil fuels will be a reduction in air pollution, acid rain, and global warming.

Jobs and Economic Development

WTE™ plants will burn (1) hardwoods that are unsalable (not wanted by other forest product firms), (2) fast-growing energy trees raised on plantations that can be harvested as often as every five to six years and add agricultural jobs, and (3) waste wood left over by other forest product firms. Harvesting overage hardwoods actually stimulates forest regeneration and often provides better habitat for wildlife. Reports suggest that there is plenty of hardwood overage, or wood not wanted by the logging, paper, and pulp industries that should be harvested.

A 100 megawatt WTE™ plant—providing enough electricity for a city of 100 000 people—will provide over 600 jobs in growing, harvesting, and transporting whole trees and in the plant producing electricity. In the search for local jobs, this is a huge benefit for economic development organizations trying to increase local employment.

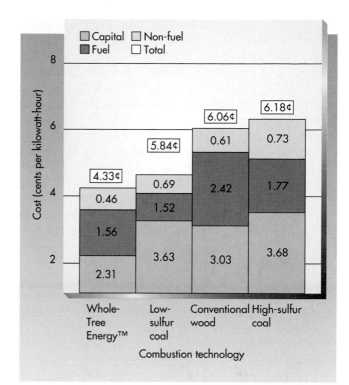

Source: Research Triangle Institute, Electric Power Research Institute and Energy Performance Systems, Inc.

COST OF PRODUCING ELECTRICITY USING FOUR DIFFERENT FUELS, CENTS/KILOWATT-HOUR

Buying Interest of Utilities

To avoid more electrical blackouts, utilities must add new electrical generating capacity. For EPS, this provides an opportunity, either (1) by retrofitting to use in WTE™ some of the coal and oil-fired plants that are operated infrequently because of their pollution problems or (2) by building new plants to use the WTE™ technology.

In an electric utility, capacity planners project the demand for electricity by industrial, commercial, and residential users and assess the utility's ability to supply the demand. The chief executive officer makes the recommendation to add new capacity, a decision reviewed by the board of directors. The vice president of power supply probably recommends the technology to be used and the site for the new power plant.

As Ostlie talks to prospective utility customers about the WTE™ technology, six concerns emerge that are covered below.

1. Can enough heat be generated by burning wood to produce electricity? "All the skeptics said we couldn't get a high enough temperature by burning wood," says Ostlie. "But in one recent heat-release test we produced values higher than those of state-of-the-art coal plants."

2. Can whole trees be loaded, transported, and dried? Forestry experts told Ostlie he couldn't load and transport whole trees on a truck because the branches wouldn't compress. So he hired a logger and did it. The WTE™ technology calls for large-scale drying of whole trees in an air-supported dome like those used in a sports stadium.

3. Are there enough trees available at reasonable cost to support commercial-size power plants? To support such a power plant, only about 0.1 percent of the land in a 80-km radius of the plant would be harvested each year. Residential biomass and waste wood from pulp and timber mill operations are potential fuel sources, as are natural stands. Ultimately, much of the tree resource may come from short-rotation, hybrid tree plantations that provide farmers with an alternative cash crop.

4. What are the environmental benefits of WTE™ for utilities? Besides being increasingly sensitive to environmental concerns, a utility retrofitting a polluting electric power plant with Whole-Tree Energy™ can gain over a million dollars a year in "SO_2 credits"—an incentive for a utility to offset power produced by its high-pollution plants with electricity produced by nonpolluting plants.

5. What will it cost to build a retrofitted or new WTE™ power plant? A major appeal of the WTE™ process is its simplicity relative to say, coal-fired power plants. To retrofit an existing 100 megawatt coal plant, it will cost about $25 million—thereby putting back into production an existing plant that is of little value. To build a new 100-megawatt WTE™ plant would take about $100 million, about 25 to 30 percent less than a new fossil fuel plant.

6. What will the cost be of electricity produced by a WTE™ plant? A recent feasibility study evaluating the WTE™ technology estimated that a WTE™ power plant could produce a kilowatt-hour of electricity for 20 to 40 percent less than today's fossil fuel plants (see figure).

"It's not far away, but we've still got to make that first sale," adds Dave Ostlie.

Questions

1. In a utility's decision whether to buy and use the WTE™ technology (*a*) who comprises the buying centre and (*b*) what aspects of the buying decision does each look at?

2. What are some of the key elements EPS should have in developing its strategy to market WTE™ to prospective utility buyers?

3. As a concerned citizen, (*a*) what do you see as the key benefits of the WTE™ technology and (*b*) what do you personally see as the potential "show stoppers" for WTE™—the critical things that can prevent it from being commercialized and becoming a reality.

4. A new product or technology like WTE™ requires educating a number of key groups, or "influencers," about the technology. Excluding the electric utilities themselves, (*a*) what groups, or market segments, should EPS try to reach, (*b*) what key benefits should be emphasized to each, and (*c*) what promotional methods or media should EPS use to reach each segment?

PART THREE

TARGETING
MARKETING
OPPORTUNITIES

Chapter 8
Collecting and Using Marketing Information

Chapter 9
Market Segmentation, Targeting, and Positioning

Chapter 10
Relationship Marketing, Information Technology, and Forecasting

Part Three describes how people with similar wants and needs become the target of marketing activities. The first step in this process, collecting information about prospective consumers, is discussed in Chapter 8. The information helps marketers focus their efforts on groups with common needs, or market segments. Chapter 9 describes how Reebok International develops specific products for diverse market segments such as runners, aerobic dancers, basketball players, walkers, and others. Chapter 9 also describes how automobile manufacturers have reduced the number of products offered to focus on selected consumer segments. Finally, Chapter 10 explains how new information technologies facilitate information collection and use and help marketers develop long-term, cost-effective relationships with individual consumers.

CHAPTER 8

Collecting and Using Marketing Information

AFTER READING THIS CHAPTER YOU SHOULD BE ABLE TO:

- Know what marketing research is and does.

- Explain the different types of marketing research.

- Understand the stages in the marketing research process.

- Know when and how to collect secondary data.

- Explain the use of surveys, experiments, and observation in marketing research.

- Identify ethical issues in the marketing research process.

- Recognize the need for ongoing marketing research.

REDUCING MOVIE RISKS: LISTENING TO CONSUMERS EARLY

"Let's return Mr. Potato Head's facial features to the default position, so it's easier for the baby to bite off his nose," John Lasseter suggests to an animator. Lasseter, director and head of creative development for the movie *Toy Story,* is charged with breathing life into Mr. Potato Head, Slinky Dog, and Buzz Lightyear, using 300 Sun Microsystem's computers to produce 110 000 individual animated frames, each taking two to five hours of computer time to transfer *Toy Story's* final movie film. (G.I. Joe missed the curtain call. Why? The filmmakers wanted to blow his head off, and Hasbro didn't want its star treated that way.)[1]

Expensive? Very! But even *Waterworld* cost $175 million to shoot—without using animation.

So with today's typical movie costing $40 million to produce and market, how can motion picture studios reduce their risk of losses? One part of the answer: use marketing research. Specifically, recruit people to attend sneak previews (test screenings) of a forthcoming movie and ask them questions that might bring about improvements in the final edit of the movie.

Without turning the page, think about answers to these questions:

- Who would you recruit for these test screenings?
- What questions would you ask them to help you in editing or modifying parts of the film?

While *Toy Story* and *Waterworld* have little else in common, they—like virtually every major movie produced today—use test screenings to modify film details to suit moviegoers's tastes. Figure 8-1 summarizes some of the key questions that are used in test screenings, both to select the people for the screenings and to obtain the key reactions of those sitting in the screenings.

FIGURE 8-1

MARKETING RESEARCH QUESTIONS
ASKED IN TEST SCREENINGS OF
MOVIES, AND HOW THEY ARE USED

POINT WHEN ASKED	KEY QUESTIONS	USE OF QUESTION(S)
Before the test screening	• How old are you? • How frequently do you pay to see movies? • What movies have you seen in the last three months?	• Decide if person fits profile of target audience for movie. If yes, invite to test screening. If not, don't invite.
After the test screening	• Were any characters too distasteful? Who? How? • Did any scenes offend you? Which ones? How? • How did you like the ending? If you didn't like it, how would you change it? • Would you recommend the movie to a friend?	• Change aspects of some characters. • Change scenes. • Change or clarify ending. • Overall indicator of liking and/or satisfaction with movie.

Here are some examples of changes to movies that have resulted from this kind of marketing research:

- *Adding more realism. Waterworld* scenes featuring an animated shark were reshot when preview audiences said it looked phony.[2]
- *Making the plot move faster.* Disney cut a duet by Pocahontas and John Smith in *Pocahontas* because it got in the way of the action and confused test audiences.[3]
- *Reaching a market segment more effectively.* More action footage was added for Kevin Costner when preview screening showed young males were less enthusiastic about *The Bodyguard* than young females.[4]
- *Changing an ending. Fatal Attraction* had probably the most commercially successful "ending-switch" of all time. In its sneak previews, audiences liked everything but the ending, which had Alex (Glenn Close) committing suicide and managing to frame Dan (Michael Douglas) as her murderer by leaving his fingerprints on the knife she used. The studio shot $1.3 million of new scenes for the ending that regular audiences eventually saw.[5]

Sometimes studios don't listen to customers and live to regret it. Test audiences said the length (3 hours and 11 minutes) of *Wyatt Earp* made the movie almost unbearable. Studio executives didn't listen, kept the original length, and the movie died at the box office.[6]

Besides test screenings, motion picture studios also use marketing research to do concept tests of proposed plots and to design and test multimillion dollar promotional campaigns that support a typical movie's introduction. These examples show how marketing research is linked to marketing strategy and decisive actions, the topic of this chapter.

WHAT MARKETING RESEARCH IS AND DOES

Marketing research is the process of defining a marketing problem or opportunity, systematically collecting and analyzing information, and recommending actions to improve an organization's marketing activities.[7] In this chapter, we focus on the basic marketing research process designed to identify and solve specific marketing problems. In Chapter 10, we discuss the important role of information systems in providing ongoing data for effective marketing decision making.

A means of reducing risk and uncertainty   Assessing the needs and wants of consumers and providing information to help design an organization's marketing program to satisfy them is the principal role that marketing research performs. This means that marketing research attempts to identify and define both marketing problems and opportunities and to generate and evaluate marketing actions. Although marketing research can provide few answers with complete assurance, it can reduce risk and uncertainty to increase the likelihood of the success of marketing decisions. It is a great help to the marketing managers who must make final decisions. Conducted properly, marketing research can solve most marketing-related problems that an executive might have. However, marketing research should not be designed to simply replace an executive's good sense, experience, or intuition but rather should be used in conjunction with those skills and as a way of taking out some of the guesswork in the marketing decision-making process.

TYPES OF MARKETING RESEARCH

To understand the variety of research activity, it is helpful to categorize different types of marketing research. Marketing research is often classified on the basis of either technique or function. Surveys, experiments, and observation are a few research techniques with which you may be familiar. However, categorizing research by its purpose or function shows how the nature of the marketing problem influences the choice of research techniques. The nature of the problem will determine whether the research is (1) exploratory, (2) descriptive, or (3) causal.

Exploratory Research

Exploratory research is preliminary research conducted to clarify the scope and nature of the marketing problem. It is generally carried out to provide the researcher with a better understanding of the dimensions of the problem. Exploratory research is often conducted with the expectation that subsequent and more conclusive research will follow. For example, the Dairy Farmers of Canada, an association representing dairy producers in the country wanted to discover why milk consumption was declining in Canada.

They conducted a search of existing literature on milk consumption, talked to experts in the field, and even conducted preliminary interviews with consumers to get

THE DAIRY FARMERS OF CANADA CONDUCTED THREE TYPES OF MARKETING RESEARCH IN AN EFFORT TO SOLVE THE DECLINE IN MILK CONSUMPTION PROBLEM. FOR DETAILS READ THE TEXT.

ideas about why consumers were drinking less milk. This exploratory research helped the association to crystallize the problem, and identify issues for more detailed follow-up research. We examine exploratory research as an integral component of the basic marketing research process later in the chapter.

Descriptive Research

Descriptive research is research designed to describe basic characteristics of a given population or to profile particular marketing situations. Unlike exploratory research, with descriptive research the researcher has a general understanding of the marketing problem and is seeking conclusive data that answers the questions necessary to determine a particular course of action. Examples of descriptive research would include the profiling product purchasers (e.g., the Canadian health food store shopper), describing the size and characteristics of markets (e.g., the Canadian pizza restaurant market), detailing product usage patterns (e.g., ATM usage by Canadian bank consumers), or outlining consumer attitudes toward particular brands (e.g., Canadian attitudes toward national, private, and generic brands).

Magazines, radio stations, and television stations almost always do descriptive research to identify the characteristics of their audiences in order to present it to prospective advertisers. As a follow-up to its exploratory research, the Dairy Farmers of Canada conducted descriptive research in order to determine the demographic characteristics of milk consumers, current usage patterns, and consumer attitudes toward milk consumption.

Causal Research

Causal research is research designed to identify cause-and-effect relationships among variables. In general, exploratory and descriptive research normally precede causal research. With causal research there is typically an expectation about the relationship to be explained, such as predicting the influence of a price change on product demand. In general, researchers attempt to establish that one event (e.g., a price change) will produce another event (e.g., a change in demand). Typical causal research studies examine the effect of advertising on sales; the relationship between price and perceived quality of a product; and the impact of a new package on product sales. When the Dairy Farmers of Canada conducted their descriptive research on milk consumers they discovered many believed milk was too fattening and too high in cholesterol. The association felt that these beliefs might be related to the overall decline in milk consumption in Canada. To test this assumption, the association ran a television advertising campaign to demonstrate that milk was a healthful product and essential to a person's diet. In their tracking studies, they found that the ad campaign did change consumer attitudes toward milk which, in turn, was causally related to a subsequent increase in milk consumption. We refer to causal research later in this chapter when we deal with experiments as a basic research technique.

CONCEPT CHECK
1. What is marketing research?
2. What is the difference between exploratory, descriptive, and causal research?

THE MARKETING RESEARCH PROCESS

Marketing research should always be conducted based on the scientific method, a process of systematically collecting, organizing and analyzing data in an unbiased, objective manner. Marketing research must meet two basic principles of the scientific method—reliability and validity. *Reliability* refers to the ability to replicate research results under identical environmental conditions. In other words, if a research project were to be conducted for the second, third or fourth time, the results should be the same. Marketers need to have reliable information to make effective decisions. If results of a study are not reliable, the research can do more harm than no research at all. *Validity* involves the notion of whether or not the research measured what was intended to be measured. In other words, does the research tell marketers what they needed to know. You should keep the concepts of reliability and validity in mind as we discuss the marketing research process.

Figure 8-2 outlines the basic marketing research process. The figure is perhaps an oversimplification of the process since marketing research does not always follow such a neat and ordered sequence of activities. However, all marketing research consists of four basic stages: (1) defining the problem, (2) determining the research

FIGURE 8-2   THE BASIC MARKETING RESEARCH PROCESS

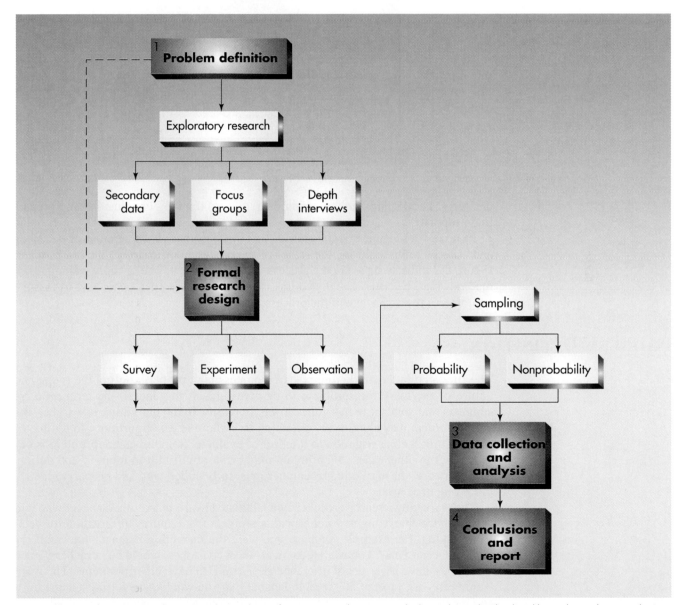

Note: Red boxes indicate stages in the process where a choice of one or more techniques or methods must be made. The dotted line indicates the researcher's choice to bypass the exploratory research stage of the process.

design, (3) collecting and analyzing data, and (4) drawing conclusions and preparing a report.

In reviewing Figure 8-2 you can see that the researcher has a number of decisions and choices to make during the stages of the process. For example, the red boxes in Figure 8-2 indicate stages in the process where a choice of one or more techniques or methods must be made. The dotted line indicates the researcher's choice to bypass the exploratory research stage of the process.

PROBLEM DEFINITION

The first step in the marketing research process is to properly define the scope and nature of the marketing problem to be investigated. In general, the term *problem* suggests that something has gone wrong. In reality, to the marketing researcher, the word *problem* may also mean something to explore or an opportunity to define, or a current marketing situation to monitor or evaluate. Sometimes the problem is obvious, but in other cases, the problem may be more difficult to identify and define. In either case, the marketing researcher must fully understand and properly identify the problem at hand.

The marketing research process is often initiated by the marketing manager who will approach the marketing researcher with a problem that requires information for decision making. For example, suppose you were the marketing manager for cranberry juice at Ocean Spray. You want to know if Asian consumers would buy cranberry juice when they have never heard of cranberries. You also have other problems. The word "cranberry" isn't part of any foreign language so you would have to find a name for it and its juice. Also, if you were going to take the product to Asia you have to find a way to encourage consumers there to try the new product.[8] The marketing researcher has to fully understand these problems. The researcher must also remember that the best place to begin a research project is at the end. In other words, the researcher must know what is to be accomplished through the research process. In this case, as the marketing manager what you really want to know is: Is there a market opportunity in Asia for cranberry juice? If so, how can it be exploited?

Proper problem definition is critical since research based on incorrect problem definition will be a waste of resources. Good marketing researchers adhere to the old adage "a problem well-defined is a problem half-solved." If the research problem is clear, the chances of collecting the necessary information to solve the problem are increased.

CONCEPT CHECK

1. What is reliability and validity?

2. What are the four basic stages in the marketing research process?

Exploratory Research

Your colleague, the marketing researcher at Ocean Spray, has to make a decision early on in the marketing research process. Should exploratory research be conducted in an attempt to help answer the question: Is there a market opportunity in Asia for cranberry juice? As we saw earlier in the chapter, exploratory research is preliminary research conducted to clarify the scope and nature of the marketing problem. In general, it is designed to provide the researcher with a better understanding of the dimensions of the problem and is often conducted with the expectation that subsequent and more conclusive research may follow.

Most researchers will usually conduct some basic exploratory research during the early stage of the research process. The extent of the exploratory research will depend on the magnitude of the problem as well as its complexity. If the researcher decides to conduct exploratory research, he or she has three basic techniques to choose from: (1) secondary data analysis, (2) focus groups, and (3) depth interviews.

Secondary data   Exploratory research almost always involves the use of **secondary data** (or historical data)—data previously collected and assembled for some project other than the one at hand. **Primary data,** on the other hand, are data gathered and assembled specifically for the project at hand. As a rule, researchers gather secondary data before collecting primary data. In general, secondary data can be obtained more quickly and at a lower cost compared to primary data. However, there can be problems with secondary data. The required information may not exist, and if it does, it may not be current or particularly pertinent to the problem at hand. Still, most researchers agree that investigating secondary data sources can save researchers from "reinventing the wheel."

Researchers examine secondary data both inside and outside the organization. Internal secondary data include financial statements, research reports, customer letters, and customer lists. What did your colleague in marketing research at Ocean Spray discover during the secondary data search efforts? She was able to discover that Ocean Spray did attempt to introduce a bland cranberry juice in Japan—named "Cranby"— and it fizzled and was pulled off the market. As a marketing manager this does provide some background information, but you still have more questions than answers about the possible marketing opportunity in Asia.

Sources of external secondary data can be wide and varied. One key source, for example, is the federal government with data made available through Statistics Canada or local libraries. Statistics Canada completes the *Census of Canada* once every decade and updates certain census data every few years. The census provides detailed information on Canadian households. Statistics Canada also prepares annual or biannual reports including the *Family Expenditure Guide* which gives a detailed breakdown of how families spend their money. These basic sources of information are used by manufacturers and retailers to identify characteristics and trends of ultimate consumers.

Statistics Canada produces many other census reports that are vital to business firms selling goods and services to organizations. Such reports include the *Census of Manufacturers* which lists the number and size of manufacturing firms by industry group as well as other information including values of shipments and wages paid.

A marketing researcher can obtain from Statistics Canada their annual *Marketing Research Handbook* or the *Canada Year Book* which includes a summary of key information often necessary to aid marketing decision making. Statistics Canada also has a database system known as CANSIM (Canadian Socio-Economic Information Management System) which marketers can access directly in order to examine aggregate data.

In addition to government-supplied data, trade associations, universities, and business periodicals provide detailed data of value. For example, one business periodical, *Sales and Marketing Management,* publishes special issues each year that provide useful data for firms selling both consumer and industrial products. The most famous publication by *S&MM* is their *Annual Survey of Buying Power. The Financial Post* produces a publication called *Canadian Markets* which provides demographic information and data on consumer spending power in provinces, cities, and towns across the country.

Companies such as Compusearch and A. C. Nielson offer both standard and customized information services to other firms on a subscription, or for-fee, basis. Compusearch can provide information on any geographic area of any size in Canada which highlights population, income and retail expenditure trends in that area. Figure 8-3

FIGURE 8-3   SOURCES OF SECONDARY DATA IN CANADA

SELECTED GUIDES, INDEXES, AND DIRECTORIES

Business Periodical Index
Canadian Almanac and Directory
Canadian Business Index
Canadian News Index
Canadian Periodical Index
Canadian Statistics Index
Canadian Trade Index
Directory of Associations in Canada
Fraser's Canadian Trade Directory
Predicasts Index
Scott's Directories
Standards Periodical Directory
Ulrich's International Periodicals Directory

SELECTED PERIODICALS AND NEWSPAPERS

Advertising Age
Adweek
American Demographics
Business Horizons
Canadian Business
Canadian Consumer
Forbes
Fortune
Harvard Business Review
Journal of Advertising
Journal of Advertising Research
Journal of Consumer Research
Journal of Marketing
Journal of Marketing Management
Journal of Marketing Research
Journal of Personal Selling and Sales Management
Journal of Retailing
Journal of Small Business
Marketing Magazine
Marketing & Media Decisions

Marketing News
Progressive Grocer
Sales and Marketing Management
The Globe and Mail
The Financial Post
The Financial Post Magazine
The Wall Street Journal

SELECTED STATISTICS CANADA PUBLICATIONS

Annual Retail Trade
Canadian Economic Observer
Canada Yearbook
Family Expenditure Guide
Market Research Handbook
Statistics Canada Catalogue

SELECTED TRADE SOURCES

A. C. Nielson
Compusearch
Conference Board of Canada
Dun & Bradstreet
Financial Post Publishing
Find/SVP
Gale Research
MacLean Hunter Research Bureau
Predicasts International
R. L. Polk

SELECTED DATABASES

CANSIM (Statistics Canada)
Dialog
Dow Jones
Infoglobe
Infomart
The Source

shows some of the secondary data sources available to the marketer in Canada. There are also hundreds of useful computerized databanks and specialized data services such as Dow Jones, Dialog, and Infoglobe that can be accessed by a telephone link from a personal computer on a marketer's desk. We discuss these services in Chapter 10.

Getting back to our marketing researcher at Ocean Spray and the cranberry juice in Asia question, she discovers some external secondary data, specifically a study on Taiwan consumers that shows increased consumption of juice beverages. Still, the study is not specific to cranberry juice, and is about four years old. As marketing manager, you realize you still have a high degree of uncertainty about the possible marketing opportunity in Asia. So you ask your colleague in marketing research to continue the exploratory stage of the marketing process.

Focus groups   A very popular exploratory research technique designed to obtain primary data is the use of focus groups. **Focus groups** are informal interview sessions in which 6 to 10 persons, relevant to the research project, are brought together in a room with a moderator to discuss topics surrounding the marketing research problem. The moderator poses questions and encourages the individuals to answer in their own words and to discuss the issues with each other. Often times, the focus group sessions are watched by observers through one-way mirrors and/or the sessions are videotaped. Of course, participants should be informed they are being observed and/or taped. Focus group sessions often provide the marketer with valuable information for decision making or can uncover other issues that should be researched in a more quantitative fashion.

Britain's Lewis Woolf Griptight, a manufacturer of infant and toddler products, conducted focus groups about possible brand names for their products before bringing a

FOCUS GROUPS IN BRITAIN GIVE THUMBS DOWN ON ONE BRAND NAME AND THUMBS UP TO ANOTHER. READ THE TEXT.

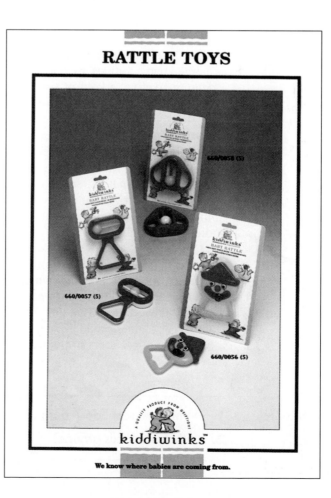

FOCUS GROUPS ENABLE A
MODERATOR TO OBTAIN
INFORMATION FROM 6–10 PEOPLE
AT THE SAME TIME.

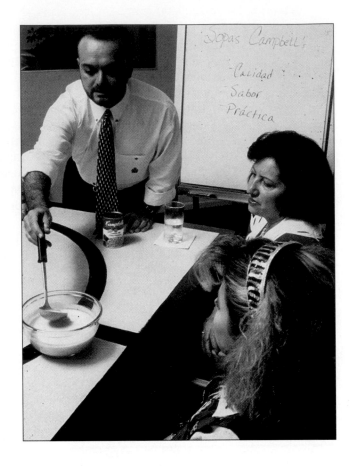

new product line to market. U.K. consumers turned thumbs down on using "Griptight" as a brand name for kids' products because they thought it sounded like "a carpet glue, a denture fixative, a kind of tire." So the firm called its product line by the name "Kiddiwinks™"—a British word for children.[9]

Depth interviews   Another exploratory research technique used to obtain primary data involves the use of depth interviews. **Depth interviews** are detailed individual interviews with people relevant to the research project. The researcher questions the individual at length in a free-flowing conversational style in order to discover information that may help solve the marketing problem being investigated. Sometimes these interviews can take a few hours and they are often recorded on audio- or videotape.

Hamburger Helper didn't fare too well with consumers when General Mills first introduced it. Initial instructions called for cooking a half pound of hamburger separately from the noodles, which were later mixed with the hamburger. Depth interviews revealed that consumers didn't think the recipe called for enough meat and that they didn't want the hassle of cooking in two different pots. So the Hamburger Helper product manager changed the recipe to call for a full pound of meat and to allow users to prepare it in one dish; this converted a potential failure into a success.

CONCEPT CHECK

    1.   What are secondary data?

    2.   What are focus groups?

FORMAL RESEARCH DESIGN

After identifying and clarifying the marketing problem, with or without exploratory research, the researcher must determine the basic framework for finding a solution to the problem. At the formal research design stage, the researcher produces a plan that outlines the method and procedures for collecting and analyzing the required information. The plan includes: the objectives of the research; the sources of information to be used; the research methods (e.g., survey, experiment); the sampling plan; and the schedule and cost of the research.

In selecting basic research methods, the researcher must make decisions. In general, the objectives of the research, the available data sources, the nature of the information required, and timing and cost considerations will determine which research method will be chosen. The basic methods the researcher can choose for descriptive and causal research include: (1) survey, (2) experiment, and (3) observation.

Survey

The most common research method of generating new or primary data is the use of surveys. A **survey** is a research technique used to generate data by asking people questions and recording their responses on a questionnaire. Surveys can be conducted by mail, telephone, or personal interview. In choosing between the three alternatives, the marketing researcher has to make important trade-offs (as shown in Figure 8-4) to balance cost against the expected quality of the information obtained. The figure shows that personal interviews have a major advantage of enabling the interviewer to be flexible in asking probing questions or getting reactions to visual materials. In contrast, mail surveys usually have the lowest cost per completed survey of the three data collection procedures. Telephone surveys lie between the other two technologies in terms of flexibility and cost.

FIGURE 8-4

COMPARISON OF MAIL, TELEPHONE AND PERSONAL INTERVIEW SURVEYS

BASIS OF COMPARISON	MAIL SURVEYS	TELEPHONE SURVEYS	PERSONAL INTERVIEW SURVEYS
Cost per completed survey	Usually the least expensive, assuming adequate return rate	Moderately expensive, assuming reasonable completion rate	Most expensive, because of interviewer's time and travel expenses
Ability to probe and ask complex questions	Little, since self-administered format must be short and simple	Some, since interviewer can probe and elaborate on questions to a degree	Much, since interviewer can show visual materials, gain rapport, and probe
Opportunity for interviewer to bias results	None, since form is completed without interviewer	Some, because of voice inflection of interviewer	Significant, because of voice and facial expressions of interviewer
Anonymity given to respondent	Complete, since no signature is required	Some, because of telephone contact	Little, because of face-to-face contact

FIGURE 8-5

TYPICAL PROBLEMS IN
WORDING QUESTIONS

PROBLEM	SAMPLE QUESTION	EXPLANATION
Leading question	Why do you like Wendy's fresh meat hamburgers better than those of competitors made with frozen meat?	Consumer is led to make statements favouring Wendy's hamburgers
Ambiguous question	Do you eat at fast-food restaurants regularly? ☐ Yes ☐ No	What is meant by word *regularly*—once a day, once a month, or what?
Unanswerable question	What was the occasion for your eating your first hamburger?	Who can remember the answer? Does it matter?
Two questions in one	Do you eat Wendy's hamburgers and chili? ☐ Yes ☐ No	How do you answer if you eat Wendy's hamburgers but not chili?
Nonexhaustive question	Where do you live? ☐ At home ☐ In dormitory	What do you check if you live in an apartment?
Nonmutually exclusive answers	What is your age? ☐ Under 20 ☐ 20-40 ☐ 40 and over	What answer does a 40-year old check?

Sometimes marketers will survey over time the same sample of people, commonly known as a survey *panel*. A panel can consist of a sample of consumers, stores, or experts from which researchers can take a series of measurements. For example, a consumer's switch from one brand of breakfast cereal to another can be measured with panel data. The use of panels is becoming more popular with marketers as they attempt to obtain ongoing information about their constituents. The use of panel data is discussed further in Chapter 10 where we deal with marketing information systems.

When marketers decide to use surveys to ask questions they assume that: (1) the right questions are being asked, (2) people will understand the questions being asked, (3) people know the answers to the questions, (4) people will answer the questions truthfully and (5) the researchers themselves will understand the answers provided. Marketers must not only concern themselves with asking the right questions but also with how to properly word those questions. Proper phrasing of a question is vital in uncovering useful marketing information.

Figure 8-5 shows typical problems to guard against in wording questions to obtain meaningful answers from respondents. For example, in a question of whether you eat at fast-food restaurants regularly, the word regularly is ambiguous. Two people might answer "yes" to the question, but one might mean "once a day" while the other means "once or twice a year." Both answers appear as "yes" to the researcher who tabulates them, but they suggest that dramatically different marketing actions be directed to each of these two prospective consumers. Therefore, it is essential that marketing research questions be worded precisely so that all respondents interpret the same question similarly. Marketing researchers must also take great care not to use "leading" questions (wording questions in a way to ensure a particular response) which can lead to a very distorted picture of the respondents' actual feelings or opinions.

In Figure 8-6 we can see the number of different formats that questions can take in a survey instrument. The questions presented are taken from a Wendy's survey that assessed fast-food preferences among present and prospective consumers. Question 1 is an example of an *open-end question,* which the respondent can answer in his or her own words. In contrast, questions in which the respondent simply checks an

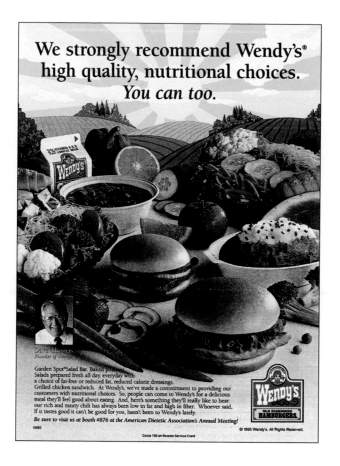

answer are *closed-end* or *fixed alternative questions.* Question 2 is an example of the simplest fixed alternative question, a *dichotomous question* that allows only a "yes" or "no" answer. A fixed alternative question with three or more choices uses a scale. Question 5 is an example of a question that uses a *semantic differential scale,* a seven-point scale in which the opposite ends have one- or two-word adjectives that have opposite meanings. For example, depending on how clean the respondent feels that Wendy's is, he or she would check the left-hand space on the scale, the right-hand space, or one of the five intervening points. Question 6 uses a *Likert scale,* in which the respondent is asked to indicate the extent to which he or she agrees or disagrees with a statement.

   The questionnaire in Figure 8-6 is an excerpt of a precisely worded survey that provides valuable information to the marketing researcher at Wendy's. Questions 1 to 8 inform him or her about the likes and dislikes in eating out, frequency of eating out at fast-food restaurants generally and at Wendy's specifically, and sources of information used in making decisions about fast-food restaurants. Question 9 gives details about the personal characteristics of the respondent's household, which can be used in trying to segment the fast-food market, a topic discussed in Chapter 9.

   Surveys of distributors—retailers and wholesalers in the marketing channel—are also very important for manufacturers. A reason given for the success of many Japanese consumer products in Canada such as Sony Walkmans and Toyota automobiles, is the stress that Japanese marketers place on obtaining accurate information from their distributors.

   Electronic technology has revolutionized the traditional concept of surveys.[10] Today, respondents can walk up to a kiosk in a shopping centre, read questions off a screen, and key their answers into a computer on a touch screen. Labatt Breweries Ltd. uses an interactive kiosk in the shape of a beer can and rewards customers with coupons

FIGURE 8-6
SAMPLE QUESTIONS FROM
WENDY'S SURVEY

1 What things are most important to you when you decide to eat out and go to a restaurant?

_____

_____

_____

_____

_____

_____

2 Have you eaten fast-food restaurant food in the past three months?
☐ Yes ☐ No

3 If you answered "yes" to Question 2, how often do you eat fast food?
☐ Once a week or more   ☐ Two or three times a month   ☐ Once a month or less

4 How important is it to you that a fast-food restaurant satisfy you on the following characteristics? Check the box that describes your feelings.

CHARAC-TERISTIC	VERY IMPOR-TANT	SOME-WHAT IMPOR-TANT	IMPOR-TANT	UN-IMPOR-TANT	SOME-WHAT IMPOR-TANT	VERY UNIMPOR-TANT
Taste of food	☐	☐	☐	☐	☐	☐
Cleanliness	☐	☐	☐	☐	☐	☐
Price	☐	☐	☐	☐	☐	☐
Variety on menu	☐	☐	☐	☐	☐	☐

5 Check the space on the scale below that describes how you feel about Wendy's on the characteristics shown.

CHARACTERISTIC		CHECK THE SPACE DESCRIBING HOW WENDY'S IS	
Taste of food	Tasty	_ _ _ _ _ _ _ _ _ _	Not tasty
Cleanliness	Clean	_ _ _ _ _ _ _ _ _ _	Not clean
Price	Inexpensive	_ _ _ _ _ _ _ _ _ _	Expensive
Variety on menu	Wide	_ _ _ _ _ _ _ _ _ _	Narrow

as a thank you for completing an electronic survey.[11] Even fully automated systems exist for conducting surveys by telephone. An automated voice questions respondents over the telephone, who key their replies on a touch-tone telephone.

Experiment

Another method that can be used by marketing researchers to generate primary data is the experiment. Marketing experiments offer the potential for establishing cause-and-effect relationships (causal research). An **experiment** involves the manipulation of an independent variable (cause) and the measurement of its effect on the dependent variable (effect) under controlled conditions.

In marketing experiments the independent variables are often one or more of the marketing mix variables, such as product features, price, or promotion used. An ideal dependent variable usually is a change in purchases of an individual, household or entire organization. If actual purchases cannot be used as a dependent variable, factors that are believed to be highly related to purchases, such as preferences in a taste test or intentions to buy, are used.

FIGURE 8-6
(CONCLUDED)

6 Check the box that describes your agreement with the statement.

STATEMENT	STRONGLY AGREE	AGREE	DON'T KNOW	DISAGREE	STRONGLY DISAGREE
Adults like to take their families to fast-food restaurants.	☐	☐	☐	☐	☐
Our children have a say in where the family eats.	☐	☐	☐	☐	☐

7 How important is this information about fast-food restaurants?

SOURCE OF INFORMATION	VERY IMPORTANT SOURCE	SOMEWHAT IMPORTANT SOURCE	NOT AN IMPORTANT SOURCE
Television	☐	☐	☐
Newspapers	☐	☐	☐
Billboards	☐	☐	☐
Mail	☐	☐	☐

8 In the past three months, how often have you eaten at each of these three fast food restaurants?

RESTAURANT	ONCE A WEEK OR MORE	TWO OR THREE TIMES A MONTH	ONCE A MONTH OR LESS
Burger King	☐	☐	☐
McDonald's	☐	☐	☐
Wendys	☐	☐	☐

9 Please answer the following questions about you and your household
  a Are you   ☐ Male   ☐ Female
  b Are you   ☐ Single   ☐ Married   ☐ Other (widowed, divorced)
  c How many children under age 18 live in your home?
     ☐ 0   ☐ 1   ☐ 2   ☐ 3   ☐ 4   ☐ 5 or more
  d What is your age?
     ☐ 24 or under   ☐ 25-39   ☐ 40 or over
  e What is your approximate total annual household income?
     ☐ Less than $15 000   ☐ $15 000-$30 000   ☐ More than $30 000

A potential difficulty with experiments is that an extraneous (or outside) variable can distort the results of an experiment and affect the dependent variable.

Experiments can be conducted in the field or in a laboratory. In *field experiments,* the research is conducted in the real world such as in a store, bank or on the street, wherever the behaviour being studied occurs naturally. Field experiments can be expensive but are a good way to determine people's reactions to changes in the elements of the marketing mix. Test marketing is probably the most common form of field experiments. Shoppers Drug Mart used taste tests in the field to determine how consumers felt about its Life Brand Cola, compared to the national brands such as Pepsi and Coke. The tests revealed that 33 percent of the consumers who participated liked Life Brand better than the competitive colas. Shoppers Drug Mart then put the product on the shelves of stores in Atlantic Canada to test the market's response to the product. A successful test market there led to a national rollout of the product in Shoppers stores across Canada.[12] Remember your problem as marketing manager for cranberry juice at Ocean Spray? You wanted to know if Asian consumers would buy cranberry juice when they had never tasted cranberries? Perhaps your marketing research colleague might recommend taste tests in Asia to gauge consumers' responses to the product.

Because marketers cannot control all the conditions in the field, they sometimes turn to a laboratory setting. Laboratories are not the real world but do offer highly controlled environments. Unlike in the field, the marketer has control over all the factors that may play a role in impacting on the behaviour under investigation. For example, in a field experiment the marketer may wish to examine the impact of a price reduction on sales of a particular product. The competition, however, may see the price reduction and offer their own price deal thus interfering with the possible results of the field experiment. This does not occur in a lab setting. Many companies are using laboratory settings where they can control conditions but can do so in a real-world fashion such as simulated supermarkets or test stores. Here they can experiment with changes in isle displays, packaging changes or other variables that may affect buyer behaviour without the fear of other extraneous factors influencing the results.

Observation

Another basic research method used to obtain primary data is observation. In general, **observation** involves watching, either mechanically or in person, how people behave. In some circumstances, the speed of events or the number of events being observed make mechanical or electronic observation more appropriate than personal observation. Retailers, for example, can use electronic cameras to count the number of customers entering or leaving a store.

A classic form of mechanical observation is A. C. Nielsen's "people meter," which is attached to television sets in selected households in Canada and the United States in order to determine the size of audiences watching television programs delivered by the networks. When a household member watches TV, he or she is supposed to push a button on the box and push it again when viewing stops. The people meter is supposed to measure who in the household is watching what program on every TV set owned.

But people meters have limitations—as with all observational data collected mechanically. Critics aren't so sure the devices are measuring what they are supposed to. They are concerned that household members, especially teenagers and the elderly, find it annoying to hit the button every time they start or stop watching TV. A "passive people meter" is now being tested which can be worn on a pin or watch to measure both TV viewing and radio listening at home, at work, or in the car and is intended to address some of the concerns about the traditional people meter.[13]

Marketers also rely on personal observations to collect primary data. For example, Proctor & Gamble observes how consumers bake cakes in its Duncan Hines kitchens to see if the baking instructions on the cake mix box are understood and followed correctly. Chrysler watches how drivers sit behind the wheel of a car to see if they can turn or operate the radio and air-conditioning buttons easily. Fisher-Price uses its licensed nursery schools to observe children use and abuse toys in order to develop better products.

CAREFUL OBSERVATION OF "TOY
TESTERS" IN FISHER-PRICE'S SCHOOL
LEADS TO BETTER PRODUCTS.

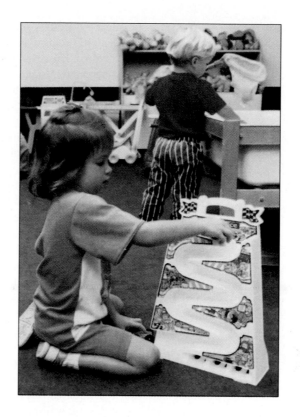

Personal observation is both useful and flexible, but it can be costly and unreliable, especially when different observers report different conclusions in watching the same activities. Also, although observation can reveal what people do, it cannot determine why they do it, such as why they are buying or not buying a product. In order to determine why consumers behave as they do, marketing researchers must talk with consumers and record their responses. This is usually accomplished through the use of surveys.

Is There an Optimal Research Design?

In short, there is no optimal research design. A researcher may choose among a variety of alternative methods for solving a particular marketing problem. A good marketing researcher understands that there is likely to be more than one way to tackle the problem. The ability to select the most appropriate research design develops with experience. Inexperienced researchers often embrace the survey method as the best design because they are most familiar with this method. More experienced researchers, on the other hand, recognize the value of other methods and can often put together creative research designs that can solve marketing problems more quickly and less expensively. Experienced researchers often note that proper definition of the marketing plays a central role in determining the most appropriate research design.

Sampling

Although sampling is an inherent component of the research design stage, it is a distinctive aspect of the research process. The researcher's sampling plan indicates who is to be sampled, how large a sample is needed, and how sampling units will be selected. Rarely does a research project involve a complete census of every person in the research population. This is because of the time and cost involved in conducting a census. Thus, sampling is used. **Sampling** is the process of gathering data from a proportion of the total population rather than from all members (census) of that particular population. A *sample,* then, is a subset from a larger population.

If proper statistical procedures are followed, a researcher does not need to select every member in a population, because a properly selected sample should be representative of the population as a whole. However, errors can and do occur in sampling and thus the reliability of the data obtained through sampling can sometimes become an issue. Thus, the first and most critical sampling question for researchers to ask is: Who is to be sampled?

Another key question concerns the sample size: How big should the sample be? As mentioned, it is usually unrealistic to expect a census of the research population be conducted. In general, larger samples are more precise than smaller ones, but proper sampling can allow a smaller proportion of the total population to provide a reliable measure of the whole.

The final question in the sampling plan concerns how to select the sampling units. There are two basic sampling techniques: probability and nonprobability sampling. **Probability sampling** involves precise rules to select the sample such that each element of the population has a specific known chance of being selected. For example, if your college wants to know how last year's 1000 graduates are doing, it can put their names in a bowl and randomly select 100 names of graduates to contact. The chance of being selected—100/1000 or 0.10—is known in advance, and all graduates have an equal chance of being contacted. This procedure helps select a sample (100 graduates) that should be representative of the entire population (the 1000 graduates) and allows conclusions to be drawn about the entire population.

Nonprobability sampling involves the use of arbitrary judgment by the marketing researcher to select the sample so that the chance of selecting a particular element of the population is either unknown or zero. If your college decided to talk to 100 of last year's graduates but only those who lived closest to the college, many class members would be arbitrarily eliminated. This has introduced a bias, or possible lack of representativeness, which may make it dangerous to draw conclusions about the entire population of the graduating class. Nonprobability samples are often used when time and budgets are limited and are most often used for exploratory research purposes. In general, marketing researchers use data from such samples with caution.

CONCEPT CHECK

1. What is a survey?

2. Which research method offers the potential for establishing cause-and-effect relationships?

3. What is sampling?

DATA COLLECTION AND ANALYSIS

Once the research design has been formalized, the process of gathering or collecting data begins. Sometimes referred to as fieldwork, data collection at this stage of the research process includes all the activities that the researcher (and staff) undertakes, to obtain data from the identified sources or respondents. Since there are several research methods that could be used by the researcher this means there may be multiple ways to collect the data. For example, with the survey method, data may be collected by telephone, mail, or personal interview.

However the data are collected, it is important to minimize errors in the process. Most research experts agree that the data collection stage of the research process is one of the major sources of error in marketing research. Some of the errors that occur are a result of a variety of problems ranging from failure to select the right respondents to incorrect recording of observations. Competent and well-trained researchers inside the organization or those employed by outside research companies can go a long way in ensuring proper data collection.

ETHICS AND SOCIAL RESPONSIBILITY ALERT

WHAT IS "TRUTH" IN REPORTING SURVEY RESULTS?

Doctors were surveyed to find out what brand of butter substitute they recommend for their patients concerned about cholesterol. The results:

- Recommend no particular brand: 80%
- Recommend Brand A: 5%
- Recommend Brand B: 4%

No other brand is recommended by more than 2 percent of the doctors. The firm owning brand A runs an ad that states: "More doctors recommend brand A than any other brand." Is this ethical? Why or why not? What kind of ethical guideline, if any, should be used to address this issue?

The next step for the marketing researcher is data analysis. Mark Twain once observed, "Collecting data is like collecting garbage. You've got to know what you're going to do with the stuff before you collect it." In essence, the marketing researcher must know *why* the data is being collected and *how* to analyze it effectively in order for it to have any value in decision making.

The level of analysis conducted on the data depends on the nature of the research and the information needed to provide a solution to the marketing problem. For survey data, frequency analysis is completed—calculating the responses question by question. The researcher may then wish to identify patterns in the data or examine how data pertaining to some questions may relate to data obtained from asking other questions. Probably the most widely used technique for organizing and analyzing marketing data is cross-tabulation. This method is particularly useful for market segmentation analysis and is discussed in Chapter 9.

CONCLUSIONS AND REPORT

At this stage of the process, the marketing researcher, often in conjunction with marketing management, must review the analysis and ask: What does this information tell us? A critical aspect of the marketing researcher's job is to interpret the information and make conclusions with regard to managerial decision making. The researcher must prepare a report to communicate the research findings. Included in this report should be suggestions for actions which might be taken by the organization to solve the marketing problem.

The researcher must be careful not to overwhelm management with technical terminology. Rather the report should highlight in a clear and concise manner the important results and conclusions. Ultimately, the marketing researcher and management must work closely together to ensure proper interpretation of the research results. In addition, management must make a commitment to act—to make decisions based on the research and their good judgment and knowledge of the situation. In other words, someone must "make something happen" to see that a solution to the marketing problems gets implemented. Failure to act on the research findings creates an appearance that the marketing research effort is of little value. Finally, once implemented, the proposed solution should be monitored to ensure intended results do occur.

ETHICAL ISSUES IN THE MARKETING RESEARCH PROCESS

Ethical issues can arise in marketing researchers' relationships with all parties involved in the research process, including respondents, the general public, their organizations, and/or their clients. Professional marketing researchers must make ethical decisions regarding the collecting, using, and reporting of research data. Examples of unethical

MARKETING NEWSNET

MARKETING RESEARCH AS SUCCESS INSURANCE

Many Canadian companies used to see marketing research as a way to gauge consumer response to their marketing programs or products. But today, many are turning to it much earlier in order to shape both what they market and how they market it.

Stephen Tile, president and COO of Goldfarb Consultants in Toronto says marketing researchers are changing their role from someone who measures the effect of things, whether products or marketing plans, to someone who helps develop these things in the first place. He suggests that formerly a marketer would brainstorm, build a marketing program or a new product, have a hypothesis about how it should work, then go and, on a limited basis, execute it somewhere and evaluate how well it did. But this method is expensive and risky. So researchers are offering what Marion Plunkett, president of Plunkett Communications Research Services of Toronto, calls "success insurance"—research done up-front to help develop a successful marketing program or product in the first place.

The Co-operators Co. of Guelph, Ontario, did extensive research before launching its DirectProtect home and car insurance, which is sold by phone. The Co-operators evaluated response to the idea of buying insurance by phone.

They discovered that consumers liked the convenience and time savings, but also found it somewhat scary because of its impersonal nature. To offset this concern, The Co-operators created a TV ad campaign featuring tiny insurance salespeople coming out of telephones, showing there really was a person on the other end of the line. The company says it has been swamped with calls and has had to add new agents.

YTV hired a marketing research firm to help it decide who to target and how to target them. The research revealed that "tweens" (children 9 to 13) like to watch television with their parents, so YTV launched a prime-time program block for tweens and adults called "YTV Shift." It chose the slot 6 to 9 p.m. because the research showed that its prime time is earlier than the traditional 7 to 11 p.m. The program block features shows like *Goosebumps* and was advertised in a magazine and radio campaign targeted at adults.

So marketing researchers are not necessarily being asked to "find out what happened." They are now being asked to "give us some information up-front so we can make better decisions." This shift to up-front research is being applauded by many industry experts and consumers are more likely to get what they want when they want it, which means real value.

---

behaviour include failure to report problems with research results because of incomplete data, reporting only favourable but not unfavourable results, using deception to collect information, and breaching the confidentiality of respondents and/or their personal data if anonymity or nondisclosure was guaranteed.[14] The Ethics and Social Responsibility Alert Box shows a classic example of an ethical issue in marketing research, the incomplete reporting of data collected.[15]

Using formal statements on ethical policies and instituting rewards and punishments can help ensure that ethical behaviour is the norm in marketing research. For example, the Professional Marketing Research Society of Canada (PMRS), and the Canadian Association of Marketing Research Organizations (CAMRO) have codes of ethics or rules of conduct to which their members must adhere. However, unethical or inappropriate behaviour by individuals or organizations cannot be regulated away. As mentioned in Chapter 4, ethical behaviour rests with the individual, but the consequences affect many.

THE NEED FOR UP-FRONT AND ONGOING MARKETING RESEARCH

In this chapter, we have established why marketers need accurate and insightful information in order to make effective marketing decisions. Unfortunately, many believe that marketing research should be used situationally and for problem-specific reasons. In other words, marketing research should be used only when problems arise, and as such, research projects should have a starting point and end point. But more and more marketers are recognizing the need for continual collection and analysis of marketing information in order to avoid "potential" problems and to uncover possible future marketing opportunities.[16] This has led to the development of marketing information systems which are discussed in Chapter 10. Moreover, as the Marketing NewsNet box points out, many Canadian firms are using marketing research as "success insurance"—research done up-front in order to help develop successful marketing programs or products in the first place.[17]

CONCEPT CHECK

1. What is the third stage of the marketing research process?

2. What is the final stage of the marketing research process?

Summary

1. Marketing research is the process of defining a marketing problem or opportunity, systematically collecting and analyzing information, and recommending actions to improve an organization's marketing activities. Marketing research assists in decision making.

2. There are three basic types of marketing research: (1) exploratory research—preliminary research conducted to clarify the scope and nature of the marketing problem, (2) descriptive research—research designed to describe basic characteristics of a given population or to profile particular marketing situations, and (3) causal research—research designed to identify cause-and-effect relationships among variables.

3. All marketing research consists of four basic stages: (1) defining the problem, (2) determining the research design, (3) collecting and analyzing data, and (4) drawing conclusions and preparing a report.

4. The first stage of the marketing research process—problem definition—is critical since research based on incorrect problem definition will be a waste of resources.

5. If the researcher decides to conduct exploratory research in the early stages of the marketing research process, he or she has three basic techniques to choose from: (1) secondary data analysis, (2) focus groups, and (3) depth interviews.

6. Secondary data (or historical data) are data previously collected and assembled for some project other than the one at hand, whereas primary data are data gathered and assembled specifically for the project at hand.

7. At the formal research design stage, the researcher produces a plan that outlines the methods and procedures for collecting and analyzing the required information. The plan includes: the objectives of the research; the sources of information to be used; the research methods; the sampling plan; and the schedule and cost of the research.

8. The basic methods the researcher can choose from for descriptive and causal research at the formal research design stage include: (1) survey, (2) experiment, and (3) observation. A survey is a research technique used to generate data by asking people questions and recording their responses on a questionnaire. An experiment involves the manipulation of an independent variable (cause) and measuring its effect on the dependent variable (effect) under controlled conditions. Observation involves watching, either mechanically or in person, how people actually behave.

9. Sampling—the process of gathering data from a proportion of the total population rather than from all members (census) of that particular population—is an inherent component of the research design stage. The researcher's sampling plan indicates who is to be sampled, how large a sample is needed, and how sampling units will be selected.

10. The third stage of the marketing research process is data collection and analysis. Sometimes referred to as fieldwork, data collection at this stage of the research process includes all the activities that the researcher (and staff) undertakes to obtain data from the identified sources or respondents. Once the data is collected, the marketing researcher must analyze and transform it into valuable information for decision making.

11. In the final stage of the process, the marketing researcher must take conclusions and prepare a research report. Included in this report should be suggestions for actions that might be taken by the organization that will solve the marketing problem.

12. Professional marketing researchers have to make ethical decisions in the collecting, using and reporting of research.

13. More and more marketers are recognizing the need for continual collection and analysis of marketing information in order to avoid "potential" problems and to uncover possible future marketing opportunities. This has led to the development of marketing information systems.

Key Terms and Concepts

marketing research p. 192
secondary data p. 197
primary data p. 197
focus groups p. 199
depth interviews p. 200
survey p. 201

experiment p. 204
observation p. 206
sampling p. 207
probability sampling p. 208
nonprobability sampling p. 208

CHAPTER PROBLEMS AND APPLICATIONS

1. Is it possible to make effective marketing decisions without marketing research?

2. Why is the problem definition stage of the marketing research process probably the most important stage?

3. You plan to open an ice cream shop in your town. What type of exploratory research would you conduct to help determine its feasibility? You find the exploratory research doesn't answer all your questions. You decide to do a survey to determine whether or not you should open the shop. What kind of questions will you ask? Who do you ask?

4. Suppose you are trying to determine the top three favourite department stores in your area. You show customers at a shopping mall a list of department stores and ask them to rank their three favourite stores from 1 to 3 (with 1 being the favourite). What problems can go wrong with the survey?

5. Your university bookstore wants to find out how students feel about the store's merchandise, prices, and customer service. What type of marketing research would you recommend to the store?

6. Before the people meter, Nielson obtained TV rating data by using "audimeters" attached to TV sets. These devices measured (1) if the TV set was turned on and (2) if so, to which channel. What are the limitations of this mechanical observation method?

7. You are a marketing researcher observing what people do when selecting bread in a supermarket. You are behind a one-way mirror and none of the customers know they are being observed. During the course of the day, you observe several people shoplifting a smaller snack product near the bread section. You know personally two of the shoplifters you see. What are the ethical problems you face in this situation?

8. You plan to open a new rent-a-car business. You have drafted a survey you want to distribute to airline passengers. The survey will be left at the airports and respondents will mail the surveys back in a prepaid envelope. Some of the questions you plan to use are shown below. Use Figure 8-5 to (a) identify the problem with each question and (b) correct it. **Note:** Some questions may have more than one problem.

a. Do you own your own car or usually rent one?
_____ Yes _____ No

b. What is your age? _____ 21–30 _____30–40 _____41–50
_____50+

c. How much did you spend on rental cars last year?
_____$100 or less _____$101–400 _____$401–800
_____$800–1000 _____$1000 or more

d. What is a good daily rental car rate? _____

CASE 8-1   Bookworms, Inc.

Late one August morning, Nancy Klein, co-owner of Bookworms, Inc., sat at her desk near the back wall of a cluttered office. With some irritation, she had just concluded that her nearby calculator could help no more. "What we still need," she thought to herself, "are estimates of demand and market share . . . but at least we have two weeks to get them."

Klein's office was located in the rear of Bookworms, Inc., an 1800-square-foot bookstore specializing in quality paperbacks. The store carries more than 10 000 titles and sold more than $520 000 worth of books last year. Titles were stocked in 18 categories, ranging from art, biography, and cooking to religion, sports, and travel.

Bookworms, Inc. was located in a small business district across the street from the boundary of Verdoon University (VU). VU currently enrolled about 12 000 undergraduate and graduate students majoring in the liberal arts, the sciences, and the professions. Despite national trends in enrollment, the VU admissions office had predicted that the number of entering students would grow at about 1 percent per year through the 1990s. The surrounding community, a city of about 350 000, was projected to grow at about twice that rate.

Bookworms, Inc. carried no texts, even though many of its customers were VU students. Both Klein and her partner, Susan Berman, felt that the VU bookstore had simply too firm a grip on the textbook market in terms of price, location, and reputation. Bookworms also carried no classical records, as of two months ago. Klein recalled with discomfort the $15 000 or so they had lost on the venture. "Another mistake like that and the bank will be running Bookworms," she thought. "And, despite what Susan thinks, the copy service could just be that final mistake."

The idea for a copy service had come from Susan Berman. She had seen the candy store next door to Bookworms (under the same roof) go out of business in July. She had immediately asked the building's owner, Ed Anderson, about the future of the 800-square-foot space. Upon learning it was available, she had met with Klein to discuss her idea for the copy service. She had spoken excitedly about the opportunity: "It can't help but make money. I could work there part-time and the rest of the time we could hire students. We could call it "Copycats" and even use a sign with the same kind of letters we do in "Bookworms." I'm sure we could get Ed to knock the wall out between the two stores, if you think it would be a good idea. Probably we could rent most of the copying equipment, so there's not much risk."

Klein was not so sure. A conversation yesterday with Anderson had disclosed his desire for a five-year lease (with an option to renew) at $1000 per month. He had promised to hold the offer open for two weeks before attempting to lease the space to anyone else. Representatives from copying-equipment firms had estimated that charges would run between $200 and $2000 per month, depending on equipment, service, and whether the equipment was bought or leased. The copy service would also have other fixed costs in terms of utility expenses, interest, insurance, and the inventory (and perhaps equipment). Klein concluded that the service would begin to make a profit at about 20 000 copies per month under the best-case assumptions, and at about 60 000 copies per month under the worst-case assumptions.

Further informal investigation had identified two major competitors. One was the copy centre located in the Krismann Library on the west side of the campus, a mile away. The other was a private firm, Kinko's, located on the south side of the campus, also one mile away. Both offered service while you wait, on several machines. The library's price was about ½ cent per copy higher than Kinko's. Both offered collating, binding, colour copying, and other services, all on a seven-days-a-week schedule.

Actually, investigation had discovered that a third major "competitor" consisted of the VU departmental machines scattered throughout the campus. Most faculty and administrative copying was done on these machines, but students were allowed the use of some, at cost. In addition, at least 20 self-service machines could be found in the library and in nearby drugstores, grocery stores, and banks.

Moving aside a stack of books on her desk, Nancy Klein picked up the telephone and dialed her partner. When Berman answered, Klein asked, "Susan, have you any idea how many copies a student might make in a semester? I mean, according to my figure, we would break even somewhere between 20 000 and 60 000 copies per month. I don't know if this is half the market or what."

"You know, I have no idea," Berman answered. "I suppose when I was going to school I probably made 10 copies a month—for articles, class notes, old tests, and so on."

"Same here," Klein said. "But some graduate students must have done that many each week. You know, I think we ought to do some marketing research before we go much further on this. What do you think?"

"Sure. Only it can't take much more time or money. What do you have in mind, Nancy?"

"Well, we could easily interview our customers as they leave the store and ask them how many copies they've made in the past week or so. Of course, we'd have to make sure they were students."

"What about a telephone survey?" Berman asked. "That way we can have a random sample. We would still ask about the number of copies, but now we would know for sure they would be students."

"Or what about interviewing students in the union cafeteria? There's always a good-sized line there around noon, as I remember, and this might be even quicker."

"Boy, I just don't know. Why don't I come in this afternoon and we can talk about it some more?"

"Good idea," Klein responded. "Between the two of us, we should be able to come up with something."

Questions

1. What sources of information should Klein and Berman use?
2. How should Klein and Berman gather data?
3. What questions should they ask?
4. How should they sample?

CHAPTER 9

Market Segmentation, Targeting, and Positioning

AFTER READING THIS CHAPTER YOU SHOULD BE ABLE TO:

• Explain what market segmentation is, when to use it, and the five steps involved in segmentation.

• Recognize the different dimensions used to segment consumer and organizational markets.

• Develop a market-product grid to use in segmenting and targeting a market.

• Interpret a cross tabulation to analyze market segments.

• Understand how marketing managers position products in the marketplace.

SNEAKER WARS: BATTLING FOR KEY MARKET SEGMENTS

Putting Reeboks on Shaq's size 22 feet probably ignited the latest sneakers war between Reebok (www.reebok.com) and Nike (www.nike.com) for key market segments. (If Shaq needs a last name, clearly basketball isn't your thing and you should probably talk to any Toronto Raptors or Vancouver Grizzlies basketball fan!) "Sneakers" here means all kinds of athletic footwear for aerobics, basketball, walking, tennis, running, and so on.

Until Reebok signed Shaq, the company's most visible market segment was women's fitness, with a product line that included a range of lower-priced casual shoes. In contrast, Nike focused largely on providing high-priced, high-quality shoes to male athletes and "wannabees." With its psychedelic "Shaqnosis" model, Reebok made a frontal attack on Nike's very loyal segment of under-18 males. Not only has Shaq become a superstar in the National Basketball Association, but his attractive, self-effacing interviews have given Reebok a powerful spokesperson to reach male athletes.[1]

But Reebok is not overlooking the female segment of the market. It considers this segment to be a very important target for its business for two reasons: (1) sales of men's sneakers are flat (not growing) and sales of high-tech basketball shoes are languishing, and (2) sales of athletic footwear (sneakers) to women 12 and older continue to grow.

The Reebok strategy—making shoes designed to satisfy needs of different customers—illustrates successful market segmentation, the main topic of this chapter. It also helps explain why Reebok's sales grew by more than 100 000 percent from the early 1980s to today. We'll study Reebok's segmentation strategy more carefully in the next few pages.

After discussing why markets need to be segmented, this chapter covers the steps a firm uses in segmenting and targeting a market and then positioning its offering in the marketplace.

WHY SEGMENT MARKETS?

A business firm segments its markets so it can respond more effectively to the wants of groups of prospective buyers and thus increase its sales and profits. Nonprofit organizations also segment the clients they serve to satisfy client needs more effectively while achieving the organization's goals. Let's use the dilemma of sneaker buyers finding their ideal Reebok shoes to describe (1) what market segmentation is and (2) when it is necessary to segment markets.

What Market Segmentation Means

People have different needs and wants, even though it would be easier for marketers if they didn't. **Market segmentation** involves aggregating prospective buyers into groups that (1) have common needs and (2) will respond similarly to a marketing action. The groups that result from this process are **market segments,** a relatively homogeneous collection of prospective buyers.

The existence of different market segments has caused firms to use a marketing strategy of **product differentiation,** a strategy that has come to have two different but related meanings. In its broadest sense, product differentiation involves a firm's using different marketing mix activities, such as product features and advertising, to help consumers perceive the product as being different and better than competing products. The perceived differences may involve physical features or nonphysical ones, such as image or price.

In a narrower sense, product differentiation involves a firm's selling two or more products with different features targeted to different market segments. A firm can get into trouble when its different products blend together in consumers' minds and don't reach distinct market segments successfully. The Reebok example discussed below shows both how a manufacturer has succeeded in using a product differentiation strategy to offer different products targeted to separate market segments and also how its success is forcing new efforts to separate two groups of its shoes in consumers' minds.

Segmentation: linking needs to actions   The definition of market segmentation first stresses the importance of aggregating—or grouping—people or organizations in a market according to the similarity of their needs and the benefits they are looking for in making a purchase. Second, such needs and benefits must be related to specific, tangible marketing actions the firm can take. These actions may involve separate products or other aspects of the marketing mix such as price, advertising or personal selling activities, or distribution strategies—the four Ps (product, price, promotion, place).

The process of segmenting a market and selecting specific segments as targets is the link between the various buyers' needs and the organization's marketing program (Figure 9-1). Market segmentation is only a means to an end: in an economist's terms, it relates supply (the organization's actions) to demand (customer needs). A basic test of the usefulness of the segmentation process is whether it leads to tangible marketing actions to increase sales and profitability.

FIGURE 9-1

MARKET SEGMENTATION LINKS MARKET NEEDS TO AN ORGANIZATION'S MARKETING PROGRAM

How Reebok's segmentation strategy developed   In 1979 Paul Fireman, who had dropped out of college to run his family's business, wandered through an international trade fair and saw Reebok's custom track shoes. He bought the North American license from the British manufacturer and started producing top-of-the-line running shoes. But Fireman then saw that the running boom had peaked and he needed other outlets for his shoes. What happened next may have affected what you have on your feet this minute.

In a brilliant marketing decision, Fireman introduced the first soft-leather aerobic-dance shoe—the Reebok "Freestyle"—in 1982. The flamboyant colours of these Reebok designer sneakers captured the attention of aerobic-dance instructors and students alike. This colour strategy still helps the sneakers get good display space in stores and attracts a lot of consumer attention.

Today known as Reebok International, Ltd., the firm successively introduced tennis shoes, children's shoes ("Weeboks"), and basketball shoes in 1984 and walking shoes in 1986 (see the columns in Figure 9-2). For those who don't want to buy four different pairs of shoes to run, play tennis, shoot baskets, and walk in, Reebok introduced—of course—"cross-trainers" in 1988. The Reebok Step Trainer appeared in 1991.

What segmentation strategy will Reebok use to take it into the twenty-first century? Suddenly the answer is a bit cloudy. Competitors are offering "retro" sneakers (nostalgic shoes taking you back to the 1960s and 1970s) and "street hockey" shoes (made to look like ice skates). And in 1995 arch-competitor Nike introduced a basketball shoe targeted at women. Reebok's strategy includes a line of hiking and outdoor gear and a possible string of fitness clubs. But, Reebok is also focusing on the global market for sneakers, a market valued at over $7 billion a year. However, learning to segment the global market and deliver customer value will not be easy for Reebok or its major competitors. One segment of interest to Reebok is the 300 million soccer players around the world.[2]

FIGURE 9-2

MARKET-PRODUCT GRID SHOWING HOW EIGHT DIFFERENT STYLES OF REEBOK SHOES REACH SEGMENTS OF CUSTOMERS WITH DIFFERENT NEEDS

GENERAL	GROUP WITH NEED	RUNNING (1981)	AEROBIC (1982)	TENNIS (1984)	BASKETBALL (1984)	CHILDREN'S (1984)	WALKING (1986)	CROSS-TRAINERS (1988)	STEP-TRAINERS (1991)	NEW PRODUCTS (1996-99)
Performance-conscious consumers (athletes)	Runners	P						P		
	Aerobic dancers		P					P		
	Tennis players			P				P		
	Basketball players				P			P		?
	Step exercisers							S	P	
Fashion-conscious consumers (nonathletes)	Comfort- and style-conscious	S	S	S	S		S	S		
	Walkers	S	S	S	S		P	P		
	Children					P				

New markets 1996-99 → ?

Key: P = primary market; S = secondary market

Using market-product grids   A **market-product grid** is a framework to relate the segments of a market to products offered or potential marketing actions by the firm. The grid in Figure 9-2 shows different markets of sneaker users as rows in the grid, while the columns show the different shoe products (or marketing actions) chosen by Reebok, so each cell in a market-product grid can show the estimated market size of a given product sold to a specific market segment.

The lightly shaded cells in Figure 9-2, labelled P, represent the primary market segment that Reebok targeted when it introduced each shoe. The darker shaded cells, labelled S, represent the secondary market segments that also started buying the shoe. In some cases, Reebok discovered that large numbers of people in a segment not originally targeted for a style of shoe bought it anyway. In fact, as many as 75 to 80 percent of the running shoes and aerobic-dance shoes are bought by nonathletes represented by the (1) comfort- and style-conscious and (2) walker segments shown in Figure 9-2—although walkers may object to being labelled "nonathletes." When this trend became apparent to Reebok in 1986, it introduced its walking shoes targeted directly at the walker segment.

Figure 9-2 also introduces one of the potential dangers of market segmentation for a firm: subdividing an entire market into two or more segments, thereby increasing the competition from other firms that focus their efforts on a single segment. Notice that Reebok's strategy is to reach both the performance (athletes) and fashion (nonathletes) segments. In the 1990s Reebok finds itself trying to clarify its identity among consumers who see Nike as a "performance shoe" and L.A. Gear as a "fashion shoe." In trying to compete in both markets, Reebok runs the danger of being first in neither. To be more responsive to both markets, Reebok has divided its operations into two separate units: "Technology," targeted at athletes, performance-oriented consumers, and children and "Lifestyle," targeted at style-conscious consumers.

When to Segment Markets

A business firm goes to the trouble and expense of segmenting its markets when this increases its sales revenue, profit, and ROI (return on investment). When its expenses more than offset the potentially increased revenues from segmentation, it should not attempt to segment its market. The specific situations that illustrate this point are the cases of (1) one product and multiple market segments and (2) multiple products and multiple market segments.

One product and multiple market segments   When a firm produces only a single product or service and attempts to sell it to two or more market segments, it avoids the extra costs of developing and producing additional versions of the product, which often entail extremely high research, engineering, and manufacturing expenses. In this case, the incremental costs of taking the product into new product segments are typically those of a separate promotional campaign or a new channel of distribution. Although these expenses can be high, they are rarely as large as those for developing an entirely new product.

Magazines and movies are single products frequently directed to two or more distinct market segments. *Time* magazine, for example, now publishes more than 100 international editions, each targeted at its own geographic and demographic segments and its own mix of advertisements. Movie companies often run different TV commercials featuring different aspects of a newly released film (love, or drama, or spectacular scenery) that are targeted to different market segments. Although multiple TV commercials for movies and separate covers or advertisements for magazines are expensive, they are minor compared with the costs of producing an entirely new movie or magazine for another market segment. Even computer software companies often market single products to multiple market segments. For example, Ottawa-based Cognos Incorporated markets its business intelligence software product—PowerPlay—to a variety of business segments, in Canada and abroad.

Multiple products and multiple market segments   Reebok's different styles of shoes, each targeted at a different type of user, are an example of multiple products aimed at multiple markets. Manufacturing these different styles of shoes is clearly more expensive than producing one but seems worthwhile if it serves customers' needs better, doesn't reduce quality or increase price, and adds to the sales revenues and profits.

3M uses a "FAB" acronym to develop different products for different market segments:

- F = Features of the product that are clear and that can be translated by R&D and manufacturing personnel into the specifications needed.
- A = Advantages of the product that make it clearly better than competitive products.
- B = Benefits of the product that are important to prospective buyers and can be communicated easily to them.

The four 3M Scotch™ videotapes shown in the ad are examples of using the FAB strategy to design four different videotapes, each designed to satisfy the unique needs of four slightly different market segments: (1) Scotch™ Re-Taping Tape to record favourite soaps and sport shows and then re-record, (2) Scotch™ Collections Tape that resists dust and can be used to build a home movie library, (3) Scotch™ Just for Kids Tape targeted at—what else?—kids, and (4) Scotch™ Archive Tape intended to record special family moments and to be saved permanently.

Product differentiation and market segmentation are generally effective strategies, as shown in the Reebok and 3M Scotch™ videotape examples, but they must be used with great care. The key is to assess how these strategies provide the organization with **synergy,** the increased customer value achieved through performing organizational functions more efficiently. The "increased customer value" can take many forms: more products, improved quality on existing products, lower prices, easier access to product through improved distribution, and so on. But the ultimate criterion is that customers should be better off as a result of the increased synergy.

Some car manufacturers have failed to achieve expected synergies as they offered many models and options to try to reach diverse market segments. They have concluded that the costs of developing, producing, marketing, and servicing dozens of slightly different models probably outweigh the higher prices that consumers are willing to pay for the wider array of choices.

As a result, many car manufacturers have reduced the number of options and simplified their product lines. For example, General Motors recently reduced the number of basic car platforms from 12 to 5—a "car platform" being small front-wheel drive cars or large rear-wheel drive cars. Although there are fewer choices, this provides two benefits to consumers: (1) lower prices through higher volume production of fewer models and (2) higher quality because of the ability to debug fewer basic designs.

CONCEPT CHECK

1. Market segmentation involves aggregating prospective buyers into groups that have two key characteristics. What are they?
2. What is product differentiation?
3. The process of segmenting and targeting markets is a bridge between what two marketing activities?

STEPS IN SEGMENTING AND TARGETING MARKETS

The process of segmenting a market and then selecting and reaching the target segments is divided into the five steps discussed in this section, as shown in Figure 9-3. Segmenting a market is not a science—it requires large doses of common sense and managerial judgment.

Market segmentation and target markets can be abstract topics, so put on your entrepreneur's hat to experience the process. Suppose you own a Wendy's fast-food restaurant next to a large urban university that offers both day and evening classes. Your restaurant specializes in the Wendy's basics: hamburgers, french fries, Frosty milkshakes, and chili. Even though you are part of a chain and have some restrictions on menu and decor, you are free to set your hours of business and to undertake local advertising. How can market segmentation help?

FIGURE 9-3

THE PROCESS OF SEGMENTING AND TARGETING MARKETS INVOLVES FIVE KEY STEPS

Form Prospective Buyers into Segments

Grouping prospective buyers into meaningful segments involves meeting some specific criteria for segmentation and finding specific variables to segment the consumer or industrial market being analyzed.[3]

Criteria to use in forming the segments   A marketing manager should develop segments for a market that meet five principal criteria:

- *Potential for increased profit and ROI.* The best segmentation approach is the one that maximizes the opportunity for future profit and ROI. If this potential is maximized through no segmentation, don't segment. For nonprofit organizations, the analogous criterion is the potential for serving client users more effectively.
- *Similarity of needs of potential buyers within a segment.* Potential buyers within a segment should be similar in terms of a marketing activity, such as product features sought or advertising media used.
- *Difference of needs of buyers among segments.* If the needs of the various segments aren't appreciably different, combine them into fewer segments. A different segment usually requires a different marketing action that, in turn, means greater costs. If increased revenues don't offset extra costs, combine segments and reduce the number of marketing actions.
- *Feasibility of a marketing action to reach a segment.* Reaching a segment requires a simple but effective marketing action. If no such action exists, don't segment.
- *Simplicity and cost of assigning potential buyers to segments.* A marketing manager must be able to put a market segmentation plan into effect. This means being able to recognize the characteristics of potential buyers and then assigning them to a segment without encountering excessive costs.

Ways to segment consumer markets   Figure 9-4 shows the main dimensions used to segment Canadian consumer markets. These include geographic, demographic, psychographic, and behavioural segmentation. By examining Figure 9-4, you can also see that there are a number of variables that can be used within each dimension for segmentation purposes. What you should remember is that segmenting markets is not a pure science—it requires large doses of common sense and managerial judgment. A marketer may have to use several dimensions and multiple variables within each dimension to form proper market segments. Let's take a look at how some marketers might segment consumer markets using the information in Figure 9-4.

- *Geographic Segmentation.* Using geographic segmentation, a marketer segments based on where consumers live. Geographic variables such as countries, regions, provinces, counties, cities, or even neighbourhoods could be used. Marketers often find Canadians differ in terms of needs or preferences based on the region in which they live. Remember, the concept of regional marketing from Chapter 3? This is a form of geographic segmentation. For example, Colgate-Palmolive markets Arctic Power, its cold-water detergent, on an energy-cost-saving dimension in Quebec, but as a clothes saver (cold-water washing is easier on clothes) in Western Canada.
- *Demographic Segmentation.* One of the most common ways to segment consumer markets is to use demographic segmentation, or segmenting a market based on population characteristics. This approach segments consumers according to variables such as age, gender, income, education, occupation and so forth. Cyanamid Canada Inc. uses age as a segmentation variable, producing and marketing its vitamins to various age groups including children, young adults, and older Canadians. Centrum Select, for instance, is specifically

MAIN DIMENSIONS	VARIABLES	TYPICAL BREAKDOWNS
Geographic segmentation	Region	Atlantic, Quebec, Ontario, Prairies, British Columbia
	City or census metropolitan area (CMA) size	Under 5000; 5000–19 999; 20 000–49 000; 50 000–99 999; 100 000–249 000; 250 000–499 999; 500 000–999 000; 1 000 000–3 999 999; 4 000 000+
	Density	Urban; suburban; rural
	Climate	East; West
Demographic segmentation	Age	Infant; under 6; 6–11; 12–17; 18–24; 25–34; 35–49; 50–64; 65+
	Gender	Male; female
	Family size	1–2; 3–4; 5+
	Stage of family life cycle	Young single; young married, no children; young married, youngest child under 6; young married, youngest child 6 or older; older married, with children; older married, no children under 18; older single; other older married
	Income	Under $10 000; $10 000–19 999; $20 000–29 999; $30 000–39 999; $40 000–54 999; $55 000–74 999; $75 000+
	Occupation	Professional; managerial; clerical; sales; labourers; students; retired; housewives; unemployed
	Education	Grade school or less; some high school; high school graduate; some college; college graduate
	Race	White; Black; Asian; Native; other
	Home ownership	Own home; rent home
Psychographic segmentation	Personality	Gregarious; compulsive; extroverted; introverted
	Lifestyle	Joiner-activists; aggressive achievers; disinterested self-indulgents; old-fashioned puritans; responsible survivors; day-to-day watchers
Behavioural segmentation	Benefits sought	Quality; service; low price
	Usage rate	Light user; medium user; heavy user
	User status	Nonuser; ex-user; prospect; first-time user; regular user
	Loyalty status	None, medium, strong

FIGURE 9-4

DIMENSIONS USED TO SEGMENT
CANADIAN CONSUMER MARKETS

designed for adults over 50. Trimark Investments of Ontario segments the financial services market by gender, targeting males and females with different products and different advertising campaigns. General Electric uses family size as a segmentation variable, targeting smaller families with compact microwaves and larger families with extra-large refrigerators. You should note, however, that a single demographic variable may not be sufficient in understanding and segmenting a given market. Thus, many marketers combine a number of demographic variables that might clearly distinguish one segment from another. For example, cosmetics companies such as Clinique combine gender, income, and occupation in order to examine market segments for different lines of cosmetic products.

• *Psychographic Segmentation.* Marketers use psychographic segmentation when they segment markets according to personality or lifestyle. It has been found that people who share the same demographic characteristics can have very different psychographic profiles. As we saw in Chapter 6, personality traits have been linked to product preferences and brand choice. In addition, a person's lifestyle (their activities, interests, and opinions) also affects the types of products, and the particular brands of products that may be purchased. Remember the Goldfarb Segments from Chapter 5? A Canadian frozen-food

LACTANTIA PURFILTRE FOR A MARKET
SEGMENT LOOKING FOR A FRESHER,
LONGER LASTING MILK.

manufacturer discovered that 80 percent of its customers fell into the disinterested self-indulgent Goldfarb segment and that convenience was more important to this segment than the taste of the food product. They pushed convenience in their advertising and were successful in attracting this market segment.[4]

- *Behavioural Segmentation.* When marketers use consumers' behaviour with or toward a product to segment the market, they are using behavioural segmentation. A powerful form of behavioural segmentation is to divide the market according to the benefits consumers seek from a product category. Using *benefits sought* the marketer examines the major benefits consumers look for in the product category, the kinds of consumers who look for each benefit, and the major brands that deliver each benefit. For example, Ontario-based Ault Foods examined the fluid milk market and discovered a segment who was looking for a fresher tasting, longer lasting product and who were prepared to pay a premium price for a product that would deliver those benefits. In response, Ault developed Lactantia PurFiltre milk for this consumer segment.[5]

Another behavioural segmentation variable often used by marketers is **usage rate**—quantity consumed or patronage during a specific period, which varies significantly among different customer groups. Air Canada, for example, focuses on usage rate for its frequent-flyer program which is designed to encourage passengers to use its airline repeatedly. Usage rate is sometimes referred to in terms of the **80/20 rule,** a concept that suggests that 80 percent of a firm's sales are obtained from 20 percent of its customers. The percentages in the 80/20 rule are not really fixed; rather, the rule suggests that a small fraction of customers provide a large fraction of sales. For example, Air Canada pays special attention to the business travel segment that comprises only 20 percent of the airline seats but 40 percent of overall revenues.[6]

Research shows that the fast-food market can also be segmented into light, medium, or heavy users. For every $1.00 spent by a light user in a fast-food restaurant, each heavy user spends over $5.00. This is the reason for the emphasis in almost all marketing strategies on effective ways to reach heavy users of products and services. Thus, as a Wendy's restaurant owner you want to keep the heavy-user segment constantly in mind. With advances in information technology (see Chapter 10), marketers are now able to conduct detailed segmentation studies. Some Canadian telecommunications companies, for example, can now segment based on more than 100 criteria, from calling patterns to promotional response.[7]

Now, in determining one or two variables to segment the market for your Wendy's restaurant, very broadly we find two main markets: students and nonstudents. To segment the students, we could try a variety of demographic variables such as age, gender, year in school, or college major, or psychographic variables such as personality or lifestyle. But none of these variables really meets the five criteria listed previously—particularly the fourth criterion about leading to a feasible marketing action to reach the various segments. Four student segments that *do* meet these criteria include the following:

- Students living in dormitories (residence halls, fraternity houses).
- Students living near the university in apartments.
- Day commuter students living outside the area.
- Night commuter students living outside the area.

FIGURE 9-5

DIMENSIONS USED TO SEGMENT
CANADIAN ORGANIZATIONAL
MARKETS

MAIN DIMENSIONS	VARIABLES	TYPICAL BREAKDOWNS
Geographic segmentation	Region	Atlantic, Quebec, Ontario, Prairies, British Columbia
	Location	In CMA; not in CMA
Demographic segmentation	NAICS code	2-digit; 3-digit; 4-digit; 5-digit categories
	Number of Employees	1–19; 20–99; 100–249; 250+
	Annual Sales Volume	Less than $1 million; $1–10 million; $10–100 million; over $100 million
Behavioural segmentation	Benefits sought	Quality; customer service; low price
	Usage rate	Light user; medium user; heavy user
	User status	Nonuser; ex-user; prospect; first-time user; regular user
	Loyalty status	None, medium, strong
	Purchase method	Centralized; decentralized; Individual; group
	Type of buy	New buy; modified rebuy; straight rebuy

These segmentation variables are really a combination of where the student lives and the time he or she is on campus (and near your restaurant). For nonstudents who might be customers, similar variables might be used:

- Faculty and staff members at the university.
- People who live in the area but aren't connected with the university.
- People who work in the area but aren't connected with the university.

Ways to segment organizational markets   Variables for segmenting organizational markets are shown in Figure 9-5. A product manager at Panasonic responsible for its new Plain Paper Laser Fax that doubles as a personal copier, answering machine, and autodial phone might segment organizational markets in the following ways:

- *Geographic segmentation.* The product manager might segment based on region or actual location of the potential customer. Firms located in a census metropolitan area (CMA) might receive a personal sales call, whereas those outside the CMA might be contacted by phone.
- *Demographic segmentation.* Firms might be categorized by the North American Industry Classification System (NAICS). Manufacturers, for example, with global customers might have different fax and answering needs than do retailers or lawyers serving local customers.
- *Behavioural segmentation.* The market might also be segmented based on benefits sought. Panasonic may decide to focus on firms looking for quality product and good customer service as opposed to those looking for simply low prices. The product manager might also segment the market based on usage rate, recognizing that larger, more globally oriented firms are more likely to be heavy users.

Form Products to Be Sold into Groups

As important as grouping customers into segments is finding a means of grouping the products you're selling into meaningful categories. If the firm has only one product or service, this isn't a problem, but when it has dozens or hundreds, these must be grouped in some way so buyers can relate to them. This is why department stores and supermarkets are organized into product groups, with the departments or aisles containing related merchandise. Likewise, manufacturers have product lines that are the groupings they use in the catalogues sent to customers.

What are the groupings for your restaurant? It could be the item purchased, such as a Frosty, chili, hamburgers, and French fries, but this is where judgment—the qualitative aspect of marketing—comes in. Students really buy an eating experience, or a meal that satisfies a need at a particular time of day, so the product grouping can be defined by meal or time of day as breakfast, lunch, between-meal snack, dinner, and after-dinner snack. These groupings are more closely related to the way purchases are actually made and permit you to market the entire meal, not just your French fries or Frosties.

Develop a Market-Product Grid and Estimate Size of Markets

Developing a market-product grid means labelling the markets (or horizontal rows) and products (or vertical columns), as shown in Figure 9-6. In addition, the size of the market in each cell, or the market-product combination, must be estimated. For your restaurant this involves estimating the number of, or sales revenue obtained from, each kind of meal that can reasonably be expected to be sold to each market segment.

The market sizes in Figure 9-6 may be simple "guesstimates" if you don't have time for formal marketing research (as discussed in Chapter 8). But even such crude estimates of the size of specific markets using a market-product grid are far better than the usual estimates of the entire market.

Select Target Markets

A firm must take care to choose its target market segments carefully. If it picks too narrow a group of segments, it may fail to reach the volume of sales and profits it needs. If it selects too broad a group of segments, it may spread its marketing efforts so thin that the extra expenses more than offset the increased sales and profits.

FIGURE 9-6

SELECTING A TARGET MARKET FOR YOUR FAST-FOOD RESTAURANT NEXT TO AN URBAN UNIVERSITY (TARGET MARKET IS SHADED)

MARKETS	BREAKFAST	LUNCH	BETWEEN-MEAL SNACK	DINNER	AFTER-DINNER SNACK
STUDENT					
Dormitory	0	1	3	0	3
Apartment	1	3	3	1	1
Day commuter	0	3	2	1	0
Night commuter	0	0	1	3	2
NONSTUDENT					
Faculty or stafff	0	3	1	1	0
Live in area	0	1	2	2	1
Work in area	1	3	0	1	0

PRODUCTS: MEALS

Key: 3, Large market; 2, medium market; 1, small market; 0, no market.

Criteria to use in picking the target segments   There are two different kinds of criteria present in the market segmentation process: (1) those to use in dividing the market into segments (discussed earlier) and (2) those to use in actually picking the target segments. Even experienced marketing executives often confuse these two different sets of criteria. The five criteria to use in actually selecting the target segments apply to your Wendy's restaurant this way:

- *Size.* The estimated size of the market in the segment is an important factor in deciding whether it's worth going after. There is really no market for breakfasts among dormitory students (Figure 9-6), so why devote any marketing effort toward reaching a small or nonexistent market?
- *Expected growth.* Although the size of the market in the segment may be small now, perhaps it is growing significantly or is expected to grow in the future. Night commuters may not look important now, but with the decline in traditional day students in many colleges, the evening adult education programs are expected to expand in the future. Thus, the future market among night commuters is probably more encouraging than the current picture shown in Figure 9-6.
- *Competitive position.* Is there a lot of competition in the segment now or is there likely to be in the future? The less the competition, the more attractive the segment is. For example, if the college dormitories announce a new policy of "no meals on weekends," this segment is suddenly more promising for your restaurant.
- *Cost of reaching the segment.* A segment that is inaccessible to a firm's marketing actions should not be pursued. For example, the few nonstudents who live in the area may not be economically reachable with ads in newspapers or other media. As a result, do not waste money trying to advertise to them.
- *Compatibility with the organization's objectives and resources.* If your restaurant doesn't have the cooking equipment to make breakfasts and has a policy against spending more money on restaurant equipment, then don't try to reach the breakfast segment.

As is often the case in marketing decisions, a particular segment may appear attractive according to some criteria and very unattractive according to others.

Choose the segments   Ultimately, a marketing executive has to use these criteria to choose the segments for special marketing efforts. As shown in Figure 9-6, let's assume you've written off the breakfast market for two reasons: too small market size

WENDY'S CAN TARGET DIFFERENT
MARKET SEGMENTS WITH DIFFERENT
ADVERTISING PROGRAMS

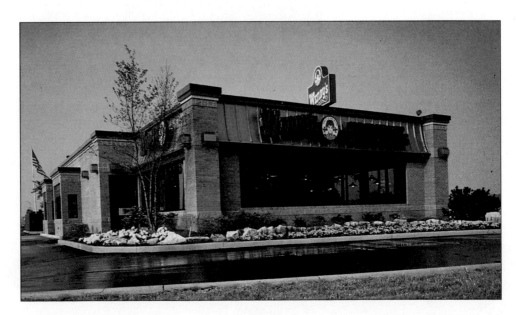

and incompatibility with your objectives and resources. In terms of competitive position and cost of reaching the segment, you choose to focus on the four student segments
and not the three nonstudent segments (although you're certainly not going to turn
away business from the nonstudent segments). This combination of market-product
segments—your target market—is shaded in Figure 9-6.

Take Marketing Actions to Reach Target Markets

The purpose of developing a market-product grid is to trigger marketing actions to increase
revenues and profits. This means that someone must develop and execute an action plan.

Your Wendy's segmentation strategy   With your Wendy's restaurant you've
already reached one significant decision: there is a limited market for breakfast, so
you won't open for business until 10:30 A.M. In fact, Wendy's first attempt at a breakfast menu was a disaster and was discontinued in 1986. Wendy's evaluates possible
new menu items continuously, not only to compete with McDonald's (and now its
chicken fajitas and pizza) but with a complex array of supermarkets, convenience
stores, and gas stations that sell reheatable packaged foods as well as new "easy-
lunch" products.

Another essential decision is where and what meals to advertise to reach specific
market segments. An ad in the student newspaper could reach all the student segments,
but you might consider this "shotgun approach" too expensive and want a more focused "rifle approach" to reach smaller segments. If you choose three segments for special actions (Figure 9-7), advertising actions to reach them might include:

- *Day commuters* (an entire market segment). Run ads inside commuter buses
  and put flyers under the windshield wipers of cars in parking lots used by day
  commuters. These ads and flyers promote all the meals at your restaurant to a
  single segment of students—a horizontal cut through the market-product grid.

FIGURE 9-7

ADVERTISING ACTIONS TO REACH
SPECIFIC STUDENT SEGMENTS

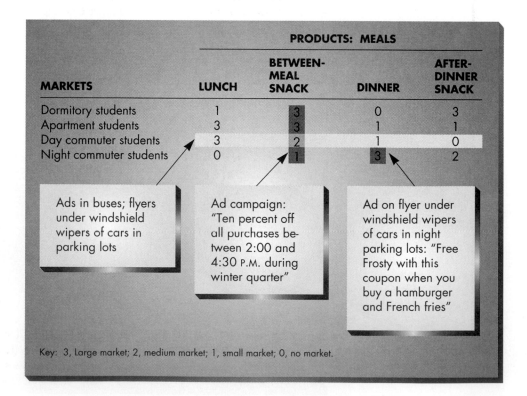

Key: 3, Large market; 2, medium market; 1, small market; 0, no market.

WHAT MARKET SEGMENTS FOR
APPLE'S COMPUTERS ARE
REPRESENTED BY THESE PHOTOS? THE
MARKETING NEWSNET BOX AND
TEXT DISCUSSION PROVIDE INSIGHTS
INTO APPLE'S MARKET
SEGMENTATION STRATEGY.

- *Between-meals snacks* (directed to all four student markets). To promote eating during this downtime for your restaurant, offer "10 percent off all purchases between 2:00 and 4:30 P.M. during winter quarter." This ad promotes a single meal to all four student segments—a vertical cut through the market-product grid.
- *Dinners to night commuters.* The most focused of all three campaigns, this ad promotes a single meal to a single student segment. The campaign might consist of a windshield flyer offering a free Frosty with the coupon when the person buys a hamburger and French fries.

Depending on how your advertising actions work, you can repeat, modify, or drop them and design new campaigns for other segments you feel warrant the effort. This example of advertising your Wendy's restaurant is just a small piece of a complete marketing program using all the elements of the marketing mix.

Apple's segmentation strategy   Steven Jobs and Stephen Wozniak didn't realize they were developing today's multibillion-dollar PC industry when they invented the Apple II in a garage in 1976. Under Jobs's inspirational leadership through the early 1980s, Apple was run with a focus on products and little concern for markets. Apple's control of its brainy, creative young engineers was likened to "Boy Scouts without adult supervision." When IBM entered the PC market in 1981, Apple lost significant market share, and many experts predicted it wouldn't survive.

MARKETING NEWSNET

Customer Value

APPLE'S SEGMENTATION STRATEGY: SEARCH FOR THE RIGHT NICHES

"Camp Runamok" was the nickname some computer industry wags gave to Apple Computer in the early 1980s because the entrepreneurial company had no coherent series of product lines directed at identifiable market segments.

Now Apple has targeted its various lines of Macintosh computers at specific market segments, as shown below.

The market-product grid below is a simplification because each "product" is really a series of Macintosh computers in that line. Each series has computers that vary by requirements of the user, such as amount of mem-

ory needed, DOS compatibility, availability of internal CD-ROM drive, and so on. There is also an overlap of likely market segments from one product line to the other.

Nevertheless, the grid suggests a market-product strategy for Apple's product lines: Performas for home, small business, and school users; PowerBooks for travellers; Power Macs for those needing more sophisticated applications; and a line of "info appliances" priced under $1000 targeted at home and small business users and running multimedia CD-ROMs and connecting to the internet.

MARKETS		PRODUCTS					
			MACINTOSH COMPUTERS				
SECTOR	SPECIFIC SEGMENT	INFO APPLI-ANCES	PER-FORMAS	POWER-BOOKS/ DUOS	POWER MACS	WORK-GROUP SERVERS	MONITORS & PRINTERS
Home	Basics, games	√	√				√
Small Business	Administration	√	√				√
School	Students/faculty		√				√
	Administration		√	√		√	√
College/ university	Students/faculty		√	√	√	√	√
	Administration			√	√	√	√
Large business	Administration			√	√	√	√
	Tech./scientific				√	√	√

In the mid-1990s Apple's now-former chief executive officer Gilbert Amelio began to formalize and give cohesiveness to Apple's market segmentation strategy and target specific Apple machines to particular market segments. The core business was to be built on Apple's line of Macintosh computers, which it continues to enhance. As in most segmentation situations, a single Apple product does not fit into an exclusive market niche. Rather, there is overlap among products in the product line and also among the markets to which they are directed. But a market segmentation strategy enables Apple to offer different products to meet the needs of the different market segments, as shown in the accompanying Marketing NewsNet box.

Recently Apple has introduced a more powerful line of Power Macs and incorporated Apple's speedy PowerPC chip in its products. At the same time, it faced some critical competitive problems:

- *Decline in market share.* Apple's market share of world sales of new personal computers fell by more than 1 percent.[8]

- *The introduction of Windows 95*™. The 1995 launch of Microsoft's Windows 95™ software system had the effect of making IBM-compatible PCs have more of the user friendliness of Apple's Macintosh line, reducing Apple's competitive advantage. Macintosh loyalists responded by noting that "Windows 95™ is Mac 89."[9]
- *Major price cuts.* Fearing a loss of market share, Apple cut the prices on some of its Macintoshes from 10 to 40 percent.[10]
- *Shortage of computers for sale.* The very appealing features on its new, high-end PowerMacs and large price cuts caused demand to surge. But Apple had not forecast this huge demand, so suppliers for its unique components could not meet Apple's production needs, causing shortages for those Macintoshes.[11]

During this time Apple also made some important strategic decisions such as signing up "clone makers"—a revolutionary step for Apple—that, in turn, gives potential software developers more incentive to write programs for use on Macintoshes.

To exploit Apple's strengths, Gilbert Amelio initiated an aggressive target marketing strategy:

- Stress its effectiveness in key applications such as desktop publishing, multimedia production, and education; also, design a "seamless" Internet capability into its new computers.[12]
- Continue to focus on market niches where it is strong—the home, school, business, and entertainment markets.[13] For example, a carefully crafted Macintosh Performa ad targets the home market by using the credibility of Apple's 18 years of experience in school computers to suggest readers "bring learning home with the Performa."
- Simplify the product line by focusing on its "best of class" products and introducing a new line of low-priced "info appliances" that are a TV-based, multimedia CD-ROM platform and Internet browser.[14]

Competition is fierce in all these areas. For example, almost all PC makers are now targeting homes without a home computer, and prices are taking a nosedive. But Apple's segmentation strategy makes it optimistic.[15]

CONCEPT CHECK

1. What are some of the variables used to segment consumer markets?

2. What are some criteria used to decide which segments to choose for targets?

ANALYZING MARKET SEGMENTS USING CROSS TABULATIONS

To do a more precise market segmentation analysis of your Wendy's restaurant, suppose you survey fast-food patrons throughout the metropolitan area where your restaurant is located, using the questionnaire shown in Chapter 8 (Figure 8-6). You want to use this information as best you can to study the market's segments and develop your strategy. Probably the most widely used approach today in marketing is to develop and interpret cross tabulations of data obtained by questionnaires.

Developing Cross Tabulations

A **cross tabulation,** or "cross tab," is a method of presenting and relating data having two or more variables. It is used to analyze and discover relationships in the data. Two important aspects of cross tabulations are deciding which of two variables to pair together to help understand the situation and forming the resulting cross tabulations.

Pairing the questions   Marketers pair two questions to understand marketing relationships and to find effective marketing actions. The Wendy's questionnaire in Chapter 8 (Figure 8-6) gives many questions that might be paired to understand the fast-food business better and help reach a decision about marketing actions to increase revenues. For example, if you want to study your hypothesis that as the age of the head of the household increases, patronage of fast-food restaurants declines, you can cross tabulate questions 9d and 3.

Forming cross tabulations   Using the answers to question 3 as the column headings and the answers to question 9d as the row headings gives a cross tabulation, as shown in Figure 9-8, using the answers 586 respondents gave to both questions. The figure shows two forms of the cross tabulation:

- The raw data or answers to the specific questions are shown in Figure 9-8A. For example, this cross tab shows that 144 households whose head was 24 years or younger ate at fast-food restaurants once a week or more.
- Answers on a percentage basis, with the percentages running horizontally, are shown in Figure 9-8B. Of the 215 households headed by someone 24 years or younger, 67.0 percent ate at a fast-food restaurant at least once a week and only 8.8 percent ate there once a month or less.

Two other forms of cross tabulation using the raw data shown in Figure 9-8A are as described in problem 7 at the end of the chapter.

Interpreting Cross Tabulations

A careful analysis of Figure 9-8 shows that patronage of fast-food restaurants is related to the age of the head of the household. Note that as the age of the head of the household increases, fast-food restaurant patronage declines, as shown by the boxed percentages

FIGURE 9-8

TWO FORMS OF A CROSS TABULATION RELATING AGE OF HEAD OF HOUSEHOLD TO FAST-FOOD RESTAURANT PATRONAGE

A. ABSOLUTE FREQUENCIES

	FREQUENCY			
AGE OF HEAD OF HOUSEHOLD (YEARS)	ONCE A WEEK OR MORE	2 OR 3 TIMES A MONTH	ONCE A MONTH OR LESS	TOTAL
24 or less	144	52	19	215
25 to 39	46	58	29	133
40 or over	82	69	87	238
Total	272	179	135	586

B. ROW PERCENTAGES: RUNNING PERCENTAGES HORIZONTALLY

	FREQUENCY			
AGE OF HEAD OF HOUSEHOLD (YEARS)	ONCE A WEEK OR MORE	2 OR 3 TIMES A MONTH	ONCE A MONTH OR LESS	TOTAL
24 or less	67.0%	24.2%	8.8%	100.0%
25 to 39	34.6	43.6	21.8	100.0
40 or over	34.4	29.0	36.6	100.0
Total	46.4%	30.6%	23.0%	100.0%

on the diagonal in Figure 9-8B. This means that if you want to reach the heavy-user segment, you should direct your marketing efforts to the segment that is 24 years old or younger.

As discussed earlier in the chapter, there are various ways to segment a consumer market besides according to age. For example, you could make subsequent cross tabulations to analyze patronage related to where students live and the meals they eat to obtain more precise information for the market-product grid in Figure 9-6.

Value of Cross Tabulations

Probably the most widely used technique for organizing and presenting marketing data, cross tabulations have some important advantages.[16] The simple format permits direct interpretation and an easy means of communicating data to management. They have great flexibility and can be used to summarize experimental, observational, and questionnaire data. Also, cross tabulations may be easily generated by today's personal computers.

Cross tabulations also have some disadvantages. For example, they can be misleading if the percentages are based on too small a number of observations. Also, cross tabulations can hide some relations because each typically only shows two or three variables. Balancing both advantages and disadvantages, more marketing decisions are probably made using cross tabulations than any other method of analyzing data.

The ultimate value of cross tabulations to a marketing manager lies in obtaining a better understanding of the wants and needs of buyers and targeting key segments. This enables a marketing manager to "position" the offering in the minds of buyers, the topic discussed next.

POSITIONING THE PRODUCT

When a company offers a product commercially, a decision critical to its long-term success is how to position it in the market on introduction. **Product positioning** refers to the place an offering occupies in consumers' minds on important attributes relative to competitive offerings. As described in the Ethics and Social Responsibility Alert, positioning strategies can also raise difficult ethical dilemmas.[17]

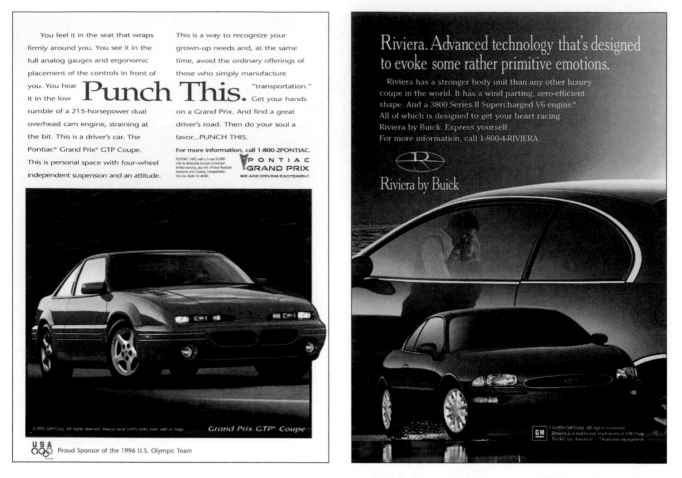

TO WHICH MARKET SEGMENTS ARE THESE GENERAL MOTORS CARS TARGETED? DO POTENTIAL BUYERS SEE THEM AS THE SAME OR DIFFERENT? FOR THE
COMPANY'S POSITIONING DILEMMA AND STRATEGY, SEE THE TEXT AND FIGURE 9-9.

Two Approaches to Product Positioning

There are several approaches to positioning a new product in the market. Head-to-head
positioning involves competing directly with competitors on similar product attributes
in the same target market. Using this strategy, Dollar competes directly with Avis and
Hertz, and Volvo pits its turbo-charged cars against Porsche.

Differentiation positioning involves avoiding direct (head-to-head) competition by
stressing unique aspects of the product. This strategy can involve positioning a product on a specific attribute, feature, or benefit. BMW, for example, positions its cars as
the "ultimate driving machines" to connote superior handling and driving performance.
Crest is positioned as the toothpaste that prevents cavities. A firm can also position its product for a particular usage situation. Arm & Hammer positions its baking soda as the one
to use when you need a refrigerator deodorant, and Gatorade is positioned as the beverage to use for replacing body fluids after athletic performances. Companies also follow a differentiation positioning strategy among brands within their own product line
to try to minimize cannibalization of a brand's sales or shares.

Product Positioning Using Perceptual Maps

A key to positioning a product effectively is the perceptions of consumers. In determining a brand's position and the preferences of consumers, companies obtain three
types of data from consumers:

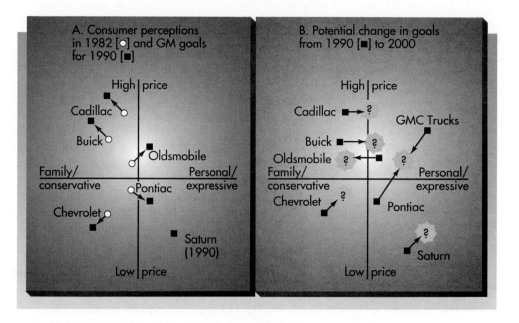

1. Evaluations of the important attributes for a product class.
2. Judgments of existing brands with the important attributes.
3. Ratings of an "ideal" brand's attributes.

From these data, it is possible to develop a **perceptual map,** a means of displaying or graphing in two dimensions the location of products or brands in the minds of consumers. The example illustrates how a manager can use perceptual maps to see how consumers perceive competing products or brands and then take actions to try to change the product offering and the image it projects to consumers.

By the 1980s General Motors (GM) was concerned that the image of its five main models of cars— Chevrolet, Pontiac, Oldsmobile, Buick, and Cadillac—had so blurred in the minds of Canadian consumers that they could not distinguish one brand from another. In fact, GM's Cadillac is still trying to overcome bad image problems from its 1981 decision to sell the Cimarron, an "economy" Cadillac that consumers saw as a thinly veiled Chevrolet Cavalier.

So in 1982 GM interviewed consumers and developed the perceptual map shown in Figure 9-9A. Note that the two dimensions on the perceptual map are (1) low price versus high price and (2) family/conservative versus personal/expressive appeal. Figure 9-9A shows that GM indeed had a problem. Although there was some variation in the vertical dimension (consumers' perception of price), there was little difference in the horizontal dimension (family/conservative appeal versus personal/expressive appeal). Then GM set new goals for where it wanted its models to be when its small car Saturn would be introduced (which turned out to be 1990). This involves **repositioning** the models, or changing the place an offering occupies in a consumer's mind relative to competitive offerings.

Figure 9-9A highlights the special 1980s problem GM faced in having its divisions sell nearly identical cars to nearly identical market segments: Pontiac went head-to-head with Chevrolet for younger buyers and Buick and Oldsmobile did the same for the sixtyish segment. So divisions were cannibalizing each others' sales. The figure shows that its 1990 goals included the following:

- Position Saturn as a low-priced, stylish import-fighter.
- Try to reposition Pontiac as a more personal/expressive (stylish) car and Chevrolet as a more family/conservative car.
- Try to reposition Buick as a higher priced, family/conservative car and Oldsmobile as a more stylish car.

Things didn't work out quite the way GM expected. One problem was the sudden love affair Canadians had with minivans, trucks, and sports utility vehicles—trends that may be permanent or just fads. To address its positioning dilemma, GM now requires every new model to be targeted at 1 of 26 precisely defined market segments. In theory, no two models are allowed to overlap, which helps separate their positioning. While these 26 market segments have not been made public, we can look at the designs and advertising for its present lines and assess where GM wants the models to be positioned in, say, the year 2000. Figure 9-9B is just such a projection. One thing is certain: Consumers of all ages want more stylish cars and are moving to the right in the positioning matrix in Figure 9-9B—especially as minivans and trucks take over more of the "family/conservative" end of the scale.[18]

Cadillac provides a case example. One question summarizes Cadillac's basic problem: how many people under 40 do you know that drive a Cadillac? The average Cadillac buyer is 63! So it's clear that Cadillac must find ways to compete with foreign rivals such as Lexus, Mercedes, and BMW. But how does Cadillac attract younger luxury-car buyers with a sleeker, smaller car without destroying its classic image and losing its present buyers?[19] One thing it didn't need was a luxury sport-utility Cadillac, which executives finally axed in 1995. Instead, Cadillac introduced the Catera, a clone of its European-produced Opel Omega MV6, to try to attract first-time luxury car buyers.

GM also made another important decision: to combine the Pontiac division (selling Bonneville, Grand Prix, Firebird, and Grand Am brands) and the GMC truck division (selling pickup trucks, vans, and sports utility vehicles). The new unit will target younger buyers wanting sportier cars, pickup trucks, and sports utility vehicles whose models will be positioned to emphasize "physical power and outdoor activity."

Looking at GM ads and styling gives the potential repositioning of Cadillac, Pontiac, and other GM cars for the coming years. Are these projections correct? Read the ads and see for yourself. Your personal car buying decisions will affect the outcome as well.

GM's future goes far beyond the North American market. It is a global automaker in search of opportunities around the world. Recently, it negotiated a joint venture with China, a country that represents a huge potential market for the twenty-first century.

CONCEPT CHECK   1. What is cross tabulation?

2. What are some advantages of cross tabulations?

3. Why do marketers use perceptual maps in product positioning decisions?

SUMMARY

1. Market segmentation is aggregating prospective buyers into groups that have common needs and will respond similarly to a marketing action.
2. A straightforward approach to segmenting, targeting, and reaching a market involves five steps: (a) form prospective buyers into segments by characteristics such as their needs, (b) form products to be sold into groups, (c) develop a market-product grid and estimate size of markets, (d) select target markets, and (e) take marketing actions to reach the target markets.
3. The main dimensions used to segment Canadian consumer markets include geographic, demographic, psychographic, and behavioural segmentation. There are a number of variables within each dimension that can be used for segmentation purposes. For example, using demographic segmentation, a marketer can use age, gender, education, or income as segmenting

variables. Organizational markets can be segmented on geographic, demographic, and behavioural dimensions. Typical variables used to segment organizational markets include NAICS codes, and size of firm.
4. Criteria used (a) to segment markets and (b) to choose target segments are related but different. The former includes potential to increase profits, similarity of needs of buyers within a segment, difference of needs among segments, and feasibility of a resulting marketing action. The latter includes market size, expected growth, the competitive position of the firm's offering in the segment, and the cost of reaching the segment.
5. A market-product grid is a useful way to display what products can be directed at which market segments, but the grid must lead to marketing actions for the segmentation process to be worthwhile.

6. Cross tabulations are widely used today in market segmentation studies to identify needs of various customer segments and the actions to reach them.

7. A company can position a product head-to-head against the competition or seek a differentiated position. A concern with positioning is often to avoid cannibalization of the existing product line. In positioning, a firm often uses consumer judgments in the form of perceptual maps to locate its product relative to competing ones.

KEY TERMS AND CONCEPTS

market segmentation p. 216
market segments p. 216
product differentiation p. 216
market-product grid p. 218
synergy p. 219
usage rate p. 223

80/20 rule p. 223
cross tabulation p. 231
product positioning p. 233
perceptual map p. 235
repositioning p. 235

CHAPTER PROBLEMS AND APPLICATIONS

1. What variables might be used to segment these consumer markets? (*a*) lawnmowers, (*b*) frozen dinners, (*c*) dry breakfast cereals, and (*d*) soft drinks.

2. What variables might be used to segment these organizational markets? (*a*) industrial sweepers, (*b*) photocopiers, (*c*) computerized production control systems, and (*d*) car rental agencies.

3. In Figure 9-6 the dormitory market segment includes students living in university-owned residence halls and fraternities. What market needs are common to these students that justify combining them into a single segment in studying the market for your Wendy's restaurant?

4. You may disagree with the estimates of market size given for the rows in the market-product grid in Figure 9-6. Estimate the market size, and give a brief justification for these market segments: (*a*) dormitory students, (*b*) day commuters, and (*c*) people who work in the area.

5. Suppose you want to increase revenues from your fast-food restaurant shown in Figure 9-7 even further. What advertising actions might you take to increase revenues from (*a*) dormitory students, (*b*) dinners, and (*c*) after-dinner snacks from night commuters?

6. Look back at Figure 8-6 in Chapter 8. Which questions would you pair to form a cross tabulation to uncover the following relationships? (*a*) frequency of fast-food restaurant patronage and restaurant characteristics important to the customer, (*b*) age of the head of household and source of information used about fast-food restaurants, (*c*) frequency of patronage of Wendy's and source of information used about fast-food restaurants, or (*d*) how much children have to say about where the family eats and number of children in the household.

7. Look back at Figure 9-8A. (*a*) Run the percentages vertically and tell what they mean. (*b*) Express all numbers in the table as a percentage of the total number of people sampled (586) and tell what the percentages mean.

8. In Figure 9-8, (*a*) what might be other names for the three patronage levels shown in the columns? (*b*) Which is likely to be of special interest to Wendy's and why?

CASE 9-1   Cantel

INTRODUCTION

Rogers Cantel Mobile Communications Inc. (Cantel) (www.rogers.com), owns and operates Canada's largest and only nationally licensed wireless (cellular) telephone company. It also operates a national paging service, a wireless data communications service, and a chain of retail service centres for the sale and service of wireless equipment. Cantel competes with the cellular subsidiaries of the "wireline" companies such as Bell Canada, Maritime Tel & Tel, Alberta Government Telephone or BC Tel, which also offer conventional telephone services via telephone wires. Cantel has spent over $1.5 billion on high-quality mobile facilities from coast to coast to provide cellular service to its customers.

HOW CELLULAR PHONES WORK

A cellular phone uses radio signals instead of wires to transmit calls. The cellular networks are connected to the public wireline phone system allowing cellular users to make calls to, or receive calls from, virtually any other phone in the world. As a cellular network service provider,

Cantel has erected hundreds of transmitters across the country; each transmitter serves an area called a "cell." As a cellular subscriber uses a phone in a moving car, or walks down the street, a switching computer "hands off" the call from one cell to another without interruption of the call.

CANTEL

Cantel first launched cellular service in July 1985 in Montreal and Toronto. In July 1987 Cantel was the first cellular company to complete continuous coverage of the 1200 kilometre corridor from Windsor, Ontario, through to Quebec City. This corridor has since almost doubled in length and now extends 2000 kilometres through to the Atlantic coast, making it the longest cellular corridor in North America. Cantel's cellular network covers cities and corridors in all ten Canadian provinces. Today more than 93 percent of the Canadian population has access to Cantel service.

In less than 10 years, cellular penetration in Canada went from 0 to 9 percent. In 1995, Cantel had over 1 million cellular subscribers and over 200 000 paging subscribers. Cantel expects wireless penetration to triple in the next five years. In 1996 Cantel began offering its customers digital personal communications services (PCS)—an innovative and superior technology for transmitting and receiving data. The service includes paging, e-mail, mobile faxing, and voice mail. Cantel also offers international cellular service that allows its customers to make and receive calls in over 40 countries. A long-term strategic alliance with AT&T Canada, including a co-branding agreement, also provides Cantel an opportunity to provide seamless availability of its services, including digital PCS throughout Canada and the United States.

In an effort to further penetrate the market, Cantel offers an all-in-one cellular service program called Amigo for as low as $19.95 per month. The package includes a lightweight cellular phone and a choice between two different calling plans.

Questions

1. Segment the market for cellular phone subscribers.
2. Who are the key target segments for cellular phones?
3. How should Cantel position its cellular service in those target segments?

EIGHT INCHES OF SNOW, WHITE OUTS AND BLACK ICE

WE SUGGEST YOU STAY OFF THE ROADS.

 SKI SEASON. AND THAT MEANS JUST GETTING TO THE SLOPES CAN BE MORE TREACHEROUS THAN ATTACKING A 60 DEGREE DOUBLE DIAMOND. OF COURSE

YOU OWN THE JEEP. GRAND CHEROKEE LIMITED 4 X 4, ALMOST NOTHING THIS SIDE OF AN AVALANCHE IS GOING TO KEEP YOU AWAY. YOU CAN MAKE YOUR OWN TRACK

WITH THE EXCLUSIVE QUADRA TRAC™ FOUR WHEEL DRIVE SYSTEM THAT SENSES WHAT TIRES OFFER THE MOST AVAILABLE GRIP AND APPLIES THE POWER ACCORDINGL

AND POWER IT HAS WITH THE AVAILABLE 5.2 LITRE V8 THAT OFFERS 220 HORSES TO PULL YOU THROUGH, OR UP JUST ABOUT ANYTHING. SO ON ONE OF THOSE BLUSTER

WINTER DAYS WHEN YOU'RE CAUGHT WAITING FOR THE SKI LIFT OPERATOR TO ARRIVE YOU CAN FIND YOUR OWN WAY TO THE TOP. OR JUST FIND YOUR OWN MOUNTAIN

THERE'S ONLY ONE

CHRYSLER CANADA ★ 1 800 361 3700

CHAPTER 10

Relationship Marketing, Information Technology, and Forecasting

AFTER READING THIS CHAPTER YOU SHOULD BE ABLE TO:

• Define and explain the use and importance of relationship marketing.

• Describe how information technology and database marketing have led to today's relationship marketing strategy.

• Describe the factors that have made relationship marketing both necessary and possible.

• Recognize structured and unstructured marketing decisions and their impact on data used in information systems.

• Recognize the top-down and buildup approaches to forecasting sales.

• Use the lost-horse and linear trend extrapolation methods to make a simple forecast.

GOOD NEWS FOR CONSUMERS: OLD-FASHIONED, PERSONALIZED RELATIONSHIPS ARE BACK!

You may have recently been surprised to receive a personal invitation to test drive a brand new Jeep (www.jeepunpaved.com), Mercedez Benz, Volvo, or BMW. How and why did these companies do that?

If you often shop from catalogues, you may have noticed that they seem to have more products that match your interests. Catalogue companies can now digitally print individualized catalogues: frequent shirt buyers get extra shirt selections, book purchasers more book options, younger consumers more sporting goods, older customers more convenience items. Similarly, credit card companies such as Royal Bank Visa and American Express send offers in your bill that are related to recent purchases.

If you read your direct-mail offerings you have probably received personal notes such as the following:

> Thanks, Ms. Hughes, for completing your payments on women's apparel. To show our thanks we are offering you up to 50 percent savings plus deferred payment until next January 6th.

You may have also read a magazine containing an ad with your name and a personal appeal in it.

Why are you receiving so much attention? Firms are trying to develop long-term, personal relationships with current customers. The actions acknowledge the potential for repeat purchases and the high cost of replacing existing customers. These one-to-one marketing activities are made possible by giant databases filled with information on a household's or individual's purchase histories, sizes, anniversary and birth dates, store patronage, and television viewing behaviour. They give companies the power to

MARKETING INFORMATION IN TODAY'S DATABASES CAN BE DISPLAYED CREATIVELY TO HELP TARGET SPECIFIC HOUSEHOLDS OR CUSTOMERS.

almost duplicate with you the kind of old-fashioned relationship small-town or neighbourhood retailers had with your grandparents![1]

Welcome to the era of relationship marketing? In this context, relationship marketing has a far more specific meaning than simply good relationships with customers. Here, the term **relationship marketing** is an organization's effort to develop a long-term, cost-effective link with individual customers for mutual benefit.[2] Relationship marketing extends the concept of market segmentation described in the last chapter to marketing actions undreamed of a decade ago. For example, when using geographic market segmentation, grocery product firms and supermarket chains have found that it isn't good enough to focus on a city or even a postal code area; they are now narrowing the target to a bull's-eye of an individual household or specific person in that household. Today's databases enable marketing strategists to identify these target customers with computer analyses and displays (like that shown above) and to reach specific households with personal, customized offers.

The result: a revolution in marketing information collection and use that will restructure the links between Canadian and international firms and their customers into the twenty-first century. This chapter first discusses customer value in the age of information and then covers what has made relationship marketing both necessary and possible, how information technology is used in marketing, and sales forecasting.

CREATING CUSTOMER VALUE AND COMPETITIVE ADVANTAGE IN THE AGE OF INFORMATION

Advances in our ability to collect and use information have led many to refer to this period as the age of information. To understand the impact of information and information technology on consumer and businesses today, let us (1) discuss the new consumer "marketspace," and (2) describe the elements of information-based marketing that can help create customer value and provide firms with a strategic competitive advantage.

The New Consumer Marketspace

Consumers and businesses today face two types of markets—the traditional *marketplace,* where physical buyers and physical sellers meet, and the new information-based electronic marketplace, or *marketspace.* For example, banks offer a physical office and on-line services, airlines sell tickets at airports and through electronic reservation systems, and some newspapers are now available in print and electronic form. Other offerings, such as voice mail, may exist only in the marketspace. While the end result of transactions in the two markets may be similar, the process of creating value is very different.

When transactions occur in the marketspace, information is accessed more easily, arranged in different ways, and available in larger amounts. In addition, consumers learn about and purchase products differently than they do in the marketplace. To provide value, companies must determine how information can be useful to consumers. At Digital Equipment Corporation, for example, a World Wide Web site is available for prospective customers to contact sales representatives or search for products. Similarly, Federal Express customers can now locate a package in transit or identify the name of the person who accepts it through the FedEx World Wide Web site. Information technology such as the World Wide Web also facilitates the development of relationships between buyers and sellers in the marketspace.[3] The Marketing NewsNet box discusses some of the possible implications of continued growth of the marketspace in the future.[4]

Three Key Elements of Information-Based Marketing

Figure 10-1 shows three elements in the structure that develop continuing, one-to-one relationships between an organization and its customers: (1) information technology, (2) database marketing, and (3) relationship marketing.

Information technology   Since the advent of computers after World War II and personal computers in the 1980s, management perceptions of the value and use of information have changed significantly. Even the terms are changing: while a decade ago managers talked about *manufacturing information systems* and *marketing information systems,* the lines of separation of information among the various departments in a firm are now disappearing. So today, all generally fall under the broader term of **information technology** (IT), which involves designing and managing a computer and communication system to satisfy an organization's requirements for information processing and access.[5]

With the existence of today's massive databases, marketing managers are able to query and analyze data almost instantaneously. For example, Sunkist used a geodemographic database developed by Compusearch of Toronto to pinpoint the postal districts of the areas of greatest orange consumption in Canada.[6]

Database marketing   The Sunkist example suggests marketing strategies at the postal district level. But many firms have discovered this is not good enough—they need to target specific households, individuals, or organizational customers. Enter database marketing, the middle step in Figure 10-1. **Database marketing** is an organization's effort to collect demographic, media, and consumption profiles of customers in order to target them more effectively.

As described later in the chapter, traditional media like TV and magazines are becoming less and less cost-effective in reaching customers, so database marketing often utilizes direct marketing tools—such as catalogues and direct mail—to target customers efficiently. A survey of the 500 major Canadian businesses revealed that over 90 percent of them use database marketing as part of their overall marketing strategy.[7] Sears Canada, for example, has a database of 4 million customers and uses it to develop

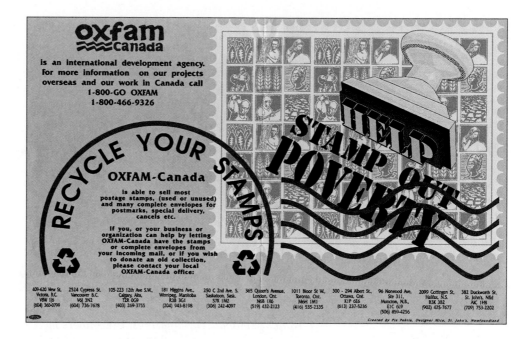

cost-efficient and well-targeted marketing programs. Many nonprofit organizations in Canada also maintain comprehensive databases on current and prospective donors to their causes. Organizations such as Oxfam-Canada, Second Harvest, and many universities use their databases for direct-mail solicitations. Oxfam-Canada, for example, used a very successful direct-mail program to generate financial donations to aid the people of Rwanda.

Relationship marketing   While database marketing is a giant step beyond the traditional market segmentation strategy, it still falls short of the ideal—a near-personal or one-to-one continuing interaction between the seller and customer.[8] As shown in the top step of Figure 10-1, this leads to today's focus on relationship marketing—an organization's effort to develop a long-term, cost-effective link with individual customers for mutual benefit. Consumers benefit in several ways. First, the marketing programs directed at them should be much more efficient, exposing them only to offerings they are very likely to want or need. Second, many consumers value the personal attention and convenience of relationship marketing. Finally, the availability of detailed information about consumer preferences should eliminate unnecessary duplication of products and services.[9] You should also remember that relationship marketing is utilized by firms who sell to organizational consumers and also by nonprofit organizations.[10] Organizations that are successful at relationship marketing create a competitive advantage over rivals who do not use information and information technology as an asset. Examples throughout the chapter will illustrate how organizations are trying to achieve this competitive advantage.

CONCEPT CHECK

1.   What is relationship marketing?

2.   How do information technology and database marketing relate to relationship marketing?

RELATIONSHIP MARKETING: THE REVOLUTION ARRIVES

As shown in Figure 10-2, relationship marketing forces today's marketing manager to be increasingly aware of many complex factors. To comprehend further how relationship marketing has revolutionized today's market segmentation and marketing mix actions, it is necessary to analyze (1) what has made relationship marketing necessary and (2) what has made relationship marketing possible.

What Makes Relationship Marketing Necessary: The Causes

Two sources of marketing problems have helped trigger the rise of relationship marketing: (1) more demanding consumers and (2) excessive business costs.

More demanding consumers   As mentioned in Chapter 3, today's consumers are constantly changing. But Box 1 in Figure 10-2 notes that one common factor remains: consumers are far more demanding than they were even five years ago. Research studies show that consumers

- *Want "personalized" offerings.* Consumers increasingly seek the combination of product and services that are tailored to their unique wants and needs. For example, 10 days after specifying their unique wants in a new car order, Japanese consumers buying a Toyota will have their built-to-order car.
- *Desire high quality and value.* Consumers are willing to pay a premium for quality, the characteristics of which consumers rank from top to bottom as: reliability, durability, ease of maintenance, ease of use, a known or trusted brand name, and (last) low price.[11]

FIGURE 10-2

COMPLEX FACTORS INFLUENCE
MARKETING MANAGERS AS THEY
DEVELOP RELATIONSHIP MARKETING
STRATEGIES

Note: Blue boxes show consumer and business factors that have made relationship marketing necessary, while green boxes show the data and data collection methods that have made relationship marketing possible.

- *Require "caring" customer service.* Effective customer service means having the seller's representatives treat customers like they want to be treated. For IBM this means an electronic customer support system that automatically diagnoses potential trouble to alert IBM service people, who sometimes show up on a customer's doorstep *before* the glitch appears on the customer's IBM equipment.[12]
- *Have reduced loyalty to sellers.* For today's consumer, the issue is not that a product, brand, or store served their needs last year but whether it will serve their needs today. Sellers have discovered that defecting customers exact a terrible price in lost revenues, which re-emphasizes the importance of the continuing customer links of relationship marketing. Studies show that reducing customer defections by 5 percent increases the future profit stream from 30 percent to 85 percent, depending on the business.

Excessive business costs   Box 2 in Figure 10-2 identifies some of the key sources of excessive business costs that have driven today's manufacturers and retailers to use relationship marketing. Poor quality can lead directly to new product failures (discussed in greater detail in Chapter 11), customer defections, and billions of dollars in lost revenues and profit. Surveys of top executives of Canadian firms show that they feel improving product and service quality is the most critical challenge facing them in the coming years.

Gaining distribution on retailers' shelves is increasingly costly and, as will be discussed in Chapter 11, may actually require manufacturers to pay for retail shelf space for new products. The cost of retail distribution has triggered relationship marketing strategies because both retailers and manufacturers now have computerized records telling them how much revenue retail shelf space should and actually does generate. Products not meeting sales targets are dropped.

In past years, large grocery product manufacturers spent hundreds of millions of dollars annually on radio, TV, and magazine advertisements. Much of this was wasted because consumers have become increasingly blasé about these messages, many of which are no longer penetrating the consumers' consciousness.[13] The result: these grocery product firms have cut back substantially on national advertising campaigns and instead use database marketing and relationship marketing strategies to select more cost-effective methods to communicate with the specific customers they want to reach. An example is the checkout-counter screen at some supermarkets (shown below) that can give customers coupons to encourage repeat purchases, buying complementary products (e.g., coupons for baby food to those buying diapers), or even switching to competing brands.

But there are two potential drawbacks in developing the huge databases often needed for relationship marketing. One is cost. The second drawback is the growing

WHAT MAY LIE IN YOUR FUTURE: PRESS A TOUCH-SENSITIVE SCREEN AT YOUR SUPERMARKET CHECKOUT COUNTER TO RECEIVE COUPONS OR RECIPES WHILE YOUR BILL IS TALLIED. THE TEXT DESCRIBES HOW CHECKOUT SCREENS LIKE THIS ARE REPLACING NATIONAL TV AND MAGAZINE ADS.

APPLYING SUNSHINE PRINCIPLES TO CONSUMER INFORMATION DATABASES

As the use of database marketing programs increases, companies are faced with increasing concerns by consumers regarding the collection and use of personal information. Legislation has addressed some of the concerns.

However, rather than rely on regulatory restrictions, two business professors suggest that companies engaged in database marketing should follow "sunshine principles." That is, database practices should be able to withstand the scrutiny of interested consumers in the light of full disclosure. Their approach includes several guidelines:

1. Data users must have the clear assent of the data subject to use personal data for database marketing purposes.
2. Companies are responsible for the accuracy of the data they use, and the data subjects should have the right to access, verify, and change information about themselves.
3. Categorizations should be based on actual behaviour as well as the more traditional criteria of attitudes, lifestyles, and demographics.

What are the advantages and disadvantages of these guidelines for consumers? For companies?

concern by consumers about the collection of personal information. The accompanying Ethics and Social Responsibility Alert describes guidelines that may address issues of privacy and reduce consumers' concerns.[14]

What Makes Relationship Marketing Possible: Information Technology

Marketing data have little value by themselves: they are simply facts or statistics. To translate data to information the data must be unbiased, timely, pertinent to the problem, accessible, and organized and presented in a way that helps the marketing manager make decisions that lead to marketing actions. This section covers key sources of information—including consumers' homes, businesses, single-source data services, and on-line databases—that have been revolutionized by technological breakthroughs in the collection, organization, and presentation of marketing data.

In-home data   To develop relationship marketing strategies, as shown in Box 3 in Figure 10-2, marketing managers need large amounts of raw data about consumers and their households—demographics and lifestyles, TV viewing habits, use of other promotional media (such as magazines, newspapers, and coupons), and their purchases. Historically, there have been two especially severe problems in collecting these data: (1) cost, and (2) the potential bias in the data collected. Breakthroughs in technology in the past decade have addressed both issues. Recently invented "smart cards" now contain detailed data on a consumer's demographics, lifestyle, and household. In-home optical scanners used by services such as Arbitron can record purchases not captured by, say, supermarket scanners. Data on TV viewing and use of other promotional media such as coupons and direct mail are captured electronically and inexpensively with little intrusion on the consumer's activities. It is important not to intrude on a consumer in order to avoid having the measurement process alter the consumer's normal behaviour. This concern is the reason Nielsen plans to replace today's people meters with "passive people meters." If this type of meter works as planned, its image-recognition computerized camera will automatically record who is watching TV without their having to push buttons to register their viewing behaviour.

At-business data   Business firms themselves (Box 4, Figure 10-2), collect huge volumes of detailed data for relationship marketing purposes. All of us have seen our supermarket checkout clerks use electronic scanners that "read" the universal product code (UPC) on our purchased items to record on our sales slip. Most supermarkets in Canada now use scanners which enable both the supermarkets and manufacturers to track performance weekly by store, product category, and brand level. Other retailers such as department stores, mass merchandisers, and clothing stores are increasingly using scanners to track purchases. Canadian information technology companies such as STS Systems of Point-Claire offer these retailers the software necessary to capture vital point-of-sale and tracking information.

Other businesses use electronic tracking of purchases, inventories, and reservations to facilitate their database marketing actions. Air Canada, for example, is linked to travel agents and airports throughout Canada through IBM's Global Network in order to track and manage passenger reservations. Travellers can use the airline's Internet site for flight schedules, frequent flyer information, even aircraft seating maps. UPS delivery people use hand-held computers that scan a special UPS label and double as data-input keyboards to collect real-time data that permit the location of packages to be identified throughout their trips. And available now at your computer store: "notepad computers" that enable you to write directly on the screen with a special stylus in order to read and manipulate handwritten letters, numbers, and drawings while working on a personal computer. Insurance companies are using these notepad computers so that a claims adjuster for auto damages can mark the damaged auto part on an exploded-view diagram and let the notepad calculate the cost of the repair.

Single-source data: putting it all together   New marketing data services have now emerged that offer **single-source data,** information provided by a single firm on household demographics and lifestyle, purchases, TV viewing behaviour, and responses to promotions like coupons, and free samples. The significant advantage of single-source data is the ability of one service to collect, analyze, and interrelate all this information.

On-line and CD-ROM databases   With a personal computer, a modem, and some communications software, you can access thousands of on-line databases (Box 5, Figure 10-2). Hence, on-line databases are no longer restricted to huge corporations and reference libraries. As shown in Figure 10-3, information in on-line databases divides into two general categories: (1) indexes to articles in publications, which are accessed through key word searches, and (2) statistical and directory data on households, products, and companies. When desired, this information can be transferred to the user's computer. Because of the cost of the telecommunications link to these on-line databases, many libraries obtain CD-ROM (compact disc, read-only memory) format. Often updated monthly, one CD-ROM disc can contain the same amount of information as an entire 20-volume encyclopedia. Many other sources of information can now be accessed through the Internet and the World Wide Web. Web sites often provide useful information or a means of requesting additional information.[15]

CONCEPT CHECK

1. What are the factors that have made relationship marketing (a) necessary and (b) possible?

2. How do consumer products firms use relationship marketing to reach individual households or consumers?

3. What is single-source data?

FIGURE 10-3

EXAMPLES OF INFORMATION IN
ON-LINE DATABASES (PROBABLY
AVAILABLE THROUGH YOUR COLLEGE
OR PUBLIC LIBRARY)

KIND OF INFORMATION	NAME	DESCRIPTION
Indexes, abstracts, and full-text information from journals and periodicals	ABI/Research*	Covers over 800 publications on business and management topics
	Wilson Business Abstracts*†	Covers 345 journals and trade publications on business and management topics
	Canadian News Index (On-line: Infoglobe)	Covers Canadian daily newspapers
	Canadian Periodical Index (On-line: Infoglobe)	Covers English and French-language magazines
	Canadian Business Index* (On-line: CAN/OLE)	Covers 200 business periodicals
Statistical and directory data on households, products, and companies	Statistics Canada Catalogue (On-line: CAN/OLE)	Lists all Statistics Canada publications
	Directory of Associations in Canada (On-line: CAN/OLE)	Lists Canadian associations of all kinds
	D&B's Canadian Key Business Directory (On-line: Dialog)	Directory of public and private Canadian companies, including financial data

*Also available on CD-ROM.
†Formerly called "Business Periodicals Index."

USING INFORMATION TECHNOLOGY IN MARKETING

Let's look at (1) when information technology is needed in marketing and (2) key elements in an information system.

When Information Technology Is Needed in Marketing

Not every firm needs information technology to help it make marketing decisions. The need for it is largely determined by (1) the value versus the cost of marketing information and (2) the kinds of decisions a marketing manager makes and how they relate to the information included in the information system.

Trade-offs: value versus cost of marketing data   Information and data can be valuable commodities, but they can also be very expensive. As mentioned earlier, the facts and figures that make up marketing information have no value by themselves. Their value comes from being organized and interpreted to help the decision maker reach better decisions.

In practice, a marketing manager (1) sets the priority of the data from most valuable to least valuable in solving a problem, (2) assesses the cost of collecting each kind of data, and (3) stops collecting more data on the list when the cost of collection outweighs their value in improving the decisions. Although these are very difficult guidelines to apply, they stress an important issue: the value of the data must be balanced

THESE AND MANY OTHER PRODUCTS ARE SOLD TO THE 100 MILLION HOUSEHOLDS IN THE *READER'S DIGEST* DATABASE. SEE THE NEXT PAGE TO LEARN WHY THIS DATABASE IS "THE BEST IN THE BUSINESS."

against their cost of collection and use. Great care is needed to use information technology that is user-friendly and that assists marketing managers in reaching decisions.

Kinds of decisions a marketing manager makes   A marketing manager makes two distinctly different kinds of decisions. One type is *structured decisions,* routine and repetitive decisions for which standard solutions exist. A product manager for a grocery products manufacturer may plan dozens of sales promotions (coupons and deals) over a five-year period. For these structured decisions the manager can access the information system to determine what will be the impact on case sales of moving the promotion up two weeks or changing a coupon's price allowance.

In contrast, *unstructured decisions* are complex decisions for which there are no standard solutions. For example, a department store manager may ask for an assessment of the impact on sales of changing the department's location within the store. Researchers have found that past experience is especially important for marketing managers in making unstructured decisions such as introducing new products, but not as important for structured decisions such as scheduling consumer promotions.[16]

Marketing consultant Regis McKenna predicts that advances in information technologies will soon allow "real-time" marketing decisions. He envisions "marketing workstations" that will draw on information from a network of databases containing graphic, video, audio, and numeric information. A marketing manager will be able to simulate concepts, obtain instant feedback from others on the network, make changes, request forecasts, write production orders, design advertising, evaluate media options, and schedule the introduction and rollout! In this scenario, information technology becomes a tool for fast and intelligent marketing decisions.[17]

The best information database in the consumer product industry
With a worldwide circulation of 20 million—more than that of *Time, Newsweek,* and *TV Guide* combined—*Reader's Digest* has the largest circulation in the world. But only 31 percent of the firm's profits come from the magazine, which has 39 foreign editions that include Russia and Hungary. The *Reader's Digest* crown jewel is its database that totals 100 million households.

Fortune magazine calls this database, simply, "the best in the business." If a household buys the book or video *A Passage to India,* it might receive another book on, perhaps, *Treasures of China,* or a video about India. The database permits relationship marketing and an inexpensive means of testing new product ideas. The firm's president says that the database tells the company the likes and dislikes of its many readers and that "our relationship with the reader is the key to the success of this company."[18]

FIGURE 10-4

STRATEGIC INFORMATION SYSTEM
FOR USE IN TODAY'S RELATIONSHIP
MARKETING DECISIONS

Note that this system captures marketing data from many sources using an array of devices. It then updates the databases and responds to the marketing manager's queries.

Key Elements in an Information System

Today's marketing managers are seeking user-friendly information systems to assist them in their decisions. As shown in Figure 10-4, today's strategic information system that helps a marketing manager develop relationship marketing strategies contains five key elements:

1. *Input devices.* These means of collecting marketing data include in-store and in-home scanners, people meters, and purchase/reservation workstations.
2. *Databases.* The marketing data collected by the input devices are stored in diverse databases containing data on households, products, retailers, media, and promotions.
3. *Models.* The models provide hypotheses about the relationships among the data contained in the databases to enable the decision maker to organize, interpret, and communicate the resulting information in order to reach marketing decisions.
4. *Computer network.* This is today's main means of collecting, processing, and updating the data coming from the input devices, databases, and models.
5. *Personal computer.* The PC on the marketing manager's desk serves as an input and output device and a means of querying the system to obtain and analyze the data it contains.

An information system such as this permits a marketing manager to reach decisions using **sensitivity analysis,** asking "what if" questions to determine how changes in a factor such as price or advertising affect marketing results such as sales revenues or profits.

CONCEPT CHECK

1. What is the difference between structured and unstructured decisions for a marketing manager?
2. What are the five elements in an information system?

MARKET AND SALES FORECASTING

Forecasting or estimating the actual size of a market is critical both in relationship marketing decisions and more traditional marketing decisions. This is because overestimating the size of a market may mean wasting research and development, manufacturing, and marketing dollars on new products that fail.[19] Underestimating it may mean missing the chance to introduce successful new products. We will discuss (1) some basic forecasting terms, (2) two major approaches to forecasting, and (3) specific forecasting techniques.

Basic Forecasting Terms

Unfortunately, there are no standard definitions for some forecasting concepts, so it's necessary to take care in defining the terms used.

Market or industry potential   The term **market potential,** or **industry potential,** refers to the maximum total sales of a product by all firms to a segment under specified environmental conditions and marketing efforts of the firms. For example, the market potential for cake mix sales to Canadian consumers in 2000 might be 2 million cases—what Pillsbury, Betty Crocker, Duncan Hines, and other cake mix producers would sell to Canadian consumers under the assumptions that (1) past patterns of dessert consumption continue and (2) the same level of promotional effort continues relative to other desserts. If one of these assumptions proves false, the estimate of market potential will be wrong. For example, if Canadian consumers suddenly become more concerned about eating refined sugar and shift their dessert preferences from cakes to fresh fruits, the estimate of market potential will be too high.

Sales or company forecast   What one firm expects to sell under specified conditions for the uncontrollable and controllable factors that affect the forecast is the **sales forecast,** or **company forecast.** For example, Duncan Hines might develop its sales forecast of 1 million cases of cake mix for Canadian consumers in 2000, assuming past dessert preferences continue and the same relative level of promotional expenditures among it, Pillsbury, and Betty Crocker. If Betty Crocker suddenly cuts its promotional spending in half, Duncan Hines's old sales forecast will probably be too low.

With both market potential estimates and sales forecasts, it is necessary to specify some significant details: the product involved (all cake mixes, only white cake mixes, or only Bundt cakes mixes); the time period (month, quarter, or year); the segment (Canada, Western Canada, upper-income buyer, or single-person households); controllable marketing factors (price and level of promotional support); uncontrollable factors (consumer tastes and actions of competitors); and the units of measurement (number of cases sold or total sales revenues).

Two Basic Approaches to Forecasting

A marketing manager rarely wants a single number for an annual forecast, such as 5000 units of $75 million in sales revenue. Rather the manager wants this total subdivided into elements the manager works with, such as sales by product line or sales by market segment. The two basic approaches to sales forecasting are (1) subdividing the total sales forecast (top-down forecast) or (2) building the total sales forecast by summing up the components (buildup forecast).

Top-down forecast   A **top-down forecast** involves subdividing an aggregate forecast into its principal components. A shoe manufacturer can use a top-down forecast to estimate the percentage of total shoe sales in a province and develop province-by-province forecasts for shoe sales for the coming year. *Canadian Markets,* published by the Financial Post, and *Sales and Marketing Management* magazine are sources that are widely used for top-down forecasting information.

FIGURE 10-5
PERCENTAGE OF CANADIAN
POPULATION, PERSONAL INCOME,
AND RETAIL SALES IN SELECTED
PROVINCES, 1997

PROVINCES	POPULATION % OF CDN. TOTAL	PERSONAL INCOME % OF CDN. TOTAL	RETAIL SALES % OF CDN. TOTAL
Newfoundland	1.9	1.3	1.6
Quebec	24.5	22.4	23.8
Ontario	37.7	40.4	36.2
British Columbia	13.0	13.3	14.4

For example, as shown in Figure 10-5, the province of Ontario has 37.7 percent of the Canadian population, 40.4 percent of the personal income in Canada, and 36.2 percent of Canadian retail sales.[20] If the shoe manufacturers wanted to use a single factor related to expected shoe sales, it would choose the factor that has been closely related to shoe sales historically, in this case the percentage of Canadian retail sales found in Ontario. The top-down forecast would then be that 36.2 percent of the firm's sales would be made in the province of Ontario.

A single factor is rarely a true indicator of sales opportunity in a given market. So, sometimes multiple factors are considered when making forecasts. The Buying Power Index (BPI) developed by *Sales and Marketing Management* magazine gives weights of 0.2, 0.5, and 0.3, respectively, to the three previously mentioned factors, as follows.

BPI = (0.2 × Percentage of national population in area) + (0.5 × Percentage of national personal income in area) + (0.3 × Percentage of national retail sales in area)

= (0.2 × 37.7) + (0.5 × 40.4) + (0.3 × 36.2)

= 7.54 + 20.20 + 10.86

= 38.6 = 38.6%

Thus, the BPI forecasts that 38.6 percent of the firm's shoe sales will occur in Ontario which is higher than if retail sales alone were used for the forecast. A marketer could also obtain data on retail sales and family expenditures from Statistics Canada and use this information to make sales forecasts.

Buildup forecast   A **buildup forecast** involves summing the sales forecasts of each of the components to arrive at the total forecast. It is a widely used method when there are identifiable components such as products, product lines, or market segments in the forecasting problem.

Figure 10-6 shows how Martin Marietta's aerospace department uses the buildup approach to develop a sales forecast involving three broad categories of projects or products: (1) work currently under contract that can be forecast precisely, (2) follow-up work that is likely to result from current contracts, and (3) new business that results from Martin Marietta's proposals for new business, which is difficult to forecast. Each of these three forecasts is the sum of a number of individual products or projects, which for simplicity are not shown. In turn, forecasts for each of the three kinds of business can be summed to give the total sales forecast for the entire department. Increasingly, with more detailed information available on all customers and segments in given markets, annual forecasting for Canadian firms has been transformed from a top-down forecast to a more buildup-oriented process.[21]

FIGURE 10-6

BUILDUP APPROACH TO A TWO-YEAR
SALES FORECAST FOR MARTIN
MARIETTA'S AEROSPACE VEHICLE
DEPARTMENT

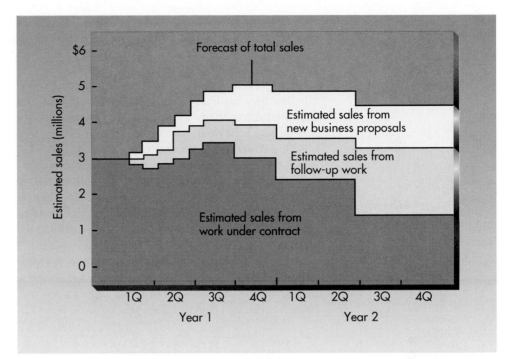

Specific Sales Forecasting Techniques

Broadly speaking, three main sales forecasting techniques are available that can lead to the forecasts used in the top-down or buildup approaches. Ordered from least costly in terms of both time and money to most costly, these are (1) judgments of the decision maker, (2) surveys of knowledgeable groups, and (3) statistical methods.

Judgments of the decision maker   Probably 99.9 percent of all sales forecasts are judgments of the person who must act on the results of the forecast—the individual decision maker. An example is the forecasts of likely sales, and hence the quantity to order, for the 13 000 items stocked in a typical supermarket that must be forecast by the stock clerk or manager. A **direct forecast** involves estimating the value to be forecast without any intervening steps. Examples appear in your daily life: How many quarts of milk should I buy? How much time should I allow to drive to the game? How much money should I get out of the automated teller machine? Your mind may go through some intervening steps but so quickly you're unaware of it.

So in estimating the amount of money to get from the automated teller machine, you probably made some unconscious (or conscious) intervening estimates (such as counting the cash in your pocket or the special events you need cash for) to obtain your direct estimate. Lost-horse forecasting does this in a more structured way. A **lost-horse forecast** involves starting with the last known value of the item being forecast, listing the factors that could affect the forecast, assessing whether they have a positive or negative impact, and making the final forecast. The technique gets its name from how you'd find a lost horse: go to where it was last seen, put yourself in its shoes, consider those factors that could affect where you might go (to the pond if you're thirsty, the hayfield if you're hungry, and so on), and go there. For example, a product manager for Wilson's tennis rackets in 1998 who needed to make a sales forecast through 2000 would start with the known value of 1998 sales and list the positive factors (more tennis courts, more TV publicity) and the negative ones (competition from other sports, high prices of graphite and ceramic rackets) to arrive at the final series of annual sales forecasts.

Surveys of knowledgeable groups   If you wonder what your firm's sales will be next year, ask people who are likely to know something about future sales. Four common groups that are surveyed to develop sales forecasts are prospective buyers, the firm's salesforce, its executives, and experts.

A **survey of buyers' intentions forecast** involves asking prospective customers whether they are likely to buy the product during some future time period. For industrial products with few prospective buyers who are able and willing to predict their future buying behaviour, this can be effective. For example, there are probably only a few hundred customers in the entire world for Boeing's largest airplanes, so Boeing simply surveys these prospects to develop its sales forecasts.

A **salesforce survey forecast** involves asking the firm's salespeople to estimate sales during a coming period. Because these people are in contact with customers and are likely to know what customers like and dislike, there is logic to this approach. However, salespeople can be unreliable forecasters—painting too rosy a picture if they are enthusiastic about a new product and too grim a forecast if their sales quota is based on it.

A **jury of executive opinion forecast** involves asking knowledgeable executives inside the firm—such as vice presidents of marketing, research and development, finance, and production—about likely sales during a coming period. Although this approach is fast and includes judgments from diverse functional areas, it can be biased by a dominant executive whose judgments are deferred to by the others.

A **survey of experts forecast** involves asking experts on a topic to make a judgment about some future event. A **Delphi forecast** is an example of a survey of experts and involves polling people knowledgeable about the forecast topic (often by mail) to obtain a sequence of anonymous estimates. The Delphi forecast gets its name from the ancient Greek oracle at Delphi who was supposed to see into the future. A major advantage of Delphi forecasting is that the anonymous expert does not have to defend his or her views or feel obliged to agree with a supervisor's estimate.

A **technological forecast** involves estimating when scientific breakthroughs will occur. In 1963, experts used the Delphi method to estimate the year by which a limited degree of weather control would occur. Their estimate: 1990! While this technological forecast looks silly today, the technique is valuable in helping managers make new product development decisions.

Statistical methods   The best-known statistical method of forecasting is **trend extrapolation,** which involves extending a pattern observed in past data into the future. When the pattern is described with a straight line, it is *linear trend extrapolation.* Suppose that in early 1987 you were a sales forecaster for the Xerox Corporation and had actual sales revenues running from 1980 to 1986 (Figure 10-7). Using linear trend extrapolation, you draw a line to fit the past data and project it into the future to give the forecast values shown for 1987 to 2000.

If in 1995 you had wanted to compare your forecasts with actual results, you would have been in for a surprise—illustrating the strength and weakness of trend extrapolation. Trend extrapolation assumes that the underlying relationships in the past will continue into the future, which is the basis of the method's key strength: simplicity. If this assumption proves correct, you have an accurate forecast. However, if this proves wrong, the forecast is likely to be wrong. In this case your forecasts from 1987 through 1993 were too low. Xerox's aggressive new product development and marketing in the late 1980s helped alter the factors underlying the linear trend extrapolation and caused the forecast to be too low. However, in 1994 the forecast and actual sales were almost identical.

In practice, marketing managers often use several of the forecasting techniques to estimate the size of markets important to them. Also, they often do three separate forecasts based on different sets of assumptions: (1) "best case" with optimistic assumptions, (2) "worst case" with pessimistic ones, and (3) "most likely case" with most reasonable assumptions.

FIGURE 10-7

LINEAR TREND EXTRAPOLATION OF
SALES REVENUES OF XEROX, MADE AT
THE START OF 1987

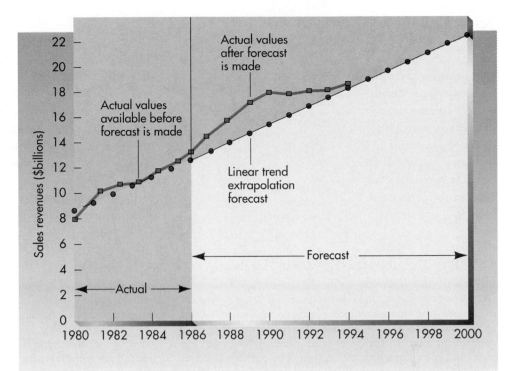

CONCEPT CHECK

1. What is the difference between the top-down and buildup approaches to forecasting sales?

2. How do you make a lost-horse forecast?

3. What is linear trend extrapolation?

SUMMARY

1. Relationship marketing is an organization's effort to develop a long-term, cost-effective link with individual customers for mutual benefit. It represents a revolutionary extension of market segmentation and, more recently, database marketing.

2. Information and information technology are increasingly seen as a means for a firm to create customer value and to obtain a competitive advantage.

3. Relationship marketing has been made necessary by more demanding consumers and excessive business and marketing costs. More than 90 percent of Canada's top 500 businesses operate database programs used for relationship marketing.

4. Relationship marketing has been made possible by breakthroughs in information technology. Key sources of information include consumers' homes, businesses, single-source data services, and on-line databases.

5. Managers generally make two kinds of decisions—structured and unstructured—and must balance the value versus the cost of information.

6. Today's strategic information system used for relationship marketing has five key elements: input devices, databases, models, computer networks, and a manager's personal computer.

7. Two basic approaches to forecasting sales are the top-down and buildup methods. Three forecasting techniques are judgments of individuals, surveys of groups, and statistical methods.

8. Individual judgments are the most widely used forecasting methods. Two common examples are direct and lost horse forecasts.

9. Asking questions of groups of people who are knowledgeable about likely future sales is another frequently used method of forecasting. Four such groups are prospective buyers, the salesforce, executives, and experts.

10. Statistical forecasting methods, such as trend extrapolation, extend a pattern observed in past data into the future.

KEY TERMS AND CONCEPTS

CHAPTER PROBLEMS AND APPLICATIONS

1. The chapter described two ways of electronically collecting information on a household's purchases: a scanner at the retailer's sales counter and an in-home scanner. How do these compare in terms of (*a*) quantity of a household's purchases measured and (*b*) possible bias reflected by consumers knowing they are being measured?

2. You walk up to the supermarket checkout counter with six cartons of yogourt you want to buy. (*a*) Describe circumstances under which the checkout procedure with electronic scanner (*1*) will measure all six items and (*2*) could miss the six items. (*b*) What problems do missing sales data cause for relationship marketing?

3. Compare the planned Nielsen passive people meter with the original people meter described in Chapter 8 in terms of (*a*) quality of information about TV viewing and (*b*) ability to get households to participate in the Nielsen TV panel.

4. Aim toothpaste runs an in-store experiment evaluating a coupon along with (*a*) in-store ads in half the stores and (*b*) no in-store ads in the other half of the stores. The results of the Aim experiment are as follows, where a sales index of 100 indicates average store sales in the weeks before the experiment.

(*a*) What are your conclusions and recommendations? (*b*) How can marketers use experiments such as this?

5. Another field experiment with coupons and in-store advertising for Wisk detergent is run. Based on the index of sales that follows, what are your conclusions and recommendations?

	WEEKS BEFORE COUPON	WEEK OF COUPON	WEEK AFTER COUPON
Without in-store ads	100	144	108
With in-store ads	100	268	203

6. In designing an information system, the format in which information is presented to a harried marketing manager is often vital. (*a*) If you were a marketing manager and interrogated your information system, would you rather see the results as they are shown in question 4 or question 5? (*b*) What are one or two strengths and weaknesses of each format?

7. What is the impact of information technology like that used by Air Canada on consumers, travel agents, corporations, and other airlines?

8. Suppose you are associate dean of your university or college's business school responsible for scheduling courses for the school year. (*a*) What repetitive information would you include in your information system to help schedule classes? (*b*) What special, one-time information might affect your schedule? (*c*) What standardized output reports do you have to provide? When?

9. Suppose you are to make a sales forecast using a top-down approach to estimate the percentage of a manufacturer's total Canadian sales going to each of the 10 provinces. You plan to use only a single factor—percentage of Canadian population, percentage of personal income, or percentage of retail sales. Which of the three factors would you use if your sales forecast were for each of the following manufacturers, and why? (*a*) Sifto salt, (*b*) Christian Dior dresses, and (*c*) Columbia records.

10. Which of the following variables would linear trend extrapolation be more accurate for? (*a*) Annual population of Canada or (*b*) annual sales of cars produced in Canada by General Motors. Why?

CASE 10-1   UPS

Reliability. Dependability. Consistency. These are the attributes that help to foster trust between buyers and sellers and provide the foundation for relationship marketing. United Parcel Service or UPS personifies this commitment to earning the customer's trust—by providing innovations that directly benefit customers in large part through the use of state-of-the-art information technology.

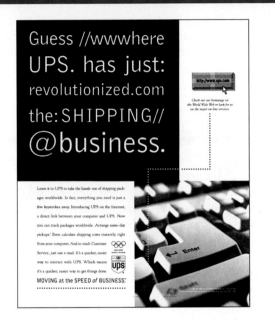

THE COMPANY

UPS was founded in 1907. Committed to serving the customer, UPS has grown to be the largest package and freight delivery service in the world. UPS serves every one of the companies listed in the Fortune 500, reaches over 80 percent of the people on earth, and handles more than 12 million packages a day from its air hub. The familiar brown trucks and vans have probably delivered packages to you or a member of your family. Today UPS is one of the largest and most profitable privately owned companies in North America with revenues exceeding $19.5 billion and net profits of $943 million.

THE SERVICE

United Parcel Service offers a wide range of services including next-day, two-day, and three-day delivery options, Saturday delivery, 24-hour tracking and immediate confirmation of delivery, and express service to more than 200 countries and territories worldwide. In addition, UPS has recently introduced a homepage on the World Wide Web (www.ups.com) to allow customers to track packages, arrange same-day pickups, and access rate information for costing out shipments. UPS also makes label printers available to its largest customers so they can do their own addressing and increase efficiency.

While UPS was founded on a premise of dependable, quality service almost 90 years ago, the basis for ensuring that service has increasingly been technology based. UPS utilizes a sophisticated computer network to not only track, trace and bill for their transportation services

but also to allow for customization of the service to suit the needs of the individual customer.

Information technology allows UPS to capture information electronically for almost immediate use. For example, the technology allows UPS to identify and contact the closest route driver for speedy pick-up of packages. A one-inch square UPS bar-code is placed on each and every package which allows the package to be tracked through the UPS system from the sender to the intended recipient. Delivery drivers even capture the signatures from those accepting the delivery with electronic clipboards. International deliveries benefit from the UPS information system that allows for packages to clear customs before the package and plane actually arrive on the ground at their foreign destination in most cases.

UPS's commitment to relationship marketing was instrumental in their gaining a five-year, $1 billion contract with J. C. Penney for their package shipments. This is not a simple agreement to carry and deliver J. C. Penney packages. Rather, it is a contract to work together to improve J. C. Penney's distribution to the mutual benefit of both parties and to create value for consumers. In the words of Ed Brockwell of UPS, "A partnership of this magnitude demands that we bring new technology and solutions to J. C. Penney which will enable them to better control costs and enhance service."

UPS, of course, benefits by obtaining what has been called "the largest distribution contract ever announced in the industry." J. C. Penney, on the other hand, benefits from UPS's expertise in the distribution business. As a result of this partnership, J. C. Penney anticipates customer service improvements and cost reductions in bar-code scanning, paperwork reduction, and increased use of electronic data interchange. So dedicated is UPS to maintaining a long-standing, mutually beneficial relationship with J. C. Penney that they assigned a full-time team, comprised of managers from Engineering, Finance, Information Services, and Customer Service to work with J. C. Penney on its distribution network.

THE COMPETITION

Federal Express is the major competitor to UPS although there are a number of other players in the delivery industry. The two major rivals have each developed their own versions of computer systems designed to provide closer links between individual business customers and the package and freight delivery service provider. Federal Express pioneered the idea with PowerShip which was followed by UPS's MaxiShip. Both are database systems given to individual business customers. These systems allow shipping customers to store addresses and shipping data, print attractive mailing labels, and track packages.

These systems also appear to encourage customer loyalty. After receiving a PowerShip system, Disney Stores increased its use of Federal Express for expedited orders from 60 to 95 percent. UPS claims that business increases at least 20 percent when a customer receives a MaxiShip system. These types of computer systems, referred to as EDI (electronic data interchange) systems because they allow the buyer and seller to share information, help to strengthen communication and the relationship between shippers and their customers.

THE ISSUES

UPS managers face a complex set of factors which are likely to influence their relationship marketing strategies in the future. First, consumers' needs are constantly changing as they try to match specific services (e.g., next day, two day, etc.) with particular products or businesses. In addition, as businesses expand their activities into the global marketplace, the demand for delivery to a growing number of global destinations will increase. Second, UPS and its customers will continue to need new methods for reducing costs. The web site, for example, will allow UPS to reduce the cost of human operators required for package-tracking inquiries. Similarly, customers will search for ways to manage their shipping function more efficiently. Third, improving methods of collecting customer-specific data and maintaining an up-to-date database will require continuous management of UPS's information technology. Finally, UPS managers must create personal customized services that will have value for individual customers.

Questions

1. What different types of information technologies does UPS employ? How do they increase customer satisfaction and reduce cost?

2. FedEx, and potentially other competitors, have EDI database systems to more closely link customers with the service provider. How can UPS develop a competitive advantage with their service?

3. What was the role of relationship marketing in UPS's $1 billion contract with J. C. Penney?

PART FOUR

SATISFYING MARKETING OPPORTUNITIES

Part Four covers the unique combination of products, price, place, and promotion that results in an offering for potential customers. How products are developed and managed is the focus of Chapters 11 and 12, and services are covered in Chapter 13. Pricing is covered in Chapters 14 and 15 and Appendix B. Three chapters address the place (distribution) element, which includes retailing innovations. Finally, three promotion chapters cover topics ranging from Pepsi's integrated marketing communications, to advertising on TSN's web site—to Julie Rasmussen's efforts to sell cosmetics in Russia, Ukraine, Kazakhstan, and the Baltics.

CHAPTER 11

Developing New Products

AFTER READING THIS CHAPTER YOU SHOULD BE ABLE TO:

• Understand the ways in which consumer and industrial products can be classified and marketed.

• Explain the implications of alternative ways of viewing "newness" in new products.

• Analyze the factors contributing to a product's success or failure.

• Recognize and understand the purposes of each step of the new-product process.

WHAT'S NEW?

What do you think about the following new products? Do you think there is a market for them? Would you be interested in buying them? How about a pair of air-conditioned shoes? Each shoe is equipped with bellows in the heel that blow in a gust of cool air with every step. What about a new type of pencil made from recycled newspaper instead of wood? How about an electric carpet designed to heat the floor under your feet? What about a watch that can track your speed down a ski slope? Finally, what about something new to drink?

Orbitz is a unique, natural fruit-flavoured beverage with colourful gel spheres that seem to defy gravity by remaining suspended in the liquid. The carbohydrate-based gel spheres in this "texturally enhanced beverage" have a delicate texture and deliver flavours that complement the flavour of the drink. Orbitz is available in a variety of flavours such as raspberry citrus, blueberry melon, strawberry, and vanilla orange.[1]

Some experts have referred to Orbitz as a beverage that looks like a little Lava Lamp. Orbitz is the very first commercialization of a technology called Levitations produced by a Bush Boake Allen, a food technology research company. Levitations is an ingredient process that allows beverage manufacturers to suspend particulates—little jelly balls in the case of Orbitz. By making the gel spheres the same density as the surrounding liquid, the particulates float evenly throughout the beverage with no settling or sedimentation. "Defy Gravity," Clearly Canadian's marketing theme for Orbitz, pretty much sums up the visual marketing power of the system.[2]

"There is no doubt that Orbitz is the most out-of-this-world beverage on the market," says Douglas Mason, President and CEO of the Clearly Canadian Beverage Corporation, the makers of Orbitz.[3] The Vancouver-based company believes Orbitz will be a hit with teenagers and young adults, or anyone looking for a beverage that is completely different. Orbitz comes in a distinctive 300 mL (10 ounce) glass bottle with a colourful logo and the address of the product's unconventional web site "Planet Orbitz" (www.orbitz.com). Check out their site! You'll also read more about Orbitz in the case that ends this chapter. So, would you drink Orbitz? A lot of people already do.

The essence of marketing is in developing products to meet buyer needs. A **product** is a good, service, or idea consisting of a bundle of tangible and intangible attributes that satisfies consumers and is received in exchange for money or some other unit of value. Tangible attributes include physical characteristics such as colour or sweetness, and intangible attributes include becoming healthier or wealthier. Hence, a product includes the breakfast cereal you eat, the accountant who fills out your tax return, or the Canadian Red Cross, which provides you self-satisfaction when you donate your blood. In many instances we exchange money to obtain the product, whereas in other instances we exchange our time and other valuables, such as our blood.

The life of a company often depends on how it conceives, produces, and markets new markets. Clearly Canadian Beverages realizes that in the beverage market consumers are always asking for new, innovative, and good tasting beverage alternatives. The company believes that Orbitz is exactly that. And, the company says it will continue to innovate this beverage by producing new and interesting flavour combinations and using multicolours in one bottle.

THE VARIATIONS OF PRODUCTS

A product varies in terms of whether it is a consumer or industrial good. For most organizations the product decision is not made in isolation because companies often offer a range of products. To better appreciate the product decision, let's first define some terms pertaining to products.

NIKE'S STRIKING ADS GAIN ATTENTION FOR ITS LINES OF SHOES AND CLOTHING.

Product Line and Product Mix

A **product line** is a group of products that are closely related because they satisfy a class of needs, are used together, are sold to the same customer group, are distributed through the same type of outlets, or fall within a given price range.[4] Polaroid has two major product lines consisting of cameras and film; Adidas's product lines are shoes and clothing; the Toronto Children's Hospital's product lines consist of inpatient hospital care, outpatient physician services, and medical research. Each product line has its own marketing strategy.

Within each product line is the *product item,* a specific product as noted by a unique brand, size, or price. For example, Downy softener for clothes comes in 360 mL and 700 mL sizes; each size is considered a separate item and assigned a distinct ordering code, or *stock keeping unit (SKU).*

The third way to look at products is by the **product mix,** or the number of product lines offered by a company. Cray Research has a single product line consisting of supercomputers, which are sold mostly to governments and large businesses. Pillsbury Canada, however, has many product lines consisting of Green Giant canned and frozen vegetables, Pillsbury refrigerated baked products, Prima Pasta, Old El Paso Mexican foods, and Underwood meat spreads.

Classifying Products

Both the federal government and companies classify products, but for different purposes. The government's classification method helps it collect information on industrial activity. Companies classify products to help develop similar marketing strategies for the wide range of products offered. Two major ways to classify products are by degree of product tangibility and type of user.

Degree of tangibility   Classification by degree of tangibility divides products into one of three categories. First is a *nondurable good,* an item consumed in one or a few uses, such as food products and fuel. A *durable good* is one that usually lasts over an extended number of uses, such as appliances, automobiles, and stereo equipment. *Services* are activities, deeds or other basic intangibles offered for sale, such as marketing research, health care, and education. According to this classification, government data indicate that Canada has become a service economy, the reason for a separate chapter (Chapter 13) on the topic.

This classification method also provides direction for marketing actions. Nondurable products such as Wrigley's gum are purchased frequently and at relatively low cost. Advertising is important to remind consumers of the item's existence, and wide distribution in retail outlets is essential. A consumer wanting Wrigley's Spearmint Gum would most likely purchase another brand of spearmint gum if Wrigley's were not available. Durable products, however, generally cost more than nondurable goods and last longer, so consumers usually deliberate longer before purchasing them. Therefore, personal selling is an important component in durable-product marketing because it assists in answering consumer questions and concerns.

Marketing is increasingly being used with services. Services are intangibles, so a major goal in marketing is to make the benefits of purchasing the product real to consumers. Thus, Canadian Airlines shows the fun of a vacation or the joy of seeing grandparents. People who provide the service are often the key to its success in the market because consumers often evaluate the product by the service provider they meet—the Hertz reservation clerk, the receptionist at the university admissions office, or the nurse in the doctor's office.

Type of user   The second major type of product classification is according to the user. **Consumer goods** are products purchased by the ultimate consumer, whereas

THE TIFFANY BRAND OF SILVER IS AN EXAMPLE OF A SPECIALTY GOOD.

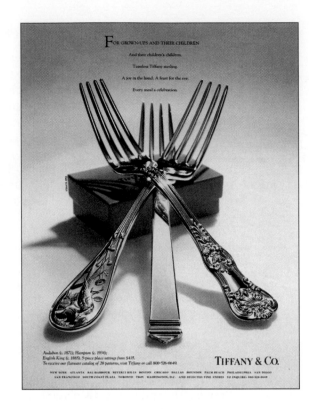

industrial goods are products used in the production of other products for ultimate consumers. In many instances the differences are distinct: Oil of Olay face moisturizer and Bass shoes are clearly consumer products, whereas DEC computers and high-tension steel springs are industrial goods used in producing other products or services.

There are difficulties, however, with this classification because some products can be considered both consumer and industrial items. A Macintosh computer can be sold to consumers as a final product or to industrial firms for office use. Each classification results in different marketing actions. Viewed as a consumer product, the Macintosh would be sold through computer stores. As an industrial product, the Macintosh might be sold by a salesperson offering discounts for multiple purchases. Classifying by the type of user focuses on the market and the user's purchase behaviour, which determine the marketing mix strategy.

CLASSIFYING CONSUMER AND INDUSTRIAL GOODS

Because the buyer is the key to marketing, consumer and industrial product classifications are discussed in greater detail.

Classification of Consumer Goods

Convenience, shopping, specialty, and unsought products are the four types of consumer goods. They differ in terms of (1) effort the consumer spends on the decision, (2) attributes used in purchase, and (3) frequency of purchase.

Convenience goods are items that the consumer purchases frequently, conveniently, and with a minimum of shopping effort. **Shopping goods** are items for which the consumer compares several alternatives on criteria, such as price, quality, or style. **Specialty goods** are items, such as Tiffany sterling silver, that a consumer makes a special effort to search out and buy. **Unsought goods** are items that the consumer either does not know about or knows about but does not initially want. Figure 11-1 shows how the classification of a consumer product into one of these four types results in different aspects of the

BASIS OF COMPARISON	TYPE OF CONSUMER GOOD			
	CONVENIENCE	**SHOPPING**	**SPECIALTY**	**UNSOUGHT**
Product	Toothpaste, cake mix, hand soap, laundry detergent	Cameras, TVs, briefcases, clothing	Rolls Royce cars, Rolex watches	Burial insurance, thesaurus
Price	Relatively inexpensive	Fairly expensive	Usually very expensive	Varies
Place (distribution)	Widespread; many outlets	Large number of selective outlets	Very limited	Often limited
Promotion	Price, availability, and awareness stressed	Differentiation from competitors stressed	Uniqueness of brand and status stressed	Awareness is essential
Brand loyalty of consumers	Aware of brand, but will accept substitutes	Prefer specific brands, but will accept substitutes	Very brand loyal; will not accept substitutes	Will accept substitutes
Purchase behaviour of consumers	Frequent purchases; little time and effort spent shopping; routine decision	Infrequent purchases; comparison shopping; uses decision time	Infrequent purchases; extensive time spent to decide and get the item	Very infrequent purchases, some comparison shopping

FIGURE 11-1   CLASSIFICATION OF CONSUMER GOODS

marketing mix being stressed. Different degrees of brand loyalty and amounts of shopping effort are displayed by the consumer for a product in each of the four classes.

The manner in which a consumer good is classified depends on the individual. One person may view a camera as a shopping good and visit several stores before deciding on a brand, whereas a friend may view cameras as a specialty good and will only buy a Nikon.

The product classification of a consumer good can change the longer a product is on the market. When first introduced, the Litton microwave oven was unique, a specialty good. Now there are competing brands on the market, and microwaves are a shopping good for many consumers.

Classification of Industrial Goods

A major characteristic of industrial goods is that their sales are often the result of *derived demand;* that is, sales of industrial products frequently result (or are derived) from the sale of consumer goods. For example, if consumer demand for Fords (a consumer product) increases, the company may increase its demand for paint-spraying equipment (an industrial product). Industrial goods are classified not only on the attributes the consumer uses but also on how the item is to be used. Thus, industrial products may be classified as production or support goods.

Production goods   Items used in the manufacturing process that become part of the final product are **production goods.** These include raw materials such as grain or lumber, as well as component parts. For example, a company that manufactures door hinges used by GM in its car doors is producing a component part. As noted in Chapter 7, the marketing of production goods is based on factors such as price, quality, delivery, and service. Marketers of these products tend to sell directly to industrial users.

Support goods   The second class of industrial goods is **support goods,** which are items used to assist in producing other goods and services. Support goods include installations, accessory equipment, supplies, and services.

- *Installations* consist of buildings and fixed equipment. Because a significant amount of capital is required to purchase installations, the industrial buyer deals directly with construction companies and manufacturers through sales representatives. The pricing of installations is often by competitive bidding.
- *Accessory equipment* includes tools and office equipment and is usually purchased in small-order sizes by buyers. As a result, instead of dealing directly with buyers, sellers of industrial accessories use distributors to contact a large number of buyers.
- *Supplies* are similar to consumer convenience goods and consist of products such as stationery, paper clips, and brooms. These are purchased with little effort, using the straight rebuy decision sequence discussed in Chapter 7. Price and delivery are key factors considered by the buyers of supplies.
- *Services* are intangible activities to assist the industrial buyer. This category can include maintenance and repair services and advisory services such as tax or legal counsel. The reputation of the seller of services is a major factor in marketing these industrial goods.

CONCEPT CHECK

1. Explain the difference between product mix and product line.

2. What are the four main types of consumer goods?

3. To which type of good (industrial or consumer) does the term *derived demand* generally apply?

NEW PRODUCTS AND WHY THEY FAIL

New products are the lifeblood of a company and keep it growing, but the financial risks are large. Before discussing how new products reach the stage of commercialization when they are available to the consumer, we'll begin by looking at *what* a new product is.

What Is a New Product?

The term *new* is difficult to define. Does changing the colour of a laundry detergent make it a new product, in the same way that a hot-air appliance which cooks like a regular oven but with the speed of a microwave is considered new? There are several ways to view the newness of a product.

Newness compared with existing products   If a product is functionally different from existing offerings, it can be defined as new. The microwave oven and automobile were once functionally new, but for most products the innovation is more a modification of an old product than a dramatic functional change.

Newness in legal terms   Consumer and Corporate Affairs Canada (CCAC) has determined that a product can be called "new" for only up to 12 months.

Newness from the company's perspective   Successful companies are starting to view newness and innovation in their products at three levels. At the lowest level, which usually involves the least risk, is a product line extension. This is an incremental improvement of an exciting or important product for the company, such as

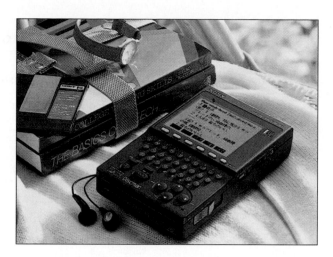

Frosted Cheerios or Diet Cherry Coke or Sensor for Women—extensions of the basic Cheerios or Diet Coke or men's Sensor product lines, respectively. At the next level is a significant jump in the innovation or technology, such as Sony's leap from the micro tape recorder to the Walkman. The third level is true innovation, a truly revolutionary new product, like the first Apple computer in 1976. Some people wonder whether Sony's Data Discman—a *portable* electronic book using a removable disc, which may lead to novels and textbooks on discs—could be such an innovation.[5] Effective new product programs in large firms deal at all three levels.

Newness from the consumer's perspective   A fourth way to define new products is in terms of their effects on consumption. This approach classifies new products according to the degree of learning required by the consumer, as shown in Figure 11-2.

With *continuous innovation,* no new behaviours must be learned. Examples include Pillsbury's Toaster Strudel that competes with Kellogg's Pop Tarts, Mercedez-Benz Canada Inc.'s SLK convertible sportscar, Cadbury Chocolate Canada's TimeOut Candy bar,

	LOW DEGREE OF CHANGE BEHAVIOUR AND LEARNING NEEDED BY CONSUMER HIGH		
BASIS OF COMPARISON	**CONTINUOUS INNOVATION**	**DYNAMICALLY CONTINUOUS INNOVATION**	**DISCONTINUOUS INNOVATION**
Definition	Requires no new learning by consumers	Disrupts consumer's normal routine but does not require totally new learning	Establishes new consumption patterns among consumers
Examples	Sensor and New Improved Tide	Electric toothbrush, compact disc player, and automatic flash unit for cameras	VCR, Jet Stream Oven, and home computer
Marketing emphasis	Generate awareness among consumers and obtain widespread distribution	Advertise benefits to consumers, stressing point of differentiation and consumer advantage	Educate consumers through product trial and personal selling

FIGURE 11-2   CONSUMPTION EFFECTS DEFINE NEWNESS

Nestle Canada's Parlour Signature line of premium ice cream, and Breathe Right nasal strips targeted toward athletes and people who snore. These innovations do not require people to change their behaviour to adopt these products. With consumer products requiring minimal consumer education, effective marketing depends on generating awareness and having strong distribution in appropriate outlets.

With *dynamically continuous innovation,* only minor changes in behaviour are required for use. An example is built-in, fold-down child seats such as those available in Chrysler minivans. Built-in car seats for children require only minor bits of education and changes in behaviour, so the marketing strategy is to educate prospective buyers on their benefits, advantages, and proper use.

A *discontinuous innovation* involves making the consumer learn entirely new consumption patterns in order to use the product. In the 1990s, a small startup firm, introduced its Jet-Stream Oven—a revolutionary cooking idea that involves moving hot air at high speeds to do the cooking. In achieving its claim of "Finally! . . . oven quality, microwave fast," the Jet-Stream Oven requires consumers to learn how to use it properly. Hence, marketing efforts involve not only gaining consumer awareness but also educating consumers on both the benefits and proper use of the innovative product. Personal selling and creative advertising are often needed to achieve this consumer education—activities that can cost millions of dollars for some discontinuous innovations.

THE JET-STREAM OVEN: A DISCONTINUOUS INNOVATION REQUIRING CONSUMER EDUCATION AND LEARNING.

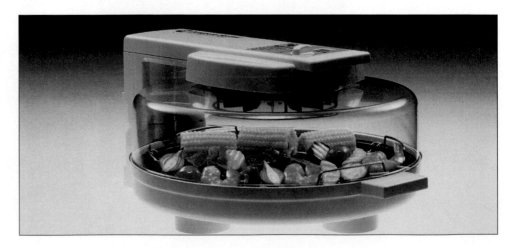

CADBURY'S TIMEOUT IS AN EXAMPLE
OF A CONTINUOUS INNOVATION.

Why Products Fail

The thousands of product failures that occur every year cost Canadian businesses millions of dollars. Some estimates place new-product failure rates as high as 80 percent. To learn marketing lessons and convert those potential failures to successes, we can analyze why new products fail and then study several failures in detail. As we go through the new-product process later in the chapter, we can identify ways such failures might have been avoided—admitting that hindsight is clearer than foresight.

Marketing reasons for new-product failures   Both marketing and non-marketing factors contribute to new-product failures.[6] Using the research results from several studies on new-product success and failure we can identify seven critical marketing factors—sometimes overlapping—that often separate new product winners and losers:[7]

1. *Insignificant "point of difference."* A distinctive "point of difference" is essential for a new product to defeat competitive ones—through having superior characteristics that deliver unique benefits to the user. Pillsbury Canada's line of low-fat refrigerated baked products fell flat with Canadian consumers who did not see these products as superior to existing products already in the freezer.[8]

FIGURE 11-3

WHY DID THESE NEW PRODUCTS
FAIL?

As explained in detail in the text, new products often fail because of one or a combination of seven reasons. Consider the two products described below, and try to identify which reason explains why they failed in the marketplace:

- Del Monte's Barbecue Ketchup that contained finely chopped onions and was aimed at the heavy ketchup-eating segment.
- Mennen's Real deodorant, a cream-like antiperspirant developed for women, that was applied like a roll-on.

Compare your insights with those in the text.

2. *Incomplete market and product definition before product development starts.* Ideally, a new product needs a precise *protocol,* a statement that, before product development begins, identifies (1) a well-defined target market; (2) specific customers' needs, wants, and preferences; and (3) what the product will be and do. Without this precision, loads of money disappear as R&D tries to design a vague product for a phantom market.

3. *Too little market attractiveness.* Market attractiveness refers to the ideal situation every new product manager looks for: a large target market with high growth and real buyer need. But often, when looking for ideal market niches, the target market is too small and competitive to warrant the R&D, production, and marketing expenses necessary to reach it. In the early 1990s Kodak discontinued its Ultralife lithium battery. Seen as a major breakthrough because of its 10-year shelf life, the battery was touted as lasting twice as long as an alkaline battery. Yet the product was only available in the 9-volt size, which accounts for less than 10 percent of the batteries sold.[9]

4. *Poor execution of the marketing mix.* Coca-Cola thought its Minute Maid Squeeze-Fresh frozen orange juice concentrate in a squeeze bottle was a hit. The idea was that consumers could make one glass of juice at a time, and the concentrate stayed fresh in the refrigerator for over a month. After two test markets, the product was finished. Consumers loved the idea, but the product was messy to use, and the advertising and packaging didn't educate them effectively on how much concentrate to mix.

5. *Poor product quality on critical factors.* Overlapping somewhat with point 1, this factor stresses that poor quality on one or two critical factors can kill the product, even though the general quality is high. For example, the Japanese, like the British, drive on the left side of the road. Until 1996 North American carmakers sent Japan few right-drive cars—unlike German carmakers who exported right-drive models in a number of their brands.[10]

6. *Bad timing.* The product is introduced too soon, too late, or at a time when consumer tastes are shifting dramatically. Good timing is a special problem with fad or fashion products (discussed in Chapter 12). Exploding sales to consumers of T-shirts and sweatshirts with names of professional sports teams turned to huge piles of unbought merchandise in 1995, following the baseball strike and hockey lockout that alienated many fans. Also, the sports fashions changed. Now hot among kids are sports-related clothes featuring in-your-face slogans like "Life is a contact sport" and "You let up, you lose."[11]

7. *No economical access to buyers.* Grocery products provide an example. Today's mega-supermarkets carry 30 000 different products (meaning they carry 30 000 different SKUs). With more than 15 000 new food products introduced each year, the fight for shelf space is tremendous in terms of costs for advertising, distribution, and shelf space.[12] Because shelf space is judged in terms of sales per

MARKETING NEWSNET

BLACK'S DEVELOPS NET PHOTOFINISHING SERVICE

Black Photo Corp. of Markham, Ontario, has launched the first Canadian Internet photofinishing service called Online Photo Centre. For $5.49 plus regular processing fees, Canadian consumers can have personal photos scanned and mounted on-line in less than five days. By using a password to access the photos, customers can then send the shots via e-mail, or order reprints and other photo services on-line.

The photos, which can also be downloaded to personal PCs, are kept on-line in Black's database for 30 days, or longer at a fee of $2.99 per month. Carol Reader, Black's vice president of marketing, says the new service is the second program this year that is a "reinforcement of Black's quality and point of difference." In April the company launched Fix Your Little Mistakes—a free photo touch-up service. Reader also says the Online Photo Centre was a result of increased consumer interest in digital cameras, and the growing trend of scanning photos to disc or CD-ROM.

The service is available at the company's web site (www.blackphoto.com), but says Reader, "This isn't just a web site, this is an opportunity of having photos scanned and being able to share them instantly, which is a true consumer benefit." The program is targeted at families, with a skew to female heads of households. A national radio and national direct-mail campaign is supporting the launch. In addition, national in-store demonstrations are being used, and Black's is also offering an MGI PC Photo Fun software kit, plus free Internet access for one month on Sympatico.

square foot, a new product must displace an existing product on the supermarket shelves. Many small manufacturers simply do not have the money to gain effective exposure for their products.

A look at some failures   Before reading further, study the product failures described in Figure 11-3, and try to identify which of the seven reasons is the most likely explanation for their failure. The two examples are discussed in greater detail below.

Del Monte aimed its Barbecue Ketchup to the heavy ketchup-using segment—children and teenagers. The problem is that most consumers in this segment hate onions, so the product's difference—onions mixed with regular ketchup—worked against it. As a result, the target market was too small. The product was subsequently reintroduced as a gourmet sauce for meat cooked on outdoor grills.

Poor execution of the marketing mix hurt Real, Mennen's deodorant. The product was introduced with a $14 million advertising campaign. One problem, though, was that customers found that if they twisted the dispenser too hard, too much cream came out, creating an instant mess. Also, the name Real gave little indication of the product or its benefits.

Developing successful new products may sometimes involve luck, but more often it involves having a product that really meets a need and has significant points of difference over competitive products. As the Marketing NewsNet box points out, Black Photo Corp. of Markham, Ontario, feels it has a winner with its new on-line photo centre because it believes the product (service) offers a significant point of difference.[13]

The likelihood of success is improved by paying close attention to the early steps of the new-product process described in the next section of the text.

CONCEPT CHECK   **1.** From a consumer's viewpoint, what kind of innovation would an improved electric toothbrush be?

2. What does "insignificant point of difference" mean as a reason for new-product failure?

THE NEW-PRODUCT PROCESS

Companies such as General Electric, Sony, or Procter & Gamble take a sequence of steps before their products are ready for market. Figure 11-4 shows the seven stages of the **new-product process,** the sequence of activities a firm uses to identify business opportunities and convert them to a saleable good or service. This sequence begins with new-product strategy development and ends with commercialization.

New-Product Strategy Development

For companies, **new-product strategy development** involves defining the role for a new product in terms of the firm's overall corporate objectives. This step in the new-product process has been added by many companies recently to provide a needed focus for ideas and concepts developed in later stages.

Objectives of the stage: identify markets and strategic roles   During this new-product strategy development stage the company uses the environmental scanning process described in Chapter 3 to identify trends that pose either opportunities or threats. Relevant company strengths and weaknesses are also identified. The outcome of new-product strategy development is not new-product ideas but identifying markets for which new products will be developed and strategic roles new products might serve—the vital protocol activity explained earlier.

Booz, Allen & Hamilton, Inc., an international consulting firm, asked firms what strategic role was served by their most successful recent product. These roles, shown in Figure 11-5, help define the direction of new-product development and divide into externally and internally driven factors.

Henry C. Yuen is an example of using an externally driven action to preempt a market segment (Figure 11-5). Not your typical TV couch potato, Yuen tried to tape a baseball game and got only snow. Unlike the rest of us who might just have mumbled, Yuen took

FIGURE 11-4

STAGES IN THE NEW-PRODUCT PROCESS

FIGURE 11-5

STRATEGIC ROLES OF MOST
SUCCESSFUL NEW PRODUCTS

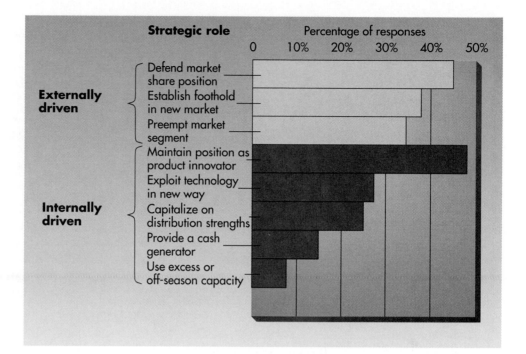

his PhD degree in mathematics and co-invented "VCR Plus"—the device millions of TV fans use to set their VCRs by punching in numbers from newspaper listings. To maintain his firm's role as a market innovator (an internally driven strategic role in Figure 11-5), in 1996 he launched "Guide Plus)," which allows viewers to use their VCR to select from the blizzard of today's programs by simply clicking one remote control button.

Cross-functional teams   A key to 3M's success in new-product development is its use of *cross-functional teams,* a small number of people from different departments in an organization who are mutually accountable to a common set of performance goals. Teams are especially important in new-product development so that individuals from R&D, marketing, manufacturing, finance, and so forth can simultaneously search together in a constructive environment for new product and market opportunities. In the past 3M and other firms often utilized these department people in sequence—possibly resulting in R&D designing new products that the manufacturing department couldn't produce economically and that the marketing department couldn't sell. A 3M cross-functional team developed a more environmentally responsible method for manufacturing an emulsifier, without compromising product quality.

Bringing people together from different departments can also lead to great synergies. At 3M the lighting technology that led to its overhead projectors 30 years ago has resulted in $800 million a year sales in lighting-related products that range from highway reflective signs to crystalline structures used on high-tech sandpapers. Marketing synergies also occur, as when a 3M cross-functional team came up with a new venue—the Home Shopping Network—to promote an extended line of 3M™ Bow Magic™ Pull Bows.[14]

3M's experiences suggest some conclusions about today's style of teamwork:

- Teams are ongoing, not just a one-shot effort.
- Teamwork takes time because the members have to learn about each other and find a comfort level.
- Team members can—and do—disagree, and that's okay.
- Teams can be informal or formal, depending on the task that needs doing.
- Teams need "champions," individuals willing and able to carry messages and requests to management and to move the project forward.

Because program and product champions are so important in marketing, they are discussed again in Chapter 22.

Idea Generation

Developing a pool of concepts as candidates for new products, or **idea generation,** must build on the previous stage's results. New-product ideas are generated by consumers, employees, basic R&D, and competitors.

Customer suggestions   Procter & Gamble surveyed Japanese parents and found that they changed their babies' diapers far more frequently than Canadian parents. In response to this market difference, P&G developed Ultra Pampers, a more absorbent diaper that makes frequent changing less necessary. Today, Ultra Pampers is the market leader in Japan.

Companies often analyze consumer complaints or problems to discover new-product opportunities. They also pose complaints to a sample of consumers, who are asked to suggest products with such deficiencies in order to identify new product opportunities. Listening to growing concerns about cholesterol and fat in its food, McDonald's reformulated its shakes with a low-fat mixture and introduced a low-fat hamburger. Black & Decker recently launched a new line of high-end small appliances in Canada called Kitchentools. Kitchentools was created after two years of consumer research into what "involved cooks" believed was lacking from the best products on the market.

Employee and co-worker suggestions   Employees may be encouraged to suggest new product ideas through suggestion boxes or contests. The idea for General Mills's $350 million-a-year Nature Valley Granola Bars came when one of its marketing managers observed co-workers bringing granola to work in plastic bags.

Research and development breakthroughs   Another source of new products is a firm's basic research, but the costs can be huge. Sony is the acknowledged world leader in new-product development in electronics. Its scientists and engineers produce an average of four new products each business day. Sony's research and development breakthroughs have led to innovative products, and its ability to manufacture and market those products has made it a legend in the electronics industry, popularizing VCRs, the Walkman, and—coming into your future?—the Data Discman. Consultants studying the new-product and innovation process say firms need a dual approach to get the most from their R&D: (1) create cultures where new ideas can thrive and (2) have systems that will sift those ideas through the development process and get them to market with lightning speed. Sony seems to have done this for four decades.

R&D's search for new-product ideas can take it to some pretty strange places. Shaman Pharmaceuticals has spent tens of millions of dollars going into the rain forests of South American jungles to observe native healers' (called "shamans") knowledge of medicinal plants to find curative compounds that could then lead to mass-produced drugs. So far it has found two chemicals that may be on your drugstore shelves in a few years. Pharmaceutical giants Merck and Eli Lilly are doing much the same thing. University research scientists can use a similar approach. For example, one scientist has patented Brazzein, a protein with 1000 times the sweetness of sugar, that has been consumed for generations by West Africans.[15]

Professional R&D laboratories also provide new-product ideas. Labs at Arthur D. Little helped put the crunch in Cap'n Crunch cereal and the flavour in Carnation Instant Breakfast. Because broccoli is increasingly felt to contain cancer-fighting properties, Little's labs are trying to find ways to make the vegetable more appealing to today's consumers. Some ideas now in test: sweetened broccoli-based vegetable juices and a chocolate-flavoured powdered broccoli-juice drink mix. An idea sent back to the drawing boards: broccoli cereal.[16]

Competitive products   New-product ideas can also be found by analyzing the competition. A six-person intelligence team from the Marriott Corporation spent six months travelling around the country staying at economy hotels. The team assessed the competition's strengths and weaknesses on everything from the soundproof qualities of the rooms to the softness of the towels. Marriott then budgeted $500 million for a new economy hotel chain, Fairfield Inns. Shortly after Neilson Dairy of Ontario began marketing Trucalcium, a new calcium-fortified milk, Natrel Inc. followed suit by launching its Ultra'lait Calcium brand in the Quebec market.

Screening and Evaluation

The third stage of the new product process is **screening and evaluation,** which involves internal and external evaluations of the new-product ideas to eliminate those that warrant no further effort.

Internal approach   Internally, the firm evaluates the technical feasibility of the proposal and whether the idea meets the new-product strategy objectives defined in step 1. In 1957 Earl Bakken, founder of Medtronic, built the first external portable heart pacemaker. Working with a team of scientists, Medtronic later built the first implantable pacemaker—a device enabling bedridden people suffering from heart problems to regain their normal, productive lives.

In the mid-1980s Medtronic concluded it had to broaden its products beyond its heart pacemaker line and embarked on a systematic search for new products. In the process it developed an astute new-product development process that reduces the likelihood of failure. Continuing internal evaluation is one key. After investing $10 million in an angioplasty catheter project, Medtronic's evaluation concluded the device was two years behind the competition and shut the project down. But Medtronic redeployed people working on that project that helped lead to four generations of implantable heart defibrillators (devices that regulate an erratic heart beat) introduced in a two-year period—keeping it well ahead of competitors.[17]

A YEAR'S WORTH OF CONSUMER
INTERVIEWS WENT INTO THE
DEVELOPMENT OF SUN CHIPS.

External approach Concept tests are external evaluations that consist of preliminary testing of the new-product idea (rather than the actual product) with consumers. Concept tests usually rely on written descriptions of the product but may be augmented with sketches, mock-ups, or promotional literature. Several key questions are asked during concept testing: How does the customer perceive the product? Who would use it? How would it be used?

For external evaluations, Medtronic often uses external panels of doctors who initially see and evaluate concepts rather than physical devices. Only after the device makes sense to the panel does Medtronic actually design and build it, which is the most expensive and risky stage of the new-product development process.

Frito-Lay spent a year interviewing 10 000 consumers about the concept of a multi-grain snack chip. The company experimented with 50 different shapes before settling on a thin, rectangular chip with ridges and a slightly salty, nutty flavour. The product, Sun Chips, is highly successful.

CONCEPT CHECK

1. What step in the new-product process has been added in recent years?

2. What are four sources of new-product ideas?

3. What is the difference between internal and external screening and evaluation approaches used by a firm in the new-product process?

Business Analysis

Business analysis involves specifying the features of the product and the marketing strategy needed to commercialize it and making necessary financial projections. This is the last checkpoint before significant capital is invested in creating a prototype of the product. Economic analysis, marketing strategy review, and legal examination of the proposed product are conducted at this stage. It is at this point that the product is analyzed relative to the firm's marketing and technological synergies.

The marketing strategy review studies the new-product idea in relation to the marketing program to support it. The proposed product is assessed to determine whether it will help or hurt sales of existing products. Likewise, the product is examined to assess whether it can be sold through existing channels or if new outlets will be needed.

After the product's important features are defined, economic considerations focus on several issues, starting with costs of R&D, production, and marketing. For financial projections, the firm must also forecast the possible revenues from future product sales and forecast market shares. In this stage the firm also estimates how many units of the product must be sold to cover the costs of production and projects a return on investment to determine the profitability.

Microsoft's Windows 95, called "one of the most strategic products ever to hit the personal-computer market" by *The Wall Street Journal,* provides an example. The initial target market for Windows 95 was the existing Microsoft operating systems, MS DOS and Windows 3.1, which run about 100 million computers around the globe and together have an 80 percent market share. Sales projections included 30 million units sold in the four months after release and possibly 100 million units a year starting in

1998. The business analysis underlying this new-product decision involved recognizing that Windows 95 required 15 000 000 lines of computer code and total R&D and marketing costs of $400 million. One reason for this complexity and cost: Microsoft imposed a huge design burden on itself by promising compatibility with past software. Hundreds of customer users in the field tried for months to get the bugs out.[18]

As an important aspect of the business analysis, the proposed new product is studied to determine whether it can be protected with a patent or copyright. An attractive new-product proposal is one in which the technology, product, or brand cannot easily be copied. This includes counterfeiting concerns, such as those discussed in the Ethics and Social Responsibility Alert.[19]

CUSTOMERS EXAMINE THE JAPANESE LANGUAGE VERSION OF WINDOWS 95™, MOMENTS AFTER IT WAS FIRST RELEASED IN JAPAN.

Development

Product ideas that survive the business analysis proceed to actual **development,** turning the idea on paper into a prototype. This results in a demonstrable, producible product in hand. Outsiders seldom understand the technical complexities of the development stage, which involves not only manufacturing the product but also performing laboratory and consumer tests to ensure that it meets the standards set. Design of the product becomes an important element.

Liquid Tide, introduced by P&G, looks like a simple modification of its original Tide detergent. However, P&G sees this product as a technological breakthrough: the first detergent without phosphates that cleans as well as existing phosphate detergents.

To achieve this breakthrough, P&G spent 400 000 hours and combined technologies from its laboratories in three countries. The new ingredient in Liquid Tide that helps suspend the dirt in wash water came out of the P&G research lab in North America. The cleaning agents in the product came from P&G scientists in Japan. Cleaning agent technology is especially advanced in Japan because consumers there wash clothes in colder water (about 70°F) than consumers in Canada (95°F) and Europe (160°F). P&G scientists thought that Liquid Tide also needed water-softening ingredients to make the cleaning agents work better. For this technology it turned to P&G's lab in Belgium, whose experience was based on European water, which has more than twice the mineral content of Canadian wash water.

The prototype product is tested in the laboratory to see if it achieves the physical standards set for it. Mattel submits its dolls and toys to rigorous tests: it clamps Barbie's foot in steel jaws, then pulls on her head with a wire to make sure her skin or head can't crack, cut, or choke future owners. Prototypes of disposable consumer goods are also subjected to consumer tests, often in-home placements of the product to see if consumers actually perceive it as a better product after they use it. In a blind test consumers preferred Liquid Tide nine to one over the detergent of their own choice tested in their washers.

Industrial products often have special, exacting test requirements. For example, jet engines for commercial aircraft have to pass a "bird strike test" and have minimal engine damage when carcasses of ducks or gulls are fired into the whirling jet engine operating on a test stand. Why this weird field test? To simulate the conditions that might occur when your plane ingests an unfortunate seagull or duck standing around

WHY DO YOU WANT GENERAL ELECTRIC TO PASS THE "BIRD STRIKE TEST" ON ITS GE90 JET ENGINE? FOR THE ANSWER, SEE THE TEXT.

on the runway at takeoff. General Electric's huge new GE90 is used to power many Boeing 777 commercial jets. As a result of tests like these GE engineers redesigned the GE 90's jet engine blades, and it passed its next bird strike test with flying colours.[20]

Market Testing

The **market testing** stage of the new-product process involves exposing actual products to prospective consumers under realistic purchase conditions to see if they will buy. Often a product is developed, tested, refined, and then tested again to get consumer reactions through either test marketing or purchase laboratories.

Test marketing   Test marketing involves offering a product for sale on a limited basis in a defined area. This test is done to determine whether consumers will actually buy the product and to try different ways of marketing it. Only about a third of the products test marketed do well enough to go on to the next phase. These market tests are usually conducted in cities that are viewed as being representative of Canadian consumers.

In examining the commercial viability of the new product, companies measure sales in the test area, often with *store audits* that measure the sales in grocery stores and the number of cases ordered by a store from the wholesaler. This gives the company an indication of potential sales volume and market share in the test area.

Market tests are also used to check other elements of the marketing mix besides the product itself such as price, level of advertising support, and distribution. In test marketing its new compact drink dispenser for small and medium offices, Coca-Cola analyzed both the distribution channel and the advertising. During the market test, Coca-Cola discovered that office managers are the people who decide whether machines are installed in break rooms. Targeting office managers, Coca-Cola introduced its successful dispenser, called BreakMate, in the early 1990s.

There are difficulties with test marketing, a primary one being how well the results can be projected. Representativeness of the test market to the target market for the product is

TEST MARKETS IN SUPERMARKETS CAN BE VALUABLE, BUT THEY ALSO ALERT COMPETITORS.

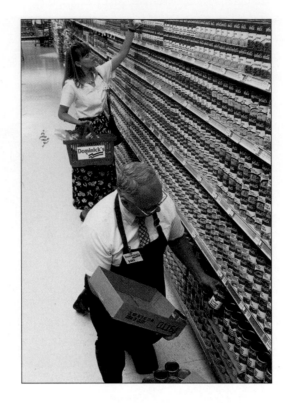

very important. Market tests also are time-consuming and expensive because production lines as well as promotion and sales programs must be set up. Costs can run over a million dollars, the exact amount depending on the size of the city and the cost of buying media time or space to advertise the product. Market tests also reveal plans to competitors, sometimes enabling them to get a product into national distribution first or to take actions to disrupt the test markets. When a product can be easily copied by a competitor, test marketing may not be used. Although Hunt-Wesson got its Prima Salsa Tomato Sauce into the test market first, Chesebrough-Pond's Ragu Extra Thick & Zesty beat it into national introduction. Competitors can also try to sabotage test markets. Pepsi ran Mountain Dew Sport Drink in a test market and Gatorade counterattacked furiously with ads and coupons. Pepsi pulled the product off the market. With such problems, some firms skip test markets completely or use simulated test markets.

Simulated test markets   Because of the time, cost, and confidentiality problems of test markets, manufacturers often turn to *simulated* (or *laboratory*) *test markets* (*STM*), a technique that simulates a full-scale test market but in a limited fashion. STMs are often run in shopping malls, where consumers are questioned to identify who uses the product class being tested. Willing participants are questioned on usage, reasons for purchase, and important product attributes. Qualified persons are then shown TV commercials or print ads for the test product along with competitors' advertising and are given money to make a decision to buy or not buy a package of the product (or the competitors') from a real or simulated store environment. If the test product is not purchased, the consumer may receive it as a free sample. Participants are interviewed later for their reactions and the likelihood of repurchase. Based on these reactions, the company may decide to proceed to the last stage of the new product process.

Market testing is a valuable step in the new-product process, but not all products can use it. Testing a service beyond the concept level is very difficult because the service is intangible and consumers can't see what they are buying. Similarly, market testing of expensive consumer products such as cars or VCRs or costly industrial products like jet engines or computers is impractical.

EFFECTIVE CROSS-FUNCTIONAL
TEAMS AT HEWLETT-PACKARD HAVE
REDUCED NEW-PRODUCT
DEVELOPMENT TIMES SIGNIFICANTLY.

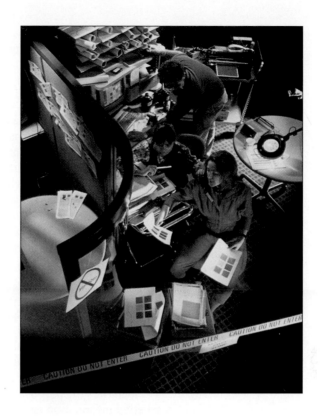

Commercialization

Finally, the product is brought to the point of **commercialization**—positioning and launching it in full-scale production and sales. Companies proceed very carefully at the commercialization stage because this is the most expensive stage for most new products, especially consumer products.

Increasing the success rate of new products   In recent years, companies have begun to recognize that speed is important in bringing a new product to market. Recent studies have shown that high-tech products coming to market on time are far more profitable than those arriving late. As a result, some companies—such as Sony, NEC, Honda, AT&T, and Hewlett-Packard—have overlapped the sequence of stages described in this chapter. With this approach, termed *parallel development* (the simultaneous development by cross-functional teams of both the product and the production process), marketing, manufacturing, and R&D personnel stay with the product from conception to production. The results are a significant reduction in new-product development times. Honda has cut car development from five years to three, while Hewlett-Packard has reduced the development time for computer printers from 54 months to 22.

The risks and uncertainties of the commercialization stage   The job is far from over when the new product gets to the commercialization stage. In fact, disasters still often occur. Some examples include the following:

- The high quality of the 5 or 50 prototypes that were handcrafted in the R&D lab with lots of tender loving care can't be replicated on the mass-production lines.
- Costs have gotten so far beyond original budgets that customers won't buy the product at the new price point that must be set to make a profit.
- Buyers can't understand the benefits of the new product without extensive, costly education activities—necessitating new training of the sales force and distributors, along with new videos and infomercials.

- Competitors introduce their new product a few weeks before the firm's own product hits the market, making the product obsolete before potential customers ever see it.

The last point in the list—bad timing—gives new product managers nightmares. IBM, for example, killed several laptop computer prototypes because competitors introduced better, more advanced machines to the market before IBM. Even well-accepted brands and products that reach the market late can represent significant lost sales. In the mid-1990s General Motors lost at least 100 000 Chevrolet Cavalier and Pontiac Sunfire sales when it couldn't simultaneously retool a factory and introduce new models. It probably lost sales, too, when it announced in 1995 that many new model launches were going to be delayed by six months to two years, extending some introductions to 1998 and 1999.[21]

Grocery products have special problems at the commercialization stage. Because space is so limited on supermarket shelves, many require manufacturers to pay a **slotting fee,** a payment a manufacturer makes to place a new item on a retailer's shelf. This can run to several million dollars for a single product. But there's even another potential expense. If a new grocery product does not achieve a predetermined sales target, some retailers require a **failure fee,** a penalty payment by a manufacturer to compensate the retailer for sales its valuable shelf space never made. To minimize the financial risk of a new product failure, many grocery product manufacturers use *regional rollouts,* introducing the product sequentially into geographical areas of Canada to allow production levels and marketing activities to build up gradually.

Figure 11-6 identifies the purpose of each stage of the new-product process and the kinds of marketing information and methods used. The figure also suggests information that might help avoid some new product failures. Although using the new-product process does not guarantee successful products, it does increase a firm's success rate.[22]

FIGURE 11-6   MARKETING INFORMATION AND METHODS USED IN THE NEW-PRODUCT PROCESS

STAGE OF PROCESS	PURPOSE OF STAGE	MARKETING INFORMATION AND METHODS USED
New product strategy development	Identify new product niches to reach in light of company objectives	Company objectives; assessment of firm's current strengths and weaknesses in terms of market and product
Idea generation	Develop concepts for possible products	Ideas from employees and co-workers, consumers, R&D, and competitors; methods of brainstorming and focus groups
Screening and evaluation	Separate good product ideas from bad ones inexpensively	Screening criteria, concept tests, and weighted point systems
Business analysis	Identify the product's features and its marketing strategy, and make financial projections	Product's key features, anticipated marketing mix strategy; economic, marketing, production, legal, and profitability analyses
Development	Create the prototype product, and test it in the laboratory and on consumers	Laboratory and consumer tests on product prototypes
Market testing	Test product and marketing strategy in the marketplace on a limited scale	Test markets, simulated test markets (STMs)
Commercialization	Position and offer product in the marketplace	Perceptual maps, product positioning, regional rollouts

CONCEPT CHECK

1. How does the development stage of the new-product process involve testing the product inside and outside the firm?

2. What is a test market?

3. What is commercialization of a new product?

SUMMARY

1. A product is a good, service, or idea consisting of a bundle of tangible and intangible attributes that satisfies consumers and is received in exchange for money or some other unit of value. A company's product decisions involve the product item, product line, and range of its product mix.

2. Products can be classified by tangibility and by user. By degree of tangibility, products divide into nondurable goods, durable goods, and services. By user, the major distinctions are consumer or industrial goods. Consumer goods consist of convenience, shopping, and specialty products. Industrial goods are for either production or support.

3. There are several ways to define a new product, such as the degree of distinction from existing products, a time base specified by Consumer and Corporate Affairs Canada, a company perspective, or effect on a consumer's usage pattern.

4. In terms of its effect on a consumer's use of a product, a discontinuous innovation represents the greatest change and a continuous innovation the least. A dynamically continuous innovation is disruptive but not totally new.

5. The failure of a new product is usually attributable to one of seven marketing reasons: insignificant point of difference, incomplete market and product definition before prod-

uct development begins, too little market attractiveness, poor execution of the marketing mix, poor product quality on critical factors, bad timing, and no economical access to buyers.

6. The new-product process consists of seven stages. Objectives for new products are determined in the first stage, new-product strategy development; this is followed by idea generation, screening and evaluation, business analysis, development, market testing, and commercialization.

7. Ideas for new products come from several sources, including consumers, employees, R&D laboratories, and competitors.

8. Screening and evaluation can be done internally or externally.

9. Business analysis involves defining the features of the new product, a marketing strategy to introduce it, and a financial forecast.

10. Development involves not only producing a prototype product but also testing it in the lab and on consumers to see that it meets the standards set for it.

11. In market testing new products, companies often rely on market tests to see that consumers will actually buy the product when it's offered for sale and that other marketing mix factors are working. Products surviving this stage are commercialized—taken to market.

KEY TERMS AND CONCEPTS

product p. 266
product line p. 267
product mix p. 267
consumer goods p. 267
industrial goods p. 268
convenience goods p. 268
shopping goods p. 268
specialty goods p. 268
unsought goods p. 268
production goods p. 269
support goods p. 270

new-product process p. 276
new-product strategy development p. 276
idea generation p. 278
screening and evaluation p. 279
business analysis p. 280
development p. 282
market testing p. 283
commercialization p. 285
slotting fee p. 286
failure fee p. 286

CHAPTER PROBLEMS AND APPLICATIONS

1. Products can be classified as either consumer or industrial goods. How would you classify the following products? (*a*) Johnson's baby shampoo, (*b*) a Black & Decker two-speed drill, and (*c*) an arc welder.

2. Are products such as Nature Valley Granola bars and Eddie Bauer hiking boots convenience, shopping, specialty, or unsought goods?

3. Based on your answer to problem 2, how would the marketing actions differ for each product and the classification to which you assigned it?

4. In terms of the behavioural effect on consumers, how would a PC, such as a Macintosh PowerBook or an IBM ThinkPad, be classified? In light of this classification, what actions would you suggest to the manufacturers of these products to increase their sales in the market?

5. Several alternative definitions were presented for a new product. How would a company's marketing strategy be affected if it used (*a*) the legal definition or (*b*) a behavioural definition?

6. What methods would you suggest to assess the potential commercial success for the following new products? (*a*) a

new, improved ketchup, (*b*) a three-dimensional television system that took the company 10 years to develop, and (*c*) a new children's toy on which the company holds a patent.

7. Look back at Figure 11-5, which outlines the roles for new products. If a company followed the role of defending market share position, what type of positioning strategy might be implemented?

8. Concept testing is an important step in the new-product process. Outline the concept tests for (*a*) an electrically powered car and (*b*) a new loan payment system for automobiles that is based on a variable rate interest. What are the differences in developing concept tests for products as opposed to services?

CASE 11-1   Orbitz

Clearly Canadian beverage Corporation of Vancouver has defied conventional wisdom with its staying power in the new age beverage market, and is now defying gravity with its newest beverage, Orbitz. Orbitz is a unique, naturally fruit-flavoured beverage with colourful gel spheres that remain suspended in the liquid. The product is sold in 10 oz (300 mL) glass bottles and carries a suggested retail price of $1.29.

WHY ORBITZ?

One of Clearly Canadian Beverages key objectives in 1996 was to diversify its portfolio of premium niche beverages. The reasons were simple. The company believed distributors and retailers would better support the company's products if a wider range of brands were offered. Similarly, consumers are still looking for "alternatives" and are willing to try new drinks with different looks, tastes, and textures. The company believed if it didn't offer the products consumers wanted, those consumers would look elsewhere. After two years of research and development and extensive consumer testing, Clearly Canadian introduced Orbitz—North America's first textually enhanced beverage. Clearly Canadian maximized the suspension technology it licensed from Bush Boake Allen Inc. Orbitz's gel spheres are designed to remain intact and in suspension in the beverage for 9 to 12 months.

TARGET MARKET

"We made it our mandate to make Orbitz appropriate for the teen market," says Jonathan Cronin, Clearly

Canadian's vice president of marketing. "We deliberately avoided developing a kid drink. We wanted to be weird, we wanted to be older, we wanted to be hip, trendy, all those things," he added. Printing a URL on the bottles and marketing materials was a deliberate tactic to raise the target age group. With a fun, interactive web site—Planet Orbitz (www.orbitz.com)—and some outrageous point-of-purchase ideas like a rocket-shaped cooler, the company clearly focused on teens and young adults. The company does believe, however, it will also attract younger kids who are trying to be cool and older adults looking for something different. But the teen market is the core consumer group.

THE APPEAL

"The initial appeal of Orbitz is visual," says Cronin. He adds, "Orbitz is a visual drink that offers theatre in a bottle. We've tried to design that into everything. The label is playful. The whole package has been designed to make you play with it." The lettering in the label winds around the bottle to encourage consumers to pick it up and read it. And all the flavours of the noncarbonated clear beverages are packaged in clear bottles—because that offers the best presentation for the naturally coloured planets or gel spheres," says Cronin.

The gel planets not only give Orbitz a unique visual appeal, they also add an extra flavour dimension to the beverage. The spheres are citrus flavoured in the Raspberry Citrus offering, strawberry in the Blueberry Melon, coconut in the Pineapple Banana Cherry Coconut, and orange in Vanilla Orange.

However, the company realized that it should not lean solely on the visual impact of the product. R&D staff at Clearly Canadian worked hard to deliver on thirst-quenching expectations. So the flavours are light and refreshing but not too sweet. The company suggests that while people are initially taken with the novelty of the product, when they do taste it, they are almost always surprised by how refreshing Orbitz is.

A SUCCESSFUL LAUNCH

Clearly Canadian launched the product into the United States market in 1996. *Rolling Stone* magazine named it the "Hot Drink of 96" and Orbitz received extensive international media attention. Consumer response to the product in the United States has been, according to the company, simply amazing. The product is available in convenience stores and supermarkets in 46 US states. The company followed up by launching the product in New Zealand in late 1996, and in Canada in 1997. The company also plans to introduce Orbitz to Europe, Asia, and the Caribbean, markets where the company already has strong distribution relationships for their existing products.

ONGOING INNOVATION

To maintain the sales momentum and generate an ongoing trial of Orbitz, Clearly Canadian has introduced new Orbitz flavours and colour combinations and announced cross promotion and sponsorship arrangements with major entertainment properties. The newest addition to the Orbitz line-up is Black Current Berry. As well as adding a new flavour, Orbitz gets even more colourful with its first "double-colour" flavour. Orbitz' Pineapple Banana Cherry Coconut now has more accent on the fruit flavour and a combination of red and white gel spheres floating in the beverage. "Consumers are constantly asking for new, innovative, and good-tasting beverage alternatives. Orbitz is exactly that. We continue to innovate this beverage by producing new and interesting flavour combinations and using multi-colours in one bottle," says Cronin.

In conjunction with BMG Entertainment, Orbitz presented an exclusive "Best New Music" CD offer including 15 alternative and dance music artists from Matthew Sweet to Treble Charger. Consumers could find the purchase offer of the CD sampler and Orbitz T-shirt in convenience and grocery stores throughout North America. Orbitz bottles with specially marked blue caps provided promotion details and consumers could visit the interactive Orbitz web site to get gravity-defying news on the promotion. Produced by BMG; every CD included a special consumer insert to join the BMG Music Club.

Clearly Canadian also announced a three-year partnership with Rollerblade Inc. The company is one of the presenting sponsors for the world's largest in-line skating event, Blade Jam and the Ultimate In-Line Challenge, one of Rollerblade's national in-line skating event series. As well as participating in these events, Rollerblade's fleet of demo vans will be carrying Orbitz beverages, offering consumers skate rental/trial opportunities while passing out samples of Orbitz.

Cronin fully expects me-too products to challenge Orbitz in the near future. But he feels that Clearly Canadian's experience in pioneering the product, its all-natural formula, and the Orbitz trademark itself will give the company a clear playing field for some time to come. He suggests, "the opportunity for this brand is virtually limitless, and we've got to stay ahead of the competition. We will not allow somebody to trump the Orbitz brand. This is just the beginning, and there's so many things we can do to add value as we mature."

Questions

1. What type of innovation is Orbitz?
2. Outline the reasons for the initial success of Orbitz.
3. Some beverage experts suggest that Orbitz will not have any staying power and that it will fizzle as did other fads before it such as Pop Rocks. What is your opinion?
4. What things can Clearly Canadian do to "add value" to the Orbitz product?

PREPARE FOR THE NEXT REVOLUTION

CLEARLY CANADIAN.
BEVERAGE CORPORATION

CHAPTER 12

Managing the Product

AFTER READING THIS CHAPTER YOU SHOULD BE ABLE TO:

• Explain the product life cycle concept and relate a marketing strategy to each stage.

• Recognize the differences in product life cycles for various products and their implications for marketing decisions.

• Understand alternative approaches to managing a product's life cycle.

• Identify the attributes of a successful brand name.

• Explain the rationale for alternative brand name strategies employed by companies.

• Understand the benefits of packaging and warranties in the marketing of a product.

CLEARLY CANADIAN REVOLUTION

As the Eighties gave way to the Nineties, the "new age" of beverages was just dawning and a little company from Vancouver was making a big splash. Clearly Canadian Beverage Corporation (www.clearly.ca) may not have produced the very first new age beverage, but its product was the first to be referred to as a new age beverage. If it did not create the category, it surely defined it, and opened the door for other new age members such as Snapple, Arizona, and Mistic.

Clearly Canadian was, if nothing else, different and hip. With a much fuller taste than an essence-based sparkling water, clear in appearance and encased in a sharp, dazzling, proprietary glass bottle, Clearly Canadian was unique, it was new age. In retrospect, it was also the first widely successful premium new age beverage. And as such, it invited many imitators.

Clearly Canadian went against the grain when the company first started out. The company went premium and very sophisticated in terms of image and packaging. But a funny thing happened to Clearly Canadian after it reached the new age summit. It atrophied. Whereas its competitors continued to innovate in terms of packaging, image, and new products—expanding the new age category beyond anyone's wildest dreams—Clearly Canadian seemed to be content to react to the market rather than being proactive.

Realizing it had to get back to its innovative roots to compete, a revamped Clearly Canadian has restructured internally and emerged with a growing portfolio of new products. It had revolutionized the beverage industry in 1988, and it was prepared to do so again.

The company created a new bottle design for its Clearly Canadian sparkling flavoured water. The new design features a bolder, more appealing blue bottle with embossing and more colourful fruit illustrations. It also introduced a new flavour, Tropical Tangerine. But in an effort to become a total beverage company, Clearly Canadian also introduced new products on both sides of the carbonation fence. The company introduced Clearly Canadian Natural Artesian Water, a premium still water, and Quenchers, a line of three preservative-free sparkling fruit beverages. On the other hand, as you read in Chapter 11, it also launched Orbitz, a natural fruit-flavoured beverage with colourful gel spheres that remain suspended in the liquid.

Clearly Canadian sparkling flavoured water remains one of the North American sales leaders in the branded sparkling water category and is distributed extensively in Canada, the United States, and numerous countries worldwide.[1]

This chapter shows how the actions taken by Clearly Canadian Beverage Corporation are typical of those made by successful marketers in managing products and brands in competitive marketing environments.

PRODUCT LIFE CYCLE

Products, like people, have been viewed as having a life cycle. The concept of the **product life cycle** describes the stages a new product goes through in the marketplace: introduction, growth, maturity, and decline (Figure 12-1).[2] There are two curves shown

FIGURE 12-1

HOW STAGES OF THE PRODUCT LIFE CYCLE RELATE TO A FIRM'S MARKETING OBJECTIVES AND MARKETING MIX ACTIONS

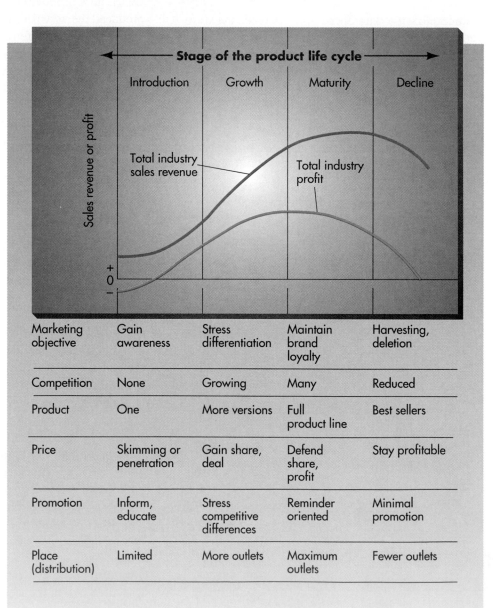

	Introduction	Growth	Maturity	Decline
Marketing objective	Gain awareness	Stress differentiation	Maintain brand loyalty	Harvesting, deletion
Competition	None	Growing	Many	Reduced
Product	One	More versions	Full product line	Best sellers
Price	Skimming or penetration	Gain share, deal	Defend share, profit	Stay profitable
Promotion	Inform, educate	Stress competitive differences	Reminder oriented	Minimal promotion
Place (distribution)	Limited	More outlets	Maximum outlets	Fewer outlets

in this figure, total industry sales revenue and total industry profit, which represent the sum of sales revenue and profit of all firms producing the product. The reasons for the changes in each curve and the marketing decisions involved are discussed in the following pages.

Introduction Stage

The introduction stage of the product life cycle occurs when a product is first introduced to its intended target market. During this period, sales grow slowly, and profit is minimal. The lack of profit is often the result of large investment costs in product development, such as the $200 million spent by Gillette to develop the Sensor razor shaving system. The marketing objective for the company at this stage is to create consumer awareness and stimulate trial—the initial purchase of a product by a consumer.

Companies often spend heavily on advertising and other promotion tools to build awareness among consumers in the introduction stage. For example, Frito-Lay spent $30 million to promote its SunChips multigrain snacks to consumers and retailers, and Gillette spent $35 million in advertising alone to introduce the Sensor razor to consumers.[3] These expenditures are often made to stimulate *primary demand,* or desire for the product class (such as multigrain snack chips), rather than for a specific brand since there are no competitors with the same product. As competitors introduce their own products and the product progresses along its life cycle, company attention is focused on creating *selective demand,* or demand for a specific brand.

Other marketing mix variables also are important at this stage. Gaining distribution is often a challenge because channel intermediaries may be hesitant to carry a new product. Moreover, in this stage a company often restricts the number of variations of the product to ensure control of product quality. For example, SunChips originally came in only two flavours and Gatorade in only one. Gillette originally offered only a single version of the Sensor razor.

During introduction, pricing can be either high or low. A high initial price may be used as part of a *skimming* strategy to help the company recover the costs of development as well as capitalize on the price insensitivity of early buyers. 3M is a master of this strategy. According to a 3M manager, "We hit fast, price high, and get the heck out when the me-too products pour in."[4] High prices also tend to attract competitors more eager to enter the market because they see the opportunity for profit. To discourage competitive entry, a company can price low, referred to as *penetration pricing.* This pricing strategy also helps build unit volume, but a company must closely monitor costs. These and other pricing techniques are covered in depth in Chapter 15.

Figure 12-2 charts the stand-alone fax machine product life cycle for business use from the early 1970s through 1996.[5] As shown, sales grew slowly in the 1970s and early 1980s after Xerox pioneered the first lightweight portable fax machine that sent and received documents. Fax machines were originally sold direct to businesses through company salespeople and were premium priced. The average price for a fax machine in 1980 was $12 700. By today's standards, those fax machines were primitive. They contained mechanical parts, not electronic circuitry, and offered few of the features seen in today's models.

Several product classes are poised to enter the introductory stage of the product life cycle or have been only recently commercialized. These include high-definition television (HDTV) and electronic imaging cameras. Electric vehicles have been in the introductory stage and are about to enter a period of rapid growth worldwide.[6]

Growth Stage

The second stage of the product life cycle, growth, is characterized by rapid increases in sales. It is in this stage that competitors appear. For example, Figure 12-2 shows the dramatic increase in sales of fax machines from 1986 to 1990. The number of companies selling fax machines was also increasing, from one in the early 1970s to

PRODUCT LIFE CYCLE FOR THE STAND-
ALONE FAX MACHINE FOR BUSINESS
USE: 1970–1996

Source: Chart drawn from Dataquest, Inc., statistics. Used with permission.

four in the late 1970s to seven manufacturers in 1983, which sold nine brands. By 1990 there were some 25 manufacturers and 60 possible brands from which to choose.

The result of more competitors and more aggressive pricing is that profit usually peaks during the growth stage. For instance, the average price for a fax machine declined from $3300 in 1985 to $1500 in 1990. At this point the emphasis of advertising shifts to stimulating selective demand, in which product benefits are compared with those of competitors' offerings.

Product sales in the growth stage grow at an increasing rate because of new people trying or using the product and a growing proportion of *repeat purchasers*—people who tried the product, were satisfied, and bought again. As a product moves through the life cycle, the ratio of repeat to trial purchasers grows. Failure to achieve substantial repeat purchasers usually means an early death for a product. Alberto-Culver introduced Mr. Culver's Sparklers, which were solid air fresheners that looked like stained glass. The product moved quickly from the introduction to the growth stage, but then sales plummeted. The problem was there were almost no repeat purchasers because buyers treated the product like cheap window decorations, left them there, and didn't buy new ones. Durable fax machines meant that replacement purchases were rare; however, it was common for more than one machine to populate a business as their use became more widespread. In 1994, there was one fax machine for every eight people in a business.

Changes start to appear in the product during the growth stage. To help differentiate a company's brand from those of its competitors, an improved version or new features are added to the original design, and product proliferation occurs. Changes in fax machines included (1) models with built-in telephones; (2) models that used plain, rather than thermal, paper for copies; (3) models that integrated telex for electronic mail purposes; and (4) models that allowed for secure (confidential) transmissions. For SunChips and Gatorade, new flavours and package sizes were added during the growth stage. Gillette introduced an advanced design of its Sensor razor, Sensor Excel, and produced a Sensor razor for women.

In the growth stage it is important to gain as much distribution for the product as possible. In the retail store, for example, this often means that competing companies fight for display and shelf space. Expanded distribution in the fax industry is an example. In 1986, early in the growth stage, only 11 percent of office machine dealers carried this equipment. By the mid-1990s, more than 70 percent of these dealers carried fax equipment, distribution was expanded to other stores selling electronic equipment, and the fight continues for which brands will be displayed.

Numerous product classes or industries are in the growth stage of the product life cycle. Examples include disposable 35-mm cameras, cellular telephones, nonalcoholic beer, and laptop computers.

Maturity Stage

The third stage, maturity, is characterized by a gradual levelling off of total industry sales or product class revenue. Also, marginal competitors begin to leave the market. Most consumers who would buy the product are either repeat purchasers of the item or have tried and abandoned it. Sales increase at a decreasing rate in the maturity stage as few new buyers enter the market. Profit declines because there is fierce price competition among many sellers and the cost of gaining each new buyer at this stage is greater than the resulting revenue.

Marketing expenses in the maturity stage are often directed toward holding market share through further product differentiation, and price competition continues through rebates and price discounting. Companies also focus on retaining distribution outlets. A major factor in a company's strategy is to reduce overall marketing costs by improving its promotional and distribution efficiency.

Stand-alone fax machines for business use entered the maturity stage in early 1991. Sixty-five percent of industry sales were captured by five producers at this time (Sharp, Muratec, Canon, Panasonic, and Ricoh), reflecting the departure of many marginal competitors. Industry sales growth had slowed in the mid-1990s compared with triple-digit average annual dollar sales increases in the late 1980s. By early 1996, there were an estimated 25 million stand-alone fax machines for business use installed throughout the world.

Numerous product classes and industries are in the maturity stage of their product life cycle. These include carbonated soft drinks, automobiles, and TVs.

Decline Stage

The decline stage occurs when sales and profits begin to drop. Frequently, a product enters this stage not because of any wrong strategy on the part of the company but because of environmental changes. New technology led to video cameras, which pushed 8-mm movie cameras into decline. Similarly, the merging of personal computer and facsimile technology began to replace the stand-alone fax machine in 1994. The decline stage for stand-alone fax machines for business use is projected for the year 2000 with the growth of e-mail. Advertising and promotional support for a product in this stage diminish as does investment in major product development. Products in the decline stage tend to consume a disproportionate share of management time and financial resources relative to their potential future worth. To handle a declining product, a company follows one of two strategies: deletion or harvesting.

Deletion   Product *deletion,* or dropping the product from the company's product line, is the most drastic strategy. Since a residual core of consumers still consume or use a product even in the decline stage, product elimination decisions are not taken lightly. When Coca-Cola decided to drop what is now known as Classic Coke, consumer objection was so intense that the company brought the product back.

Harvesting   A second strategy, *harvesting,* is when a company retains the product but reduces marketing support costs.[7] The product continues to be offered, but salespeople do not allocate time in selling nor are advertising dollars spent. The purpose of harvesting is to maintain the ability to meet customer requests. For example, Gillette continues to sell its Liquid Paper correction fluid for use with typewriters in the era of word-processing equipment.

Some Dimensions of the Product Life Cycle

Some important aspects of product life cycles are (1) their length, (2) the shape of their curves, and (3) how they vary with different levels of the products.

Length of the product life cycle   There is no exact time that a product takes to move through its life cycle. As a rule, consumer products have shorter life cycles than industrial products. For example, many new consumer food products such as SunChips move from the introduction stage to maturity in 18 months. The availability of mass communication vehicles informs consumers faster and shortens life cycles. Also, the rate of technological change tends to shorten product life cycles as new product innovation replaces existing products. This is happening with stand-alone fax machines.

The shape of the product life cycle   The product life cycle curve shown in Figure 12-1 might be referred to as a *generalized life cycle,* but not all products have the same shape to their curve. In fact, there are several different life cycle curves, each type suggesting different marketing strategies. Figure 12-3 shows the shape of life cycle curves for four different types of products: high-learning, low-learning, fashion, and fad products.

A *high-learning product* is one for which significant education of the customer is required and there is an extended introductory period (Figure 12-3A). Products such as home computers had this type of life cycle curve because consumers have to understand the benefits of purchasing the product or be educated in a new way of performing a familiar task. Convection ovens, for example, necessitate that the consumer learn a new way of cooking and alter familiar recipes.

In contrast, for a *low-learning product* sales begin immediately because little learning is required by the consumer, and the benefits of purchase are readily understood (Figure 12-3B). This product often can be easily imitated by competitors, so the marketing strategy is to broaden distribution quickly. In this way, as competitors rapidly enter, most retail outlets already have the innovator's product. It is also important to have the manufacturing capacity to meet demand. A recent example of a successful low-learning product is Frito-Lay's SunChips, discussed earlier. SunChips achieved $100 million in sales the first year it was introduced.

A *fashion product* (Figure 12-3C), such as hemline lengths on skirts or lapel widths on sports jackets, is introduced, declines, and then seems to return. Life cycles for

FIGURE 12-3

ALTERNATIVE PRODUCT LIFE CYCLES

fashion products most often appear in women's and men's clothing styles. The length of the cycles may be years or decades.

A *fad*, such as wall walkers or toe socks, experiences rapid sales on introduction and then an equally rapid decline (Figure 12-3D). These products are typically novelties. Japan's latest novelty craze recently hit the Canadian market. Tamagotchi is a "virtual pet" that comes in an egg-sized plastic oval with a digital screen on which the pet exists. Bandai Canada says the Tamagotchi is targeted to pre-teen girls.[8]

The product level: class, form, and brand   The product life shown in Figure 12-1 is a total industry or product class curve. Yet, in managing a product it is important to often distinguish among the multiple life cycles (class, form, and brand) that may exist. **Product class** refers to the entire product category or industry, such as video games.[9] **Product form** pertains to variations within the class. For video games, product form exists in the computing capability of game players such as 8-, 16- and 32/64-bit machines. Game players have a life cycle of their own and typically move from the introduction stage to maturity in six years. A final type of life cycle curve can represent a video game brand. Sales of these brands are driven by the purchase of their game players and the number and quality of their games. A new product form and brand cycle began in 1995 with the introduction of 32/64-bit machines and a new competitor, Sony's PlayStation game player. Sony will compete with Sega's Saturn and Nintendo's Ultra 64 game players and games.

The life cycle and consumers   The life cycle of a product depends on sales to consumers. Not all consumers rush to buy a product in the introductory stage, and the shapes of the life cycle curves indicate that most sales occur after the product has been on the market for some time. In essence, a product diffuses, or spreads, through the population, a concept called the *diffusion of innovation*.[10]

Some people are attracted to a product early, while others buy it only after they see their friends with the item. Figure 12-4 shows the consumer population divided into five categories of product adopters based on when they adopt a new product. Brief profiles

FIGURE 12-4

FIVE CATEGORIES AND PROFILES OF PRODUCT ADOPTERS

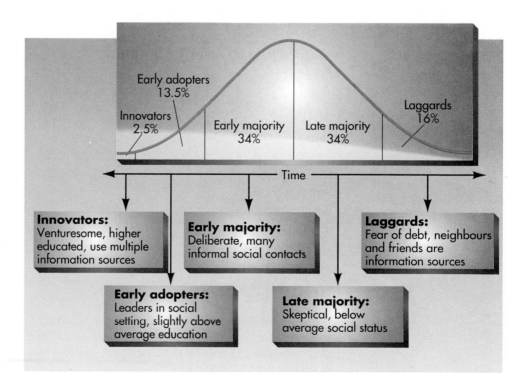

accompany each category. For any product to be successful, it must be purchased by innovators and early adopters. This is why manufacturers of new pharmaceuticals try to gain adoption by leading hospitals, clinics, and physicians that are widely respected in the medical field. Once accepted by innovators and early adopters, the adoption of new products moves on to the early majority, late majority, and laggard categories.

Several factors affect whether a consumer will adopt a new product or not. Common reasons for resisting a product in the introduction stage are usage barriers (the product is not compatible with existing habits), value barriers (the product provides no incentive to change), risk barriers (physical, economic, or social), and psychological barriers (cultural differences or image).[11]

Companies attempt to overcome these barriers in numerous ways. When Procter & Gamble launched its Oil of Olay Moisturizing Body Wash and Moisturizing Bath Bar into a very competitive soap category, it had to give Canadian consumers an incentive to change their current soap. How? The company used a major advertising campaign, large-scale sampling, and in-store demonstrations. The company now has 12 percent market share in the category.[12]

CONCEPT CHECK

1. Advertising plays a major role in the _____ stage of the product life cycle, and _____ plays a major role in maturity.

2. How do high-learning and low-learning products differ?

3. What does the life cycle for a fashion product look like?

MANAGING THE PRODUCT LIFE CYCLE

An important task for a firm is to manage its products through the successive stages of their life cycles. This section discusses the role of the product manager, who is usually responsible for this, and analyzes three ways to manage a product through its life cycle: modifying the product, modifying the market, and repositioning the product.

Role of a Product Manager

The product manager (sometimes called *brand manager*) manages the marketing efforts for a close-knit family of products or brands.[13] Introduced by P&G in 1928, the product manager style of marketing organization is used by consumer goods firms such as General Foods and Frito-Lay and by industrial firms such as Intel and Hewlett-Packard. General Motors of Canada and Pillsbury Canada also use product managers as well. All product managers are responsible for managing existing products through the stages of the life cycle, and some are also responsible for developing new products. Product managers' marketing responsibilities include developing and executing a marketing program for the product line described in an annual marketing plan and approving ad copy, media selection, and package design. The role of product managers in planning, implementing, and controlling marketing strategy is covered in depth in Chapter 22.

Modifying the Product

Product modification involves altering a product's characteristic, such as its quality, performance, or appearance, to try to increase and extend the product's sales. Wrinkle-free cotton slacks sold by Levi Strauss revitalized sales of men's casual pants and now accounts for 60 percent of the men's cotton pants product class sales. Iced tea, in dry mix or ready-to-serve formats has enjoyed a revival in recent years. But a new modification of iced tea, frozen iced tea, is now showing impressive sales increases. The Minute Maid Company of Canada Inc., which markets Nestea frozen iced tea calls it "the biggest new product we've launched in the '90s".[14]

New features, packages, or scents can be used to change a product's characteristics and give the sense of a revised product. Procter & Gamble revamped Pantene shampoo and conditioner with a new vitamin formula and relaunched the brand with a multi-million dollar advertising and promotion campaign. The result? Pantene, a brand first introduced in the 1940s, became the top-selling shampoo and conditioner in an industry with more than 1000 competitors.[15]

Modifying the Market

With **market modification** strategies, a company tries to increase a product's use among existing customers, create new use situations, or find new customers.

Increasing use   Promoting more frequent usage has been a strategy of Campbell Soup Company. Since soup consumption rises in the winter and declines during the summer, the company now advertises more heavily in warm months to encourage consumers to think of soup as more than a cold-weather food. Similarly, The Florida Orange Growers Association advocates drinking orange juice throughout the day rather than for breakfast only.

Creating new use situation   Finding new uses for an existing product has been the strategy behind Woolite, a laundry soap. Originally intended for the hand washing of woolen material, Woolite now promotes itself for use with all fine clothing items. Mars, Inc. suggests a new-use situation when it markets its M&M's candy as a replacement for chocolate chips in baked goods.

Finding new users   To prevent sales declines in wall-to-wall carpeting, carpet manufacturers found new user groups such as schools and hospitals. To expand company sales, Nautilus, a manufacturer of fitness equipment for gyms, entered the home market. Commercial accounts represented 95 percent of the company's sales, but the

MARS, INC. SUCCESSFULLY EXTENDS THE LIFE CYCLE OF ITS M&M'S CANDY BY FINDING NEW USE SITUATIONS.

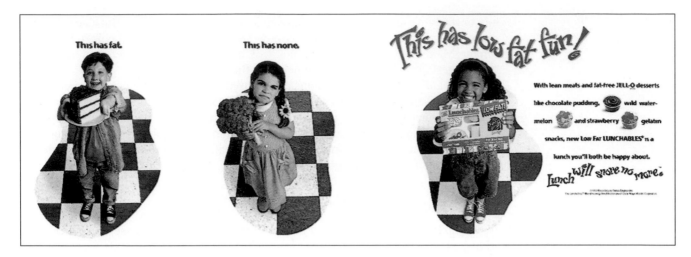

OSCAR MAYER CAPITALIZES ON THE POPULARITY OF THE "BETTER-FOR-YOU" TREND IN THE FOOD INDUSTRY WITH ITS NEW LOW FAT LUNCHABLES®
PRODUCT LINE.

home market has a $1 to $5 billion sales potential. Pharmacia & Upjohn, Inc. first targeted men for its Rogaine Topical Solution, a drug to restore hair growth, but later marketed this product to women.

Repositioning the Product

Often a company decides to reposition its product or product line in an attempt to prevent sales decline. *Product repositioning* is changing the place a product occupies in a consumer's mind relative to competitive products. A firm can reposition a product by changing one or more of the four marketing mix elements. Four factors that trigger a repositioning action are discussed next.

Reacting to a competitor's position   One reason to reposition a product is because a competitor's entrenched position is adversely affecting sales and market share. Procter & Gamble recently repositioned its venerable Ivory soap bar in response to the success of Lever 2000, sold by Lever Brothers. Lever 2000, a bar soap that moisturizes, deodorizes, and kills bacteria, eroded P&G's dominance of the bar soap market. P&G responded with its own triple-threat soap called New Ivory Ultra Safe Skin Care Soap. The problem? The new Ivory doesn't float![16]

Reaching a new market   Dannon Yogurt introduced Yop, a liquid yogurt, in France. The product flopped because the French were not interested in another dairy product. When Dannon repositioned Yop as a soft drink for the health-conscious French consumer, sales soared.[17]

Repositioning can involve more than changing advertising copy. The New Balance Company changed its product's position as a running shoe for the serious runner to a shoe for the mass market. The distribution strategy was altered from selling only through specialty running stores to selling through discount and department stores as well.

Catching a rising trend   Changing consumer trends can also lead to repositioning. The recent popularity of low-fat or fat-free foods is an example.[18] Today, many consumers say that a food's fat content is a concern to them. Nabisco's SnackWell line of cookies and crackers and Oscar Mayer Low-Fat Lunchables were among the first to capitalize on this "better-for-you" trend in the food industry. At Kraft-General Foods, fat-free and reduced-fat versions of its existing products total millions in sales annually.

ETHICS AND SOCIAL RESPONSIBILITY ALERT

CONSUMERS ARE PAYING MORE FOR LESS IN DOWNSIZED PACKAGES

For more than 30 years, Starkist put 6.5 ounces of tuna into its regular-sized can. Today, Starkist puts 6.125 ounces of tuna into its can but charges the same price. Colgate-Palmolive's Ajax king-size laundry detergent package has remained the same size, but the contents have been cut from 61 ounces to 55 ounces and the package price increased from $2.59 to $2.79. Procter & Gamble cut the number of Pampers disposable diapers in its packages while leaving the price the same. The price of Mennen Speed Stick deodorant has not changed, but it now comes in a larger package with 2.25 ounces of deodorant versus 2.5 ounces in the previous, smaller package.

Consumer advocates charge that "downsizing" packages while maintaining or increasing prices is a subtle and unannounced way of taking advantage of consumer's buying habits. Manufacturers argue that this practice is a way of keeping prices from rising beyond psychological barriers for their products.

Is downsizing an unethical practice if manufacturers do not inform consumers that the package contents are less than they were previously?

Changing the value offered   In repositioning a product, a company can decide to change the value it offers buyers and trade up or down. **Trading up** involves adding value to the product (or line) through additional features or higher-quality materials. Japanese automakers built their reputations with reliable and affordable cars. Many have since traded up, as evidenced by Honda's Acura, Toyota's Lexus, and Nissan's Infiniti, to compete in the luxury sedan market historically occupied by Mercedes-Benz and Cadillac. Dog food manufacturers also have traded up by offering super premium foods based on "life-stage nutrition." Mass merchandisers can trade up by adding a designer clothes section to their store, as shown by recent actions by Sears Canada and The Bay.

Trading down involves reducing the number of features, quality, or price. For example, airlines have added more seats, thus reducing leg room, and eliminated extras, such as snack service and food portions. Trading down often exists when companies engage in **downsizing**—reducing the content of packages without changing package size and maintaining or increasing the package price. For instance, Fabergé's Brut antiperspirant deodorant spray comes in its regular-size can at the same price, but the content has been reduced from five ounces to four.[19] Firms have been criticized for this practice, as described in the accompanying Ethics and Social Responsibility Alert.[20]

CONCEPT CHECK

1. How does a product manager help manage a product's life cycle?
2. What does "creating new use situations" mean in managing a product's life cycle?
3. Explain the difference between trading up and trading down in repositioning.

BRANDING

A basic decision in marketing products is **branding,** in which an organization uses a name, phrase, design, symbols, or combination of these to identify its products and distinguish them from those of competitors. A **brand name** is any word, "device"

FIGURE 12-5

EXAMPLES OF WELL-KNOWN
TRADEMARKS, BRAND NAMES, AND
TRADE NAMES.

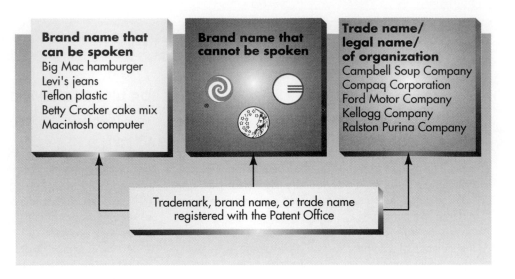

(design, sound, shape, or colour), or combination of these used to distinguish a seller's goods or services. Some brand names can be spoken, such as a Gatorade. Other brand names cannot be spoken, such as the rainbow-coloured apple (the *logotype* or *logo*) that Apple Computer puts on its machines and in its ads. A **trade name** is a commercial, legal name under which a company does business. The Campbell Soup Company is the trade name of that firm.

A **trademark** identifies that a firm has legally registered its brand name or trade name so the firm has its exclusive use, thereby preventing others from using it. In Canada, trademarks are registered under the Trademarks Act with Consumer and Corporate Affairs Canada. A well-known trademark can help a company advertise its offerings to customers and develop their brand loyalty. Figure 12-5 shows examples of well-known trademarks.

Because a good trademark can help sell a product, *product counterfeiting,* which involves low-cost copies of popular brands not manufactured by the original producer, has been a growing problem. Counterfeit products can steal sales from the original manufacturer or hurt the company's reputation.

Trademark protection is a significant issue in global marketing. For instance, the transformation of the Soviet Union into individual countries has meant that many firms, such as Xerox, have had to reregister trademarks in each of the republics to prohibit misuse and generic use ("xeroxing") of their trademarks by competitors and consumers.

The Value of Brands

Branding policy is important not only for manufacturers but also for retailers and consumers. Retailers value branding because consumers shop at stores that carry their desired brands. Some retailers have created their own store brands to further enhance loyalty from their customers. Sears exclusively offers the Kenmore brand for its appliance line and Craftsman as the brand for tools.

A good brand name is of such importance to a company that it has led to a concept called **brand equity,** the added value a given brand name gives to a product beyond the functional benefits provided.[21] This value has two distinct advantages. First, brand equity provides a competitive advantage, such as the Sunkist label that implies quality fruit and the Gatorade name that defines sport drinks. A second advantage is that consumers are often willing to pay a higher price for a product with brand equity. Brand equity, in this instance, is represented by the premium a consumer will pay for one brand over another when the functional benefits provided are identical. Intel microchips, Kodak film, Duracell batteries, Microsoft computer software, and Louis Vuitton luggage all enjoy a price premium arising from brand equity.

MARKETING NEWSNET

ACA UNVEILS NEW BRAND

ACA Co-operative, a 50-year-old Annapolis Valley, Nova Scotia, company has adopted a new brand name—Eden Valley Farms. Even though ACA is the tenth largest company in Nova Scotia (400 employees and annual sales of $75 million), and holds a one-third market share in the Maritimes in the chicken and egg categories, research showed that fewer than 5 percent of consumers recognized the ACA brand.

ACA realized it had to build a brand and offer consumers unique choices if it was to remain competitive. The 81 farmers who comprise the co-op settled on Eden Valley Farms for the new brand name. It is not an actual place but according to the co-op it says the right things: freshness, quality, and heritage. These factors, particularly heritage, are emphasized in the new logo, which features a

traditional-looking barn in a verdant pasture. The Eden Valley packaging sports a "50 + Years of Excellence" badge, although the brand itself is less than a year old.

A major ad campaign including TV and billboards supports the brand launch. In addition, the co-op has expanded its product line to include flavoured chicken breasts. Packaging touts the co-op's chickens as grain-fed and wholesome, and includes cooking suggestions and recipes. ACA is packaging its eggs in cartons of 8, 12 and 18 to answer consumer demand for more choice and is marketing The Good Morning Egg, which is an egg enhanced with Omega-3 polyunsaturates.

ACA competes with some very big brands such as Maple Leaf and Maple Lodge Farms, but feels with the new brand name it will be better able to hold and enhance its market share.

Consumers, however, may benefit most from branding. Recognizing competing products by distinct trademarks allows them to be more efficient shoppers. Consumers can recognize and avoid products with which they are dissatisfied, while becoming loyal to other, more satisfying brands. As discussed in Chapter 6, brand loyalty often eases consumers' decision making by eliminating the need for an external search. CanWest Global TV System adopted a Canada-wide identity with a new logo and single brand "Global." CanWest says the new brand should make it easier for viewers to identify the network's stations and find the schedule they have. In another case, as the Marketing NewsNet box points out, ACA Co-operative of Nova Scotia adopted a new brand name after it discovered fewer than 5 percent of consumers recognized the ACA brand.[22]

Licensing

The value of brand equity is evident in the strategy of licensing. **Licensing** is a contractual agreement whereby a company allows another firm to use its brand name, patent, trade secret, or other property for a royalty or a fee. Licensing can be very profitable to the licensor and the licensee.[23]

Licensing also assists companies in entering global markets with minimal risk as Clearly Canadian Beverages of Vancouver has done in several markets including Japan and the United States. Similarly, PepsiCo Foods International licensed Elite Foods in Israel to produce and market Frito-Lay's Ruffles potato chips and Cheetos cheese-flavoured corn puffs. These brands capture 15 percent of the salty snack market in Israel.[24]

Picking a Good Brand Name

We take brand names such as Dial, Sanyo, Porsche, and Danskin for granted, but it is often a difficult and expensive process to pick a good name. Five criteria are mentioned most often in selecting a good brand name.[25]

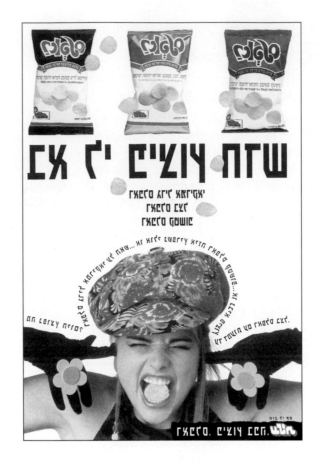

The name should suggest the product benefits. For example, Accutron (watches), Easy Off (oven cleaner), Glass Plus (glass cleaner), Cling-Free (antistatic cloth for drying clothes), and Tidy Bowl (toilet bowl cleaner) all clearly describe the benefits of purchasing the product.

The name should be memorable, distinctive, and positive. In the auto industry, when a competitor has a memorable name, others quickly imitate. When Ford named a car the Mustang, Pintos, Colts, Mavericks, and Broncos soon followed. The Thunderbird name led to the Phoenix, Eagle, Sunbird, and Firebird.

The name should fit the company or product image. Sharp is a name that can apply to audio and video equipment. Excedrin, Anacin, and Nuprin are scientific-sounding names, good for an analgesic. However, naming a personal computer PCjr, as IBM did with its first computer for home use, neither fit the company nor the product. PCjr, sounded too much like a toy and stalled IBM's initial entry into the home-use market. Also, the name should have no legal or regulatory restrictions. Legal restrictions produce trademark infringement suits, and regulatory restrictions arise through improper use of words.

Finally, the name should be simple (such as Bold laundry detergent, Sure deodorant, and Bic pens) and should be emotional (such as Joy and My Sin perfumes). In the development of names for international use, having a nonmeaningful brand name has been considered a benefit. A name such as Exxon does not have any prior impressions or undesirable images among a diverse world population of different languages and cultures. The 7Up name is another matter. In Shanghai, China, the phrase means "death through drinking" in the local dialect, and sales have suffered as a result.[26]

Branding Strategies

In deciding to brand a product, companies have several possible strategies, including manufacturer branding, reseller branding, or mixed branding approaches.

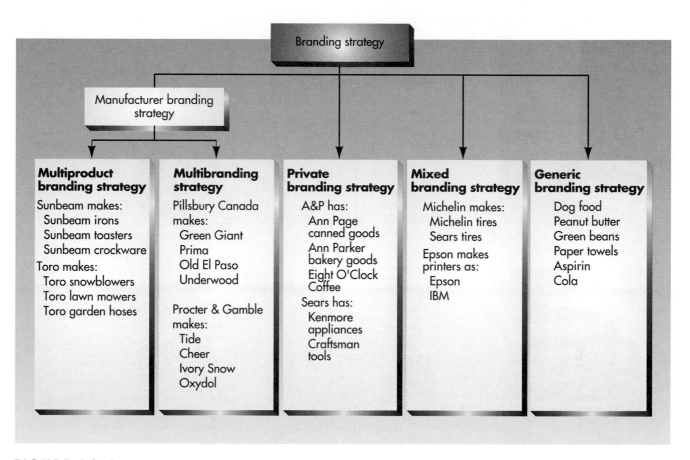

FIGURE 12-6   ALTERNATIVE BRANDING STRATEGIES

Manufacturer branding   With **manufacturer branding,** the producer dictates the brand name using either a multiproduct or multibrand approach. **Multiproduct branding** is when a company uses one name for all its products. This approach is often referred to as a *blanket* or *family* branding strategy (Figure 12-6).

There are several advantages to multiproduct branding. Capitalizing again on brand equity, consumers who have a good experience with the product will transfer this favourable attitude to other items in the product class with the same name. Therefore, this brand strategy makes possible *line extensions,* the practice of using a current brand name to enter a new market segment in its product class. Campbell Soup Company effectively employs a multiproduct branding strategy with soup line extensions. It offers regular Campbell soup, home-cooking style, chunky, and "healthy request" varieties and more than 100 soup flavours. This strategy can also result in lower advertising and promotion costs because the same name is used on all products, thus raising the level of brand awareness.

A strong brand equity also allows for *brand extension,* the practice of using a current brand name to enter a completely different product class.[27] For instance, the equity in the Tylenol name as a trusted pain reliever allowed Johnson & Johnson to successfully extend this name to Tylenol Cold & Flu and Tylenol PM, a sleep aid. Fisher-Price, an established name in children's toys, was able to extend this name to children's shampoo and conditioners and baby bath and lotion products.

However, there is a risk with brand extensions. Too many uses for one brand name can dilute the meaning of a brand for consumers. Marketing experts claim this has happened to the Arm & Hammer brand given its use for toothpaste, laundry detergent, cat litter, air freshener, carpet deodorizer, and anti-perspirant.[28]

A recent variation on brand extensions is the practice of **co-branding,** the pairing of two brand names of two manufacturers for joint-marketing purposes. Co-branding can

BLACK & DECKER USES A MULTIBRANDING STRATEGY TO REACH DIFFERENT MARKET SEGMENTS. BLACK & DECKER MARKETS ITS LINE OF TOOLS FOR THE DO-IT-YOURSELFER MARKET WITH THE BLACK & DECKER NAME, BUT USES THE DEWALT NAME FOR ITS PROFESSIONAL TOOL LINE.

benefit firms by allowing them to enter new product classes, capitalize on an already established brand name in a product class, or reach new market segments. For example, Volkswagen and Trek co-brand to market the Jetta automobile and the Trek mountain bike. Second Cup of Toronto has a co-branding agreement with Air Canada, while rival Starbucks co-brands with Canadian Airlines.[29] Probably one of the major co-branding agreements in recent history in Canada is the one between Rogers Cantel Communications and AT&T Canada Inc. Both companies suggest that together they will be able to provide seamless and expanded wireless telecommunications services to their respective customers throughout North America.[30]

An alternative manufacturer's branding strategy, **multibranding,** involves giving each product a distinct name. Multibranding is a useful strategy when each brand is intended for a different market segment. P&G makes Camay soap for those concerned with soft skin and Safeguard for those who want deodorant protection. Black & Decker markets its line of tools for the household do-it-yourselfer segment with the Black & Decker name, but uses the DeWalt name for its professional tool line. Disney uses the Touchstone Pictures name for films directed at adults and its Disney name for children's films.

Multibranding strategies become more complex in the global marketplace. As an example, P&G uses multiple brand names for the same product when competing internationally. For instance, PertPlus shampoo is sold as Rejoice in Hong Kong, PertPlus in the Middle East, and Vidal Sassoon in the United Kingdom. However, international branding strategies do differ. In Japan, where corporate names are important, P&G markets the company's name prominently with the brand name of the product.

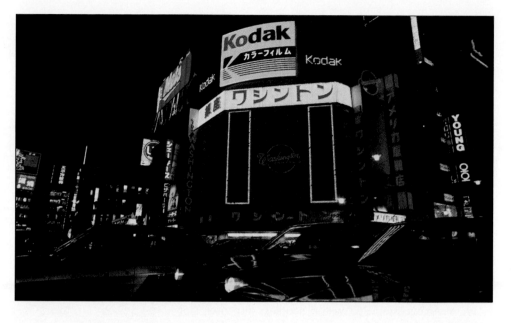

Compared with the multiproduct approach, promotional costs tend to be higher with multibranding. The company must generate awareness among consumers and retailers for each new brand name without the benefit of any previous impressions. The advantages of this approach are that each brand is unique to each market segment and there is no risk that a product failure will affect other products in the line.

The multibranding approach in Europe is slowly being replaced by **euro-branding,** the strategy of using the same brand name for the same product across all countries in the 15-nation European Union. This strategy has many of the benefits linked with multiproduct branding in addition to making Pan-European advertising and promotion programs possible.

Private branding   A company uses **private branding,** often called *private labelling* or *reseller branding,* when it manufactures products but sells them under the brand name of a wholesaler or retailer. Radio Shack, Sears, and Kmart are large retailers that have their own brand names. Food products are often private labelled for supermarkets.

Matsushita of Japan manufactures VCRs for Magnavox, GE, Sylvania, JCPenney, and Curtis Mathes. The advantage to the manufacturer is that promotional costs are shifted to the retailer or other company, and the manufacturer can often sell more units through others than by itself. There is a risk, though, because the manufacturer's sales depend heavily on the efforts of others.

Mixed branding   A compromise between manufacturer and private branding is **mixed branding,** where a firm markets products under its own name and that of a reseller because the segment attracted to the reseller is different from their own market. Sanyo and Toshiba manufacture television sets for Sears as well as for themselves. This process is similar to Michelin's, which manufactures tires for Sears as well as under its own name. Kodak recently adopted a mixed branding approach in Japan to increase its sales of 35-mm film. In addition to selling its Kodak brand, the company now makes "COOP" private label film for the Japanese Consumer Cooperative Union, which is a group of 2500 stores. Priced 38 percent below its Kodak brand, the private label seeks to attract the price-sensitive Japanese consumer.[31]

Generic branding   An alternative branding approach is the **generic brand,** which is a no-brand product such as dog food, peanut butter, or green beans. There is no identification other than a description of the contents. The major appeal is that the

MARKETING NEWSNET

CREATING CUSTOMER VALUE THROUGH PACKAGING: PEZ HEADS DISPENSE MORE THAN CANDY

Customer value can assume numerous forms. For Pez Candy, Inc., customer value manifests itself in some 250 Pez character candy dispensers. Each 99 cent refillable dispenser ejects tasty candy tablets in a variety of flavours that delight preteen and teens alike.

Pez was formulated in 1927 by Austrian food mogul Edward Haas III and successfully sold in Europe as an adult breath mint. Pez, which comes from the German word for peppermint, *pfefferminz,* was originally packaged in a hygienic, headless plastic dispenser. Pez first appeared in North America in 1953 with a headless dispenser, marketed to adults. After conducting extensive marketing research, Pez was repositioned with fruit flavours, repackaged with licensed character heads on top of the dispenser, and remarketed as a children's product in the mid-1950s. Since then, most top-level licensed characters and hundreds of other characters have become Pez heads. Consumers eat more than 1 billion Pez tablets annually, and company sales growth exceeds that of the candy industry as a whole.

The unique Pez package dispenses a "use experience" for its customers beyond the candy itself, namely, fun. And fun translates into a 98 percent awareness level for Pez among teenagers and 89 percent among mothers with children. Pez has not advertised its product for years. With that kind of awareness, who needs advertising?

price is up to one-third less than that of branded items. Generic brands account for less than 1 percent of total grocery sales.[32] The limited appeal of generics has been attributed to the popularity of private brands and greater promotional efforts for manufacturer brand-name items. Consumers who use generics see these products as being as good as brand-name items, and, in light of what they expect, users of these products are relatively pleased with their purchases.

PACKAGING

The **packaging** component of a product refers to any container in which it is offered for sale and on which information is communicated. To a great extent, the customer's first exposure to a product is the package, and it is an expensive and important part of the marketing strategy. For Pez Candy, Inc., the character head-on-a-stick plastic container that dispenses a miniature brick candy is the central element of its marketing strategy as described in the accompanying Marketing NewsNet.[33]

Creating Customer Value through Packaging

Today's packaging costs millions of dollars, and an estimated 10 cents of every dollar spent by a consumer goes to packaging. Despite the cost, packaging is essential because packages provide important benefits for the manufacturer, retailer, and ultimate consumer.

Communication benefits   A major benefit of packaging is the information on it convcycd to thc consumcr, such as directions on how to use the product and the composition of the product, which is needed to satisfy legal requirements of product disclosure. For example, a new labelling system for packaged and processed foods created a uniform format for nutritional and dietary information. Other information consists of seals and symbols, either government required or commercial seals of approval (such as the Good Housekeeping seal).

Functional benefits   Packaging often plays an important functional role, such as convenience, protection, or storage. Quaker State has changed its oil containers to eliminate the need for a separate spout, and Borden has changed the shape of its Elmer's Wonder Bond adhesive to prevent clogging of the spout. Molson brought Canadian Draft to Calgary beer drinkers in new packaging called the Home Draft Unit which takes up the space of 12 cans but holds 17 cans worth of beer and lasts for 21 days after it is opened.[34]

Consumer protection has become an important function of packaging, including the development of tamper-resistant containers. Today, companies commonly use safety seals or pop-tops that reveal previous opening. Nevertheless, no package is truly tamper resistant.

Another functional value of packaging is in extending storage and *shelf life* (the time a product can be stored before it spoils). New technology allows products requiring refrigeration to be packaged in paper-sealed containers, which dramatically increases their shelf life.

Perceptual benefits   A third component of packaging is the perception created in the consumer's mind. Just Born Inc., a candy manufacturer of such brands as Jolly Joes and Mike and Ike Treats, discovered the importance of this component of packaging. For many years the brands were sold in old-fashioned black and white packages, but when the packaging was changed to four colour, with animated grape

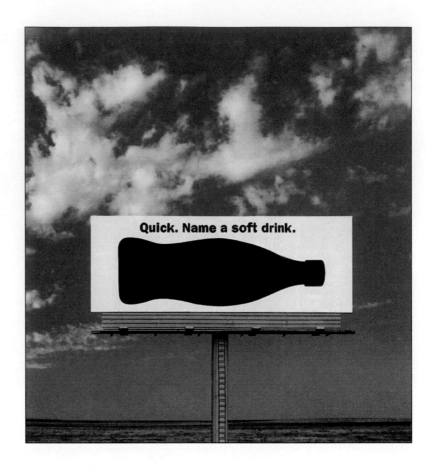

and cherry characters, sales increased 25 percent. Procter & Gamble changes the packaging for Clearasil every year to give the appearance of a new cream, which is important to the target market of teenagers who purchase the product. Coca-Cola has brought back its famous pale-green, contoured bottle to attract consumers who remember drinking soft drinks from glass bottles, not from aluminum cans and large plastic bottles. A worldwide sales increase of 8 percent was linked to the new-old bottle. In Japan and Spain, sales increases were 23 percent and 30 percent, respectively.[35]

The popularity of the contoured bottle has led Coca-Cola to experiment with a contoured aluminum can in Europe.

A package can connote status, economy, or even product quality. Equally fresh potato chips were wrapped in two different types of bags: wax paper and polyvinyl. Consumers rated the chips in the polyvinyl as crisper and even tastier, even though the chips were identical.[36]

In the past, the colour of packages was selected subjectively. For example, the famous Campbell's soup can was the inspiration of a company executive who liked Cornell University's red-and-white football uniforms. Today, there is greater recognition that colour affects consumers' perceptions. When the colour of the can of Barrelhead Sugar-Free Root Beer changed to beige from blue, consumers said it tasted more like old-fashioned root beer.[37] And Owens-Corning judged the pink colour of its fiber insulation to be so important that the colour was given trademark status by the courts.[38]

Global Trends in Packaging

Two global trends in packaging originating in the mid-1990s will continue into the twenty-first century. One trend involves the environmental effects of packaging, the other focuses on packaging health and safety concerns.

Environmental sensitivity   Because of widespread worldwide concern about the growth of solid waste and the shortage of viable landfill sites, the amount, composition, and disposal of packaging material continues to receive much attention.[39] Recycling packaging material is a major thrust. Procter & Gamble now uses recycled cardboard in 70 percent of its paper packaging and is packaging Tide, Cheer, Era, and Dash detergents in jugs that contain 25 percent recycled plastic. Spic and Span liquid cleaner is packaged in 100 percent recycled material. Other firms, such as the large U.K. retailer Gainsbury, emphasize the use of less packaging material. Gainsbury examines every product it sells to ensure that each uses only the minimum material necessary for shipping and display.

European countries have been trendsetters concerning packaging guidelines and environmental sensitivity. Many of these guidelines now exist in provisions governing trade to and within the European Union. In Germany, for instance, 80 percent of packaging material must be collected, and 80 percent of this amount must be recycled or reused to reduce solid waste in landfills. North American firms marketing in Europe have responded to these guidelines, and ultimately benefited North American consumers. The history of Procter & Gamble's Downy Refill liquid fabric softener is an example. The product's plastic bottle is reusable, and the refill carton uses 75 percent less packaging material. First introduced in Germany in 1987, the product moved to Canada in 1989, and then to the United States in late 1990. Downy Refill now accounts for more than 40 percent of Downy's sales.[40]

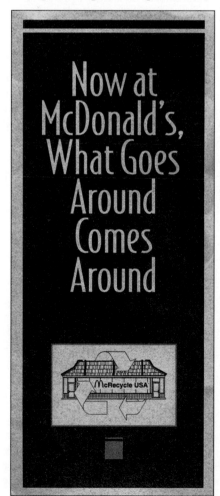

Increasingly, firms are using life cycle analysis (LCA) to examine the environmental effect of their packaging at every stage from raw material sources and production through distribution and disposal. A classic use of LCA was the decision by McDonald's to abandon the polystyrene clam-shells it used to package its hamburger. LCA indicated that the environment would be better served if the amount of solid waste packaging was reduced than if the polystyrene shells were recycled. McDonald's elected to package its hamburgers in a light wrap made of paper and polyethylene and eliminate the polystyrene package altogether.

Health and safety concerns   A second trend involves the growing health and safety concerns of packaging materials. Today, a majority of Canadian and European consumers believe companies should make sure products and their packages are safe, regardless of the cost, and companies are responding to this view in numerous ways.[41] For instance, studies suggest that microwave heating of some packages can lead to potentially cancer-causing agents seeping into food products. The major concern relates to packaging that contains heat susceptors—thin, metalicized plastic film strips that help brown microwaveable food. Du Pont and 3M, among other firms, are working to develop alternatives in anticipation of regulatory changes regarding packaging.[42] Most butane lighters sold today, such as those made by BIC, contain a child-resistant safety latch to prevent misuse and accidental fire.

PRODUCT WARRANTY

A final component for product consideration is the **warranty,** which is a statement indicating the liability of the manufacturer for product deficiencies. There are various degrees of product warranties with different implications for manufacturers and customers.

The Variations of a Warranty

Some companies offer *express warranties,* which are written statements of liabilities. In recent years the government has required greater disclosure on express warranties to indicate whether the warranty is a limited-coverage or full-coverage alternative. A *limited-coverage warranty* specifically states the bounds of coverage and, more important, areas of noncoverage, whereas a *full warranty* has no limits of noncoverage. Cadillac is a company that boldly touts its warranty coverage.

With greater frequency, manufacturers are being held to *implied warranties,* which assign responsibility for product deficiencies to the manufacturer. Studies show that warranties are important and affect a consumer's product evaluation. Brands that have limited warranties tend to receive less positive evaluations compared with full-warranty items.

The Growing Importance of Warranties

Warranties are important in light of increasing product liability claims. In the early part of this century the courts protected companies, but the trend now is toward "strict liability" rulings, where a manufacturer is liable for any product defect, whether it followed reasonable research standards or not. This issue is hotly contested by companies and consumer advocates.

Warranties represent much more to the buyer than just protection from negative consequences—they can hold a significant marketing advantage for the producer. Sears has built a strong reputation for its Craftsman tool line with a simple warranty: if you break a tool, it's replaced with no questions asked. Zippo has an equally simple guarantee: "If it ever fails, we'll fix it free."

CONCEPT CHECK

1. How does a generic brand differ from a private brand?
2. Explain the role of packaging in terms of perception.
3. What is the difference between an expressed and an implied warranty?

SUMMARY

1. Products have a finite life cycle consisting of four stages: introduction, growth, maturity, and decline. The marketing objectives for each stage differ.

2. In the introductory stage the need is to establish primary demand, whereas the growth stage requires selective demand strate-

gies. In the maturity stage the need is to maintain market share; the decline stage necessitates a deletion or harvesting strategy.

3. There are various shapes to the product life cycle. High-learning products have a long introductory period, and low-learning products rapidly enter the growth stage. There are also

different curves for fashions and fads. Different product life cycle curves can exist for the product class, product form, and brand.

4. In managing a product's life cycle, changes can be made in the product itself or in the target market. Product modification approaches include changes in the quality, performance, or appearance. Market modification approaches entail increasing a product's use among existing customers, creating new use situations, or finding new users.

5. Product repositioning can come about by reacting to a competitor's position, reaching a new market, capitalizing on a rising trend, or changing the value offered in a product.

6. Branding enables a firm to distinguish its product in the marketplace from those of its competitors. A good brand name should suggest the product benefits, be memorable, fit the company or product image, be free of legal restrictions, and be simple and emotional. A good brand name is of such importance that it has led to a concept of brand equity, the added value a given brand name gives to a product beyond the functional benefits provided.

7. Licensing of a brand name is being used by many companies. The company allows the name to be used without having to manufacture the product.

8. Manufacturers can follow one of three branding strategies: a manufacturer's brand, a reseller brand, or a mixed brand approach. With a manufacturer's branding approach, the company can use the same brand name for all products in the line (multiproduct, or family, branding) or can give products different brands (multibranding).

9. A reseller, or private, brand is used when a firm manufactures a product but sells it under the brand name of a wholesaler or retailer. A generic brand is a product with no identification of manufacturer or reseller that is offered on the basis of price appeal.

10. Packaging provides communication, functional, and perceptual benefits. The two global emerging trends in packaging are greater concerns regarding the environmental impact and the health and safety of packaging materials.

11. The warranty, a statement of a manufacturer's liability for product deficiencies, is an important aspect of a manufacturer's product strategy.

KEY TERMS

product life cycle p. 292
product class p. 297
product form p. 297
product modification p. 298
market modification p. 299
trading up p. 301
trading down p. 301
downsizing p. 301
branding p. 301
brand name p. 301
trade name p. 302
trademark p. 302

brand equity p. 302
licensing p. 303
manufacturer branding p. 305
multiproduct branding p. 305
co-branding p. 305
multibranding p. 306
euro-branding p. 307
private branding p. 307
mixed branding p. 307
generic brand p. 307
packaging p. 308
warranty p. 312

CHAPTER PROBLEMS AND APPLICATIONS

1. Listed here are three different products in various stages of the product life cycle. What marketing strategies would you suggest to these companies? (*a*) GTE cellular telephone company—growth stage, (*b*) Mountain Stream tap-water purifying systems—introductory stage, and (*c*) hand-held manual can openers—decline stage.

2. It has often been suggested that products are intentionally made to break down or wear out. Is this strategy a planned product modification approach?

3. The product manager of GE is reviewing the penetration of trash compactors in Canadian homes. After more than a decade in existence, this product is in relatively few homes.

What problems can account for this poor acceptance? What is the shape of the trash compactor life cycle?

4. For several years Ferrari has been known as the manufacturer of expensive luxury automobiles. The company plans to attract the major segment of the car-buying market who purchase medium-priced automobiles. As Ferrari considers this trading-down strategy, what branding strategy would you recommend? What are the trade-offs to consider with your strategy?

5. The nature of product warranties has changed as the court system reassesses the meaning of warranties. How does the regulatory trend toward warranties affect product development?

CASE 12-1   Polaroid Canada

When Polaroid (www.polaroid.com) first introduced instant photography in 1947, it was a remarkable breakthrough in consumer photography. Polaroid prints were of comparable quality to other camera systems of the time, but the unique aspect of Polaroid pictures was that they developed instantly.

Instant photography became very popular with consumers and very profitable for Polaroid. However, in the 1980s the advent of newer technology and a changing and more sophisticated consumer began to change the marketplace. New, compact, fully automatic 35-mm cameras provided high-quality prints never before achieved with easy-to-use cameras. Meanwhile, rapidly declining processing time—to as low as one hour—further contributed to the popularity of 35-mm cameras. This development began to undermine Polaroid's competitive advantage: immediacy.

In the late 1980s, 35-mm cameras and film became the standard in consumer photography for traditional photographic uses. The new 35-mm prints forced comparisons with instant pictures and consumers perceived that there were some differences in terms of colour and resolution. In addition, an instant print was typically twice as expensive as a 35-mm print. As the photographic marketplace changed, Polaroid remained committed to the instant segment even though instant photography's competitive advantage of immediacy was slowly eroding. With the advent of 35-mm point-and-shoot cameras, there was a concern that consumers would be less likely to use Polaroid instant cameras in traditional photographic situations since they now had more camera options.

The key issue facing Polaroid in the 1990s was how to make "instant" important to consumers once again. Polaroid had to begin to reposition the camera and rejuvenate what consumers saw as a mature brand.

Questions

1. How can Polaroid revitalize their instant photography business?
2. Who should Polaroid target?
3. What message should Polaroid communicate to the target(s)?

CHAPTER 13

Managing Services

- Describe the four unique elements of services.

- Explain the service continuum.

- Understand the way in which consumers purchase and evaluate services.

- Understand the important role of internal marketing in service organizations.

- Explain the special nature of the marketing mix for services.

SKI RESORTS'S NEW TARGET MARKET: HOT DOGS!

Like many other businesses, Canadian ski resorts are always looking for new ways to increase sales. These resorts investigate marketing actions ranging from pursuing new products (in this case new services) and new markets to changing their pricing and promotion practices.

The range of new services offered by ski resorts in Canada has increased dramatically over the years. Some resorts offer day-long back-country expeditions. Others have introduced guided tours called "woods skiing." Some resorts put together total vacation packages including skiing, and off-site entertainment. Others have opened new natural-state terrain and have added snowboarding to their offerings.

Some ski resorts have decided to focus on select target markets. Such targets include "extreme" skiers and "hot dogs" who are bored with the gentler runs found at many resorts. Other niches include children, the over-50 age group, European skiers, and snowboarders.

Ski resorts—and all service organizations—face another special challenge: matching demand and capacity. Historically, ski areas could attract consumers only during the winter months, leaving their resorts idle the rest of the year. Many ski areas, however, are now learning to attract enthusiasts of other sports, such as mountain bikers and hikers, in order to keep their resorts open during the summer months.

As the actions of the ski industry illustrate, the marketing of services is unique and challenging. In this chapter, we discuss how services differ from traditional products (goods), how service consumers make purchase decisions, and the important aspects of developing and managing the marketing mix for services.

THE SERVICE ECONOMY

As defined in Chapter 1, **services** are activities, deeds, or other basic intangibles offered for sale to consumers in exchange for money or something else of value. One services-marketing expert suggests that services permeate every aspect of our lives.[1] We use transportation services when we travel; we use restaurant services to feed us and hotels to put roofs over our heads. At home, we rely on services such as electricity and telephones. At work, we need postal, courier, and maintenance services to keep our workplaces running. We use the services of hairstylists to maintain our personal self-image. Our employers use public relations and advertising firms to maintain their corporate images. Lawyers, physicians, dentists, stockbrokers, and insurance agents look after our personal and financial health. In our leisure time, we use a variety of services ranging from cinemas to theme parks for amusement and relaxation. And when we do buy goods, such as a new car or a washing machine, we rely on services to keep them running and repair them when they break down.

Services have become one of the most important components of the Canadian as well as world economy. The services sector now accounts for close to 60 percent of global gross national product, and with many service firms operating internationally, exports of services are also increasing. In Canada, over 60 cents out of every consumer dollar is spent on buying services. More than 7 out of 10 Canadians work in the service sector. In other words, more Canadians are doing things (performing services) than making things (producing goods). Experts predict that nearly all new employment in the future will be created by the service sector. They suggest that if current trends continue, almost all Canadians will be working in services by 2025.[2] Much of this employment is expected to be created by small service companies, particularly those offering personal, professional, and informational services. In fact, one of the fastest growing segments of the Canadian services economy is information technology services which includes computer training.

THE UNIQUENESS OF SERVICES

As we noted in Chapter 11, when consumers buy products they are purchasing a bundle of tangible and intangible attributes that deliver value and satisfaction. In general, it is very difficult to define a pure good or a pure service. A pure good implies that the consumer obtains benefits from the good alone without any added value from service; conversely, a pure service assumes there is no "goods" element to the service which the customer receives. In reality, most services contain some goods element. For example, at McDonald's you receive a hamburger; at the Royal Bank you are provided with a bank statement. And most goods offer some service—even if it is only delivery. In fact, many goods-producing firms are adding service offerings as a way to differentiate their products from those of their competitors.

But there are certain commonalities between *services as products* that set them apart from tangible goods. The four unique elements to services are: intangibility, inconsistency, inseparability, and inventory. These elements are sometimes referred to as the **four I's of services.**

Intangibility   Services are intangible; that is, they can't be held, touched, or seen before the purchase decision. In contrast, before purchasing a traditional product, a consumer can touch a box of laundry detergent, kick the tire of an automobile, or sample a new breakfast cereal. A major marketing need for services is to make them tangible or show the benefits of using a service. American Express emphasizes the gifts available to cardholders through its Membership Rewards program; and a leading insurance company says, "You're in Good Hands with Allstate"; and Canadian Pacific Hotels tells business travellers that they'll have the convenience of their offices away from their offices, including computer hook-ups and portable phones.

Inconsistency   Developing, pricing, promoting, and delivering services is challenging because the quality of a service is often inconsistent. Since services depend on the people who provide them, their quality varies with each person's capabilities and day-to-day job performance. Inconsistency is much more of a problem with services than it is with tangible goods. Tangible products can be good or bad in terms of quality, but with modern production lines the quality will at least be consistent. On the other hand, the Toronto Maple Leafs hockey team may look like potential Stanley Cup winners on one day, but lose by 10 goals the next day. Or a cello player with the Vancouver Symphony may not be feeling well and give a less-than-average performance. Whether the service involves tax assistance at Ernst & Young or guest relations at the Sheraton, organizations attempt to reduce inconsistency through standardization and training. Standardization through automation is becoming increasingly popular in many service industries including banking. Marathon Buildings Group of Toronto uses both highly trained personnel and technology to ensure the tenants in their office buildings receive prompt and effective customer service.

Inseparability   A third difference between services and goods is inseparability. There are two dimensions to inseparability. The first is inseparability of production and consumption. Whereas goods are first produced, then sold, and then consumed, services are sold first, and then produced and consumed simultaneously. For example, you can buy a ticket at the Canadian Airlines ticket office, then fly and consume in-flight service as it is being produced. The second dimension of inseparability is that, in most cases, the consumer cannot (and does not) separate the deliverer of the service from the service itself. For example, to receive an education, a person may attend a university. The quality of the education may be high, but if the student has difficulty interacting with instructors, finds counselling services poor, or does not receive adequate library or computer assistance, he or she may not be satisfied with the educational experience. In short, a student's evaluations of education will be influenced primarily by the perceptions of instructors, counsellors, librarians, and other people at the university responsible for delivering the education.

PEOPLE AND TECHNOLOGY PLAY AN
IMPORTANT ROLE IN DELIVERING
MANY SERVICES.

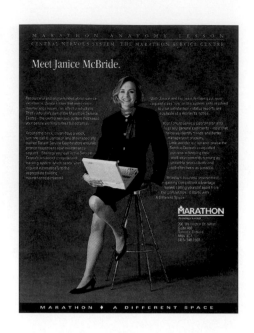

Inventory   Inventory of services is different from that of goods. Inventory problems exist with goods because many items are perishable and because there are costs associated with handling inventory. With services, inventory carrying costs are more subjective and are related to **idle production capacity,** which is when the service provider is available but there is no demand. The inventory cost of a service is the cost of paying the person used to provide the service along with any needed equipment. If a physician is paid to see patients but no one schedules an appointment, the fixed cost of the idle physician's salary is a high inventory carrying cost. In some service businesses, however, the provider is on commission (a Merrill Lynch stockbroker) or is a part-time employee (a counterperson at McDonald's). In these businesses, inventory carrying costs can be significantly lower or nonexistent because the idle production capacity can be cut back by reducing hours or having no salary to pay because of the commission compensation system.

Figure 13-1 shows a scale of inventory carrying costs represented on the high side by airlines and hospitals and on the low end by real estate agents and hair stylists. The inventory carrying costs of airlines is high because of high-salaried pilots and very expensive equipment. In contrast, real estate agents and hairstylists work on commission and need little expensive equipment to conduct business.

FIGURE 13-1   INVENTORY CARRYING COSTS OF SERVICES

FIGURE 13-2

SERVICE CONTINUUM

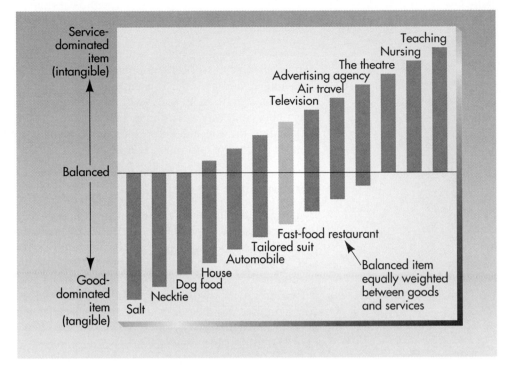

The Service Continuum

The four I's differentiate services from goods in most cases, but as we mentioned earlier, most products sold cannot be defined as pure goods or pure services. For example, does IBM Canada sell goods or services? While the company sells computers and software, a major component of its business is information technology services. Does McLean Hunter provide only goods when it publishes *Marketing* magazine, or does it consider itself a service because it presents up-to-date Canadian business information? As companies look at what they bring to the market, there is a range from tangible to the intangible or good-dominant to service-dominant offerings referred to as the **service continuum** (Figure 13-2).

Teaching, nursing, and the theatre are intangible, service-dominated activities, and intangibility, inconsistency, inseparability, and inventory are major concerns in their marketing. Salt, neckties, and dog food are tangible goods, and the problems represented by the four I's are not relevant in their marketing. However, many businesses are a mix of intangible-service and tangible-good factors. A clothing tailor provides a service but also a good, the finished suit. How pleasant, courteous, and attentive the tailor is to the customer is an important component of the service, and how well the clothes fit is an important part of the good. As shown in Figure 13-2, a fast-food restaurant is about half tangible goods (the food) and half intangible services (courtesy, cleanliness, speed, convenience).

CONCEPT CHECK

1. What are the four I's of services?

2. Would inventory carrying costs for an accounting firm employing chartered accountants be (*a*) high, (*b*) low, or (*c*) nonexistent?

3. To eliminate inconsistencies, organizations rely on _____ and _____.

HOW CONSUMERS PURCHASE SERVICES

Universities, hospitals, hotels, and lawyers are facing an increasingly competitive environment. Successful service organizations, like successful goods-producing firms, must understand how the consumer makes a purchase decision and a postpurchase evaluation. Service companies will be better able to position themselves effectively if they understand why a consumer chooses to use a particular service. Moreover, by understanding the consumer's postpurchase evaluation process, service companies can identify sources of customer satisfaction or dissatisfaction.

Purchasing a Service

Because of their intangible nature, it is generally more difficult for consumers to evaluate services before purchase than it is to evaluate goods (see Figure 13-3). Tangible goods such as clothes, jewellry and furniture have *search* qualities, such as colour, size, and style, which can be determined before purchase. But rarely can a consumer inspect, try out, or test a service in advance. This is because some services such as restaurants and child care have *experience* qualities, which can only be discerned after purchase or consumption. Other services provided by specialized professionals such as medical diagnosis and legal services have *credence* qualities, or characteristics that the consumer may find impossible to evaluate even after purchase and consumption.[3]

The experience and credence qualities of services forces consumers to make a prepurchase examination of the service by assessing the tangible characteristics that are part of, or surround, the service.[4] In other words, consumers will evaluate what they cannot see by what they can see. For example, you might consider the actual appearance of the dentist's office, or its physical location when making a judgment about the possible quality of dental services that might be supplied there. Many service organizations go to great lengths to ensure that the tangible aspects of the services convey the appropriate image and serve as surrogate indicators of the intangible service to be provided. Proper management of the tangible aspects of services is sometimes called *impression management.*

FIGURE 13-3

SERVICES ARE MORE DIFFICULT TO EVALUATE THAN GOODS BEFORE A PURCHASE

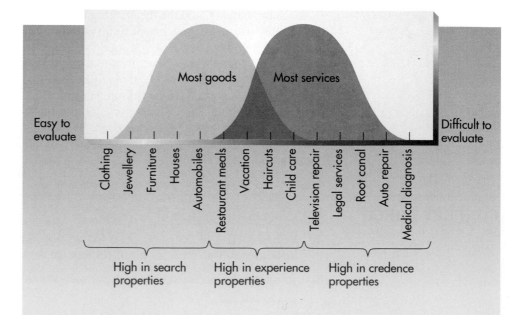

Service marketers must also recognize that because of the uncertainty created by experience and credence qualities, consumers turn to personal sources of information such as early adopters, opinion leaders, and reference group members during the purchase decision process.[5] Accordingly, services marketers must ensure customer satisfaction in order to ensure positive word-of-mouth referral.

Postpurchase Evaluation

Once a consumer tries a service, how is it evaluated? The primary method is by comparing expectations about the service offering with the actual experience a consumer has with the service.[6] Differences between a consumer's expectations and experience are often identified through **gap analysis.** This type of analysis asks consumers to assess their expectations and experiences on various dimensions of service quality. Expectations are influenced by word-of-mouth communications, personal needs, past experience, and marketing communications activities, while actual experiences are determined by the way an organization delivers the service.

One popular instrument developed by researchers to measure service quality and to conduct gap analysis is called SERVQUAL.[7] Researchers measure consumers expectations and their actual service experience using a multi-item instrument. Consumers are asked to rate the importance of various dimensions of service quality and to score the service in terms of their expectations and actual experience. SERVQUAL provides the services marketer with a consumer rating of service quality and an indication of where improvements can be made.

Researchers using SERVQUAL have found that consumers judge service quality along five key dimensions: tangibles, reliability, responsiveness, assurance, and empathy (see Figure 13-4).[8] However, the relative importance of these various dimensions of service quality has been found to vary by type of service.[9]

Service marketers must understand what dimensions consumers use in judging service quality, recognize the relative importance of each dimension, find out how they

FIGURE 13-4

DIMENSIONS OF SERVICE QUALITY

DIMENSION	DEFINITION	QUESTIONS USED TO ASSESS
Tangibles	Appearance of physical facilities, equipment, personnel, and communications materials.	Do our employees dress appropriately?
Reliability	Ability to perform the promised service dependably and accurately.	Did we perform the service right the first time?
Responsiveness	Willingness to help customers and provide prompt service.	Do our employees provide you with prompt service?
Assurance	Respectful, considerate personnel who listen to customers and answer their questions.	Do our employees treat you courteously? Do they answer all your questions?
Empathy	Knowing the customer and understanding their needs. Approachable and available.	Do our employees understand your needs? Are our operating hours convenient for you?

ETHICS AND SOCIAL RESPONSIBILITY ALERT

THE CONSUMERS' ROLE IN IMPROVING SERVICE QUALITY

Research has shown that many consumers are reluctant to provide feedback to organizations about the quality of their services. Moreover, one study found that only 1 in 27 service customers offered feedback that might be important in improving service quality.

Most services marketers want to know if customers are happy or satisfied with the services provided, and many try a variety of methods (e.g., customer response or comment cards) to obtain or encourage an answer. However,

most consumers do not take the time to respond, even if they *are* dissatisfied. In general, consumers, if unhappy, will simply not return. But, while they will not take the time to tell the organization about the problem, they *will* take the time to tell their friends and co-workers. The question is— why? If you have a problem with an organization that markets a service, whether it is inconvenient hours or rude employees, wouldn't it be better to tell the organization? Is it ethical for you to complain to your friends without informing the organization?

rate in terms of service quality, and take actions to deliver service quality that is consistent with consumer expectations. As a consumer, you play an important role in ensuring organizations deliver service quality. However, as the Ethics and Social Responsibility box points out, sometimes consumers do not provide the feedback necessary to improve service quality.

CONCEPT CHECK

1. What are the differences between search, experience, and credence qualities?
2. What is gap analysis?
3. An instrument or approach used to measure service quality is
   _____.

MANAGING THE MARKETING OF SERVICES

Just as the unique aspects of services necessitate changes in the consumer's purchase process, the marketing management process requires special adaptation.[10] In services marketing, the employee often plays a central role in attracting, building, and maintaining relationships with customers.[11] This aspect of services marketing has led to a new concept: internal marketing.[12]

Internal marketing is based on the notion that in order for a service organization to serve its customers well, it must care for and treat its employees like valued customers. In short, it must focus on its employees (or its "internal market") before successful marketing efforts can be directed at customers.[13] Internal marketing involves creating an organizational climate in general, and jobs in particular, that lead to the right service personnel performing the service in the right way. The organization must train and motivate all its employees to work together to provide service quality and customer satisfaction. Research has shown that service organizations who want to be truly customer-oriented must be employee-oriented.[14]

In addition to employees, services organizations must also focus on the proper management of the marketing mix. Let's now discuss the special nature of the marketing mix for services.

LOGOS CREATE SERVICE IDENTITIES.

Product (Service)

To a large extent, the concepts of the product component of the marketing mix discussed in Chapters 11 and 12 apply equally to Cheerios (a good) and to Royal Bank Visa (a service). Yet there are three aspects of the good/service element of the mix that warrant special attention: exclusivity, brand name, and capacity management.

Exclusivity   Chapter 11 pointed out that one favourable dimension in a new product (a good) is its ability to be patented. Remember that a patent gives the manufacturer of a good exclusive rights to its production. A major difference between products and services is that services cannot be patented. Hence the creator of a successful fast-food chain could quickly discover the concept being copied by others. Domino's Pizza, for example, has seen competitors copy the quick delivery advantage that propelled the company to success.

Branding   An important aspect of marketing goods is the branding strategy used. However, because services are intangible and, therefore, more difficult to describe, the brand name or identifying logo of the service organization is particularly important when a consumer makes a purchase decision. Many companies in the Canadian financial services industry, such as banks, trust companies, brokerage firms, and insurance companies, use branding in order to distinguish themselves in the minds of the consumers. Canada Trust, Bank of Montreal, and the Royal Bank are three prime examples. Strong brand names and symbols are important for service marketers, not only for differentiation purposes but also for conveying an image of quality. A service firm with a well-established brand reputation will also find it easier to market new services than firms without such brand reputations.[15]

Take a look at the figures at the top of this page to determine how successful some companies have been in branding their service by name, logo, or symbol.

Capacity management   Most services have a limited capacity due to the inseparability of the service from the service provider and the perishable nature of the service. For example, a patient must be in the hospital at the same time as the surgeon to "buy" an appendectomy, and only one patient can be helped at that time. Similarly, no additional surgery can be conducted tomorrow because of an unused operating room or an available surgeon today—the service capacity is lost if it is not used. So the service component of the mix must be integrated with efforts to influence consumer demand.[16] This is referred to as **capacity management.**

Service organizations must manage the availability of the offering so that (1) demand matches capacity over the duration of the demand cycle (for example, one day, week, month, year) and (2) the organization's assets are used in ways that will maximize the return on investment (ROI).[17] Figure 13-5 shows how a hotel tries to

FIGURE 13-5

MANAGING CAPACITY IN A HOTEL

* Employees of corporations called upon by salesforce (pay full price and book rooms through special reservations line).
† Individual customers paying full price but reserving rooms via publicized telephone number or by just "walking in."

manage its capacity during the high and low seasons. Differing price structures are assigned to each segment of consumers to help moderate or adjust demand for the service. Airline contracts fill a fixed number of rooms throughout the year. In the slow season, when more rooms are available, tour packages at appealing prices are used to attract groups or conventions, such as an offer for seven nights at a reduced price. Weekend packages are also offered to buyers. In the high-demand season, groups are less desirable because more individual guests will be available and willing to pay higher prices.

Pricing

In service industries, *price* is often referred to in many ways. Hospitals refer to charges; consultants, lawyers, physicians, and accountants to fees; airlines to fares; and hotels to rates.

Role of pricing   In services marketing, pricing plays two essential roles: (1) to affect consumer perceptions and (2) to be used in capacity management. Because of the intangible nature of services, price is often perceived by consumers as a possible indicator of the quality of the service. For example, would you be willing to risk a $10 dental surgery? Or a $50 divorce lawyer? In many instances, there may be few other available cues for the customer to use to judge a service, so price becomes very important as a quality indicator.[18]

The capacity management role of price is very important to a number of service operations including movie theatres, hairstylists, restaurants, hotels, and airlines. Many service businesses use **off-peak pricing,** which consists of charging different prices during different times of the day or days of the week to reflect variations in demand for the service. For example, airlines offer discounts for weekend travel, and movie theatres offer matinee prices.

Place (Distribution)

Place or distribution is a major factor in developing a service marketing strategy because of the inseparability of services from the producer. Rarely are intermediaries involved in the distribution of a service; the distribution site and the service deliverer are the tangible components of the service.

Historically, in professional services marketing, little attention was paid to distribution. But increased competition has forced many professional firms to consider the value of convenient distribution. Hairstyling chains, legal firms, and accounting firms such as Deloitte & Touche all use multiple locations for the distribution of services. In the banking industry, customers of participating banks using the Interac system can access any one of thousands of automated teller machines across Canada.

As mentioned in Chapter 10, many goods marketers have extended their distribution via the electronic marketplace. Similarly, service marketers are also recognizing the potential of the electronic marketplace or marketspace. The Internet, for example, is now used by many service organizations as an alternative distribution channel. More and more often, customers are moving from face-to-face contacts with suppliers in fixed locations to "anywhere, anytime" marketspace transactions.[19]

Promotion

The value of promotion, especially advertising, for many services is to show consumers the benefits of purchasing the service. For example, advertising can be an effective way to demonstrate attributes such as availability, location, consistent quality, efficient and courteous service, and assurances of satisfaction.[20] While many service firms are using the Internet as an alternative distribution channel, they are also using it as an advertising medium. Many colleges and universities, for example, have their own web sites and well-designed home pages to convey their messages to prospective students.

Public relations is an important promotional tool for services firms. It is particularly useful in conveying a proper image and in helping to support a firm's positioning

SERVICES NEED PROMOTIONAL
PROGRAMS.

The Global Marketplace. It's No
Place To Go It Alone.

What you need is an expert guide. Someone who knows the place
like a native. With nearly 60,000 people in over 100 countries, from
Eastern Europe to the Pacific Rim, we're at your side. To listen to your
concerns. To deliver timely, workable solutions. Wherever
you have opportunities or problems.

We're one of the world's top accounting, tax
and consulting firms. Our people understand the
global marketplace because our clients have to.

**Deloitte &
Touche**

Accounting, Tax and Consulting Services

W e   L i s t e n .   W e   D e l i v e r .

Deloitte Touche Tohmatsu International

strategy. Public relations tools such as events sponsorship, or public-service activities are very popular among service firms. This is particularly true for professional services companies, which are often restricted in the use of advertising by their professional governing bodies.

Personal selling also plays an important role in services marketing. It has been said that when a consumer buys a service, they are buying the person selling the service. Personal selling is valuable not only in attracting customers but also in retaining them. Increasingly, many service marketers are following the path set by packaged-goods firms, that is, they are developing integrated marketing communications plans.[21]

SERVICES IN THE FUTURE

What can we expect from the services industry in the future? New and better services, of course, and an unprecedented variety of suppliers—changes that will largely be driven by deregulation, technological developments, and consumer interests.

Deregulation in telecommunications, financial services, professional services and other service industries have led to a greater variety of services, and in some cases, to a convergence of many of the suppliers of services. Many financial services suppliers, for example, are moving toward a one-stop-shopping environment where consumers can obtain loans, credit cards, mortgages, and insurance all under one roof.

Technological advances are also changing many service industries. Perhaps the most dramatic is the trend toward "pay-for-use" services. The information super-highway will make it possible to obtain movies, software programs, video games, photographs, and virtually all digital information electronically for a fee. Electronic banking, e-mail, and on-line services are already taking advantage of the changes. Technology is also changing the way some services operate. Air Canada, for example, offers electronic tickets called e-tickets that replace traditional paper tickets, and many stock brokerage firms now encourage customers to buy and sell stock electronically. In the near future, readers of this book may simply use their computer

TECHNOLOGICAL CHANGES HAVE
EXPANDED THE VARIETY OF SERVICES
AVAILABLE AND CHANGED THE WAY
SOME SERVICES OPERATE.

MARKETING NEWSNET

DELIVERING CUSTOMER SATISFACTION

Many service experts agree that in order for services firms to grow and prosper in the future, they must focus on delivering customer satisfaction. From the customers' perspective, satisfaction occurs when a service firm meets or exceeds customer expectations. So the starting point in designing efforts to deliver customer satisfaction is determining the customers' expectations about the service. To accomplish this, service firms must spend time listening to customers to find out what they want and then deliver it. This is the most fundamental step that service firms can take to ensure customer satisfaction.

In general, service marketing experts suggest that customers expect service companies to keep their promises (reliability), to offer honest communications materials and clean, comfortable facilities (tangibles), to provide prompt service (responsiveness), to be competent and courteous (assurance) and to provide caring, individualized attention (empathy). What is most important, according to experts, is that service firms focus on delivering a highly reliable service. Research shows that little else matters to customers when service is unreliable. Friendly staff and sincere apologies do not compensate for unreliable service. Although most customers appreciate an apology, the apology does not erase the memory of that service.

The goal, then, is to focus on no mistakes in the first place. An internal "double checking" system ensures that if a mistake does occur, it gets corrected *before* it reaches the customer. By focusing on "zero defects" (mistakes), service firms can move toward "zero defections"—no lost customers due to dissatisfaction.

and a cable or telephone connection to read assigned pages or to download a copy of the book to a compact disc![22]

Other changes in services are being driven by changes in consumer interests. Experts suggest that "time will be the currency of the future." Consumers will search for new services that reduce the time needed to go to the post office, bank, or supermarket or to prepare food, clean clothes, or maintain their homes. Consumers will put increased demand on services companies, expecting greater choice, convenience, information, responsiveness, and access. Technology will play a key role in satisfying those demands. Many banking customers, for example, prefer to visit their bank as little as possible and many are now doing more business by phone. It is very possible that an all-telephone or completely virtual bank is on the horizon for Canadian consumers. Consumers will have a choice to do everything electronically or to deal with a real person 24 hours a day, every day of the year for all their financial needs including loans and mortgages.

Still, experts suggest that many services organizations are currently failing to satisfy their customers. They argue that customers are often overheard saying, "if this is a service economy, where the heck's the service." Unless services marketers start today to focus on delivering customer satisfaction, experts predict service companies will be facing increased numbers of aggravated, stressed, and unhappy consumers in the future.[23] The Marketing NewsNet discusses how service firms can better deliver customer satisfaction.[24]

CONCEPT CHECK

1. Matching demand with capacity is the focus of _____ management.

2. What factors will influence future changes in services?

SUMMARY

1. Services are activities, deeds, or other basic intangibles offered for sale to consumers in exchange for money or something else of value. Services have become one of the most important components of the Canadian and world economy.

2. Services share four commonalities that set them apart from goods: intangibility, inconsistency, inseparability, and inventory.

3. Intangibility refers to the difficulty in communicating service benefits. Inconsistency refers to the difficulty of providing the same level of quality each time a service is purchased. Inseparability means services are produced and consumed simultaneously and that consumers cannot separate the service deliverer from the service itself. Inventory costs for services are related to the cost of maintaining production capacity.

4. Many companies are not clearly service-based or goods-based organizations. As companies look at what they bring to the market, there is a range from tangible to the intangible or good-dominant to service-dominant offerings referred to as the service continuum.

5. Consumers can evaluate goods by the search properties, but must evaluate services by their experience and credence properties.

6. A gap analysis determines if consumers' expectations are different from their actual experiences. Gap analysis usually measures dimensions of service quality including: tangibles, reliability, responsiveness, assurance, and empathy.

7. Internal marketing is based on the notion that in order for a service organization to serve its customers well, it must care for and treat its employees like valued customers. In short, it must focus on its employees, or internal market, before successful programs can be directed at customers.

8. Because services are intangible, branding a service is particularly important in order to differentiate the service and to convey an image of quality. The brand name or identifying logo helps "tangiblize" the service for the consumer.

9. The inseparability of production and consumption of services means capacity management is important in services marketing. Capacity management involves smoothing demand to meet capacity.

10. The intangible nature of services makes price an important cue to service quality.

11. Distribution is important as a tangible component of a service offering. Technology is allowing service firms to expand their distribution including the use of marketspace.

12. Promotion is important in services marketing in order to demonstrate to consumers the benefits of purchasing a service.

13. Three factors are driving changes in the services industry: deregulation, technology, and consumer interests.

KEY TERMS AND CONCEPTS

services p. 318
four I's of services p. 318
idle production capacity p. 320
service continuum p. 321

gap analysis p. 323
internal marketing p. 324
capacity management p. 325
off-peak pricing p. 326

CHAPTER PROBLEMS AND APPLICATIONS

1. Explain how the four I's of services would apply to a branch office of the Royal Bank.

2. Idle production capacity may be related to inventory or capacity management. How would the pricing component of the marketing mix reduce idle production capacity for (a) a car wash, (b) a stage theatre group, and (c) a university?

3. What are the search, experience, and credence qualities of an airline for the business traveller and the pleasure traveller? What qualities are most important to each group?

4. This chapter showed that consumers judge service quality along five key dimensions: tangibles, reliability, responsiveness, assurance, and empathy. Indicate the "one" dimension which is most important to you in judging service quality of each of the following services: (a) physicians, (b) banking, (c) car rental companies, and (d) dry cleaning.

5. The text suggests that internal marketing is necessary before a successful marketing effort can be directed at consumers. Why is this particularly true for service organizations?

6. Outline the capacity management groups and strategies that an airline must consider.

7. Draw the channel of distribution for the following services: (a) a restaurant, (b) a hospital, and (c) a hotel.

8. How does off-peak pricing influence demand for services?

9. In recent years, many service businesses have begun to provide their employees with uniforms. Explain the rationale behind this strategy in terms of the concepts discussed in this chapter.

10. Look at the service continuum in Figure 13-2. Explain how the following points in the continuum differ in terms of consistency: (a) salt, (b) automobile, (c) advertising agency, and (d) teaching.

CASE 13-1   National Hockey League

The National Hockey League (www.nhl.com) traces its beginnings to November 22, 1917, and as such is the second oldest league of four major team sports in North America, with only professional baseball predating it. Throughout its history, the NHL has been recognized for its ideas and innovations. For example, the NHL was the first major sports league to introduce a play-off system, one that has been adopted by all other major sports.

However, historically, the NHL and many of the team owners had a negative mindset toward marketing. Marketing was actually considered unseemly. The general approach was to simply open the doors at the arenas and wait for customers to come. But with NHL costs, particularly player salaries on the rise, the NHL needed a bigger audience, both at the games and on television. The league now fully embraces marketing and it starts at the top. NHL Commissioner Gary Bettman, the former vice-president of the NBA (National Basketball Association) leads the marketing effort of the NHL.

The league is heavily involved in product licensing. It even has an on-line or cyberspace store where fans can purchase official NHL merchandise. Fans can also obtain an NHL mastercard complete with the logo of their favourite team. Corporate involvement and sponsorship in the NHL is also a priority with the league. Several teams have built new arenas and have attracted major corporate sponsors to be associated with the new complexes (e.g., General Motors Place, home of the Vancouver Canucks, and the Molson Centre, home to the Montreal Canadiens).

The NHL has also penetrated the European television market with ESPN broadcasting NHL games on prime-time Swedish TV. Europe is also seen as a good market for licensing. In an effort to improve the entertainment value of the game for television viewers, the league has worked to improve how the games are televised, from the use of different camera angles to a computer-enhanced puck that is easier to follow.

Marketing professional hockey in the United States became a little easier in 1993–94 when entertainment giants Disney and Blockbuster Entertainment bought the league's Anaheim and Miami franchises. Blockbuster now offers NHL merchandise in its video outlets across Canada and the United States. Cross-marketing possibilities with Disney appear endless. For example, the Mighty Ducks arena, The Pond, is close to Disneyland, so vacation packages and other tie-ins with the theme park are being utilized.

The NHL believes that other strong franchises in the US including Denver and Phoenix are helping to sell the game to a new generation of fans. Strong fan support and media interest in the United States has led to the awarding of new franchises in Nashville, Atlanta, Columbus, and St. Paul. The NHL believes a strong presence in the United States market will ensure the league's long-term prosperity.

By the year 2000, only six teams will be Canadian-based, with the other 24 teams being located across the United States. The NHL believes hockey is clearly an international game with only soccer being played in more countries. It hopes that with great players and great teams, consumers around the world will support and patronize professional hockey as a wholesome form of entertainment.

Questions

1. What is the "product" that the National Hockey League is really marketing to prospective fans?
2. Who is the NHL competing with in terms of fan attendance?
3. How does marketing "hockey" differ from marketing a consumer product like breakfast cereal?

CHAPTER 14

Pricing: Relating Objectives to Revenues and Costs

AFTER READING THIS CHAPTER YOU SHOULD BE ABLE TO:

• Identify the elements that make up a price.

• Recognize the constraints on a firm's pricing latitude and the objectives a firm has in setting prices.

• Explain what a demand curve is and how it affects a firm's total and marginal revenue.

• Recognize what price elasticity of demand means to a manager facing a pricing decision.

• Explain the role of costs in pricing decisions.

• Calculate a break-even point for various combinations of price, fixed cost, and unit variable cost.

THE CASE OF THE $660 MILLION PRICE CUT

By all conventional measures Boeing (www.boeing.com) is the world leader in the design, manufacture, and marketing of commercial jet aircraft: after ushering in jet-age air travel with the Boeing 707 three decades ago, it has built almost 8000 jetliners—more than all other manufacturers in the world combined.[1]

Still, when it comes to setting price, Boeing sweats the details like small and large organizations the world over. Consider some of the problems it faces today in the 1990s:

• Deregulation of airlines and open sky treaties between nations. This has led to intense competition and cost controls among airlines.

• High operating costs on many international airlines. The costs of operating a jetliner plus the recessions in Japan and Europe have made airline executives frantic in these countries. Because the recession and the strong yen have grounded many of its core first-class customers, Japan Airlines (JAL) has sought ways to drastically cut costs. For instance, on a JAL flight to Hawaii, foreign crew members were substituted for the Japanese crew. The newly hired Thai flight attendants earn about five percent of the annual salary of their Japanese counterparts, and the Irish pilot and Canadian co-pilot earn about half as much.[2]

• Competition from the Airbus Industrie consortium. Composed of key aerospace partners from France, Great Britain, Germany, and Spain, Airbus Industrie is a formidable international competitor that bids on jetliner purchases around the world.

The effect of all of this on Boeing? Annual revenues began to fall as sales of jetliners plummeted.

MARKETING NEWSNET

JETLINER CROSS-FUNCTIONAL TEAMS AND CUSTOMER VALUE: NO LONGER SLEEPY IN SEATTLE

The new economics of jetliner production and use has awakened Boeing. In recent years Boeing utilized a variety of cross-functional teams to add genuine value for its customers—both the airlines that buy Boeing jetliners and the passengers that ride in them.

Boeing's cross-functional teams blend not only employees from different functional areas within the firm but also its suppliers and customers as well. Here are some actions triggered by these teams:

- Introduction of a new 737-800 model. This upgrade of the 737 series—the best selling jetliner in aviation history—offers the airline customers more range, more speed, and better operating economics.
- Next-day shipment on routine spare parts. This was a drastic improvement over the previous 10-day Boeing standard, which, in turn, was three times better than the industry standard.
- Reduction of order cycle time by 45 percent. This means that the time from receiving a jetliner order until delivery has been reduced from 18 months to 10—with a new target of 8 months.

More recently, Boeing's flagship customer, United Airlines, put the Boeing 777 into service. Listening to passengers like you, the Boeing Triple-7 provides some great customer-value innovations: 1.9 m of centre aisle head-

room, a 14.25 cm TV screen in the seatback in front of each passenger, and most seats that are 46.25 cm wide—3.75 cm wider than most economy jetliner seats.

But the airlines wanted customer value, too, in the form of the flexibility to reconfigure seats to handle different uses for the plane, which generates a conflict between the customer value of the airlines and that of passengers. Until things change, you might avoid seats in rows 16, 31, 40, and 43. They're still only 42.5 cm wide! So delivering customer value for all of a firm's customers often requires some difficult trade-offs.

So what's a company to do? Boeing's answer: cut price . . . big time! Working with General Electric (GE), its jet-engine supplier, Boeing faced intense competition with McDonnell Douglas and Airbus Industrie for a 55-plane order from Scandinavian Airline System (SAS). Boeing won the order by agreeing to sell its 100-passenger 737-600 jetliners to SAS for $20 million each, a $12 million (38 percent) reduction from its regular price. And for 55 jetliners that adds up to a $660 million price cut![3]

Cutting price isn't always the solution. As we'll see in this chapter, a firm can go bankrupt if, in the long run, the prices customers pay don't cover its production and marketing expenses and also provide some profit. In fact, cutting price didn't succeed when Boeing sought an order for 40 new upgraded 737s from Northwest Airlines for a $50 million "list" price each. Instead, Northwest decided to refurbish 40 of its old DC-9s for $5 million apiece and operate them for another 15 years.[4]

Innovative companies now recognize that value for their customers is more than simply a low price. As shown in the Marketing NewsNet above,[5] Boeing has utilized cross-functional teams to improve jetliner designs as well as to speed up jetliner and spare parts delivery to customers. But as the box shows, sometimes what is seen as greater customer value for one group (reconfiguration flexibility for airlines) can conflict with that for another (wider seats for all the passengers).[6]

Welcome to the fascinating—and intense—world of pricing, where myriad forces come together in the specific price prospective buyers are asked to pay. This chapter and Chapter 15 cover important factors used in setting prices.

NATURE AND IMPORTANCE OF PRICE

The price paid for goods and services goes by many names. You pay *tuition* for your education, *rent* for an apartment, *interest* on a bank credit card, and a *premium* for car insurance. Your dentist or physician charges you a *fee,* a professional or social organization charges *dues,* and airlines flying their Boeing—or other—jetliners charge a *fare.* In business, a consultant may require a *retainer* for services rendered, an executive is given a *salary,* a salesperson receives a *commission,* and a worker is paid a *wage.* Of course, what you pay for clothes or a haircut is termed a *price.*

What Is a Price?

These examples highlight the many varied ways that price plays a part in our daily lives. From a marketing viewpoint, **price** is the money or other considerations (including other goods and services) exchanged for the ownership or use of a good or service. For example, Shell Oil exchanged 1 million pest control devices for sugar from a Caribbean country, and Wilkinson Sword exchanged some of its knives for advertising used to promote its razor blades. This practice of exchanging goods and services for other goods and services rather than for money is called **barter.** These transactions account for billions of dollars annually in domestic and international trade.

For most products and services, money is exchanged, although the amount is not always the same as the list or quoted price, because of the discounts, allowances, and extra fees shown in Figure 14-1. Suppose you decide to buy two identical Lamborghini

FIGURE 14-1   THE PRICE OF FOUR DIFFERENT PURCHASES

| ITEM PURCHASED | PRICE EQUATION | | | |
	PRICE	= LIST PRICE	DISCOUNTS AND – ALLOWANCES	+ EXTRA FEES
New car bought by an individual	Final price	= List price	– Quantity discount Cash discount Trade-ins	+ Financing charges Special accessories
Term in college bought by a student	Tuition	= Published tuition	– Scholarship Other financial aid Discounts for number of credits taken	+ Special activity fees
Bank loan obtained by a small business	Principal and interest	= Amount of loan sought	– Allowance for collateral	+ Premium for uncertain creditworthiness
Merchandise bought from a wholesaler by a retailer	Invoice price	= List price	– Quantity discount Cash discount Seasonal discount Functional or trade discount	+ Penalty for late payment

HOW DO CONSUMERS RELATE *VALUE* TO *PRICE*, AS IN THE NEW KOHLER WALK-IN BATHTUB THAT IS SAFE FOR CHILDREN AND ELDERLY ALIKE? FOR A DISCUSSION OF THIS IMPORTANT ISSUE, SEE THE TEXT.

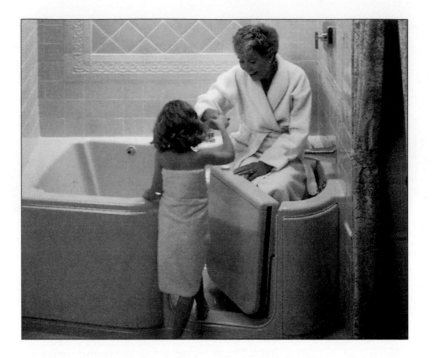

Diablo VTs because their 492-horsepower engines can move you from 0 to 60 mph in 4.1 seconds.[7] (You need *two,* in case one is in the shop.) The list price is $255 000 each. As a quantity discount for buying two, you get $28 000 off the list price for each. You agree to pay half down and the other half when the cars are delivered, which results in a financing fee of $15 000 per car. You are allowed $1000 for your only trade—your 1985 Honda—amounting to $500 off the price of each Diablo VT.

Applying the "price equation" (as shown in Figure 14-1) to your purchase, your price per car is:

Price = List price − Discounts and allowances + Extra fees

      = $255 000 − ($20 000 + $500) + $15 000

      = $249 500

Are you still interested? Perhaps you might look at the Dodge Viper or Aston Martin to compare prices. Figure 14-1 also illustrates how the price equation applies to a variety of different products and services.

Price as an Indicator of Value

From a consumer's standpoint, price is often used to indicate value when it is paired with the perceived benefits of a product or service. Specifically, **value** can be defined as the ratio of perceived benefits to price, or:[8]

$$\text{Value} = \frac{\text{Perceived benefits}}{\text{Price}}$$

This relationship shows that for a given price, as perceived benefits increase, value increases. Also, for a given price, value decreases when perceived benefits decrease. Creative marketers engage in **value-pricing,** the practice of simultaneously increasing product and service benefits and maintaining or decreasing price.

For some products, price influences the perception of overall quality, and ultimately value, to consumers.[9] For example, in a survey of home furnishing buyers, 84 percent agreed with the following statement: "The higher the price, the higher the quality." For professional services, such as dental services it has been shown that many Canadian consumers believe a low price often implies poor quality.[10]

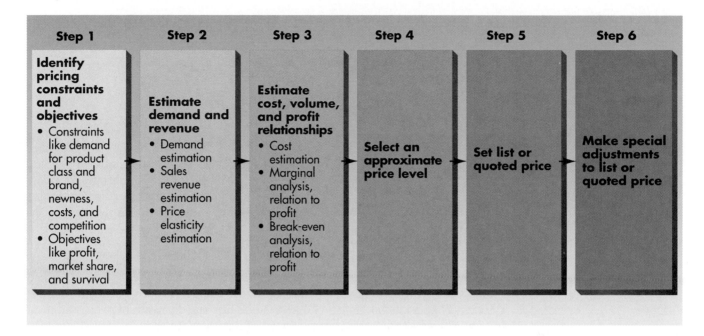

Step 1	Step 2	Step 3	Step 4	Step 5	Step 6
Identify pricing constraints and objectives • Constraints like demand for product class and brand, newness, costs, and competition • Objectives like profit, market share, and survival	**Estimate demand and revenue** • Demand estimation • Sales revenue estimation • Price elasticity estimation	**Estimate cost, volume, and profit relationships** • Cost estimation • Marginal analysis, relation to profit • Break-even analysis, relation to profit	**Select an approximate price level**	**Set list or quoted price**	**Make special adjustments to list or quoted price**

FIGURE 14-2   STEPS IN SETTING PRICE

Consumer value assessments are often comparative. Here value involves the judgment by a consumer of the worth and desirability of a product or service relative to substitutes that satisfy the same need. In this instance a "reference value" emerges, which involves comparing the costs and benefits of substitute items. For example, Kohler introduced a walk-in bathtub that is safe for children and the elderly. Although priced higher than conventional step-in bathtubs, it has proven very successful because buyers place great "value" on the extra safety.

Price in the Marketing Mix

Pricing is also a critical decision made by a marketing executive because price has a direct effect on a firm's profits. This is apparent from a firm's **profit equation:**

Profit = Total revenue − Total cost

or

Profit = (Unit price × Quantity sold) − Total cost

What makes this relationship even more important is that price affects the quantity sold, as illustrated with demand curves later in this chapter. Furthermore, since the quantity sold sometimes affects a firm's costs because of efficiency of production, price also indirectly affects costs. So pricing decisions influence both total revenue and total cost, which makes pricing one of the most important decisions marketing executives face.

The importance of price in the marketing mix necessitates an understanding of six major steps involved in the process organizations go through in setting prices (Figure 14-2):

- Identify pricing constraints and objectives.
- Estimate demand and revenue.
- Determine cost, volume, and profit relationships.
- Select an approximate price level.
- Set list or quoted price.
- Make special adjustments to list or quoted price.

The first three steps are covered in this chapter and the last three in Chapter 15.

STEP 1: IDENTIFYING PRICING CONSTRAINTS AND OBJECTIVES

Let's first review the pricing constraints so that we can better understand the nature of pricing alternatives.

Identifying Pricing Constraints

Factors that limit the latitude of prices a firm may set are **pricing constraints.** Consumer demand for the product clearly affects the price that can be charged. Other constraints on price are set by factors within the organization: newness of the product, whether it is part of a product line, and cost of and flexibility in changing a price. Competitive factors such as the nature of competition and price set by competitors also restrict the latitude of an organization's ability to set price. Legal and regulatory constraints on pricing are discussed in Chapter 15.

Demand for the product class, product, and brand   The number of potential buyers for the product class (such as cars), product (sports cars), and brand (Lamborghini) clearly affects the price a seller can charge. So does whether the item is a luxury—like a Lamborghini—or a necessity—like bread and a roof over your head. In fact, when a consumer is in urgent need of a particular necessity, a marketer may command a premium price. In this situation, there may be ethical issues involved (see the Ethics and Social Responsibility Alert).[11] The nature of demand is discussed later in the chapter.

Newness of the product: stage in the product life cycle   The newer a product and the earlier it is in its life cycle, the higher is the price that can usually be charged. When NutraSweet was introduced in 1983, it was the only nonartificial sugar substitute that was safe to use, contained few calories, and was sweeter than sugar. The newness of the product coupled with patent protection meant that a premium price of $92 per pound could be charged. However, once its patent expired in 1992, rivals emerged (such as Johnson & Johnson's sweetener Sucralose), which affected the pricing latitude for NutraSweet. NutraSweet's price per pound has fallen by about half.

Single product versus a product line   When Sony introduced its CD player, not only was it unique and in the introductory stage of its product life cycle but also it

was the *only* CD player Sony sold, so the firm had great latitude in setting a price. Now, with a line of CD player products, the price of individual models has to be consistent with the others based on features provided and meaningful price differentials that communicate value to consumers.

Cost of producing and marketing the product   In the long run, a firm's price must cover all the costs of producing and marketing a product. If the price doesn't cover the cost, the firm will fail, so in the long run a firm's costs set a floor under its price.

Cost of changing prices and time period they apply   If Canadian Airlines asks General Electric (GE) to provide spare jet engines to power the new Boeing 737 it just bought, GE can easily set a new price for the engines to reflect its latest information

ETHICS AND SOCIAL RESPONSIBILITY ALERT

GETTING AN UNFAIR PREMIUM PRICE?

The drug Clozapine is one of the most significant advances in antipsychotic drugs in two decades. But few of the people who really need this drug get it since the drug costs about $9000 a year. Pharmaceutical companies have been accused of price-gouging with respect to this drug and critical life-saving drugs, such as those used in AIDS treatment.

Some consumer advocates argue that many industries have a tendency to command premium prices for necessary products or services knowing that consumers usually have little choice but to pay them. Oil companies, for example, are often criticized for raising prices on home-heating oil during the cold Canadian winters. The oil companies argue it is simply a supply and demand issue. Many consumers, however, feel they are being gouged unfairly because oil companies realize the consumer has little choice but to pay

the price. Price-gouging claims are also levied against major airlines during peak travel periods. Individual companies are sometimes accused of price gouging during shortages. For example, during water shortages bottled water suppliers have sometimes increased the price of their product by two to three times its original price. College students often report paying high and unfair prices for off-campus housing when demand is high, and supply is low.

The practice of commanding premium prices for luxuries and necessities appears to be gaining acceptability with marketers. A recent survey of Canadian MBA students found that 30 percent of them stated they would charge higher than normal prices if they believed the consumer would pay the higher price.

Is the use of premium pricing for necessities fair? Is it ethical? What should be done about this practice?

---

since only one buyer has to be informed. But if Sears Canada decides that sweater prices are too low in its winter catalogues after thousands of catalogues have been mailed to customers, it has a big problem. It can't easily inform thousands of potential buyers that the price has changed, so Sears Canada must consider the cost of changing prices and the time period for which they apply in developing the price list for its catalogue items. In actual practice, research indicates that most firms change the price for their major products once a year.[12]

Type of competitive markets   The seller's price is constrained by the type of market in which it competes. Economists generally delineate four types of competitive markets: pure monopoly, oligopoly, monopolistic competition, and pure competition. Figure 14-3 shows that the type of competition dramatically influences the latitude of price competition and, in turn, the nature of product differentiation and extent of advertising. A firm must recognize the general type of competitive market it is in to understand the latitude of both its price and nonprice strategies. For example,

- *Pure monopoly.* Ontario Hydro, an electric power company, receives approval from the public utility commission for the rates it can charge Ontario consumers. In most areas of the province it is the only source of electricity for consumers and runs public-service ads to show them how to conserve electricity.
- *Oligopoly.* The few sellers of aluminum (Alcan, Alcoa) or mainframe computers try to avoid price competition because it can lead to disastrous price wars in which all lose money. Yet firms in such industries stay aware of a competitor's price cuts or increases and may follow suit. The products can be undifferentiated (aluminum) or differentiated (mainframe computers), and informative advertising that avoids head-to-head price competition is used.

STRATEGIES AVAILABLE	TYPE OF COMPETITIVE MARKET			
	PURE MONOPOLY (One seller who sets the price for a unique product)	**OLIGOPOLY** (Few sellers who are sensitive to each other's prices)	**MONOPOLISTIC COMPETITION** (Many sellers who compete on nonprice factors)	**PURE COMPETITION** (Many sellers who follow the market price for identical, commodity products)
Price competition	None: sole seller sets price	Some: price leader or follower of competitors	Some: compete over range of prices	Almost none: market sets price
Product differentiation	None: no other producers	Various: depends on industry	Some: differentiate products from competitors'	None: products are identical
Extent of advertising	Little: purpose is to increase demand for product class	Some: purpose is to inform but avoid price competition	Much: purpose is to differentiate firm's products from competitors'	Little: purpose is to inform prospects that seller's products are available

FIGURE 14-3   PRICING, PRODUCT, AND ADVERTISING STRATEGIES AVAILABLE TO FIRMS IN FOUR TYPES OF COMPETITIVE MARKETS

- *Monopolistic competition.* Dozens of regional, private brands of peanut butter compete with national brands like Skippy and Jif. Both price competition (regional, private brands being lower than national brands) and nonprice competition (product features and advertising) exist.
- *Pure competition.* Hundreds of local grain elevators sell corn whose price per bushel is set by the marketplace. Within strains, the corn is identical, so advertising only informs buyers that the seller's corn is available.

Competitors' prices   A firm must know or anticipate what specific price its present and potential competitors are charging now or will charge. When the NutraSweet Company planned the market introduction of Simplesse® all natural fat substitute, it had to consider the price of fat replacements already available as well as potential competitors including Procter & Gamble's Olestra and Pfizer Inc.'s VeriLo.

Identifying Pricing Objectives

Expectations that specify the role of price in an organization's marketing and strategic plans are **pricing objectives.** To the extent possible, these organizational pricing ob-

jectives are also carried to lower levels in the organization, such as in setting objectives for marketing managers responsible for an individual brand. H. J. Heinz, for example, has specific pricing objectives for its Heinz ketchup brand that vary by country. Chapter 2 discussed several broad objectives that an organization may pursue, which tie in directly to the organization's pricing policies.

Profit   Three different objectives relate to a firm's profit, usually measured in terms of return on investment (ROI) or return on assets. One objective is *managing for long-run profits,* which is followed by many Japanese firms that are willing to forgo immediate profit in cars, TV sets, or computers to develop quality products that can penetrate competitive markets in the future. A *maximizing current profit* objective, such as during this quarter or year, is common in many firms because the targets can be set and performance measured quickly. Canadian firms are sometimes criticized for this short-run orientation. A *target return* objective involves a firm such as Irving Oil or Mohawk setting a goal (such as 20 percent) for pretax ROI. These three profit objectives have different implications for a firm's pricing objectives.

Sales   Given that a firm's profit is high enough for it to remain in business, its objectives may be to increase sales revenue. The hope is that the increase in sales revenue will in turn lead to increases in market share and profit. Cutting price on one product in a firm's line may increase its sales revenue but reduce those of related products. Objectives related to sales revenue or unit sales have the advantage of being translated easily into meaningful targets for marketing managers responsible for a product line or brand—far more easily than with an ROI target, for example.

Market share   Market share is the ratio of the firm's sales revenues or unit sales to those of the industry (competitors plus the firm itself). Companies often pursue a market share objective when industry sales are flat or declining and they want to get a larger share. Molson and Labatt Breweries have adopted this objective in the beer market while Pepsi-Cola Canada and Coca-Cola Canada battle for market share in the soft drink category using a variety of tactics including sales promotions and heavy advertising.[13] Although increased market share is a primary goal of some firms, others see it as a means to an end: increasing sales and profits.

Unit volume   Many firms use unit volume, the quantity produced or sold, as a pricing objective. These firms often sell multiple products at very different prices and are sensitive to matching production capacity with unit volume. Using unit volume as an objective, however, can sometimes be misleading from a profit standpoint. Volume can be increased by employing sales incentives (such as lowering prices, giving rebates, or offering lower interest rates). By doing this the company chooses to lower profits in the short run to quickly sell its product. This happened recently when Fiat offered $1600 rebates and zero-interest financing in Italy on its $10 000 Uno compact car.[14]

Survival In some instances, profits, sales, and market share are less important objectives of the firm than mere survival. Continental Airlines has struggled to attract passengers with low fares, no-penalty advance-booking policies, and aggressive promotions to improve the firm's cash flow. This pricing objective has helped Continental to stay alive in the competitive airline industry.

Social responsibility A firm may forgo higher profit on sales and follow a pricing objective that recognizes its obligations to customers and society in general. Medtronics followed this pricing policy when it introduced the world's first heart pacemaker. Gerber supplies a specially formulated product free of charge to children who cannot tolerate foods based on cow's milk. Government agencies, which set many prices for services they offer, use social responsibility as a primary pricing objective.

CONCEPT CHECK

1. What do you have to do to the list price to determine the final price?

2. How does the type of competitive market a firm is in affect its latitude in setting price?

STEP 2: ESTIMATING DEMAND AND REVENUE

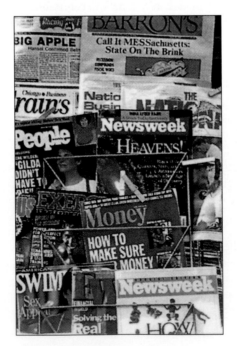

Basic to setting a product's price is the extent of customer demand for it. Marketing executives must also translate this estimate of customer demand into estimates of revenues the firm expects to receive.

Fundamentals of Estimating Demand

Newsweek decided to conduct a pricing experiment at newsstands in 11 cities.[15] In one city, newsstand buyers paid $2.25. In five cities, newsstand buyers paid the regular price $2.00. In another city, the price was $1.50, and in four other cities it was only $1.00. By comparison, the regular newsstand price for *Time* was $1.95. Why did *Newsweek* conduct the experiment? According to a *Newsweek* executive, "We wanted to figure out what the demand curve for our

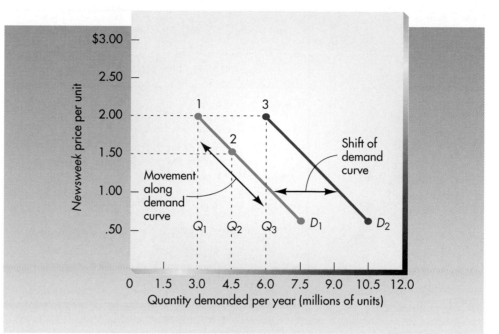

magazine at the newsstand was." And you thought that demand curves only existed to confuse you on the test in basic economics!

The demand curve   A **demand curve** shows a maximum number of products consumers will buy at a given price. Demand curve D_1 in Figure 14-4 shows the newsstand demand for *Newsweek* under present conditions. Note that as price falls, people buy more. But price is not the complete story in estimating demand. Economists stress three other key factors:

1. *Consumer tastes.* As we saw in Chapter 3, these depend on many factors such as demographics, culture, and technology. Because consumer tastes can change quickly, up-to-date marketing research is essential.
2. *Price and availability of other products.* As the price of close substitute products falls (the price of *Time*) and their availability increases, the demand for a product declines (the demand for *Newsweek*).
3. *Consumer income.* In general, as real consumer income (allowing for inflation) increases, demand for a product also increases.

The first of these two factors influences what consumers *want* to buy, and the third affects what they *can* buy. Along with price, these are often called **demand factors,** or factors that determine consumers' willingness and ability to pay for goods and services.

Movement along versus shift of a demand curve   Demand curve D_1 in Figure 14-4 shows that as the price is lowered from $2 to $1.50, the quantity demanded increases from 3 million (Q_1) to 4.5 million (Q_2) units per year. This is an example of a movement along a demand curve and assumes that other factors (consumer tastes, price and availability of substitutes, and consumer income) remain unchanged.

What if some of these factors change? For example, if advertising causes more people to want *Newsweek,* newsstand distribution is increased, and consumer incomes double, then the demand increases. This is shown in Figure 14-4 as a shift of the demand curve to the right, from D_1 to D_2. This increased demand means that more *Newsweek* magazines are wanted for a given price: at a price of $2, the demand is 6 million units per year (Q_3) on D_2 rather than 3 million units per year (Q_1) on D_1.

FIGURE 14-5

FUNDAMENTAL REVENUE CONCEPTS

Total revenue (TR) is the total money received from the sale of a product. If:

 TR = Total revenue
  P = Unit price of the product
  Q = Quantity of the product sold

then:

 TR = P × Q

Average revenue (AR) is the average amount of money received for selling one unit of the product, or simply the price of that unit. Average revenue is the total revenue divided by the quantity sold:

$$AR = \frac{TR}{Q} = P$$

Marginal revenue (MR) is the change in total revenue obtained by selling one additional unit:

$$MR = \frac{\text{Change in TR}}{\text{1 unit increase in Q}} = \frac{\Delta TR}{\Delta Q} = \text{slope of TR curve}$$

Fundamentals of Estimating Revenue

While economists may talk about "demand curves," marketing executives are more likely to speak in terms of "revenues generated." Demand curves lead directly to three related revenue concepts critical to pricing decisions: **total revenue, average revenue,** and **marginal revenue** (Figure 14-5).

Demand curves and revenue Figure 14-6A again shows the demand curve for *Newsweek,* but it is now extended to intersect both the price and quantity axes. The demand curve shows that as price is reduced, the quantity of *Newsweek* magazines sold increases. This relationship holds whether the price is reduced from $3 to $2.50 on the demand curve or is reduced from $1 to $0 on the curve. In the former case the market demands no *Newsweek* magazines, whereas in the latter case 9 million could be given away at $0 per unit.

It is likely that if *Newsweek* was given away, more than 9 million would be demanded. This fact illustrates two important points. First, it can be dangerous to extend a demand curve beyond the range of prices for which it really applies. Second, most demand curves are rounded (or convex) to the origin, thereby avoiding an unrealistic picture of what demand looks like when a straight-line curve intersects either the price axis or the quantity axis.

Figure 14-6B shows the total revenue curve for *Newsweek* calculated from the demand curve shown in Figure 14-6A. The total revenue curve is developed by simply multiplying the unit price times the quantity for each of the points on the demand curve. Total revenue starts at $0 (point *A*), reaches a maximum of $6 750 000 at point *D,* and returns to $0 at point *G*. This shows that as price is reduced in the *A*-to-*D* segment of the curve, total revenues are increased. However, cutting price in the *D*-to-*G* segment results in a decline in total revenue.

Marginal revenue, which is the slope of the total revenue curve, is positive but decreasing when the price lies in the range from $3 to above $1.50 per unit. But below $1.50 per unit, marginal revenue is actually negative, so the extra quantity of magazines sold is more than offset by the decrease in the price per unit.

For any downward-sloping, straight-line demand curve, the marginal revenue curve always falls at a rate twice as fast as the demand curve. As shown in Figure 14-6A, the marginal revenue becomes $0 per unit at a quantity sold of 4.5 million units—the very point at which total revenue is maximum (see Figure 14-6B). Because a

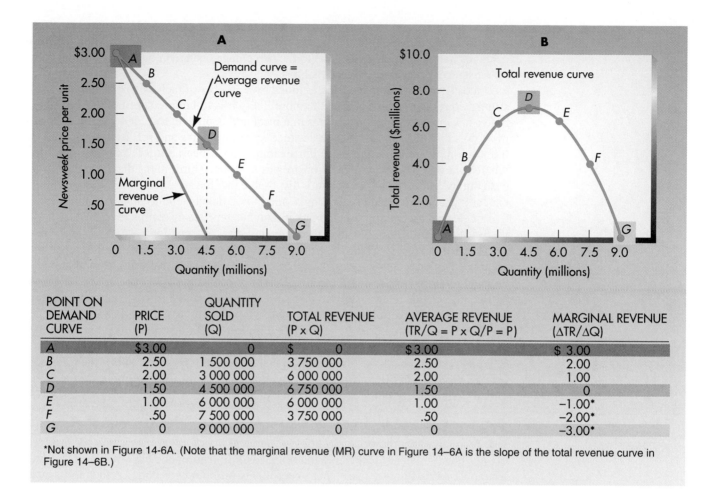

POINT ON DEMAND CURVE	PRICE (P)	QUANTITY SOLD (Q)	TOTAL REVENUE (P x Q)	AVERAGE REVENUE (TR/Q = P x Q/P = P)	MARGINAL REVENUE (ΔTR/ΔQ)
A	$3.00	0	$ 0	$3.00	$ 3.00
B	2.50	1 500 000	3 750 000	2.50	2.00
C	2.00	3 000 000	6 000 000	2.00	1.00
D	1.50	4 500 000	6 750 000	1.50	0
E	1.00	6 000 000	6 000 000	1.00	−1.00*
F	.50	7 500 000	3 750 000	.50	−2.00*
G	0	9 000 000	0	0	−3.00*

*Not shown in Figure 14-6A. (Note that the marginal revenue (MR) curve in Figure 14–6A is the slope of the total revenue curve in Figure 14–6B.)

FIGURE 14-6   HOW A DOWNWARD-SLOPING DEMAND CURVE AFFECTS TOTAL, AVERAGE, AND MARGINAL REVENUE.

rational marketing manager would never operate in the region of the demand curve in which marginal revenue is negative, only the positive portion is shown in typical graphs of demand curves, as is done in Figure 14-6A.

What price did *Newsweek* select after conducting its experiment? It kept the price at $2.00. However, through expanded newsstand distribution and more aggressive advertising, *Newsweek* was later able to shift its demand curve to the right and charge a price of $2.50 without affecting its newsstand volume.

Price elasticity of demand   With a downward-sloping demand curve, we have been concerned with the responsiveness of demand to price changes. This can be conveniently measured by **price elasticity of demand,** or the percentage change in quantity demanded relative to a percentage change in price. Price elasticity of demand (E) is expressed as follows:

$$E = \frac{\text{Percentage change in quantity demanded}}{\text{Percentage change in price}}$$

Because quantity demanded usually decreases as price increases, price elasticity of demand is usually a negative number. However, for the sake of simplicity and by convention, elasticity figures are shown as positive numbers.

Price elasticity of demand assumes three forms: elastic demand, inelastic demand, and unitary demand elasticity. *Elastic demand* exists when a small percentage decrease in price produces a larger percentage increase in quantity demanded. Price elasticity is greater than 1 with elastic demand. *Inelastic demand* exists when a small percentage decrease in price produces a smaller percentage increase in quantity demanded. With inelastic demand, price elasticity is less than 1. *Unitary demand* exists when the percentage change in price is identical to the percentage change in quantity demanded. In this instance, price elasticity is equal to 1.

Price elasticity of demand is determined by a number of factors. First, the more substitutes a product or service has, the more likely it is to be price elastic. For example, butter has many possible substitutes in a meal and is price elastic, but gasoline has almost no substitutes and is price inelastic. Second, products and services considered to be necessities are price inelastic. For example, open-heart surgery is price inelastic, whereas airline tickets for a vacation are price elastic. Third, items that require a large cash outlay compared with a person's disposable income are price elastic. Accordingly, cars and yachts are price elastic; books and movie tickets tend to be price inelastic.

Price elasticity is important to marketing managers because of its relationship to total revenue. For example, with elastic demand, total revenue increases when price decreases, but decreases when price increases. With inelastic demand, total revenue increases when price increases and decreases when price decreases. Finally, with unitary demand total revenue is unaffected by a slight price change.

Because of this relationship between price elasticity and a firm's total revenue, it is important that marketing managers recognize that price elasticity of demand is not the same over all possible prices of a product. Figure 14-6B illustrates this point using the *Newsweek* demand curve shown in Figure 14-6A. As the price decreases from $2.50 to $2, total revenue increases, indicating an elastic demand. However, when the price decreases from $1 to 50 cents, total revenue declines, indicating an inelastic demand. Unitary demand elasticity exists at a price of $1.50.

Price elasticities for brands and product classes   Marketing executives also recognize that the price elasticity of demand is not always the same for product classes (such as stereo receivers) and brands within a product class (such as Sony and Marantz). For example, marketing experiments on brands of cola, coffee, and snack and specialty foods generally show elasticities of 1.5 to 2.5, indicating they are price elastic. By comparison, entire product classes of fruits and vegetables have elasticities of about 0.8—they are price inelastic.[16]

CONCEPT CHECK

1. What is the difference between a movement along and a shift of a demand curve?

2. What does it mean if a product has a price elasticity of demand that is greater than 1?

STEP 3: ESTIMATING COST, VOLUME, AND PROFIT RELATIONSHIPS

While revenues are the moneys received by the firm from selling its products or services to customers, costs or expenses are the moneys the firm pays out to its employees and suppliers. Marketing managers often use marginal analysis and break-even analysis to relate revenues and costs at various levels of units sold, topics covered in this section.

The Importance of Controlling Costs

The profit equation described at the beginning of the chapter showed that Profit = Total revenue − Total cost. Therefore, understanding the role and behaviour of costs is critical for all marketing decisions, particularly pricing decisions. Four cost con-

FIGURE 14-7

FUNDAMENTAL COST CONCEPTS

Total cost (TC) is the total expense incurred by a firm in producing and marketing the product. Total cost is the sum of fixed cost and variable cost.

Fixed cost (FC) is the sum of the expenses of the firm that are stable and do not change with the quantity of product that is produced and sold. Examples of fixed costs are rent on the building, executive salaries, and insurance.

Variable cost (VC) is the sum of the expenses of the firm that vary directly with the quantity of product that is produced and sold. For example, as the quantity sold doubles, the variable cost doubles. Examples are the direct labour and direct materials used in producing the product and the sales commissions that are tied directly to the quantity sold. As mentioned above:

$$TC = FC + VC$$

Variable cost expressed on a per unit basis is called *unit variable cost (UVC)*.
Marginal cost (MC) is the change in total cost that results from producing and marketing one additional unit:

$$MC = \frac{\text{Change in TC}}{\text{1 unit increase in Q}} = \frac{\Delta TC}{\Delta Q} = \text{slope of TC curve}$$

cepts are important in pricing decisions: **total cost, fixed cost, variable cost,** and **marginal cost** (Figure 14-7).

Many firms go bankrupt because their costs get out of control, causing their total costs to exceed their total revenues over an extended period of time. This is why sophisticated marketing managers make pricing decisions that balance both their revenues and costs. By controlling costs and attending to critical pricing details companies can provide genuine value to consumers. In many cases, controlling costs may enable a firm to sell products at prices below those of competitors and in doing so attract new customers to its products.

Marginal Analysis and Profit Maximization

A basic idea in business, economics, and indeed everyday life is marginal analysis. In personal terms, marginal analysis means that people will continue to do something as long as the incremental return exceeds the incremental cost. This same idea holds true in marketing and pricing decisions. In this setting, **marginal analysis** means that as long as revenue received from the sale of an additional product (marginal revenue) is greater than the additional cost of production and selling it (marginal cost), a firm will expand its output of that product.[17]

Marginal analysis is central to the concept of maximizing profits. In Figure 14-8A, marginal revenue and marginal cost are graphed. Marginal cost starts out high at lower quantity levels, decreases to a minimum through production and marketing efficiencies, and then rises again due to the inefficiencies of overworked labour and equipment. Marginal revenue follows a downward slope. In Figure 14-8B, total cost and total revenue curves corresponding to the marginal cost and marginal revenue curves are graphed. Total cost initially rises as quantity increases but increases at the slowest rate at the quantity where marginal cost is lowest. The total revenue curve increases to a maximum and then starts to decline, as shown in Figure 14-6B.

The message of marginal analysis, then, is to operate up to the quantity and price level where marginal revenue equals marginal cost (MR = MC). Up to the output quantity at which MR = MC, each increase in total revenue resulting from selling one additional unit exceeds the increase in the total cost of producing and marketing that unit. Beyond the point at which MR = MC, however, the increase in total revenue from selling one more unit is less than the cost of producing and marketing that unit. At the quantity at which MR = MC, the total revenue curve lies farthest above the total cost curve, they are parallel, and profit is a maximum.

FIGURE 14-8

PROFIT MAXIMIZATION PRICING

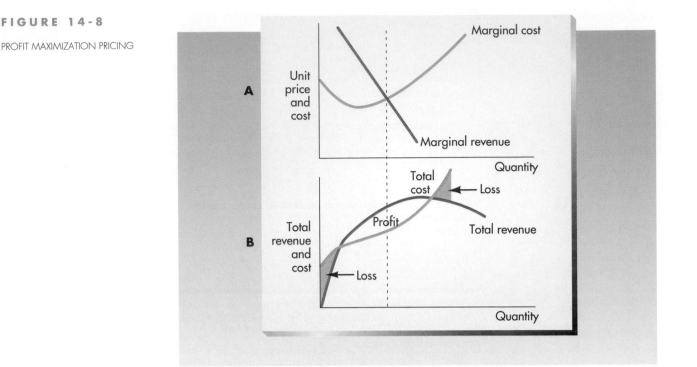

Break-Even Analysis

Marketing managers often employ a simpler approach for looking at cost, volume, and profit relationships, which is also based on the profit equation.[18] **Break-even analysis** is a technique that analyzes the relationship between total revenue and total cost to determine profitability at various levels of output. The **break-even point** (BEP) is the quantity at which total revenue and total cost are equal and beyond which profit occurs. In terms of the definitions in Figure 14-7:

$$BEP_{Quantity} = \frac{\text{Fixed cost}}{\text{Unit price} - \text{Unit variable cost}}$$

Calculating a break-even point   Consider, for example, a corn farmer who wishes to identify how many bushels of corn he must sell to cover his fixed cost at a given price. Suppose the farmer had a fixed cost (FC) of $2000 (for real estate taxes, interest on a bank loan, and other fixed expenses) and a unit variable cost (UVC) of $1 per bushel (for labour, corn seed, herbicides, and pesticides). If the price (P) is $2 per bushel, his break-even quantity is 2000 bushels:

$$BEP_{Quantity} = \frac{FC}{P - UVC} = \frac{\$2000}{\$2 - \$1} = 2000 \text{ bushels}$$

The shaded row in Figure 14-9 shows that the break-even quantity at a price of $2 per bushel is 2000 bushels since, at this quantity, total revenue equals total cost. At less than 2000 bushels the farmer incurs a loss, and at more than 2000 bushels he makes a profit. Figure 14-10 shows a graphic presentation of the break-even analysis, called a **break-even chart.**

Applications of break-even analysis   Because of its simplicity, break-even analysis is used extensively in marketing, most frequently to study the impact on profit of changes in price, fixed cost, and variable cost. The mechanics of break-even analysis are the basis of the widely used electronic spreadsheets offered by computer

QUANTITY SOLD (Q)	PRICE PER BUSHEL (P)	TOTAL REVENUE (TR) (P × Q)	UNIT VARIABLE COST (UVC)	TOTAL VARIABLE COSTS (TVC) (UVC × Q)	FIXED COST (FC)	TOTAL COST (TC) (FC + VC)	PROFIT (TR − TC)
0	$2	$ 0	$1	$ 0	$2 000	$2 000	−$2 000
1 000	2	2 000	1	1 000	2 000	3 000	−1 000
2 000	2	4 000	1	2 000	2 000	4 000	0
3 000	2	6 000	1	3 000	2 000	5 000	1 000
4 000	2	8 000	1	4 000	2 000	6 000	2 000
5 000	2	10 000	1	5 000	2 000	7 000	3 000
6 000	2	12 000	1	6 000	2 000	8 000	4 000

FIGURE 14-9   CALCULATING A BREAK-EVEN POINT

programs such as Microsoft Excel or Lotus 1-2-3 that permit managers to answer hypothetical "what if . . ." questions about the effect of changes in price and cost on their profit.

An example will show the power of break-even analysis. As described in Figure 14-11, if an electronic calculator manufacturer automates its production, thereby increasing fixed cost and reducing variable cost by substituting machines for workers, this increases the break-even point from 333 333 to 500 000 units per year.

But what about the impact of the higher level of fixed cost on profit? Remember, profit at any output quantity is given by:

Profit = Total revenue − Total cost

$$= (P \times Q) - [FC + (UVC \times Q)]$$

FIGURE 14-10

BREAK-EVEN ANALYSIS CHART

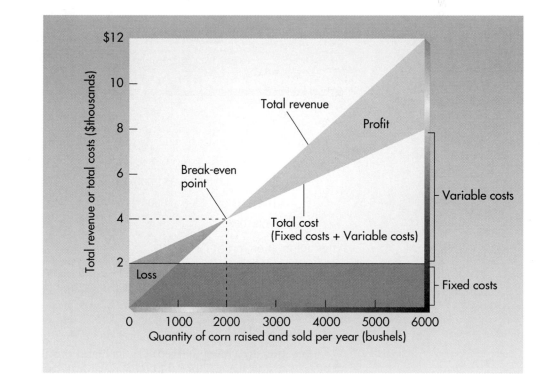

FIGURE 14-11

THE COST TRADE-OFF: FIXED VERSUS
VARIABLE COSTS

Executives in virtually every mass-production industry—from locomotives and cars to electronic calculators and breakfast cereals—are searching for ways to increase quality and reduce production costs to remain competitive in world markets. Increasingly they are substituting robots, automation, and computer-controlled manufacturing systems for blue- and white-collar workers.

To understand the implications of this on the break-even point and profit, consider this example of an electronic calculator manufacturer:

BEFORE AUTOMATION

$$P = \$10 \text{ per unit}$$
$$FC = \$1\,000\,000$$
$$UVC = \$7 \text{ per unit}$$
$$BEP_{Quantity} = \frac{FC}{P - UVC}$$
$$= \frac{\$1\,000\,000}{\$10 - \$7}$$
$$= 333\,333 \text{ units}$$

AFTER AUTOMATION

$$P = \$10 \text{ per unit}$$
$$FC = \$4\,000\,000$$
$$UVC = \$2 \text{ per unit}$$
$$BEP_{Quantity} = \frac{FC}{P - UVC}$$
$$= \frac{\$4\,000\,000}{\$10 - \$2}$$
$$= 500\,000 \text{ units}$$

The automation increases the fixed cost and increases the break-even quantity from 333 333 to 500 000 units per year. So if annual sales fall within this range, the calculator manufacturer will incur a loss with the automated plant, whereas it would have made a profit it if had not automated.

But what about its potential profit if it sells 1 million units a year? Look carefully at the two break-even charts below, and see the text to check your conclusions:

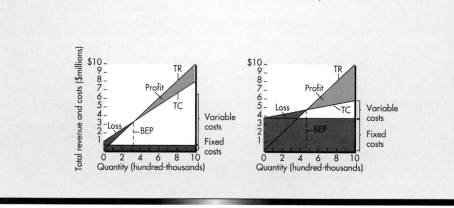

So profit at 1 million units of sales before automation is:

Profit = (P × Q) − [FC + (UVC × Q)]

= ($10 × 1 000 000) − [$1 000 000 + ($7 × 1 000 000)]

= $10 000 000 − $8 000 000

= $2 000 000

After automation, profit is:

Profit = (P × Q) − [FC + (UVC × Q)]

= ($10 × 1 000 000) − [$4 000 000 + ($2 × 1 000 000)]

= $10 000 000 − $6 000 000

= $4 000 000

Automation, by adding to fixed cost, increases profit by $2 million at 1 million units of sales. Thus, as the quantity sold increases for the automated plant, the potential increase or leverage on profit is tremendous. This is why with large production and sales volumes, automated plants for GM cars or Texas Instruments calculators produce large profits. Also, firms in other industries, such as airline, railroad, and hotel and motel industries, that require a high fixed cost can reap large profits when they go even slightly beyond the break-even point.

CONCEPT CHECK

1. What is the difference between fixed cost and variable cost?

2. What is a break-even point?

Summary

1. Price is the money or other considerations exchanged for the ownership or use of a product or service. Although price typically involves money, the amount exchanged is often different from the list or quoted price because of allowances and extra fees.

2. Consumers use price as an indicator of value when it is paired with the perceived benefits of a good or service. Sometimes price influences consumer perceptions of quality itself and at other times consumers make value assessments by comparing the costs and benefits of substitute items.

3. Pricing constraints such as demand, product newness, costs, competitors, other products sold by the firm, and the type of competitive market restrict a firm's pricing latitude.

4. Pricing objectives, which specify the role of price in a firm's marketing strategy, may include pricing for profit, sales revenue, market share, unit sales, survival, or some socially responsible price level.

5. A demand curve shows the maximum number of products consumers will buy at a given price and for a given set of

(*a*) consumer tastes, (*b*) price and availability of other products, and (*c*) consumer income. When any of these change, there is a shift of the demand curve.

6. Important revenue concepts include total revenue, average revenue, and marginal revenue.

7. Price elasticity of demand measures the sensitivity of units sold to a change in price. When demand is elastic, a reduction in price is more than offset by an increase in units sold, so that total revenue increases.

8. It is necessary to consider cost behaviour when making pricing decisions. Important cost concepts include total cost, variable cost, fixed cost, and marginal cost.

9. Break-even analysis shows the relationship between total revenue and total cost at various quantities of output for given conditions of price, fixed cost, and variable cost. The break-even point is where total revenue and total cost are equal.

Key Terms and Concepts

price p. 335
barter p. 335
value p. 336
value-pricing p. 336
profit equation p. 337
pricing constraints p. 338
pricing objectives p. 341
demand curve p. 343
demand factors p. 343
total revenue p. 344
average revenue p. 344

marginal revenue p. 344
price elasticity of demand p. 345
total cost p. 347
fixed cost p. 347
variable cost p. 347
marginal cost p. 347
marginal analysis p. 347
break-even analysis p. 348
break-even point p. 348
break-even chart p. 348

Chapter Problems and Applications

1. How would the price equation apply to the purchase price of (*a*) gasoline, (*b*) an airline ticket, and (*c*) a chequing account?

2. What would be your response to the statement, "Profit maximization is the only legitimate pricing objective for the firm"?

3. How is a downward-sloping demand curve related to total revenue and marginal revenue?

4. A marketing executive once said, "If the price elasticity of demand for your product is inelastic, then your price is probably too low." What is this executive saying in terms of the economic principles discussed in this chapter?

5. A marketing manager reduced the price on a brand of cereal by 10 percent and observed a 25 percent increase in quantity sold. The manager then thought that if the price were reduced by another 20 percent, a 50 percent increase in quantity sold would occur. What would be your response to the marketing manager's reasoning?

6. A student theatre group at a university has developed a demand schedule that shows the relationship between ticket prices and demand based on a student survey, as follows:

TICKET PRICE	NUMBER OF STUDENTS WHO WOULD BUY
$1	300
2	250
3	200
4	150
5	100

a. Graph the demand curve and the total revenue curve based on these data. What ticket price might be set based on this analysis?

b. What other factors should be considered before the final price is set?

7. Touché Toiletries, Inc. has developed an addition to its Lizardman Cologne line tentatively branded Ode d'Toade Cologne. Unit variable costs are 45 cents for a 75-g bottle, and heavy advertising expenditures in the first year would result in total fixed costs of $900 000. Ode d'Toade Cologne is priced at $7.50 for a 75-g bottle. How many bottles of Ode d'Toade must be sold to break even?

8. Suppose that marketing executives for Touché Toiletries reduced the price to $6.50 for a 75-g bottle of Ode d'Toade and the fixed costs were $1 100 000. Suppose further that the unit variable cost remains at 45 cents for a 75-g bottle. (*a*) How many bottles must be sold to break even? (*b*) What dollar profit level would Ode d'Toade achieve if 200 000 bottles were sold?

9. Executives of Random Recordings, Inc. produced an album entitled *Sunshine/Moonshine* by the Starshine Sisters Band. The cost and price information was as follows:

Album cover	$ 1.00	per album
Songwriter's royalties	0.30	per album
Recording artists' royalties	0.70	per album
Direct material and labour costs to produce the album	1.00	per album
Fixed cost of producing an album (advertising, studio fee, etc.)	100,000.00	
Selling price	7.00	per album

a. Prepare a chart like that in Figure 14-10 showing total cost, fixed cost, and total revenue for album quantity sold levels starting at 10 000 albums through 100 000 albums at 10 000 album intervals, that is, 10 000, 20 000, 30 000, and so on.

b. What is the break-even point for the album?

CASE 14-1   Washburn International, Inc.

"The relationship between musicians and their guitars is something really extraordinary—and is a fairly strange one," says Brady Breen in a carefully understated tone of voice. Breen has the experience to know. He's production manager of Washburn International (www.washburn.com) one of the most prestigious guitar manufacturers in the world. Washburn's instruments range from one-of-a-kind, custom-made acoustic and electric guitars and basses to less-expensive, mass-produced ones.

THE COMPANY AND ITS HISTORY

The modern Washburn International started in 1977 when a small firm bought the century-old Washburn brand name and a small inventory of guitars, parts, and promotional supplies. At that time annual revenues of the company were $300 000 for the sale of about 2500 guitars. Washburn's first catalogue, appearing in 1978, told a frightening truth:

Our designs are translated by Japan's most experienced craftsmen, assuring the consistent quality and craftsmanship for which they are known.

At that time the North American guitar-making craft was at an all-time low. Guitars made by Japanese firms such as Ibane and Yamaha were in use by an increasing number of professionals.

Times have changed for Washburn. Today the company sells about 250 000 guitars a year. Annual sales exceed $50 million. All this resulted from Washburn's aggressive marketing strategies to develop product lines with different price points targeted at musicians in distinctly different market segments.

THE PRODUCTS AND MARKET SEGMENTS

Arguably the most trendsetting guitar developed by the modern Washburn company appeared in 1980. This was the Festival Series of cutaway, thin-bodied flattops, with built-in bridge pickups and controls, which went on to become the virtual standard for live performances. John Lodge of the Moody Blues endorsed the 12-string version—his gleaming white guitar appearing in both concerts and ads for years. In the time since the Festival Series appeared, countless rock and country stars have used these instruments including Bob Dylan, Dolly Parton, Greg Allman, John Jorgenson, and George Harrison.

Until 1991 all Washburn guitars were manufactured in Asia. That year Washburn started building its high-end guitars in North America. Today Washburn marketing executives divide its product line into four levels. From high-end to low-end these are:

- One-of-a-kind, custom units
- Batch-custom units
- Mass-customized units
- Mass-produced units

The one-of-a-kind custom units are for the many stars that use Washburn instruments. The mass-produced units targeted at first-time buyers are still manufactured in Asian factories.

PRICING ISSUES

Setting prices for its various lines presents a continuing challenge for Washburn. Not only do the prices have to reflect the changing tastes of its various segments of musicians, but the prices must also be competitive with the prices set for guitars manufactured and marketed globally. In fact, Washburn and other well-known guitar manufacturers have a prestige-niche strategy. For Washburn this involves endorsements by internationally known musicians who play its instruments and lend their names to lines of Washburn signature guitars. This has the effect of reducing the price elasticity or price sensitivity for these guitars. Stars playing Washburn guitars like Nuno Bettencourt, David Gilmour of Pink Floyd, Joe Perry of Aerosmith, and Darryl Jones of the Rolling Stones have their own lines of signature guitars—the "batch-custom" units mentioned above.

Joe Baksha, Washburn's executive vice president, is responsible for reviewing and approving prices for the company's lines of guitars. Setting a sales target of 2000 units for a new line of guitars, he is considering a suggested retail price of $329 per unit for customers at one of the hundreds of retail outlets carrying the Washburn line. For planning purposes, Baksha estimates half of the final retail price will be the price Washburn nets when it sells its guitar to the wholesalers and dealers in its channel of distribution.

Looking at Washburn's financial data for its present North American plant, Baksha estimates that this line of guitars must bear these fixed costs:

Rent and taxes	= $12 000
Depreciation of equipment	= $ 4 000
Management and quality control program	= $20 000

In addition, he estimates the variable costs for each unit to be:

Direct materials	= $25/unit
Direct labour	= 8 hours/unit @ $14/hour

Carefully kept production records at Washburn's North American plant make Baksha believe that these are reasonable estimates. He explains, "Before we begin a production run, we have a good feel for what our costs will be. The North American-built N-4, for example, simply costs more than one of our foreign-produced Mercury or Wing series electrics."

Caught in the global competition for guitar sales, Washburn searches for ways to reduce and control costs. After much agonizing, the company decided to move to Nashville, Tennessee. In this home of country music, Washburn expects to lower its manufacturing costs because there are many skilled workers in the region, and its fixed costs will be reduced by avoiding some of the expenses of having a big city location. Specifically, Washburn projects that it will reduce its rent and taxes expense by 40 percent and the wage rate it pays by 15 percent in relocating from its current plant to Nashville.

Questions

1. What factors are most likely to affect the demand for the lines of Washburn guitars (*a*) bought by a first-time guitar buyer and (*b*) bought by a sophisticated musician who wants a signature model signed by David Gilmour or Joe Perry?

2. For Washburn what are examples of (*a*) shifting the demand curve to the right to get a higher price for a guitar line (movement *of* the demand curve) and (*b*) pricing decisions involving moving *along* a demand curve?

3. In Washburn's current North American plant what is the break-even point for the new line of guitars if the retail price is (*a*) $329, (*b*) $359, and (*c*) $299? Also, (*d*) if Washburn achieves the sales target of 2000 units at the $329 retail price, what will its profit be?

4. Assume that Washburn moves its production to Nashville and that the costs are reduced as projected in the case. Then, what will be the (*a*) new break-even point at a $329 retail price for this line of guitars and (*b*) the new profit if it sells 2000 units?

5. If for competitive reasons, Washburn eventually has to move all its production back to Asia, (*a*) which specific costs might be lowered and (*b*) what additional costs might it expect to incur?

CHAPTER 15

Pricing: Arriving at the Final Price

AFTER READING THIS CHAPTER YOU SHOULD BE ABLE TO:

• Understand how to establish the initial "approximate price level" using demand-oriented, cost-oriented, profit-oriented, and competition-oriented approaches.

• Identify the major factors considered in deriving a final list or quoted price from the approximate price level.

• Describe adjustments made to the approximate price level based on geography, discounts, and allowances.

• Prepare basic financial analyses useful in evaluating alternative prices and arriving at the final sales price.

• Describe the principal laws and regulations affecting pricing practices.

VIDEOPHONE 2500: A PICTURE IS WORTH . . . ?

How much would you pay to see the person you are talking to on the telephone? Executives responsible for VideoPhone 2500 really needed to know the answer to this question. VideoPhone 2500 was an incarnation of a technology dating back to the 1960s when AT&T (now Lucent Technologies) launched its PicturePhone. The company reportedly spent $500 million on PicturePhone, expecting it would become a $1 billion business in 1980. These expectations were not met, and the product was discontinued in 1978. PicturePhone was resurrected in 1992 as VideoPhone 2500. This time a senior company executive predicted there would be "millions" of these phones in use by 1994. However, by mid-1994, only about 30 000 units had been sold worldwide. By 1997, only 40 000 units were in use.

Why didn't VideoPhone 2500 sales skyrocket? The problem appears to reside in its perceived value marked by (1) the quality of the picture and (2) the price of the product. Engineers continue to work on picture quality. Adopting recent breakthroughs in what are called compression technologies, engineers believe they can deliver a still clearer video picture over conventional telephone lines. As for price, a senior company executive suggests the right retail price for the VideoPhone is probably under $500, or about half the retail price in 1997, and one-third the $1499 price when it was introduced in 1992.[1]

The challenge with the VideoPhone 2500 involved the imaginative application of technology at a price point that created value for the consumer. Marketers recognize that consumer demand, cost, competition, and profit considerations all play a part in a pricing decision. Unfortunately, things did not work out for VideoPhone 2500—the product has now been shelved.

This chapter describes how companies select an approximate price level, highlights important considerations in setting a list or quoted price, and identifies

FIGURE 15-1   STEPS IN SETTING PRICE

various price adjustments that can be made to prices set by the firm—the last three steps an organization uses in setting price (Figure 15-1). In addition, an overview of legal and regulatory aspects of pricing is provided.

STEP 4: SELECT AN APPROXIMATE PRICE LEVEL

A key to a marketing manager's setting a final price for a product is to find an "approximate price level" to use as a reasonable starting point. Four common approaches to helping find this approximate price level are (1) demand-oriented, (2) cost-oriented, (3) profit-oriented, and (4) competition-oriented approaches (Figure 15-2). Although these approaches are discussed separately below, some of them overlap, and an effective marketing manager will consider several in searching for an approximate price level.

Demand-Oriented Approaches

Demand-oriented approaches weigh factors underlying expected customer tastes and preferences more heavily than such factors as cost, profit, and competition when selecting a price level.

Skimming pricing   A firm introducing a new or innovative product can use **skimming pricing,** setting the highest initial price that customers really desiring the product are willing to pay. These customers are not very price sensitive because they weigh the new product's price, quality, and ability to satisfy their needs against the same characteristics of substitutes. As the demand of these customers is satisfied, the firm lowers the price to attract another, more price-sensitive segment. Thus, skimming pricing gets its name from skimming successive layers of "cream," or customer segments, as prices are lowered in a series of steps.

Skimming pricing is an effective strategy when (1) enough prospective customers are willing to buy the product immediately at the high initial price to make these sales profitable, (2) the high initial price will not attract competitors, (3) lowering price has only a minor effect on increasing the sales volume and reducing the unit costs, and (4) customers interpret the high price as signifying high quality. These four con-

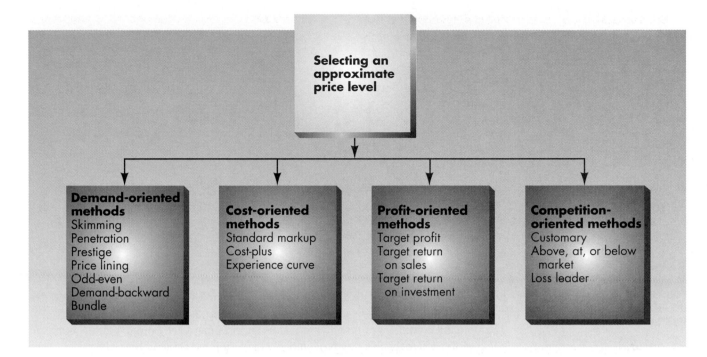

FIGURE 15-2   FOUR APPROACHES FOR SELECTING AN APPROXIMATE PRICE LEVEL

ditions are most likely to exist when the new product is protected by patents or copyrights or its uniqueness is understood and valued by customers. Brian Lyttle from East Longview, Alberta, is a bladesmith who manufactures specialty knives. His exotic knives are made out of meteorite, fossilized woolly mammoth ivory, and whale teeth. He charges up to $6000 per knife, a price his clients like Bruce Cockburn and Brad Pitt are prepared to pay because of the uniqueness of the knives.[2]

Penetration pricing   Setting a low initial price on a new product to appeal immediately to the mass market is **penetration pricing,** the exact opposite of skimming pricing. Sony Corporation consciously chose a penetration strategy when it introduced its PlayStation video-game player for under $300, about $100 dollars less than the list prices of its competitors' products. Sony's penetration strategy quickly made it a front-runner in the latest generation of video games.[3] Nintendo, however, responded and released its Nintendo 64, at a suggested retail price of under $250.[4]

The conditions favouring penetration pricing are the reverse of those supporting skimming pricing: (1) many segments of the market are price sensitive, (2) a low initial price discourages competitors from entering the market, and (3) unit production and marketing costs fall dramatically as production volumes increase. A firm using penetration pricing may (1) maintain the initial price for a time to gain profit lost at its low introductory level, or (2) lower the price further, counting on the new volume to generate the necessary profit.

In some situations penetration pricing may follow skimming pricing. A company might initially price high to attract price-insensitive consumers and recoup initial research and development costs and introductory promotional expenditures. Once this is done, penetration pricing is used to appeal to a broader segment of the population and increase market share.[5] Apple Computer and Digital Equipment did this in Japan when each cut their personal computer prices to increase their respective market shares.[6]

Prestige pricing   As noted in Chapter 14, consumers may use price as a measure of the quality or prestige of an item so that as price is lowered beyond some point,

FIGURE 15-3

DEMAND CURVES FOR TWO TYPES
OF DEMAND-ORIENTED APPROACHES

demand for the item actually falls. **Prestige pricing** involves setting a high price so that status-conscious consumers will be attracted to the product and buy it (Figure 15-3A). The demand curve slopes downward and to the right between points A and B but turns back to the left between points B and C since demand is actually reduced between points B and C. From A to B buyers see the lowering of price as a bargain and buy more; from B to C they become dubious about the quality and prestige and buy less. A marketing manager's pricing strategy here is to stay above price P_0 (the initial price). Heublein, Inc. successfully repositioned its Popov brand of vodka to make it a prestige brand. It increased price by 8 percent, which led to a 1 percent decline in market share but a whopping 30 percent increase in profit.[7]

Rolls-Royce cars, diamonds, perfumes, fine china, Swiss watches, and crystal have an element of prestige pricing appeal in them and may sell worse at lower prices than at higher ones. The recent success of Swiss watchmaker TAG Heuer is an example. The company raised the average price of its watches from $250 to $1000, and its sales volume increased sevenfold![8]

Price lining   Often a firm that is selling not just a single product but a line of products may price them at a number of different specific pricing points, which is called **price lining.** For example, a discount department store manager may price a line of women's dresses at $59, $79, and $99. As shown in Figure 15-3B, this assumes that demand is elastic at each of these price points but inelastic between these price points. In some instances all the items might be purchased for the same cost and then marked up at different percentages to achieve these price points based on colour, style, and expected demand. In other instances manufacturers design products for different price points, and retailers apply approximately the same markup percentages to achieve the three or four different price points offered to consumers. Sellers often feel that a limited number (such as three or four) of price points is preferable to 8 or 10 different ones, which may only confuse prospective buyers.[9]

Odd-even pricing   Sears Canada offers a Craftsman radial saw for $499.99, the suggested retail price for VideoPhone 2500 is $999.99, and Kmart sells Windex glass cleaner on sale for 99 cents. Why not simply price these items at $500, $1000, and $1, respectively? These firms are using **odd-even pricing,** which involves setting prices a few dollars or cents under an even number. The presumption is that consumers see the Sears radial saw as priced at "something over $400" rather than "about $500." In theory, demand increases if the price drops from $500 to $499.99. There is some evidence to suggest this does happen. However, consumers may interpret these odd-ending prices as meaning lower quality.[10]

Demand-backward pricing   Manufacturers sometimes estimate the price that consumers would be willing to pay for a relatively expensive item, such as a shopping good. They then work backward through the markups taken by retailers and wholesalers to determine what price they can charge wholesalers for the product. This practice, called **demand-backward pricing,** results in the manufacturer deliberately adjusting the composition and quality of the component parts in the product to achieve the target price. This pricing practice is used with great success by Compaq Computer Corporation as illustrated in the accompanying Marketing NewsNet.[11]

Bundle pricing   A frequently used demand-oriented pricing practice is **bundle pricing**—the marketing of two or more products in a single "package" price. For example, Canadian Airlines offers vacation packages that include airfare, car rental, and lodging. Bundle pricing is based on the idea that consumers value the package more than the individual items. This is due to benefits received from not having to make separate purchases and enhanced satisfaction from one item given the presence of another. Moreover, bundle pricing often provides a lower total cost to buyers and lower marketing costs to sellers.[12] For example, Cantel offers an all-in-one cellular phone and service package that includes a Motorola cellular phone and a calling plan for less than $20 a month.[13]

CONCEPT CHECK

1. What are the circumstances in pricing a new product that might support skimming or penetration pricing?

2. What is odd-even pricing?

Cost-Oriented Approaches

With cost-oriented approaches the price setter stresses the supply or cost side of the pricing problem, not the demand side. Price is set by looking at the production and marketing costs and then adding enough to cover direct expenses, overhead, and profit.

Standard markup pricing   Managers of supermarkets and other retail stores have such a large number of products that estimating the demand for each product as a means of setting price is impossible. Therefore, they use **standard markup pricing,** which entails adding a fixed percentage to the cost of all items in a specific product class. This percentage markup varies depending on the type of retail store (such as furniture, clothing, or grocery) and on the product involved. High-volume products usually have smaller markups than do low-volume products. Supermarkets such as Sobey's Safeway, and Loblaws have different markups for staple items and discretionary items. The markup on staple items like sugar, flour, and dairy products varies from 10 percent to 23 percent, whereas markups on discretionary items like snack foods and candy ranges from 27 percent to 47 percent. These markups must cover all expenses of the store, pay for overhead costs, and contribute something to profits. For supermarkets these markups, which may appear very large, result in only a 1 percent profit on sales revenue if the store is operating efficiently. By comparison, consider the markups on snacks and beverages purchased at your local movie theatre. The markup on soft drinks is 87 percent, 65 percent on candy bars, and a whopping 90 percent on popcorn! An explanation of how to compute a markup, along with operating statement data and other ratios, is given in Appendix B to this chapter.

Figure 15-4 shows the way standard markups combine to establish the selling price of the manufacturer to the wholesaler, the wholesaler to the retailer, and the retailer to the ultimate consumer. For example, the markups on a home appliance (for simplicity, sold to consumers for exactly $100) can increase as the product gets closer to the ultimate consumers; that is, the manufacturer has a 15 percent markup on its cost, the wholesaler 20 percent, and the retailer 40 percent.

FIGURE 15-4

MARKUPS ON COST FOR THE
MANUFACTURER, WHOLESALER, AND
RETAILER ON A HOME APPLIANCE
SOLD TO THE CONSUMER FOR $100

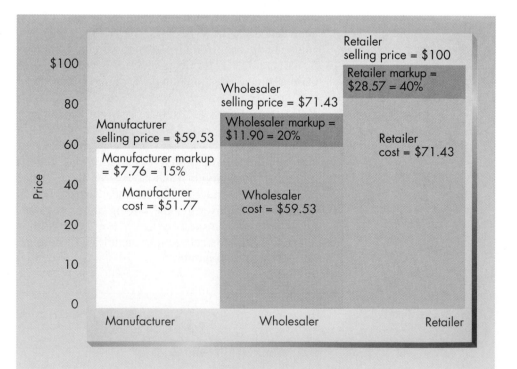

These larger markups later in the channel reflect the fact that as the product gets closer to the ultimate consumer, the seller has a smaller volume of the product and must provide a greater number of services or amount of individual attention to the buyer. The manufacturer gets $59.53 for selling the appliance to the wholesaler, who gets $71.43 from the retailer, who gets $100 from the ultimate consumer. As noted in the discussion of demand-backward pricing, if the manufacturer targets the price to the ultimate consumer at $100, it must verify that this includes adequate markups for the retailer, wholesaler, and itself.

Cost-plus pricing   Many manufacturing, professional services, and construction firms use a variation of standard markup pricing. **Cost-plus pricing** involves summing the total unit cost of providing a product or service and adding a specific amount to the cost to arrive at a price. Cost-plus pricing generally assumes two forms. With *cost-plus percentage-of-cost pricing,* a fixed percentage is added to the total unit costs. This is often used to price one- or few-of-a-kind items, as when an architectural firm charges a percentage of construction costs of, say, the multimillion dollar Molson Centre, home of the Montreal Canadiens. In buying highly technical, few-of-a-kind products such as hydroelectric power plants, or space satellites, buyers, particularly government agencies, have found that general contractors are reluctant to specify a formal, fixed price for the procurement. Therefore, they use *cost-plus fixed fee pricing,* which means that a supplier is reimbursed for all costs, regardless of what they turn out to be, but is allowed only a fixed fee as profit that is independent of the final cost of the project. For example, suppose the Department of National Defence agreed to pay a manufacturer $1.2 billion as the cost of a new military satellite and agreed to a $100 million fee for providing the satellite. Even if the manufacturer's cost increased to $2 billion for the satellite, its fee would remain $100 million.

The rising cost of legal fees has prompted some law firms to adopt a cost-plus pricing approach. Rather than billing clients on an hourly basis, lawyers and their clients agree on a fixed fee based on expected costs plus a profit for the law firm.[14] Many advertising agencies also use this approach. Here, the client agrees to pay the agency a fee based on the cost of its work plus some agreed-on profit, which is often a percentage of total cost.[15]

Experience curve pricing   The method of **experience curve pricing** is based on the learning effect, which holds that the unit cost of many products and services declines by 10 percent to 30 percent each time a firm's experience at producing and selling them doubles.[16] This reduction is regular or predictable enough that the average cost per unit can be mathematically estimated. For example, if the firm estimates that costs will fall by 15 percent each time volume doubles, then the cost of the 100th unit produced and sold will be about 85 percent of the cost of the 50th unit, and the 200th unit will be 85 percent of the 100th unit. Therefore, if the cost of the 50th unit is $100, the 100th unit would cost $85, the 200th unit would be $72.25, and so on. Since prices often follow costs with experience curve pricing, a rapid decline in price is possible. Japanese firms in the electronics industry often adopt this pricing approach. This cost-oriented pricing approach complements the demand-oriented pricing strategy of skimming followed by penetration pricing. For example, CD player prices have decreased from $900 to less than $200, fax machine prices have declined from $1000 to under $300, and cellular telephones that sold for $4000 are now priced below $99. Figure 15-5 displays the relationship between volume increases in cellular phone sales and the average cost of the least expensive model.[17]

Profit-Oriented Approaches

A price setter may choose to balance both revenues and costs to set price using profit-oriented approaches. These might either involve a target of a specific dollar volume of profit or express this target profit as a percentage of sales or investment.

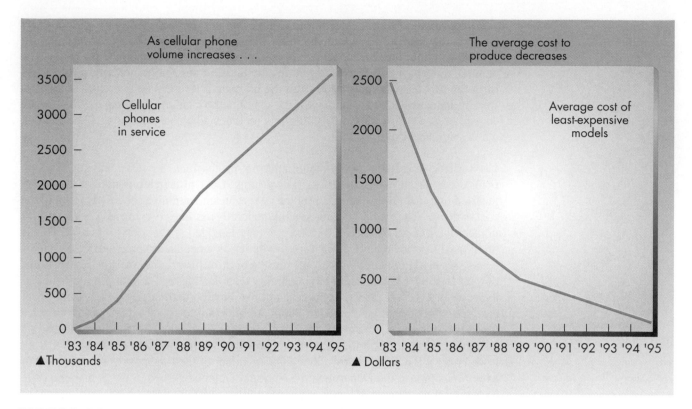

FIGURE 15-5 CELLULAR PHONE UNIT SALES AND AVERAGE COST

Target profit pricing A firm may set an annual target of a specific dollar volume of profit, which is called **target profit pricing.** Suppose a picture framing store owner wishes to use target profit pricing to establish a price for a typical framed picture and assumes the following:

- Variable cost is a constant $22 per unit.
- Fixed cost is a constant $26 000.
- Demand is insensitive to price up to $60 per unit.
- A target profit of $7000 is sought at an annual volume of 1000 units (framed pictures).

The price can be calculated as follows:

Profit = Total revenue − Total cost

Profit = (P × Q) − [FC + (UVC × Q)]

$7000 = (P × 1000) − [$26 000 + ($22 × 1000)]

$7000 = 1000P − ($26 000 + $22 000)

1000P = $7000 + $48 000

P = $55

Note that a critical assumption is that this higher average price of a framed picture will not cause the demand to fall.

Target return-on-sales pricing A difficulty with target profit pricing is that although it is simple and the target involves only a specific dollar volume, there is no benchmark of sales or investment used to show how much of the firm's effort is needed to achieve the target. Firms such as supermarket chains often use

target return-on-sales pricing to set typical prices that will give the firm a profit that is a specified percentage, say, 1 percent, of the sales volume. Suppose the owner decides to use target return-on-sales pricing for the frame shop and makes the same first three assumptions shown previously. The owner now sets a target of 20 percent return on sales at an annual volume of 1250 units. This gives

$$\text{Target return on sales} = \frac{\text{Target profit}}{\text{Total revenue}}$$

$$20\% = \frac{\text{TR} - \text{TC}}{\text{TR}}$$

$$0.20 = \frac{\text{P} \times \text{Q} - [\text{FC} + (\text{UVC} - \text{Q})]}{\text{TR}}$$

$$0.20 = \frac{\text{P} \times 1250 - [26\,000 + (\$22 \times 1250)]}{\text{P} \times 1250}$$

$$\text{P} = \$53.50$$

So at a price of $53.50 per unit and an annual quantity of 1250 frames,

TR = P × Q = $53.50 × 1250 = $66 875

TC = FC + (UVC × Q) = 26 000 + (22 × 1250) = $53 500

Profit = TR − TC = $66 875 − $53 500 = $13 375

As a check,

$$\text{Target return on sales} = \frac{\text{Target profit}}{\text{Total revenue}} = \frac{\$13\,375}{\$66\,875} = 20\%$$

Target return-on-investment pricing   Firms such as GM and many public utilities set annual return-on-investment (ROI) targets such as ROI of 20 percent. **Target return-on-investment pricing** is a method of setting prices to achieve this target.

Suppose the store owner sets a target ROI of 10 percent, which is twice that achieved the previous year. She considers raising the average price of a framed picture to $54 or $58—up from last year's average of $50. To do this, she might improve product quality by offering better frames and higher-quality matting, which will increase the cost but will probably offset the decreased revenue from the lower number of units that can be sold next year.

To handle this wide variety of assumptions, today's managers use computerized spreadsheets to project operating statements based on a diverse set of assumptions. Figure 15-6 shows the results of computerized spreadsheet simulation, with assumptions shown at the top and the projected results at the bottom. A previous year's operating statement results are shown in the column headed "Last Year," and the assumptions and spreadsheet results for four different sets of assumptions are shown in columns A, B, C, and D.

In choosing a price or another action using spreadsheet results, the decision maker must (1) study the results of the computer simulation projections and (2) assess the realism of the assumptions underlying each set of projections. For example, the store owner sees from the bottom row of Figure 15-6 that all four spreadsheet simulations exceed the after-tax target ROI of 10 percent. But, after more thought, she judges it to be more realistic to set an average price of $58 per unit, allow the unit variable cost to increase by 20 percent to account for more expensive framing and matting, and settle for the same unit sales as the 1000 units sold last year. She selects simulation D in this computerized spreadsheet approach to target ROI pricing and has a goal of 14 percent after-tax ROI. Of course, these same calculations can be done by hand, but this is far more time-consuming.

ASSUMPTIONS OR RESULTS	FINANCIAL ELEMENT	LAST YEAR	SIMULATION			
			A	B	C	D
Assumptions	Price per unit (P)	$50	$54	$54	$58	$58
	Units sold (Q)	1 000	1 200	1 100	1 100	1 000
	Change in unit variable cost (UVC)	0%	+10%	+10%	+20%	+20%
	Unit variable cost	$ 22.00	$ 24.20	$ 24.20	$ 26.40	$ 26.40
	Total expenses	$8 000	Same	Same	Same	Same
	Owner's salary	$18 000	Same	Same	Same	Same
	Investment	$20 000	Same	Same	Same	Same
	Provincial and federal taxes	50%	Same	Same	Same	Same
Spreadsheet simulation results	Net sales (P × Q)	$50 000	$64 800	$59 400	$63 800	$58 000
	Less: COGS (Q × UVC)	22 000	29 040	26 620	29 040	26 400
	Gross margin	$28 000	$35 760	$32 780	$34 760	$31 600
	Less: total expenses	8 000	8 000	8 000	8 000	8 000
	Less: owner's salary	18 000	18 000	18 000	18 000	18 000
	Net profit before taxes	$ 2 000	$ 9 760	$ 6 780	8 760	$ 5 600
	Less: taxes	4 000	4 880	3 390	4 380	2 800
	Net profit after taxes	$ 1 000	$ 4 880	$ 3 390	$ 4 380	$ 2 800
	Investment	$20 000	$20 000	$20 000	$20 000	$20 000
	Return on investment	5.0%	24.4%	17.0%	21.9%	14.0%

FIGURE 15-6

RESULTS OF COMPUTER SPREADSHEET SIMULATION TO SELECT PRICE TO ACHIEVE A TARGET RETURN ON INVESTMENT

Competition-Oriented Approaches

Rather than emphasize demand, cost, or profit factors, a price setter can stress what competitors or "the market" is doing.

Customary pricing   For some products where tradition, a standardized channel of distribution, or other competitive factors dictate the price, **customary pricing** is used. Tradition prevails in the pricing of Swatch watches. The $40 customary price for the basic model has not changed in 10 years.[18] Candy bars offered through standard vending machines have a customary price of 50 cents, and a significant departure from this price may result in a loss of sales for the manufacturer. Hershey typically has changed the amount of chocolate in its candy bars depending on the price of raw chocolate rather than vary its customary retail price so that it can continue selling through vending machines.

Above-, at-, or below-market pricing   For most products it is difficult to identify a specific market price for a product or product class. Still, marketing managers often have a subjective feel for the competitors' price or market price. Using this benchmark, they then may deliberately choose a strategy of **above-, at-, or below-market pricing.**

Among watch manufacturers, Rolex takes pride in emphasizing that it makes one of the most expensive watches you can buy—a clear example of above-market pricing. Manufacturers of national brands of clothing such as Alfred Sung and Christian Dior and retailers such as Holt Renfrew deliberately set premium prices for their products.

Large mass-merchandise chains such as Sears Canada and The Bay generally use at-market pricing. These chains often establish the going market price in the minds of competitors. Similarly, Revlon generally prices its products "at market." These companies also provide a reference price for competitors that use above- and below-market pricing.

In contrast, a number of firms use a strategy of below-market pricing. Manufacturers of all generic products and retailers who offer their own private brands of products ranging from peanut butter to shampoo deliberately set prices for these products about 8 percent to 10 percent below the prices of nationally branded competitive products such as Skippy peanut butter, Vidal Sassoon shampoo, or Crest toothpaste. Below-market pricing also exists in business-to-business marketing. Hewlett-Packard, for instance, consciously prices its line of office personal computers below Compaq and IBM to promote a value image among corporate buyers.[19]

Loss-leader pricing   For a special promotion many retail stores deliberately sell a product below its customary price to attract attention to it. For example, supermarkets will often use produce or paper goods as loss leaders. The purpose of **loss-leader pricing** is not to increase sales of that particular product but to attract consumers in hopes they will buy other products as well, particularly discretionary items carrying large markups.

CONCEPT CHECK

1. What is standard markup pricing?

2. What profit-oriented pricing approach should a manager use if he or she wants to reflect the percentage of the firm's resources used in obtaining the profit?

3. What is the purpose of loss-leader pricing when used by a retail firm?

STEP 5: SET THE LIST OR QUOTED PRICE

The first four steps in setting price in Chapter 14 and in this chapter result in an approximate price level for the product that appears reasonable. But it still remains for the manager to set a specific list or quoted price in light of all relevant factors.

One-Price versus Flexible-Price Policy

A seller must decide whether or not to follow a one-price or flexible-price policy. A **one-price policy** is setting the same price for similar customers who buy the same product and quantities under the same conditions. For example, the regular passenger vehicle charge to use The Confederation Bridge (or The Link)—the bridge that connects Prince Edward Island and New Brunswick—is $35 whether you are a tourist or a resident, and whether there is one or five persons in the passenger vehicle. Similarly, Saturn Corporation uses a "no haggle, one-price" policy for both new and used Saturn cars. In contrast, a **flexible-price policy** is offering the same product and quantities to similar customers but at different prices. As noted at the end of this chapter, flexible pricing carried to the extreme could be considered price discrimination and is a practice prohibited under the Competition Act.

Prices paid by an ultimate consumer illustrate the differences in these two policies, although the same principles apply to manufacturers and wholesalers as well. When you buy a Wilson Sting tennis racket from a discount store, you are offered the product at a single price. You can buy it or not, but there is no variation in the price under the seller's one-price policy. But with a house, the seller generally uses a flexible-price policy, and you might negotiate a purchase at a price that lies within a range of prices. Flexible prices give sellers greater discretion in setting the final price in light of demand, cost, and competitive factors.

Company, Customer, and Competitive Effects

As the final list or quoted price is set, the effects on the company, customers, and competitors must be assessed.

Company effects   For a firm with more than one product, a decision on the price of a single product must consider the price of other items in its product line or related product lines in its product mix. Within a product line or mix there are usually some products that are substitutes for one another and some that complement each other. Frito-Lay recognizes that its tortilla chip product line consisting of Baked Tostitos, Tostitos, and Doritos brands are partial substitutes for one another and its bean and cheese dip line and salsa sauces complement the tortilla chip line.

A manager's challenge when marketing multiple products is **product-line pricing,** the setting of prices for all items in a product line. When setting prices, the manager seeks to cover the total cost and produce a profit for the complete line, not necessarily for each item. For example, the $299 penetration price for Sony's PlayStation video-game player was likely below its cost, but the price of its video games (complementary products) was set high enough to cover the loss and deliver a handsome profit for the PlayStation product line.[20]

Product-line pricing involves determining (1) the lowest priced product and price, (2) the highest priced product and price, and (3) price differentials for all other products in the line.[21] The lowest and highest priced items in the product line play important roles. The highest priced item is typically positioned as the premium item in quality and features. The lowest priced item is the traffic builder designed to capture the attention of the hesitant or first-time buyer. Price differentials between items in the line should make sense to customers and reflect differences in their perceived value of the products offered. Behavioural research also suggests that the price differentials should get larger as one moves up the product line.

Customer effects   In setting price, retailers weigh factors heavily that satisfy the perceptions or expectations of ultimate consumers, such as the customary prices for a variety of consumer products. Retailers have found that they should not price their store brands 20 to 25 percent below manufacturers' brands. When they do, consumers often view the lower price as signalling lower quality and don't buy.[22] Manufacturers and wholesalers must choose prices that result in profit for resellers in the channel to gain their cooperation and support. Toro failed to do this on its lines of lawn mowers and snow throwers. It decided to augment its traditional hardware outlet distribution by also selling through big discoun-

FRITO-LAY RECOGNIZES THAT ITS
TORTILLA CHIP PRODUCTS ARE PARTIAL
SUBSTITUTES FOR ONE ANOTHER AND
ITS BEAN AND CHEESE DIPS AND
SALSA SAUCES COMPLEMENT TORTILLA
CHIPS. THIS KNOWLEDGE IS USED FOR
FRITO-LAY PRODUCT-LINE PRICING.

ters such as Kmart and Wal-Mart. To do so, it set prices for the discounters substantially below those for its traditional hardware outlets. Many unhappy hardware stores abandoned Toro products in favour of mowers and snow throwers from other manufacturers.

Competitive effects   A manager's pricing decision is immediately apparent to most competitors, who may retaliate with price changes of their own. Therefore, a manager who sets a final list or quoted price must anticipate potential price responses from competitors. Regardless of whether a firm is a price leader or follower, it wants to avoid cutthroat price wars in which no firm in the industry makes a satisfactory profit. For example, price wars in the airline industry usually result in losses for all players. Similarly, in the residential long-distance telephone industry, even price reductions as little as 1 percent can have a significant effect in a highly competitive environment. In general, each time a competitor lowers its per-minute charge and is matched by the other players, revenues tend to tumble for everyone. A recent price war between Molson's and Labatt's trimmed millions off the bottom lines of both companies.[23]

Balancing Incremental Costs and Revenues

When a price is changed or new advertising or selling programs are planned, their effect on the quantity sold must be considered. This assessment, called *marginal analysis* (Chapter 14), involves a continuing, concise trade-off of incremental costs against incremental revenues.

Do marketing and business managers really use marginal analysis? Yes, they do, but they often don't use phrases like *marginal revenue, marginal cost,* and *elasticity of demand.*

Think about these managerial questions:

- How many extra units do we have to sell to pay for that $1000 advertisement?
- How much savings on unit variable cost do we have to get to keep the break-even point the same if we invest in a $10 000 labour-saving machine?
- Should we hire three more salespeople or not?

All these questions are a form of managerial or incremental analysis, even though these exact words are not used.

Figure 15-7 shows the power—and some limitations—of marginal analysis applied to a marketing decision. Note that the frame store owner must either conclude that a simple advertising campaign will more than pay for itself in additional sales or not undertake the campaign. The decision could also have been made to increase the average

FIGURE 15-7

THE POWER OF MARGINAL ANALYSIS IN REAL-WORLD DECISIONS

Suppose the owner of a picture framing store is considering buying a series of magazine ads to reach her up-scale target market. The cost of the ads is $1000, the average price of a framed picture is $50, and the unit variable cost (materials plus labour) is $30.

This is a direct application of marginal analysis that an astute manager uses to estimate the incremental revenue or incremental number of units that must be obtained to at least cover the incremental cost. In this example, the number of extra picture frames that must be sold is obtained as follows:

$$\text{Incremental number of frames} = \frac{\text{Extra fixed cost}}{\text{Price} - \text{Unit variable cost}}$$
$$= \frac{\$1000 \text{ of advertising}}{\$50 - \$30}$$
$$= 50 \text{ frames}$$

So unless there are some other benefits of the ads, such as long-term goodwill, she should only buy the ads if she expects they will increase picture frame sales by at least 50 units.

price of a framed picture to cover the cost of the campaign, but the principle still applies: expected incremental revenues from pricing and other marketing actions must more than offset incremental costs.

The example in Figure 15-7 shows both the main advantage and difficulty of marginal analysis. The advantage is its common-sense usefulness, and the difficulty is obtaining the necessary data to make decisions. The owner can measure the cost quite easily, but the incremental revenue generated by the ads is difficult to measure. She could partly solve this problem by offering $2 off the purchase price with use of a coupon printed in the ad to see which sales resulted from the ad.

STEP 6: MAKE SPECIAL ADJUSTMENTS TO THE LIST OR QUOTED PRICE

When you pay 50 cents for a bag of M&Ms in a vending machine or receive a quoted price of $5000 from a contractor to build a new kitchen, the pricing sequence ends with the last step just described: setting the list or quoted price. But when you are a manufacturer of M&M candies or gas grills and sell your product to dozens or hundreds of wholesalers and retailers in your channel of distribution, you may need to make a variety of special adjustments to the list or quoted price. Wholesalers also must adjust list or quoted prices they set for retailers. Three special adjustments to the list or quoted price are (1) discounts, (2) allowances, and (3) geographical adjustments (Figure 15-8).

Discounts

Discounts are reductions from list price that a seller gives a buyer as a reward for some activity of the buyer that is favourable to the seller. Four kinds of discounts are especially important in marketing strategy: (1) quantity, (2) seasonal, (3) trade (functional), and (4) cash discounts.

Quantity discounts   To encourage customers to buy larger quantities of a product, firms at all levels in the channel of distribution offer **quantity discounts,** which are reductions in unit costs for a larger order.[24] For example, an instant photocopying service might set a price of 10 cents a copy for 1 to 25 copies, 9 cents a copy for 26 to 100, and

FIGURE 15-8

THREE SPECIAL ADJUSTMENTS TO LIST
OR QUOTED PRICE

8 cents a copy for 101 or more. Because the photocopying service gets more of the buyer's business and has longer production runs that reduce its order-handling costs, it is willing to pass on some of the cost savings in the form of quantity discounts to the buyer.

Quantity discounts are of two general kinds: noncumulative and cumulative. *Noncumulative quantity discounts* are based on the size of an individual purchase order. They encourage large individual purchase orders, not a series of orders. This discount is used by Federal Express to encourage companies to ship a large number of packages at one time. *Cumulative quantity discounts* apply to the accumulation of purchases of a product over a given time period, typically a year. Cumulative quantity discounts encourage repeat buying by a single customer to a far greater degree than do noncumulative quantity discounts. A decision by Burger King to replace Pepsi-Cola with Coca-Cola in its outlets was based on the cumulative quantity discounts offered by Coca-Cola on its syrup.[25]

Seasonal discounts   To encourage buyers to stock inventory earlier than their normal demand would require, manufacturers often use seasonal discounts. A firm such as Toro that manufactures lawn mowers and snow throwers offers seasonal discounts to encourage wholesalers and retailers to stock up on lawn mowers in January and February and on snow throwers in July and August—five or six months before the seasonal demand by ultimate consumers. This enables Toro to smooth out seasonal manufacturing peaks and troughs, thereby contributing to more efficient production. It also rewards wholesalers and retailers for the risk they accept in assuming increased inventory carrying costs and having supplies in stock at the time they are wanted by customers.

Trade (functional) discounts   To reward wholesalers and retailers for marketing functions they will perform in the future, a manufacturer often gives trade, or functional, discounts. These reductions off the list or base price are offered to resellers in the channel of distribution on the basis of (1) where they are in the channel and (2) the marketing activities they are expected to perform in the future.

TORO USES SEASONAL DISCOUNTS
TO STIMULATE CONSUMER DEMAND.

FIGURE 15-9

THE STRUCTURE OF TRADE
DISCOUNTS

Suppose a manufacturer quotes price in the following form: list price—$100 less 30/10/5. The first number in the percentage sequence always refers to the retail end of the channel, and the last number always refers to the wholesaler or jobber closest to the manufacturer in the channel. The trade discounts are simply subtracted one at a time. This price quote shows $100 is the manufacturer's suggested retail price; 30 percent of the suggested retail price is available to the retailer to cover costs and provide a profit of $30 ($100 × 0.3 = $30); wholesalers closest to the retailer in the channel get 10 percent of their selling price ($70 × 0.1 = $7); and the final group of wholesalers in the channel (probably jobbers) that are closest to the manufacturer get 5 percent of their selling price ($63 × 0.05 = $3.15). Thus, starting with the manufacturer's retail price and subtracting the three trade discounts shows that the manufacturer's selling price to the wholesaler or jobber closest to it is $59.85 (Figure 15-9).

Traditional trade discounts have been established in various product lines such as hardware, food, and pharmaceutical items. Although the manufacturer may suggest the trade discounts shown in the example just cited, the sellers are free to alter the discount schedule depending on their competitive situation.

Cash discounts   To encourage retailers to pay their bills quickly, manufacturers offer them cash discounts. Suppose a retailer receives a bill quoted at $1000, 2/10 net 30. This means that the bill for the product is $1000, but the retailer can take a 2 percent discount ($1000 × 0.02 = $20) if payment is made within 10 days and send a cheque for $980. If the payment cannot be made within 10 days, the total amount of $1000 is due within 30 days. It is usually understood by the buyer that an interest charge will be added after the first 30 days of free credit.

Naive buyers may think that the 2 percent discount offered is not substantial. What this means is that the buyer pays 2 percent on the total amount to be able to use that amount an extra 20 days—from day 11 to day 30. In a 360-day business year, this is an effective annual interest rate of 36 percent (2% × 360/20 = 36%). Because the effective interest rate is so high, firms that cannot take advantage of a 2/10 net 30 cash discount often try to borrow money from their local banks at rates far lower than the 36 percent they must pay by not taking advantage of the cash discount.

Retailers provide cash discounts to consumers as well to eliminate the cost of credit granted to consumers. These discounts take the form of discount-for-cash policies. Canadian Tire is famous for its discount-for-cash policy where consumers receive 3 percent off for cash purchases in the form of cash-bonus coupons that can be used against future purchases.

Allowances

Allowances—like discounts—are reductions from list or quoted prices to buyers for performing some activity.

Trade-in allowances   A new car dealer can offer a substantial reduction in the list price of that new Ford Taurus by offering you a trade-in allowance of $500 for your 1985 Chevrolet. A trade-in allowance is a price reduction given when a used product is part of the payment on a new product. Trade-ins are an effective way to lower the price a buyer has to pay without formally reducing the list price.

Promotional allowances   Sellers in the channel of distribution can qualify for **promotional allowances** for undertaking certain advertising or selling activities to promote a product. Various types of allowances include an actual cash payment or an extra amount of "free goods" (as with a free case of pizzas to a retailer for every dozen cases purchased). Frequently, a portion of these savings is passed on to the consumer by retailers.

Some companies, such as Procter & Gamble, have chosen to reduce promotional allowances for retailers by using everyday low pricing. **Everyday low pricing** (EDLP) is the practice of replacing promotional allowances with lower manufacturer list prices. EDLP promises to reduce the average price to consumers while minimizing promotional allowances that cost manufacturers millions of dollars every year.

Geographical Adjustments

Geographical adjustments are made by manufacturers or even wholesalers to list or quoted prices to reflect the cost of transportation of the products from seller to buyer. The two general methods for quoting prices related to transportation costs are (1) FOB origin pricing and (2) uniform delivered pricing.

FOB origin pricing   FOB means "free on board" some vehicle at some location, which means the seller pays the cost of loading the product onto the vehicle that is used (such as a barge, railroad car, or truck). **FOB origin pricing** usually involves the seller's naming the location of this loading as the seller's factory or warehouse (such as "FOB Toronto" or "FOB factory"). The title to the goods passes to the buyer at the point of loading, so the buyer becomes responsible for picking the specific mode of transportation, for all the transportation costs, and for subsequent handling of the product. Buyers farthest from the seller face the big disadvantage of paying the higher transportation costs.

Uniform delivered pricing   When a **uniform delivered pricing** method is used, the price the seller quotes includes all transportation costs. It is quoted in a contract as "FOB buyer's location," and the seller selects the mode of transportation, pays the freight charges, and is responsible for any damage that may occur since the seller retains title to the goods until delivered to the buyer. Although they go by various names, four kinds of uniform delivered pricing methods are (1) single-zone pricing, (2) multiple-zone pricing, (3) FOB with freight-allowed pricing, and (4) basing-point pricing.

In *single-zone pricing* all buyers pay the same delivered price for the products, regardless of their distance from the seller. So although a store offering free delivery in a metropolitan area has lower transportation costs for goods shipped to customers nearer the store than for those shipped to distant ones, customers pay the same delivered price.

In *multiple-zone pricing* a firm divides its selling territory into geographic areas or zones. The delivered price to all buyers within any one zone is the same, but prices across zones vary depending on the transportation cost to the zone and the level of competition and demand within the zone. This system is also used in setting prices on long

ETHICS AND SOCIAL RESPONSIBILITY ALERT

FLEXIBLE PRICING OR PRICE DISCRIMINATION: IS THERE ETHNIC OR GENDER DISCRIMINATION IN BARGAINING FOR A NEW CAR?

Many buyers dread the prospect of buying a new automobile. Why? They dread negotiating the price. Price bargaining, however, has a more serious side and demonstrates the potential pitfalls of flexible pricing: possible price discrimination based on ethnicity or gender. Research shows that some car dealers offer females higher prices on vehicles than males. Similarly, nonwhite buyers, male or female, may also be offered higher prices on cars than white buyers. This occurs despite the fact that all buyers used identical bargaining strategies when negotiating the price of a new car. Even if the practice cannot be proved as systematic price discrimination, it raises an ethical question: should car dealers be allowed to charge higher prices to some buyers for the identical vehicle? Some car dealers argue that the price is largely determined based on how well the consumer negotiates. They add, some buyers are simply better at haggling than others. However, there have been some indications that some dealers have taken advantage of newly arrived immigrants who do not understand the car buying process, particularly the concept of price negotiation. Similarly, some females argue that after purchasing a new car, they discovered that they paid more than a male counterpart who had purchased an identical vehicle under similar terms and conditions. Saturn Corporation has eliminated new car price negotiating and offers a no haggle, one-price policy. According to a Saturn executive, "People don't want to dicker on price, period, whether it's a house, suit of clothes, or a car. When you have to dicker, you feel uncomfortable because you always feel you paid too much." In certain instances, some consumers do. Many times, however, it tends to be female buyers, and nonwhite purchasers. What is your feeling on this situation?

distance phone calls. And, when Sable Gas comes on shore in 1999, Maritime and northeast natural gas customers will be charged prices based on their proximity to the gas pipeline. The closer the customer is to the gas, the lower the price.[26]

With *FOB with freight-allowed pricing,* also called *freight absorption pricing,* the price is quoted by the seller as "FOB plant—freight allowed." The buyer is allowed to deduct freight expenses from the list price of the goods, so the seller agrees to pay, or "absorbs," the transportation costs.

Basing-point pricing involves selecting one or more geographical locations (basing point) from which the list price for products plus freight expenses are charged to the buyer. For example, a company might designate Montreal as the basing point and charge all buyers a list price of $100 plus freight from Montreal to their location. Basing-point pricing methods have been used in the steel, cement, and lumber industries where freight expenses are a significant part of the total cost to the buyer and products are largely undifferentiated.

Legal and Regulatory Aspects of Pricing

Arriving at a final price is clearly a complex process. The task is further complicated by legal and regulatory restrictions. Chapter 3 described the regulatory environment of companies. Here we elaborate on the specific laws and regulations affecting pricing decisions. Five pricing practices have received the most scrutiny: (1) price fixing, (2) price discrimination, (3) deceptive pricing, (4) predatory pricing, and (5) delivered pricing.

Price fixing   A conspiracy among firms to set prices for a product is termed **price fixing.** Price fixing is illegal per se under the Competition Act (*per se* means in and of itself). When two or more competitors explicitly or implicitly set prices, this practice is called *horizontal price fixing.*

FIGURE 15-10

FIVE MOST COMMON DECEPTIVE
PRICING PRACTICES

- *Bait and switch.* A deceptive practice exists when a firm offers a very low price on a product (the bait) to attract customers to a store. Once in the store, the customer is persuaded to purchase a higher-priced item (the switch) using a variety of tricks, including (1) downgrading the promoted item and (2) not having the item in stock or refusing to take orders for the item.
- *Bargains conditional on other purchases.* This practice may exist when a buyer is offered "1-Cent Sales," "Buy 1, Get 1 Free," and "Get 2 for the Price of 1." Such pricing is legal only if the first items are sold at the regular price, not a price inflated for the offer. Substituting lower-quality items on either the first or second purchase is also considered deceptive.
- *Comparable value comparisons.* Advertising such as "Retail Value $100.00, Our Price $85.00," is deceptive if a verified and substantial number of stores in the market area did not price the item at $100.
- *Comparisons with suggested prices.* A claim that a price is below a manufacturer's suggested or list price may be deceptive if few or no sales occur at that price in a retailer's market area.
- *Former price comparisons.* When a seller represents a price as reduced, the item must have been offered in good faith at a higher price for a substantial previous period. Setting a high price for the purpose of establishing a reference for a price reduction is deceptive.

Vertical price fixing involves controlling agreements between independent buyers and sellers (a manufacturer and a retailer) whereby sellers are required not to sell products below a minimum retail price. This practice, called resale price maintenance, is also illegal under the provisions of the Competition Act.

It is important to recognize that a manufacturer's "suggested retail price" is not illegal per se. The issue of legality arises only when manufacturers enforce such a practice by coercion. Furthermore, there appears to be a movement toward a "rule of reason" in price fixing cases. This rule holds that circumstances surrounding a practice must be considered before making a judgment about its legality. The "rule of reason" perspective is the direct opposite of the per se rule, which holds that a practice is illegal in and of itself.

Price discrimination   The Competition Act prohibits **price discrimination**—the practice of charging different prices to different buyers for goods of like grade and quality. The Competition Act also covers promotional allowances. To legally offer promotional allowances to buyers, sellers must do so on a proportionally equal basis to all buyers distributing the seller's products. In general, this rule of reason is applied frequently in price discrimination cases and is often applied to cases involving flexible pricing policies of firms. It is not easy to prove price discrimination has actually taken place especially when firms practice flexible-price policies.

Under the Competition Act, the legislation requires that there be a "practice" of price discrimination, implying more than one instance, or even two or three instances. However, some suggest that the use of flexible pricing may create the potentiality for some firms to engage in price discrimination. Even if the practice cannot be proved legally as price discrimination, there may be some ethical issues involved (see the Ethics and Social Responsibility Alert).[27]

Deceptive pricing   Price deals that mislead consumers fall into the category of deceptive pricing. Deceptive pricing is outlawed by the Competition Act. The five most common deceptive pricing practices are described in Figure 15-10. Over the past few years, companies from Newfoundland to British Columbia have been found guilty and fined for deceptive pricing practices including Suzy Shier Ltd., Kmart, and Colour Your World. However, as you examine Figure 15-10, you should remember that it is often difficult for the government to police and enforce all these laws. So it is essential to rely on ethical standards of those making and publicizing pricing decisions.

Predatory pricing   Two types of predatory pricing are defined within the Competition Act. The first is called *geographic predatory pricing*. Sellers are prohibited from engaging in a policy of selling products or services in one region in Canada at a price lower than another region with the intent or effect of lessening competition or of eliminating a competitor.

The second type of predatory pricing offence is committed when a business engages in a policy of selling products or services at "unreasonably low" prices in an attempt to substantially lessen competition. In many cases, the very low prices are designed to drive competitors out of business. Once competitors have been driven out, the firm raises its prices.

Delivered pricing   Delivered pricing is the practice of refusing a customer delivery of an article on the same trade terms as other customers in the same location. It is a noncriminal offense, but the Competition Tribunal can prohibit suppliers from engaging in such a practice.

CONCEPT CHECK

1. Why would a seller choose a flexible-price policy over a one-price policy?

2. If a firm wished to encourage repeat purchases by a buyer throughout a year, would a cumulative or noncumulative quantity discount be a better strategy?

3. Which pricing practices are covered by the Competition Act?

SUMMARY

1. Four general methods of finding an approximate price level for a product or service are demand-oriented, cost-oriented, profit-oriented, and competition-oriented pricing approaches.

2. Demand-oriented pricing approaches stress consumer demand and revenue implications of pricing and include seven types: skimming, penetration, prestige, price lining, odd-even, demand-backward, and bundle pricing.

3. Cost-oriented pricing approaches emphasize the cost aspects of pricing and include three types: standard markup, cost-plus, and experience curve pricing.

4. Profit-oriented pricing approaches focus on a balance between revenues and costs to set a price and include three types: target profit, target return-on-sales, and target return-on-investment pricing.

5. Competition-oriented pricing approaches stress what competitors or the marketplace are doing and include three types: customary; above-, at-, or below-market; and loss-leader pricing.

6. Given an approximate price level for a product, a manager must set a list or quoted price by considering factors such as one-price versus a flexible-price policy; the effects of the proposed price on the company, customer, and competitors; and balancing incremental costs and revenues.

7. List or quoted price is often modified through discounts, allowances, and geographical adjustments.

8. Legal and regulatory issues in pricing focus on price fixing, price discrimination, deceptive pricing, predatory pricing and delivered pricing.

KEY TERMS AND CONCEPTS

skimming pricing p. 356
penetration pricing p. 357
prestige pricing p. 358
price lining p. 358
odd-even pricing p. 358
demand-backward pricing p. 359
bundle pricing p. 359
standard markup pricing p. 360

cost-plus pricing p. 361
experience curve pricing p. 361
target profit pricing p. 362
target return-on-sales pricing p. 363
target return-on-investment pricing p. 363
customary pricing p. 364
above-, at-, or below-market pricing p. 364
loss-leader pricing p. 365

CHAPTER PROBLEMS AND APPLICATIONS

1. Under what conditions would a camera manufacturer adopt a skimming price approach for a new product? A penetration approach?

2. What are some similarities and differences between skimming pricing, prestige pricing, and above-market pricing?

3. A producer of microwave ovens has adopted an experience curve pricing approach for its new model. The firm believes it can reduce the cost of producing the model by 20 percent each time volume doubles. The cost to produce the first unit was $1000. What would be the approximate cost of the 4096th unit?

4. The Hesper Corporation is a leading manufacturer of high-quality upholstered sofas. Current plans call for an increase of $600 000 in the advertising budget. If the firm sells its sofas for an average price of $850 and the unit variable costs are $550, then what dollar sales increase will be necessary to cover the additional advertising?

5. Suppose executives estimate that the unit variable cost for their VCR is $100, the fixed cost related to the product is $10 million annually, and the target volume for next year is 100 000 recorders. What sales price will be necessary to achieve a target profit of $1 million?

6. A manufacturer of motor oil has a trade discount policy whereby the manufacturer's suggested retail price is $30 per case with the terms of 40/20/10. The manufacturer sells its products through jobbers, who sell to wholesalers, who sell to gasoline stations. What will the manufacturer's sale price be?

7. What are the effective annual interest rates for the following cash discount terms? (*a*) 1/10 net 30, (*b*) 2/10 net 30, and (*c*) 2/10 net 60.

8. Suppose a manufacturer of exercise equipment sets a suggested price to the consumer of $395 for a particular piece of equipment to be competitive with similar equipment. The manufacturer sells its equipment to a sporting goods wholesaler who receives a 25 percent markup and a retailer who receives a 50 percent markup. What demand-oriented pricing approach is being used, and at what price will the manufacturer sell the equipment to the wholesaler?

CASE 15-1   My Own Meals

"The kids generally like the fast-food meals. I tend to not like them because I try to stay away from the high fat," says Angela Harmon, mother of three young girls. "I have to have something that is nutritious and fast," remarks Mary Champlain, mother of two. Comments like these and her own experiences led Mary Anne Jackson to conclude that there was an opportunity to provide parents with better children's food options. As Mary explains, "being a busy working mother, I knew that there was a need for this type of product in the marketplace."

- About 90 percent of children under the age of 7 eat at McDonald's at least 4 times per month.
- More than 80 percent of homes in Canada now have microwave ovens.
- Women already represent almost half of the total workforce. By the year 2000, two out of three new entrants into the labour force will be women.

With this evidence, some food industry experience and business education, and a lot of entrepreneurial spirit, Mary Anne Jackson set out to satisfy the need for nutritious, convenient children's meals. Her idea: develop a line of healthy, microwaveable meals for children 2 to 10 years old.

THE IDEA

Mary's insight about the marketplace was supported by several socioeconomic trends. For example:

- More than 65 percent of working mothers now have school-age children, the highest percentage ever.

THE COMPANY

Ms. Jackson started by founding a company, My Own Meals, Inc., with a line of five healthy microwaveable meals. The meals were offered in shelf-stable "retort" packages, which are like flexible cans. This created a whole new category of prepared foods, and raised more than a few eyebrows among the major food companies. Mary observed that "The need for children's meals was not being addressed in the past, and I think this was because most major food companies are run by men." Eventually, however, the big companies challenged My Own Meals with their own entries into the new category. The competition reinforced Mary's efforts, "Having competitors come into the marketplace justified the existence of the category," she explains.

The product line was developed using a lot of marketing research—hundreds of busy mothers provided input about product quality, usage rates, and price. The results indicated that customers would serve their children high-quality meals between 3 and 4 times each month and that they would be willing to pay approximately $2.30 for each meal.

THE ISSUE: SETTING RETAIL PRICES

"We were trying to decide if we were priced appropriately and competitively for the marketplace, and we decided that we would look at the price elasticity for our product line," observes Mary Anne Jackson. "We found that the closer we came to $3.00 a unit, the lower the volume was, and overall we were losing revenues and profits," said Jackson.

To arrive at final retail prices for her company's products Mary Anne Jackson considered factors related to demand, cost, profit, and competition. For example, because lower-quality brands had entered the market, My Own Meals needed a retail price that reflected the superior quality of its products. "We're premium priced because we're a higher-quality product than any of our competitors. If we weren't, our quality image would be lowered to the image that they have," explains Jackson. At some stores, however, prices approached $3.00 and consumer demand decreased.

To estimate the prices consumers would see on their shelves, Jackson needed to estimate the cost of producing the meals and add My Own Meal's markup. Then she determined the markup of each of the distribution channels—retail grocery stores, mass merchants, day care centres, and military commissaries—would add to reach the retail price. The grocery stores were very concerned about profitability and used a concept called direct product profitability (DPP) to determine prices and shelf space. "They want to know how much money they make on each square foot of the shelf dedicated to each product line. I had to do a DPP analysis to show them why they were making more on our products for our space than the competition," remarks Mary Anne Jackson. Finally, Mary considered competitors' prices which were:

- Looney Toons $2.49
- Kid Cuisine $1.89
- Kid's Kitchen $1.19

Mary knew that it was important to consider all of these factors in her pricing decisions. The price would influence the interest of consumers and retailers, the reactions of competitors, and ultimately the success of My Own Meals!

Questions

1. In what ways are the demand factors of (*a*) consumer tastes, (*b*) price and availability of substitute products, and (*c*) consumer income important in influencing consumer demand for My Own Meals products?

2. How can (*a*) demand-oriented, (*b*) cost-oriented, (*c*) profit-oriented, and (*d*) competition-oriented approaches be used to help My Own Meals arrive at an approximate price level?

3. Why might the retail price of My Own Meal's products be different in grocery stores, mass merchants, day care centres, and cafeterias?

Financial Aspects of Marketing

Basic concepts from accounting and finance provide valuable tools for marketing executives. This appendix describes an actual company's use of accounting and financial concepts and illustrates how they assist the owner in making marketing decisions.

THE CAPLOW COMPANY

An accomplished artist and calligrapher, Jane Westerlund, decided to apply some of her experience to the picture framing business. She bought an existing retail frame store, The Caplow Company, from a friend who owned the business and wanted to retire. She avoided the do-it-yourself end of the framing business and chose three kinds of business activities: (1) cutting the frame, mats, and glass for customers who brought in their own pictures or prints to be framed, (2) selling prints and posters that she had purchased from wholesalers, and (3) restoring high-quality frames and paintings.

To understand how accounting, finance, and marketing relate to each other, let's analyze (1) the operating statement for her frame shop, (2) some general ratios of interest that are derived from the operating statement, and (3) some ratios that pertain specifically to her pricing decisions.

The Operating Statement

The operating statement (also called an *income statement* or *profit-and-loss statement*) summarizes the profitability of a business firm for a specific time period, usually a month, quarter, or year. The title of the operating statement for The Caplow Company shows it is for a one-year period (Figure B-1). The purpose of an operating statement is to show the profit of the firm and the revenues and expenses that led to that profit. This information tells the owner or manager what has happened in the past and suggests actions to improve future profitability.

The left side of Figure B-1 shows that there are three key elements to all operating statements: (1) sales of the firm's goods and services, (2) costs incurred in making

and selling the goods and services, and (3) profit or loss, which is the difference between sales and costs.

Sales elements   The sales element of Figure B-1 has four terms that need explanation:

- *Gross sales* are the total amount billed to customers. Dissatisfied customers or errors may reduce the gross sales through returns or allowances.
- *Returns* occur when a customer gives the item purchased back to the seller, who either refunds the purchase price or allows the customer a credit on subsequent purchases. In any event, the seller now owns the item again.
- *Allowances* are given when a customer is dissatisfied with the item purchased and the seller reduces the original purchase price. Unlike returns, in the case of allowances the buyer owns the item.
- *Net sales* are simply gross sales minus returns and allowances.

The operating statement for The Caplow Company shows that

Gross sales	$80 500
Less: Returns and allowances	500
Net sales	$80 000

The low level of returns and allowances shows the shop generally has done a good job in satisfying customers, which is essential in building the repeat business necessary for success.

Cost elements   The *cost of goods sold* is the total cost of the products sold during the period. This item varies according to the kind of business. A retail store purchases finished goods and resells them to customers without reworking them in any way. In contrast, a manufacturing firm combines raw and semifinished materials and parts, uses labour and overhead to rework these into finished goods, and then sells them to customers. All these activities are reflected in the cost of goods sold item on a manufacturer's operating statement. Note that the frame shop has some features of a pure retailer (prints

THE CAPLOW COMPANY
Operating Statement
For the Year Ending December 31, 1997

Sales	Gross sales			$80 500
	Less: Returns and allowances			500
	Net sales			$80 000
Costs	Cost of goods sold:			
	Beginning inventory at cost		$ 6 000	
	Purchases at billed cost	$21 000		
	Less: Purchase discounts	300		
	Purchases at net cost	20 700		
	Plus freight-in	100		
	Net cost of delivered purchases		20 800	
	Direct labour (framing)		14 200	
	Cost of goods available for sale		41 000	
	Less: Ending inventory at cost		5 000	
	Cost of goods sold			36 000
	Gross margin (gross profit)			$44 000
	Expenses:			
	Selling expenses:			
	Sales salaries	2 000		
	Advertising expense	3 000		
	Total selling expense		5 000	
	Administrative expenses:			
	Owner's salary	18 000		
	Bookkeeper's salary	1 200		
	Office supplies	300		
	Total administrative expense		19 500	
	General expenses:			
	Depreciation expense	1 000		
	Interest expense	500		
	Rent expense	2 100		
	Utility expenses (heat, electricity)	3 000		
	Repairs and maintenance	2 300		
	Insurance	2 000		
	Employment insurance and CPP	2 200		
	Total general expense		13 100	
	Total expenses			37 600
Profit or loss	Profit before taxes			$ 6 400

and posters it buys that are resold without alteration) and a pure manufacturer (assembling the raw materials of molding, matting, and glass to form a completed frame).
Some terms that relate to cost of goods sold need clarification:

- *Inventory* is the physical material that is purchased from suppliers, may or may not be reworked, and is available for sale to customers. In the frame shop inventory includes molding, matting, glass, prints, and posters.
- *Purchase discounts* are reductions in the original billed price for reasons such as prompt payment of the bill or the quantity bought.
- *Direct labour* is the cost of the labour used in producing the finished product. For the frame shop this is the cost of producing the completed frames from the molding, matting, and glass.
- *Gross margin (gross profit)* is the money remaining to manage the business, sell the products or services, and give some profit. Gross margin is net sales minus cost of goods sold.

JANE WESTERLUND (LEFT) AND AN
ASSISTANT ASSESS THE RESTORATION
OF A GOLD FRAME FOR REGILDING.

The two right-hand columns in Figure B-1 between "Net sales" and "Gross margin" calculate the cost of goods sold:

Net sales		$80 000
Cost of goods sold		
Beginning inventory at cost	$ 6 000	
Net cost of delivered purchases	20 800	
Direct labour (framing)	14 200	
Cost of goods available for sale	41 000	
Less: ending inventory at cost	5 000	
Cost of goods sold		36 000
Gross margin (gross profit)		$44 000

This section considers the beginning and ending inventories, the net cost of purchases delivered during the year, and the cost of the direct labour going into making the frames. Subtracting the $36 000 cost of goods sold from the $80 000 net sales gives the $44 000 gross margin.

Three major categories of expenses are shown in Figure B-1 below the gross margin:

- *Selling expenses* are the costs of selling the product or service produced by the firm. For The Caplow Company there are two such selling expenses: sales salaries of part-time employees waiting on customers and the advertising expense of simple newspaper ads and direct-mail ads sent to customers.
- *Administrative expenses* are the costs of managing the business, and, for The Caplow Company, include three expenses: the owner's salary, a part-time bookkeeper's salary, and office supplies expense.
- *General expenses* are miscellaneous costs not covered elsewhere; for the frame shop these include seven items: depreciation expense (on her equipment), interest expense, rent expense, utility expenses, repairs and maintenance expense, insurance expense, and employment insurance and Canada Pension plan.

As shown in Figure B-1, selling, administrative, and general expenses total $37 600 for The Caplow Company.

Profit element   What the company has earned, the *profit before taxes,* is found by subtracting cost of goods sold and expenses from net sales. For The Caplow Company, Figure B-1 shows that profit before taxes is $6400.

General Operating Ratios to Analyze Operations

Looking only at the elements of Caplow's operating statement that extend to the right-hand column highlights the firm's performance on some important dimensions. Using operating ratios such as *expense-to-sales-ratios* for expressing basic expense or profit elements as a percentage of net sales gives further insights:

ELEMENT IN OPERATING STATEMENT	DOLLAR VALUE	PERCENTAGE OF NET SALES
Gross sales	$80 500	
Less: Returns and allowances	500	
Net sales	80 000	100%
Less: Cost of goods sold	36 000	45
Gross margin	44,000	55
Less: Total expenses	37 600	47
Profit (or loss) before taxes	$6 400	8%

Westerlund can use this information to compare her firm's performance from one time period to the next. To do so, it is especially important that she keep the same definitions for each element of her operating statement, also a significant factor in using the electronic spreadsheets discussed in Chapter 15. Performance comparisons between periods are more difficult if she changes definitions for the accounting elements in the operating statement.

She can use either the dollar values or the operating ratios (the value of the element of the operating statement divided by net sales) to analyze the firm's performance. However, the operating ratios are more valuable than the dollar values for two reasons: (1) the simplicity of working with percentages rather than dollars and (2) the availability of operating ratios of typical firms in the same industry, which are published by Dun & Bradstreet and trade associations. Thus, Westerlund can compare her firm's performance not only with that of *other* frame shops but also with that of *small* frame shops that have annual net sales, for example, of under $100 000. In this way she can identify where her operations are better or worse than other similar firms. For example, if trade association data showed a typical frame shop of her size had a ratio of cost of goods sold to net sales of 37 percent, compared with her 45 percent, she might consider steps to reduce this cost through purchase discounts, reducing inbound freight charges, finding lower cost suppliers, and so on.

Ratios to Use in Setting and Evaluating Price

Using The Caplow Company as an example, we can study four ratios that relate closely to setting a price: (1) markup, (2) markdown, (3) stockturns, and (4) return on investment. These terms are defined in Figure B-2 and explained below.

Markup   Both markup and gross margin refer to the amount added to the cost of goods sold to arrive at the selling price, and they may be expressed either in dollar or percentage terms. However, the term *markup* is more commonly used in setting retail prices. Suppose the average price Westerlund charges for a framed picture is $80. Then in terms of the first two definitions in Figure B-2 and the earlier information from the operating statement,

NAME OF FINANCIAL ELEMENT OR RATIO	WHAT IT MEASURES	EQUATION
Selling price ($)	Price customer sees	Cost of goods sold (COGS) + Markup
Markup ($)	Dollars added to COGS to arrive at selling price	Selling price − COGS
Markup on selling price (%)	Relates markup to selling price	$\frac{Markup}{Selling\ price} \times 100 = \frac{Selling\ price - COGS}{Selling\ Price} \times 100$
Markup on cost (%)	Relates markup to cost	$\frac{Markup}{COGS} \times 100 = \frac{Selling\ price - COGS}{COGS} \times 100$
Markdown (%)	Ability of firm to sell its products at initial selling price	$\frac{Markdowns}{Net\ sales} \times 100$
Stockturn rate	Ability of firm to move its inventory quickly	$\frac{COGS}{Average\ inventory\ at\ cost}$ or $\frac{Net\ sales}{Average\ inventory\ at\ selling\ price}$
Return on investment (%)	Profit performance of firm compared with money invested in it	$\frac{Net\ profit\ after\ taxes}{Investment} \times 100$

FIGURE B-2   HOW TO CALCULATE SELLING PRICE, MARKUP, MARKDOWN, STOCKTURN, AND RETURN ON INVESTMENT

ELEMENT OF PRICE	DOLLAR VALUE
Cost of goods sold	$36
Markup (or gross margin)	44
Selling price	$80

The third definition in Figure B-2 gives the percentage markup on selling price:

$$Markup\ on\ selling\ price\ (\%) = \frac{Markup}{Selling\ price} \times 100$$

$$= \frac{44}{80} \times 100 = 55\%$$

And the percentage markup on cost is obtained as follows:

$$Markup\ on\ cost\ (\%) = \frac{Markup}{Cost\ of\ goods\ sold} \times 100$$

$$= \frac{44}{36} \times 10 = 122.2\%$$

Inexperienced retail clerks sometimes fail to distinguish between the two definitions of markup, which (as the preceding calculations show) can represent a tremendous difference, so it is essential to know whether the base is cost or selling price. Marketers generally use selling price as the base for talking about "markups" unless they specifically state that they are using cost as a base.

Retailers and wholesalers that rely heavily on markup pricing (discussed in Chapter 15) often use standardized tables that convert markup on selling price to markup on cost, and vice versa. The two equations below show how to convert one to the other:

$$Markup\ on\ selling\ price\ (\%) = \frac{Markup\ on\ cost\ (\%)}{100\% + Markup\ on\ cost\ (\%)} \times 100$$

$$Markup\ on\ cost\ (\%) = \frac{Markup\ on\ selling\ price\ (\%)}{100\% - Markup\ on\ selling\ price\ (\%)} \times 100$$

Using the data from The Caplow Company gives

$$\text{Markup on selling price (\%)} = \frac{\text{Markup on cost (\%)}}{100\% + \text{Markup on cost (\%)}} \times 100$$

$$= \frac{122.2}{100 + 122.2} \times 100 = 55\%$$

$$\text{Markup on cost (\%)} = \frac{\text{Markup on selling price (\%)}}{100\% - \text{Markup on selling price (\%)}} \times 100$$

$$= \frac{55}{100 - 55} \times 100 = 122.2\%$$

The use of an incorrect markup base is shown in Westerlund's business. A markup of 122.2 percent on her cost of goods sold for a typical frame she sells gives 122.2% × $36 = $44 of markup. Added to the $36 cost of goods sold, this gives her selling price of $80 for the framed picture. However, a new clerk working for her who erroneously priced the framed picture at 55 percent of cost of goods sold set the final price at $55.80 ($36 of cost of goods sold plus 55% × $36 = $19.80). The error, if repeated, can be disastrous: frames would be accidentally sold at $55.80, or $24.20 below the intended selling price of $80.

Markdown   A markdown is a reduction in a retail price that is necessary if the item will not sell at the full selling price to which it has been marked up. The item might not sell for a variety of reasons: the selling price was set too high or the item is out of style or has become soiled or damaged. The seller "takes a markdown" by lowering the price to sell it, thereby converting it to cash to buy future inventory that will sell faster.

The markdown percentage cannot be calculated directly from the operating statement. As shown in the fifth item of Figure B-2, the numerator of the markdown percentage is the total dollar markdowns. Markdowns are reductions in the prices of goods that are purchased by customers. The denominator is net sales.

Suppose The Caplow Company had a total of $700 in markdowns on the prints and posters that are stocked and available for sale. Since the frames are custom made for individual customers, there is little reason for a markdown there. Caplow's markdown percent is then

$$\text{Markdown (\%)} = \frac{\text{Markdowns}}{\text{Net sales}} \times 100$$

$$= \frac{\$700}{\$80\ 000} \times 100$$

$$= 0.875\%$$

Other kinds of retailers often have markdown ratios several times this amount. For example, women's dress stores have markdowns of about 25 percent, and menswear stores have markdowns of about 2 percent.

Stockturn rate   A business firm is anxious to have its inventory move quickly, or "turn over." Stockturn rate, or simply stockturns, measures this inventory movement. For a retailer a slow stockturn rate may show it is buying merchandise customers don't want, so this is a critical measure of performance. When a firm sells only a single product, one convenient way to measure stockturn rate is simply to divide its cost of goods sold by average inventory at cost. The sixth item in Figure B-2 shows how to calculate stockturn rate using information in the following operating statement:

$$\text{Stockturn rate} = \frac{\text{Cost of goods sold}}{\text{Average inventory at cost}}$$

The dollar amount of average inventory at cost is calculated by adding the beginning and ending inventories for the year and dividing by 2 to get the average. From Caplow's operating statement, we have

A CUSTOMER DISCUSSES CHOICES OF FRAMING AND MATTING FOR HER PRINT WITH JANE WESTERLUND.

$$\text{Stockturn rate} = \frac{\text{Cost of goods sold}}{\text{Average inventory at cost}}$$

$$= \frac{\text{Cost of goods sold}}{\dfrac{\text{Beginning inventory} + \text{Ending inventory}}{2}}$$

$$= \frac{\$36\,000}{\dfrac{\$6000 + \$5000}{2}}$$

$$= \frac{\$36\,000}{\$5500}$$

$$= 6.5 \text{ stockturns per year}$$

What is considered a "good stockturn" varies by the kind of industry. For example, supermarkets have limited shelf space for thousands of new products from manufacturers each year, so they watch stockturn carefully by product line. The stockturn rate in supermarkets for breakfast foods is about 17 times per year, for pet food about 22 times, and for paper products about 25 times per year.

Return on investment   A better measure of the performance of a firm than the amount of profit it makes in a year is its ROI, which is the ratio of net income to the investment used to earn that net income. To calculate ROI, it is necessary to subtract income taxes from profit before taxes to obtain net income, then divide this figure by the investment that can be found on a firm's balance sheet (another accounting statement that shows the firm's assets, liabilities, and net worth). While financial and accounting experts have many definitions for "investment," an often-used definition is "total assets."

For our purposes, let's assume that Westerlund has total assets (investment) of $20 000 in The Caplow Company, which covers inventory, store fixtures, and framing equipment. If she pays $1000 in income taxes, her store's net income is $5400, so her ROI is given by the seventh item in Figure B-2:

Return on investment = Net income/investment $\times$ 100

$$= \$5400/\$20\ 000 \times 100$$

$$= 27\%$$

If Westerlund wants to improve her ROI next year, the strategies she might take are found in this alternative equation for ROI:

ROI = Net sales/investment $\times$ Net income/net sales

= Investment turnover $\times$ Profit margin

This equation suggests that The Caplow Company's ROI can be improved by raising turnover or increasing profit margin. Increasing stockturns will accomplish the former, whereas lowering cost of goods sold to net sales will cause the latter.

CHAPTER 16

Marketing Channels and Wholesaling

AFTER READING THIS CHAPTER YOU SHOULD BE ABLE TO:

• Explain what is meant by a marketing channel of distribution and why intermediaries are needed.

• Recognize differences between marketing channels for consumer and industrial products and services.

• Describe the types and functions of firms that perform wholesaling activities.

• Distinguish among traditional marketing channels and different types of vertical marketing systems.

• Describe factors considered by marketing executives when selecting and managing a marketing channel.

REIGNING CATS AND DOGS WAG PET INDUSTRY MARKETING CHANNELS

Fido's bark and Fifi's purr are a nurturing pet owner's sound of music. Pet pampering has the sound of money for companies that market pet foods, toys, clothing, accessories, and furniture.

About half of Canadian households care for dogs, cats, fish, birds, and hamsters, all of whom get hungry. Annual pet food sales run into hundreds of millions of dollars; hundreds of millions more is spent for pet supplies and health care. Surprised? Don't be. A recent survey revealed that one-half of pet owners consider themselves "Mom and Dad" to their animal companions.

A decade ago, supermarkets sold 95 percent of pet products; small pet stores sold the rest. But the 1990s witnessed a distribution revolution that took a huge bite out of supermarket sales. Superpremium pet brands, such as Hill's Science Diet, Iams, and Nutro Pet Food, posed the first challenge to supermarkets. These and similar brands, which now capture 20 percent of the pet food market, were initially sold only at veterinarians' offices and pet stores. The next assault came from nongrocery outlets such as Wal-Mart. The latest bite has come from pet superstores—PetsMart, Petco, Petstuff, and Pet Food Warehouse—which now capture more than 40 percent of pet product sales.

Pet superstores cater to pets and their adoptive parents. Animals and their companions prowl aisles filled with everything a discriminating shopper could want—doggy dental floss, bones, purple aquarium gravel, hamster starter kits, and bins of toys, balls, stuffed playthings, and treats—many at a pet's eye level to stimulate impulse purchases. Pet food and supplements are plentiful as are sweaters, hats, and colourful collars and leashes. Some stores offer pet grooming and in-house veterinary services.

The distribution revolution in the pet products industry is illustrative of changes in marketing channels occurring in other industries, including home-improvement supplies (Home Depot), office equipment (Business Depot), and children's toys (Toys "Я" Us), where the superstore concept has emerged. In each instance, product manufacturers and intermediaries that supply these stores have had to adjust their marketing practices in ways described later in this chapter.[1]

This chapter focuses on marketing channels of distribution and why they are an important component in the marketing mix. It then shows how such channels benefit consumers and the sequence of firms that make up a marketing channel. Finally, it describes factors that influence the choice and management of marketing channels, including channel conflict and legal restrictions.

NATURE AND IMPORTANCE OF MARKETING CHANNELS

Reaching prospective buyers, either directly or indirectly, is a prerequisite for successful marketing. At the same time, buyers benefit from distribution systems used by firms.

Defining Marketing Channels of Distribution

You see the results of distribution every day. You may have purchased Frito-Lay's Potato Chips at the 7-Eleven store, your lunch at McDonald's, and Levi's jeans at Sears. Each of these items was brought to you by a marketing channel of distribution, or simply a **marketing channel,** which consists of individuals and firms involved in the process of making a product or service available for use or consumption by consumers or industrial users.

Marketing channels can be compared with a pipeline through which water flows from a source to terminus. Marketing channels make possible the flow of goods from a producer, through intermediaries, to a buyer. Intermediaries go by various names (Figure 16-1) and perform various functions.[2] Some intermediaries actually purchase items from the seller, store them, and resell them to buyers. For example, Sunshine Biscuits produces cookies and sells them to food wholesalers. The wholesalers then sell the cookies to supermarkets and grocery stores, which, in turn, sell them to consumers. Other intermediaries such as brokers and agents represent sellers but do not actually take title to products—their role is to bring a seller and buyer together. Century 21 real estate agents are examples of this type of intermediary. The importance of intermediaries is made even clearer when we consider the functions they perform and the value they create for buyers.

FIGURE 16-1

TERMS USED FOR MARKETING
INTERMEDIARIES

TERM	DESCRIPTION
Middleman	Any intermediary between manufacturer and end-user markets
Agent or broker	Any intermediary with legal authority to act on behalf of the manufacturer
Wholesaler	An intermediary who sells to other intermediaries, usually to retailers; usually applies to consumer markets
Retailer	An intermediary who sells to consumers
Distributor	An imprecise term, usually used to describe intermediaries who perform a variety of distribution functions, including selling, maintaining inventories, extending credit, and so on; a more common term in industrial markets but may also be used to refer to wholesalers
Dealer	An even more imprecise term that can mean the same as distributor, retailer, wholesaler, and so forth

Value Created by Intermediaries

Few consumers appreciate the value created by intermediaries; however, producers recognize that intermediaries make selling goods and services more efficient because they minimize the number of sales contacts necessary to reach a target market. Figure 16-2 shows a simple example of how this comes about in the personal computer industry. Without a retail intermediary (such as Future Shop), IBM, Apple, Compaq, and AST would each have to make four contacts to reach the four buyers shown who are in the target market. However, each producer has to make only one contact when Future Shop acts as an intermediary. Equally important from a macromarketing perspective, the total number of industry transactions is reduced from 16 to 8, which reduces producer cost and hence benefits the consumer. This simple example also illustrates why computer manufacturers constantly compete with each other to gain access to computer retailers such as Future Shop and Business Depot.

Functions performed by intermediaries   Intermediaries make possible the flow of products from producers to buyers by performing three basic functions (Figure 16-3).[3] Most prominently, intermediaries perform a transactional function that involves buying, selling, and risk taking because they stock merchandise in anticipation of sales. Intermediaries perform a logistical function evident in the gathering, storing, and dispersing of products (see Chapter 17 on physical distribution). Finally, intermediaries perform facilitating functions, which assist producers in making goods and services more attractive to buyers.

All three groups of functions must be performed in a marketing channel, even though each channel member may not participate in all three. Channel members often negotiate about which specific functions they will perform. Sometimes conflict results, and a breakdown in relationships among channel members occurs. This happened recently when PepsiCo, Inc. terminated its marketing and distribution arrangement with its bottler in France, citing poor performance. However, because all channel functions had to be performed, PepsiCo could eliminate this intermediary but not the functions

FIGURE 16-2   HOW INTERMEDIARIES MINIMIZE TRANSACTIONS

Contacts with no intermediaries
4 Producers x 4 Buyers = 16 Contacts

Contacts with one intermediary
4 Producers + 4 Buyers = 8 Contacts

FIGURE 16-3

MARKETING CHANNEL FUNCTIONS
PERFORMED BY INTERMEDIARIES

Type of function	Activities related to function
Transactional function	• *Buying.* Purchasing products for resale or as an agent for supply of a product • *Selling.* Contacting potential customers, promoting products, and soliciting orders • *Risk taking.* Assuming business risks in the ownership of inventory that can become obsolete or deteriorate
Logistical function	• *Assorting.* Creating product assortments from several sources to serve customers • *Storing.* Assembling and protecting products at a convenient location to offer better customer service • *Sorting.* Purchasing in large quantities and breaking into smaller amounts desired by customers • *Transporting.* Physically moving a product to customers
Facilitating function	• *Financing.* Extending credit to customers • *Grading.* Inspecting, testing, or judging products, and assigning them quality grades • *Marketing information and research.* Providing information to customers and suppliers, including competitive conditions and trends

it performed. So PepsiCo either had to find another bottler (which it did) or set up its own bottling operation to perform the channel functions.[4]

Consumer benefits from intermediaries   Consumers also benefit from intermediaries. Having the goods and services you want, when you want them, where you want them, and in the form you want them is the ideal result of marketing channels. In more specific terms, marketing channels help create value for consumers through the four utilities described in Chapter 1: time, place, form, and possession. Time utility refers to having a product or service when you want it. For example, Federal Express provides next-morning delivery. Place utility means having a product or service available where consumers want it, such as having a Gulf gas station located on a long stretch of lonely highway. Form utility involves enhancing a product or service to make it more appealing to buyers, for example, tailoring services provided by Holt Renfrew. Possession utility entails efforts by intermediaries to help buyers take possession of a product or service, such as having airline tickets delivered by a travel agency.

CONCEPT CHECK

1. What is meant by a marketing channel?

2. What are the three basic functions performed by intermediaries?

FIGURE 16-4

COMMON MARKETING CHANNELS
FOR CONSUMER GOODS AND
SERVICES

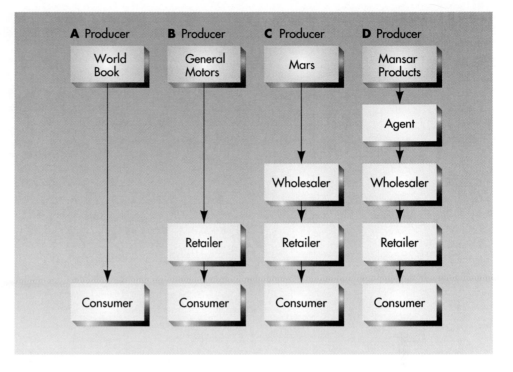

CHANNEL STRUCTURE AND ORGANIZATION

A product can take many routes on its journey from a producer to buyers, and marketers search for the most efficient route from the many alternatives available.

Marketing Channels for Consumer Goods and Services

Figure 16-4 shows the four most common marketing channels for consumer goods and services. It also shows the number of levels in each marketing channel, as evidenced by the number of intermediaries between a producer and ultimate buyers. As the number of intermediaries between a producer and buyer increases, the channel is viewed as increasing in length. Thus the producer → wholesaler → retailer → consumer channel is longer than the producer → consumer channel.

Channel A represents a **direct channel** because a producer and ultimate consumers deal directly with each other. Many products and services are distributed this way. A number of insurance companies sell their financial services using a direct channel and branch sales offices, and World Book Educational Products sells its encyclopedias door-to-door. Schwan's Sales Enterprises markets a full line of frozen foods using door-to-door salespeople who sell from refrigerated trucks. Because there are no intermediaries with a direct channel, the producer must perform all channel functions.

The remaining three channel forms are **indirect channels** because intermediaries are inserted between the producer and consumers and perform numerous channel functions.

Channel B, with a retailer added, is most common when a retailer is large and can buy in large quantities from a producer or when the cost of inventory makes it too expensive to use a wholesaler. Manufacturers such as GM, Ford, and Chrysler use this channel, and a local car dealer acts as a retailer. Why is there no wholesaler? So many variations exist in the product that it would be impossible for a wholesaler to stock all the models required to satisfy buyers; in addition, the cost of maintaining an inventory would be too high. However, large retailers such as Sears, 7-Eleven, Safeway, and The

FIGURE 16-5

COMMON MARKETING CHANNELS
FOR INDUSTRIAL GOODS AND
SERVICES

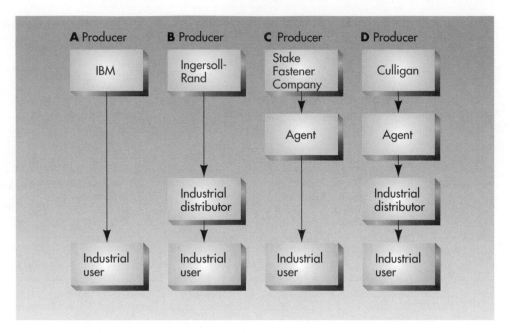

Bay buy in sufficient quantities to make it cost-effective for a producer to deal with only a retail intermediary.

Adding a wholesaler in Channel C is most common for low-cost, low-unit value items that are frequently purchased by consumers, such as candy, confectionary items, and magazines. For example, Mars sells its line of candies to wholesalers in case quantities; then they can break down (sort) the cases so that individual retailers can order in boxes or much smaller quantities.

Channel D, the most indirect channel, is employed when there are many small manufacturers and many small retailers and an agent is used to help coordinate a large supply of the product. Mansar Products, Ltd. is a Belgian producer of specialty jewellery that uses agents to sell to wholesalers which then sell to many small retailers.

Marketing Channels for Industrial Goods and Services

The four most common channels for industrial goods and services are shown in Figure 16-5. In contrast with channels for consumer products, industrial channels typically are shorter and rely on one intermediary or none at all because industrial users are fewer in number, tend to be more concentrated geographically, and buy in larger quantities (see Chapter 7).

Channel A, represented by IBM's large, mainframe computer business, is a direct channel. Firms using this channel maintain their own salesforce and are responsible for all channel functions. This channel arrangement is employed when buyers are large and well defined, the sales effort requires extensive negotiations, and the products are of high unit value and require hands-on expertise in terms of installation or use.

Channels B, C, and D are indirect channels with one or more intermediaries to reach industrial users. In Channel B an **industrial distributor** performs a variety of marketing channel functions, including selling, stocking, and delivering a full product assortment and financing. In many ways, industrial distributors are like wholesalers in consumer channels. Ingersoll-Rand, for example, uses industrial distributors to sell its line of pneumatic tools.

Channel C introduces a second intermediary, an *agent,* who serves primarily as the independent selling arm of producers and represents a producer to industrial users. For example, Stake Fastener Company, a producer of industrial fasteners, has an agent call on industrial users rather than employing its own salesforce.

Channel D is the longest channel and includes both agents and distributors. For instance, Culligan, a producer of water treatment equipment, uses agents to call on distributors who sell to industrial users.

Multiple Channels and Strategic Alliances

In some situations producers use **dual distribution,** an arrangement whereby a firm reaches different buyers by employing two or more different types of channels for the same basic product.[5] For example, GE sells its large appliances directly to home and apartment builders but uses retail stores to sell to consumers. In some instances, firms use multiple channels when a multibrand strategy is employed (see Chapter 12). Hallmark sells its Hallmark greeting cards through Hallmark stores and select department stores, and its Ambassador brand of cards through discount and drugstore chains. In other instances, a firm will distribute modified products through different channels.

A recent innovation in marketing channels is the use of **strategic channel alliances,** whereby one firm's marketing channel is used to sell another firm's products.[6] An alliance between Pepsi-Cola and Thomas J. Lipton Company is a case in point. Lipton relies on Pepsi-Cola's extensive bottling network to distribute Lipton Original, a ready-to-drink iced tea sold only in bottles. Strategic alliances are very popular in global marketing, where the creation of marketing channel relationships is expensive and time-consuming. For example, General Motors distributes the Swedish Saab through its dealers in Canada. And Kraft-General Foods uses the distribution system of Ajinomoto, a major Japanese food company, to market its Maxwell House coffee in Japan.

These examples illustrate the creative routes to the marketplace available through dual distribution and strategic channel alliances. They also show how innovative firms can reach more buyers and increase sales volume. Read the Marketing NewsNet on the following page so you won't be surprised when you are served Nestlé (not General Mills) Cheerios in Europe, Mexico, and parts of Asia.[7]

Direct Marketing Channels

Increasingly, many firms are using direct marketing to reach buyers. **Direct marketing** allows consumers to buy products by interacting with various advertising media without a face-to-face meeting with a salesperson.[8] Direct marketing includes mail-order selling, direct-mail sales, catalogue sales, telemarketing, video-text such as Prodigy, and televised home shopping (for example, the Canadian Home Shopping Network).[9]

Some firms sell products almost entirely through direct marketing. These firms include L. L. Bean (apparel), Sharper Image (expensive gifts and novelties), and Gateway 2000 (personal computers). Manufacturers such as Nestlé and Sunkist, in addition to using traditional channels composed of wholesalers and retailers, employ direct marketing through catalogues and telemarketing to reach more buyers. At the same time, retailers such as Sears Canada use direct marketing techniques to augment conventional store merchandising activities. Direct marketing is covered in greater depth in Chapter 18.

A Closer Look at Channel Intermediaries

Channel structures for consumer and industrial products assume various forms based on the number and type of intermediaries. Knowledge of the roles played by these intermediaries is important for understanding how channels operate in practice.

MARKETING NEWSNET

NESTLÉ AND GENERAL MILLS: CEREAL PARTNERS WORLDWIDE

Can you say Nestlé Cheerios *miel aman-des*? Millions of French start their day with this European equivalent of General Mills's Honey Nut Cheerios, made possible by Cereal Partners Worldwide (CPW). CPW is the food industry's first strategic alliance designed to be a global business; it joined the cereal manufacturing and marketing capability of General Mills with the worldwide distribution clout of Nestlé.

From its headquarters near Lake Geneva, Switzerland, CPW first launched General Mills cereals under the Nestlé label in France, the United Kingdom, Spain and Portugal in 1991, and recorded sales of $250 million. In 1992, distribution moved to include Mexico, Italy, and Germany. Asia—particularly the Phillipines and Thailand—was targeted in 1993 and 1994. CPW expects to achieve its goal of $1 billion in sales by 2000. The General Mills-Nestlé strategic alliance is also likely to increase the ready-to-eat worldwide market share of these companies,

which are already rated as the two best-managed firms in the world.

The terms *wholesaler, agent,* and *retailer* have been used in a general fashion consistent with the meanings given in Figure 16-1. However, on closer inspection, a variety of specific types of intermediaries emerges. Figure 16-6 shows a common classification of intermediaries that engage in wholesaling activities—those activities involved in selling products and services to those who are buying for the purposes of resale or business use. Intermediaries engaged in retailing activities are discussed in detail in Chapter 18. Figure 16-7 describes the functions performed by major types of independent wholesalers.[10]

FIGURE 16-6   TYPES OF WHOLESALING INTERMEDIARIES

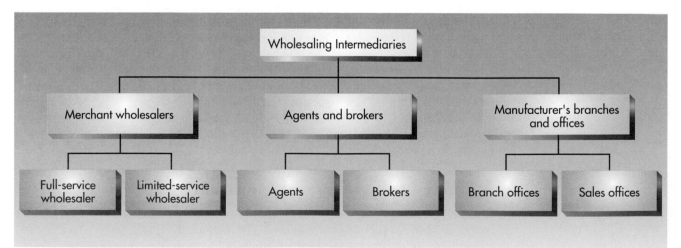

Merchant wholesalers   Merchant wholesalers are independently owned firms that take title to the merchandise they handle. They go by various names, including industrial distributor (described earlier). About 83 percent of the firms engaged in wholesaling activities are merchant wholesalers.

Merchant wholesalers are classified as either full-service or limited-service wholesalers, depending on the number of functions performed. Two major types of full-service wholesalers exist. **General merchandise** (or *full-line*) **wholesalers** carry a broad assortment of merchandise and perform all channel functions. This type of wholesaler is most prevalent in the hardware, drug, and clothing industries. However, these wholesalers do not maintain much depth of assortment within specific product lines. **Specialty merchandise** (or *limited-line*) **wholesalers** offer a relatively narrow range of products but have an extensive assortment within the product lines carried. They perform all channel functions and are found in the health foods, automotive parts, and seafood industries.

FIGURE 16-7   FUNCTIONS PERFORMED BY INDEPENDENT WHOLESALER TYPES

| | MERCHANT WHOLESALERS | | | | | | AGENTS AND BROKERS | | |
| | FULL SERVICE | | LIMITED SERVICE | | | | | | |
FUNCTIONS PERFORMED	GENERAL MERCHANDISE	SPECIALTY MERCHANDISE	RACK JOBBERS	CASH AND CARRY	DROP SHIPPERS	TRUCK JOBBERS	MANUFACTURER'S AGENTS	SELLING AGENTS	BROKERS
TRANSACTIONAL FUNCTIONS									
Buying	Yes★	Yes	Yes	Yes	Yes	Yes	No	No	No
Sales calls on customers	Yes	Yes	Yes	No	Yes	Yes	Yes	Yes	Yes
Risk taking (taking title to products)	Yes	Yes	Yes	Yes	Yes	Yes	No	No	No
LOGISTICAL FUNCTIONS									
Creates product assortments	Yes	Yes	Yes	Yes	No	Yes	Sometimes	No	Yes
Stores products (maintains inventory)	Yes	Yes	Yes	Yes	No	Yes	No	No	No
Sorts products	Yes	Yes	Yes	Yes	Yes	Yes	No	No	No
Transports products	Yes	Yes	Yes	No	No	Yes	No	No	No
FACILITATING FUNCTIONS									
Provides financing (credit)	Yes	Yes	Yes	No	Yes	No	Sometimes	Sometimes	Sometimes
Provides market information and research	Yes	Yes	Sometimes	Sometimes	Yes	Sometimes	Yes	Yes	Yes
Grading	Yes	Yes	Sometimes	Sometimes	Sometimes	Sometimes	No	No	Yes

★ Key: ● , Yes; ◐ , sometimes; ○ , no.

Four major types of limited-service wholesalers exist. **Rack jobbers** furnish the racks or shelves that display merchandise in retail stores, perform all channel functions, and sell on consignment to retailers, which means they retain the title to the products displayed and bill retailers only for the merchandise sold. Familiar products such as hosiery, toys, housewares, and health and beauty aids are sold by rack jobbers. **Cash and carry wholesalers** take title to merchandise but sell only to buyers who call on them, pay cash for merchandise, and furnish their own transportation for merchandise. They carry a limited product assortment and do not make deliveries, extend credit, or supply market information. This wholesaler is common in electric supplies, office supplies, hardware products, and groceries. **Drop shippers,** or *desk jobbers,* are wholesalers who own the merchandise they sell but do not physically handle, stock, or deliver it. They simply solicit orders from retailers and other wholesalers and have the merchandise shipped directly from a producer to a buyer. Drop shippers are used for bulky products such as coal, lumber, and chemicals, which are sold in extremely large quantities. **Truck jobbers** are small wholesalers who have a small warehouse from which they stock their trucks for distribution to retailers. They usually handle limited assortments of fast-moving or perishable items that are sold for cash directly from trucks in their original packages. Truck jobbers handle products such as bakery items, dairy products, meat, and tobacco.

Agents and brokers   Unlike merchant wholesalers, agents and brokers do not take title to merchandise and typically provide fewer channel functions. They make their profit from commissions or fees paid for their services, whereas merchant wholesalers make their profit from the sale of the merchandise they own.

Manufacturer's agents and selling agents are the two major types of agents used by producers. **Manufacturer's agents,** or *manufacturer's representatives,* work for several producers and carry noncompetitive, complementary merchandise in an exclusive territory. Manufacturer's agents act as a producer's sales arm in a territory and are principally responsible for the transactional channel functions, primarily selling. They are used extensively in the automotive supply, footwear, and fabricated steel industries. However, Swank Jewelry, Japanese computer firms, and Apple have used manufacturer's agents as well. By comparison, **selling agents** represent a single producer and are responsible for the entire marketing function of that producer. They design promotional plans, set prices, determine distribution policies, and make recommendations on product strategy. Selling agents are used by small producers in the textile, apparel, food, and home furnishing industries.

Brokers are independent firms or individuals whose principal function is to bring buyers and sellers together to make sales. Brokers, unlike agents, usually have no continuous relationship with the buyer or seller but negotiate a contract between two parties and then move on to another task. Brokers are used extensively by producers of seasonal products (such as fruits and vegetables) and in the real estate industry.

A unique broker that acts in many ways like a manufacturer's agent is a food broker, representing buyers and sellers in the grocery industry. Food brokers differ from conventional brokers because they act on behalf of producers on a permanent basis and receive a commission for their services. For example, Nabisco uses food brokers to sell its candies, margarine, and Planters peanuts, but it sells its line of cookies and crackers directly to retail stores. Do agents and brokers create value for customers? The accompanying Marketing NewsNet describes how Mr. Coffee used both manufacturer's agents and brokers to become a leader in the electric-drip coffee maker market.[11]

Manufacturer's branches and offices   Unlike merchant wholesalers, agents, and brokers, manufacturer's branches and offices are wholly owned extensions of the producer that perform wholesaling activities. Producers will assume wholesaling functions when there are no intermediaries to perform these activities,

MARKETING NEWSNET

MR. COFFEE + AGENTS + BROKERS = CUSTOMER VALUE

Vincent Marotta hated the way coffee tasted, but he was convinced that its poor taste was caused not by bad coffee but by the machines that brewed it. In 1972, he developed the prototype for what is now known as Mr. Coffee, the first electric-drip coffee maker. By 1996 more than 50 million Mr. Coffees had been sold, as well as billions of coffee filters. Was Mr. Coffee's success only a result of a high-quality product that satisfied a need? Not quite. Distribution played an integral role in creating value for customers.

Mr. Coffee and its filters were sold by manufacturer's agents who called on appliance mass merchandise stores. In time, however, it became apparent that Mr. Coffee users found it inconvenient to visit appliance and mass merchandise stores to buy replacement filters. These customers would benefit by having filters in the stores where they bought their coffee. Therefore, a national network of food brokers was hired to sell Mr. Coffee filters to supermarkets and grocery stores. The result? It is estimated that about 75 percent of Mr. Coffee's filter sales come from retail food outlets.

When the company introduced the Ice Tea Pot by Mr. Coffee, it used its network of manufacturer's agents to call on appliance and mass merchandise stores. Filters were sold by food brokers to retail food outlets, and another success was brewed.

customers are few in number and geographically concentrated, or orders are large or require significant attention. Wholesaling activities performed by producers are conducted by means of a branch office or sales office. A *manufacturer's branch office* carries a producer's inventory, performs the functions of a full-service wholesaler, and is an alternative to a merchant wholesaler. A *manufacturer's sales office* does not carry inventory, typically performs only a sales function, and serves as an alternative to agents and brokers.

Vertical Marketing Systems and Channel Partnerships

The traditional marketing channels described so far represent a loosely knit network of independent producers and intermediaries brought together to distribute goods and services. However, new channel arrangements have emerged for the purpose of improving efficiency in performing channel functions and achieving greater marketing effectiveness. These new arrangements are called vertical marketing systems and channel partnerships. **Vertical marketing systems** are professionally managed and centrally coordinated marketing channels designed to achieve channel economies and maximum marketing impact.[12] Figure 16-8 depicts the major types of vertical marketing systems: corporate, contractual, and administered.

Corporate systems   The combination of successive stages of production and distribution under a single ownership is a *corporate vertical marketing system.* For example, a producer might own the intermediary at the next level down in the channel. This practice, called *forward integration,* is exemplified by Polo/Ralph Lauren, which manufactures clothing and also owns apparel shops. Other examples of forward integration include Goodyear, Singer, Sherwin Williams, and Irving Oil.

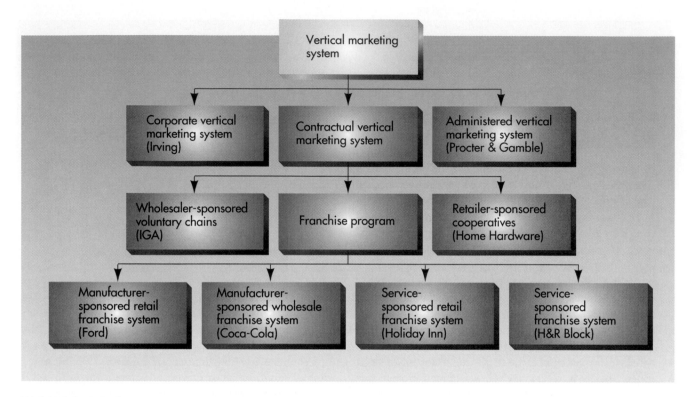

FIGURE 16-8   TYPES OF VERTICAL MARKETING SYSTEMS

Alternatively, a retailer might own a manufacturing operation, a practice called *backward integration.* For example, Safeway supermarkets operate their own bakeries.

Contractual systems   Under a *contractual vertical marketing system,* independent production and distribution firms integrate their efforts on a contractual basis to obtain greater functional economies and marketing impact than they could achieve alone. Contractual systems are the most popular among the three types of vertical marketing systems and are estimated to account for about 40 percent of all retail sales.

Three variations of contractual systems exist. *Wholesaler-sponsored voluntary chains* involve a wholesaler that develops a contractual relationship with small, independent retailers to standardize and coordinate buying practices, merchandising programs, and inventory management efforts. With the organization of a large number of independent retailers, economies of scale and volume discounts can be achieved to compete with chain stores. IGA stores represent wholesaler-sponsored voluntary chains. *Retailer-sponsored cooperatives* exist when small, independent retailers form an organization that operates a wholesale facility cooperatively. Member retailers then concentrate their buying power through the wholesaler and plan collaborative promotional and pricing activities. An example of retailer-sponsored cooperative includes Home Hardware.

The most visible variation of contractual systems is **franchising,** a contractual arrangement between a parent company (a franchisor) and an individual or firm (a franchisee) that allows the franchise to operate a certain type of business under an established name and according to specific rules. Four types of franchise arrangements are most popular. Manufacturer-sponsored retail franchise systems are most prominent in the automobile industry, where a manufacturer such as Ford licenses dealers to sell its cars subject to various sales and service conditions. Manufacturer-sponsored wholesale systems are evident in the soft-drink industry, where Pepsi-Cola licenses wholesalers (bottlers) who purchase concentrate from Pepsi-Cola and then carbonate, bottle, promote, and distribute its products to supermarkets and restaurants. Service-sponsored retail franchise systems are provided by firms that have designed a unique approach for performing a service and wish to profit by selling the franchise to others. Holiday Inn, Avis, and McDonald's represent this franchising approach. Service-sponsored franchise systems exist when franchisors license individuals or firms to dispense a service under a trade name and specific guidelines. An example is H&R Block tax services. Service-sponsored franchise arrangements are the fastest-growing type of franchise in the 1990s.[13] Franchising is discussed further in Chapter 18.

Administered systems   In comparison, *administered vertical marketing systems* achieve coordination at successive stages of production and distribution by the size and influence of one channel member rather than through ownership. P&G, given its broad product assortment ranging from disposable diapers to detergents, is able to obtain cooperation from supermarkets in displaying, promoting, and pricing its products. Wal-Mart can obtain cooperation from manufacturers in terms of product specifications, price levels, and promotional support, given its position as the world's largest retailer.

Channel partnerships   Increasingly, channel members are forging channel partnerships akin to supply partnerships described in Chapter 7. A **channel partnership** consists of agreements and procedures among channel members for ordering and physically distributing a producer's products through the channel to the ultimate consumer.[14] A central feature of channel partnerships is the collaborative use of modern information and communication technology to better serve customers and reduce the time and cost of performing channel functions.

The partnership Levi Strauss & Company has with Modell's Sporting Goods is a case in point.[15] By using point-of-sale scanning equipment and direct electronic linkage to Levi Strauss, Modell's can instantaneously inform Levi Strauss what styles and sizes of jeans are needed, create purchase orders, and convey shipping instructions without any human involvement. The result? The costs of performing transaction, logistic, and facilitating functions are substantially reduced, and the customer is virtually assured of having his or her preferred 501 Levi jeans in stock. The role of information and communication technology in the management of physical distribution and logistics is discussed further in Chapter 17.

CONCEPT CHECK

1. What is the difference between a direct and an indirect channel?

2. Why are channels for industrial products typically shorter than channels for consumer products?

3. What is the principal distinction between a corporate vertical marketing system and an administered vertical marketing system?

CHANNEL CHOICE AND MANAGEMENT

Marketing channels not only link a producer to its buyers but also provide the means through which a firm implements various elements of its marketing strategy. Therefore, choosing a marketing channel is a critical decision.

Factors Affecting Channel Choice and Management

The final choice of a marketing channel by a producer depends on a number of factors that often interact with each other.

Environmental factors   The changing environment described in Chapter 3 has an important effect on the choice and management of a marketing channel. For example, the Fuller Brush and Avon names synonymous with door-to-door selling, now use catalogues and telemarketing to reach customers. Rising employment among women, resulting in fewer being at home during working hours, prompted this action. Advances in the technology of growing, transporting, and storing perishable cut flowers as well as telecommunications technology is helping Flowers Online grow globally.[16]

Consumer factors   Consumer characteristics have a direct bearing on the choice and management of a marketing channel. Determining which channel is most appropriate is based on answers to fundamental questions such as: Who are potential customers? Where do they buy? When do they buy? How do they buy? What do they buy? These answers also indicate the type of intermediary best suited to reaching target buyers. For example, Ricoh Company, Ltd. studied the serious (as opposed to recreational) camera user and concluded that a change in marketing channels was necessary. The company terminated its contract with a wholesaler who sold to mass merchandise stores and began using manufacturer's agents who sold to photo specialty stores. These stores agreed to stock and display Ricoh's full line and promote it prominently, and sales volume tripled within 18 months.[17]

Product factors   In general, highly sophisticated products such as large, scientific computers, unstandardized products such as custom-built machinery, and products of high unit value are distributed directly to buyers. Unsophisticated, standardized products with low unit value, such as table salt, are typically distributed through indirect channels. A product's stage in the life cycle also affects marketing channels. Figure 16-9 shows the dominant retail marketing channel for personal computers since their introduction in the 1970s.[18]

FIGURE 16-9

DOMINANT RETAIL MARKETING
CHANNEL FOR PERSONAL
COMPUTERS OVER THE PC LIFE CYCLE

Company factors   A firm's financial, human, or technological capabilities affect channel choice. For example, firms that are unable to employ a salesforce might use manufacturer's agents or selling agents to reach wholesalers or buyers. If a firm has multiple products for a particular target market, it might use a direct channel, whereas firms with a limited product line might use intermediaries of various types to reach buyers.

Company factors also apply to intermediaries. For example, personal computer hardware and software producers wishing to reach business users might look to value-added resellers such as Future Shop, which has its own salesforce.

Channel Design Considerations

Recognizing that numerous routes to buyers exist and also recognizing the factors just described, marketing executives typically consider three questions when choosing a marketing channel and intermediaries:

1. Which channel and intermediaries will provide the best coverage of the target market?
2. Which channel and intermediaries will best satisfy the buying requirements of the target market?
3. Which channel and intermediaries will be the most profitable?

Target market coverage   Achieving the best coverage of the target market requires attention to the density and type of intermediaries to be used at the retail level of distribution. Three degrees of distribution density exist: intensive, exclusive, and selective. **Intensive distribution** means that a firm tries to place its products and services in as many outlets as possible. Intensive distribution is usually chosen for convenience products or services; for example, chewing gum, automatic teller machines, and soft drinks. Increasingly, medical services are distributed in this fashion.

Exclusive distribution is the extreme opposite of intensive distribution because only one retail outlet in a specified geographical area carries the firm's product. Exclusive distribution is typically chosen for specialty products or services; for example, automobiles, some women's fragrances, men's suits, and yachts. Sometimes manufacturers sign exclusive distribution agreements with retail chain stores. Hewlett-Packard originally sold its personal computers for home use only through a few retailers, but it has since broadened its distribution.

Selective distribution lies between these two extremes and means that a firm selects a few retail outlets in a specific area to carry its products. This is the most common form of distribution intensity and is usually associated with shopping goods or services such as Rolex watches, and Taylor-Made golf clubs.

The type or availability of a retail outlet will also influence whether a target market is reached. For example, the L'eggs division of the Hanes Corporation distributes fashionable white pantyhose to nurses through catalogues because supermarkets and department stores do not typically carry these items.

Satisfying buyer requirements   A second consideration in channel design is gaining access to channels and intermediaries that satisfy at least some of the interests buyers might want fulfilled when they purchase a firm's products or services. These interests fall into four categories: (1) information, (2) convenience, (3) variety, and (4) attendant services.

Information is an important requirement when buyers have limited knowledge or desire specific data about a product or service. Properly chosen intermediaries communicate with buyers through in-store displays, demonstrations, and personal selling. Computer stores originally grew in popularity as a source for small computers because they provided such information. Similarly, direct sales firms such as Amway, Avon, and

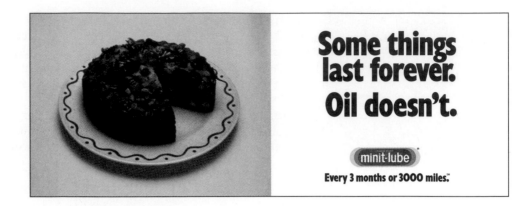

Tupperware have been able to identify the unique information needs of Japanese women and successfully communicate the benefits of their products and method of selling. Amway is one of the fastest-growing firms in Japan, and Avon records more than $350 million in Japanese sales each year through direct selling.[19]

Convenience has multiple meanings for buyers, such as proximity or driving time to a retail outlet. For example, 7-Eleven stores with outlets nationwide satisfy this interest for buyers, and candy and snack food firms benefit by gaining display space in these stores. For other consumers, convenience means a minimum of time and hassle. The rapid growth of Jiffy Lube and Minit-Lube, which promise to change engine oil and filters in less than 10 minutes, appeal to this aspect of convenience.

Variety reflects buyers' interest in having numerous competing and complementary items from which to choose. Variety is evident in both the breadth and depth of products and brands carried by intermediaries, which enhances their attraction to buyers. Thus, manufacturers of pet food and supplies seek distribution through pet superstores such as Petco and PetsMart, which offer a wide array of pet products.

Attendant services provided by intermediaries are an important buying requirement for products such as appliances that require delivery, installation, and credit. Therefore, Whirlpool seeks dealers that provide such services.

Profitability   The third consideration in designing a channel is profitability, which is determined by the margins earned (revenues minus cost) for each channel member and for the channel as a whole. Channel cost is the critical dimension of profitability. These costs include distribution, advertising, and selling expenses associated with different types of marketing channels. The extent to which channel members share these costs determines the margins received by each member and by the channel as a whole.

Global Dimensions of Marketing Channels

Marketing channels around the world reflect traditions, customs, geography, and the economic history of individual countries and societies. Even so, the basic marketing channel functions must be performed. But differences do exist, and are illustrated by highlighting marketing channels in Japan—the world's second-largest economy.

Intermediaries outside Western Europe and North America tend to be small, numerous, and often owner operated. Japanese marketing channels tend to include many intermediaries based on tradition and lack of storage space. As many as five intermediaries are involved in the distribution of soap in Japan compared with one or two in North America (see Figure 16-10).[20]

Understanding marketing channels in global markets is often a prerequisite to successful marketing. For example, Gillette attempted to sell its razors and blades through company salespeople in Japan as it does in North America, thus eliminating wholesalers

FIGURE 16-10   MARKETING CHANNEL FOR SOAP IN JAPAN

traditionally involved in marketing toiletries. Warner-Lambert Company sold its Schick razors and blades through the traditional Japanese channel involving wholesalers. The result? Gillette holds 10 percent of the Japanese razor and blade market, and Schick holds 62 percent.[21]

Channel relationships also must be considered. In Japan, the distribution *keiretsu* (translated as "alignments") bonds producers and intermediaries together.[22] The bond, through vertical integration and social and economic ties, ensures that each channel member benefits from the distribution alignment. The dominant member of the distribution *keiretsu,* which is typically a producer, has considerable influence over channel member behaviour, including which competing products are sold by other channel members. Well-known Japanese companies such as Matsushita (electronics), Nissan and Toyota (automotive products), Nippon Gakki (musical instruments), and Kirin (and other brewers and distillers) employ the distribution *keiretsu* extensively. Shiseido and Kanebo, for instance, influence the distribution of cosmetics through Japanese department stores.

Channel Relationships: Conflict, Cooperation, and Law

Unfortunately, because channels consist of independent individuals and firms, there is always potential for disagreements concerning who performs which channel functions, how profits are allocated, which products and services will be provided by whom, and who makes critical channel-related decisions. These channel conflicts necessitate measures for dealing with them. Sometimes they result in legal action.

Conflict in marketing channels   Channel conflict arises when one channel member believes another channel member is engaged in behaviour that prevents it from achieving its goals.[23] Two types of conflict occur in marketing channels: vertical conflict and horizontal conflict.

Vertical conflict occurs between different levels in a marketing channel; for example, between a manufacturer and a wholesaler or retailer or between a wholesaler and a retailer. Three sources of vertical conflict are most common. First, conflict arises when a channel member bypasses another member and sells or buys products direct. This conflict emerged when Jenn-Air, a producer of kitchen appliances, decided to terminate its distributors and sell direct to retailers. Conflict also arose when Wal-Mart elected to purchase products direct from manufacturers rather than through manufacturer's agents.[24] Second, disagreements over how profit margins are distributed among channel members produce conflict. This happened when Businessland and Compaq Computer Corporation disagreed over how price discounts were applied in the sale of Compaq's products. Compaq Computer stopped selling to Businessland for 13 months until the issue was resolved.[25] A third conflict situation arises when manufacturers believe wholesalers or retailers are not giving their products adequate attention. For example, H. J. Heinz Company found itself in a conflict situation with its supermarkets in Great Britain when the supermarkets promoted and displayed private brands at the expense of Heinz brands.[26]

Horizontal conflict occurs between intermediaries at the same level in a marketing channel, such as between two or more retailers (Zellers and Kmart) or two or more wholesalers that handle the same manufacturer's brands. Two sources of horizontal conflict are most common. First, horizontal conflict arises when a manufacturer increases its distribution coverage in a geographical area. For example, a franchised Cadillac dealer in Toronto might complain to GM that another franchised Cadillac dealer has located too close to its dealership. Second, dual distribution causes conflict when different types of retailers carry the same brands. For instance, the launch of Elizabeth Taylor's Black Pearls fragrance by Elizabeth Arden was put on hold when some up-scale department store chains refused to stock the item once they learned that mass merchants would also carry the brand. Elizabeth Arden subsequently introduced the brand only through the up-scale department stores in 1996.[27]

Cooperation in marketing channels   Conflict can have destructive effects on the workings of a marketing channel, so it is necessary to secure cooperation among channel members. One means is through a **channel captain,** a channel member that coordinates, directs, and supports other channel members. Channel captains can be producers, wholesalers, or retailers. P&G assumes this role because it has a strong consumer following in brands such as Crest, Tide, and Pampers. Therefore, it can set policies or terms that supermarkets will follow. Wal-Mart is a retail channel captain because of its strong consumer image, number of outlets, and purchasing volume.

A firm becomes a channel captain because it is typically the channel member with the ability to influence the behaviour of other members.[28] Influence can take four forms. First, economic influence arises from the ability of a firm to reward other members given its strong financial position or customer franchise. Microsoft Corporation and Toys "Я" Us have such influence. Expertise is a second source of influence over other channel members. Third, identification with a particular channel member may also create influence for that channel member. For instance, retailers may compete to carry the Ralph Lauren line, or clothing manufacturers may compete to be carried by Eaton's or The Bay. In both instances the desire to be associated with a channel member gives that firm influence over others. Finally, influence can arise from the legitimate right of one channel member to dictate the behaviour of other members. This situation would occur under contractual vertical marketing systems where a franchisor could legitimately direct how a franchisee behaves. Other means for securing cooperation in marketing channels rest in the different variations of vertical marketing systems.

Channel influence can be used to gain concessions from other channel members. For instance, some large supermarket chains expect manufacturers to pay allowances, in the form of cash or free goods, to stock and display their products. Some manufacturers call these allowances "extortion" as described in the Ethics and Social Responsibility Alert.[29]

Legal considerations   Conflict in marketing channels is typically resolved through negotiation or the exercise of power by channel members. Sometimes conflict produces legal action. Therefore, knowledge of legal restrictions affecting channel strategies and practices is important. Some restrictions were described in Chapter 14, namely, price fixing and price discrimination. However, other legal considerations unique to marketing channels warrant attention.

In general, suppliers do have the right to choose the intermediaries who carry or represent their products. However, suppliers can run into legal difficulty over *refusing to deal* with customers who can meet the usual trade terms offered by the supplier. The Competition Act looks seriously at cases where a supplier withholds or withdraws products from a customer if such behaviour will adversely affect that customer.

Dual distribution is a situation where a manufacturer distributes through its own vertically integrated channel in direct competition with wholesalers and retailers that also sell its products. If the manufacturer's behaviour is viewed as an attempt to unduly

ETHICS AND SOCIAL RESPONSIBILITY ALERT

THE ETHICS OF SLOTTING ALLOWANCES

How firms acquire and use influence in marketing channels has often prompted legal restrictions. Nevertheless, influence gained through the economic strength, expertise, identification with others, and legitimate rights of channel members can be used in numerous ways.

Some supermarket chains demand slotting allowances from manufacturers, paid in the form of money or free goods, to stock and display products. The allowances, which can range from $100 for a single store to upwards of $25 000 for a supermarket chain, have been labelled "ransom" and "extortional allowances" by manufacturers. Supermarket operators see these allowances as a reasonable cost of handling business for manufacturers.

Is the practice of charging slotting allowances unethical behaviour?

lessen competition by eliminating wholesalers or retailers, then such action may violate the Competition Act and would be examined by the Bureau of Competition Policy.

Vertical integration is viewed in a similar light. Like dual distribution, it is not illegal, but the practice could be subject to legal action if such integration were designed to eliminate or lessen competition unduly.

Exclusive dealing and tied selling are prohibited under the Competition Act if they are found to unduly lessen competition or create monopolies. *Exclusive dealing* exists when a supplier requires channel members to sell only its products or restricts distributors from selling directly competitive products. *Tied selling* occurs when a supplier requires a distributor purchasing some products to buy others from the supplier. These arrangements often arise in franchising. Tied selling would be investigated by the Bureau of Competition Policy if the tied products could be purchased at fair market value from other suppliers at desired standards of the franchisor and if the arrangements were seen as restricting competition. Full-line forcing is a special kind of tied selling. This is a supplier's requiring that a channel member carry its full line of products to sell a specific item in the supplier's line.

Resale or market restrictions refer to a supplier's attempt to stipulate to whom distributors may resell the supplier's products and in what specific geographical areas or territories they may be sold. These practices could be subject to review under the Competition Act if such restrictions were deemed to be restraining or lessening competition.

CONCEPT CHECK

1. What are the three degrees of distribution density?

2. What are the three questions marketing executives consider when choosing a marketing channel and intermediaries?

3. What is meant by "exclusive dealing?"

SUMMARY

1. A marketing channel consists of individuals and firms which are involved in the process of making a product or service available for use or consumption by consumers or industrial users.

2. Intermediaries make possible the flow of products and services from producers to buyers by performing transactional, logistical, and facilitating functions. At the same time, intermediaries create time, place, form, and possession utility.

3. Channel structure describes the route taken by products and services from producers to buyers. Direct channels represent the shortest route because producers interact directly with buyers. Indirect channels include intermediaries between producers and buyers.

4. In general, marketing channels for consumer products and services contain more intermediaries than do channels for industrial products and services. In some situations, producers use multiple channels and strategic channel alliances.

5. Numerous types of wholesalers can exist within a marketing channel. The principal distinction between the various types of wholesalers lies in whether they take title to the items they sell and the channel functions they perform.

6. Vertical marketing systems are channels designed to achieve channel function economies and marketing impact. A vertical marketing system may be one of three types: corporate, administered, or contractual.

7. Marketing managers consider environmental, consumer, product, and company factors when choosing and managing marketing channels.

8. Channel design considerations are based on the target market coverage sought by producers, the buyer requirements to be satisfied, and the profitability of the channel. Target market coverage comes about through one of three levels of distribution density: intensive, exclusive, and selective distribution. Buyer requirements are evident in the amount of information, convenience, variety, and service sought by consumers. Profitability relates to the margins obtained by each channel member and the channel as a whole.

9. Marketing channels in the global marketplace reflect traditions, customs, geography, and the economic history of individual countries and societies. These factors influence channel structure and relationships among channel members.

10. Conflicts in marketing channels are inevitable. Vertical conflict occurs between different levels in a channel. Horizontal conflict occurs between intermediaries at the same level in the channel.

11. Legal issues in the management of marketing channels typically arise from six practices: refusal to deal, dual distribution, vertical integration, exclusive dealing, tied selling, and resale or market restrictions.

KEY TERMS AND CONCEPTS

marketing channel p. 388
direct channel p. 391
indirect channels p. 391
industrial distributor p. 392
dual distribution p. 393
strategic channel alliances p. 393
direct marketing p. 393
general merchandise wholesalers p. 395
specialty merchandise wholesalers p. 395
rack jobbers p. 396
cash and carry wholesalers p. 396
drop shippers p. 396

truck jobbers p. 396
manufacturer's agents p. 396
selling agents p. 396
brokers p. 396
vertical marketing systems p. 397
franchising p. 398
channel partnership p. 399
intensive distribution p. 401
exclusive distribution p. 401
selective distribution p. 401
channel captain p. 404

CHAPTER PROBLEMS AND APPLICATIONS

1. A distributor for Celanese Chemical Company stores large quantities of chemicals, blends these chemicals to satisfy requests of customers, and delivers the blends to a customer's warehouse within 24 hours of receiving an order. What utilities does this distributor provide?

2. Suppose the president of a carpet manufacturing firm has asked you to look into the possibility of bypassing the firm's wholesalers (who sell to carpet, department, and furniture stores) and selling direct to these stores. What caution would you voice on this matter, and what type of information would you gather before making this decision?

3. What type of channel conflict is likely to be caused by dual distribution, and what type of conflict can be reduced by direct distribution? Why?

4. How does the channel captain idea differ among corporate, administered, and contractual vertical marketing systems with particular reference to the use of the different forms of influence available to firms?

5. Comment on this statement: "The only distinction among merchant wholesalers and agents and brokers is that merchant wholesalers take title to the products they sell."

6. How do specialty, shopping, and convenience goods generally relate to intensive, selective, and exclusive distribution? Give a brand name that is an example of each goods-distribution matchup.

CASE 16-1   Creston Vineyards

Larry Rosenbloom's customers include individuals, retail stores, restaurants, and hotels. Because of the many types and large numbers of customers, distribution is as important as production at Creston Vineyards. As Larry explains, "We need distributors in our business . . . as most other [businesses] do, to get the product to the end user, to the consumer."

THE COMPANY

In 1980, Stephanie and Larry Rosenbloom purchased an abandoned ranch and started Creston Vineyards. Because it takes several years for vines to grow and produce grapes, Creston did not sell its first wine until 1982. Today, the 569 acre ranch has 155 acres of planted vineyards and produces over 55 000 cases of eight varieties of wines. The production facilities include a 15 000 square foot winery and 2000 square feet of laboratory and office space.

Since 1982 Creston wines have won over 500 awards in wine tasting events and competitions.

THE INDUSTRY AND DISTRIBUTION CHANNELS

The wine industry is undergoing several very interesting changes. First, sales have increased in recent years after a general decline since 1984. The decline was attributed to changing consumer demographics, shifting buying habits, and concerns about the economy. At least some of the recent interest in wine is related to the press reports suggesting the possible health benefits of red wine. A second change is the significant increase in the price of wine due to a low supply of good international wines and changing exchange rates, and an infestation of vine-eating insects (phylloxera). Finally, many wine producers are trying to change the image of wine from a beverage only for special occasions and gourmet foods to a beverage for any occasion.

The industry also faces several distribution challenges. The large number of wine producers and the variety of consumers requires a sophisticated system of distribution channels. By combining different types of intermediaries the industry is able to meet the requirements of many customers. In addition, because the sale of wine is regulated, the use of multiple distribution channels facilitates the sale of wine in many locations.

One of the most common channels of distribution involves a distributor buying wine directly from the vineyard and reselling it to retail stores and restaurants within a geographic area. Some distributors, however, may not need quantities large enough to warrant purchasing directly from the vineyard. They usually purchase several brands at the same time from a warehouse. A broker may facilitate sales by providing information to distributors, training the distributor's salesforce, and even assisting in sales calls to retailers. John Drady, one of twelve brokers for Creston Vineyards explains: "It's very important that we translate our knowledge and our selling skills to the distributor's salespeople so they can, in turn, go out and [sell] more readily on their own."

Other channels are also used by Creston. For example, in some markets Creston can sell directly to any customer. The vineyard also sells directly to some large retailers. Another channel of distribution is through wine clubs which provide club members with information about wines and an average of six wines per year. The popularity of wine clubs has been increasing and they now account for 15 percent of Creston's sales. The newest type of distribution channel is through on-line services. Creston now has a page on the World Wide Web (www.wines.com) that provides information about its wines and allows orders to be shipped directly to consumers. Customers will also find greetings from Alex Trebek, the Canadian-born game-show host, who now is the current owner of Creston Vineyards.

THE ISSUES

In an industry with thousands of products and hundreds of producers, Creston is relatively new and small. Selecting and managing its distribution channels to best meet the needs of many constituents is a key task. Providing marketing assistance, product information, and appropriate assortment, transportation, storage, and credit are just a few of the functions the warehouse, brokers, distributors, and retailers may provide as the product moves from the vineyard to the end user.

Creston also faces a situation where new, and possibly more efficient, channels are becoming available. Direct sales, wine clubs, and on-line services have generated substantial sales for Creston. Other channels, or new variations of existing channels, may also be available in the future. Overall, Creston must continue to utilize distribution channels to provide value to customers ranging from large retailers, to hotels and restaurants, and to individuals.

Questions

1. What functions must be performed by intermediaries in the wine industry?
2. What intermediaries and distribution channels are currently used by Creston Vineyards?
3. How do different channels of distribution reach different segments? Are there any segments Creston does not reach with its current channels?

CHAPTER 17

Physical Distribution and Logistics Management

AFTER READING THIS CHAPTER YOU SHOULD BE ABLE TO:

• Explain what physical distribution and logistics management are and how they relate to the marketing mix.

• Understand the nature of logistics trade-offs among transportation, inventory, and other logistics elements.

• Understand how managers trade off different "logistics costs" relative to customer service in order to reach a logistics decision.

• Recognize how customer service in logistics decisions contributes to customer value and successful marketing programs.

• Describe the major logistics functions of transportation, warehousing and materials handling, order processing, and inventory management.

$500 MILLION TO $1 BILLION LOST SALES . . . AND NO. 1, TOO!

The year 1994 was a red-letter year for Compaq Computer (www.compaq.com). It became the world's No. 1 producer of PCs, but the company estimates it lost $500 million to $1 billion during the year because its hot-selling laptops and desktops weren't available when and where its customers—31 000 distributors, wholesalers, and retailers around the world—wanted them! Compaq's chief financial officer, Daryl White, told *Fortune* magazine:

> We've done most of what we need to do to be more competitive. We've changed the way we develop products, manufacture, market, and advertise. The one piece of the puzzle we haven't addressed is logistics. It's the next source of competitive advantage. The possibilities are just astounding.[1]

We can excuse Mr. White, however, for being just a little too modest about Compaq's logistics actions over the past three years. Consider, in fact, that Compaq

• *Quintupled* production from 1991 to 1994 *without* expanding factory space, partly due to cooperation with suppliers to reduce inventories of unassembled components.
• Took an idea from Wal-Mart and moved the component inventories off its factory floor to a warehouse 12 miles away and leased by 35 of its suppliers.
• Cut the average time a computer spends on the floor of its distribution centre from four weeks to two weeks.

Still, Compaq isn't out of the woods, logistically speaking. Like most computer companies, observes *Fortune* magazine, Compaq's 40 percent on-time delivery record to its customers could put it into bankruptcy court if it were an airline.[2]

To address this problem Compaq initiated a program to avoid building computers for inventory. By the time you read this, Compaq expects that its production facilities will be linked to its distributors so that *every* computer it produces will be built to the specifications of an ultimate buyer or user.

Welcome to the very unglamorous—but increasingly critical—world of physical supply, physical distribution, and logistics management. The essence of the problem is simple: it makes no sense to have brilliant marketing programs to sell world-class products if the products aren't available at the right time, at the right place, and in the right form and condition that customers want them. It's finding the continuing solutions through time that's always the problem. This chapter examines the physical distribution process, which moves products from producer to consumer, and how a firm balances distribution costs against the need for effective customer service.

SIGNIFICANCE OF PHYSICAL DISTRIBUTION AND LOGISTICS MANAGEMENT

We often hear the term *physical distribution,* but may rarely hear the term *logistics.* In this section we contrast the two concepts, describe the increasing importance of logistics and how these activities vary among firms, and relate logistics to marketing strategy decisions.

Relating Physical Supply, Physical Distribution, and Logistics

Generally, marketing managers use **physical distribution management** to mean organizing the movement and storage of a finished product to the customer. Logistics implies a broader view and attempts to coordinate both the inbound flow of raw materials *and* the outbound flow of finished product. Because these two flows are not simply mirror images of each other, we prefer to discuss the broader term of logistics, or *logistics management,* in this chapter. **Logistics management** is organizing the cost-effective *flow* of raw materials, in-process inventory, finished goods, and related information from point-of-origin to point-of-consumption to satisfy *customer requirements.*[3]

Three elements of this definition deserve emphasis. First, logistics deals with decisions needed to move a product from the source of raw materials to consumption, or the *flow* of the product. Second, those decisions have to be made in a *cost-effective* manner. While it is important to drive down the costs of a firm's logistics system, there is a limit—the third point of emphasis. A firm needs to drive down logistics costs as long as it can deliver expected *customer service,* which means satisfying customer requirements. In other words, customer needs determine the outputs of the logistics system, and hence the role of management is to see that those needs are satisfied in the most cost-effective manner.

Figure 17-1 demonstrates the relation of physical supply, physical distribution, and logistics to the operations of a manufacturing firm. This chart shows how the firm receives its physical supply in the form of raw materials and parts from its suppliers, converts these to finished products, and then engages in the distribution of these products to its customers. Note that these concepts also apply to nonmanufacturing firms, such as retailers and wholesalers, for which the inbound activities include the finished goods that are resold to customers without physical modification.

Increasing Importance of Logistics Systems

Several factors account for the trend of increased emphasis on logistics systems. There has been a large growth in the differentiation of products in order to respond to consumer demands. The effect of this increased product differentiation is that inventory control has become more complex, and thus there are many more things to keep track of. Consider,

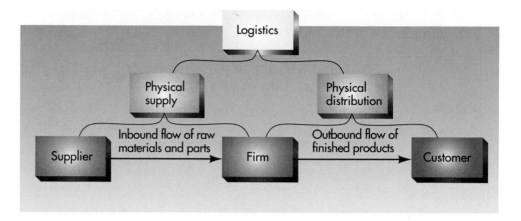

for example, that L. L. Bean must track more than 50 000 separate items when each product is divided by size, colour, and other distinguishing features.[4] In today's environment, the increasing costs of carrying inventory make it clear that inventories cannot grow unchecked. Thus, while firms are under pressure to provide high levels of customer service by having many items available, they need to control the cost of such service.

Such dramatic savings in inventory are possible when efficient transportation systems and information technology can be substituted for inventory. A significant development allowing this substitution to take place has been the increased competition between and among available transportation systems. This permits manufacturers, wholesalers, and retailers to benefit from increased flexibility, particularly when dealing with railroads and truck lines. Also, continuously upgraded computer and information technology has permitted efficient tracking of the thousands of items manufacturers produce.

In the 1990s, industries outside the manufacturing sector have discovered the importance of powerful distribution networks—sectors as diverse as banking and entertainment. In fact, strategists are concluding that control of the distribution networks is often more important than producing the original good or service. Some examples of powerful distribution networks and some guiding principles of today's competitive environment seeking creative ways to add customer value appear in the Marketing NewsNet box on the next page.[5]

How Movement and Storage Activities Vary among Firms

For firms that don't physically move or store many items, logistics costs will be minor. For example, insurance companies and banks distribute mainly paperwork, and most of their inbound materials are supplies. At the other end of the spectrum are firms that produce many products from diverse raw materials at widely separated plants, and which, in turn, distribute products to widely dispersed markets. For large consumer product companies that compete both nationally and internationally, such as Procter & Gamble, the range of logistics problems can be enormous. For example, P&G produces approximately 80 different brands, all of which require a different mix of raw materials. The logistics system has to move all the raw materials to the appropriate manufacturing plant, and then distribute the finished products (brands) to the marketplace. This involves moving products to thousands of wholesalers and retailers around the world. In addition, P&G's logistics managers must also control a number of information flows, including how much inventory is where, the order processing system for customers, the reordering process from the factories, and the level of customer service that the logistics system is delivering. Because of the scope of P&G's logistics problems, it has learned to simplify matters by working closely with its major distributors or customers, such as Wal-Mart where it has located a dozen P&G employees.

Technology   MARKETING NEWSNET

DESIGNING DISTRIBUTION NETWORKS TO ENSURE ACCESS TO CUSTOMERS: EASIER SAID THAN DONE!

In many industries the "small is beautiful" era of the 1970s and 1980s is gone. Its replacement: a drive to control strong distribution networks to ensure continuing access to important target market customers for producers of goods and services. Although the industries may differ, some common threads emerge. Let's look at (1) some industry examples and (2) some guiding principles.

Industry Examples

"Distribution networks" here can mean either the physical transportation of goods or electronic transmission of services, such as

- *Mass merchandise chains.* Wal-Mart, for example, gains access to customers by moving both products and inventory information very efficiently.
- *Banks and financial institutions.* Putting your card into an automated teller machine (ATM) a few years ago may have been a problem: The ATM may not have talked to your bank. Now they connect—often globally—so large banks and other financial institutions have been acquiring smaller ones.
- *Movie producers and TV/cable/telephone systems.* The Walt Disney acquisition of Capital Cities/ABC is but the first of a complex series of corporate combinations directed at linking Hollywood's entertainment

to an electronic delivery system—from TV and cable companies to telephone companies.

Guiding Principles

Some principles seem to emerge from the 1990s experiences. Specifically, huge distribution networks

- *Demand centralized control.* In this age of decentralization, delegation, and empowerment, the opposite is true for distribution networks: a centralized system is essential to achieve the synergies needed.
- *Require efficient electronic links, such as software and telecommunications systems.* This applies whether the distribution network is in retailing, banking, or entertainment.
- *Transcend departmental, corporate, and often national boundaries.* This means many different groups, with different orientations, need "buy-in" for success. Technology (the preceding bullet) is the easy part. Changing people's ingrained behaviour is much harder.

Across dozens of industries, the close of the 1990s will see these guiding principles take on new meanings in very diverse forms. But the goal is clear: organizations are increasingly seeking ways to provide genuine values to customers in order to gain their loyalty.

The relative importance of logistics to a firm can be evaluated on a number of key factors:

- Number, weight, volume, and perishability of raw materials and final products.
- Number of material supply points.
- Number of material processing points.
- Number of product consumption points.

As the number of any of these factors increases, the complexity and cost of the logistics system increase as well. The total logistics costs to wrap, bundle, load, store, unload, sort, reload, and transport goods is enormous.[6]

For all firms (including manufacturers, wholesalers, and retailers), for every dollar of sales about 8 cents is spent on distribution costs.

Relation of Logistics to Marketing Strategy

Recalling your own shopping experiences can show the critical relationship between marketing and logistics. Consider your disappointment after travelling to a store—in response to an advertised sale—only to find that the items were out of stock or had been lost or damaged in transit. Imagine how a manufacturer such as Compaq (described at the start of the chapter) reacts upon learning that the product was not on the shelf, after spending huge

HAND-HELD COMPUTERS AND BAR CODING HAVE REDUCED DELAY AND LOST SHIPMENTS AND IMPROVED CUSTOMER SERVICE SIGNIFICANTLY.

sums on its extensive promotional campaign. The bottom line is that poorly executed logistics can do serious damage to an otherwise excellent marketing strategy. To demonstrate the importance of logistics' relationship to marketing, consider how logistics impacts the 4 Ps—product factors, pricing factors, promotional factors, and place factors.

Product factors   The physical characteristics of the product, as well as its raw materials, will often dictate what kinds of transportation can be used, the length of time inventory can be accumulated, and whether markets can be served from one or many

A LOGISTICS MANAGER'S NIGHTMARE: HOW TO GET THIS DUAL-PACK ON A RETAILER'S SHELF WHILE BALANCING LOGISTICS AND MARKETING BENEFITS AND COSTS.

locations. One physical characteristic that has important logistics implications is the perishability of the product, or its *shelf life*. For example, the distribution of fresh foods requires timely transportation and low inventories to minimize spoilage. Time-dated food materials must be kept fresh on the store shelves and not allowed to spoil in the warehouse. These products may require specialized transport and storage facilities, such as refrigerated vehicles. Other products have a very short time frame in which to retain their freshness, such as fresh cut flowers, fresh seafoods, or out-of-town newspapers. These require premium transportation, such as air freight, and, in some cases, they can only be distributed to a regional market. For example, some newspapers such as *The Globe & Mail* are printed in a number of cities around the country for regional distribution the same day.

ETHICS AND SOCIAL RESPONSIBILITY ALERT

WHAT ARE THE SOCIAL COSTS OF PACKAGING?

Some experts believe that the logistic systems of many firms depend too heavily on packaging. While efficient packaging materials allow a firm to use cheaper modes of transportation or less specialized warehouse services, these benefits are offset by costs imposed on society in general. Specifically, what should society do with the excessive packaging that comes with the product? In many cases, the packaging material is difficult to dispose of or is quickly filling landfills. Further, the focus on recycled products is a complicated issue and has its own costs and benefits. For example, Procter & Gamble has just introduced a plastic bottle for its Ultra Downy fabric softener that is made of 100 percent recycled plastic. However, because P&G will colour the bottle as part of its marketing program, the bottle will be difficult to recycle once it is used.

What are the benefits and costs to society of such packaging trends? What should communities do to counter the trend of overpackaging? What are the responsibilities of global citizens to counteract the trend of overpackaging?

One of the most important links between a product's physical characteristics and logistics is the product package. On the one hand, the marketer views the package as an important point-of-purchase promotional device. On the other hand, there are many logistical implications associated with the packaging decision. Does the protective packaging reduce the density of the products so that less product can be loaded into the transport vehicle or warehouse? If so, logistics costs will increase. Does the product's package require it to be placed in an exterior package or carton? In this case, additional handling will be required at the retail level to prepare the product for sale. As described in the accompanying Ethics and Social Responsibility Alert, package features can make handling, stacking, filling, or disposing of the package more difficult, and once again logistics costs will increase.[7]

When the computerized inventory monitoring network in a logistics system breaks down, major problems can occur. For example, Rubbermaid, which makes dozens of products, such as containers and toys, got in hot water with Wal-Mart—its most important distributor. Rubbermaid offered an end-of-quarter deep discount price cut to some customers, but not Wal-Mart. Needless to say, Wal-Mart was furious when it found out and proceeded to feature promotional materials for Sterilite, one of Rubbermaid's rising competitors.[8]

Pricing factors   Pricing interacts with logistics in several ways. As mentioned in the discussion of geographical pricing adjustments in Chapter 15, price quotations such as FOB origin assign responsibility for arranging and paying for transportation services to the buyer. Logistics costs are also important for determining quantity discounts. Transportation rate structures generally contain a quantity discount provided by the carrier such that lower rates are available for larger shipments.

Promotional factors   Promotion interacts with logistics in the areas of advertising, sales promotion, and personal selling. Advertising and promotional campaigns must be planned and coordinated with the logistics system to ensure product availability at the appropriate time. For example, General Motors learned that an eight-week wait was a big turn-off for some customers thinking about buying a Cadillac, 11 percent of whom then bought a car from a competitor rather than wait for delivery. Cadillac is testing the feasibility of customer responsiveness as a competitive differentiator with the objective of delivering popularly configured Cadillacs to customers immediately from dealers' lots, with overnight delivery if the vehicle isn't available on site. For those customers who desire a more custom configuration, Cadillac is taking their orders, assembling and delivering their exact Cadillacs within three weeks under the "Cadillac Custom Rapid Delivery" process.[9] So distribution can and must be synchronized to ensure timely and efficient handling of orders.

Place factors   It is the responsibility of logistics to get the product to the right place at the right time in usable conditions. Logistics also plays an important part in determining where a firm locates its plants and distribution centres relative to markets. Such decisions must consider transportation costs as well as the ability of the product to be transported long distances and be stored for long periods of time.

Effective logistics can also help gain access to key distribution outlets. In the Nike-Reebok "sneaker war," two critical market segments are teens and Generation X buyers, who are often willing to pay $80, $90, or more for a pair of shoes. These segments are core customers of the Foot Locker chain. Recently, Nike has been winning in Foot Locker sales because—among other things—Reebok needs to overhaul its information-tracking system and fix its distribution snags, which have resulted in limited customer exposure to its lines in Foot Locker outlets. If Reebok fixes these problems—and with "Shaq" in its ads—it will remain a formidable competitor for Nike.[10]

CONCEPT CHECK

1. What are the three important characteristics of the logistics concept?

2. Why are distribution networks in industries as diverse as retailing and banking increasingly important in the 1990s?

3. How does logistics interact with the product element of the marketing mix?

OBJECTIVES OF THE LOGISTICS SYSTEM

The objective of a logistics system is to minimize relevant logistics costs while delivering maximum customer service. Recently, firms have begun to realize that logistics costs are also dependent on their relationship with suppliers, carriers, and customers. This has led to the practice of forming "strategic alliances" among buyers, sellers, and the transportation system that connects them.[11]

Such strategic alliances are often supported by sophisticated information systems that involve shared databases of customer information and **electronic data interchange (EDI),** computers linked in two different firms to transmit documents such as purchase orders, bills of lading, and invoices. For example, Canadian Tire uses EDI to track inventory and to communicate with suppliers. This ensures product availability and facilitates planning shipments to lower distribution costs.[12]

Total Logistics Cost Concept

For our purposes **total logistics cost** includes expenses associated with transportation, materials handling and warehousing, inventory, stockouts (being out of inventory), and order processing. A more complete list of decisions that are associated with the flow of product and make up total logistics cost includes the following:

- Traffic and transportation.
- Warehousing and storage.
- Packaging.
- Materials handling.
- Inventory control.

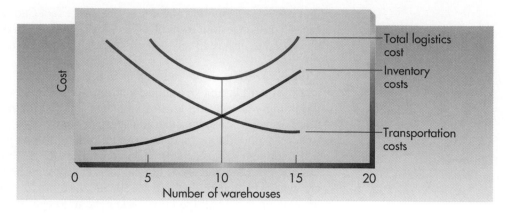

- Order processing.
- Customer service level.
- Plant and warehouse site location.
- Return goods handling.

Note that many of these costs are interrelated so that changes in one will impact the others. For example, as the firm attempts to minimize its transportation costs by shipping in larger quantities, it will also experience an increase in inventory levels. Larger inventory levels will not only increase inventory costs but should also reduce stockouts. It is important, therefore, to study the impact on all of the logistics decision areas when considering a change.

Figure 17-2 provides a graphic example. An oft-used logistics strategy is for a firm to have a number of warehouses, which receive shipments in large quantities and then redistribute smaller shipments to local customers. As the number of warehouses increases, inventory costs rise and transportation costs fall. That is, more inventory is warehoused, but it is transported in volume closer to customers. The net effect is to minimize the total costs of the logistics system shown in Figure 17-2 by having 10 warehouses. This means the total cost curve is minimized at a point where neither of the two individual cost elements is at a minimum but the overall system is.

Studying its total logistics cost has had revolutionary consequences for National Semiconductor, which produces computer chips. In two years it cut its standard delivery time 47 percent, reduced distribution costs 2.5 percent, and increased sales 34 percent by shutting down six warehouses around the world and air-freighting its microchips from its huge distribution centre in Singapore. It does this even though it has six factories around the world. National also discovered that a lot of its chips were actually profit-losers, and it cut the number of products it sells by 45 percent, thereby simplifying logistics and increasing profits.[13]

Customer Service Concept

If logistics is a *flow,* the end of it—or *output*—is the service delivered to customers. However, service can be expensive. One firm found that to increase on-time delivery from a 95 percent rate to a 100 percent rate tripled total logistics costs. Higher levels of service require tactics such as more inventory to reduce stockouts, more expensive transportation to improve speed and lessen damage, and double or triple checking of orders to ensure correctness. A firm's goal should be to provide adequate customer service while controlling logistics costs. Customer service is now seen not merely as an expense but as a strategic tool for increasing customer satisfaction and sales. For example, a 3M survey about customer service among 18 000 European customers in 16 countries revealed surprising agreement in all countries about the importance of customer service. Respondents stressed factors such as condition of product delivered, on-time delivery, quick delivery after order placement, and effective handling of problems.[14]

Within the context of logistics, **customer service** is the ability of a logistics system to satisfy users in terms of time, dependability, communication, and convenience.[15] As suggested by Figure 17-3, a logistics manager's key task is to balance these four customer service factors against total logistics cost factors.

Time   In a logistics setting, time refers to **lead time** for an item, which means the lag from ordering an item until it is received and ready for use. This is also referred to as **order cycle time** or **replenishment time** and may be more important to retailers or wholesalers than consumers. The various elements that make up the typical order cycle include recognition of the need to order, order transmittal, order processing, documentation, and transportation. A current emphasis on logistics is to reduce lead time so that the inventory levels of customers may be minimized. Another emphasis is to make the process of reordering and receiving products as simple as possible, often through electronic data interchange and other computer-based ordering and inventory systems. The order processing portion of lead time is discussed later in this chapter.

Dependability   Dependability is the consistency of replenishment. This is important to both intermediaries and consumers. It can be broken into three elements: consistent lead time, safe delivery, and complete delivery. Consistent service allows planning (such as appropriate inventory levels), whereas inconsistencies create surprises. Intermediaries may be willing to accept longer lead times if they know about them in advance and can thus make plans. While surprise delays may shut down a production line, early deliveries will be almost as troublesome because of the problems of storing the extra inventory. Dependability is essential for the just-in-time strategies discussed at the end of the chapter.

Communication   Communication is a two-way link between buyer and seller that helps in monitoring service and anticipating future needs. Status reports on orders are a typical example of improved communication between buyer and seller. The increased communication capability of transportation carriers has enhanced the accuracy of such tracing information and improved the ability of buyers to schedule shipments. Note, however, that such information is still reactive and is not a substitute for

FIGURE 17-4

EXAMPLES OF CUSTOMER SERVICE
STANDARDS

TYPE OF FIRM	CUSTOMER SERVICE STANDARD
Wholesaler	At least 98% of orders filled accurately
Manufacturer	Order cycle time of no more than 5 days
Retailer	Returns accepted within 30 days
Airline	At least 90% of arrivals on time
Trucker	A maximum of 5% loss and damage per year
Restaurant	Lunch served within 5 minutes of order

consistent on-time deliveries. Therefore, some firms have established strategic alliances in an effort to institutionalize a more proactive flow of useful information that, in turn, improves on-time deliveries. Hewlett-Packard (HP), a high-tech computer printer manufacturer, turned its inbound raw materials over to a logistics firm. HP lets this firm manage the warehousing and coordinate parts delivery so that HP can focus on its printer business. In the process, HP estimates it has cut its warehouse operating costs by about 10 percent.[16]

Convenience   The concept of convenience for a logistics manager means that there should be a minimum of effort on the part of the buyer in doing business with the seller. Is it easy for the customer to order? Are the products available from many outlets? Does the buyer have to buy huge quantities of the product? Will the seller arrange all necessary details, such as transportation? The seller must concentrate on removing unnecessary barriers to customer convenience.

Customer Service Standards

Firms that operate effective logistics systems usually develop a set of written customer service standards. These serve as objectives and provide a benchmark against which results can be measured for control purposes. In developing these standards, information is collected on customers' needs. It is also necessary to know what competitors offer as well as the willingness of customers to pay a bit more for better service. After these and similar questions are answered, realistic standards are set and an ongoing monitoring program is established. Note that the examples in Figure 17-4 suggest that customer service standards will differ by type of firm.

CONCEPT CHECK

1. What is a current strategy adopted by firms attempting to squeeze costs from their logistics system while delivering customer service?

2. In what ways do key customer service factors differ between a manufacturer and a retailer?

3. What is the relationship between transportation costs and volume shipped? What impact does it have on the pricing of the firm?

MAJOR LOGISTICS FUNCTIONS

Four key elements in a logistics system include (1) transportation, (2) warehousing and materials handling, (3) order processing, and (4) inventory management. These are described in more detail in the following sections.

FIGURE 17-5

ADVANTAGES AND
DISADVANTAGES
OF FIVE MODES OF
TRANSPORTATION

MODE	RELATIVE ADVANTAGES	RELATIVE DISADVANTAGES
Rail	Full capability Extensive routes Low cost	Some reliability, damage problems Not always complete pickup and delivery Sometimes slow
Truck	Complete pickup and delivery Extensive routes Fairly fast	Size and weight restrictions Higher cost More weather-sensitive
Air	Fast Low damage Frequent departures	High cost Limited capabilities
Pipeline	Low cost Very reliable	Limited routes (accessibility) Slow
Water	Low cost Huge capacities	Slow Limited routes and schedules More weather-sensitive

Transportation

Transportation provides the movement of goods necessary in a logistics system. There are five basic modes of transportation: railroads, motor carriers, air carriers, pipelines, and water carriers, and modal combinations involving two or more modes, such as highway trailers on a rail flatcar.

All modes can be evaluated on six basic service criteria:

- *Cost.* Charges for transportation.
- *Time.* Speed of transit.
- *Capability.* What can be realistically carried with this mode.
- *Dependability.* Reliability of service regarding time, loss, and damage.
- *Accessibility.* Convenience of the mode's routes (such as pipeline availability).
- *Frequency.* Scheduling.

Figure 17-5 summarizes service advantages and disadvantages of five of the modes of transportation available.

Railroads   Railroads carry heavy, bulky items over long distances. Of the commodities tracked by the rail industry, coal, farm products, chemicals, and nonmetallic minerals represent the majority of the total tonnage. Railroads have the ability to carry larger shipments than trucks (in terms of total weight per vehicle), but their routes are less extensive. Service innovations include unit trains and intermodal service. A *unit train* is dedicated to one commodity (often coal), using permanently coupled cars that run a continuous loop from a single origin to a single destination and back. Even though the train returns empty, the process captures enough operating efficiencies to make it one of the lowest cost transportation alternatives available. Unit trains are held to a specific schedule so that the customers can plan on reliable delivery and usually carry products that can be loaded and unloaded quickly and automatically.

Railroads have been able to apply the unit train concept to **intermodal transportation,** which involves combining different transportation modes to get the best features of each. The result is a service that attracts high-valued freight, which would normally go by truck. The most popular combination is truck-rail, also referred to as *piggyback* or *trailer on flatcar (TOFC).* The other popular use of an intermodal combination is

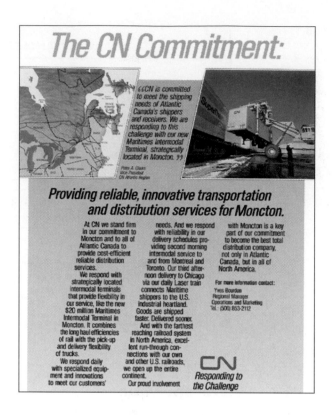

associated with export/import traffic and uses containers in place of trailers. These containers can be loaded on ships, trains, and truck trailers, so in terms of the on-land segment of international shipments, a container is handled the same way as a trailer. Containers are used in international trade because they take up less space on ocean-going vessels.

Motor carriers   In contrast to the railroad industry, the for-hire motor carrier industry is composed of many small firms, including many independent truckers and firms that own their own trucks for transporting their own products.

The greatest advantage of motor carriers is the complete door-to-door service. Trucks can go almost anywhere there is a road, and with the design of specialized equipment they can carry most commodities. Their physical limitations are size and weight restrictions enforced by the provinces. Trucks have the reputation for maintaining a better record than rail for loss and damage and providing faster, more reliable service, especially for shorter distances. As a result, trucks carry higher-valued goods that are time-sensitive and expensive to carry in inventory. The trade-off is that truck rates are substantially higher than rail rates.

Air carriers and express companies   Air freight is costly, but its speed may create savings in lower inventory. The items that can be carried are limited by space constraints and are usually valuable, time-sensitive, and lightweight, such as perishable flowers, clothing, and electronic parts. Products moved in containers are especially amenable to this mode of shipment. Specialized firms provide ground support in terms of collecting shipments and delivering them to the air terminal. When air freight is handled by the major airlines—such as Air Canada and Canadian Airlines—it is often carried as cargo in the luggage space of scheduled passenger flights. This strategy allows the airline to utilize excess capacity that would otherwise be lost.

IF SPEED IS IMPORTANT, THEN SHIPPING BY AIR IS APPROPRIATE.

Freight forwarders   **Freight forwarders,** already mentioned a number of times, are firms that accumulate small shipments into larger lots and then hire a carrier to move them, usually at reduced rates. Recall that transportation companies provide rate incentives for larger quantities. Forwarders collect many small shipments consigned to a common destination and pay the carrier the lower rate based on larger volume, so they often convert shipments that are less-than-truckload (LTL) into full truckloads, thereby receiving better shipping rates. The rates charged by the forwarder to the individual shippers, in turn, are somewhat less than the small quantity rate, and the difference is the forwarder's margin. In general, the shipment receives improved service at lower cost. While forwarders may specialize in a particular mode—such as air freight—they are available for all modes of transportation. International freight forwarders play an equally important role in the export/import trades.

Air freight forwarders are an example of specialization in one transportation mode. In some cases, airlines will subcontract excess space to *air freight forwarders* or *express companies,* which are firms that market air express services to the general public. Where markets are large enough, major airlines have responded with pure air freight service between specific airports—often involving international destinations.

CONCEPT CHECK

1. What are some new kinds of train service offered by railroads to compete more effectively with other modes of transportation?

2. What is intermodal transportation?

3. What are the inherent advantages of truck transportation?

FLY-BY-NIGHT IDEA + CUSTOMER SERVICE + KISS = FEDERAL EXPRESS

Armed with one of his college term papers, which got a C– grade, Frederick W. Smith didn't build a better mousetrap and wait for the world to beat a path to his door. Instead, he set out to show the world that with his simple new innovation *he* could beat a path to everybody else's door.

He gave the name *Federal Express* to his door-to-door parcel service that uses orange, white, and purple jets. And he advertised "absolutely, positively overnight" delivery for his small-parcel service—limited to 70 pounds, the weight one person can carry. "I figured we had to be enormously reliable," says Smith, "since our service is frequently used for expensive spare parts, live organs, or other emergency shipments."

But Federal Express (FedEx) isn't your typical "fly-by-night" outfit. After all, Smith *did* write his term paper at Yale, and he *did* use a family trust of $4 million to get started—and Federal Express *did* lose $27 million in its first 26 months of operation.

What Smith had was a good idea, a good understanding of customer service, and the tenacity and resources to stick with it. First, Smith reasoned, he had to own his own jet aircraft so *all* parcels could be picked up early in the evening, flown to a single sorting centre (Memphis), and rerouted to their final destination before dawn. The KISS (keep it simple, stupid) concept worked to

the company's advantage in the early years. Always looking for a better idea, FedEx recently introduced "FedEx Ship"—a shipping software solution in both Mac and Windows™ versions that lets any customer order pickups, print their shipping labels, and track their express deliveries without touching a telephone. Of course, FedEx benefits, too, by cutting telephone traffic and package pickup costs, and also eliminating paperwork errors that might impact sorting. This is essential in the competitive domestic marketplace.

And in its international segment, FedEx is turning a profit after losing $1 billion over an eight-year period.

Warehousing and Materials Handling

Warehouses may be classified in one of two ways: (1) storage warehouses and (2) distribution centres. In *storage warehouses* the goods are intended to come to rest for some period of time, as in the aging of products or in storing household goods. *Distribution centres,* on the other hand, are designed to facilitate the timely movement of goods and represent a very important part of the logistics system. Distribution centres are the focus of the following discussion and represent the second most significant cost for logistics systems.

Distribution centres not only allow firms to hold their stock in decentralized locations but are also used to facilitate sorting and consolidating products from different plants or different suppliers. Some physical transformation can also take place in distribution centres such as mixing or blending different ingredients, labelling, and repackaging. They may also serve as sales offices and order processing centres.

Wal-Mart uses its distribution centres and information systems to lower retail prices, thereby increasing customer value. Kmart's specialty stores and private brands, on the other hand, come in a distant second to Wal-Mart's strategy. Today, Wal-Mart's sales are nearly $50 billion a year more than Kmart's.[17]

Materials handling, which involves moving goods over short distances into, within, and out of warehouses and manufacturing plants, is a key part of warehouse operations.

STORAGE WAREHOUSES OFTEN
STOCK A LARGE, STABLE VOLUME
OF GOODS.

The two major problems with this activity are high labour costs and high rates of loss and damage. Every time an item is handled, there is a chance for loss or damage. Common materials handling equipment includes forklifts, cranes, and conveyors. Recently, materials handling in warehouses has been automated by using computers and robots to reduce the cost of holding, moving, and recording the inventories of stores.

Order Processing

There are several stages in the processing of an order, and a failure at any one of them can cause a problem with the customer. The process starts with transmitting the order by a variety of means such as computer or electronic data interchange (EDI). This is followed by entering the order in the appropriate databases and sending the information to those needing it. For example, a regional warehouse is notified to prepare an order. After checking inventory, a new quantity may need to be reordered from the production line, or purchasing may be requested to reorder from a vendor. If the item is currently out of stock, a "backorder" is created, and the whole process of keeping track of a small part of the original order must be managed. In addition, credit may have to be checked for some customers, all paperwork associated with the order must be prepared, transportation must be arranged, and a confirmation of the order must be sent. Order processing systems are generally evaluated in terms of speed and accuracy.

Inventory Management

Inventory management is one of the primary responsibilities of the logistics manager. The major problem is maintaining the delicate balance between too little and too much. Too little inventory may result in poor service, stockouts, brand switching, and loss of market share; too much leads to higher costs because of the money tied up in inventory and the chance that it may become obsolete.

Creative inventory management practices can make possible cost savings elsewhere in the logistics system. For example, IBM has begun closing many of its parts warehouses because Federal Express's reliable overnight delivery (see the Marketing

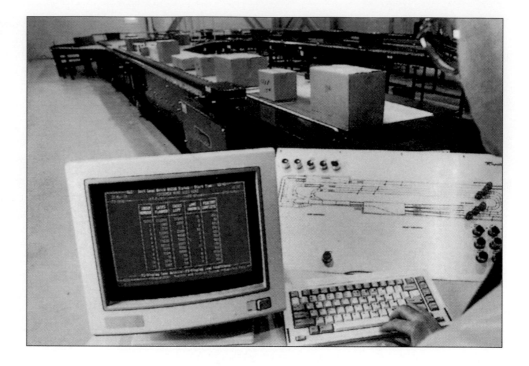

NewsNet box) enables FedEx to inventory high-priced IBM parts at its sorting hubs and deliver them quickly to IBM customers.[18]

Reasons for inventory   Traditionally, carrying inventory has been justified on several grounds: (1) to offer a buffer against variations in supply and demand, often caused by uncertainty in forecasting demand; (2) to provide better service for those customers who wish to be served on demand; (3) to promote production efficiencies; (4) to provide a hedge against price increases by suppliers; (5) to promote purchasing and transportation discounts; and (6) to protect the firm from contingencies such as strikes and shortages.

Inventory costs   Specific inventory costs are often hard to detect because they are difficult to measure and occur in many different parts of the firm. A classification of inventory costs includes the following:

- *Capital costs.* The opportunity costs resulting from tying up funds in inventory instead of using them in other, more profitable investments; these are related to interest rates.
- *Inventory service costs.* Items such as insurance and taxes that are present in many provinces.
- *Storage costs.* Warehousing space and materials handling.
- *Risk costs.* Possible loss, damage, pilferage, perishability, and obsolescence.

Storage costs, risk costs, and some service costs vary according to the characteristics of the item inventoried. For example, perishable products or highly seasonal items have higher risk costs than a commodity type product such as lumber. Capital costs are always present and are proportional to the *values* of the item and prevailing interest rates. The costs of carrying inventory vary with the particular circumstances but quite easily could range from 10 to 35 percent for different firms.

Newer inventory strategies   Conventional wisdom during the 1970s and 1980s was that a firm should protect itself against uncertainty by maintaining a reserve inventory at each of its production and stocking points. This has been describe as a "just-in-case" philosophy of inventory management and led to unnecessarily high levels of inventory. In contrast is the **just-in-time (JIT) concept,** which is an inventory supply system that operates with very low inventories and requires fast, on-time delivery. When parts are needed for production, they arrive from suppliers "just in time," which means neither before nor after they are needed. Note that JIT is used in situations where demand forecasting is reliable, such as when supplying a production line, and is not suitable for inventories that are to be stored over significant periods of time.

Ryder System, a large logistics management firm, is charged with making Saturn's JIT system work smoothly. Ryder long-haul trucks and their drivers are the most expensive part of the system. The key—very literally—to this JIT system is a computer disk in the form of a plastic key that drivers plug into an on-truck computer. The computer screen then tells the driver where to go, the route to use, and how much time to spend getting there.[19]

Proponents cite several advantages to JIT. First, there are the financial advantages that come from lower inventory levels and faster turnover. Second, the Japanese experience suggests that JIT yields better reliability in production scheduling and product quality. However, for JIT to work properly, suppliers must be able to provide fast, reliable deliveries or there will be failures relative to customer service. Consequently, with JIT the supplier assumes more responsibility and risk for inventory, quality products, and on-time delivery than formerly.

CONCEPT CHECK

1. What are the basic trade-offs between the modes of transportation?

2. What types of inventory should use storage warehouses and which type should use distribution centres?

3. What are the strengths and weaknesses of a just-in-time system?

SUMMARY

1. Logistics management includes the coordination of the flows of both inbound and outbound goods, an emphasis on making these flows cost-effective, and customer service.

2. The importance of logistical activities varies among firms. The complexity of the system increases with the width of the product line, number of supply points, and number of geographic markets served.

3. Although some marketers may pay little attention to logistics, they do so at their own peril. Logistics directly affects the success of the marketing program and all areas of the marketing mix. In the 1990s powerful distribution networks to control access to customers through efficient logistics systems are gaining strategic importance.

4. The total logistics cost concept suggests that a system of interrelated costs is present such as transportation, materials handling and warehousing, inventory, and stockout costs.

5. Minimizing total logistics cost is irrelevant without specifying an acceptable customer service level that must be maintained. The importance of customer service varies among industries.

6. Although key customer service factors depend on the situation, important elements of the customer service program are likely to be time-related dependability, communications, and convenience.

7. The modes of transportation (e.g., railroads, motor carriers, air carriers, and trucks) offer shippers different service benefits. Better service often costs more, although it should result in savings in other areas of the logistics system.

8. The function of warehousing in a logistics system is to facilitate storage and movement of goods. Distribution centres provide flexibility and facilitate sorting and consolidating products from different plants or different suppliers.

9. Inventory management is critical since too much inventory greatly increases costs and too little may result in stockouts. Various methods are available to manage inventory. A currently popular approach is the just-in-time concept, which attempts to minimize inventory in the system.

10. Some buyers and sellers have developed strategic alliances designed to make the logistics transaction as efficient as possible.

...D CONCEPTS

CHAPTER PROBLEMS AND APPLICATIONS

1. List several companies to which logistical activities are unimportant. Also list several whose focus is only on the inbound or outbound side.

2. Give an example of how logistical activities might affect trade promotion strategies.

3. What are some types of businesses in which order processing may be among the paramount success factors?

4. What behavioural problems might arise to negate the logistics concept within the firm?

5. List the customer service factors that would be vital to buyers in the following types of companies: (*a*) manufacturing, (*b*) retailing, (*c*) hospitals, and (*d*) construction.

6. Name some cases when extremely high service levels (e.g., 99 percent) would be warranted.

7. Name the mode of transportation that would be the best for the following products: (*a*) farm machinery, (*b*) cut flowers, (*c*) frozen meat, and (*d*) coal.

8. The auto industry is a heavy user of the just-in-time concept. Why? What other industries would be good candidates for its application? What do they have in common?

9. Look again at Figure 17-2. Explain why as the number of warehouses increases, (*a*) inventory costs rise and (*b*) transportation costs fall.

10. How has Wal-Mart's investment in (*a*) regional distribution centres and (*b*) computerized inventory systems contributed to its low retail prices?

CASE 17-1   Navistar International

How important is logistics management in today's business environment? Just ask managers at the Navistar International Corporation (www.navistar.com), which produces up to 400 customized trucks each day!

THE COMPANY

Navistar International is one of the largest manufacturers of medium and heavy trucks in the world. Much of its success can be attributed to the sophisticated use of database marketing actions (described in Chapter 10) that deliver a customized truck equipped with features designed to improve the productivity of each specific customer. This strategy, however, created a problem—a huge inventory of parts. Tailoring a truck to the unique needs of each buyer requires that Navistar keep 80 000 parts, some of which are needed by only one or just a few customers.

Navistar's success is also the result of superior product quality. The manufacturing department focuses much of its effort on ensuring that there are few defects in

Navistar trucks. This attention to quality, however, slowed the manufacturing process so that Navistar's order cycle time reached 100 days. In fact, one measure of manufacturing efficiency, the percentage of trucks delivered to the customer on time, indicated that 40 percent of Navistar's deliveries were late.

Managers at Navistar realized that to satisfy customer requirements they needed to reduce order cycle time and inventory costs while maintaining high-quality customized products. Logistics management approaches, which balance the needs of the sales, engineering, and manufacturing departments, were an obvious potential solution.

LOGISTICS MANAGEMENT AT NAVISTAR

In response to these issues, Navistar developed an elaborate material requirement planning (MRP) system to manage the purchase of parts and components from its many suppliers. Navistar also developed an electronic data interchange (EDI) with its major suppliers that allowed specifications, quotes, purchase orders, invoices, and even payments to be made electronically. The system was responsible for the elimination of millions of pieces of paper and the errors and inefficiencies caused by the manual processing of thousands of orders. Finally, a just-in-time system (JIT) was added to match deliveries of supplies with its manufacturing requirements.

These systems have helped Navistar begin to integrate the many complex tasks of producing custom-built trucks. In addition, the systems have helped dealers to improve their customer service. Dealers can now submit their orders electronically and receive information about the lead time of the specified components and the probable delivery date of the completed truck. In the future, as Navistar continues to improve its systems, current status of orders, delivery schedule adjustments, and other important information should be available to dealers.

Navistar has set challenging goals for its logistics management systems. First, it hopes to achieve 100 per-

cent on-time delivery ("slot credibility"). Second, managers hope that Navistar can reduce its order cycle time to 30–45 days. Finally, the company is determined to minimize inventory. Overall, Navistar believes these changes will represent increased value for its customers and allow Navistar to maintain its dominant position in the truck market.

Questions

1.   What factors helped Navistar managers realize that logistics management approaches might help them better satisfy customer requirements?

2.   What systems did Navistar develop to improve its production process? How can Navistar measure their impact?

3.   Explain how the new systems have improved Navistar's customer service.

Canadian Internet Mall

[**Mall Directory** | **Search The Mall** | **Join the Mall**]

Canadian Internet Mall Wins Business Hot Site Award!

CHAPTER 18

Retailing

AFTER READING THIS CHAPTER YOU SHOULD BE ABLE TO:

• Identify retailers in terms of the utilities they provide.

• Explain the alternative ways to classify retail outlets.

• Understand the many methods of nonstore retailing.

• Classify retailers in terms of the retail positioning matrix.

• Develop retailing mix strategies over the life cycle of a retail store.

VIRTUAL RETAILING MAY SOON LET YOU SHOP WHILE YOU FLOP!

Imagine that you are watching "Seinfeld" on TV and you like the shirt Jerry or Elaine is wearing. You click on it with your remote control, and a windows-style menu asks if you want to buy it. You click on "yes," and another menu asks for your colour preference—you choose blue. Additional menus list your credit cards and your campus, home, and work addresses—you indicate how to pay for and where to send your purchase. Because your computer knows your size information, it sends the data electronically to the factory where a shirt is custom-made for you. An overnight service delivers the shirt to your door the next morning—possibly before you are awake![1]

Sound unlikely? Only if you haven't been watching the extraordinary boom in electronic shopping. Popular TV shopping channels such as QVC and Canadian Home Shopping Network are being joined by a wide variety of on-line shopping services. Canadian Internet Mall (www.cdn-mall.com), B.C. Storefronts (www. bcstorefronts.com) and many other "virtual shopping malls" allow shoppers to review product information, place orders, and select next-day delivery times with a few computer keystrokes. Other forms of interactive merchandising such as video-on-demand and on-line services are increasing the likelihood that we may soon just "click" to buy.[2]

The dramatic growth of electronic shopping is just one example of the dynamic and exciting nature of retailing today. This chapter examines the critical role retailing plays as a component of many distribution channels and the challenging decisions retailers face as they strive to create value for their customers.

What types of products will consumers buy directly through catalogues, the mail, computers, or telephone? In what type of store will consumers look for products they don't buy directly? How important is the location of the store? Will customers expect services such as alterations, delivery, installation, or repair? What price should be charged for each product? These are difficult and important questions that are an integral part of retailing. In the channel of distribution, retailing is where the customer meets the product. It is through retailing that exchange (a central aspect of marketing) occurs. **Retailing** includes all activities involved in selling, renting, and providing goods and services to ultimate customers for personal, family, or household use.

THE VALUE OF RETAILING

Retailing is an important marketing activity. Not only do producers and consumers meet through retailing actions, but retailing also creates customer value and has a significant impact on the economy. To consumers, the value of retailing is in the form of utilities provided. Retailing's economic value is represented by the people employed in retailing as well as by the total amount of money exchanged in retail sales.

Consumer Utilities Offered by Retailing

The utilities provided by retailers create value for consumers. Time, place, possession, and form utilities are offered by most retailers in varying degrees, but one utility is often emphasized more than others. Look at Figure 18-1 to see how well you can match the retailer with the utility being emphasized in the description.

Providing ATMs and banking by phone as the Royal Bank does puts the bank's products and services close to the consumer, providing place utility. By providing financing or leasing and taking used cars as trade-ins, Saturn makes the purchase easier and provides possession utility. Form utility—production or alteration of a product—is offered by Levi Strauss & Co. as it creates "Personal Pair" Jeans for Women to meet each customer's specifications. Finding toy shelves stocked in May is the time utility dreamed about by every child (and many parents) who enters Toys "Я" Us. Many retailers offer a combination of the four basic utilities. Some supermarkets, for example, offer convenient locations (place utility) and are open 24 hours (time utility). In addition, consumers may seek additional utilities such as entertainment, recreation, or information.[3]

FIGURE 18-1

WHICH COMPANY BEST REPRESENTS
WHICH UTILITIES?

Royal Bank	One of the leaders in automated banking, the Royal Bank provides customers with convenience and 24 hour access to their banking sources.
Saturn	Saturn dealers have adopted a one-price strategy that eliminates the need for negotiating. Instead, all customers are offered the same price. Test drives, financing, trade-ins, leasing are all offered to encourage customers to purchase a Saturn.
Levi Strauss	In the next five years, Levi Strauss & Co. will open 100 Original Levi's Stores where in-store computers are used to create personal-fit jeans. An order for Levi's "Personal Pair" Jeans for Women specifies the customer's measurements, style, and colour preferences and can be delivered in approximately three weeks.
Toys "Я" Us	A distinctive toy store with a backwards Я, this company is what every kid dreams about. Walking into a Toys "Я" Us store is like living under a Christmas tree. Unlike most stores, which reduce their space allotted to toys after the holiday season, a huge selection of toys is always available at Toys "Я" Us.

Can You Match Them?

Time	Place	Possession	Form
_____	_____	_____	_____

Global MARKETING NEWSNET

MEGAMERCHANTS ARE BUSTING BORDERS!

Around the world, customer wants and needs are converging, and retailers are responding with frenzied global expansion. Experts estimate that retailers will spend $5 billion during the next two years opening new stores in foreign countries. Wal-Mart, for example, has plans to open stores in Brazil, Argentina, Hong Kong, and China. Home Depot will open 50 stores in Canada, while Office Depot, Saks Fifth Avenue, and JCPenney are expanding into Mexico. Italy's Bennetton already has stores in 120 countries, and Britain's Marks & Spencer has grown to 150 stores around the world.

Why are retailers expanding so rapidly? One reason is that the many markets are saturated with retailers. Therefore, large merchants are looking for new places to invest. A second reason, however, is that retailers would like to transform their store names into global brands—a move that will allow them to sell higher-margin private-label goods, avoid price wars, and better negotiate with suppliers. Keith Oates of Marks & Spencer says, "we'll be a global brand in time, like Coca-Cola."

The Global Economic Impact of Retailing

Retailing is important to the Canadian and global economies. Retail sales in Canada are estimated to reach almost $250 billion in 1999.[4] The retail sector also employs over 1.8 million people in Canada, or approximately 15 percent of the total employed labour force. Just three major retail categories—food stores, automotive, and clothing stores represent over 65 percent of the total retail trade in Canada.

The magnitude of retail sales is hard to imagine. Some of Canada's top retailers, for example, have annual sales revenues that surpass the GDP of several small nation-states. A study on global retailing found that the top 100 retailers in the world take in more than $1 trillion (US) in sales annually. These global retail companies operate more than 185 000 stores and have their head offices based in 15 countries. Just the top 10 global retailers, including Wal-Mart and Metro-Kaufhof International have annual sales of over $270 billion.[5] The Marketing NewsNet describes the incredible expansion of retailers on a global scale.[6] In the Arabian Gulf, Dubai is promoting itself as a gateway to the Middle East with the "Dubai Shopping Festival." More than 3000 retail outlets participate by offering sales, discounts, special offers and other promotions. Each day the festival also holds a free drawing for a $16 000 bar of gold and a raffle for two Lexus automobiles. Because the event attracts more than 2 million shoppers, retailers are eager to expand their global participation in Dubai and other growing markets.

CONCEPT CHECK

1. When Levi Strauss makes jeans cut to a customer's exact measurements, what utility is provided?

2. Two measures of the importance of retailing in the global economy are _____ and _____ .

FIGURE 18-2

CLASSIFYING RETAIL OUTLETS

METHOD OF CLASSIFICATION	DESCRIPTION OF RETAIL OUTLET
Form of ownership	Independent retailer Corporate chain Contractual system • Retailer-sponsored cooperative • Wholesaler-sponsored voluntary chain • Franchise
Level of service	Self-service Limited-service Full-service
Merchandise line	Depth • Single-line • Limited-line Breadth • General merchandise • Scrambled merchandising

CLASSIFYING RETAIL OUTLETS

For manufacturers, consumers, and the economy, retailing is an important component of marketing that has several variations. Because of the large number of alternative forms of retailing, it is easier to understand the differences among retail institutions by recognizing that outlets can be classified in several ways:

- **Form of ownership.** Who owns the outlet.
- **Level of service.** The degree of service provided to the customer.
- **Merchandise line.** How many different types of products a store carries and in what assortment.

Within each method of classification there are several alternative types of outlets, as shown in Figure 18-2 and explained in the following pages.

Form of Ownership

Independent retailer   One of the most common forms of retail ownership is the independent business, owned by an individual. Small retailers tend to dominate employment in hardware, sporting goods, jewellery, and gift stores. They are also popular retailers of auto supplies, books, paint, cameras, and women's accessories. The advantage of this form of ownership for the owner is that he or she can be his or her own boss. For customers, the independent store can offer convenience, quality, personal service, and lifestyle compatibility.[7]

Corporate chain   A second form of ownership, the corporate chain, involves multiple outlets under common ownership. If you've ever shopped at The Bay, Zeller's, Eaton's, or Loblaw's, you've shopped at a chain outlet.

In a chain operation, centralization in decision making and purchasing is common. Chain stores have advantages in dealing with manufacturers, particularly as the size of the chain grows. A large chain can bargain with a manufacturer to obtain good service or volume discounts on orders. Kmart's and Wal-Mart's large volumes make them strong negotiators with manufacturers of most products. Consumers also benefit in dealing with chains because there are multiple outlets with similar merchandise and consistent management policies.

Retailing has become a high-tech business for many large chains. Wal-Mart, for example, has developed a sophisticated inventory management and cost control system that allows rapid price changes for each product in every store. Although the technology requires a substantial investment, it is a necessary competitive tool today—a lesson illustrated by Mexico's largest drugstore chain. When Wal-Mart, Price Club, and other discounters opened stores in Mexico, Formacias Benavides used its state-of-the-art computer system to match prices on popular pharmaceutical products that were also available in the new competitors' stores.[8]

Contractual system   Contractual systems involve independently owned stores that band together to act like a chain. The three kinds described in Chapter 16 are retailer-sponsored cooperatives, wholesaler-sponsored voluntary chains, and franchises. One retailer-sponsored cooperative is Guardian Drugs, which consists of neighbourhood pharmacies that all agree with several other independent grocers to buy their products from the same wholesaler. In this way, members can take advantage of volume discounts commonly available to chains and also give the impression of being a large chain, which may be viewed more favourably by some consumers. Wholesaler-sponsored voluntary chains such as Independent Grocers' Alliance (IGA) try to achieve similar benefits.

As noted in Chapter 16, in a franchise system an individual or firm (the franchisee) contracts with a parent company (the franchisor) to set up a business or retail outlet.

McDonald's, Holiday Inn, Midas, and H&R Block all involve some level of franchising. The franchisor usually assists in selecting the store location, setting up the store, advertising, and training personnel. The franchisee pays a one-time franchise fee and an annual royalty, usually tied to the store's sales. Although this might be seen as a relatively new phenomenon, this ownership approach has been used with gas stations since the early 1900s.[9] Franchising is attractive because of the opportunity for people to enter a well-known, established business where managerial advice is provided. Also, the franchise fee may be less than the cost of setting up an independent business. The International Franchise Association recently reported that franchising is one of the strongest segments of the economy.[10]

Franchise fees paid to the franchisor can range from as little as $10 000 for a Dominos Pizza franchise to $50 000 for a TGI Friday restaurant franchise.[11] When the fees are combined with other costs such as real estate and equipment, however, the total investment can be substantial. By selling franchises, an organization reduces the cost of expansion but loses some control. A good franchisor, however, will maintain strong control of the outlets in terms of delivery and presentation of merchandise.

Level of Service

Even though most customers perceive little variation in retail outlets by form of ownership, differences among retailers are more obvious in terms of level of service. In some department stores, such as The Bay, very few services are provided. Some grocery stores, such as LoFoods, have customers bag the food themselves.

Other outlets, such as Holt Renfrew, provide a wide range of customer services from gift wrapping to wardrobe consultation.

Self-service   Self-service is at the extreme end of the level of service continuum because the customer performs many functions and little is provided by the outlet. Home building supply outlets, discount stores, and gas stations are often self-service. Warehouse stores, usually in buildings several times larger than a conventional store, are self-service with all nonessential customer services eliminated. Several new forms of self-service include a self-service scanning system called the Portable Personal Shopper now used by some grocery stores in The Netherlands.[12]

Limited service   Limited-service outlets provide some services, such as credit, merchandise return and telephone ordering, but not others, such as custom-made clothes. Department stores typically are considered limited-service outlets.

Full-service   Full-service retailers, which include most specialty stores and some department stores, provide many services to their customers. Services can include more salespeople on the floor or delivering purchases to customers' homes. Often this full-service strategy is a competitive advantage for such stores.[13]

Merchandise Line

Retail outlets also vary by their merchandise lines, the key distinction being the breadth and depth of the items offered to customers (Figure 18-3). **Depth of product line** means that the store carries a large assortment of each item, such as a shoe store that offers running shoes, dress shoes, and children's shoes. **Breadth of product line** refers to the variety of different items a store carries.

Depth of line   Stores that carry a considerable assortment (depth) of a related line of items are limited-line stores. Black's photography stores carry considerable depth in photography equipment. Stores that carry tremendous depth in one primary line of merchandise are single-line stores. Victoria's Secret carries great depth in women's lingerie. Both limited- and single-line stores are often referred to as *specialty outlets*. A new specialty store in the Canadian retail sector is Abbotsford, BC-based Columbo's which specializes in cigars and smoking-related accessories.

FIGURE 18-3   BREADTH VERSUS DEPTH OF MERCHANDISE LINES

Specialty discount outlets focus on one type of product, such as electronics, business supplies or books at very competitive prices. These outlets are referred to in the trade as *category killers* because they often dominate the market. Toys " Я " Us, for example, controls a significant share of the toy market.[14]

Breadth of line   Stores that carry a broad product line, with limited depth, are referred to as *general merchandise stores.* For example, a large department store carries a wide range of different types of products but not unusual sizes. The breadth and depth of merchandise lines are important decisions for a retailer. Traditionally, outlets carried related lines of goods. Today, however, **scrambled merchandising,** offering several unrelated product lines in a single store, is common. The modern drugstore carries food, camera equipment, magazines, paper products, toys, small hardware items, and pharmaceuticals. Supermarkets rent video tapes, develop film, and sell flowers.

A form of scrambled merchandising, the **hypermarket,** has been successful in Europe since the late 1960s. These hypermarkets are large stores (more than 200 000 square feet) offering a mix of 40 percent food products and 60 percent general merchandise. Prices are typically 5 to 20 percent below discount stores. The general concept behind the stores is simple: offer consumers everything in a single outlet, eliminating the need to stop at more than one location.

Despite their success in Europe, hypermarkets have not been popular in North America. Many shoppers are uncomfortable with the huge size of the stores. In addition, the competitive environment is tough: warehouse stores beat hypermarkets on price, category killers beat them on selection, and discounters beat them on location.

Searching for a better concept, some retailers are trying new stores, called *super-centres,* which combine a typical merchandise store with full-size grocery. Quebec grocery giant Provigo Inc. operates Maxi & Co., a combination of grocery and department store. The stores offer a complete selection of groceries as well as stationery, hardware, linens, kitchen items, videos, books, computer programs, beauty products, etc.[15]

Scrambled merchandising is convenient for consumers because it eliminates the number of stops required in a shopping trip. However, for the retailer this merchandising policy means there is competition between very dissimilar types of retail outlets, or **intertype competition.** A local bakery may compete with a department store, discount outlet, or even a local gas station. Scrambled merchandising and intertype competition make it more difficult to be a retailer.

CONCEPT CHECK

1. Centralized decision making and purchasing are an advantage of _____ ownership.

2. What are some examples of new forms of self-service retailers?

3. Would a shop for big men's clothes carrying pants in sizes 40 to 60 have a broad or deep product line?

NONSTORE RETAILING

Most of the retailing examples discussed earlier in the chapter, such as corporate chains, department stores, and limited- and single-line specialty stores, involve store retailing. Many retailing activities today, however, are not limited to sales in a store. Nonstore retailing occurs outside a retail outlet such as through direct marketing (described in Chapter 16), direct selling, and automatic vending.[16]

Direct Marketing

Few areas of retailing have grown as rapidly as direct marketing. What was once a specialized activity is now a set of fashionable tools used by virtually every type of business. Direct marketing includes direct-mail, telemarketing, and in-home shopping.

Direct mail   Direct-mail retailing is attractive because it eliminates the cost of a store and clerks. In addition, it improves marketing efficiency through segmentation and targeting and creates customer value by providing a fast and convenient means of making a purchase.

As the number of direct-mail purchases have increased, the number of catalogues and products sold through catalogues has skyrocketed. The competition combined with higher paper and postal costs, however, have hurt some large catalogue merchants. A successful approach now used by many catalogue retailers is to send specialty catalogues to market niches identified in their databases. L. L. Bean, a long-standing catalogue retailer, for example, has developed an individual catalogue for fly fishing enthusiasts.[17]

Creative forms of catalogue retailing are also being developed. Victoria's Secret mails as many as 45 catalogues a year to its customers to generate mail-order and 800-number business and to increase traffic in its 600 stores.[18]

Telemarketing   Another form of direct marketing, called **telemarketing,** involves using the telephone to interact with and sell directly to consumers. Compared with direct mail, telemarketing is often viewed as a more efficient means of targeting consumers, although the two techniques are often used together. Telemarketing has grown in popularity as companies search for ways to cut costs but still provide convenient access to their customers.[19]

As the use of telemarketing grows, consumer privacy has become a topic of discussion among consumers, government and businesses. Issues such as industry standards, ethical guidelines, and privacy are evolving to provide a balance between the varying perspectives. The accompanying Ethics and Social Responsibility Alert offers some of the details of the debate.[20]

In-home shopping   In-home shopping includes several relatively new forms of nonstore retailing—television-assisted retailing and computer-assisted retailing. TV shopping is possible when consumers watch a shopping channel on which products are displayed; orders are then placed over the telephone. Two popular programs, Home Shopping Network and QVC, reach millions of Canadian households. A limitation of TV shopping has been the lack of buyer-seller interaction and the inability of consumers to control the items they see. But two new technologies—fiber optics and digital compression—will soon allow consumers to choose from as many as 500 channels and interact with the program source.[21]

Consumers can also shop at home via the Internet and its World Wide Web. Many retailers all across Canada have set up web sites to allow the customer to "browse" at home. Even the NHL has an on-line store called "Hot Off the Ice" where customers can view and order a variety of NHL merchandise.[22] Also, as the chapter opener also indicated, there has been major growth in the development of cyberspace or virtual malls, some containing as many as 600 stores, where customers can shop without ever leaving their homes. There are already close to 30 million Internet users, worldwide. Future growth in on-line shopping will likely follow the penetration of computers into homes. However, owning a computer will not be a necessity for everyone. Many "on-line cafes" are now available for consumers without their own computers.[23]

Direct Selling

Direct selling, sometimes called door-to-door retailing, involves direct sales of goods and services to consumers through personal interactions and demonstrations in their home or office. A variety of companies, including familiar names such as Fuller Brush, Avon, World Book, and Mary Kay Cosmetics, have created an industry with more than $16 billion in sales by providing consumers with personalized service and convenience. However, sales have been declining as retail chains such as Wal-Mart begin to carry similar products at discount prices and as the increasing number of dual-career households reduces the number of potential buyers at home.

In response to changes in the marketplace, many direct selling retailers are expanding into other markets. Avon, for example, already has 1.3 million sales representatives in 26 countries including Mexico, Poland, Argentina, and China. Similarly, other retailers such as Amway and Electrolux are rapidly expanding in Europe. Direct selling is likely to continue to grow in markets where the lack of effective distribution channels increases the importance of door-to-door convenience and where the lack of consumer knowledge about products and brands will increase the need for a person-to-person approach.[24]

Automatic Vending

Direct marketing also encompasses vending machines, which make it possible to serve customers when and where stores cannot. Maintenance and operating costs are high, so product prices tend to be higher than those in stores. Typically, small convenience products are available in vending machines. Improved technology, however, now allows these machines to accept credit cards—a change that will permit more expensive items to be sold through this form of retailing. Some airports, for example, now have vending machines that sell software to commuters with laptop computers. Another improvement in vending machines is the use of modems to notify retailers when their machines are empty.[25]

VENDING MACHINES SERVE
CUSTOMERS WHEN AND WHERE
STORES CANNOT.

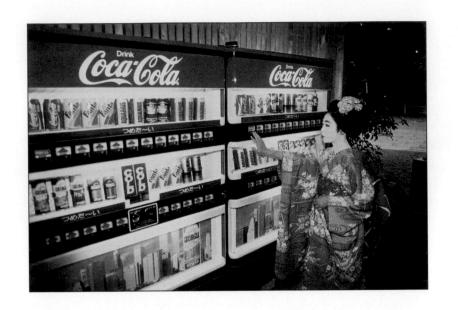

CONCEPT CHECK

1. Successful catalogue retailers often send _____ catalogues to _____ markets identified in their databases.

2. How are on-line shopping services and the Internet changing retailing?

3. Where are direct selling retail sales growing? Why?

RETAILING STRATEGY

This section identifies how a retail store positions itself and describes specific actions it can take to develop a retailing strategy.

Positioning a Retail Store

The classification alternatives presented in the previous sections help determine one store's position relative to its competitors.

Retail positioning matrix   The **retail positioning matrix** is a matrix developed by the MAC Group, Inc., a management consulting firm.[26] This matrix positions retail outlets on two dimensions: breadth of product line and value added. As defined previously, breadth of product line is the range of products sold through each outlet. The second dimension, *value-added,* includes elements such as location (as with 7-Eleven stores), product reliability (as with Holiday Inn or McDonald's), or prestige (as with Birk's).

The retail positioning matrix in Figure 18-4 shows four possible positions. An organization can be successful in any position, but unique strategies are required within each quadrant. Consider the four stores shown in the matrix:

1. Eaton's has high value-added and a broad product line. Retailers in this quadrant pay great attention to store design and product lines. Merchandise often has a high margin of profit and is of high quality. The stores in this position typically provide high levels of service.

2. Kmart has low value-added and a broad line. Kmart and similar firms typically trade a lower price for increased volume in sales. Retailers in this position focus on price with low service levels and an image of being a place for good buys.

FIGURE 18-4

RETAIL POSITIONING MATRIX

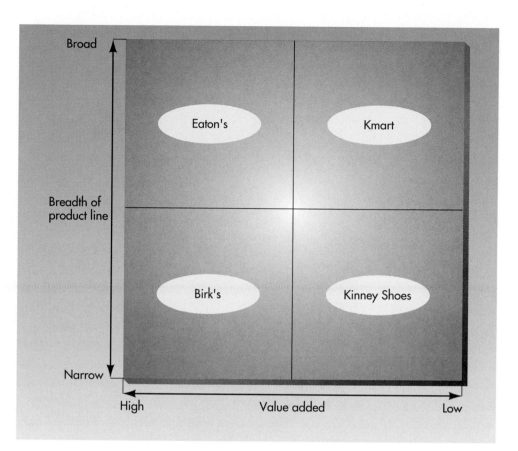

3. Birk's has high value-added and a narrow line. Retailers of this type typically sell a very restricted range of products that are of high-status quality. Customers are also provided with high levels of service.
4. Kinney has low value-added and a narrow line. Such retailers are specialty mass merchandisers. Kinney, for example, carries attractively priced shoes for the entire family. These outlets appeal to value-conscious consumers. Economies of scale are achieved through centralized advertising, merchandising, buying, and distribution. Stores are usually the same in design, layout, and merchandise; hence they are often referred to as "cookie-cutter" stores.

Keys to positioning   To successfully position a store, it must have an identity that has some advantages over the competitors yet is recognized by consumers. A company can have outlets in several positions on the matrix, but this approach is usually done with different store names. Hudson's Bay Company, for example, owns The Bay department stores (with high value-added and a broad line) and Zellers stores (low value-added and a broad line). Shifting from one box in the retail positioning matrix to another is also possible, but all elements of retailing strategy must be reexamined.

Retailing Mix

In developing retailing strategy, managers work with the **retailing mix,** which includes the (1) goods and services, (2) physical distribution, and (3) communications tactics chosen by a store (Figure 18-5).[27] Decisions relating to the mix focus on the consumer. Each of the areas shown is important, but we will cover only three basic areas: (1) pricing, (2) store location, and (3) image and atmosphere. The communications and promotion components are discussed in Chapter 20 on advertising and Chapter 21 on personal selling.

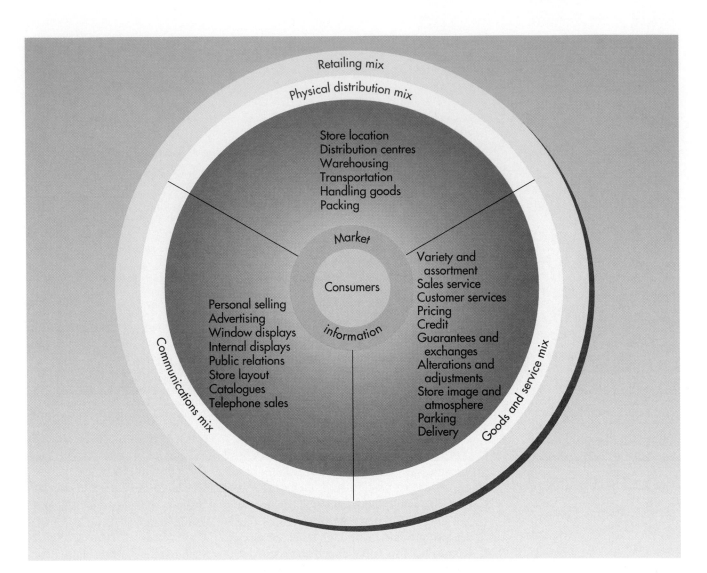

Retailing mix

Physical distribution mix

Store location
Distribution centres
Warehousing
Transportation
Handling goods
Packing

Market

Consumers

information

Variety and
  assortment
Sales service
Customer services
Pricing
Credit
Guarantees and
  exchanges
Alterations and
  adjustments
Store image and
  atmosphere
Parking
Delivery

Personal selling
Advertising
Window displays
Internal displays
Public relations
Store layout
Catalogues
Telephone sales

Communications mix

Goods and service mix

FIGURE 18-5

THE RETAILING MIX

Retail pricing   In setting prices for merchandise, retailers must decide on the markup, markdown, and timing for markdowns. As mentioned in the appendix to Chapter 15, the *markup* refers to how much should be added to the cost the retailer paid for a product to reach the final selling price. Retailers decide on the *original markup,* but by the time the product is sold, they end up with a *maintained markup.* The original markup is the difference between retailer cost and initial selling price. When products do not sell as quickly as anticipated, their price is reduced. The difference between the final selling price and retailer cost is the maintained markup, which is also called the *gross margin.*

Discounting a product, or taking a *markdown,* occurs when the product does not sell at the original price and an adjustment is necessary. Often new models or styles force the price of existing models to be marked down. Discounts may also be used to increase demand for complementary products. For example, retailers might take a markdown on stereos to increase sales of CDs or reduce the price of cake mix to generate frosting purchases.

Although most retailers plan markdowns, many retailers use price discounts as part of their regular merchandising policy. Emphasizing consistently low prices (everyday low pricing strategy) and eliminating most markdowns or sales has become a successful strategy for retailers like Wal-Mart. Because consumers often use price as an indicator of product quality, however, the brand name of the product and the image of the store become important decision factors in these situations.

A final issue, *timing,* involves deciding when to discount the merchandise. Many retailers take a markdown as soon as sales fall off to free up valuable selling space and cash. However, other stores delay markdowns to discourage bargain hunters and maintain an image of quality. There is no clear answer, but retailers must consider how the timing might affect future sales.

Off-price retailing is a retail pricing practice that is most commonly found in clothing sales. **Off-price retailing** involves selling brand-name merchandise at lower than regular prices.[28] The difference between the off-price retailer and a discount store is that off-price merchandise is bought by the retailer from manufacturers with excess inventory at prices below wholesale prices, while the discounter buys at full wholesale price (but takes less of a markup than do traditional department stores). Because of this difference in the way merchandise is purchased by the retailer, selection at an off-price retailer is unpredictable, and searching for bargains has become a popular activity for many consumers. Savings to the consumer at off-price retailers are reported as high as 70 percent off the prices of a traditional department store.

There are two variations of off-price retailing. One is the warehouse club. These large stores (more than 100 000 square feet) began as rather stark outlets with no elaborate displays, customer service, or home delivery. They require an annual membership fee (usually $25) for the privilege of shopping there. While a typical Kmart store stocks 100 000 items, warehouse clubs carry about 3500 items and usually stock one brand name of appliances or food product. Service is minimal, and customers usually must pay by cash or cheque. However, the extremely competitive pricing of merchandise makes warehouse clubs attractive. Traditional grocers, especially in Quebec, Ontario, Alberta, and BC have lost sales to warehouse club stores. Sam's Club and Price Club are popular warehouse clubs that you may be familiar with.

A second variation is the factory outlet store. These outlets, such as Bass Shoe Outlet, Levi Strauss Factory Outlet, and Oneida Factory Store, offer products for 25 to 30 percent off the suggested retail price. Manufacturers use the stores to clear excess merchandise and to reach customers who focus on value shopping. Some experts expect the next trend to combine outlet stores, off-price retailers, and department store clearance centres in "value-retail centres."[29]

Store location   A second aspect of the retailing mix involves deciding where to locate the store and how many stores to have. Department stores, which started downtown in most cities, have followed customers

to the suburbs, and in recent years more stores have been opened in large regional malls. Most stores today are near several others in one of five settings: the central business district, the regional shopping centre, the community shopping centre, the strip, or the power centre.

The **central business district** is the oldest retail setting, the community's downtown area. Until the regional outflow to the suburbs, it was the major shopping area, but the suburban population has grown at the expense of the downtown shopping area.

Regional shopping centres are the suburban malls of today, containing up to 100 stores. The typical drawing distance of a regional centre is 8 to 16 kilometres from the mall. These large shopping areas often contain two or three anchor stores, which are well-known national or regional stores such as Sears, Eaton's, or The Bay. The largest variation of a regional shopping centre is the West Edmonton Mall. The shopping centre is a conglomerate of 600 stores, six amusement centres, 110 restaurants, and a 355-room Fantasyland hotel.[30] Other large regional shopping centres are being planned for the Canadian market. These centres will not be as big as the West Edmonton Mall, but will offer consumers approximately 250 stores under one roof as well as entertainment and food service establishments.[31]

A more limited approach to retail location is the **community shopping centre,** which typically has one primary store (usually a department store branch) and often about 20 to 40 smaller outlets. Generally, these centres serve a population base of about 100 000.

Not every suburban store is located in a shopping mall. Many neighbourhoods have clusters of stores, referred to as a **strip location,** to serve people who are within a 5-to-10-minute drive and live in a population base of under 30 000. Gas station, hardware, laundry, and grocery outlets are commonly found in a strip location. Unlike the larger shopping centres, the composition of these stores is usually unplanned. A variation of the strip shopping location is called the **power centre,** which is a huge shopping strip with multiple anchor (or national) stores. Power centres are seen as having the convenient location found in many strip centres and the additional power of national stores. These large strips often have two to five anchor stores and often contain a supermarket, which brings the shopper to the power centre on a weekly basis.

Several new types of retail locations include carts, kiosks, and wall units. These forms of retailing have been popular in airports and mall common areas because they provide consumers with easy access and rental income for the property owner. Retailers benefit from the relatively low cost compared with a regular store.

Retail image and atmosphere   Deciding on the image of a retail outlet is an important retailing mix factor that has been widely recognized and studied since the late 1950s. Pierre Martineau described image as "the way in which the store is defined in the shopper's mind," partly by its functional qualities and partly by an aura of psychological attributes.[32] In this definition, *functional* refers to mix elements such as price ranges, store layouts, and breadth and depth of merchandise lines. The psychological attributes are the intangibles such as a sense of belonging, excitement, style, or warmth. Image has been found to include impressions of the corporation that operates the store, the category or type of store, the product categories in the store, the brands in each category, merchandise and service quality, and the marketing activities of the store.[33]

Closely related to the concept of image is the store's atmosphere or ambiance. Many retailers believe that sales are affected by layout, colour, lighting, scent, and music in the store as well as by how crowded it is. In addition, the physical surroundings that influence customers may affect the store's employees.[34]

In creating the right image and atmosphere, a retail store tries to identify its target audience and what the target audience seeks from the buying experience so the store will fortify the beliefs and the emotional reactions buyers are seeking.

CONCEPT CHECK

1. What are the two dimensions of the retail positioning matrix?

2. How does original markup differ from maintained markup?

3. A huge shopping strip with multiple anchor stores is a _____ centre.

FIGURE 18-6

THE WHEEL OF RETAILING

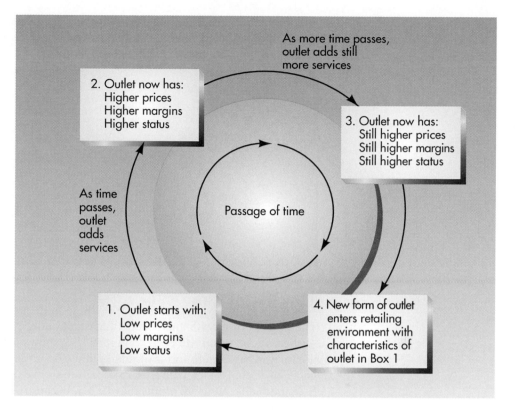

THE CHANGING NATURE OF RETAILING

Retailing is the most dynamic aspect of a channel of distribution. Stores such as factory outlets show that new retailers are always entering the market, searching for a new position that will attract customers. The reason for this continual change is explained by two concepts: the wheel of retailing and the retail life cycle.

The Wheel of Retailing

The **wheel of retailing** describes how new forms of retail outlets enter the market.[35] Usually they enter as low-status, low-margin stores such as a drive-in hamburger stand with no indoor seating and a limited menu (Figure 18-6, box 1). Gradually these outlets add fixtures and more embellishments to their stores (in-store seating, plants, and chicken sandwiches as well as hamburgers) to increase the attractiveness for customers. With these additions, prices and status rise (box 2). As time passes, these outlets add still more services and their prices and status increase even further (box 3). These retail outlets now face some new form of retail outlet that again appears as low-status, low-margin operator (box 4), and the wheel of retailing turns as the cycle starts to repeat itself.

In the 1950s, McDonald's and Burger King had very limited menus of hamburgers and french fries. Most stores had no inside seating for customers. Over time, the wheel of retailing for fast-food restaurants has turned. These chains have changed by altering their stores and expanding their menus. Today, McDonald's has new products such as pizza and pasta and new formats such as the McDonald's Cafe, and new decor options such as the 50s-style store opened in Chicago. The changes are leaving room for new forms of outlets that offer only the basics—burgers, fries, and cola, a drive-through window, and no inside seating. For still others, the wheel has come full circle. Taco Bell is now opening small, limited-offering outlets in gas stations, discount stores, or "wherever a burrito and a mouth might possibly intersect."

Discount stores were a major new retailing form in the 1960s and priced their products below those of department stores. As prices in discount stores rose, in the 1980s they found themselves overpriced compared with a new form of retail outlet—the warehouse retailer. Today, off-price retailers and factory outlets are offering prices even lower than warehouses!

The Retail Life Cycle

The process of growth and decline that retail outlets, like products, experience is described by the **retail life cycle**.[36] Figure 18-7 shows the retail life cycle and the position of various current forms of retail outlets on it. Early growth is the stage of emergence of a retail outlet, with a sharp departure from existing competition. Market share rises gradually, although profits may be low because of startup costs. In the next stage, accelerated development, both market share and profit achieve their greatest growth rates. Usually multiple outlets are established as companies focus on the distribution

FIGURE 18-7

THE RETAIL LIFE CYCLE

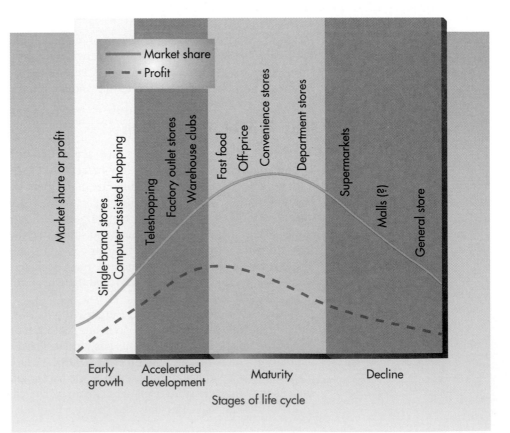

element of the retailing mix. In this stage some later competitors may enter. Wendy's, for example, appeared on the hamburger chain scene almost 20 years after McDonald's had begun operation. The key goal for the retailer in this stage is to establish a dominant position in the fight for market share.

The battle for market share is usually fought before the maturity phase, and some competitors drop out of the market. New retail forms enter in the maturity phase, stores try to maintain their market share, and price discounting occurs. In the early 1990s, major fast-food chains such as Wendy's and McDonald's began to aggressively discount their prices. McDonald's introduced its Extra Value Meal, a discounted package of burger, fries, and drink, while Wendy's followed with a kid's Value Menu.

The challenge facing retailers is to delay entering the decline stage in which market share and profit fall rapidly. Specialty apparel retailers, such as the Gap, Limited, Benetton, and Ann Taylor have noticed a decline in market share after a decade of growth. To prevent further decline, these retailers will need to find ways of discouraging their customers from moving to low-margin, mass-volume outlets or high-price, high-service boutiques.

FUTURE CHANGES IN RETAILING

Three exciting trends in retailing—the increasing impact of technology, the dramatic changes in the way we shop, and the growing importance of brands—are likely to lead to many changes for retailers and consumers in the future.

The Impact of Technology

Technology has already enabled consumers to shop or bank at home and this is changing the face of retailing in Canada. Another significant change retailers face in the future is the way consumers pay for purchases. Credit cards, for example, are likely to be replaced by smart cards, which look the same as credit cards but store information on computer chips instead of magnetic strips. They will hold information about bank accounts and amounts of available funds, and they will contain customer purchase information such as airline seat preferences and clothing sizes. The idea is already popular in Europe and Asia. Benefits for consumers include faster service—a smart card transaction is much faster than having a cheque or credit card approved—and they are a convenient method of paying for small dollar-amount transactions. Merchants will also benefit because they will save the 5 to 7 percent usually paid to credit card companies or lost in handling.[37]

Changing Shopping Behaviour

In recent years consumers have become precision shoppers. The number of stores consumers visit and the number of times they visit those stores each month is declining. Shoppers are demanding convenient hours and locations, outstanding service, selection, and reasonable prices from retailers. As a result, familiar forms of retailers such as supermarkets, travel agencies, car dealerships, and hardware stores are likely to change or be replaced by new types of retailers. For example, local car dealers and neighbourhood hardware stores will be challenged by what are referred to as "big-box" retailers. Car Canada Group, for example, is considered a big-box car dealer that offers over 400 reconditioned vehicles, warranties, financing, and fast transaction times. Big-box home improvement centres are also experiencing growth, from zero market share in 1992 to over 11 percent in 1997.[38] Some retail experts suggest that consumers like these new types of retailers because they are often fast, focused, and flexible.

Another response to the changes in consumers' preferences is a form of co-branding where two retailers share a location. For example, McDonald's has developed partnerships with Wal-Mart that will lead to thousands of satellite outlets in the retail stores.

Starbucks Coffee Co. has opened cafes in conjunction with Chapters Bookstores. And KFC, which attracts a strong dinner crowd, will partner with Taco Bell, which is stronger in the lunch market, at 800 of its stores. Retailers hope that consumers will appreciate the convenience of the new locations.

The Importance of Brands

The use of brands is also changing dramatically. Many retailers have developed their own private-label brands to increase customer loyalty. As a result, many manufacturers have opened their own stores. Single-brand, or company, stores allow manufacturers to display their entire product line in a controlled "showcase."

Two of the most successful variations of the company store trend are the Disney and Warner studio stores. The Disney stores and the Warner stores market characters such as Mickey Mouse, Peter Pan, Bugs Bunny, and the Tasmanian Devil directly to the public. While both companies are fortunate to have several characters to promote, they have discovered that preferences vary throughout the world. In British stores, for example, Winnie the Pooh is the top seller, while Bambie and Thumper are preferred in France, and Mickey and Minnie are the first choices in Japan![39]

Most consumers associate strong brand names with specific products such as Coke or Tide, or particular companies such as Microsoft or Motorola. In the future, however, many large merchants will be trying to turn their store names into brands. For example, Sears Canada suggests its recent strong revenue growth is due to its new philosophy of "thinking like a brand and acting like a retailer."[40] The changing role of products, stores, and manufacturers as popular, well-known brands is likely to generate many more changes in the dynamic practice of retailing!

CONCEPT CHECK

1. According to the wheel of retailing, when a new retail form appears, how would you characterize its image?

2. Market share is usually fought out before the _____ stage of the retail life cycle.

3. What is a smart card?

SUMMARY

1. Retailing provides a number of values to the consumer in the form of various utilities: time, place, possession, and form. Economically, retailing is important in terms of the people employed and money exchanged in retail sales.

2. Retailing outlets can be classified along several dimensions: the form of ownership, level of service, or merchandise line.

3. There are several forms of ownership: independent, chain, retailer-sponsored cooperative, wholesaler-sponsored chain or franchise.

4. Stores vary in the level of service, being self-service, limited-service, or full-service.

5. Retail outlets vary in terms of the breadth and depth of their merchandise lines. Breadth refers to the number of different items carried, and depth refers to the assortment of each item offered.

6. Nonstore retailing includes direct marketing, direct selling, and automatic vending. Direct marketing includes direct-mail, telemarketing, and in-home shopping.

7. A retail store positions itself on two dimensions: breadth of product line and value added, which includes elements such as location, product reliability, and prestige.

8. Retailing strategy is based on the retailing mix, consisting of goods and services, physical distribution, and communication tactics.

9. In retail pricing, retailers must decide on the markup, markdown, and timing for the markdown. Off-price retailers offer brand-name merchandise at lower than regular prices. This retailing form is most common in the clothing industry.

10. Retail store location is an important retail mix decision. The common alternatives are the central business district, a regional shopping centre, a community shopping centre, or a strip location. A variation of the strip location is the power centre, which is a strip location with multiple national anchor stores and a supermarket.

11. Retail image and atmosphere help retailers create the appropriate buying experience for their target market.

12. New retailing forms are explained by the wheel of retailing. Stores enter as low-status, low-margin outlets. Over time, they add services and raise margins, which allows a new form of low-status, low-margin retailing outlet to enter.
13. Like products, retail outlets have a life cycle consisting of four stages: early growth, accelerated development, maturity, and decline.
14. Technology will change the way consumers pay for purchases in the future. Smart cards may lead to a cashless society.

KEY TERMS AND CONCEPTS

retailing p. 430
form of ownership p. 432
level of service p. 432
merchandise line p. 432
depth of product line p. 434
breadth of product line p. 434
scrambled merchandising p. 435
hypermarket p. 435
intertype competition p. 435
telemarketing p. 436

retail positioning matrix p. 438
retailing mix p. 439
off-price retailing p. 441
central business district p. 441
regional shopping centres p. 441
community shopping centre p. 442
strip location p. 442
power centre p. 442
wheel of retailing p. 443
retail life cycle p. 444

CHAPTER PROBLEMS AND APPLICATIONS

1. Discuss the impact of the growing number of dual-income households on (a) nonstore retailing and (b) the retail mix.
2. How does value-added affect a store's competitive position?
3. In retail pricing, retailers often have a maintained markup. Explain how this maintained markup differs from original markup and why it is so important.
4. What are the similarities and differences between the product and retail life cycles?
5. How would you classify Kmart in terms of its position on the wheel of retailing versus that of an off-price retailer?
6. Develop a chart to highlight the role of each of the three main elements of the retailing mix across the four stages of the retail life cycle.

7. In Figure 18-4 Kinney Shoes was placed on the retail positioning matrix. What strategies should Kinney follow to move itself into the same position as Birks?
8. Breadth and depth are two important components in distinguishing among types of retailers. Discuss the breadth and depth implications of the following retailers discussed in this chapter: (a) Levi Strauss, (b) Wal-Mart, (c) L. L Bean, and (d) Future Shop.
9. According to the wheel of retailing and the retail life cycle, what will happen to factory outlet stores?
10. The text discusses the development of television-assisted retailing and computer-assisted retailing in Canada. How does the development of each of these retailing forms agree with the implications of the retail life cycle?

CASE 18-1   IKEA

IKEA began as a mail-order firm in Sweden in the 1940s. Today it is one of the largest retail home furnishings chains with outlets in more than two dozen countries and sales exceeding $5 billion. IKEA has 19 stores in North America, 7 in Canada and 12 in the United States. Sales in these outlets totalled more than $530 million in 1997, up over 9 percent from the previous 12-month period.

THE IKEA CONCEPT

Founded by Swedish catalogue king Ingvar Kamprad, IKEA is an acronym for his name and hometown, Elmtaryd Agunnaryd. IKEA is guided by a corporate philosophy spelled out in Kamprad's "Testament of a Furniture Retailer." The basic philosophy can be summed up as "form, function, price = attractive, useful and affordable furniture." Specifically, IKEA's promise is "to offer a wide range of home furnishing items of good design and function, at prices so low, that the majority of people can afford to buy them." The corporate values of thrift, inventiveness, informality, and hard work are deeply rooted in the company.

Instead of traditional stores, IKEA stores are a combination of gallery and warehouse. Sales staff on the floor are kept to a minimum. Products are displayed in rooms that are fully furnished, allowing consumers to visualize how they would look in a home setting. Products are stored in flat cartons, which the consumer picks up and takes home for final assembly. In essence, IKEA's consumers are really "prosumers" (half producers, half consumers) since they assume responsibility for assembly of the products. The consumers are also active players in the distribution process since they must transport the products to their homes.

While the key to the IKEA concept is self-service and self-assembly, IKEA does offer its customers some services. For example, home delivery is available in most stores at an extra charge. If delivery is not available, IKEA will refer customers to a delivery service company in the area. IKEA will even rent out automobile roof racks to the customers to transport their purchases home. Many IKEA stores offer a home decoration service if customers wish to furnish an entire room or home, and most also offer a kitchen planning service. Using computer simulations, trained kitchen planners work with the customer to plan and choose the right kitchen. IKEA's products are easy to assemble and require no skills or tools. But if customers desire, IKEA will refer them to assembly companies who will come to the customer's home to assemble the products.

There are about 12 000 products in the total IKEA product range. Each store carries a selection of the products depending on store size. The core products are the same worldwide. IKEA contracts more than 2000 suppliers in over 60 countries to manufacture their products. The manufacturers ship the components to large warehouses or distribution centres which, in turn, supply the various stores. The suppliers must provide well-designed and high-quality products that are distinctively Scandinavian. They must also be able to provide the product at a low price and ensure continuity of supply.

IKEA's key promotion vehicle is its catalogue. The catalogue is produced in 30 editions, in 17 languages for 31 countries. The company also uses attention-getting and often provocative advertising designed to generate additional word-of-mouth publicity. For example, the company was the first to feature gay consumers in mainstream TV ads. The company also uses quirky and humorous ad appeals to reach customers. And, of course, IKEA also has its own World Wide Web site to communicate with its customers (www.IKEA.com).

The primary target market of IKEA are young (if not in age, at least in thought), educated, liberal-minded professionals who are not overly concerned with status symbols. This target market is similar across countries and regions where IKEA is located. However, because of changing demographics, especially the aging of the population in many countries, IKEA is attempting to broaden its target market to include the "older customer." IKEA is also offering a line of business furnishings for the first time in North America in an attempt to reach out to the commercial market segment.

IKEA takes a managed growth perspective in terms of retail expansion. Globally, only five new stores are planned for in 1997–98, including Bologna, Hong Kong, Shanghai, Gdansk, and Stuttgart.

Questions

1. Outline IKEA's basic marketing mix.

2. Why do you think IKEA has been successful in a highly competitive retail furnishings market?

3. From the consumer's perspective, what makes IKEA's approach to retailing an attractive alternative to traditional furniture shopping?

CHAPTER 19

Integrated Marketing Communications, Sales Promotion, and Public Relations

AFTER READING THIS CHAPTER YOU SHOULD BE ABLE TO:

- Explain the communication process and its elements.

- Understand the promotional mix and the uniqueness of each component.

- Select the promotional approach appropriate to a product's life cycle stage and characteristics.

- Differentiate between the advantages of push and pull strategies.

- Understand the alternative strengths and weaknesses of consumer-oriented and trade-oriented sales promotions.

- Appreciate the value of public relations as part of an integrated communications program.

WHY IS JAMES BOND DRIVING A BMW?

Since 1963, in a series of 16 movies including box-office hits *Dr. No, You Only Live Twice, Diamonds Are Forever,* and *License to Kill,* James Bond, British secret agent 007, has driven his signature automobile—the sporty Aston-Martin. In the most recent Bond thriller, *Goldeneye,* however, Bond drives the new BMW Z3 roadster.

Why the switch after more than 30 years? Primarily because of a promotional agreement between movie studio Metro-Goldwyn-Mayer and automaker BMW (www.bmw.com). In exchange for the on-screen exposure, BMW promoted the film on TV, in car showrooms, and on airplanes. The agreement provided benefits for both partners: the marketing efforts reached new audiences and almost guaranteed the success of the movie, and BMW received more than 6000 orders for the new automobile.

Other movies have also used brand-name products. It was Steven Speilberg's placement of Hershey's Reese's Pieces in *E.T.* that brought a lot of interest to the concept. Similarly, when Tom Cruise wore Bausch and Lomb's Ray-ban sunglasses in *Risky Business* and its Aviator sunglasses in *Top Gun*—and sales skyrocketed from 100 000 to 7 000 000 pairs in five years—the potential impact of "product placement" was recognized. Ray-ban's Predator series of sunglasses also got a sales bounce when Tom Cruise wore a pair in *Jerry McGuire,* and when Will Smith sported a pair in *Men in Black.* Other examples of product placement include Tom Hanks wearing a pair of Nike running shoes in *Forrest Gump,* and Jim Carey passing a Subway billboard while driving through Africa in *Ace Ventura: When Nature Calls.*

It's not just movies, though. Other outlets include music videos, television shows, game shows, and even other companies' commercials. NBC's top-rated "Seinfeld" has included Junior Mints, Clearly Canadian, Rold Gold pretzels, and diet Coke in its episodes. "Baywatch" receives Adidas shoes and Speedo swimsuits that are often used on the program. "Home Improvement" actors have modelled Logo Athletic jackets, and "ER" actors use Compaq computers. Mazda recently placed a Miata in a gasoline ad.[1]

Placement of products in the many media alternatives available today is becoming an important part of marketing and promotion. Applications of the technique demonstrate the importance of creativity in communicating with potential customers. In addition, to ensure that a consistent message is delivered through product placement and all promotional activities, a process that integrates marketing communications is a necessity.

Promotion represents the fourth element in the marketing mix. The promotional element comprises a mix of tools available for the marketer called the *promotional mix,* which consists of advertising, personal selling, sales promotion, and public relations. All of these elements can be used to (1) inform prospective buyers about the benefits of the product, (2) persuade them to try it, and (3) remind them later about the benefits they enjoyed by using the product. This chapter first gives an overview of the communication process and the promotional elements used in marketing and then discusses sales promotion and public relations. Chapter 20 covers advertising, and Chapter 21 discusses personal selling.

THE COMMUNICATION PROCESS

Communication is the process of conveying a message to others and requires six elements: a source, a message, a channel of communication, a receiver, and the processes of encoding and decoding[2] (Figure 19-1). The **source** may be a company or person who has information to convey. The information sent by a source, such as a description of a new weight reduction drink, forms the **message.** The message is conveyed by means of a **channel of communication** such as a salesperson, advertising media, or public relations tools. Consumers who read, hear, or see the message are the **receivers.**

FIGURE 19-1

THE COMMUNICATION PROCESS

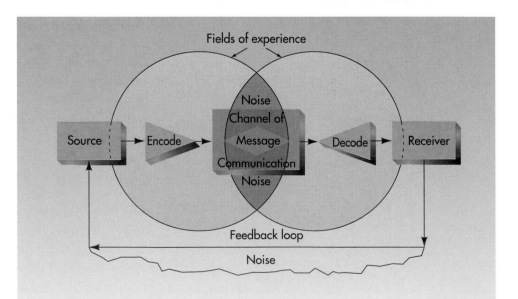

Encoding and Decoding

Encoding and decoding are essential to communication. **Encoding** is the process of having the sender transform an abstract idea into a set of symbols. **Decoding** is the reverse, or the process of having the receiver take a set of symbols, the message, and transform them back to an abstract idea. Look at the accompanying automobile advertisement: who is the source, and what is the message?

Decoding is performed by the receivers according to their own frame of reference: their attitudes, values, and beliefs.[3] In the ad, Lexus is the source and the message is this advertisement, which appeared in *Forbes* magazine (the channel). How would you interpret (decode) this advertisement? The picture and text in the advertisement show that the source's intention is to introduce a unique product and to position Lexus as a company in "the relentless pursuit of perfection"—a position the source believes will appeal to the upper-income readers of the magazine.

The process of communication is not always a successful one. Errors in communication can happen in several ways. The source may not adequately transform the abstract idea into an effective set of symbols, a properly encoded message may be sent through the wrong channel and never make it to the receiver, the receiver may not properly transform the set of symbols into the correct abstract idea, or finally, feedback may be so delayed or distorted that it is of no use to the sender. Although communication appears easy to perform, truly effective communication can be very difficult.

For the message to be communicated effectively, the sender and receiver must have a mutually shared **field of experience**—similar understanding and knowledge. Figure 19-1 shows two circles representing the fields of experience of the sender and receiver,

A SOURCE AND A MESSAGE.

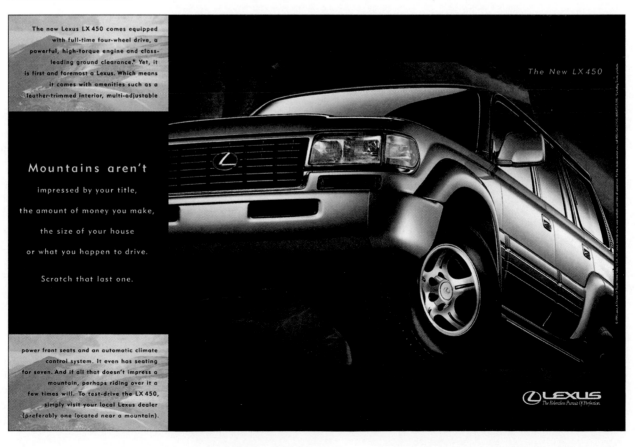

The new Lexus LX 450 comes equipped with full-time four-wheel drive, a powerful, high-torque engine and class-leading ground clearance.* Yet, it is first and foremost a Lexus. Which means it comes with amenities such as a leather-trimmed interior, multi-adjustable

The New LX 450

Mountains aren't

impressed by your title,

the amount of money you make,

the size of your house

or what you happen to drive.

Scratch that last one.

power front seats and an automatic climate control system. It even has seating for seven. And if all that doesn't impress a mountain, perhaps riding over it a few times will. To test-drive the LX 450, simply visit your local Lexus dealer (preferably one located near a mountain).

LEXUS
The Relentless Pursuit Of Perfection.

which overlap in the message. Some of the better-known communication problems have occurred when Canadian companies have taken their messages to cultures with different fields of experience. Many misinterpretations are merely the result of bad translations. For example, General Motors made a mistake when its "Body by Fisher" claim was translated into Flemish as "Corpse by Fisher."[4]

Feedback

Figure 19-1 shows a line labelled *feedback loop*. **Feedback** is the communication flow from receiver back to sender and indicates whether the message was decoded and understood as intended. Chapter 20 reviews approaches called *pretesting* that ensure that advertisements are decoded properly.

Noise

Noise includes extraneous factors that can work against effective communication by distorting a message or the feedback received (Figure 19-1). Noise can be a simple error, such as a printing mistake that affects the meaning of a newspaper advertisement, or using words or pictures that fail to communicate the message clearly. Noise can also occur when a salesperson's message is misunderstood by a prospective buyer, such as when a salesperson's accent, use of slang terms, or communication style make hearing and understanding the message difficult.

CONCEPT CHECK

1. What are the six elements required for communication to occur?

2. A difficulty for Canadian companies advertising in international markets is that the audience does not share the same _____ .

3. A misprint in a newspaper ad is an example of _____ .

THE PROMOTIONAL ELEMENTS

To communicate with consumers, a company can use one or more of four promotional alternatives: advertising, personal selling, sales promotion, and public relations. Figure 19-2 summarizes the distinctions among these four elements. Three of these elements—advertising, sales promotion, and public relations—are often said to use *mass selling* because they are used with groups of prospective buyers. In contrast, personal selling uses *person-to-person interaction* between a seller and a prospective buyer. Personal selling activities include face-to-face, telephone, and interactive electronic communication.

Advertising

Advertising is any paid form of nonpersonal communication about an organization, good, service, or idea by an identified sponsor. The *paid* aspect of this definition is important because the space for the advertising message normally must be bought. An occasional exception is the public service announcement, where the advertising time or space is donated. A full-page, four-colour ad in *Chatelaine*, for example, costs about $30 000, while a full-page, four colour ad in *L'Actualité* costs about $12 000. The nonpersonal component of advertising is also important. Advertising involves mass media (such as TV, radio, and magazines), which are nonpersonal and do not have an immediate feedback loop as does personal selling. So before the message is sent, marketing

PROMOTIONAL ELEMENT	MASS VERSUS PERSON-TO-PERSON	PAYMENT	STRENGTHS	WEAKNESSES
Advertising	Mass	Fees paid for space or time	• Efficient means for reaching large numbers of people	• High absolute costs • Difficult to receive good feedback
Personal selling	Person-to-person	Fees paid to salespeople as either salaries or commissions	• Immediate feedback • Very persuasive • Can select audience • Can give complex information	• Extremely expensive per exposure • Messages may differ between salespeople
Public relations	Mass	No direct payment to media	• Often most credible source in the consumer's mind	• Difficult to get media cooperation
Sales promotion	Mass	Wide range of fees paid, depending on promotion selected	• Effective at changing behaviour in short run • Very flexible	• Easily abused • Can lead to promotion wars • Easily duplicated

FIGURE 19-2   THE PROMOTIONAL MIX

research plays a valuable role; for example, it determines that the message is understood by the target market and that the target market will actually see the medium chosen.

AN ATTENTION-GETTING ADVERTISEMENT.

There are several advantages to a firm using advertising in its promotional mix. It can be attention-getting—as with this Eastpak ad—and also communicate specific product benefits to prospective buyers. By paying for the advertising space, a company can control *what* it wants to say and, to some extent, to *whom* the message is sent. If a stereo company wants college students to receive its message about CD players, advertising space is purchased in a college campus newspaper. Advertising also allows the company to decide *when* to send its message (which includes how often). The nonpersonal aspect of advertising also has its advantages. Once the message is created, the same message is sent to all receivers in a market segment. If the message is properly pretested, the company can trust that the same message will be decoded by all receivers in the market segment.

Advertising has some disadvantages. As shown in Figure 19-2 and discussed in depth in Chapter 20, the costs to produce and place a message are significant, and the lack of direct feedback makes it difficult to know how well the message was received.

Personal Selling

The second major promotional alternative is **personal selling,** defined as the two-way flow of communication between a buyer and seller, designed to influence a person's or group's purchase decision. Unlike advertising, personal selling is usually face-to-face communication between the sender and receiver (although telephone and electronic sales are growing). Why do companies use personal selling?

There are important advantages to personal selling, as summarized in Figure 19-2. A salesperson can control to *whom* the presentation is made. Although some control is available in advertising by choosing the medium, some people may read the college newspaper, for example, who are not in the target audience for CD players. For the CD-player manufacturer, those readers outside the target audience are *wasted coverage.* Wasted coverage can be reduced with personal selling. The personal component of selling has another advantage over advertising in that the seller can see or hear the potential buyer's reaction to the message. If the feedback is unfavourable, the salesperson can modify the message.

The flexibility of personal selling can also be a disadvantage. Different salespeople can change the message so that no consistent communication is given to all customers. The high cost of personal selling is probably its major disadvantage. On a cost-per-contact basis, it is generally the most expensive of the four promotional elements.

Public Relations

Public relations is a form of communication management that seeks to influence the feelings, opinions, or beliefs held by customers, prospective customers, shareholders, suppliers, employees, and other publics about a company and its products or services.[5] Many tools such as special events, lobbying efforts, annual reports, and image management may be used by a public relations department,[6] although publicity often plays the most important role. **Publicity** is a nonpersonal, indirectly paid presentation of an organization, good, or service. It can take the form of a news story, editorial, or product announcement. A difference between publicity and both advertising and personal selling is the "indirectly paid" dimension. With publicity a company does not pay for space in a mass medium (such as television or radio) but attempts to get the medium to run a favourable story on the company. In this sense there is an indirect payment for publicity in that a company must support a public relations staff.

An advantage of publicity is credibility. When you read a favourable story about a company's product (such as a glowing restaurant review), there is a tendency to believe it. Travellers throughout the world have relied on Arthur Frommer's guides such as *Ireland on $25 a Day.* These books outline out-of-the-way, inexpensive restaurants, hotels, inns, and bed-and-breakfast rooms, giving invaluable publicity to these establishments. Such businesses do not (nor can they) buy a mention in the guide, which in recent years has sold millions of copies.

The disadvantages of publicity relate to the lack of the user's control over it. A company can invite a news team to preview its innovative exercise equipment and hope for a favourable mention on the 6 p.m. newscasts. But without buying advertising time, there is no guarantee of any mention of the new equipment or that it will be aired when the target audience is watching. The company representative who calls the station and asks for a replay of the story may be told, "Sorry, it's only news once." With publicity there is little control over what is said, to whom, or when. As a result, publicity is rarely the main component of a promotional campaign.

Sales Promotion

A fourth promotional element is **sales promotion,** a short-term inducement of value offered to arouse interest in buying a good or service. Used in conjunction with advertising or personal selling, sales promotions are offered to intermediaries as well as to ultimate consumers. Coupons, rebates, samples, and sweepstakes are just a few examples of sales promotions discussed later in this chapter.

The advantage of sales promotion is that the short-term nature of these programs (such as a coupon or sweepstakes with an expiration date) often stimulates sales for their duration. Offering value to the consumer in terms of a cents-off coupon or rebate provides an incentive to buy.

Sales promotions cannot be the sole basis for a campaign because gains are often temporary and sales drop off when the deal ends. Advertising support is often needed to convert the customer who tried the product because of a sales promotion into a long-term buyer. If sales promotions are conducted continuously, they lose their effectiveness. Customers begin to delay purchase until a coupon is offered, or they question the product's value. Some aspects of sales promotions also are regulated by the federal government. These issues are reviewed in detail later in this chapter.

CONCEPT CHECK

1. Explain the difference between advertising and publicity when both appear on television.

2. Which promotional element should be offered only on a short-term basis?

3. Cost per contact is high with the _____ element of the promotional mix.

INTEGRATED MARKETING COMMUNICATIONS—DEVELOPING THE PROMOTIONAL MIX

A firm's **promotional mix** is the combination of one or more of the promotional elements it chooses to use. In putting together the promotional mix, a marketer must consider several issues. First, the balance of the elements must be determined. Should advertising be emphasized more than personal selling? Should a promotional rebate be offered? Would public relations activities be effective? Several factors affect such decisions: the target audience for the promotion, the stage of the product's life cycle, characteristics of the product, decision stage of the buyer, and even the channel of distribution. Second, because the various promotional elements are often the responsibility of different departments, coordinating a consistent promotional effort is necessary. A promotional planning process designed to ensure integrated marketing communications can facilitate this goal.

The Target Audience

Promotional programs are directed to the ultimate consumer, to an intermediary (retailer, wholesaler, or industrial distributor), or to both. Promotional programs directed to buyers of consumer products use mass media. Geographical dispersion and the number of potential buyers are the primary reasons for a mass approach. Personal selling is used at the place of purchase, generally the retail store.

Advertising directed to industrial buyers is used selectively in trade publications, such as *Fence* magazine for buyers of fencing material. Because industrial buyers often have specialized needs or technical questions, personal selling is particularly important. The salesperson can provide information and the necessary support after sales.

Intermediaries are often the focus of promotional efforts. As with industrial buyers, personal selling is the major promotional ingredient. The salespeople inform retailers about future advertising campaigns directed at ultimate users, for example, and they assist retailers in making a profit. Intermediaries' questions often pertain to the allowed markup, merchandising support, and return policies, which are best handled by a salesperson.

F I G U R E   1 9 - 3

PROMOTIONAL TOOLS USED OVER
THE PRODUCT LIFE CYCLE OF PURINA
PUPPY CHOW

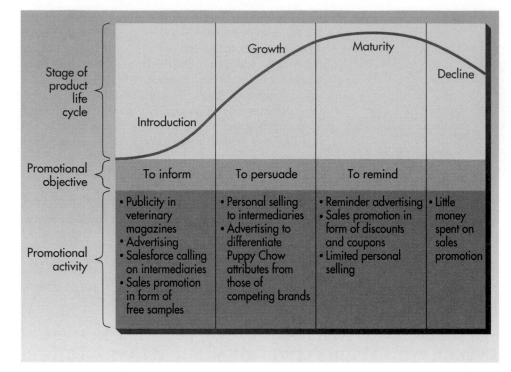

The Product Life Cycle

All products have a product life cycle (see Chapter 12), and the composition of the promotional mix changes over the four life cycle stages, as shown for Purina Puppy Chow in Figure 19-3.

Introduction stage   Informing consumers in an effort to increase their level of awareness is the primary promotional objective in the introduction stage of the product life cycle. In general, all the promotional mix elements are used at this time, although the use of specific mix elements during any stage depends on the product and situation. Stories on Purina's new nutritional food are placed in *Dog World* magazine, trial samples are sent to registered dog owners in 10 major cities, advertisements are placed during reruns of the TV show "Lassie," and the salesforce begins to approach supermarkets to get orders. Advertising is particularly important as a means of reaching as many people as possible to build up awareness and interest. Publicity may even begin slightly before the product is commercially available.

Growth stage   The primary promotional objective of the growth stage is to persuade the consumer to buy the product—Purina Puppy Chow—rather than substitutes, so the marketing manager seeks to gain brand preference and solidify distribution. Sales promotion assumes less importance in this stage, and publicity is not a factor because it depends on novelty of the product. The primary promotional element is advertising, which stresses brand differences. Personal selling is used to solidify the channel of distribution. For consumer products such as dog food, the salesforce calls on the wholesalers and retailers in hopes of increasing inventory levels and gaining shelf space. For industrial products, the salesforce often tries to get contractual arrangements to be the sole source of supply for the buyer.

Maturity stage   In the maturity stage the need is to maintain existing buyers, and advertising's role is to remind buyers of the product's existence. Sales promotion, in the form of discounts and coupons offered to both ultimate consumers and intermedi-

IBM MUST CONSIDER PRODUCT CHARACTERISTICS SUCH AS COMPLEXITY, RISK, AND ANCILLARY SERVICES WHEN DESIGNING ITS PROMOTIONAL MIX.

aries, is important in maintaining loyal buyers. Price cuts and discounts can also significantly increase a mature brand's sales. The salesforce at this stage seeks to satisfy intermediaries. An unsatisfied customer who switches brands is hard to replace.

Decline stage   The decline stage of the product life cycle is usually a period of phaseout for the product, and little money is spent in the promotional mix—especially in sales promotions.

Product Characteristics

The proper blend of elements in the promotional mix also depends on the type of product. Three specific characteristics should be considered: complexity, risk, and ancillary services. *Complexity* refers to the technical sophistication of the product and hence the amount of understanding required to use it. It's hard to provide much information in a one-page magazine ad or 30-second television ad, so the more complex the product, the greater the emphasis on personal selling.

A second element is the degree of *risk* represented by the product's purchase. Risk for the buyer can be assessed in terms of financial risk, social risk, and physical risk. A hair transplant procedure, for example, might represent all three risks—it may be expensive, people can see and evaluate the purchase, and there may be a chance of physical harm. Although advertising helps, the greater the risk, the greater the need for personal selling.

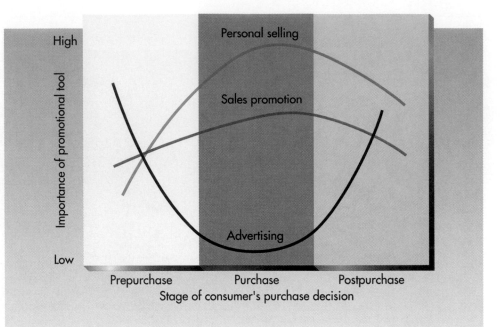

The level of *ancillary services* required by a product also affects the promotional strategy. Ancillary services pertain to the degree of service or support required after the sale. This characteristic is common to many industrial products and consumer purchases. Who will repair your automobile or VCR? Advertising's role is to establish the seller's reputation. However, personal selling is essential to build buyer confidence and provide evidence of customer service.

Stages of the Buying Decision

Knowing the customer's stage of decision making can also affect the promotional mix. Figure 19-4 shows how the importance of the three directly paid promotional elements varies with the three stages in a consumer's purchase decision.

Prepurchase stage   In the prepurchase stage advertising is more helpful than personal selling because advertising informs the potential customer of the existence of the product and the seller. Sales promotion in the form of free samples also can play an important role to gain low-risk trial. When the salesperson calls on the customer after heavy advertising, there is some recognition of what the salesperson represents. This is particularly important in industrial settings in which sampling of the product is usually not possible.

Purchase stage   At the purchase stage the importance of personal selling is highest, whereas the impact of advertising is lowest. Sales promotion in the form of coupons, deals, point-of-purchase displays, and rebates can be very helpful in encouraging demand. In this stage, although advertising is not an active influence on the purchase, it is the means of delivering the coupons, deals, and rebates that are often important.

Postpurchase stage   In the postpurchase stage the salesperson is still important. In fact, the more personal contact after the sale, the more the buyer is satisfied. Advertising is also important to assure the buyer that the right purchase was made. Advertising and personal selling help reduce the buyer's postpurchase anxiety.[7]

Sales promotion in the form of coupons can help encourage repeat purchases from satisfied first-time triers.

Channel Strategies

Chapter 16 discussed the channel flow from producer to intermediaries to consumer. Achieving control of the channel is often difficult for the manufacturer, and promotional strategies can assist in moving a product through the channel of distribution. This is where a manufacturer has to make an important decision about whether to use a push strategy, pull strategy, or both in its channel of distribution.

Push strategy   Figure 19-5A shows how a manufacturer uses a **push strategy,** directing the promotional mix to channel members to gain their cooperation in ordering and stocking the product. In this approach, personal selling and sales promotions play major roles. Salespeople call on wholesalers to encourage orders and provide sales assistance. Sales promotions, such as case discount allowances (20 percent off the regular case price), are offered to stimulate demand. By pushing the product through the channel, the goal is to get channel members to push it to their customers.

Canadian firms such as Pepsi-Cola Canada and Clearly Canadian Beverages spend a significant amount of their marketing resources on maintaining their relationships with their distributors, and through them, with retailers. In general, Canadian consumer goods firms are allocating greater percentages of their promotional budgets toward intermediaries. In some cases, as much as 60 percent of the promotional budget is being allocated to personal selling and sales promotions designed to reach intermediaries, while 40 percent is spent on promotional activities directed toward ultimate consumers.[8]

Pull strategy   In some instances manufacturers face resistance from channel members who do not want to order a new product or increase inventory levels of an existing brand. As shown in Figure 19-5B, a manufacturer may then elect to implement a

MARKETING NEWSNET

PEPSI USES INTEGRATED MARKETING COMMUNICATIONS APPROACH IN HONDURAS

New owners and an aggressive integrated marketing communications campaign has put the pep back into Pepsi in Honduras, doubling market share in less than a year and catching Coca-Cola off-guard. Mariposa Corp. of Guatemala injected new life into the sluggish Pepsi franchise by boosting communications expenditures by 30 percent, making Pepsi the pick of a new generation of Honduran cola drinkers. Daniel Alvarez, Pepsi's marketing manager says marketing is the most important thing in Honduras. People consume what they see, hear, or read about. So Pepsi launched a massive communications campaign with a common theme, "Try Pepsi Today." On television, radio, and in the newspapers—all the time, people are reading, hearing, and seeing "Try Pepsi Today." Billboards and banners from atop of bridges, streets and storefronts in-

vite Hondurans to "Try Pepsi Today." To further heighten Pepsi's image, the company sponsors town fairs and concerts and helps support schools and colleges. Pepsi is also the official sponsor of the country's number-one soccer team. The company has also taken charge of publicity, increased merchandising efforts, and undertaken major sampling programs in the streets. Twenty shiny new trucks painted with the Pepsi logo have also been added to the fleet and are seen daily by consumers as they wind through the narrow streets. And the campaign is working. Market share has shot up 20–30 percent in just nine months. Along with the integrated marketing communications effort, the company has focused on better service to vendors. The company also made an investment in refrigeration. The number of coolers has risen from 800 to 4000—a key move in a sweltering country where most pop is drunk lukewarm.

pull strategy by directing its promotional mix at ultimate consumers to encourage them to ask the retailer for the product. Seeing demand from ultimate consumers, retailers order the product from wholesalers and thus the item is pulled through the intermediaries. Pharmaceutical companies, for example, historically marketed only to doctors. Now they spend millions to advertise prescription drugs directly to consumers. The strategy is designed to encourage consumers to ask their physicians for a specific drug by name—pulling it through the channel. Successful advertising strategies, such as Nicoderm's "Ask your doctor . . ." campaign, can have dramatic effects on the sales of a product.[9]

Integrated Marketing Communications

In the past the promotional elements were regarded as separate functions handled by experts in separate departments. The salesforce designed and managed its activities independently of the advertising department, and sales promotion and public relations were often the responsibility of outside agencies or specialists. The result was often an overall communication effort that was uncoordinated and, in some cases, inconsistent. Moreover, organizations lost opportunities to combine techniques that could have improved the effectiveness of their promotional activities and maximized their finite budgets. Today, the concept of designing marketing communications programs that coordinate all promotional activities—advertising, personal selling, sales promotion, and public relations—to provide a consistent message across all audiences and to maximize the promotional budget is referred to as **integrated marketing communications** (IMC).

The key to developing successful IMC programs is to create a process that facilitates their design and use. A tool used to evaluate a company's current process is the IMC audit. The audit analyzes the internal communication network of the company, identifies key audiences, evaluates customer databases, assesses messages in recent ads, public relations releases, packaging, video news releases, signage, sales promotion pieces, and direct mail and determines managers' knowledge of IMC.[10] While many organizations are interested in improving their IMC process, a recent survey suggests that fewer than one-third have been successful at implementing IMC. The reasons include lack of expertise, lack of budget, and lack of management approval.[11]

Once the IMC process is implemented, most organizations want to assess its benefits. The tendency is to try to determine which element of promotion "works" better. In an integrated program, however, media advertising might be used to build awareness, sales promotion to generate an inquiry, direct mail to provide additional information to individual prospects, and a personal sales call to complete the transaction. The tools are used for different reasons, and their combined use creates a synergy that should be the focus of the assessment.[12] The accompanying Marketing NewsNet box describes Pepsi's successful integrated marketing communications program in Honduras.[13]

CONCEPT CHECK

1. For consumer products, why is advertising emphasized more than personal selling?

2. Explain the differences between a push strategy and a pull strategy.

3. Integrated marketing communications programs provide a _____ message across all audiences.

SALES PROMOTION

The Importance of Sales Promotion

At one time, sales promotion was considered by many to be a supplemental ingredient of the promotional mix. But more recently the use of sales promotion has increased, and so has its perceived importance to marketers. In fact, in Canada, more money is now spent on sales promotion than on advertising.[14]

There are several reasons for the growth in importance of sales promotion. For one, many marketers are looking for measurable results from their promotional efforts. Sales promotion is viewed as an effective tool in this regard. Second, consumers and the trade (e.g., retailers) have become more value-conscious and thus more responsive to sales promotion activities. Third, some suggest that the use of sales promotion has grown because it has become contagious. In short, many marketers are simply responding to the increased use of sales promotion by competitors. Finally, the availability of information technology such as computerized scanning equipment has also served as a stimulus for the growth of sales promotion.

While sales promotion techniques have grown in use and in stature, they are rarely used in isolation or as a stand-alone promotional tool. With the trend toward integrated marketing communications, sales promotion techniques are used more commonly in conjunction with other promotional activities. However, the selection and integration of the many sales promotion techniques requires a good understanding of the relative advantages and disadvantages of each kind of sales promotion.[15]

Consumer-Oriented Sales Promotions

Directed to ultimate consumers, **consumer-oriented sales promotions,** or simply consumer promotions, are sales tools used to support a company's advertising and personal selling efforts. The alternative consumer-oriented sales promotion tools include coupons, deals, premiums, contests, sweepstakes, samples, continuity programs, point-of-purchase displays, rebates, and product placement (see Figure 19-6).

KIND OF SALES PROMOTION	OBJECTIVES	ADVANTAGES	DISADVANTAGES
Coupons	Stimulate demand	Encourage retailer support	Consumers delay purchases
Deals	Increase trial; retaliate against competitor's actions	Reduce consumer risk	Consumers delay purchases; reduce perceived product value
Premiums	Build goodwill	Consumers like free or reduced-price merchandise	Consumers buy for premium, not product
Contests	Increase consumer purchases; build business inventory	Encourage consumer involvement with product	Require creative or analytical thinking
Sweepstakes	Encourage present customers to buy more; minimize brand switching	Get customer to use product and store more often	Sales drop after sweepstakes
Samples	Encourage new product trial	Low risk for consumer	High cost for company
Continuity programs	Encourage repeat purchases	Help create loyalty	High cost for company
Point-of-purchase displays	Increase product trial; provide in-store support for other promotions	Provide good product visibility	Hard to get retailer to allocate high-traffic space
Rebates	Encourage customers to purchase; stop sales decline	Effective at stimulating demand	Easily copied; steal sales from future; reduce perceived product value
Product placement	Introduce new products; demonstrate product use	Positive message in a noncommercial setting	Little control over presentation of product

FIGURE 19-6   SALES PROMOTION ALTERNATIVES

FRIDAY'S ATTRACTS NEW
CUSTOMERS WITH COUPONS.

Coupons   Coupons are typically printed certificates that give the bearer a saving or a stated price reduction when they purchase a specific product. Coupons can be used to stimulate demand for mature products, or promote the early trial of a new brand. In 1997, an estimated 17 billion coupons were distributed in Canada, including direct-to-consumer and retailer-initiated coupons. Consumers redeemed over 268 million of these coupons having an average face value of 68 cents. This means that Canadians saved about $180 million on products as a result of using coupons.[16]

Studies show that when coupons are used, a company's market share does increase during the period immediately after they are distributed.[17] There are indications, however, that couponing can reduce gross revenues by lowering the price paid by already-loyal consumers.[18] Therefore, manufacturers and retailers are particularly interested in coupon programs directed at potential first-time buyers. One means of focusing on these potential buyers is through electronic in-store coupon machines that match coupons to your most recent purchases.[19]

Deals   Deals are short-term price reductions, commonly used to increase trial among potential customers or to retaliate against a competitor's actions. There are two basic types of deals: cents-off deals and price-pack deals. Cents-off deals offer a brand at less than a regular price, and the reduced prices are generally marked directly on the label or package. Cents-off deals can be very effective, even more so than coupons in stimulating short-term sales.

Price-pack deals offer consumers something extra such as "20 percent more for the same price," or "two packages for the price of one." Price-pack deals can be very effective in retaliating against or preempting a competitor's actions. For example, if a rival manufacturer introduces a new cake mix, the company could respond with the price-pack deal (e.g., 2 for 1) building up the stock on the kitchen shelves of cake mix buyers and making the competitor's introduction more difficult. Marketers must be careful, however, from overusing deals. If consumers expect a deal they may delay a purchase until the deal occurs. Moreover, frequent deals may erode the perceived value of the brand to the consumer.

Premiums   Premiums are items offered free or at a significant savings as incentives to buy a product. A premium offered at below its normal price is known as *self-liquidating* because the cost charged to the consumers covers the cost of the item. For example, Burger King, recently offered *Lost World* watches at a nominal price to their customers. Offering premiums at no-cost or at low-cost encourage customers to return frequently or to use more of the product. However, the company must be careful that the consumer doesn't just buy the premium.

Contests   A fourth sales promotion in Figure 19-6, the contest, is where consumers apply their analytical or creative thinking to try to win a prize. Most often a consumer submits an entry to be judged by a panel. Many companies use contests not only to increase consumer purchases, but to obtain the names and addresses of consumers for use in database marketing purposes. Gillette's Cavalcade of Sports 25-week hockey pool contest awarded a $1 million weekly cash prize to each week's winner.

Sweepstakes   A sweepstakes requires participants to submit some kind of entry form but are purely games of chance requiring no analytical or creative effort by the consumer. *Reader's Digest* and Publisher's Clearing House are two of the better-known sweepstakes. Canada has federal and provincial regulations covering sweepstakes, contests, and games regarding fairness, to ensure that the chance of winning is represented honestly and to guarantee that the prizes are awarded.

Samples   Another common consumer sales promotion is sampling, or offering the product free or at a greatly reduced price. Often used for new products, sampling puts the product in the consumer's hands. A trial size is generally offered that is smaller than the regular package size. If the consumers like the sample, it is hoped they will remember and buy the product. Coty Canada launched its Universo fragrance for men with an extensive sampling program in theatres that were running their 30-second commercial about the product.[20] Kimberly-Clark used sampling to promote its UltraTrim diapers. It undertook a personally addressed sample mailing to 235 000 Canadian households using a database of mothers provided by Welcome Wagon. The sampling program was backed by TV advertising developed specifically for the Canadian market, as well as newspaper and magazine ads with coupons.[21] Shoppers Drug Mart of Toronto recently handed out 18 000 samples of Life brand health & beauty products on Toronto Transit Commission buses, while EMI Music Canada is offering customers a free CD sampler featuring new Canadian bands.

Continuity programs   Continuity programs are a sales promotion tool used to encourage and reward repeat purchases by acknowledging each purchase made by a consumer and offering a premium as purchases accumulate. Trading stamps, which were first introduced by supermarkets and gas stations in the 1960s and 1970s, are an example. More recently airlines and hotels have used frequent-flyer and frequent-traveller programs to reward customers. Even GM has a continuity program—a credit card that allows consumers to accumulate up to $3500 in "points" toward the purchase of a new Chevrolet, Pontiac, Oldsmobile, Buick, or Cadillac. Of course, you might be more familiar with Pepsi-Cola Canada's continuity program called "Pepsi-Stuff" where you collect points off especially marked packages of Pepsi products and redeem them for merchandise in the Pepsi-Stuff catalogue.[22]

Point-of-purchase   In a store aisle, you often encounter a sales promotion called a point-of-purchase display. These product displays take the form of advertising signs,

A GRAVITY-FEED BIN THAT DOUBLES AS A POINT-OF-PURCHASE DISPLAY.

which sometimes actually hold or display the product, and are often located in high-traffic areas near the cash register or the end of an aisle. The accompanying picture shows gravity-feed bins that Nabisco uses for its animal crackers; it helps ensure product freshness, provides storage, and captures the consumer's attention as an end-aisle, point-of-purchase display.

Some studies estimate that two-thirds of a consumer's buying decisions are made in the store. This means that grocery product manufacturers want to get their message to you at the instant you are next to their brand in your supermarket aisle—perhaps through a point-of-purchase display. At many supermarkets this may be done through Actmedia's in-store marketing network. Supermarket shopping cart displays, video screens in the aisles, and audio messages remind shoppers about products they might consider buying. The advantage of these methods of promotion is that they do not rely on the consumers' ability to remember the message for long periods of time. Other in-store promotions such as interactive kiosks are also becoming popular.[23]

Rebates   Another consumer sales promotion in Figure 19-6, the cash rebate, offers the return of money based on proof of purchase. This tool has been used heavily by car manufacturers facing increased competition. Turner Home Entertainment offered purchasers of its home video *The Swan Princess,* a $5 rebate through a collaborative agreement, or *tie-in,* with Pillsbury, which printed the offer on 20 million packages.[24] When the rebate is offered on lower-priced items, the time and trouble of mailing in a proof-of-purchase to get the rebate cheque means that many buyers—attracted by the rebate offer—never take advantage of it. However, this "slippage" is less likely to occur with frequent users of rebate promotions.[25]

Product placement   A final consumer promotion, **product placement,** involves the use of a brand-name product in a movie, television show, video, or a commercial for another product. Companies are usually eager to gain exposure for their products, and the studios believe that product placements add authenticity to the film or program. The studios also receive fees—usually $40 000—although merchandise may be offered instead of cash. Ford Explorers appeared in *Jurassic Park* because Ford agreed to supply 10 of the vehicles and sell them at wholesale to the production company members after the filming was completed. How are product placements arranged? Many companies simply send brochures and catalogues to the studio resource departments; others are approached by agents who review scripts to find promising scenes where a product might be used.[26]

Trade-Oriented Sales Promotions

Trade-oriented sales promotions, or simply trade promotions, are sales tools used to support a company's advertising and personal selling directed to wholesalers, retailers, or distributors. Some of the sales promotions just reviewed are used for this purpose, but there are three other common approaches targeted uniquely to these intermediaries: (1) allowances and discounts, (2) cooperative advertising, and (3) training of distributors' salesforces.

Allowances and discounts   Trade promotions often focus on maintaining or increasing inventory levels in the channel of distribution. An effective method for encouraging such increased purchases by intermediaries is the use of allowances and discounts. However, overuse of these "price reductions" can lead to retailers changing their ordering patterns in the expectation of such offerings. Although there are many variations that manufacturers can use with discounts and allowances, three common approaches include the merchandise allowance, the case allowance, and the finance allowance.[27]

Reimbursing a retailer for extra in-store support or special featuring of the brand is a *merchandise allowance.* Performance contracts between the manufacturer and trade member usually specify the activity to be performed, such as a picture of the product in a newspaper with a coupon good at only one store. The merchandise allowance then consists of a percentage deduction from the list case price ordered during the promotional period. Allowances are not paid by the manufacturer until it sees proof of performance (such as a copy of the ad placed by the retailer in the local newspaper).

A second common trade promotion, a *case allowance,* is a discount on each case ordered during a specific time period. These allowances are usually deducted from the invoice. A variation of the case allowance is the "free goods" approach, whereby retailers receive some amount of the product free based on the amount ordered, such as 1 case free for every 10 cases ordered.[28]

A final trade promotion, the *finance allowance,* involves paying retailers for financing costs or financial losses associated with consumer sales promotions. This trade promotion is regularly used and has several variations. One type is the floor stock protection program—manufacturers give retailers a case allowance price for products in their warehouse, which prevents shelf stock from running down during the promotional period. Also common are freight allowances, which compensate retailers that transport orders from the manufacturer's warehouse.

Cooperative advertising   Resellers often perform the important function of promoting the manufacturer's products at the local level. One common sales promotional activity is to encourage both better quality and greater quantity in the local advertising efforts of resellers through **cooperative advertising.** These are programs by which a manufacturer pays a percentage of the retailer's local advertising expense for advertising the manufacturer's products.

Usually the manufacturer pays a percentage, often 50 percent, of the cost of advertising up to a certain dollar limit, which is based on the amount of the purchases the retailer makes of the manufacturer's products. In addition to paying for the advertising, the manufacturer often furnishes the retailer with a selection of different ad executions, sometimes suited for several different media. A manufacturer may provide, for example, several different print layouts as well as a few broadcast ads for the retailer to adapt and use.[29]

Training of distributors' salesforces   One of the many functions the intermediaries perform is customer contact and selling for the producers they represent. Both retailers and wholesalers employ and manage their own sales personnel. A manufacturer's success often rests on the ability of the reseller's salesforce to represent its products.

Thus, it is in the best interest of the manufacturer to help train the reseller's salesforce. Because the reseller's salesforce is often less sophisticated and knowledgeable about the products than the manufacturer might like, training can increase their sales performance. Training activities include producing manuals and brochures to educate the reseller's salesforce. The salesforce then uses these aids in selling situations. Other activities include national sales meetings sponsored by the manufacturer and field visits to the reseller's location to inform and motivate the salesperson to sell the products. Manufacturers also develop incentive and recognition programs to motivate reseller's salespeople to sell their products.

CONCEPT CHECK
1. Which sales promotional tool is most common for new products?
2. What's the difference between a coupon and a deal?
3. Which trade promotion is used on an ongoing basis?

PUBLIC RELATIONS

As noted previously, public relations is a form of communication management that seeks to influence the image of an organization and its products and services. Public relations efforts may utilize a variety of tools and may be directed at many distinct audiences. While public relations personnel usually focus on communicating positive aspects of the business, they may also be called on to minimize the negative impact of a problem or crisis. Intel, for example, had already shipped millions of its Pentium microprocessor chips when it was revealed that the chip had a flaw that caused mathematical errors.[30] Unfortunately, the company initially denied the seriousness of the problem, creating a more difficult situation for the public relations department.

Public Relations Tools

In developing a public relations campaign, several tools and tactics are available to the marketer. The most frequently used public relations tool is publicity which we defined earlier in the chapter as a nonpersonal, indirectly paid presentation of an organization, good, or service. Publicity usually takes the form of a *news release,* consisting of an announcement regarding changes in the company, or the product line.

The objective of a news release is to inform a newspaper, radio station, or other medium of an idea for a story. A study found that more than 40 percent of all free mentions of a brand name occur during news programs.[31] A second common publicity tool is the *news conference.* Representatives of the media are all invited to an informational meeting, and advance materials regarding the content are sent. This tool is often used when negative publicity—as in the cases of the Tylenol poisonings and the Audi 5000 acceleration problem—requires a company response.[32]

Nonprofit organizations rely heavily on publicity to spread their messages. PSAs (*public service announcements*), where free space or time is donated by the media is a common use of publicity for these organizations. The Canadian Red Cross, for example, depends on PSAs on radio and television to announce their needs.

A growing area of public relations involves the creation, or support, and publicizing of *special events* such as company-sponsored seminars, conferences, sports competitions, entertainment events, or other celebrations. The goal of events sponsorship is to create a forum to disseminate company information or to create brand identification to members of

ETHICS AND SOCIAL RESPONSIBILITY ALERT

PUBLIC RELATIONS: WHAT SHOULD WE BELIEVE?

Many organizations realize that most consumers view public relations, particularly news-oriented publicity, as more credible than advertising per se. As such, many organizations have turned to well-managed public relations programs in order to influence the perceptions that relevant publics have toward them or their causes. Many organizations disseminate information that will cast them only in the best possible light or ensure that their view on a particular issue is conveyed to the public. However, there is growing concern that the public relations function is being used to disseminate misinformation, or least, an outrageous distortion of reality. Take, for example, the battle over salmon farming in British Columbia. On one side, op-

ponents of salmon farming are using publicity to suggest that the farmed salmon are raised on artificial hormones and antibodies. They also argue that these mostly-Atlantic salmon are raised in offshore pens and compete with and threaten Pacific salmon species. The BC Salmon Farmers Association is countering with a public and community relations blitz which they feel addresses the misinformation campaigns by its opponents. For now, the BC government has imposed a moratorium on new salmon-farming sites pending an environmental review. For the consumer, it is a question of who to believe.

What are the dangers when organizations with conflicting views on an issue market their positions via public relations activities? What role does the media have in this situation?

the target audience. College sports events such as the CIAU hockey and football championships are sponsored by Coca-Cola and General Motors, while AT&T Canada is the official sponsor of the Calgary Stampede, and the Canadian Senior Golf Championship. Western Union, EMI's Beat Factory, Loblaw's and the Toronto Raptors sponsor Toronto's Caribana Caribbean Music Festival, and Chrysler Canada, Canada Trust and others sponsor the development of the Canadian Trail project.[33]

Another public relations tool is for the organization to engage in *public-service activities* such as establishing or supporting community-based initiatives that benefit the well-being of society. For example, Ciba-Geigy Canada sponsors Health & Welfare Canada's Quit 4 Life Program, which encourages teens to quit smoking.

Finally, the development of *collateral materials* such as annual reports, brochures, newsletters, or video presentations about the company and its products are also basic public relations tools. These materials provide information to target publics and often generate publicity.

Good public relations activities should be planned and made part of an organization's integrated marketing communications effort. However, public relations activities must be used wisely and in an ethical and socially responsible manner (see the accompanying Ethics and Social Responsibility Alert).[34]

INCREASING THE VALUE OF PROMOTION

Today's customers seek value from companies that provide leading-edge products, hassle-free transactions at competitive prices, and customer intimacy.[35] Promotion practices have changed dramatically to improve transactions and increase customer intimacy by (1) emphasizing long-term relationships, and (2) increasing self-regulation.

Building Long-Term Relationships with Promotion

In 1970 manufacturers offered retailers promotional discounts of approximately 4 percent to encourage special purchases of a product; more recently, as managers have been pressured to produce short-term sales increases, the discounts have averaged about 15 percent.

Although this sounds like good news, consumers didn't always receive the discount. The reason: in a practice called *forward buying* supermarkets often purchased more merchandise than they planned to sell during the promotion, only to sell the remaining stock at a regular price later, or the retailer would often "divert" part of the shipment by selling it to a supermarket that had not been offered the manufacturer's discount. In either case, only 30 percent of the discount actually reached the consumer. Over time, retailers began to focus on products offered with discounts, and consumers learned to shop for what was on sale.

In an effort to increase the customer value of trade promotions, consumer goods manufacturers such as P&G are trying to put an end to the discount war. Their first action was to reduce the number of discounts that they offer stores. Second, wholesale prices have been reduced, in some cases by 25 percent. Finally, manufacturers are searching for new promotional activities that may provide more value to consumers.[36] Overall, they hope that these changes will build customer loyalty for the long term—emphasizing a lifetime of purchases rather than a single transaction.

Self-Regulation

Unfortunately, over the years many consumers have been misled—or even deceived—by some promotions. Examples include sweepstakes in which the gifts were not awarded, rebate offers that were a terrible hassle, and advertisements whose promises were great, until the buyer read the small print.

Promotions targeted at special groups such as children and the elderly also raise ethical concerns. For example, providing free samples to children in elementary schools or linking product lines to TV programs and movies have led to questions about the need for greater restrictions on promotional activities. Although there are many federal and provincial rules and regulations governing promotional practices in Canada, some observers believe more government regulation is warranted.

To rely on formal regulation by federal, provincial, and local governments of all promotional activities would be very expensive. As a result, there are increasing efforts by advertising agencies, trade associations, and marketing organizations at *self-regulation.*[37] By imposing standards that reflect the values of society on their promotional activities, marketers can (1) facilitate the development of new promotional methods, (2) minimize regulatory constraints and restrictions, and (3) help consumers gain confidence in the communication efforts used to influence their purchases. As organizations strive for effective self-regulation, marketing executives will need to make sound ethical judgments about the use of existing and new promotional practices.

CONCEPT CHECK   1. What is a news release?
2. What is the difference between government regulation and self-regulation?

SUMMARY

1. Communication is the process of conveying a message to others and requires a source, a message, a channel of communication, a receiver, and the processes of encoding and decoding.
2. For effective communication to occur, the sender and receiver must have a shared field of experience. Feedback from receiver to sender helps determine whether decoding has occurred or noise has distorted the message.
3. The promotional elements consist of advertising, personal selling, sales promotion, and public relations. These tools vary according to whether they are personal; can be identified

with a sponsor; and can be controlled with regard to whom, when, where, and how often the message is sent.
4. In selecting the appropriate promotional mix, marketers must consider the target audience, the stage of the product's life cycle, characteristics of the product, decision stage of the buyer, and the channel of distribution.
5. The target for promotional programs can be the ultimate consumer, an intermediary, or both. Ultimate consumer programs rely more on advertising, whereas personal selling is more important in reaching industrial buyers and intermediaries.

6. The emphasis on the promotional tools varies with a product's life cycle. In introduction, awareness is important. During growth, creating brand preference is essential. Advertising is more important in the former stage and personal selling in the latter. Sales promotion helps maintain buyers in the maturity stage.

7. The appropriate promotional mix depends on the complexity of the product, the degree of risk associated with its purchase, and the need for ancillary services.

8. In the prepurchase stage of a customer's purchase decision advertising is emphasized; at the purchase stage personal selling is most important; and during the postpurchase stage advertising, personal selling, and sales promotion are used to reduce postpurchase anxiety.

9. When a push strategy is used, personal selling and sales promotions directed to intermediaries play major roles. In a pull strategy, advertising and sales promotions directed to ultimate consumers are important.

10. Integrated marketing communications programs coordinate all promotional activities to provide a consistent message across all audiences and to maximize the promotional budget.

11. More money is spent on sales promotion than on advertising. Selecting sales promotions requires a good understanding of the advantages and disadvantages of each option.

12. There is a wide range of consumer-oriented sales promotions: coupons, deals, premiums, contests, sweepstakes, samples, continuity programs, point-of-purchase displays, rebates, and product placements.

13. Trade-oriented promotions consist of allowances and discounts, cooperative advertising, and training of distributors' salesforces. These are used at all levels of the channel.

14. The most frequently used public relations tool is publicity— a nonpersonal, indirectly paid presentation of an organization, good, or service conducted through news releases, news conferences, or public service announcements.

15. Efforts to improve the value of promotion include emphasizing long-term relationships and increasing self-regulation.

KEY TERMS AND CONCEPTS

communication p. 452
source p. 452
message p. 452
channel of communication p. 452
receivers p. 452
encoding p. 453
decoding p. 453
field of experience p. 453
feedback p. 454
noise p. 454
advertising p. 454
personal selling p. 455

public relations p. 456
publicity p. 456
sales promotion p. 456
promotional mix p. 457
push strategy p. 461
pull strategy p. 462
integrated marketing communications p. 462
consumer-oriented sales promotions p. 463
product placement p. 466
trade-oriented sales promotions p. 467
cooperative advertising p. 467

CHAPTER PROBLEMS AND APPLICATIONS

1. After listening to a recent sales presentation, Mary Smith signed up for membership at the local health club. On arriving at the facility, she learned there was an additional fee for racquetball court rentals. "I don't remember that in the sales talk; I thought they said all facilities were included with the membership fee," complained Mary. Describe the problem in terms of the communication process.

2. Develop a matrix to compare the four elements of the promotional mix on three criteria—to *whom* you deliver the message, *what* you say, and *when* you say it.

3. Explain how the promotional tools used by an airline would differ if the target audience were (*a*) consumers who travel for pleasure and (*b*) corporate travel departments that select the airlines to be used by company employees.

4. Suppose you introduced a new consumer food product and invested heavily both in national advertising (pull strategy) and in training and motivating your field salesforce to sell the product to food stores (push strategy). What kinds of feedback would you receive from both the advertising and your salesforce? How could you increase both the quality and quantity of each?

5. Fisher-Price Company, long known as a manufacturer of children's toys, has introduced a line of clothing for children. Outline a promotional plan to get this product introduced in the marketplace.

6. Many insurance companies sell health insurance plans to companies. In these companies the employees pick the plan, but the set of offered plans is determined by the company. Recently Blue Cross–Blue Shield, a health insurance company, ran a television ad stating, "If your employer doesn't offer you Blue Cross–Blue Shield coverage, ask why." Explain the promotional strategy behind the advertisement.

7. Identify the sales promotion tools that might be useful for (*a*) Tastee Yogourt—a new brand introduction, (*b*) 3M self-sticking Post-it notes, and (*c*) Wrigley's Spearmint Gum.

8. Design an integrated marketing communications program—using each of the four promotional elements—for Music Boulevard, an on-line music store.

9. The Toronto Raptors basketball team has asked you to advise them as to which consumer-oriented sales promotion techniques could be best to improve home game attendance. What will you tell them?

10. Describe a self-regulation guideline you believe would improve the value of (*a*) an existing form of promotion and (*b*) a new promotional practice.

CASE 19-1   Vitality Health Food Store

Vitality Health Food Store will open for business in the fall of 1998. It will be an independently owned retail store run by John Carter, a university graduate with a degree in business. It will be located in a strip mall in a growing, upscale suburban neighbourhood. Carter decided to open the business because of his interest in health food and because of the impressive sales growth that has occurred in the sector over the past decade (9 percent annually). Vitality has no other specialty health food stores to compete within its trade area. However, many supermarkets in the area do offer some health food sections in their stores in response to consumer demand for health food.

Carter has projected sales of $500 000 for his first year of business, which is about average for a store of this type and size. His basic marketing strategy is to penetrate the market by positioning the store as the one-stop shop for the consumers' health food needs. Customer service, convenience, and variety will be integral elements of the marketing strategy. Carter and all employees will be knowledgeable, friendly, and are committed to the concept of "relationship marketing."

Carter conducted some research on the health food shopper. He has determined that his primary (potential) customer will have the profile outlined in Exhibit 1. He selected his location given the numbers of potential customers living within close proximity to the store who fit the profile. But Carter realizes that customers must be made aware of the store, be persuaded to visit and make purchases. Moreover, those customers must be reminded to return and encouraged to become regular shoppers. He strongly believes that the promotional element of the marketing mix will play a major role in the success of the business. Accordingly, he has allocated about $25 000 for promotion activities, excluding the costs of retail sales personnel. However, he still has to determine how to spend this money.

Questions

1. Using Figure 19-4 as a guide, outline the appropriate promotional mix for Vitality Health Food Store for each of the three stages in the consumer's purchase decision.

2. What specific sales promotion activities would you recommend for the store? Why?

3. What specific public relations activities would you recommend for the store? Why?

EXHIBIT 1

PROFILE OF POTENTIAL SHOPPER

CATEGORY	CHARACTERISTICS
Demographics	Female, aged 25–49, college educated, working in professional occupations, earning over $30 000 per year
Lifestyle	Health and fitness oriented, environmentally conscious, and concerned about preservatives and additives in food
Benefits sought	Wants high-quality, safe, and healthy food, product variety, and knowledgeable and helpful retail staff.
Media habits	Most likely to read consumer magazines, the Sunday edition of the newspaper, listen to FM radio, and watch late-night television

Headlines
Television
Results
Standings
Events
Teams
History
Sites/Venues
Tickets
Official Site

1997 Canada GAMES

Brought to you in part by:

Everything We Do Is Built Around You

Parade of athletes ends 1997 Canada Games

The torch is off to Cornerbrook

The competitions are finished and the athletes have gone their separate ways. Two weeks ago, all of Canada gathered in Brandon, Manitoba to give their best shot. Now all that remains are the memories of some great accomplishments.

There was Nova Scotia's dominance in the canoeing competitions and Manitoba's Sara Alroubaie exciting the hometown fans with multiple medals in the pool. The team competitions belonged to British Columbia as they won gold in rugby, field hockey, men's and women's basketball, women's soccer and women's softball. In the diving pool, it was Quebec that led the way. On the track, Ontario's Troy Dos Santos made everyone stand up and take notice that he will be heard from again.

The final medal standings showed Ontario on top with 64 gold and 154 medals overall. Quebec finished up second with 46 gold and 126 medals, while British Columbia ended the Games with 31 gold and a total of 99 medals. The Centennial Cup was awarded to Alberta for showing the most improvement over their showing in the 1993 Canada Games.

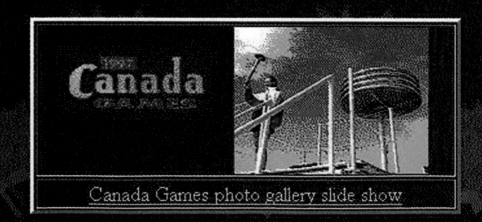
Canada Games photo gallery slide show

TSN had over 54 hours of live coverage of the Games from Brandon.

Canada Games Facts

Each province has now hosted at least one Games.

CHAPTER 20

Advertising

AFTER READING THIS CHAPTER YOU SHOULD BE ABLE TO:

• Explain the differences between product advertising and institutional advertising and the variations within each type.

• Understand the steps used to develop, execute, and evaluate an advertising program.

• Understand alternative ways to set an advertising budget.

• Explain the advantages and disadvantages of alternative advertising media.

WHO IS ADVERTISING IN CYBERSPACE? WHO ISN'T?

For thousands of businesses, the past year has been a race to advertise their products and services in cyberspace—the network of World Wide Web sites on the Internet. From virtually nothing only a few years ago, experts now predict that "on-line advertising" expenditures will run into millions of dollars.[1] It seems like everyone is advertising on-line including Pizza Hut, IBM Canada, Cantel, CompuSmart, Magnotta Winery Corporation, and Nestlé Canada Ltd., to name a few.[2]

How does it work? Generally, businesses start by creating a web site, or web page, that contains information in text, audio, and graphical form. Consumers can often view the products, and make purchases by credit card. Thousands of Canadian businesses have established web sites for advertising purposes.

Many firms with web sites also advertise on other sites. For example, TSN's popular web site—www.tsn.ca—allows advertisers or sponsors to appear on its web pages. When sports fans access www.tsn.ca they will find advertisers on the site. ESPN also provides space for advertisers on their SportsZone web site (www.espnet.sportszone.com). Many other web sites and on-line service providers such as Yahoo Canada also sell advertising space.

To direct consumers to a particular web site, businesses are developing customized software packages called web browsers. Volkswagen, for example, will soon place discs with customized software in the glove compartments of its new cars. In addition to facilitating purchases, encouraging use of a web site provides direct contact with customers, creates an opportunity for relationship marketing, and improves customer service.

What does the future hold? A recent survey of Canada's biggest food and beverage processors found that almost one-quarter of them were currently using the Internet for marketing and advertising purposes, and another 7 percent said they plan to be on the Internet within a year. And, they will find consumers in cyberspace since research shows that 20 percent of Canadians access the Internet regularly. In the words of one marketing expert, "To not be on the Internet in the 90s is going to be like not having a phone."[3]

On-line advertising is one example of the many exciting changes taking place in the field of advertising today. Chapter 19 described **advertising** as any *paid* form of *nonpersonal* communication about an organization, good, service, or idea, by an identified sponsor. This chapter describes alternative types of advertisements, the advertising decision process, and other important changes in advertising.

TYPES OF ADVERTISEMENTS

As you look through any magazine, watch television, listen to the radio, or browse on the web, the variety of advertisements you see or hear may give you the impression that they have few similarities. Advertisements are prepared for different purposes, but they basically consist of two types: product and institutional.

Product Advertisements

Focused on selling a good or service, **product advertisements** take three forms: (1) pioneering (or informational), (2) competitive (or persuasive), and (3) reminder. Look at the ads by AT&T, Corel, and Godiva, and determine the type and objective of each ad.

Used in the introductory stage of the life cycle, *pioneering* advertisements tell people what a product is, what it can do, and where it can be found. The key objective of a pioneering ad (such as that for the AT&T wireless wrist telephone) is to inform the target market. Informative ads have been found to be interesting, convincing, and effective.[4]

ADVERTISEMENTS SERVE VARYING PURPOSES. WHICH AD WOULD BE CONSIDERED (1) PIONEERING, WHICH IS (2) COMPETITIVE, AND WHICH IS USED AS A (3) REMINDER?

Advertising that promotes a specific brand's features and benefits is *competitive.* The objective of these messages is to persuade the target market to select the firm's brand rather than that of a competitor. An increasingly common form of competitive advertising is *comparative* advertising, which shows one brand's strengths relative to those of competitors.[5] The Corel ad, for example, highlights the competitive advantage of CorelFlow 3 over its primary competitor, Visio 4. Firms such as P&G, which began

DIAL SOAP USES REINFORCEMENT
ADS TO ENCOURAGE CONSUMERS
TO KEEP USING THE PRODUCT.

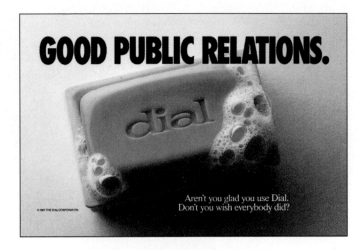

using comparative ads for the first time in 1993, are attracted by studies showing that comparative ads attract more attention and increase the perceived quality of the advertiser's brand.[6] But firms that use comparative advertising need market research and test results to provide legal support for their claims.[7]

Reminder advertising is used to reinforce previous knowledge of a product. The Godiva ad shown reminds consumers about the association between its product and a special event—in this case, your birthday. Reminder advertising is good for products that have achieved a well-recognized position and are in the mature phase of their product life cycle. Another type of reminder ad, *reinforcement,* is used to assure current users they made the right choice. One example: "Aren't you glad you use Dial? Don't you wish everybody did?"

Institutional Advertisements

The objective of **institutional advertisements** is to build goodwill or an image for an organization, rather than promote a specific good or service. Institutional advertising has been used by companies to build confidence in the company name.[8] Often this form of advertising is used to support the public relations plan or counter adverse publicity. Four alternative forms of institutional advertisements are often used:

1. *Advocacy* advertisements state the position of a company on an issue. Molson places ads encouraging the responsible use of alcohol, as shown on the next page.
2. *Pioneering institutional* advertisements, like the pioneering ads for products discussed earlier, are used for announcement about what a company is, what it can do, or where it is located. Recent Bayer ads stating "We cure more headaches than you think" are intended to inform consumers that the company produces many products in addition to aspirin.
3. *Competitive institutional* advertisements promote the advantages of one product class over another and are used in markets where different product classes compete for the same buyers. The Steel Alliance, for example, made up of major North American steel producers, including Stelco, Dofasco, and Ipsco, are spending $100 million on a TV and print campaign promoting steel's many uses.
4. *Reminder institutional* advertisements, like the product form, simply bring the company's name to the attention of the target market again.

AN ADVOCACY ADVERTISEMENT
ABOUT THE RESPONSIBLE USE OF
ALCOHOL BY MOLSON.

"Planning every run
is the mark of a good skier,
even the run home. So think ahead,
and don't drink and drive."

Brian Stemmle
NATIONAL SKI TEAM MEMBER

Take Care.
MOLSON Ⓜ

CONCEPT CHECK   1. What is the difference between pioneering and competitive ads?

2. What is the purpose of an institutional advertisement?

DEVELOPING THE ADVERTISING PROGRAM

Because media costs are high, advertising decisions must be made carefully, using a systematic approach. Paralleling the planning, implementation, and control steps described in the strategic marketing process (Chapter 2), the advertising decision process is divided into (1) developing, (2) executing, and (3) evaluating the advertising program (Figure 20-1). Development of the advertising program focuses on the four *W*s:

- *Who* is the target audience?
- *What* are (1) the advertising objectives, (2) the amounts of money that can be budgeted for the advertising program, and (3) the kinds of copy to use?
- *Where* should the advertisements be run?
- *When* should the advertisements be run?

FIGURE 20-1

THE ADVERTISING DECISION PROCESS

Identifying the Target Audience

The first decision in developing the advertising program is identifying the *target audience,* the group of prospective buyers toward which an advertising program is directed. To the extent that time and money permit, the target audience for the advertising program is the target market for the firm's product, which is identified from marketing research and market segmentation studies. The more a firm knows about its target audience's profile—including their lifestyle, attitudes, and values—the easier it is to develop an advertising program. If a firm wanted to reach you with its ads, it would need to know what TV shows you watch and what magazines you read.

Specifying Advertising Objectives

After the target audience is identified, a decision must be reached on what the advertising should accomplish. Consumers can be said to respond in terms of a **hierarchy of effects,** which is the sequence of stages a prospective buyer goes through from initial awareness of a product to eventual action (either trial or adoption of the product).[9]

- *Awareness.* The consumer's ability to recognize and remember the product or brand name.
- *Interest.* An increase in the consumer's desire to learn about some of the features of the product or brand.
- *Evaluation.* The consumer's appraisal of the product or brand on important attributes.
- *Trial.* The consumer's actual first purchase and use of the product or brand.
- *Adoption.* Through a favourable experience on the first trial, the consumer's repeated purchase and use of the product or brand.

For a totally new product the sequence applies to the entire product category, but for a new brand competing in an established product category it applies to the brand itself. These steps can serve as guidelines for developing advertising objectives.

Although sometimes an objective for an advertising program involves several steps in the hierarchy of effects, it often focuses on a single stage. Regardless of what the specific objective might be, from building awareness to increasing repeat purchases,[10] advertising objectives should possess three important qualities. They should (1) be designed for a well-defined target audience, (2) be measurable, and (3) cover a specified time period.

Setting the Advertising Budget

Advertising costs money and sometimes companies spend enormous amounts of it to reach their customers. Global advertising expenditures are estimated at over $437 billion (US) in 1998. In Canada, advertising expenditures are estimated at $12 billion.[11] Some of the top advertisers in Canada include Procter & Gamble, General Motors of Canada, Unilever, and the Royal Bank. But many other firms, large and small make an investment in advertising. Determining the ideal amount for the ad budget is difficult because there is no precise way to measure the exact results of spending advertising dollars. However, there are several methods used to set the advertising budget.[12]

Percentage of sales   In the **percentage of sales budgeting** approach, funds are allocated to advertising as a percentage of past or anticipated sales, in terms of either dollars or units sold. A common budgeting method,[13] this approach is often stated in terms such as, "Our ad budget for this year is 3 percent of last year's gross sales." The advantage of this approach is obvious: it's simple and provides a financial safeguard by tying the advertising budget to sales. However, there is a major fallacy in this approach, which implies that sales cause advertising. Using this method, a company may reduce its advertising budget because of a downturn in past sales or an anticipated downturn in future sales—situations where it may need advertising the most.

Competitive parity   A second common approach, **competitive parity budgeting,** is matching the competitor's absolute level of spending or the proportion per point of market share. This approach has also been referred to as *matching competitors* or *share of market*. It is important to consider the competition in budgeting.[14] Consumer responses to ads are affected by competing ads, so if a competitor runs 30 radio ads each week, it may be difficult for a firm to get its message across with only five messages.[15] The competitor's budget level, however, should not be the only determinant in setting a company's budget. The competition might have very different advertising objectives, which require a different level of advertising expenditures.

All you can afford   Common to many small businesses is **all you can afford budgeting,** in which money is allocated to advertising only after all other budget items are covered. As one company executive said in reference to this budgeting process, "Why, it's simple. First, I go upstairs to the controller and ask how much they can afford to give us this year. He says a million and a half. Later, the boss comes to me and asks how much we should spend, and I say 'Oh, about a million and a half.' Then we have our advertising appropriation."[16]

Fiscally conservative, this approach has little else to offer. Using this budgeting philosophy, a company acts as though it doesn't know anything about an advertising–sales relationship or what its advertising objectives are.

Objective and task   The best approach to budgeting is **objective and task budgeting,** whereby the company (1) determines its advertising objectives, (2) outlines the tasks to accomplish these objectives, and (3) determines the advertising cost of performing these tasks.[17]

This method takes into account what the company wants to accomplish and requires that the objectives be specified.[18] Strengths of the other budgeting methods are integrated into this approach because each previous method's strength is tied to the objectives. For example, if the costs are beyond what the company can afford, ob-

FIGURE 20-2

THE OBJECTIVE AND TASK APPROACH

OBJECTIVE

To increase awareness among college students for a new CD player. Awareness at the end of one semester should be 20 percent of all students from the existing 0 percent today.

TASKS	COSTS
Advertisements once a week for a semester in 500 college papers	$280 000
Advertisements weekly for a semester on the nationally syndicated "Rockline" radio show	25 000
Three monthly, full-page ads in *Audio* magazine	9 000
Total Budget	$314 000

jectives are reworked and the tasks revised. The difficulty with this method is the judgment required to determine the tasks needed to accomplish objectives. Would two or four insertions in *MacLean's* magazine be needed to achieve a specific awareness level? Figure 20-2 shows a sample media plan with objectives, tasks, and budget outlined. The total amount to be budgeted is $314 000. If the company can only afford $200 000, the objectives must be reworked, tasks redefined, and the total budget recalculated.

Designing the Advertisement

The central element of an advertising program is the ad itself. Advertising messages consist of advertising copy and the artwork (including audio) that the target audience is intended to see (as in magazines, newspapers, and TV) or hear (as on radio and TV). The message usually focuses on the key benefits of the product that are important to a prospective buyer in making trial and adoption decisions.

Message content   Most advertising messages are made up of both informational and persuasional elements. These two elements, in fact, are so intertwined that it is sometimes difficult to tell them apart. For example, basic information contained in many ads such as the product name, benefits, features, and price are presented in a way that tries to attract attention and encourage purchase. On the other hand, even the most persuasive advertisements have to contain at least some basic information to be successful.

Information and persuasive content can be combined in the form of an appeal to provide a basic reason for the consumer to act. Although the marketer can use many different types of appeals, common advertising appeals include fear appeals, sex appeals, and humorous appeals.

Fear appeals suggest to the consumer that he or she can avoid some negative experience through the purchase and use of a product or through a change in behaviour. Insurance companies often try to show the negative effects of premature death on the relatives of those who don't carry enough life or mortgage insurance. Food producers encourage the purchase of low-fat, high-fiber products as a means of reducing cholesterol levels and the possibility of a heart attack.[19] When using fear appeals, the advertiser must be sure that the appeal is strong enough to get the audience's attention and concern, but not so strong that it will lead them to "tune out" the message. The accompanying Marketing NewsNet suggests some guidelines for developing an ad with a fear appeal.[20]

MARKETING NEWSNET

DESIGNING ADS THAT DEAL WITH NEGATIVE ISSUES

Have you ever developed anxiety over a message you've received from an advertisement? If your answer is yes, chances are that your reaction was the result of what advertisers call a *fear appeal*. Examples you may be familiar with include fire or smoke detector ads that depict a family home burning, political candidate endorsements that warn against the rise of other unpopular ideologies, or social cause ads warning of the serious consequences of drug use, alcoholism, or AIDS. This approach is based on three steps—the creation of a fearful situation by giving the audience information about the severity of the threat and the probability of its occurrence, describing the effectiveness of a solution or coping response, and suggesting how the solution can be implemented.

How individuals react to fear appeals, though, varies significantly with their prior knowledge and experience. Indeed, the varying levels of anxiety that result from the ads suggest several ethical concerns for the psychological well-being of consumers. Therefore, advertisers need to consider four guidelines when developing their ads:

1. Whenever possible, use low or moderate (rather than high) levels of fear.
2. Offer more than one alternative as a solution.
3. Avoid deceptive implications (e.g., that a product will completely eliminate a fearful condition).
4. Pretest each ad to ensure a balance between the message and the associated level of anxiety.

In contrast, *sex appeals* suggest to the audience that the product will increase the attractiveness of the user. Sex appeals can be found in almost any product category, from automobiles to toothpaste. The accompanying Ethics and Social Responsibility Alert discusses the use of sex appeals in clothing ads.[21] Unfortunately, many commercials that use sex appeals are only successful at gaining the attention of the audience; they have little impact on how consumers think, feel, or act. Some advertising experts even argue that such appeals get in the way of successful communication by distracting the audience from the purpose of the ad.

Humorous appeals imply either directly or more subtly that the product is more fun or exciting than competitors' offerings. As with fear and sex appeals, the use of humour is widespread in advertising and can be found in many product categories. Unfortunately for the advertiser, humour tends to wear out quickly, thus boring the consumer. Eveready ads, featuring the Energizer battery bunny, frequently change to avoid this advertising "wearout." Another problem with humorous appeals is that their effectiveness may vary across cultures if used in a global campaign.[22]

Creating the actual message   The "creative people" in an advertising agency—copywriters and art directors—have the responsibility to turn appeals and features such as quality, style, dependability, economy, and service into attention-getting, believable advertisements.

Advertising agency DDB Needham Worldwide was recently designated as *Advertising Age* magazine's advertising Agency of the Year for infiltrating "the consumers' vernacular with its ad copy." Robert Scarpelli, the agency's creative director, says, "We try to do advertising that gets into the language, is remembered, and talked about." An example of DDB Needham's approach is the television campaign for Frito-Lay's Rold Gold pretzels. In the commercials, "Seinfeld's" Jason Alexander fantasizes about all the feats he can accomplish while eating the fat-free pretzels. Not only has "Prove it, Pretzel Boy" become part of the consumers' lexicon, the product's market share has increased from 11 percent to 25 percent! Other successful campaigns with memorable taglines include Lotto ads that proclaim, "Hey, you never know," and Bud Light ads, in which "everyman" falsifies his identity to get a Bud Light by claiming, "Yes, I am."[23]

ETHICS AND SOCIAL RESPONSIBILITY ALERT

THE USE OF SEX APPEALS

Over the years, many companies have used sex appeals in their advertising programs. Calvin Klein, for example, has built a reputation for this type of campaign. The use of sex appeals can be seen in everything from cosmetics to automobiles and banking to airline travel. Firms believe the appeals attract attention. However, some question whether or not the practice has gone too far. Some critics suggest that the do-anything-to-get-noticed mentality cul-minated in the recent Molson Dry "Lesbian Kiss" TV spot. The spot was pitched at young heterosexual males by offering up a fantasy akin to an X-rated movie. Others suggest that Labatt also may have pushed the envelope too far with its use of Iggy Pop's "Lust for Life" song in its Labatt's Blue commercials.

Why are ad campaigns that use sex appeals often so controversial? What is your opinion about the use of sex appeals?

DDB Needham's use of television actor Jason Alexander is an example of a very popular form of advertising today—the use of a celebrity spokesperson. In homes across Canada, sports heros, rock stars, and movie stars are talking directly to consumers through ads in all of today's many media options. Advertisers who use a celebrity spokesperson believe that the ads are more likely to influence sales. A campaign may also encourage consumers to associate a product with a celebrity.[24]

A CREATIVE ADVERTISEMENT WITH A CATCHY PHRASE ("PROVE IT, PRETZEL BOY!") FOR ROLD GOLD PRETZELS.

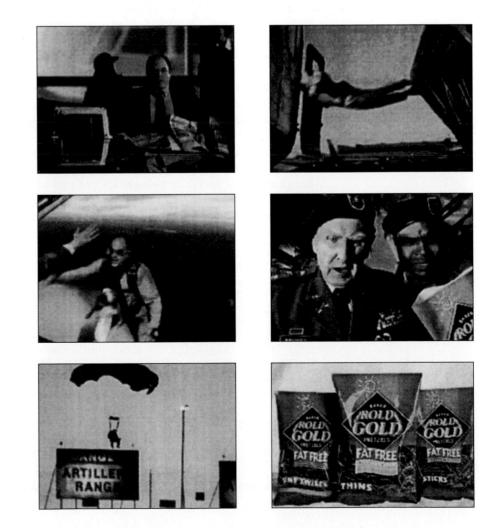

Translating the copywriter's ideas into an actual advertisement is a complex process. Designing quality artwork, layout, and production for the advertisements is costly and time-consuming. High-quality TV commercials typically cost over $200 000 to produce a 30-second ad. High-visibility commercials can be even more expensive: two 15-second Rolaids commercials involved $500 000 and 75 people over a six-month period. About 70 "takes" are necessary, and typical, to get things "right."[25]

CONCEPT CHECK

1. What are characteristics of good advertising objectives?

2. What is the weakness of the percentage of sales budgeting approach?

Selecting the Right Media

Every advertiser must decide where to place its advertisements. The alternatives are the *advertising media,* the means by which the message is communicated to the target audience. Newspapers, magazines, radio, and TV are examples of advertising media. This "media selection" decision is related to the target audience, type of product, nature of the message, campaign objectives, available budget, and the costs of the alternative media.

Choosing a medium and a vehicle within that medium   In deciding where to place advertisements, a company has several media to choose from and a number of alternatives, or vehicles, within each medium. Often advertisers use a mix of media forms and vehicles to maximize the exposure of the message to the target audience while at the same time minimizing costs. These two conflicting goals of (1) maximizing exposure and (2) minimizing costs are of central importance to media planning.

Basic terms   Media buyers speak a language of their own, so every advertiser involved in selecting the right media for their campaigns must be familiar with some common terms used in the advertising industry. Figure 20-3 shows the most common terms used in media decisions.

Because advertisers try to maximize the number of individuals in the target market exposed to the message, they must be concerned with reach. **Reach** is the number of different people or households exposed to an advertisement. The exact definition of reach sometimes varies among alternative media. Newspapers often use reach to describe their total circulation or the number of different households that buy the paper. Television and radio stations, in contrast, describe their reach using the

---

FIGURE 20-3

THE LANGUAGE OF THE MEDIA BUYER

TERM	WHAT IT MEANS
Reach	The number of different people or households exposed to an advertisement.
Rating	The percentage of households in a market that are tuned to a particular TV show or radio station.
Frequency	The average number of times an individual is exposed to an advertisement.
Gross rating points (GRPs)	Reach (expressed as a percentage of the total market) multiplied by frequency.
Cost per thousand (CPM)	The cost of advertising divided by the number of thousands of individuals or households who are exposed.

term **rating**—the percentage of households in a market that are tuned to a particular TV show or radio station. In general, advertisers try to maximize reach in their target market at the lowest cost.

Although reach is important, advertisers are also interested in exposing their target audience to a message more than once. This is because consumers often do not pay close attention to advertising messages, some of which contain large amounts of relatively complex information. When advertisers want to reach the same audience more than once, they are concerned with **frequency,** the average number of times a person in the target audience is exposed to a message or advertisement. Like reach, greater frequency is generally viewed as desirable.[26]

When reach (expressed as a percentage of the total market) is multiplied by frequency, an advertiser will obtain a commonly used reference number called **gross rating points** (GRPs). To obtain the appropriate number of GRPs to achieve an advertising campaign's objectives, the media planner must balance reach and frequency. The balance will also be influenced by cost. **Cost per thousand** (CPM) refers to the cost of reaching 1000 individuals or households with the advertising message in a given medium (*M* is the Roman numeral for 1000).

Different Media Alternatives

Figure 20-4 summarizes the advantages and disadvantages of the important advertising media, which are described in more detail below.

FIGURE 20-4

ADVANTAGES AND DISADVANTAGES OF MAJOR ADVERTISING MEDIA

MEDIUM	ADVANTAGES	DISADVANTAGES
Television	Reaches extremely large audience; uses picture, print, sound, and motion for effect; can target specific audiences.	High cost to prepare and run ads; short exposure time and perishable message; difficult to convey complex information.
Radio	Low cost; can target specific audiences; ads can be placed quickly; can use sound, humour, and intimacy effectively.	No visual excitement; short exposure time and perishable message; difficult to convey complex information.
Magazines	Can target specific audiences; high-quality colour; long life of ad; ads can be clipped and saved; can convey complex information.	Long time needed to place ad; limited control of ad position; relatively high cost; competes for attention with other magazine features.
Newspapers	Excellent coverage of local markets; ads can be placed and changed quickly; ads can be saved; quick consumer response; low cost.	Ads compete for attention with other newspaper features; can't control ad position on page; short life span; can't target specific audiences.
Direct mail	Best for targeting specific audiences; very flexible (3-D, pop-up ads); ad can be saved; measurable.	Relatively high cost; audience often sees it as "junk mail"; no competition with editorial matter.
Outdoor	Low cost; local market focus; high visibility; opportunity for repeat exposures.	Message must be short and simple; low selectivity of audience; criticized as a traffic hazard, eyesore.

Sources: William F. Arens, *Contemporary Advertising,* 6th ed. (Homewood, Ill.: Richard D. Irwin, 1996), p. 241; and William G. Nickels, James M. McHugh, and Susan M. McHugh, *Understanding Business,* 4th ed. (Homewood, Ill.: Richard D. Irwin, 1996), p. 495.

TV STORYBOARDS LEAD TO COMMERCIALS, WHICH COMMUNICATE WITH SIGHT, SOUND, AND MOTION.

Television   Television is a valuable medium because it communicates with sight, sound, and motion. Print advertisements alone could never give you the sense of a sports car cornering at high speed or communicate Ford's excitement about its new Probe. In addition, network television is the only medium that can reach 99 percent of the homes in Canada.[27]

Television's major disadvantage is cost: the average price of a prime-time 30-second spot on a Canadian national network can cost $30 000.[28] Because of these high charges, many advertisers have reduced the length of their commercials from 30 seconds to 15 seconds. This practice, referred to as *splitting 30s,* reduces costs but severely restricts the amount of information and emotion that can be conveyed. Research indicates, however, that two different versions of a 15-second commercial, run back-to-back, will increase recall over long intervals.[29]

Another problem with television is the likelihood of *wasted coverage*—having people outside the market for the product see the advertisement. In recent years the cost and wasted coverage problems of TV have been reduced through the introduction of cable TV. Advertising time is often less expensive on cable channels than on the major networks. In addition, there are currently many cable channels—such as TSN, Much Music, and CNN—that reach very narrowly defined audiences.[30]

A relatively new, and increasingly popular, form of television advertising is the infomercial. **Infomercials** are program-length (30-minute) advertisements that take an educational approach to communication with potential customers. Volvo, Club Med, General Motors, Saturn, Mattel, Revlon, Texaco, and many other companies are using infomercials as a means of providing information that is relevant, useful, and entertaining to prospective customers.[31]

Radio   There are approximately 700 radio stations in Canada.[32] The major advantage of radio is that it is a segmented medium. There are jazz stations, classic music stations, all-talk shows, and hard rock stations, all listened to by different market segments. The average university or college student is a surprisingly heavy radio listener and spends more time during the day listening to radio than watching network television—2.2 hours versus 1.6 hours. Thus, advertisers with university and college students as their target market must consider radio.

The disadvantage of radio is that it has limited use for products that must be seen. Another problem is the ease with which consumers can tune out a commercial by switching stations. Radio is a medium that competes for people's attention as they do other activities such as driving, working, or relaxing. Peak radio listening time is during the drive times (6 to 10 A.M. and 4 to 7 P.M.).

STRONG IMAGES INCREASE AN AD'S
EFFECTIVENESS.

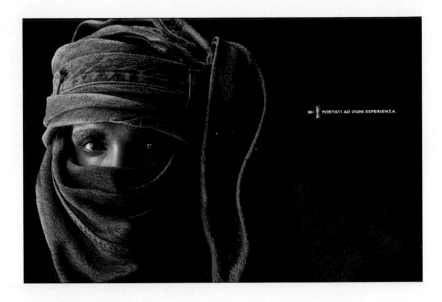

Magazines   Magazines are becoming a very specialized medium. There are about 500 consumer magazines in Canada.[33] The marketing advantage of this medium is the great number of special-interest publications that appeal to narrowly defined segments. Runners read *Runner's World,* sailors buy *Sail,* gardeners subscribe to *Gardening Life,* and children peruse *Sports Illustrated for Kids.* Each magazine's readers often represent a unique profile. In addition to the distinct audience profiles of magazines, good colour production is an advantage that allows magazines to create strong images. The image created by the Levi's ad used in Italy (shown above) helped it win the International Advertising Festival print advertising award in Cannes.

The cost of advertising in national magazines is a disadvantage, but many national publications publish regional and even metro editions, which reduce the absolute cost and wasted coverage. In addition to cost, a limitation to magazines is their infrequency. At best, magazines are printed on a weekly basis, with many specialized publications appearing only monthly or less often.

Newspapers   Newspapers are an important local medium with excellent reach potential. Because of the daily publication of most papers, they allow advertisements to focus on specific current events, such as a "24-hour sale." Local retailers often use newspapers as their sole advertising medium.

Newspapers are rarely saved by the purchaser, so companies are generally limited to ads that call for an immediate customer response (although customers can clip and save ads they want). Companies also cannot depend on newspapers for colour reproduction as good as that in most magazines.

National advertising campaigns rarely include this medium except in conjunction with local distributors of their products. In these instances both parties often share the advertising costs using a cooperative advertising program, which was described in Chapter 19. Another exception is the use of newspapers such as *The Globe* and *Mail* which has national distribution.

In an effort to deliver timely news coverage, many newspapers are delivering online and this is opening up new advertising potential for such newspapers.

Direct mail   Direct mail allows the greatest degree of audience selectivity. Direct-mail companies can provide advertisers with a mailing list of their target market, such as students who live within two miles of the store, product managers in Toronto, or people who own mobile homes. Direct mail has an advantage in providing complete product information, compared with that provided in 15-second, 30-second, or 60-second television

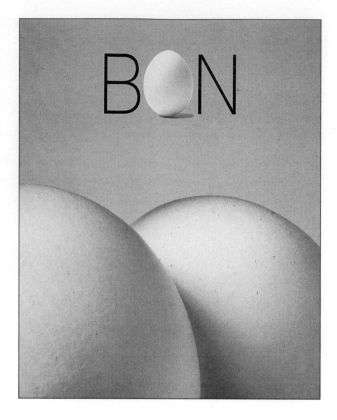

or radio spots. Many advertisers now use direct mail in combination with other media to create *integrated marketing communications programs.* Mass media are used to create awareness, while direct mail builds a relationship and facilitates a purchase.

One disadvantage of direct mail is that rising postal costs are making it more expensive. In fact, many direct-mail advertisers are beginning to use private delivery services, which sometimes charge less than Canada Post for catalogues and other mailers. The major limitation is that people often view direct mail as junk, and the challenge is to get them to open a letter. Databases, which help marketers send their target market only mail that is relevant to them, are improving consumers' response to advertising they receive in the mail.

Outdoor   A very effective medium for reminding consumers about your product is outdoor advertising. The most common form of outdoor advertising, called *billboards,* often results in good reach and frequency and has been shown to increase purchase rates.[34] The visibility of this medium is good supplemental reinforcement for well-known products, and it is a relatively low-cost, flexible alternative. A company can buy space just in the desired geographical market. A disadvantage to billboards, however, is that no opportunity exists for lengthy advertising copy. Also, a good billboard site depends on traffic patterns and sight lines. In many areas environmental laws have limited the use of this medium.

If you have ever lived in a metropolitan area, chances are you might have seen another form of outdoor advertising, transit advertising. This medium includes messages on the interior and exterior of buses, subway cars, and taxis. As use of mass transit grows, transit advertising may become increasingly important. Selectivity is available to advertisers, who can buy space by neighbourhood or bus route. For example, Shoppers Drug Mart of Toronto used two Toronto Transit Commission buses wrapped with Life labels and slogans and selected Toronto-area bus routes with possible high-traffic morning and evening rush hours.[35] One disadvantage to this medium is that the heavy travel times, when audiences are the largest, are not conducive to reading advertising copy.

Other media   As traditional media have become more expensive and cluttered, advertisers have been attracted to a variety of nontraditional advertising options, called *place-based media.* Messages are placed in locations that attract a specific target audience such as airports, doctors' offices, health clubs, or theatres (where ads are played on the screen before the movies are shown). Also, as referred to in the chapter opener, electronic advertising, particularly on-line advertising via the Internet is showing tremendous growth as advertisers attempt to reach customers more effectively and efficiently. A new twist on Internet advertising is the targeted use of *e-mail advertising* where companies can contact customers specifically via their e-mail addresses. Air Canada, for example, uses e-mail advertising to reach their frequent flyer members.[36]

Selection criteria   Choosing between these alternative media is difficult and depends on several factors. First, knowing the media habits of the target audience is essential to deciding among the alternatives. Second, occasionally product attributes necessitate that certain media be used. For example, if colour is a major aspect of product appeal, radio is excluded. Newspapers allow advertising for quick actions to confront competitors, and magazines are more appropriate for complicated messages because the reader can spend more time reading the message. The final factor in selecting a medium is cost. When possible, alternative media are compared using a common denominator that reflects both reach and cost—a measure such as CPM.

Scheduling the Advertising

There is no correct schedule to advertise a product, but three factors must be considered. First is the issue of *buyer turnover,* which is how often new buyers enter the market to buy the product. The higher the buyer turnover, the greater is the amount of advertising required. A second issue in scheduling is the *purchase frequency;* the more frequently the product is purchased, the less repetition is required. Finally, companies must consider the *forgetting rate,* the speed with which buyers forget the brand if advertising is not seen.

Setting schedules requires an understanding of how the market behaves. Most companies tend to follow one of three basic approaches:

1. *Steady ("drip") schedule.* When seasonal factors are unimportant, advertising is run at a steady or regular schedule throughout the year.
2. *Flighting ("intermittent") schedule.* Periods of advertising are scheduled between periods of no advertising to reflect seasonal demand.
3. *Pulse ("burst") schedule.* A flighting schedule is combined with a steady schedule because of increases in demand, heavy periods of promotion, or introduction of a new product.

For example, products such as dry breakfast cereals have a stable demand throughout the year and would typically use a steady schedule of advertising. In contrast, products such as snow skis and suntan lotions have seasonal demands and receive flighting-schedule advertising during the seasonal demand period. Some products such as toys or automobiles require pulse-schedule advertising to facilitate sales throughout the year and during special periods of increased demand (such as holidays or new car introductions). Some evidence suggests that pulsing schedules are superior to other advertising strategies.[37]

CONCEPT CHECK

1. You see the same ad in *Time* and *MacLean's* magazines and on billboards and TV. Is this an example of reach or frequency?

2. What is the most selective medium available?

3. What factors must be considered when choosing among alternative media?

EXECUTING THE ADVERTISING PROGRAM

As shown earlier in Figure 20-1, executing the advertising program involves pretesting the advertising copy and actually carrying out the advertising program. An advertiser once remarked, "I know half my advertising is wasted, but I don't know what half." By evaluating advertising efforts marketers can try to ensure that their advertising expenditures are not wasted.[38] Evaluation is done usually at two separate times: before and after the advertisements are run in the actual campaign. Several methods used in the evaluation process at the stages of idea formulation and copy development are discussed below. Posttesting methods are reviewed in the section on evaluation.

Pretesting the Advertising

To determine whether the advertisement communicates the intended message or to select among alternative versions of the advertisement, **pretests** are conducted before the advertisements are placed in any medium.

Portfolio tests   Portfolio tests are used to test copy alternatives. The test ad is placed in a portfolio with several other ads and stories, and consumers are asked to read through the portfolio. Afterward subjects are asked for their impressions of the ads on several evaluative scales, such as from "very informative" to "not very informative."

Jury tests   Jury tests involve showing the ad copy to a panel of consumers and having them rate how they liked it, how much it drew their attention, and how attractive they thought it was. This approach is similar to the portfolio test in that consumer reactions are obtained. However, unlike the portfolio test, a test advertisement is not hidden within other ads.

Theatre tests   Theatre testing is the most sophisticated form of pretesting. Consumers are invited to view new television shows or movies in which test commercials are also shown. Viewers register their feelings about the advertisements either on hand-held electronic recording devices used during the viewing or on questionnaires afterward.

Carrying Out the Advertising Program

The responsibility for actually carrying out the advertising program can be handled in one of three ways, as shown in Figure 20-5. The **full-service agency** provides the most complete range of services, including market research, media selection, copy development, artwork, and production. Agencies that assist a client by both developing and placing advertisements have traditionally charged a commission of 15 percent of media costs. As corporations have reorganized and cut costs, however, new methods

FIGURE 20-5

ALTERNATIVE STRUCTURES OF ADVERTISING AGENCIES USED TO CARRY OUT THE ADVERTISING PROGRAM

TYPE OF AGENCY	SERVICES PROVIDED
Full-service agency	Does research, selects media, develops copy, and produces artwork
Limited-service agency	Specializes in one aspect of creative process; usually provides creative production work; buys previously unpurchased media space
In-house agency	Provides range of services, depending on company needs

of paying agencies have been introduced. About 45 percent of advertisers now pay less than 15 percent, while others pay preset fees. A small but growing number of advertisers pay performance-based fees. Advertising agency Young and Rubicam, Inc., for example, actually earned more than 15 percent from Sears because its "Softer Side of Sears" campaign has been so successful.[39] **Limited-service agencies** specialize in one aspect of the advertising process such as providing creative services to develop the advertising copy or buying previously unpurchased media space. Limited-service agencies that deal in creative work are compensated by a contractual agreement for the services performed. Finally, **in-house agencies** made up of the company's own advertising staff may provide full services or a limited range of services.

EVALUATING THE ADVERTISING PROGRAM

The advertising decision process does not stop with executing the advertising program. The advertisements must be posttested to determine whether they are achieving their intended objectives, and results may indicate that changes must be made in the advertising program.

Posttesting the Advertising

An advertisement may go through **posttests** after it has been shown to the target audience to determine whether it accomplished its intended purpose. Five approaches common in posttesting are discussed here.[40]

STARCH SCORES AN ADVERTISEMENT.

Aided recall (recognition-readership) After being shown an ad, respondents are asked whether their previous exposure to it was through reading, viewing, or listening. The Starch test shown in the accompanying photo uses aided recall to determine the percentage (1) who remember seeing a specific magazine ad *(noted),* (2) who saw or read any part of the ad identifying the product or brand *(seen-associated),* and (3) who read at least half of the ad *(read most).* Elements of the ad are then tagged with the results, as shown in the picture.

Unaided recall A question such as, "What ads do you remember seeing yesterday?" is asked of respondents without any prompting to determine whether they saw or heard advertising messages.

Attitude tests Respondents are asked questions to measure changes in their attitudes after an advertising campaign, such as whether they have a more favourable attitude toward the product advertised.[41]

Inquiry tests Additional product information, product samples, or premiums are offered to an ad's readers or viewers. Ads generating the most inquiries are presumed to be the most effective.

Sales tests Sales tests involve studies such as controlled experiments (e.g., using radio ads in one market and newspaper ads in another and comparing the results) and consumer purchase tests (measuring retail sales that result from a given advertising campaign). The most sophisticated experimental methods today allow a manufacturer, a distributor, or an advertising agency to manipulate an advertising variable (such as schedule or copy) through cable systems and observe subsequent sales effects by monitoring data collected from checkout scanners in supermarkets.[42]

Making Needed Changes

Results of posttesting the advertising copy are used to reach decisions about changes in the advertising program. If the posttest results show that an advertisement is doing poorly in terms of awareness or cost efficiency, it may be dropped and other ads run in its place in the future. On the other hand, sometimes an advertisement may be so successful it is run repeatedly or used as the basis of a larger advertising program, as with Colgate's "White on White" laundry detergent commercials now used in 30 countries.

IMPORTANT CHANGES IN ADVERTISING AND SOCIETY

Several aspects of advertising are likely to change in the near future. First, in place of traditional mass media, new media such as CD-ROMs, the Internet, and interactive channels are evolving. Some experts suggest that the success of these media may reduce the number and effectiveness of mass media advertising opportunities. In response, some large marketers have begun to produce their own programs to guarantee an outlet for their ads. Procter & Gamble, for example, is working with Paramount Television Group to produce "Frazier" and "Wings." Similarly, Hallmark invested $365 million to purchase a company to produce its "Hall of Fame" programs.[43]

Second, new technologies may change how advertising is created. One company has developed a product that can place a corporate logo or message in a television transmission electronically. Fans watching a baseball game on television, for example, would see an ad on the wall behind the batter even though the wall is blank for fans at the game. One advantage of this form of advertising will be that viewers will only see ads that are relevant to them.[44]

Another change is the declining difference between advertising and editorial material. You may have noticed special advertising sections in newspapers and magazines with nonadvertising content, called *advertorials.* Like infomercials, the advertorials provide large amounts of relevant information in a form that readers may find entertaining. The growth of on-line advertising has created an electronic variation of the advertorial. At New Balance Athletic Shoe's web site, for example, consumers can find tips on exercise, diet and running, content provided by *Runner's World, Men's Health,* and *Women's Sport and Fitness* and, of course, information on New Balance products and events.[45]

CONCEPT CHECK

1. Explain the difference between pretesting and posttesting advertising copy.

2. What is the difference between aided and unaided recall posttests?

SUMMARY

1. Advertising may be classified as either product or institutional. Product advertising can take three forms: pioneering, competitive, or reminder. Institutional ads are one of these three or advocacy.

2. The advertising decision process involves developing, executing, and evaluating the advertising program. Developing the advertising program focuses on determining who is the target audience, what to say, where the message should be said, and when to say it.

3. Setting advertising objectives is based on the hierarchy of effects. Objectives should be measurable, have a specified time period, and state the target audience.

4. Budgeting methods often used are percentage of sales, competitive parity, and the all you can afford approaches. The best budgeting approach is based on the objectives set and tasks required.

5. Copywriters and art directors have the responsibility of identifying the key benefits of a product and communicating them to the target audience with attention-getting advertising. Common appeals include fear, sex, and humour.

6. In selecting the right medium, there are distinct trade-offs among television, radio, magazines, newspapers, direct mail, outdoor, and other media. The decision is based on media habits of the target audience, product characteristics, message requirements, and media costs.

7. In determining advertising schedules, a balance must be made between reach and frequency. Scheduling must take into account buyer turnover, purchase frequency, and the rate at which consumers forget.

8. Advertising is evaluated before and after the ad is run. Pretesting can be done with portfolio, jury, or theatre tests. Posttesting is done on the basis of aided recall, unaided recall, attitude tests, inquiry tests, and sales tests.

9. To execute an advertising program, companies can use several types of advertising agencies. These firms can provide a full range of services or specialize in creative or placement activities. Some firms use their own in-house agency.

10. Important future changes in advertising include the growth of new media, the development of new advertising technologies, and the use of advertorials.

KEY TERMS AND CONCEPTS

advertising p. 476
product advertisements p. 476
institutional advertisements p. 477
hierarchy of effects p. 479
percentage of sales budgeting p. 480
competitive parity budgeting p. 480
all you can afford budgeting p. 480
objective and task budgeting p. 480
reach p. 484
rating p. 485

frequency p. 485
gross rating points p. 485
cost per thousand p. 485
infomercials p. 486
pretests p. 490
full-service agency p. 490
limited-service agencies p. 491
in-house agencies p. 491
posttests p. 491

CHAPTER PROBLEMS AND APPLICATIONS

1. How does competitive product advertising differ from competitive institutional advertising?

2. Suppose you are the advertising manager for a new line of children's fragrances. Which form of media would you use for this new product?

3. You have recently been promoted to be director of advertising for the Timkin Tool Company. In your first meeting with Mr. Timkin, he says, "Advertising is a waste! We've been advertising for six months now and sales haven't increased. Tell me why we should continue." Give your answer to Mr. Timkin.

4. A large life insurance company has decided to switch from using a strong fear appeal to a humorous approach. What are the strengths and weaknesses of such a change in message strategy?

5. Some national advertisers have found that they can have more impact with their advertising by running a large number of ads for a period and then running no ads at all for a period. Why might such a flighting schedule be more effective than a steady schedule?

6. Which medium has the lowest cost per thousand?

MEDIUM	COST	AUDIENCE
TV show	$5 000	25 000
Magazine	2 200	6 000
Newspaper	4 800	7 200
FM radio	420	1 600

7. Each year managers at Bausch and Lomb evaluate the many advertising media alternatives available to them as they develop their advertising program for contact lenses. What advantages and disadvantages of each alternative should they consider? Which media would you recommend to them?

8. The Royal Bank has just developed two versions of an advertisement to encourage senior citizens to direct deposit their Canada Pension cheques with the bank. Direct deposit means the government sends the funds directly to the bank, so that the consumer does not have to go and deposit the cheques. Suggest how the bank can evaluate the two ads.

9. The Toro Company has a broad product line. What timing approach would you recommend for the advertising of (*a*) the lawn mower line and (*b*) the new line of lawn and garden furniture?

10. What are two advantages and two disadvantages of the advertising posttests described in the chapter?

CASE 20-1   Lysol

L&F is a North American business unit of the Kodak Corporation. An important brand for L&F is the Lysol product line. Most Canadian consumers are familiar with Lysol Spray, but L&F wants to increase sales of not only the spray product, but the entire line of Lysol products. It is attempting to develop a strategy in Canada in order to market more of the entire line of Lysol products.

Lysol, primarily the spray, has a long brand heritage in Canada. The disinfectant benefit of the product is very distinctive. In the early 1990s, Lysol spray had 44 percent household penetration in Canada, but the other Lysol products—Lysol Basin, Tub & Tile Cleaner; Lysol Toilet Bowl Cleaner; and Lysol Liquid (All-Purpose) Cleaner—had much lower penetration. With little existing synergy between the products within the line, L&F wanted to bring these disparate products together. In doing so, L&F could achieve economies of scale in terms of marketing expenses. The company believed that by combining the marketing budgets for the four separate products, it could achieve a greater impact on the market. It was felt that one way to link the products together was through the unifying benefit of disinfection.

L&F wanted to achieve a greater market penetration with all four products. However, the overall household cleaning product category was not growing and in some areas was actually declining. Some industry people felt that one reason for this was that many households were cleaning less. They also felt that the recession was impacting on sales in the category. Therefore, new growth for Lysol would have to come at the expense of existing competitors.

While all competitors were using advertising and couponing, the intensity of the battle was at the shelf level. Competitive firms were literally battling it out for shelf space in order to capture market share. This meant that trade sales promotions were being used extensively, often in the form of price discounting. L&F felt it shouldn't get more involved in trade discounts because of the squeeze it put on margins. It did believe, however, that limited use of consumer coupons should be part of its overall consumer-focused marketing communications activity.

L&F believed that the Lysol brand probably had a rather tired personality. The company wanted to give it a 1990s contemporary, interesting, and even provocative image. The problem was that to most consumers, household cleaning products were really an uninteresting category. As such, building consumer awareness of the entire line would not be possible without increasing the level of consumer involvement. The question was how to create interest or involvement with the product line. A way had to be found to demonstrate the line and to have consumers pay attention.

L&F knew that timing would be important. For example, interest in the category would be highest just before or during traditional spring cleaning time in Canada, which ran between late February to early May. Interest would also be high again in late fall or early winter. But if the product line itself could not be made interesting or more involving, even good timing wouldn't help.

L&F had to determine an appropriate creative message for the consumer, select an appropriate communications medium, and consider other ways to build sales and market share for the line.

Questions

1. What would be the most appropriate advertising medium for L&F to use in order to communicate with its market?

2. What would be a creative way to build consumer involvement with the product line? What would be the specific message and execution?

3. Besides the specific advertising medium you recommended to L&F in question 1, what other promotional activities would you recommend to build sales and market share for the Lysol line?

4. What type of advertising schedule would you recommend L&F use during the year?

CHAPTER 21

Personal Selling and Sales Management

AFTER READING THIS CHAPTER YOU SHOULD BE ABLE TO:

- Recognize different types of personal selling.

- Describe the stages in the personal selling process.

- Specify the functions and tasks in the sales management process.

- Determine whether a firm should use manufacturer's representatives or a company salesforce and the number of people needed in a company's salesforce.

- Understand how firms recruit, select, train, motivate, compensate, and evaluate salespeople.

- Describe recent applications of salesforce automation.

MARY KAY COSMETICS: SELLING BEAUTY IN RUSSIA

What images come to mind when you hear the words "sales" and "sales management" mentioned as a career? Whatever they are, they would surely change after meeting Julie Rasmussen (shown on the opposite page).

Ms. Rasmussen exudes the entrepreneurial spirit sought in today's challenging global world of cosmetic and skin care marketing. After arriving in Moscow in 1992 with nothing more than a suitcase and an American Express Corporate Card, she employed a mixture of persistence and creativity to build the Russian subsidiary of Mary Kay Cosmetics (www.marykay.com) from nothing to an all-female salesforce of independent representatives stretching across Russia, Ukraine, Kazakhstan, and the Baltics. Today she is president of the venture, which fills as many as 500 orders a day.

Drawing on her education as a Russian literature major with a master's degree in international relations, plus fluency in the Russian language, Ms. Rasmussen recruited, selected, and trained a salesforce that has since grown to 7000. Ms. Rasmussen attributes the success of Mary Kay, in a region where people have been denied access to Western beauty products for almost 70 years, to an abundance of intelligent women who are "amazingly entrepreneurial." Mary Kay salespeople make an average of $350 a month, which is significantly more than Russia's $90 average monthly salary. Sales directors, who organize their own sales team, average as much as $6000 a month, says Ms. Rasmussen.

Ms. Rasmussen acknowledges the challenges of sales and marketing in Russia, including inflation and political instability. But she adds, "In terms of fast-moving consumer goods, Russia is where it is happening."[1]

This chapter examines the scope and significance of personal selling and sales management in marketing. It first highlights many forms of personal selling and outlines the selling process. The functions of sales management are then described, including recent advances in salesforce automation.

SCOPE AND SIGNIFICANCE OF PERSONAL SELLING AND SALES MANAGEMENT

Chapter 19 described personal selling and management of the sales effort as being part of the firm's promotional mix. Although it is important to recognize that personal selling is a useful vehicle for communicating with present and potential buyers, it is much more. Take a moment to answer the questions in the personal selling and sales management quiz in Figure 21-1. As you read on, compare your answers with those in the text.

Nature of Personal Selling and Sales Management

Personal selling involves the two-way flow of communication between a buyer and seller, often in a face-to-face encounter, designed to influence a person's or group's purchase decision. However, with advances in telecommunications, personal selling also takes place over the telephone, through video teleconferencing and interactive computer links between buyers and sellers. For example, customers of Haggar Apparel Company can enter purchase orders into their computer, have it contact Haggar's computer, and find out when the requested products can be shipped.[2]

Personal selling remains a highly human-intensive activity despite the use of technology. Accordingly, the people involved must be managed. **Sales management** involves planning the selling program and implementing and controlling the personal selling effort of the firm. Numerous tasks are involved in managing personal selling, including setting objectives; organizing the salesforce; recruiting, selecting, training, and compensating salespeople; and evaluating the performance of individual salespeople.

Pervasiveness of Selling

"Everyone lives by selling something," wrote author Robert Louis Stevenson a century ago. His observation holds true today. In Canada, over 1 million people are employed in sales positions.[3]

Included in this number are manufacturing sales personnel, real estate brokers, stockbrokers, and salesclerks who work in retail stores. In reality, however, virtually every occupation that involves customer contact has an element of personal selling. For example, lawyers, accountants, bankers, and company personnel recruiters perform sales-related activities, whether or not they acknowledge it.

Many executives in major companies have held sales positions at some time in their careers. For example, Victor Kiam, the flamboyant chair and chief executive officer of Remington Products, Inc., previously held a sales position at Lever Brothers. It might be said that today Kiam is Remington's most visible salesperson. It is no accident that these individuals rose from sales and marketing positions to top management. Thus, selling often serves as a stepping-stone to top management, as well as being a career path in itself.

FIGURE 21-1

PERSONAL SELLING AND SALES MANAGEMENT QUIZ

> 1. About how much does it cost for a consumer product salesperson to make a single personal sales call? (check one)
> $100 _____ $150 _____ $200 _____
> $125 _____ $175 _____ $225 _____
> 2. "A salesperson's job is finished when a sale is made." True or false? (circle one)
> True   False
> 3. On average, sales training programs devote about what percentage of time to sales techniques? (check one)
> 20% _____   40% _____   60% _____
> 30% _____   50% _____   70% _____

Personal Selling in Marketing

Personal selling serves three major roles in a firm's overall marketing effort. First, salespeople are the critical link between the firm and its customers. This role requires that salespeople match company interests with customer needs to satisfy both parties in the exchange process. Second, salespeople *are* the company in a consumer's eyes. They represent what a company is or attempts to be and are often the only personal contact a customer has with the company. For example, the "look" projected by salespeople for Avon Products, Inc. is an important factor in communicating the benefits of the company's cosmetic line. Third, personal selling may play a dominant role in a firm's marketing program. This situation typically arises when a firm uses a push marketing strategy, described in Chapter 19. Avon, for example, pays almost 40 percent of its total sales dollars for selling expenses.[4] Pharmaceutical firms and office and educational equipment manufacturers also rely heavily on personal selling in the marketing of their products.

Creating Customer Value through Salespeople: Relationship Selling

As the critical link between the firm and its customers, salespeople can create customer value in many ways.[5] For instance, by being close to the customer, salespeople can identify creative solutions to customer problems. Salespeople can create value by easing the customer buying process, offering instructions and advice. Customer value is also created by salespeople who follow through after the sale to ensure that customers are satisfied or whether or not they need any further assistance.

Customer value creation is made possible by **relationship selling,** the practice of building ties to customers based on a salesperson's attention and commitment to customer needs over time. It focuses on creating long-term customers, not a one-time sale[6] and involves mutual respect and trust among buyers and sellers. Surveys of senior sales executives reveal that over 95 percent consider "building long-term relationships with customers" to be the most important activity affecting sales performance.[7] Companies such as Merck Frosst Canada, IBM Canada, National Bank, Bell Canada, and Kraft-General Foods Canada have made relationship building a core focus on their sales effort. Relationship selling, in essence, is one way in which an organization can implement the relationship marketing concept, which as you know from Chapter 10 is an organization's effort to develop a long-term, cost-effective link with individual customers for mutual benefit.

CONCEPT CHECK

1. What is personal selling?

2. What is involved in sales management?

THE MANY FORMS OF PERSONAL SELLING

Personal selling assumes many forms based on the amount of selling done and the amount of creativity required to perform the sales task. Broadly speaking, three types of personal selling exist: order taking, order getting, and sales support activities.[8] While

FIGURE 21-2

COMPARING ORDER TAKERS AND
ORDER GETTERS

BASIS OF COMPARISON	ORDER TAKERS	ORDER GETTERS
Objective	Handle routine product orders or reorders	Identify new customers and uncover customer needs
Purchase situation	Focus on straight rebuy or simple purchase situations	Focus on new buy and modified rebuy purchase situations
Activity	Perform order processing functions	Act as creative problem solvers
Training	Require significant clerical training	Require significant sales, product, and customer training

some firms use only one of these types of personal selling, others use a combination of all three. Figure 21-2 compares order getters and order takers to illustrate some important differences between them.

Order Taking

Typically, an **order taker** processes routine orders or reorders for products that were already sold by the company. The primary responsibility of order takers is to preserve an ongoing relationship with existing customers and maintain sales. Two types of order takers exist. *Outside order takers* visit customers and replenish inventory stocks of resellers, such as retailers or wholesalers. For example, Frito-Lay salespeople call on supermarkets, neighbourhood grocery stores, and other establishments to ensure that the company's line of snack products (such as Doritos and Tostitos) is in adequate supply. In addition, outside order takers typically provide assistance in arranging displays. *Inside order takers*, also called *order* or *salesclerks*, typically answer simple questions, take orders, and complete transactions with customers. Many retail clerks are inside order takers. Inside order takers are often employed by companies that use *inbound telemarketing*, the use of toll-free telephone numbers that customers can call to obtain information about products or services and make purchases. In industrial settings, order taking arises in straight rebuy situations. Order takers, for the most part, do little selling in a conventional sense and engage in little problem solving with customers. They often represent simple products that have few options, such as confectionary items, magazine subscriptions, and highly standardized industrial products. Inbound telemarketing is also an essential selling activity for service-based firms who market intangibles such as credit card or long-distance telephone companies. Order takers in such firms often undergo extensive training so that they can better assist callers with their purchase decisions.

Order Getting

An **order getter** sells in a conventional sense and identifies prospective customers, provides customers with information, persuades customers to buy, closes sales, and follows up on customers' use of a product or service. Like order takers, order getters can be inside (an automobile salesperson) or outside (an IBM salesperson). Order getting involves a high degree of creativity and customer empathy and is typically required for selling complex or technical products with many options, so considerable product knowledge and sales training are necessary. In modified rebuy or new buy purchase situations in industrial selling, an order getter acts as a problem solver who identifies how

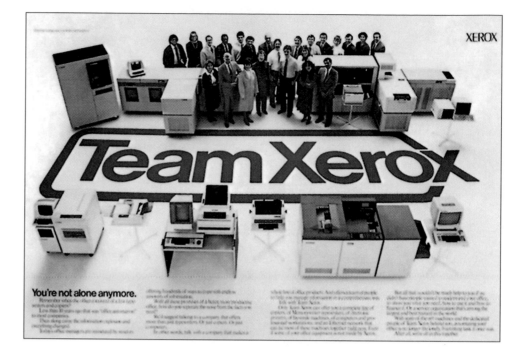

a particular product may satisfy a customer's need. Similarly, in the purchase of a service, such as insurance, a Canada Life insurance agent can provide a mix of plans to satisfy a buyer's needs depending on income, stage of the family's life cycle, and investment objectives.

Order getting is an expensive process.[9] It is estimated that the median direct cost of a single sales call for an industrial product is $198.67; for a consumer product, $210.43; and for a service, $193.58. (What amount did you check for question 1 in Figure 21-1?) These costs illustrate why outbound telemarketing is so popular today. *Outbound telemarketing* is the practice of using the telephone rather than personal visits to contact customers. A significantly lower cost per sales call (in the range of $20 to $25) and little or no field expense accounts for its widespread appeal. Inbound and outbound telemarketing usage has grown about 25 percent per year.[10]

Sales Support Personnel

Sales support personnel augment the selling effort of order getters by performing a variety of services. For example, **missionary salespeople** do not directly solicit orders but rather concentrate on performing promotional activities and introducing new products. They are used extensively in the pharmaceutical industry, where they persuade physicians to prescribe a firm's product. Actual sales are made through wholesalers or directly to pharmacists who fill prescriptions. A **sales engineer** is a salesperson who specializes in identifying, analyzing, and solving customer problems and brings know-how and technical expertise to the selling situation but often does not actually sell products and services. Sales engineers are popular in selling industrial products such as chemicals and heavy equipment.

In many situations firms engage in cross-functional **team selling,** the practice of using an entire team of professionals in selling to and servicing major customers.[11] Team selling is used when specialized knowledge is needed to satisfy the different interests of individuals in a customer's buying centre. For example, a selling team might consist of a salesperson, a sales engineer, a service representative, and a financial executive, each of whom would deal with a counterpart in the customer's firm. Team selling takes different forms. In **conference selling,** a salesperson and other company resource people meet with buyers to discuss problems and opportunities. In **seminar selling,** a company team conducts an educational program for a customer's technical staff, describing state-of-the-art developments. IBM Canada and Xerox Canada Corporation pioneered cross-functional team selling in working with prospective buyers. Other firms have embraced this practice and created and sustained value for their customers, as described in the accompanying Marketing NewsNet.[12]

CONCEPT CHECK

1. What is the principal difference between an order taker and an order getter?
2. What is team selling?

THE PERSONAL SELLING PROCESS: BUILDING RELATIONSHIPS

Selling, and particularly order getting, is a complicated activity that involves building buyer-seller relationships. Although the salesperson-customer interaction is essential to personal selling, much of a salesperson's work occurs before this meeting and continues after the sale itself. The **personal selling process** consists of six stages: (1) prospecting, (2) preapproach, (3) approach, (4) presentation, (5) close, and (6) follow-up (Figure 21-3).

Prospecting

Personal selling begins with *prospecting*—the search for and qualification of potential customers.[13] For some products that are one-time purchases such as encyclopedias, continual prospecting is necessary to maintain sales. There are three types of prospects. A *lead* is the name of a person who may be a possible customer. A *prospect* is a customer who wants or needs the product. If an individual wants the product, can afford to buy it, and is the decision maker, this individual is a *qualified prospect.*

FIGURE 21-3

STAGES AND OBJECTIVES OF THE
PERSONAL SELLING PROCESS

STAGE	OBJECTIVE	COMMENTS
Prospecting	Search for and qualify prospects	Start of the selling process; prospects produced through advertising, referrals, and cold canvassing.
Preapproach	Gather information and decide how to approach the prospect	Information sources include personal observation, other customers, and own salespeople.
Approach	Gain prospect's attention, stimulate interest, and make transition to the presentation	First impression is critical; gain attention and interest through reference to common acquaintances, a referral, or product demonstration.
Presentation	Begin converting a prospect into a customer by creating a desire for the product or service	Different presentation formats are possible; however, involving the customer in the product or service through attention to particular needs is critical; important to deal professionally and ethically with prospect skepticism, indifference, or objections.
Close	Obtain a purchase commitment from the prospect and create a customer	Salesperson asks for the purchase; different approaches include the trial close and assumptive close.
Follow-up	Ensure that the customer is satisfied with the product or service	Resolve any problems faced by the customer to ensure customer satisfaction and future sales possibilities.

Leads and prospects are generated using several sources. For example, advertising may contain a coupon or a toll-free number to generate leads. Some companies use exhibits at trade fairs, professional meetings, and conferences to generate leads or prospects. Staffed by salespeople, these exhibits are used to attract the attention of prospective buyers and disseminate information. Another approach for generating leads is through *cold canvassing* in person or by telephone. This approach simply means that a salesperson may open a telephone directory, pick a name, and visit or call that individual. Although the refusal rate is high with cold canvassing, this approach can be successful.[14]

However, cold canvassing is frowned upon in most Asian and Latin American societies. Personal visits, based on referrals, are expected.[15] Cold canvassing is also often criticized by Canadian consumers. Many consumers see cold canvassing as an intrusion to their privacy, and many find it simply distasteful.[16] Many trade associations have codes of ethics for dealing with this issue such as adhering to consumers' "do not call," "do not mail," or "do not visit" requests. The Canadian government has also attempted to more closely regulate cold canvassing with the CRTC requiring telemarketers to inform consumers that they have the right to say no to such solicitations.[17]

With the development and growth in database marketing (Chapter 10), prospecting has become a little easier, and often the response rates are much higher since the databases allow for greater precision when targeting. Database marketing also ensures that fewer consumers who are really nonprospects receive unwanted solicitations.

Preapproach

Once a salesperson has identified a qualified prospect, preparation for the sale begins with the preapproach. The *preapproach* stage involves obtaining further information on the prospect and deciding on the best method of approach. Knowing how the prospect prefers to be approached, and what the prospect is looking for in a product or service, is essential regardless of cultural setting. For example, a Merrill Lynch stockbroker will need information on a prospect's discretionary income, investment objectives, and preference for discussing brokerage services over the telephone or in person. For industrial products the preapproach involves identifying the buying role of a prospect (for example, influencer or decision maker), important buying criteria, and the prospect's receptivity to a formal or informal presentation. Identifying the best time to contact a prospect is also important. For example, insurance companies have discovered the best times to call people in different occupations: dentists before 9:30 A.M., lawyers between 11:00 A.M. and 2:00 P.M., and college professors between 7:00 and 8:00 P.M.[18]

This stage is very important in international selling where customs dictate appropriate protocol. In many South American countries, for example, buyers expect salespeople to be punctual for appointments. However, prospective buyers are routinely 30 minutes late. South Americans take negotiating seriously and prefer straightforward presentations, but a hard-sell approach will not work.[19]

Approach

The *approach* stage involves the initial meeting between the salesperson and prospect, where the objectives are to gain the prospect's attention, stimulate interest, and build the foundation for the sales presentation itself and the basis for a working relationship. The first impression is critical at this stage, and it is common for salespeople to begin the conversation with a reference to common acquaintances, a referral, or even the product or service itself. Which tactic is taken will depend on the information obtained in the prospecting and preapproach stages.

The approach stage is very important in international settings. In many societies outside Canada, considerable time is devoted to nonbusiness talk designed to establish a rapport between buyers and sellers. For instance, it is common that two or three meetings occur before business matters are discussed in the Middle East and Asia. Gestures are also very important. Business cards should be printed in English on one side and the language of the prospective customer on the other. Knowledgeable Canadian salespeople know that their business cards should be handed to Asian customers using both hands, with the name facing the receiver. In Asia, anything involving names demands respect.[20]

Presentation

The *presentation* is at the core of the order-getting selling process, and its objective is to convert a prospect into a customer by creating a desire for the product or service. Three major presentation formats exist: (1) stimulus-response format, (2) formula selling format, and (3) need-satisfaction format.

Stimulus-response format   The **stimulus-response presentation** format assumes that given the appropriate stimulus by a salesperson, the prospect will buy. With this format the salesperson tries one appeal after another, hoping to "hit the right button." A counter clerk at McDonald's is using this approach when he or she asks whether you'd like an order of french fries or a dessert with your meal. The counter clerk is engaging in what is called *suggestive selling.* Although useful in this setting, the stimulus-response format is not always appropriate, and for many products a more formalized format is necessary.

Formula selling format   A more formalized presentation, the **formula selling presentation** format, is based on the view that a presentation consists of information that must be provided in an accurate, thorough, and step-by-step manner to inform the prospect. A popular version of this format is the *canned sales presentation,* which is a memorized, standardized message conveyed to every prospect.[21] Used frequently by firms in telephone and door-to-door selling of consumer products (for example, Fuller Brush Company and Encyclopaedia Britannica), this approach treats every prospect the same, regardless of differences in needs or preference for certain kinds of information. Canned sales presentations can be advantageous when the differences between prospects are unknown or with novice salespeople who are less knowledgeable about the product and selling process than experienced salespeople. Although it guarantees a thorough presentation, it often lacks flexibility and spontaneity and, more important, does not provide for feedback from the prospective buyer—a critical component in the communication process and the start of a relationship.

Need-satisfaction format   The stimulus-response and formula selling formats share a common characteristic: the salesperson dominates the conversation. By comparison, the **need-satisfaction presentation** format emphasizes probing and listening by the salesperson to identify needs and interests of prospective buyers. Once these are identified, the salesperson tailors the presentation to the prospect and highlights product benefits that may be valued by the prospect. The need-satisfaction format, which emphasizes problem solving, is the most consistent with the marketing concept. Two selling styles are associated with this format. **Adaptive selling** involves adjusting the presentation to fit the selling situation, such as knowing when to offer solutions and when to ask for more information. **Consultative selling** focuses on problem identification, where the salesperson serves as an expert on problem recognition and resolution.[22] Both styles are used for industrial products such as computers and heavy equipment. Many consumer service firms such as brokerage and insurance firms and consumer product firms like AT&T Canada and Gillette also subscribe to these selling styles.

Handling objections   A critical concern in the presentation stage is handling objections. *Objections* are excuses for not making a purchase commitment or decision. Some objections are valid and are based on the characteristics of the product or service or price. However, many objections reflect prospect skepticism or indifference. Whether valid or not, experienced salespeople know that objections do not put an end to the presentation. Rather, techniques can be used to deal with objections in a courteous, ethical, and professional manner. The following six techniques are the most common:[23]

1. *Acknowledge and convert the objection.* This technique involves using the objection as a reason for buying. For example, a prospect might say, "The price is too high." The reply: "Yes, the price is high because we use the finest materials. Let me show you. . . ."

2. *Postpone.* The postpone technique is used when the objection will be dealt with later in the presentation: "I'm going to address that point shortly. I think my answer would make better sense then."

3. *Agree and neutralize.* Here a salesperson agrees with the objection, then shows that it is unimportant. A salesperson would say, "That's true and others have

Global

MARKETING NEWSNET

THE SUBTLETY OF SAYING YES IN EAST ASIA

By the year 2000, the economies of East Asia—spanning from Japan to Indonesia—will rival the North American economy under NAFTA as well as the economy of the European Union.

The marketing opportunities in East Asia are great, but effective selling in these countries will require a keen cultural ear. Seasoned global marketers know that in many Asian societies it is impolite to say *no,* and *yes* has multiple meanings.

Yes in Asian societies can have at least four meanings. It can mean that listeners are simply acknowledging that a speaker is talking to them even though they don't understand what is being said, or it can mean that a speaker's words are understood, but not that they are agreed with. A third meaning of *yes* conveys that a presentation is understood, but other people must be consulted before any commitment is possible. Finally, *yes* can also mean that a proposal is understood and accepted. However, experienced negotiators also note that this *yes* is subject to change if the situation is changed.

This one example illustrates why savvy salespeople are sensitive to cultural underpinnings when engaged in cross-cultural sales negotiations.

said the same. However, they concluded that issue was outweighed by the other benefits."

4. *Accept the objection.* Sometimes the objection is valid. Let the prospect express such views, probe for the reason behind it, and attempt to stimulate further discussion on the objection.

5. *Denial.* When a prospect's objection is based on misinformation and clearly untrue, it is wise to meet the objection head on with a firm denial.

6. *Ignore the objection.* This technique is used when it appears that the objection is a stalling mechanism or is clearly not important to the prospect.

Each of these techniques requires a calm, professional interaction with the prospect and is most effective when objections are anticipated in the preapproach stage. Handling objections is a skill requiring a sense of timing, appreciation for the prospect's state of mind, and adeptness in communication. Objections also should be handled ethically. Lying or misrepresenting product or service features are grossly unethical practices.

Close

The *closing* stage in the selling process involves obtaining a purchase commitment from the prospect. This stage is the most important and the most difficult because the salesperson must determine when the prospect is ready to buy. Telltale signals indicating a readiness to buy include body language (prospect reexamines the product or contract closely), statements ("This equipment should reduce our maintenance costs"), and questions ("When could we expect delivery?"). The close itself can take several forms. Three closing techniques are used when a salesperson believes a buyer is about ready to make a purchase: (1) trial close, (2) assumptive close, and (3) urgency close. A *trial close* involves asking the prospect to make a decision on some aspect of the purchase: "Would you prefer the blue or gray model?" An *assumptive close* entails asking the prospect to consider choices concerning delivery, warranty, or financing terms under the assumption that a sale has been finalized. An *urgency close* is used to commit the prospect quickly by making reference to the timeliness of the purchase: "The low interest financing ends next week," or, "That is the last model we have in stock." Of course, these statements should be used only if they accurately reflect the situation; otherwise, such claims would be unethical. When a prospect is clearly ready to buy, the final close is used, and a salesperson asks for the order.

Knowing when the prospect is ready to buy becomes even more difficult in cross-cultural buyer-seller negotiations where societal customs and language play a large role. Read the accompanying Marketing NewsNet to understand the multiple meanings of *yes* in Japan and other societies in East Asia.[24]

Follow-Up

The selling process does not end with the closing of a sale; rather, professional selling requires customer follow-up. One marketing authority equated the follow-up with courtship and marriage,[25] by observing, ". . . the sale merely consummates the courtship. Then the marriage begins. How good the marriage is depends on how well the relationship is managed." The *follow-up* stage includes making certain the customer's purchase has been properly delivered and installed and difficulties experienced with the use of the item are addressed. Attention to this stage of the selling process solidifies the buyer-seller relationship. Moreover, research shows that the cost and effort to obtain repeat sales from a satisfied customer is roughly half of that necessary to gain a sale from a new customer.[26] In short, today's satisfied customers become tomorrow's qualified prospects or referrals. (What was your answer to question 2 in the quiz in Figure 21-1?)

CONCEPT CHECK

1. What are the six stages in the personal selling process?

2. What is the distinction between a lead and a qualified prospect?

3. Which presentation format is most consistent with the marketing concept? Why?

THE SALES MANAGEMENT PROCESS

Selling must be managed if it is going to contribute to a firm's overall objectives. Although firms differ in the specifics of how salespeople and the selling effort are managed, the sales management process is similar across firms. Sales management consists of three interrelated functions: (1) sales plan formulation, (2) sales plan implementation, and (3) evaluation and control of the salesforce (Figure 21-4).

FIGURE 21-4

THE SALES MANAGEMENT PROCESS

ETHICS AND SOCIAL RESPONSIBILITY ALERT

THE ETHICS OF ASKING CUSTOMERS ABOUT COMPETITORS

Salespeople are a valuable source of information about what is happening in the marketplace. By working closely with customers and asking good questions, salespeople often have first-hand knowledge of customer problems and wants. They also are able to spot the activities of competitors. However, should salespeople explicitly ask customers about competitor strategies such as pricing practices, product development efforts, and trade and promotion programs?

Gaining knowledge about competitors by asking customers for information is a ticklish ethical issue. Research indicates that 25 percent of salespeople engaged in business-to-business selling consider this practice unethical, and their companies have explicit guidelines for this practice. It is also noteworthy that Japanese salespeople consider this practice to be more unethical than do salespeople in North America.

Do you believe that asking customers about competitor practices is unethical? Why or why not?

Sales Plan Formulation

Formulating the sales plan is the most basic of the three sales management functions. According to one vice president of sales for a manufacturer of electronics products, "If a company hopes to implement its marketing strategy, it really needs a detailed sales planning process."[27] The **sales plan** is a statement describing what is to be achieved and where and how the selling effort of salespeople is to be deployed. Formulating the sales plan involves three tasks: (1) setting objectives, (2) organizing the salesforce, and (3) developing account management policies.

Setting objectives   Setting objectives is central to sales management because this task specifies what is to be achieved. In practice, objectives are set for the total salesforce and for each salesperson. Selling objectives can be output related and focus on dollar or unit sales volume, number of new customers added, and profit. Alternatively, they can be input related and emphasize the number of sales calls and selling expenses. Output- and input-related objectives are used for the salesforce as a whole and for each salesperson. A third type of objective that is behaviourally related is typically specific for each salesperson and includes his or her product knowledge, customer service, and selling and communication skills. Increasingly, firms are also emphasizing knowledge of competition as an objective since salespeople are calling on customers and should see what competitors are doing. But should salespeople explicitly ask their customers for information about competitors? Read the accompanying Ethics and Social Responsibility Alert to see how salespeople view this practice.[28]

Whatever objectives are set, they should be precise and measurable and specify the time period over which they are to be achieved. Once established, these objectives serve as performance standards for the evaluation of the salesforce—the third function of sales management.

Organizing the salesforce   Establishing a selling organization is the second task in formulating the sales plan. Three questions are related to organization. First, should the company use its own salesforce, or should it use independent agents such as manufacturer's representatives? Second, if the decision is made to employ

FIGURE 21-5

BREAK-EVEN CHART FOR COMPARING
INDEPENDENT AGENTS AND A
COMPANY SALESFORCE

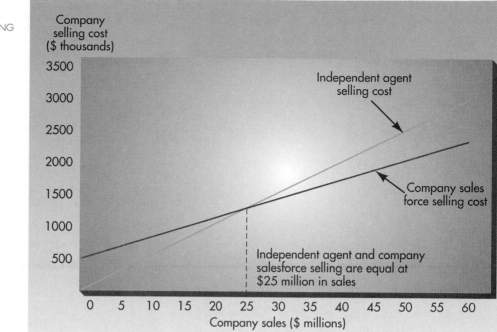

company salespeople, then should they be organized according to geography, customer type, or product or service? Third, how many company salespeople should be employed?

The decision to use company salespeople or independent agents is made infrequently. However, Apple Computer switched from using agents to its own salesforce, and Coca-Cola's Food Division replaced its salesforce with independent agents (food brokers). The Optoelectronics Division of Honeywell, Inc. has switched back and forth between agents and its own salesforce over the last 25 years. The decision is based on an analysis of economic and behavioural factors. An economic analysis examines the costs of using both types of salespeople and is a form of break-even analysis.

Consider a situation in which independent agents would receive a 5 percent commission on sales, and company salespeople would receive a 3 percent commission, salaries, and benefits. In addition, with company salespeople, sales administration costs would be incurred for a total fixed cost of $500 000 per year. At what sales level would independent or company salespeople be less costly? This question can be answered by setting the costs of the two options equal to each other and solving for the sales level amount, as shown in the following equation:

$$\frac{\text{Total cost of company salespeople}}{0.03(X) + \$500\,000} = \frac{\text{Total cost of independent agents}}{0.05(X)}$$

where X = sales volume. Solving for X, sales volume equals $25 million, indicating that below $25 million in sales independent agents would be cheaper, but above $25 million a company salesforce would be cheaper. This relationship is shown in Figure 21-5.

Economics alone does not answer this question, however. A behavioural analysis is also necessary and should focus on issues related to the control, flexibility, effort, and availability of independent and company salespeople.[29] Figure 21-6 shows the com-

FIGURE 21-6

THE CASE FOR USING COMPANY
SALESPEOPLE VERSUS INDEPENDENT
AGENTS

CRITERIA	CASE FOR COMPANY SALESFORCE	CASE FOR INDEPENDENT AGENTS
Control	Company selects, trains, supervises, and can use multiple rewards to direct salespeople.	Agents are equally well selected, trained, and supervised by the representative organization.
Flexibility	Company can transfer salespeople, change customer selling practices, and otherwise direct its own salesforce.	Little fixed cost is present with agents; mostly there are variable costs; therefore, firm is not burdened with overhead.
Effort	Sales effort is enhanced because salespeople represent one firm, not several; firm loyalty is present; there is better customer service because salespeople receive salary as well as commission.	Agents might work harder than salespeople because compensation is based solely on commissions; customer service is good, since it builds repeat business.
Availability	Knowledgeable agents might not be available where and when needed.	Entrepreneurial spirit of agents will make them available where a marketing opportunity exists.

mon behavioural arguments for independent agents versus a company salesforce. An individual firm must weigh the pros and cons of the economic and behavioural considerations before making this decision.

If a company elects to employ its own salespeople, then it must choose an organizational structure based on (1) geography, (2) customer, or (3) product (Figure 21-7). A geographical structure is the simplest organization, where Canada or indeed the globe, is first divided into regions and each region is divided into districts or territories. Salespeople are assigned to each district with defined geographical boundaries and call on all customers and represent all products sold by the company. The principal advantage of this structure is that it can minimize travel time, expenses, and duplication of selling effort. However, if a firm's products or customers require specialized knowledge, then a geographical structure is not suitable.

When different types of buyers have different needs, a customer sales organizational structure is used. In practice this means that a different salesforce calls on each separate type of buyer or marketing channel. For example, Kodak switched from a geographical to a marketing channel structure with different sales teams serving specific retail channels: mass merchandisers, photo specialty outlets, and food and drug stores. The rationale for this approach is that more effective, specialized customer support and knowledge are provided to buyers. However, this structure often leads to higher administrative costs and some duplication of selling effort, since two separate salesforces are used to represent the same products.

A variation of the customer organizational structure is **major account management,** the practice of using team selling to focus on important customers so as to build mutually beneficial, long-term, cooperative relationships.[30] Major account management involves teams of sales, service, and often technical personnel who work with purchasing, manufacturing, engineering, logistics, and financial executives in customer organizations. This approach, which often assigns company personnel to a customer account, results in "customer specialists" who can provide exceptional service. Procter & Gamble uses this approach with Wal-Mart as does Black & Decker with Home Depot.

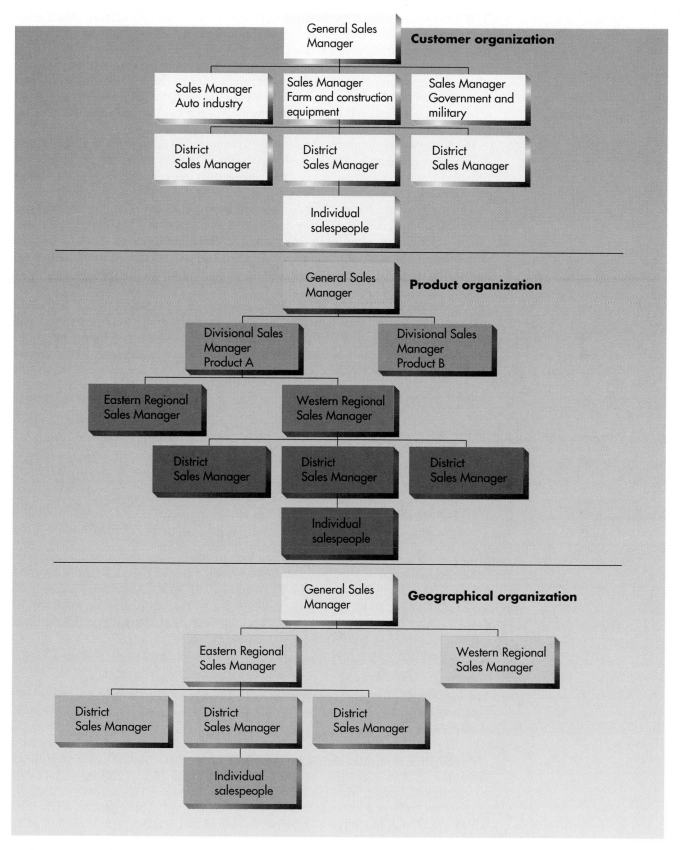

FIGURE 21-7

ORGANIZING THE SALESFORCE BY CUSTOMER, PRODUCT, AND GEOGRAPHY

When specific knowledge is required to sell certain types of products, then a product sales organization is used. For example, Procter & Gamble has a salesforce that sells household products and another that sells food products.

The primary advantage of this structure is that salespeople can develop expertise with technical characteristics, applications, and selling methods associated with a particular product or family of products. However, this structure also produces high administrative costs and duplication of selling effort since two company salespeople may call on the same customer.

In short, there is no one best sales organization for all companies in all situations. Rather, the organization of the salesforce should reflect the marketing strategy of the firm. Each year about 10 percent of firms change their sales organizations to implement new marketing strategies.

The third question related to salesforce organization involves determining the size of the salesforce. For example, why does Frito-Lay have about 13 500 salespeople who call on supermarkets, grocery stores, and other establishments to sell snack foods? The answer lies in the number of accounts (customers) served, the frequency of calls on accounts, the length of an average call, and the amount of time a salesperson can devote to selling.

A common approach for determining the size of a salesforce is the **workload method.** This formula-based method integrates the number of customers served, call frequency, call length, and available selling time to arrive at a figure for the salesforce size. For example, Frito-Lay needs about 13 500 salespeople according to the following workload method formula:

$$NS = \frac{NC \times CF \times CL}{AST}$$

where:

NS = Number of salespeople

NC = Number of customers

CF = Call frequency necessary to service a customer each year

CL = Length of an average call

AST = Average amount of selling time available per year

Frito-Lay sells its products to 400 000 supermarkets, grocery stores, and other establishments. Salespeople should call on these accounts at least once a week, or 52 times a year. The average sales call lasts 55 minutes (0.91 hour). An average salesperson works 2000 hours a year (50 weeks × 40 hours a week), but 12 hours a week are devoted to nonselling activities such as travel, leaving 1400 hours a year. Using these guidelines, Frito-Lay would need

$$NS = \frac{400\ 000 \times 52 \times 0.91}{1400} = 13\ 520 \text{ salespeople}$$

The value of this formula is apparent in its flexibility; a change in any one of the variables will affect the number of salespeople needed. Changes are determined, in part, by the firm's account management policies.

Developing account management policies   The third task in formulating a sales plan involves developing **account management policies** specifying whom salespeople should contact, what kinds of selling and customer service activities should be engaged in, and how these activities should be carried out.[31] These policies might state which individuals in a buying organization should be contacted, the amount of sales and service effort that different customers should receive, and the kinds of information salespeople should collect before or during a sales call.

An example of an account management policy in Figure 21-8 shows how different accounts or customers can be grouped according to level of opportunity and the firm's

	COMPETITIVE POSITION OF SALES ORGANIZATION	
	HIGH	**LOW**
High	1 *Attractiveness.* Accounts offer good opportunity, since they have high potential and sales organization has a strong position. *Account management policy.* Accounts should receive high level of sales calls and service to retain and possibly build accounts.	3 *Attractiveness.* Accounts may offer good opportunity if sales organization can overcome its weak position. *Account management policy.* Emphasize a heavy sales organization position or shift resources to other accounts if stronger sales organization position impossible.
Low	2 *Attractiveness.* Accounts are somewhat attractive since sales organization has a strong position, but future opportunity is limited. *Account management policy.* Accounts should receive moderate level of sales and service to maintain current position of sales organization.	4 *Attractiveness.* Accounts offer little opportunity, and sales organization position is weak. *Account management policy.* Consider replacing personal calls with telephone sales or direct mail to service accounts. Consider dropping account.

(Left axis label: **ACCOUNT OPPORTUNITY**)

FIGURE 21-8

ACCOUNT MANAGEMENT POLICY
GRID

competitive sales position. When specific account names are placed in each cell, salespeople clearly see which accounts should be contacted, with what level of selling and service activity, and how to deal with them. Accounts in cells 1 and 2 might have high frequencies of personal sales calls and increased time spent on a call. Cell 3 accounts will have lower call frequencies, and cell 4 accounts might be contacted through telemarketing or direct mail rather than in person.

Sales Plan Implementation

The sales plan is put into practice through the tasks associated with sales plan implementation. Whereas sales plan formulation focuses on "doing the right things," implementation emphasizes "doing things right." The three major tasks involved in implementing a sales plan are (1) salesforce recruitment and selection, (2) salesforce training, and (3) salesforce motivation and compensation.

Salesforce recruitment and selection   Effective recruitment and selection of salespeople is one of the most crucial tasks of sales management. It entails finding people who match the type of sales position required by a firm. Recruitment and selection practices would differ greatly between order-taking and order-getting sales positions, given the differences in the demands of these two jobs. Therefore, recruitment and selection begin with a carefully crafted job analysis and job description followed by a statement of job qualifications.[32]

A *job analysis* is a study of a particular sales position, including how the job is to be performed and the tasks that make up the job. Information from a job analysis is used to write a *job description,* a written document that describes job relationships and requirements that characterize each sales position. It explains (1) to whom a salesperson reports, (2) how a salesperson interacts with other company personnel, (3) the customers to be called on, (4) the specific activities to be carried out, (5) the physical and mental demands of the job, and (6) the types of products and services to be sold. The job description is then translated into a statement of job qualifications, including the aptitudes, knowledge, skills, and a variety of behavioural characteristics considered necessary to perform the job successfully. Qualifications for order-getting sales positions often mirror the expectations of buyers: (1) problem-solving ability, (2) honesty, (3) intimate product knowledge, and (4) attentiveness reflected in responsiveness to buyer needs and customer follow-up.[33] Firms use a variety of methods for evaluating prospective salespeople. Personal interviews, reference checks, and background information provided on application forms are the most frequently used methods.[34]

Salesforce training   Whereas recruitment and selection of salespeople is a one-time event, salesforce training is an ongoing process that affects both new and seasoned salespeople. For example, Microsoft offers nearly 100 training courses annually for its experienced salespeople alone.[35] Sales training covers much more than selling practices. On average, training programs devote 35 percent of time to product information, 30 percent to sales techniques, 25 percent to market and company information, and 10 percent to other topics, including ethical practices.[36] (What was your answer to question 3 on the quiz in Figure 21-1?)

Training new salespeople is an expensive and time-consuming process.[37] The average cost of training a new industrial product salesperson (including salary during the training period) is $9763 and takes four months. Training a new consumer product salesperson costs $4995 and takes about three months, and training new salespeople in service industries costs $6610 and takes almost four months. On-the-job training is the most popular type of training, followed by individual instruction taught by experienced salespeople. Formal classes and seminars taught by sales trainers are also popular.

Salesforce motivation and compensation   A sales plan cannot be successfully implemented without motivated salespeople. Research on salesperson motivation suggests that (1) a clear job description, (2) effective sales management practices, (3) a sense of achievement, and (4) proper compensation, incentives, or rewards will produce a motivated salesperson.[38]

The importance of compensation as a motivating factor means that close attention must be given to how salespeople are financially rewarded for their efforts. Salespeople are paid using one of three plans: (1) straight salary, (2) straight commission, or (3) a combination of salary and commission. Under a *straight salary compensation plan* a salesperson is paid a fixed fee per week, month, or year. With a *straight commission compensation plan* a salesperson's earnings are directly tied to the sales or profit generated. For example, an insurance agent might receive a 2 percent commission of $2000 for selling a $100 000 life insurance policy. A *combination compensation plan* contains a specified salary plus a commission on sales or profit generated.

Each compensation plan has its advantages and disadvantages. A straight salary plan is easy to administer and gives management a large measure of control over how salespeople allocate their efforts.

MARY KAY COSMETICS RECOGNIZES A TOP SALESPERSON AT ITS ANNUAL SALES MEETING.

However, it provides little incentive to expand sales volume. This plan is used when salespeople engage in many nonselling activities, such as account servicing. A straight commission plan provides the maximum amount of selling incentive but can detract salespeople from providing customer service. This plan is common when nonselling activities are minimal. Combination plans are most preferred by salespeople and attempt to build on the advantages of salary and commission plans while reducing potential shortcomings of each. Today, 68 percent of companies use combination plans, 19 percent use straight salary, and 13 percent rely solely on commissions. The popularity of combination plans is evident in the recent decision by Digital Equipment Corporation to convert its 10 000 computer salespeople from straight salary to a salary plus commission plan.

Nonmonetary rewards are also given to salespeople for meeting or exceeding objectives. These rewards include trips, honour societies, distinguished salesperson awards, and letters of commendation. Some unconventional rewards include the new pink Cadillacs, fur coats, and jewellery given by Mary Kay Cosmetics to outstanding salespeople.

Effective recruitment, selection, training, motivation, and compensation programs combine to create a productive salesforce. Ineffective practices often lead to costly salesforce turnover. Canadian and U.S. firms experience an annual 27 percent turnover rate, which means that about one of every four salespeople are replaced each year. The expense of replacing and training a new salesperson, including the cost of lost sales, can be as high as $75 000.[39] Moreover, new recruits are often less productive than established salespeople.

Salesforce Evaluation and Control

The final function in the sales management process involves evaluating and controlling the salesforce. It is at this point that salespeople are assessed as to whether sales objectives were met and account management policies were followed. Both quantitative and behavioural measures are used.

Quantitative assessments   Quantitative assessments, called quotas, are based on input- and output-related objectives set forth in the sales plan. Input-related measures focus on the actual activities performed by salespeople such as those involving sales calls, selling expenses, and account management policies. The number of sales calls made, selling expense related to sales made, and the number of reports submitted to superiors are frequently used input measures.

Output measures focus on the results obtained and include sales produced, accounts generated, profit achieved, and orders produced compared with calls made. Dollar sales volume, last year/current year sales ratio, the number of new accounts, and sales of specific products are frequently used measures when evaluating salesperson output.

Behavioural evaluation   Behavioural measures are also used to evaluate salespeople. These include assessments of a salesperson's attitude, attention to customers, product knowledge, selling and communication skills, appearance, and professional demeanor. Even though these assessments are sometimes subjective, they are frequently considered, and, in fact, inevitable, in salesperson evaluation. Moreover, these factors are often important determinants of quantitative outcomes.

Many Canadian companies now include customer satisfaction as a behavioural measure of salesperson performance. IBM Canada has been very aggressive in using this behavioural measure. Hotels, like the Ritz-Carlton, also use customer satisfaction measures as part of an employee's evaluation.[40]

Salesforce Automation

Personal selling and sales management are undergoing a technological revolution in the form of salesforce automation. **Salesforce automation** (SFA) is the use of technology designed to make the sales function more effective and efficient. SFA applies to a wide range of activities including each stage in the personal selling process and management of the salesforce itself. Computer and communication technologies have and will continue to play a central role in salesforce automation.[41]

Salesforce computerization   Computer technology has become an integral part of field selling through innovations such as laptop, notebook, palmtop, pad, and tablet computers. Salespeople can use this technology to process orders, plan time allocations, forecast sales, and communicate with co-workers and customers. Toshiba Medical System's salespeople use laptop computers with built-in CD-ROM capabilities to provide interactive presentations for their computerized tomography (CT) and magnetic resonance imaging (MRI) scanners. In it the customer sees elaborate three-dimensional animations, high-resolution scans, and video clips of the company's products in operation as well as narrated testimonials from satisfied customers. Toshiba has found this application to be effective both for sales presentations and for training its salespeople.[42]

Salesforce communication   Technology also has changed the way salespeople communicate with customers, other salespeople and sales support personnel, and management. Facsimile, electronic mail, and voice mail are three common communication technologies used by salespeople today. Cellular (phone) technology, which now allows

salespeople to exchange data as well as voice transmissions, is equally popular. Whether travelling or in a customer's office, these technologies provide information at the salesperson's fingertips to answer customer questions and solve problems.

Advances in communication and computer technologies have made possible the mobile sales office. Some salespeople now equip minivans with a fully functional desk, swivel chair, light, computer, printer, fax machine, cellular phone, and a satellite dish.

Sales management in the age of automation   Salesforce automation represents both an opportunity and a challenge for sales management. Examples of SFA applications include computer hardware and software for account analysis, time management, order processing and follow-up, sales presentations,

THE MOBILE OFFICE FOR SALESPEOPLE HAS GROWN IN POPULARITY WITH THE ADVENT OF COMPUTER AND COMMUNICATION TECHNOLOGY.

proposal generation, and product and sales training. But applications are not free. It is estimated that equipment, software, and training costs for automating a salesforce ranges from $2500 to $5000 or more per person. However, companies such as Tandem Computer report that savings from SFA by its 1700 national and international field salespeople amount to $2 million annually.[43]

Some companies are using SFA to eliminate the need for field sales offices. Compaq Computer Corporation is a case in point. The company shifted its entire salesforce into home offices, closed three regional sales offices, and saved $10 million in staff salaries and office rent. A fully equipped home office for each salesperson costs the company about $8000 and includes a notebook computer, fax/copier, cellular phone, two phone lines, and office furniture.[44]

Salesforce automation is clearly changing how selling is done and how salespeople are managed. Its numerous applications promise to boost selling productivity, improve customer service, and decrease selling cost. As applications increase, SFA has the potential to transform selling and sales management in the twenty-first century.

CONCEPT CHECK

1. What are the three types of selling objectives?

2. What three factors are used to structure sales organizations?

3. Sales training typically focuses on what two sales-related issues?

SUMMARY

1. Personal selling involves the two-way flow of communication between a buyer and a seller, often in a face-to-face encounter, designed to influence a person's or group's purchase decision. Sales management involves planning the sales program and implementing and controlling the personal selling effort of the firm.

2. Personal selling is pervasive since virtually every occupation that involves customer contact has an element of selling attached to it.

3. Personal selling plays a major role in a firm's marketing effort. Salespeople occupy a boundary position between buyers and sellers; they *are* the company to many buyers and account for a major cost of marketing in a variety of industries; and they can create value for customers.

4. Three types of personal selling exist: order taking, order getting, and sales support activities. Each type differs from the others in terms of actual selling done and the amount of creativity required to perform the job.

5. The personal selling process, particularly for order getters, is a complex activity involving six stages: (1) prospecting, (2) preapproach, (3) approach, (4) presentation, (5) close, and (6) follow-up.

6. The sales management process consists of three interrelated functions: (1) sales plan formulation, (2) sales plan implementation, and (3) evaluation of the salesforce.

7. A sales plan is a statement describing what is to be achieved and where and how the selling effort of salespeople is to be deployed. Sales planning involves setting objectives, organizing the salesforce, and developing account management policies.

8. Effective salesforce recruitment and selection efforts, sales training that emphasizes selling skills and product knowledge, and motivation and compensation practices are necessary to successfully implement a sales plan.

9. Salespeople are evaluated using quantitative and behavioural measures that are linked to selling objectives and account management policies.

10. Salesforce automation involves the use of technology designed to make the sales function more effective and efficient. It applies to a wide range of activities including each stage in the personal selling process and management of the salesforce itself.

KEY TERMS AND CONCEPTS

personal selling p. 498
sales management p. 498
relationship selling p. 499
order taker p. 500
order getter p. 500
missionary salespeople p. 501
sales engineer p. 501
team selling p. 501
conference selling p. 502
seminar selling p. 502
personal selling process p. 502

stimulus-response presentation p. 505
formula selling presentation p. 505
need-satisfaction presentation p. 505
adaptive selling p. 505
consultative selling p. 505
sales plan p. 508
major account management p. 510
workload method p. 512
account management policies p. 512
salesforce automation p. 512

CHAPTER PROBLEMS AND APPLICATIONS

1. Jane Dawson is a new sales representative for the Charles Schwab brokerage firm. In searching for clients, Jane purchased a mailing list of subscribers to *The Financial Post* and called them all regarding their interest in discount brokerage services. She asked if they have any stocks and if they have a regular broker. Those people without a regular broker were asked their investment needs. Two days later Jane called back with investment advice and asked if they would like to open an account. Identify each of Jane Dawson's actions in terms of the steps of selling.

2. For the first 50 years of business the Johnson Carpet Company produced carpets for residential use. The salesforce was structured geographically. In the past five years a large percentage of carpet sales has been to industrial users, hospitals, schools, and architects. The company also has broadened its product line to include area rugs, Oriental carpets, and wall-to-wall carpeting. Is the present salesforce structure appropriate, or would you recommend an alternative?

3. Where would you place each of the following sales jobs on the order taker/order getter continuum shown below? (*a*) Burger King counter clerk, (*b*) automobile insurance salesperson, (*c*) IBM computer salesperson, (*d*) life insurance salesperson, and (*e*) shoe salesperson.

|---|---|
| **Order taker** | **Order getter** |

4. Listed here are three different firms. Which compensation plan would you recommend for each firm, and what reasons would you give for your recommendations? (*a*) A newly formed company that sells lawn care equipment on a door-to-door basis directly to consumers; (*b*) the Nabisco Company, which sells heavily advertised products in supermarkets by having the salesforce call on these stores and arrange shelves, set up displays, and make presentations to store buying committees; and (*c*) the Wang word-processing division, which makes word-processing system presentations to company buying committees consisting of purchasing agents and future users.

5. The TDK tape company services 1000 audio stores throughout Canada. Each store is called on 12 times a year, and the average sales call lasts 30 minutes. Assuming a salesperson works 40 hours a week, 50 weeks a year, and devotes 75 percent of the time to actual selling, how many salespeople does TDK need?

6. A furniture manufacturer is currently using manufacturer's representatives to sell its line of living room furniture. These representatives receive an 8 percent commission. The company is considering hiring its own salespeople and has estimated that the fixed cost of managing and paying their salaries would be $1 million annually. The salespeople would also receive a 4 percent commission on sales. The company has sales of $25 million dollars, and sales are expected to grow by 15 percent next year. Would you recommend that the company switch to its own salesforce? Why or why not?

7. Suppose someone said to you, "The only real measure of a salesperson is the amount of sales produced." How might you respond?

CASE 21-1   Contemporary Developments in Selling Today

Salespeople today often can no longer afford to behave like the pushy, stereotypical salesperson often portrayed in the media. More sophisticated customers, changes in technology, and a changing selling environment have meant that the "old-fashioned" salesperson of the past is increasingly becoming obsolete.

Three contempory developments in selling are changing how the sales function is being performed. These developments include (1) changes in sales motivation and compensation programs, (2) the introduction of salesforce automation, and (3) higher expectations for ethics in selling.

CHANGES IN MOTIVATION AND COMPENSATION PROGRAMS

One of the areas where selling has changed has been in the way salespeople are motivated and compensated. Marshall Industries, an electronics firm, operated until 1988 with a sales compensation and motivation program that encouraged a competitive environment between members of the sales force. In such an environment, salespeople were not interested in helping one another and the company as a whole. Rather, salespeople were primarily concerned with *their* customers and *their* territory. Compensation and motivation programs that produce winners and losers tend to have this effect. Since 1988, however, a new compensation and motivation program has been in place that encourages and rewards salesperson cooperation by eliminating commissions and other individual bonuses. Marshall Industries' sales compensation program was redesigned to reward group performance. Salespeople focused more on serving the customer rather than on achieving quotas. The results have been dramatic. Sales have increased from $400 million to $700 million within a five-year period, salesperson turnover was cut by 50 percent, and the company's stock price rose from $10 to $42 per share.

INTRODUCTION OF SALESFORCE AUTOMATION

Improvements and innovations in salesforce automation have had a dramatic impact on the tools available to the salesforce as well as improving salesforce effectiveness. Navistar has turned to technology to gain an advantage in their markets by developing a selling tool that allows potential customers to compare its brand of International trucks against competitors on a component-by-component basis. For example, a potential customer can learn how the turn radius for an International truck compares to that of a competitive truck, or how gas consumption varies, or how engine efficiency differs. This approach helps identify specific customer needs and highlight the implications of the purchase decision; that is, how does the purchase of this truck impact operating and maintenance costs? It's an extremely powerful tool for helping the salesforce show the benefits of the International truck in a very quantitive and useful manner on the criteria of importance to a given buyer.

SELLING ETHICS

The ethics of the personal selling profession has long been criticized by the public and the media. But, while the ethical conduct of salespeople is receiving increased attention and closer scrutiny, ethical conflicts continue to be an inherent part of the salesperson's job for a number of reasons. First, there is always some amount of pressure on the sales force to close the sale and "make the numbers." Where the payoff is large, and the chances of detection small, ethical corners may be cut to make the sale. Second, to be successful, a salesperson must be regarded by the company and the customer as a strong and loyal advocate for each party. However, it is usually impossible to maximize simultaneously the payoff to both the company and the customer. Thus, salespeople often encounter ethical dilemmas when fulfilling the expectations of one party serves to penalize the other. Third, salespeople in the field tend to be more autonomous than other company personnel. Removed from the corporate culture and continuous supervision, the salesperson often acts like an independent entrepreneur. As such, the salesperson is given a level of resources and decision-making authority that can create opportunities to engage in unethical practices. Finally, many experts argue that personal selling is inherently unethical because it causes the individual to promulgate what he or she is *paid* to believe, rather than what is truly believed. Under these conditions, the argument goes, real trust between parties is not possible. College students, in particular, have criticized personal selling on this point, maintaining that selling requires the individual to convey a pretense of sincerity.

Questions

1. What are the pros and cons of various salesforce compensation programs? What types of behaviour are encouraged under each?

2. Describe how salesforce automation can be used at different stages of the selling process to facilitate the salesperson's efforts.

3. There are many types of ethical conflicts that are faced by the salesforce due to the nature of the selling job. What steps can a salesperson and his/her company take to minimize the potential for ethical dilemmas?

MANAGING THE MARKETING PROCESS

Chapter 22
The Strategic Marketing Process

Part Five discusses issues and techniques related to the planning, implementation, and control phases of the strategic marketing process. Chapter 22 explains how marketing executives search for a competitive advantage and allocate the firm's resources to maximize the effects of marketing efforts. Frameworks for improving marketing planning, guidelines for creating an effective marketing plan, and alternatives for organizing a marketing department are also discussed.

The Strategic Marketing Process

AFTER READING THIS CHAPTER YOU SHOULD BE ABLE TO:

- Explain how marketing managers allocate their limited resources, both in theory and in practice.

- Describe three marketing planning frameworks: Porter's generic strategies, profit enhancement options, and market-product synergies.

- Describe what makes an effective marketing plan and some problems that often exist with them.

- Describe the alternatives for organizing a marketing department and the role of a product manager.

- Schedule a series of tasks to meet a deadline using a Gantt chart.

- Understand how sales and profitability analyses and marketing audits are used to evaluate and control marketing programs.

MARKETING STRATEGY AT GENERAL MILLS: A RETURN TO ITS ROOTS

General Mills' (www.generalmills.com) marketing strategists faced tough times in the mid-1990s. Its flagship Cheerios and Wheaties breakfast cereals and its Betty Crocker cake mixes were competing in a food industry growing at only 1 percent each year. Also, private brands were becoming tougher competitors, requiring General Mills to cut its prices, thereby hurting its margins and profits.[1] General Mills's restaurant chains—Red Lobster, Olive Garden, and China Coast—were growing fast but were constantly competing with its food lines for limited corporate resources.

In the end the corporate cultures—discussed in Chapter 2—in the General Mills food and restaurant sectors were far different, and real synergies between the two sectors didn't materialize. Therefore, corporate and marketing planners made a big decision: divide the original company into two new separate, focused companies:[2]

- General Mills, Inc.—a $5.5 billion consumer foods company that includes foods such as cereals, Betty Crocker cake mixes and desserts, Hamburger Helper, Yoplait yogourt, and Fruit by the Foot.
- Darden, Inc.—a $3.2 billion multiunit restaurant company that includes the Red Lobster, Olive Garden, and China Coast chains.

Marketing strategists planning the breakup hoped that the split would enable each new company to plan, implement, and control marketing efforts that would achieve higher growth in sales revenues and profits in their separated units than in the past. The breakup had at least one immediate result: the new product introduction of Frosted Cheerios—industry analysts have called it the most successful product launch of a ready-to-eat cereal in history.[3]

This chapter discusses issues and techniques related to the planning, implementation, and control phases of the strategic marketing process, the kind of topics marketing strategists at General Mills and Darden face in growing their businesses. The individual elements of the strategic marketing process were introduced in Chapter 2.

STRATEGIC MARKETING'S GOAL: EFFECTIVE RESOURCE ALLOCATION

As noted in Chapter 2, corporate and marketing executives search continuously to find a competitive advantage—a unique strength relative to competitors, often based on quality, time, cost, innovation, or customer intimacy. Having identified this competitive advantage, they must allocate their firm's resources to exploit it.[4] The timing of product and market actions may also influence the magnitude and duration of a firm's competitive advantage.[5]

Allocating Marketing Resources Using Sales Response Functions

A **sales response function** relates the expense of marketing effort to the marketing results obtained.[6] For simplicity in the examples that follow, only the effects of annual marketing effort on annual sales revenue will be analyzed, but the concept applies to other measures of marketing success—such as profit, units sold, or level of awareness—as well.

Maximizing incremental revenue minus incremental cost   Economists give managers a specific guideline for optimal resource allocation: allocate the firm's marketing, production, and financial resources to the markets and products where the excess of incremental revenues over incremental costs is greatest. This parallels the marginal revenue–marginal cost analysis of Chapter 14.

Figure 22-1 illustrates this resource allocation principle. The firm's annual marketing effort, such as sales and advertising expenses, is plotted on the horizontal axis. As this annual marketing effort increases, so does the resulting annual sales revenue. The relationship is assumed to be S-shaped, showing that an additional $1 million of marketing effort results in far greater increases of sales revenue in the mid-range (such as $4 million) than at either end (such as $2 million or $7 million).

A numerical example of resource allocation   Suppose Figure 22-1 shows the situation for a recently introduced General Mills product such as Gushers. Also assume the sales revenue response function doesn't change through time. Point A shows the position of the firm in year 1, and point B shows it three years later in year 4. Marketing effort in the form of advertising and other promotions has increased from $3 million to $6 million a year, while sales revenue has increased from $30 million to $70 million a year.

Let's look at the major resource allocation question: what are the probable increases in sales revenue in years 1 and 4 for an extra $1 million of marketing effort? As Figure 22-1 reveals:

Year 1

Increase in marketing effort from $3 million to $4 million = $1 million

Increase in sales revenue from $30 million to $50 million = $20 million

Ratio of incremental sales revenue to effort = $20 000 000:$1 000 000 = 20:1

Year 4

Increase in marketing effort from $6 million to $7 million = $1 million

Increase in sales revenue from $70 million to $73 million = $3 million

Ratio of incremental sales revenue to effort = $3 000 000:$1 000 000 = 3:1

Thus, in year 1 a dollar of extra marketing effort returned $20 in sales revenue, whereas in year 4 it returned only $3. If no other expenses are incurred, it might make sense to spend $1 million in year 4 to gain $3 million in incremental sales revenue. However, it may be far wiser for General Mills to invest the money in products in one of its other business units, such as its new lighter texture Whipped Deluxe Frosting or its new Pop Secret Popcorn Bars. The essence of resource allocation is simple: put incremental resources where the incremental returns are greatest over the foreseeable future.

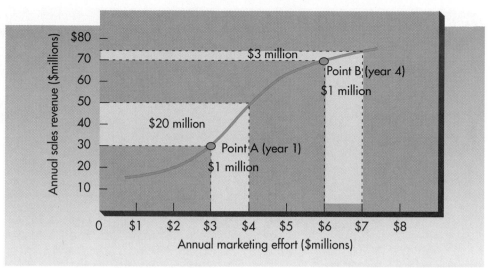

Allocating Marketing Resources in Practice

General Mills, like many firms in these businesses, does extensive analysis using **share points,** or percentage points of market share, as the common basis of comparison to allocate marketing resources effectively. This allows it to seek answers to the question "How much is it worth to us to try to increase our market share by another 1 (or 2, or 5, or 10) percentage point?"

This also enables higher-level managers to make resource allocation trade-offs among different kinds of business units owned by the company. To make these resource allocation decisions, marketing managers must estimate (1) the market share for the product, (2) the revenues associated with each point of market share (the present-day $82 million for a share point in breakfast cereals[7] may be five times what it is in cake mixes), and (3) the contribution to overhead and profit (or gross margin) of each share point.

The resource allocation process helps General Mills choose wisely from among the many opportunities that exist in its various products and markets.

Resource Allocation and the Strategic Marketing Process

Company resources are allocated effectively in the strategic marketing process by converting marketing information into marketing actions. Figure 22-2 summarizes the strategic marketing process introduced in Chapter 2, along with some details of the marketing actions and information that compose it. Figure 22-2 is really a simplification of the actual strategic marketing process: while the three phases of the strategic marketing process have distinct separations in the figure and the marketing actions are separated from the marketing information, in practice these blend together and interact.

The upper half of each box in Figure 22-2 highlights the actions involved in that part of the strategic marketing process, and the lower half summarizes the information and reports used. Note that each phase has an output report:

PHASE	OUTPUT REPORT
Planning	Marketing plans (or programs) that define goals and the marketing mix strategies to achieve them
Implementation	Results (memos or computer outputs) that describe the outcomes of implementing the plans
Control	Corrective action memos, triggered by comparing results with plans, that (1) suggest solutions to problems and (2) take advantage of opportunities

	Planning Phase			Implementation Phase	Control Phase
	Step 1	Step 2	Step 3		
Action	**Situation (SWOT) analysis** • Identify industry trends • Analyze competitors • Assess own company • Research customers	**Market-product focus and goal setting** • Set market and product goals • Select target markets • Find points of difference • Position the product	**Marketing program** • Develop the program's marketing mix • Develop the budget, by estimating revenues, expenses, and profits	• Obtain resources • Design marketing organization • Develop schedules • Execute marketing program	• Compare results with plans to identify deviations • Correct negative deviations; exploit positive ones
				Plans →	**Results** →
Information	• Determine trend in past and current revenues: For industry and competitors in total and by segment • Project future revenues, expenses and profits: For own product in total and by segment	• Market potential By industry By segment • Market-product grids, with ranked targets • Product positioning that stresses key features, advantages, benefits	• Characteristics and timing of: Product actions Price actions Promotion actions Place actions • Projected marketing expenses • Detailed plans to execute the marketing program	• Memos assigning responsibilities for actions and deadlines; Gantt charts • Organizational charts and job descriptions	• Tracking reports measuring results of the marketing actions • Deviation reports comparing actual results with plans • Action memos to try to correct problems and exploit opportunities
	← Corrective actions →			← Corrective actions →	

FIGURE 22-2

THE STRATEGIC MARKETING PROCESS;
ACTIONS AND INFORMATION

The corrective action memos become "feedback loops" in Figure 22-2 that help improve decisions and actions in earlier phases of the strategic marketing process.

THE PLANNING PHASE OF THE STRATEGIC MARKETING PROCESS

Three aspects of the strategic marketing process deserve special mention: (1) the varieties of marketing plans, (2) marketing planning frameworks that have proven useful, and (3) some marketing planning and strategy lessons.

The Variety of Marketing Plans

The planning phase of the strategic marketing process usually results in a marketing plan that sets the direction for the marketing activities of an organization. As noted earlier in Appendix A, a marketing plan is the heart of a business plan. Like business plans, marketing plans aren't all from the same mould; they vary with the length of the planning period, the purpose, and the audience. Let's look briefly at three kinds: long-range, annual, and new-product marketing plans.

Long-range marketing plans   Typically, long-range marketing plans cover marketing activities from two to five years into the future. Except for firms in industries such as autos, steel, or forest products, marketing plans rarely go beyond five years into the future because the tremendous number of uncertainties present make the

STEPS IN ANNUAL MARKETING PLANNING PROCESS	WEEKS BEFORE APPROVAL OF PLAN					
	50	40	30	20	10	0
1. Obtain up-to-date marketing information from marketing research study of product users.	▲					
2. Brainstorm alternatives to consider in next year's plan with own marketing research and outside advertising agency personnel.	◢▲					
3. Meet with internal media specialists to set long-run guidelines in purchase of media.			◢▲			
4. Obtain sales and profit results from last fiscal year, which ended 16 weeks earlier.			◢▲			
5. Identify key issues (problems and opportunities) to address in next year's plan by talks with marketing researchers, advertising agency, and other personnel.			◢▲			
6. Hold key issues meeting with marketing director; form task force of line managers if significant product, package, or size change is considered.				▲		
7. Write and circulate key issues memo; initiate necessary marketing research to reduce uncertainty.				◢▲		
8. Review marketing mix elements and competitors' behaviour with key managers, keeping marketing director informed.					◢▲	
9. Draft marketing plan, review with marketing director, and revise as necessary.					◢▲	
10. Present plan to marketing director, advertising agency, division controller, and heads of responsible line departments (product, packaging, sales, etc.) and make necessary changes.					▲	
11. Present marketing plan to division general manager for approval, 10 weeks before start of fiscal year.						▲

KEY: ◢ Planned period of work, ▲ Planned completion date

FIGURE 22-3

STEPS A LARGE CONSUMER PACKAGE GOODS FIRM TAKES IN DEVELOPING ITS ANNUAL MARKETING PLAN

benefits of planning less than the effort expended. Such plans are often directed at top-level executives and the board of directors.

Annual marketing plans   Usually developed by a product manager (discussed later in the chapter) in a consumer products firm such as General Mills, annual marketing plans deal with marketing goals and strategies for a product, product line, or entire firm for a single year. Typical steps that firms such as Kellogg, Coca-Cola, and Johnson & Johnson take in developing their annual marketing plans for their existing products are shown in Figure 22-3.[8] This annual planning cycle typically starts with a detailed marketing research study of current users and ends after 48 weeks with the approval of the plan by the division general manager—10 weeks before the fiscal year starts. Between these points there are continuing efforts to uncover new ideas through brainstorming and key-issues sessions with specialists both inside and outside the firm. The plan is fine-tuned through a series of often excruciating reviews by several levels of management, which leaves few surprises and little to chance.

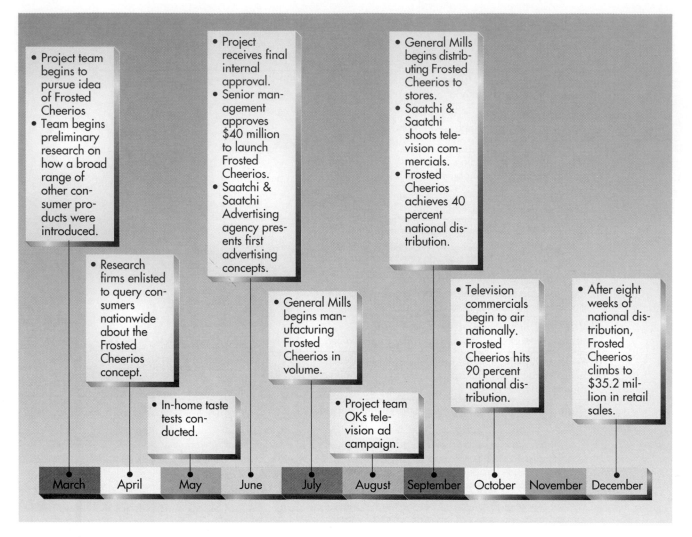

FIGURE 22-4

FROSTED CHEERIOS: FROM IDEA TO
GROCERY SHELF IN SIX MONTHS

Marketing plans for new-product launches: Frosted Cheerios   Planning and implementing the introduction of Frosted Cheerios by a General Mills team shows the interactions of marketing strategy and tactics with the information, actions, and people needed for success. Central to all of this activity is a new-product marketing plan. As noted in Chapter 11, during 1993 and 1994 General Mills introduced a series of breakfast cereals that did poorly in the market. So when Mark Addicks was named director of marketing for new cereal products in March 1995, he knew the company needed a big winner. Figure 22-4 shows a time line of actions in the marketing plan that led to the shipment of Frosted Cheerios to stores in September 1995. The time from the new-product idea in March 1995 to first shipment in September took six months—half the normal new launch time for a new cereal product at General Mills.[9]

Figure 22-4 illustrates many key marketing concepts developed throughout this book:

- *Cross-functional teams.* The first thing Addicks did was recruit a team with a representative from every pertinent department: marketing, sales, research and development (R&D), marketing research, product development, and manufacturing.
- *Corporate goals.* Frosted Cheerios must contribute to General Mills's corporate targets of increasing earnings per share 12 percent annually and growth of unit volume 5 percent annually.
- *Marketing goals.* The new product must not cannibalize sales of the existing brands of Cheerios (plain Cheerios alone had 1995 sales of $289 million) or hurt their images. Also, 0.5 percent market share is considered a success.

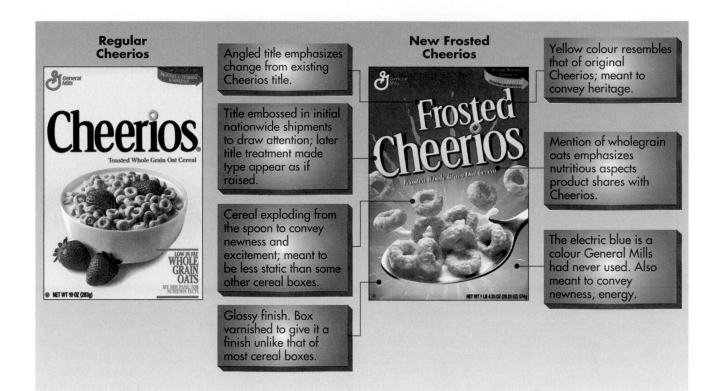

FIGURE 22-5

THE CROSS-FUNCTIONAL TEAM'S
THINKING BEHIND THE FROSTED
CHEERIOS NEW PACKAGE

- *Marketing budget.* Top management allocated $40 million for the launch, the most of any product in its history.
- *Target market.* The target market is kids (60 percent) and baby-boomer adults (40 percent) who do not have the sugared cereals hangup that their parents do.
- *Benchmarking.* The team studied successful product launches of all kinds, including Disney movies and Nickelodeon TV programs, to learn lessons for its cereal launch.
- *Marketing research on consumers.* In April (see Figure 22-4) consumers were asked about the Frosted Cheerios concept; 88 percent of the kids saying they would eat them. In-home taste tests in May bore this out and identified the best from among three formulations.
- *Competitive advantages/points of difference.* A big concern was copycat imitations. So Addicks's team targeted these unique elements: complex enough to avoid copying, sweet enough to appeal to the target market, and grainy enough to maintain the Cheerios taste and image.
- *Product strategy.* Manufacturing Frosted Cheerios was a lot more complex than dipping regular Cheerios in sugar. R&D scientists found they had to blend corn flour in with the regular oat flour to give their new product the proper Cheerios "crunch." The final package, shown in Figure 22-5, was selected from seven competing designs. The figure shows the detailed planning needed to position the product favourably in the eyes and minds of consumers.
- *Pricing strategy.* The team set a price consistent with other Cheerios brands and competitive with other sugared cereals, like Kellogg's Frosted Flakes.
- *Promotion strategy.* Working with the team, its advertising agency shot the TV commercials in September (Figure 22-4), using contemporary and campy characters such as Underdog, rap artist Latifah, and loud-mouth comedian Gilbert Gottfried.[10]
- *Place strategy.* As shown in Figure 22-4, General Mills started shipping to stores in September and had 90 percent distribution the next month.

In terms of implementation, Frosted Cheerios was on retailer shelves when the TV ad campaigns started, always a huge concern with new grocery product introductions.

After eight weeks, sales were $35.2 million, about 2.5 percent market share. At $82 million per share point, sales revenue projections for 1996 were more than $200 million. This market share was five times the minimum level needed to support the brand. Clearly Frosted Cheerios is a huge success by any standard—a success attributable to a cohesive cross-functional team's attention to detail and deadlines in its new-product marketing plan.

CONCEPT CHECK

1. What is the significance of the S-shape of the sales response function in Figure 22-1?

2. What are the main output reports from each phase of the strategic marketing process?

3. What are three kinds of marketing plans?

Frameworks to Improve Marketing Planning

Marketing planning for a firm with many products competing in many markets—a multiproduct, multimarket firm—is a complex process. Three techniques that are useful in helping corporate and marketing executives in such a firm make important resource allocation decisions are (1) Porter's generic business strategies, (2) profit enhancement options, and (3) market-product synergies. All of these techniques are based on elements introduced in earlier chapters.

Porter's generic business strategies   As shown in Figure 22-6, Michael E. Porter has developed a framework in which he identifies four basic, or "generic," strategies.[11] A **generic business strategy** is one that can be adopted by any firm, regardless of the product or industry involved, to achieve a competitive advantage. Some current research suggests that a firm needs several major competencies, not just one, to sustain its competitive advantage over longer periods;[12] other research suggests that the preferred strategy is to focus on a single discipline—such as operational excellence, product leadership, or customer intimacy.[13]

Although all of the techniques discussed here involve generic strategies, the phrase is most often associated with Porter's framework. In this framework the columns identify the two fundamental alternatives firms can use in seeking competitive advantage: (1) becoming the low-cost producer within the markets in which it competes or (2) differentiating itself from competitors through developing points of difference in its product offerings or marketing programs. In contrast, the rows

FIGURE 22-6

PORTER'S FOUR GENERIC BUSINESS STRATEGIES

		SOURCE OF COMPETITIVE ADVANTAGE	
		LOWER COST	**DIFFERENTIATION**
COMPETITIVE SCOPE	**BROAD TARGET**	1. Cost leadership	2. Differentiation
	NARROW TARGET	3. Cost focus	4. Differentiation focus

identify the competitive scope: (1) a broad target by competing in many market segments or (2) a narrow target by competing in only a few segments or even a single segment. The columns and rows result in four business strategies, any one of which can provide a competitive advantage among similar business units in the same industry:

1. A **cost leadership strategy** (cell 1) requires a serious commitment to reducing expenses that, in turn, lowers the price or the items sold in a relatively broad array of market segments. Sometimes significant investments in capital equipment may be necessary to improve the production process to give these low unit costs. The cost leader still must have adequate quality levels. The original Model T Ford and today's South Korean shipbuilders are examples of a cost leadership strategy. By mass producing only black Model T's, Henry Ford drove the price down to where the typical family could buy a car. South Korean shipbuilders now dominate Asian competitors because of their cost efficiencies.

2. A **differentiation strategy** (cell 2) requires innovation and significant points of difference in product offerings, higher quality, advanced technology, or superior service in a relatively broad array of market segments. This allows a price premium. General Motors used this strategy against Ford in the 1920s when it developed an array of models with different colours and features in contrast to Ford's black Model T. It has taken Ford half a century to approach a similar level of differentiation through offering multiple product lines and, in some cases, higher quality.

3. A **cost focus strategy** (cell 3) involves controlling expenses and, in turn, lowering prices, in a narrow range of market segments. Retail chains targeting only a few market segments in a restricted group of products have used a cost focus strategy successfully. The 1-2-3 Dollar Store is a cost focused retailer.

4. Finally, a **differentiation focus strategy** (cell 4) utilizes significant points of difference to one or only a few market segments. Enterprise Rent-A-Car ("The Company that Picks You Up") has achieved spectacular success by offering to pick up or drop off their car renters at their homes or offices.

These strategies also form the foundation for Michael Porter's theory about what makes a nation's industries successful, as discussed in Chapter 5. But entire industries are becoming increasingly commoditized as technological and operational advantages become short-lived. Accordingly, more Canadian companies are attempting to gain a competitive advantage by developing a relationship with their customers that the competition cannot break. Nowhere is this becoming more of a reality than in the Canadian telecommunications equipment and services market. Challenges faced by Canadian telecom companies are a sign of things for most industries that face growing competition and a limited number of customers. In essence, if everyone sells the same product at the same prices to the same customers, a customer-intimacy or relationship marketing program can serve as a competitive advantage for a particular company. Often technology is the enabler in this situation. For example, many firms are using their web sites as a two-way information forum between themselves and their customers.

Profit enhancement options   If a business wants to increase, or "enhance," its profits, it can (1) increase revenues, (2) decrease expenses, or (3) do both. Among these "profit enhancement options," let's look first at the strategy options of increasing revenues and then at those for decreasing expenses.

The strategy option of increasing revenues can only be achieved by using one or a combination of four ways to address present or new markets and products (Figure 22-7): (1) market penetration, (2) product development, (3) market development, and (4) diversification (which are described in Chapter 2).

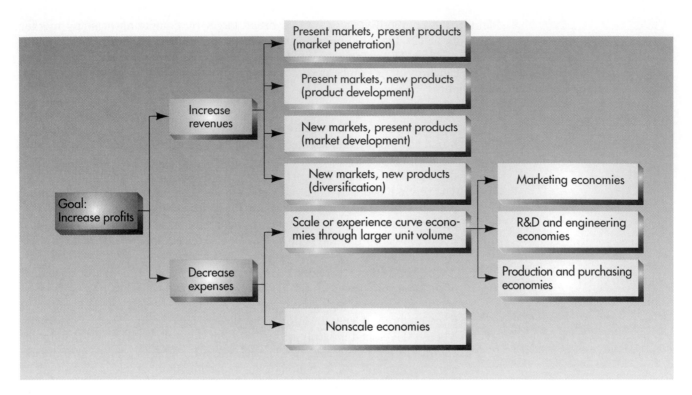

FIGURE 22-7   GENERIC MARKETING STRATEGIES FOR INCREASING A FIRM'S PROFITS

Procter & Gamble has followed a successful strategy of market penetration (present markets, present products) by concentrating its effort on becoming the market leader in each of its 39 product categories. It is currently first in market share in more than half these product categories. Recent research, however, suggests that while market share may be directly related to profitability in some industries, this is not true for all. Corporate goals such as increasing customer satisfaction may be more successful than simply maximizing market share.[14]

In contrast, Johnson & Johnson has succeeded with a product development strategy—finding new products for its present markets—to complement popular brands such as Tylenol pain reliever and Accuvue contact lenses. To compete with Bristol-Meyers and other companies, Johnson & Johnson developed Tylenol PM—a combination pain killer and sleeping pill—and Surevue—a long-lasting disposable contact lens.

Walt Disney Co. has pursued a market development strategy (new market, present product) since the success of the original Disneyland in Anaheim, California. The first market expansion, of course, was to Orlando, Florida, and more recently Disney has built theme parks in Tokyo and Paris.

Disney has also pursued a diversification strategy by entering into the motion picture business with the development of Touchstone Pictures, and by buying and operating an NHL franchise, the Mighty Ducks.

Strategy options for decreasing expenses fall into two broad categories (Figure 22-7). One is relying on scale economies or experience curve benefits from an increased volume of production to drive unit costs down and gross margins up, the best-known examples being electronic devices such as fax or voice-mail machines whose prices fell by half in a few years. Scale economies may occur in marketing, as well as in R&D, engineering, production, and purchasing.

The other strategy option to decrease expenses is simply finding other ways to reduce costs, such as cutting the number of managers, increasing the effectiveness of

MARKETING NEWSNET

THE STRATEGY ISSUE OF THE 1990S: FINDING SYNERGIES

CIBC buys Oppenheimer & Co. of New York for "synergy." Time Warner buys Turner Broadcasting "to get synergy." Both Sun Microsystems and Sony considered buying Apple for the purpose of "getting synergy." With the current go-go days of giant mergers and acquisitions, the partners in these ventures are looking for synergies that have often proven elusive or impossible to achieve. For example, AT&T finally spun off its NCR computer group that it had bought only a few years earlier—to find synergies—after losing more than $1 billion.

To try your hand in this multibillion dollar synergy game, let's assume you are vice president of marketing for Great Lawns Corporation, whose product lines are nonpowered lawnmowers and powered walking mowers. A market-

product grid for your business is shown below. You distribute your nonpowered mowers in the three market segments shown and your powered, walking mowers in suburban markets—but you don't yet sell your powered walking mowers in cities or rural areas.

Here are your strategy dilemmas:

1. Where are the marketing synergies (efficiencies)?
2. Where are the R&D and manufacturing synergies (efficiencies)?
3. What would a market-product grid look like for an ideal company for Great Lawns to merge with?

For the answers to these questions, read the text and study Figures 22-8 and 22-9.

the salesforce through more training, or reducing the product rejects by inspectors. In an effort to decrease costs, IBM Canada and Xerox Canada have downsized through layoffs.

Market-product synergies   Let's use the market-product grid framework introduced in Chapter 9 to study two kinds of synergy that are critical in developing corporate and marketing strategies: (1) marketing synergy and (2) R&D–manufacturing synergy. While the following example involves external synergies through mergers and acquisitions, the concepts apply equally well to internal synergies sought in adding new products or seeking new markets.

A critical step in the external analysis is to assess how these merger and acquisition strategies provide the organization with **synergy,** the increased customer value achieved through performing organizational functions more efficiently. The "increased customer value" can take many forms: more products, improved quality on existing products, lower prices, improved distribution, and so on. But the ultimate criterion is

FIGURE 22-8

MARKET-PRODUCT GRID OF
ALTERNATIVE STRATEGIES FOR A
LAWNMOWER MANUFACTURER

that customers should be better off as a result of the increased synergy. The firm, in turn, should be better off by gaining more satisfied customers.

A market-product grid helps identify important trade-offs in the strategic marketing process. As noted in the Marketing NewsNet, assume you are vice president of marketing for Great Lawns Corporation's line of nonpowered lawnmowers and powered walking mowers sold to the consumer market. You are looking for new product and new market opportunities to increase your revenues and profits.

You conduct a market segmentation study and develop a market-product grid to analyze future opportunities. You identify three major segments in the consumer market based on geography: (1) city, (2) suburban, and (3) rural households. These market segments relate to the size of lawn a consumer must mow. The product clusters are (1) nonpowered, (2) powered walking, and (3) powered riding mowers. Five alternative marketing strategies are shown in the market-product grids in Figure 22-8.

As mentioned in Chapter 9, the important marketing efficiencies—or synergies—run horizontally across the rows in Figure 22-8. Conversely, the important R&D and production efficiencies—or synergies—run vertically down the columns. Let's look at the synergy effects for the five combinations in Figure 22-8:

A. *Market-product concentration.* The firm benefits from "focus" on a single product line and market segment, but it loses opportunities for significant synergies in both marketing and R&D–manufacturing.

B. *Market specialization.* The firm gains marketing synergy through providing a complete product line, but R&D–manufacturing have the difficulty of developing and producing two new products.

C. *Product specialization.* The firm gains R&D–manufacturing synergy through production economies of scale, but gaining market distribution in the three different geographic areas will be costly.

D. *Selective specialization.* The firm doesn't get either marketing or R&D–manufacturing synergies because of the uniqueness of the market-product combinations.

E. *Full coverage.* The firm has the maximum potential synergies in both marketing and R&D–manufacturing. The question: Is it spread too thin?

The Marketing NewsNet posed the question of what the ideal partner would be, given the market-product combinations shown in the box. If, as vice president of marketing, you want to follow a full-coverage strategy, then the ideal merger partner is

FIGURE 22-9

AN IDEAL MERGER FOR GREAT
LAWNS TO OBTAIN FULL MARKET-
PRODUCT COVERAGE

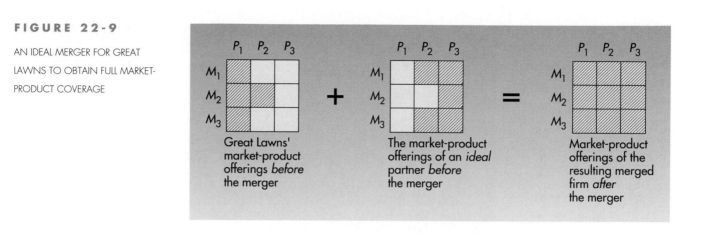

shown in Figure 22-9. This would give the maximum potential synergies—if you are not spreading your merged companies too thin. Marketing gains by having a complete product line in all regions, and R&D–manufacturing gains by having access to new markets that can provide production economies of scale through producing larger volumes of its existing products.

CONCEPT CHECK	**1.** Describe Porter's four generic business strategies.
	2. What are four alternative ways to increase a firm's profits when considering profit enhancement options strategies?
	3. Where do (*a*) marketing synergies and (*b*) R&D–manufacturing synergies appear in a market-product grid framework?

Some Planning and Strategy Lessons

Applying these frameworks is not automatic but requires a great deal of managerial judgment. Commonsense requirements of an effective marketing plan are discussed next, followed by problems that can arise.

Guidelines for an effective marketing plan   Dwight D. Eisenhower, when he commanded Allied armies in World War II, made his classic observation, "Plans are nothing; planning is everything." It is the process of careful planning that focuses an organization's efforts and leads to success. The plans themselves, which change with events, are often secondary. Effective planning and plans are inevitably characterized by identifiable objectives, specific strategies or courses of action, and the means to execute them. Here are some guidelines in developing effective marketing plans:

- *Set measurable, achievable goals.* Ideally, goals should be quantified and measurable in terms of what is to be accomplished and by when. So, "Increase market share from 18 percent to 22 percent by December 31, 1998" is preferable to "Maximize market share given our available resources." Also, to motivate people the goals must be achievable.
- *Use a base of facts and valid assumptions.* The more a marketing plan is based on facts and valid assumptions, rather than guesses, the less uncertainty and risk are associated with executing it. Good marketing research helps.

DOMINO'S, A LEGEND IN EFFECTIVE IMPLEMENTATION, STAYED WITH ITS BASIC PIZZA-AND-COKE MENU INTO THE 1990S. FOR THE RESULT, SEE THE TEXT.

- *Utilize simple, but clear and specific, plans.* Effective execution of plans requires that people at all levels in the firm understand what, when, and how they are to accomplish their tasks.
- *Have complete and feasible plans.* Marketing plans must incorporate all the key marketing mix factors and be supported by adequate resources.
- *Make plans controllable and flexible.* Marketing plans must enable results to be compared with planned targets, which allows replanning—the flexibility to update the original plans.

Problems in marketing planning and strategy   From postmortems on company plans that did work and on those that did not work, a picture emerges of where problems occur in the planning phase of a firm's strategic marketing process. The following list explores these problems:

1. Plans may be based on very poor assumptions about environmental factors, especially changing economic conditions and competitors' actions. Canadians used to equate the name Listerine with mouthwash. But Scope started an anti-Listerine campaign and successfully convinced Canadians that mouthwash didn't have to taste bad to work. The result? Listerine lost its position as market leader.
2. Planners and their plans may have lost sight of their customers' needs. Domino's Pizza is a legend for its implementation efficiency in home-delivered pizzas. But in the early 1990s it refused to recognize that its customers wanted a broader selection than its pizza-and-Coke menu, and its profits plummeted. The successful additions of buffalo wings and thin-crust pizza are helping it rebound.[15]
3. Too much time and effort may be spent on data collection and writing the plans. Westinghouse has cut its planning instructions for operating units "that looked like an auto repair manual" to five or six pages.
4. Line operating managers often feel no sense of ownership in implementing the plans. Andy Grove, CEO of Intel, observed, "We had the very ridiculous system . . . of delegating strategic planning to strategic planners. The strategies these [planners] prepared had no bearing on anything we actually did."[16] The solution is to assign more planning activities to line operating managers—the people who actually carry them out.

ETHICS AND SOCIAL RESPONSIBILITY ALERT

HOW TO ADD NEW VALUES TO STRATEGIC MARKETING PLANS

How can companies change their strategic marketing process to reflect the interests of the many stakeholders they serve—such as the community, customers, employees, shareholders, and suppliers? Although many approaches have had success, several actions are critical:

1. Identify, define, and prioritize critical values.
2. Measure employee perceptions of the values.
3. Assess customer perceptions of the degree to which company actions conform to these values.
4. Audit current management practices and modify them to reflect values.
5. Use a reward system that reinforces values.

Using these guidelines can help companies develop appropriate value-driven strategies. For example, Johnson & Johnson faced the cyanide crisis with its Tylenol brand by using its primary value—trust—that led to media cooperation and total recall of the product.

Ford Motor Company recently specified three values—people, products, and profits—to guide its attempts to become more competitive. Why are people first? "Because people are our most important asset. Everything that we are and can accomplish can only be done by people," says Ford chairman and CEO Donald Peterson. Ford's strategies now focus first on employees and their work environment.

What values would you specify for Ford? For your current employer?

Balancing value and values in strategic marketing plans   Two important trends are likely to influence the strategic marketing process in the future. The first, value-based planning, combines marketing planning ideas and financial planning techniques to assess how much a division or strategic business unit (SBU) contributes to the price of a company's stock (or shareholder wealth). Value is created when the financial return of a strategic activity exceeds the cost of the resources allocated to the activity.

The second trend is the increasing interest in value-driven strategies, which incorporate concerns for ethics, integrity, employee health and safety, and environmental safeguards with more common corporate values such as growth, profitability, customer service, and quality. Some experts have observed that although many corporations cite broad corporate values in advertisements, press releases, and company newsletters, they have not yet changed their strategic plans to reflect the stated values. Because plans depend on goals, the next step will require that organizations learn to specify value-based objectives. See the accompanying Ethics and Social Responsibility Alert for guidelines that help add new values to the planning process.[17]

THE IMPLEMENTATION PHASE OF THE STRATEGIC MARKETING PROCESS

The Monday morning diagnosis of a losing football coach often runs something like "We had an excellent game plan: we just didn't execute it."

Is Planning or Implementation the Problem?

The planning-versus-execution issue applies to the strategic marketing process as well: a difficulty when a marketing plan fails is determining whether the failure is due to a poor plan or poor implementation. Figure 22-10 shows the outcomes of (1) good and bad marketing planning and (2) good and bad marketing implementation.[18] Good planning and good implementation in cell 1 spell success, as with the Swiss

FIGURE 22-10

RESULTS OF GOOD AND BAD
MARKETING PLANNING AND
IMPLEMENTATION

	MARKETING PLANNING AND STRATEGY	
MARKETING IMPLEMENTATION	**GOOD (APPROPRIATE)**	**BAD (INAPPROPRIATE)**
GOOD (EFFECTIVE)	1 *Success:* Marketing program achieves its objectives.	2 *Trouble:* Solution lies in recognizing that only the strategy is at fault and correcting it.
BAD (INEFFECTIVE)	3 *Trouble:* Solution lies in recognizing that only implementation is at fault and correcting it.	4 *Failure:* Marketing program flounders and fails to achieve its objectives.

firm that combined a strong product—its Swatch brand watches—with excellent advertising, distribution, and pricing. NeXT Computer, Inc. fell into the "bad-bad" cell 4 with its workstation that used a proprietary hardware strategy that discouraged many potential customers and a salesforce "just too small and strapped for cash to reach many prospects." NeXT has now closed its computer factory to focus on its software business.

Cells 2 and 3 indicate trouble because either the marketing planning *or* marketing implementation—not both—is bad. A firm or product does not stay permanently in cell 2 or 3. If the problem is solved, the result can be success (cell 1); if not, it is failure (cell 4).

Toyota used good implementation on a bad marketing strategy (cell 2) when it applied its superior automobile marketing skills to the introduction of its T100 pickup truck. Consumer response was well below forecasts because the truck was too big to compete with smaller "compact" pickups and too small and underpowered to compete with full-size options. Goodyear Tire and Rubber Co. found itself in cell 3 after it successfully developed all-season radial tires but created problems with the dealer distribution network by raising wholesale prices. The poor implementation led to a two-point decline in market share—a drop of 3 million tires.

Increasing Emphasis on Marketing Implementation

In the 1990s, the implementation phase of the strategic marketing process has emerged as a key factor to success by moving many planning activities away from the duties of planners to those of line managers.

GE reorganized to reduce the size of its corporate strategic planning staff and also reduced the number of layers of middle managers and pushed decision-making authority lower in the organization. Some experts argue that in the future "boundaryless organizations" in which technology, information, managers, and managerial practices are shared across traditional organizational structures will be necessary.[19] The Marketing NewsNet box describes how implementation activities may occur in tomorrow's organizations.[20]

Improving Implementation of Marketing Programs

No magic formula exists to guarantee effective implementation of marketing plans. In fact, the answer seems to be equal parts of good management skills and practices, from which have come some guidelines for improving program implementation.

SWATCH WATCHES HAVE BENEFITED FROM HAVING BOTH GOOD MARKETING PLANNING AND IMPLEMENTATION.

Communicate goals and the means of achieving them   Those called on to implement plans need to understand both the goals sought and how they are to be accomplished. Everyone in Domino's Pizza—-from founder Tom Monaghan to telephone order takers, make-line people, and drivers—is clear on what the firm's goal is: to deliver tasty, hot pizzas quickly to homes of customers who order them by telephone. All Domino's personnel are trained in detail to perform their respective jobs to help achieve that goal.

Have a responsible program champion willing to act   Successful programs almost always have a **product or program champion** who is able and willing to cut red tape and move the program forward.[21] Such people often have the uncanny ability to move back and forth between big-picture strategy questions and specific details when the situation calls for it. Product or program champions are often brash in overcoming organizational hurdles. In many cases, they adhere to the axiom, "Better to ask forgiveness than permission." Using this strategy, 3M's Art Fry championed Post-it Notes to success, an idea he got when looking for a simple way to mark his hymnal while singing in his church choir.

Reward successful program implementation   When an individual or a team is rewarded for achieving the organization's goal, they have maximum incentive to see a program implemented successfully because they have personal ownership and a stake in that success. At a General Electric surge protector plant, employees receive a bonus each quarter that the facility meets plantwide performance goals.

MARKETING NEWSNET

Cross Functional

IMPLEMENTATION IN THE ORGANIZATION OF TOMORROW

In today's global marketplace, corporations struggle to reduce their response time to windows of opportunity. One of the reasons is that few companies have the complete expertise necessary to quickly launch new products in diverse and changing markets. To excel at implementation of marketing strategies, the organization of tomorrow will emphasize adaptability by taking advantage of information technology and acting, as Peter Drucker suggests, like a symphony orchestra.

Frank Ostroff and Doug Smith at the consulting firm McKinsey & Co. have suggestions for firms making the transition, including:

1. Organize around process, not task.
2. Flatten the hierarchy.
3. Give leaders responsibility for process performance.
4. Link performance to customer satisfaction.
5. Create teams that have managerial and nonmanagerial responsibilities.
6. Reward team performance.

In addition, companies will need to utilize networks of suppliers, customers, and even competitors to create *strategic alliances*.

These developments are described by many terms today, including the *boundaryless company*, the *virtual corporation*, and *capabilities-based competition*, but regardless of the terminology, you can bet that the future will bring exciting changes in the way marketing plans are implemented. Organizations as diverse as GE, Hallmark Cards, Eastman Kodak, and Clearly Canadian Beverages are already trying many of these ideas!

Drivers delivering Domino's pizza take their job seriously—because it may lead directly to their owning a franchise in a few years.

Take action and avoid "paralysis by analysis" Management experts warn against paralysis by analysis, the tendency to excessively analyze a problem instead of taking action. To overcome this pitfall, they call for a "bias for action" and recommend a "do it, fix it, try it" approach.[22] Conclusion: Perfectionists finish last, so getting 90 percent perfection and letting the marketplace help in the fine tuning makes good sense in implementation.

Lockheed Aircraft's Skunk Works got its name from the comic strip *L'il Abner* and its legendary reputation from achieving superhuman technical feats with a low budget and ridiculously short deadlines by stressing teamwork. Under the leadership of Kelly Johnson, in 35 years the Skunk Works turned out a series of world-class aircraft from the first jet airplane (the P-80) to the most untrackable aircraft (the F-117 Stealth fighter). Two of Kelly Johnson's basic tenets: (1) make decisions promptly and (2) avoid paralysis by analysis. Chris Haney and Scott Abbott, the Canadian inventors of Trivial Pursuit, took only 45 minutes to develop the basic concept. Then, they quickly developed the prototype and test-marketed the product. By making prompt decisions and avoiding paralysis by analysis, these entrepreneurs created the biggest-selling adult game in Canada.[23]

Foster open communication to surface the problems Success often lies in fostering a work environment that is open enough so employees are willing to speak out when they see problems without fear of recrimination. The focus is placed on trying to solve the problem as a group rather than finding someone to blame. Solutions are solicited from anyone who has a creative idea to suggest—from the janitor to the president—without regard to status or rank in the organization.

FOR THE UNUSUAL WAY GM DEVELOPED ITS SATURN, SEE THE TEXT.

Two more Kelly Johnson axioms from Lockheed's Skunk Works apply here: (1) when trouble develops, surface the problem immediately, and (2) get help; don't keep the problem to yourself. This latter point is important even if it means getting ideas from competitors.

Saturn is GM's attempt to create a new company where participatory management and improved communications lead to a successful product. For example, to encourage discussion of possible cost reductions, each employee receives 100 to 750 hours of training, including balance sheet analysis. To avoid the "NIH syndrome"—the reluctance to accept ideas "not invented here" or not originated inside one's own firm—Saturn engineers bought 70 import cars to study for product design ideas and selected options that would most appeal to their target market.

Schedule precise tasks, responsibilities, and deadlines   Successful implementation requires that people know the tasks for which they are responsible and the deadline for completing them. To implement the tasks required to carry out its marketing plans, the Royal Canadian Mint prepares an **action item list** that has three columns: (1) the task, (2) the name of the person responsible for accomplishing that task, and (3) the date by which the task is to be finished. Action item lists are forward-looking, clarify the targets, and put strong pressure on people to achieve their designated tasks by the deadline.

Related to the action item lists are formal *program schedules,* which show the relationships through time of the various program tasks. Scheduling an action program involves (1) identifying the main tasks, (2) determining the time required to complete each, (3) arranging the activities to meet the deadline, and (4) assigning responsibilities to complete each task.

FIGURE 22-11

TASKS IN COMPLETING A TERM
PROJECT

Shown below are the tasks you might face as a member of a student team to complete a marketing research study using a mail questionnaire. Elapsed time to complete all the tasks is 15 weeks. How do you finish the project in an 11-week quarter? For an answer, see the text.

TASK	TIME (WEEKS)
1. Construct and test a rough-draft questionnaire for clarity (in person, not by mail) on friends.	2
2. Type and copy a final questionnaire.	2
3. Randomly select the names of 200 students from the school directory.	1
4. Address and stamp envelopes; mail questionnaires.	1
5. Collect returned questionnaires.	3
6. Tabulate and analyze data from returned questionnaires.	2
7. Write final report.	3
8. Type and submit final report.	1
Total time necessary to complete all activities	15

Suppose, for example, that you and two friends are asked to do a term project on the problem, "How can the college increase attendance at its performing arts concerts?"[24] And suppose further that the instructor limits the project in the following ways:

1. The project must involve a mail survey of the attitudes of a sample of students.
2. The term paper with the survey results must be submitted by the end of the 11-week quarter.

To begin the assignment, you need to identify all the project tasks and then estimate the time you can reasonably allocate to each one. As shown in Figure 22-11, it would take 15 weeks to complete the project if you did all the tasks sequentially; so to complete it in 11 weeks, your team must work on different parts at the same time, and some activities must be independent enough to overlap. This requires specialization and cooperation. Suppose that of the three of you (A, B, and C), only student C can type. Then you (student A) might assume the task of constructing the questionnaire and selecting samples, and student B might tabulate the data. This division of labour allows each student to concentrate on and become expert in one area, but you should also cooperate. Student C might help A and B in the beginning, and A and B might help C later on.

You must also figure out which activities can be done concurrently to save time. In Figure 22-11 you can see that task 2 must be completed before task 4. However, task 3 might easily be done before, at the same time as, or after task 2. Task 3 is independent of task 2.

Scheduling production and marketing activities—from a term project to a new product rollout to a space shuttle launch—can be done efficiently with Gantt charts. Figure 22-12 shows one variation of a Gantt chart used to schedule the class project, demonstrating how the concurrent work on several tasks enables the students to finish the project on time. Developed by Henry L. Gantt, this method is the basis for the scheduling techniques used today, including elaborate computerized methods. The key to all scheduling techniques is to distinguish tasks that *must* be done sequentially from those that *can* be done concurrently. As in the case of the term project, scheduling tasks concurrently often reduces the total time required for a project.

TASK DESCRIPTION	STUDENTS INVOLVED IN TASK	WEEK OF QUARTER 1 2 3 4 5 6 7 8 9 10 11
1. Construct and test a rough-draft questionnaire for clarity (in person, not by mail) on friends.	A	
2. Type and copy the final questionnaire.	C	
3. Randomly select the names of 200 students from the school directory.	A	
4. Address and stamp envelopes; mail questionnaires.	C	
5. Collect returned questionnaires.	B	
6. Tabulate and analyze data from returned questionnaires.	B	
7. Write final report.	A, B, C	
8. Type and submit final report.	C	

KEY: ▲ Planned completion date   ▢ Planned period of work   Current date
     ▲ Actual completion date   ▢ Actual period of work

FIGURE 22-12   GANTT CHART FOR SCHEDULING THE TERM PROJECT

CONCEPT CHECK

1. Why is it important to include line operating managers in the planning process?

2. What is the meaning and importance of a program champion?

3. Explain the difference between sequential and concurrent tasks in a Gantt chart.

Organizing for Marketing

A marketing organization is needed to implement the firm's marketing plans. Basic issues in today's marketing organizations include understanding (1) how line versus staff positions and divisional groupings interrelate to form a cohesive marketing organization and (2) the role of the product manager.

Line versus staff and divisional groupings   Although simplified, Figure 22-13 shows the organization of Pillsbury's Prepared Dough Products Business Unit in detail and highlights the distinction between line and staff positions in marketing. People in **line positions,** such as group marketing managers, have the authority and responsibility to issue orders to the people who report to them, such as marketing managers. In this organizational chart, line positions are connected with solid lines. Those in **staff positions** (shown by dotted lines) have the authority and responsibility to advise people in line positions but cannot issue direct orders to them.

Most marketing organizations use divisional groupings—such as product line, functional, geographical, and market-based—to implement plans and achieve their organizational objectives. Three of these appear in some form in Pillsbury's organizational chart in Figure 22-13. At the top of its organization, Pillsbury organizes by **product**

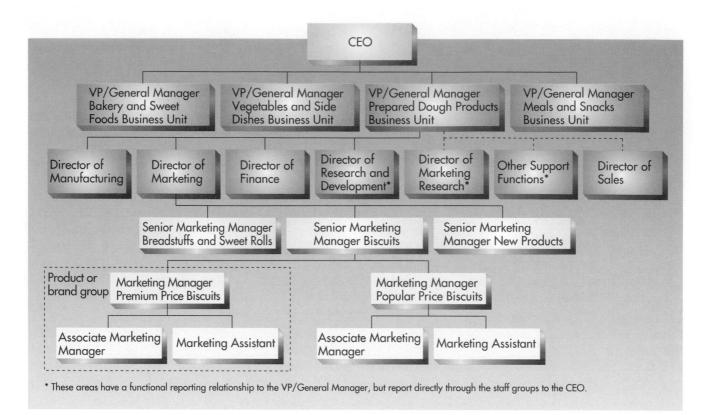

* These areas have a functional reporting relationship to the VP/General Manager, but report directly through the staff groups to the CEO.

FIGURE 22-13   ORGANIZATION OF THE PILLSBURY COMPANY

line groupings, in which a unit is responsible for specific product offerings. For example, Pillsbury has four main product lines: Bakery & Sweet Foods, Vegetables & Side Dishes, Prepared Dough Products, and Meals & Snacks.

The Prepared Dough Products Business Unit is organized by **functional groupings** such as manufacturing, marketing, and finance, which are the different business activities within a firm.

Pillsbury uses **geographical groupings** for its field sales representatives. Each director of sales has several regional sales managers reporting to him or her, such as

PRODUCTS FROM PILLSBURY'S LINE OF
PREPARED DOUGH PRODUCTS.

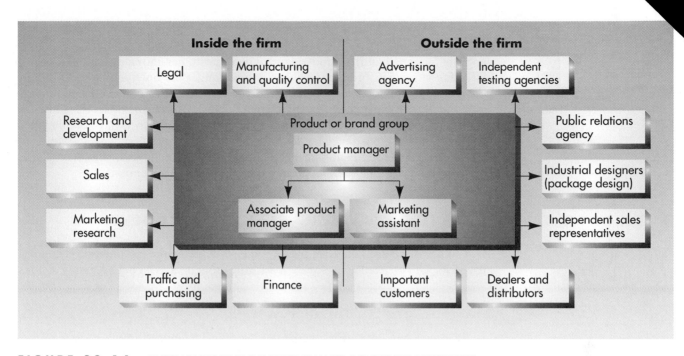

FIGURE 22-14   UNITS WITH WHICH THE PRODUCT MANAGER AND PRODUCT GROUP WORK

Western, Eastern, and so on. These, in turn, have district managers reporting to them (although for simplicity these are not shown in the chart).

A fourth method of organizing a company is to use **market-based groupings,** which utilize specific customer segments, such as the banking, health care, or manufacturing segments. When this method of organizing is combined with product groupings, the result is a *matrix organization.*

A relatively new position in consumer products firms is the *category manager* (senior marketing manager in Figure 22-13). Category managers have profit-and-loss responsibility for an entire product line—all biscuit brands, for example. They attempt to reduce the possibility of one brand's actions hurting another brand in the same category. The popularity of category management among packaged goods manufacturers has increased rapidly as supermarket buyers have become responsible for purchasing, merchandising, and promoting entire categories.

Role of the product manager   The key person in the product or brand group shown in Figure 22-14 is the manager who heads it. As mentioned in Chapter 12, this person is often called the *product manager* or *brand manager,* but in Pillsbury he or she carries the title *marketing manager.* This person and the assistants in the product group are the basic building blocks in the marketing department of most consumer and industrial product firms. The function of a product manager is to plan, implement, and control the annual and long-range plans for the products for which he or she is responsible.

There are both benefits and dangers to the product manager system. On the positive side, product managers become strong advocates for the assigned products, cut red tape to work with people in various functions both inside and outside the organization (Figure 22-14), and assume profit-and-loss responsibility for the performance of the product line. On the negative side, even though product managers have major responsibilities, they have relatively little direct authority, so most groups and functions shown in Figure 22-14 must be coordinated to meet the product's goals.[25] To coordinate the many units, product managers must use persuasion rather than orders. But as Canadian firms move toward more customer-intimacy and relationship marketing strategies, product managers are no longer the only ones responsible for managing the product or customer base. Some Canadian firms have created new positions such as "manager of student segment" or "VP of financial services clients" which shadow the traditional product manager roles. These firms have divided their organizations into "customer-facing roles" (such as a segment manager). More and more often it is the segment managers, not the product managers, who make the final decisions on product, price, promotion, and place (distribution).[26]

THE CONTROL PHASE OF THE STRATEGIC MARKETING PROCESS

The essence of control, the final phase of the strategic marketing process, is comparing results with planned goals for the marketing program and taking necessary actions.

The Marketing Control Process

Ideally, quantified goals from the marketing plans developed in the planning phase have been accomplished by the marketing actions taken in the implementation phase (Figure 22-15) and measured as results in the control phase. A marketing manager then uses *management by exception,* which means identifying results that deviate from plans to diagnose their causes and take new actions. Often results fall short of plans, and a corrective action is needed. For example, after 50 years of profits Caterpillar accumulated losses of $1 billion. To correct the problem, Caterpillar focused its marketing efforts on core products and reduced its manufacturing costs. At other times the comparison shows that performance is far better than anticipated, in which case the marketing manager tries to identify the reason and move quickly to exploit the unexpected opportunity.

Measuring results   Without some quantitative goal, no benchmark exists with which to compare actual results. Manufacturers of both consumer and industrial products are increasingly trying to develop marketing programs that have not only specific action programs but also specific procedures for monitoring key measures of performance. Today marketing executives are measuring not only tangible financial targets

FIGURE 22-15

THE CONTROL PHASE OF THE

STRATEGIC MARKETING PROCESS

such as sales revenues and profits, but also less tangible ones such as customer satisfaction, new-product development cycle time, and salesforce motivation.

Taking marketing actions   When results deviate significantly from plans, some kind of action is essential. Deviations can be the result of the process used to specify goals or can be due to changes in the marketplace. Timex Canada was losing market share because it didn't have the strategies or the people in place to keep pace with a quickly changing industry. Timex rethought its strategies, product lines, and executions. In doing so, the company was able to recapture its number-one position in the industry.

Sales Analysis

For controlling marketing programs, **sales analysis**—using the firm's sales records to compare actual results with sales goals and identify areas of strength and weakness—is critical. All the variables that might be used in market segmentation may be used in **sales component analysis** (also called *microsales analysis*), which traces sales revenues to their sources, such as specific products, sales territories, or customers. Common breakdowns include the following:

- *Customer characteristics:* demographics, NAICS code, size, reason for purchase, and type of reseller (retailer or wholesaler).
- *Product characteristics:* model, package size, and colour.
- *Geographical region:* sales territory, city, province, and region.
- *Order size.*
- *Price or discount class.*
- *Commission to the sales representative.*

Today's computers can easily produce these breakdowns, provided the input data contain these classifications. Therefore, it is critical that marketing managers specify the breakdowns they require from the accounting and information systems departments.

The danger is that marketing managers or chief executive officers get overwhelmed by the volume of computerized reports. This can lead to a situation where they cannot spot the key performance numbers in the report needed for control and subsequent action.

Profitability Analysis

To their surprise, marketing managers often discover the 80/20 principle the hard way, on the job. **Profitability analysis** enables the manager to measure the profitability of the firm's products, customer groups, sales territories, channels of distribution, and even order sizes. This leads to decisions to expand, maintain, reduce, or eliminate specific products, customer groups, or channels.

For example, following the 80/20 principle, a marketing manager will try to find the common characteristics among the 20 percent of the customers (or products, brands, sales districts, salespeople, or kinds of orders) that are generating 80 percent (or the bulk) of revenues and profits to find more like them to exploit competitive advantages. Conversely, the 80 percent of customers, products, brands, and so on that are generating few revenues and profits may need to be reduced or even dropped entirely unless a way is found to make them profitable.

The Marketing Audit

Often a broader marketing perspective is needed than is given by sales or profitability analyses, one that covers a longer time horizon and relates the marketing mix factors to environmental variables. This is the role of a **marketing audit,** which is a

...RVICES: THE REASON FOR

...t/service free from deadwood?
2. What is the life cycle stage?
3. How will user demands or trends affect you?
4. Are you a leader in new-product innovation?
5. Are inexpensive methods used to estimate new product potentials before considerable amounts are spent on R&D and market introduction?
6. Do you have different quality levels for different markets?
7. Are packages/brochures effective salespeople for the products/services they present?
8. Do you present products/services in the most appealing colours (formats) for markets being served?
9. Are there features or benefits to exploit?
10. Is the level of customer service adequate?
11. How are quality and reliability viewed by customers?

CUSTOMER: USER PROFILES

1. Who is the current and potential customer?
2. Are there geographic aspects of use: regional, rural, urban?
3. Why do people buy the product/service; what motivates their preferences?
4. Who makes buying decisions; when; where?
5. What is the frequency and quality of use?

MARKETS: WHERE PRODUCTS/SERVICES ARE SOLD

1. Have you identified and measured major segments?
2. Are small, potential market segments overlooked in trying to satisfy the majority?
3. Are the markets for the products/services expanding or declining?
4. Should different segments be developed; are there gaps in penetration?

COMPETITORS: THEIR INFLUENCE

1. Who are the principal competitors, how are they positioned, and where are they headed?
2. What are their market shares?
3. What features of competitor's products/services stand out?
4. Is the market easily entered or dominated?

PRICING: PROFITABILITY PLANNING

1. What are the objectives of current pricing policy: acquiring, defending, or expanding?
2. Are price policies set to produce volume or profit?
3. How does pricing compare with competition in similar levels of quality?
4. Does cost information show profitability of each item?
5. What is the history of price deals, discounts, and promotions?

FIGURE 22-16   MARKETING AUDIT QUESTIONS

comprehensive, unbiased, periodic review of the strategic marketing process of a firm or SBU. The purpose of the marketing audit, which serves as both a planning and control technique, is to identify new problems and opportunities that warrant an action plan to improve performance.

Many firms undertaking a marketing audit use a checklist such as that shown in Figure 22-16 as a part of their situation analysis in their strategic marketing process. The checklist used covers factors ranging from the marketing mix factors and customer profiles to markets and competitors.

For a meaningful, comprehensive marketing audit, the individual or team conducting the audit must have a free rein to talk to managers, employees, salespeople, distributors, and customers, as well as have access to all pertinent internal and external reports and memoranda. They need to involve all levels of the organization in the process to ensure that resulting action recommendations have widespread support.

CONCEPT CHECK

1. What is the difference between a line and a staff position in a marketing organization?
2. What are four groupings used within a typical marketing organization?
3. What two components of the strategic marketing process are compared to control a marketing program?

SUMMARY

1. Marketing managers use the strategic marketing process to allocate their resources as effectively as possible. Sales response functions help them assess what the market's response to additional marketing effort will be.

2. The planning phase of the strategic marketing process usually results in a marketing plan that sets the direction for the marketing activities of an organization. Three kinds of marketing plans are long-range, annual, and new-product plans.

3. Three useful frameworks to improve marketing planning are (1) Porter's generic business strategies, (2) profit enhancement options, and (3) market-product synergies.

4. An effective marketing plan has measurable, achievable goals; uses facts and valid assumptions; is simple, clear, and specific; is complete and feasible; and is controllable and flexible.

5. The implementation phase of the strategic marketing process is concerned with executing the marketing program developed in the planning phase and has achieved increased attention the past decade.

6. Essential to good scheduling is separating tasks that can be done concurrently from those that must be done sequentially. Gantt charts are a simple, effective means of scheduling.

7. Organizing marketing activities necessitates recognition of two different aspects of an organization: (a) line and staff positions and (b) product line, functional, geographical, and market-based groupings.

8. The product manager performs a vital marketing role in both consumer and industrial product firms, interacting with numerous people and groups both inside and outside the firm.

9. The control phase of the strategic marketing process involves measuring the results of the actions from the implementation phase and comparing them with goals set in the planning phase. Sales analyses, profitability analyses, and marketing audits are used to control marketing programs.

KEY TERMS AND CONCEPTS

sales response function p. 524
share points p. 525
generic business strategy p. 530
cost leadership (generic) strategy p. 531
differentiation (generic) strategy p. 531
cost focus (generic) strategy p. 531
differentiation focus (generic) strategy p. 531
synergy p. 533
product or program champion p. 539
action item list p. 541

line positions p. 543
staff positions p. 543
product line groupings pp. 543–544
functional groupings p. 544
geographical groupings p. 544
market-based groupings p. 545
sales analysis p. 547
sales component analysis p. 547
profitability analysis p. 547
marketing audit p. 547

CHAPTER PROBLEMS AND APPLICATIONS

1. Assume a firm faces an S-shaped sales response function. What happens to the ratio of incremental sales revenue to incremental marketing effort at the (a) bottom, (b) middle, and (c) top of this curve?

2. What happens to the ratio of incremental sales revenue to incremental marketing effort when the sales response function is an upward-sloping straight line?

3. In 1998 General Mills plans to invest millions of dollars in expanding its cereal and cake mix businesses. To allocate this money between these two businesses, what information would General Mills like to have?

4. Suppose your Great Lawns mower company has the market-product concentration situation shown in Figure 22-8A. What are both the synergies and potential pitfalls of following expansion strategies of (a) market specialization and (b) product specialization?

5. Are value-driven strategies inconsistent with value-based planning? Give an example that supports your position.

6. The first Domino's Pizza restaurant was near a college campus. What implementation problems are (a) similar and (b) different for restaurants near a college campus versus a military base?

7. A common theme among managers who succeed repeatedly in program implementation is fostering open communication. Why is this so important?

8. Parts of tasks 6 and 7 in Figure 22-11 are done both concurrently and sequentially. How can this be? How does it help the students meet the term paper deadline?

9. In Pillsbury's organizational chart in Figure 22-13, where do product line, functional, and geographical groupings occur?

10. Why are quantified goals in the planning phase of the strategic marketing process important for the control phase?

CASE 22-1   Clearly Canadian

Clearly Canadian Beverage Corporation, based in Vancouver is a leading producer in the $6 billion new age or alternative beverage industry with a portfolio of premium beverages. The company's product line includes its flagship brand, Clearly Canadian sparkling flavoured water, Clearly Canadian Natural Artesian Water (a premium still water), Orbitz (a natural fruit-flavoured beverage with colourful spheres that remain suspended in the liquid), and Quenchers (a line of preservative-free sparkling fruit beverages). The company distributes its products in Canada, the United States, and numerous countries around the world. Clearly Canadian had sales revenues in excess of $68 million in 1997.

HISTORY

When Clearly Canadian entered the beverage market in the late 1980s, it was an instant success with consumers looking for something different. Clearly Canadian sparkling flavoured water may not have been the first new age or alternative beverage, but it was the first product *referred to* as a new age or alternative beverage. If it did not create the category, it did define it, and opened the doors for countless other new age members such as Snapple, Mistic, and Arizona. The company went against the grain when it started out. It wanted to carve out a niche using a premium product, a very sophisticated image, and distinctive packaging. Clearly Canadian sparkling water had a much fuller taste than an essence-based sparkling water. The product was clear in appearance and was packaged in an appealing blue-glass bottle. Millions of consumers bought the product and by 1992, the company was selling about 22 million cases of the beverage.

The company had entered the market early and capitalized on the emerging consumer trend toward flavoured waters. Innovative packaging allowed the product to stand out on the crowded shelves. Premium pricing also helped position Clearly Canadian as a high-quality product. But the company's distribution system was also integral to its early success. Whereas many other companies failed to achieve widespread distribution, Clearly Canadian did so in Canada *and* the United States. The company also pursued an aggressive market development strategy and expanded into Mexico, England, Ireland, Japan, and other regions.

But by 1993 growth in the new age or alternative beverage category began to slow and company sales declined. In fact, sales of Clearly Canadian dropped to 7 million cases, down from 22 million the year before. Experts suggested that consumers' capricious tastes and the growing competition were the primary reasons for the decline. Others insisted that with the growing number of new brands, the so-called upscale new age beverages could no longer command the premium prices being charged. In fact, many new brands used low-price strategies to secure market share, and this had undermined the premium niche positioning of the entire category. Clearly Canadian had definitely lost market share to "knock off" products, but also to new alternative beverages such as iced tea.

CLEARLY CANADIAN'S REACTION

Clearly Canadian recognized that it had contributed to its decline by being content to react to the market rather than being proactive. Whereas competitors continued to innovate in terms of packaging, image, and new products, Clearly Canadian atrophied. The company realized it had to get back to its innovative roots to compete. By 1994, the company added new flavours to the line and introduced a multiserving bottle as well as a four-pack concept. It also launched a 200 mL bottle for the hospitality industry. The company undertook new consumer promotion activities and a systemwide sales incentive program for its sales representatives. Still, these efforts did not significantly boost sales, and Clearly Canadian appeared to be a company whose time had passed.

CONTINUING TO REINVENT ITSELF

Undaunted, Clearly Canadian had established a five-year strategic blueprint and continued to move ahead with its implementation. The company restructured internally and emerged with a growing portfolio of new products. Doug Mason, chair and chief executive officer of Clearly Canadian stated that "we've gone from a company that sold a beverage to a beverage company."

The company introduced Clearly Canadian Natural Artesian Water, a premium still water, and Quenchers, a line of preservative-free sparkling fruit beverages. The company also launched Orbitz, a texturally modified beverage that features fruit-flavoured gel spheres suspended in a clear fruit drink. The company also relaunched its flagship brand with a new deeper-blue bottle, and more colourful design. There are also three new flavours.

Ultimately the company's goal is to have 50 percent of the company's sales from products other than the flagship brand. The company continues a program to reacquire the distribution rights for the company's products. Distributors and licensees were crucial to the early market penetration efforts, but now the company views them as a layer of insulation between the products and the ultimate customers. By reacquiring these rights, Clearly Canadian gains direct involvement over the distribution and marketing efforts for its products. The company is now in direct control of more than 80 percent of North American distribution.

The company believes its success will be based on its ability to respond quickly to consumer needs with new products, sizes, flavours, and packaging. The company believes that as a niche player, it can continue to be a source of innovation for the entire new age or alternative beverage industry. By developing and creating interest in new products the company suggests it will help grow the entire category and not just take share away from existing brands.

By 1997, Clearly Canadian had retained its status as one of the top 10 ranked alternative beverage companies in terms of sales revenue. With the 1996 introduction of Orbitz and the relaunch of its flagship brand in 1997, Clearly Canadian reestablished itself as a leader in innovation. The product continues to be one of the most popular sparkling waters in Canada and the United States. In addition to the glass bottle, Clearly Canadian is also packaged in aluminum cans and in a one-litre PET package. Orbitz is considered the most successful product launch in the North American alternative beverage category.

THE FUTURE

The company recognizes that the dynamics will continue to shift in the industry. What won't change, according to Clearly Canadian, is the need for products to deliver on convenience, price, quality, and taste. The company's goals for the future are to continue to innovate by marketing brands that consumers want. Accordingly, Clearly Canadian believes there are a growing number of consumers who are seeking beverages made from natural ingredients that provide tangible health and nutrition benefits. The challenge, the company argues, is to produce healthier beverages that taste good. Clearly Canadian is monitoring and responding to these consumer trends. The company is currently researching and developing new product lines, including "nutraceutical" or functional beverages as well as a "super-oxygenated" drink. Also, in an effort to better communicate with their consumers and shareholders, Clearly Canadian recently introduced a new web site (www.clearly.ca).

Questions

1. Which of the four generic business strategies shown in Figure 22-6 does Clearly Canadian Beverage Corporation appear to be pursuing?
2. What are the basic generic marketing strategies (Figure 22-7) that new age or alternative beverage companies can use to increase their profitability?
3. Clearly Canadian Beverage Corporation says part of its new strategy is to compete "as close to the cooler door as possible." What do you think this means? Why is this an appropriate strategy for a niche marketer?

APPENDIX C

Career Planning in Marketing

GETTING A JOB: THE PROCESS OF MARKETING YOURSELF

Getting a job is usually a lengthy process, and it is exactly that—a *process* that involves careful planning, implementation, and control. You may have everything going for you: a respectable grade point average (GPA), relevant work experience, several extracurricular activities, superior communication skills, and demonstrated leadership qualities. Despite these, you still need to market yourself systematically and aggressively; after all, even the best products lie dormant on the retailer's shelves unless marketed effectively.

The process of getting a job involves the same activities marketing managers use to develop and introduce products into the marketplace.[1] The only difference is that you are marketing yourself, not a product. You need to conduct marketing research by analyzing your personal qualities (performing a self-audit) and by identifying job opportunities. Based on your research results, select a target market—those job opportunities that are compatible with your interests, goals, skills, and abilities—and design a marketing mix around that target market. *You* are the "product"; you must decide how to "position" yourself in the job market. The price component of the marketing mix is the salary range and job benefits (such as health and life insurance, vacation time, and retirement benefits) that you hope to receive. Promotion involves communicating with prospective employers through written correspondence (advertising) and job interviews (personal selling). The place element focuses on how to reach prospective employers—at the campus placement centre or job fairs, for example.

This appendix will assist you in career planning by (1) providing information about careers in marketing and (2) outlining a job search process.

CAREERS IN MARKETING

The diversity of marketing opportunities is reflected in the many types of marketing jobs, ranging from purchasing to marketing research to public relations to product management. The growing interest in marketing by service and nonprofit organizations—such as hospitals, financial institutions, the performing arts, and government—has added to the numerous opportunities offered by traditional employers such as manufacturers, retailers, consulting firms, and advertising agencies. Examples of Canadian companies that have opportunities for graduates with degrees in marketing include Ford of Canada, Royal Bank, Nortel, Procter & Gamble, IBM Canada, Pillsbury Canada, Deloitte Consulting, Angus Reid Group, and many others. Most of these career opportunities offer the chance to work with interesting people on stimulating and rewarding problems.

Studies of career paths and salaries suggest that marketing careers can also provide an excellent opportunity for advancement and substantial pay. Surveys of chief executive officers (CEOs) of publicly held companies reveal that marketing and finance were the most common career paths to their positions. Similarly, reports of average starting salaries of university graduates indicate that salaries in marketing compare favourably with those in many other fields. The future is likely to be even better. A recent Canadian survey has pegged marketing as well as information technology departments as the areas where most of the hiring will occur over the next few years. In fact, the survey revealed that 65 percent of hiring by for-profit companies will be in marketing.[2]

Figure C-1 describes marketing occupations in six major categories: product management and physical distribution, advertising, retailing, sales, marketing research, and nonprofit marketing. One of these may be right for you! (Additional sources of marketing career information are provided at the end of this appendix.)

PRODUCT MANAGEMENT AND PHYSICAL DISTRIBUTION

Product manager for consumer goods develops new products that can cost millions of dollars, with advice and consent of management—a job with great responsibility.

Administrative manager oversees the organization within a company that transports products to consumers and handles customer service.

Operations manager supervises warehousing and other physical distribution functions and often is directly involved in moving goods on the warehouse floor.

Traffic and transportation manager evaluates the costs and benefits of different types of transportation.

Inventory control manager forecasts demand for stockpiled goods, coordinates production with plant managers, and keeps track of current levels of shipments to keep customers supplied.

Administrative analyst performs cost analyses of physical distribution systems.

Customer service manager maintains good relations with customers by coordinating sales staffs, marketing management, and physical distribution management.

Physical distribution consultant is an expert in the transportation and distribution of goods.

SALES

Direct salesperson (door-to-door) calls on consumers in their homes to make sales.

Trade salesperson calls on retailers or wholesalers to sell products for manufacturers.

Industrial or semitechnical salesperson sells supplies and services to businesses.

Complex or professional salesperson sells complicated or custom-designed products to business. This requires understanding of the technology of a product.

NONPROFIT MARKETING

Marketing manager for nonprofit organizations develops and directs mail campaigns, fundraising, and public relations.

ADVERTISING

Account executive maintains contact with clients while coordinating the creative work among artists and copywriters. In full-service ad agencies, account executives are considered partners with the client in promoting the product and helping to develop marketing strategy.

Media buyer deals with media sales representatives in selecting advertising media and analyzes the value of media being purchased.

Copywriter works with art director in conceptualizing advertisements and writes the text of print or radio ads or the storyboards of television ads.

Art director handles the visual component of advertisements.

Sales promotion manager designs promotions for consumer products and works at an ad agency or a sales promotion agency.

Public relations manager develops written or filmed messages for the public and handles contacts with the press.

Specialty advertising manager develops advertising for the sales staff and customers or distributors.

RETAILING

Buyer selects products a store sells, surveys consumer trends, and evaluates the past performance of products and suppliers.

Store manager oversees the staff and services at a store.

MARKETING RESEARCH

Project manager for the supplier coordinates and oversees the market studies for a client.

Account executive for the supplier serves as a liaison between client and market research firm, like an advertising agency account executive.

In-house project director acts as project manager (see above) for the market studies conducted by the firm for which he or she works.

Marketing research specialist for an advertising agency performs or contracts for market studies for agency clients.

Source: David W. Rosenthal and Michael A. Powell, *Careers in Marketing,* © 1984, pp. 352–54. Adapted by permission of Prentice Hall, Englewood Cliffs, N.J.

FIGURE C-1

TWENTY-SIX MARKETING OCCUPATIONS

Product Management and Physical Distribution

Many organizations assign one manager the responsibility for a particular product. For example, P&G has separate managers for Tide, Ivory, and Crisco. Product or brand managers are involved in all aspects of a product's marketing program, such as marketing research, sales, sales promotion, advertising, and pricing, as well as manufacturing. Managers of similar products typically report to a category manager and may be part of a *product management team.*[3]

University graduates with bachelor's and master's degrees—often in marketing and business—enter P&G as brand assistants, the only starting position in its product or brand group. Each year students from campuses across Canada accept positions with P&G. As brand assistants, their responsibilities consist primarily of selling and sales training.

After one to two years of good performance, the brand assistant is promoted to assistant brand manager and after about the same period to brand (product) manager. These promotions often involve several brand groups. For example, a new employee might start as brand assistant for P&G's soap products, be promoted to assistant brand manager for Crest toothpaste, and subsequently become brand manager for Pampers. The reason, as recruiter Henry de Montebello explains, is that "in the future everybody will have strategic alliances with everybody else, and the executives who thrive will be well-rounded."[4]

Several other jobs related to product management (Figure C-1) deal with physical distribution issues such as storing the manufactured product (inventory), moving the product from the firm to the customers (transportation), maintaining good relations with customers (customer service), and engaging in many other aspects of the manufacture and sale of goods. Prospects for these jobs are likely to increase as wholesalers increase their involvement with selling and distribution activities and begin to take advantage of overseas opportunities.[5]

Advertising

Although we may see hundreds of advertisements in a day, what we can't see easily is the fascinating and complex advertising profession. The entry-level advertising positions filled every year include jobs with a variety of firms. Advertising professionals often remark that they find their jobs appealing because the days are not routine and they involve creative activities with many interesting people.

Advertising positions are available in three kinds of organizations: advertisers, media companies, and agencies. Advertisers include manufacturers, retail stores, service firms, and many other types of companies. Often they have an advertising department responsible for preparing and placing their own ads. Advertising careers are also possible with the media: television, radio stations, magazines, and newspapers. Finally, advertising agencies offer job opportunities through their use of account management, research, media, and creative services.

Starting positions with advertisers and advertising agencies are often as assistants to employees with several years of experience. An assistant copywriter facilitates the development of the message, or copy, in an advertisement. An assistant art director participates in the design of visual components of advertisements. Entry-level media positions involve buying the media that will carry the ad or selling air time on radio or television or page space in print media. Advancement to supervisory positions requires planning skills, a broad vision, and an affinity for spotting an effective advertising idea. Students interested in advertising should develop good communication skills and try to gain advertising experience through summer employment opportunities or internships.

Retailing

There are two separate career paths in retailing: merchandise management and store management (Figure C-2). The key position in merchandising is that of a buyer, who is responsible for selecting merchandise, guiding the promotion of the merchandise, setting prices, bargaining with wholesalers, training the salesforce, and monitoring the competitive environment. The buyer must also be able to organize and coordinate many critical activities under severe time constraints. In contrast, store management involves the supervision of personnel in all departments and the general management of all facilities, equipment, and merchandise displays. In addition, store managers are responsible for the financial performance of each department and for the store as a whole. Typical positions beyond the store manager level include district manager, regional manager, and divisional vice president.[6]

Most starting jobs in retailing are trainee positions. A trainee is usually placed in a management training program and then given a position as an assistant buyer or assis-

FIGURE C-2

TYPICAL RETAILING CAREER PATHS

tant department manager. Advancement and responsibility can be achieved quickly because there is a shortage of qualified personnel in retailing and because superior performance of an individual is quickly reflected in sales and profits—two visible measures of success.

Sales

College graduates from many disciplines are attracted to sales positions because of the increasingly professional nature of selling jobs and the many opportunities they can provide. A selling career offers benefits that are hard to match in any other field: (1) the opportunity for rapid advancement (into management or to new territories and accounts); (2) the potential for extremely attractive compensation; (3) the development of personal satisfaction, feelings of accomplishment, and increased self-confidence; and (4) independence—salespeople often have almost complete control over their time and activities. Many companies now offer two sales career paths—one for people who want to go into management, and another for those who want to remain in sales for their entire career.

Employment opportunities in sales occupations are found in a wide variety of organizations, including insurance agencies, retailers, and financial service firms. Activities in sales jobs include *selling duties,* such as prospecting for customers, demonstrating the product, or quoting prices; *sales-support duties,* such as handling complaints and helping solve technical problems; and *nonselling duties,* such as preparing reports, attending sales meetings, and monitoring competitive activities. Salespeople who can deal with these varying activities are critical to a company's success.

One of the fastest areas of growth in sales positions is in the direct marketing industry. Interest in information technology, relationship marketing, and integrated marketing has increased the demand for contact with customers. For many firms this means new or additional telemarketing efforts; for other firms it means increasing the amount of time salespeople spend with clients.

Marketing Research

Marketing researchers play important roles in many organizations today. They are responsible for obtaining, analyzing, and interpreting data to facilitate making marketing decisions. This means marketing researchers are basically problem solvers. Success in the area requires not only an understanding of statistics and computers but also a broad base of marketing knowledge[7] and an ability to communicate with management. Individuals who are inquisitive, methodical, analytical, and solution-oriented find the field particularly rewarding.

The responsibilities of the men and women currently working in the market research industry include defining the marketing problem, designing the questionnaire, selecting the sample, collecting and analyzing the data, and, finally, reporting the re-sults of the research. These jobs are available in three kinds of organizations. *Marketing research consulting firms* contract with large companies to provide re-search about their products or services.[8] *Advertising agencies* may provide research services to help clients with questions related to advertising and promotional prob-lems. Finally, some companies have an *in-house research staff* to design and execute their research projects. Typical positions would include director, statistician, analyst, field work director, and interviewer.[9]

Although marketing researchers may start as assistants performing routine tasks, they quickly advance to broader responsibilities. Survey design, interview-ing, report writing, and all aspects of the research process create a challenging ca-reer. In addition, research projects typically deal with such diverse problems as consumer motivation, pricing, forecasting, and competition. A survey of research organizations suggested that, to be successful in marketing research positions, stu-dents should develop skills in written, oral, and interpersonal communication; sta-tistics and analysis; research design; and logic. The survey also suggested that practical work experience (e.g., internships) provides a useful supplement to class-room education.[10]

International Careers

Many of the careers just described can be found in global or international settings—in multinational corporations, small- to medium-sized firms with export business, and franchises. The international public relations firm Burson-Marstellar, for example, has offices in New York, Sydney, Copenhagen, and Bangkok. Similarly, franchises such as Blockbuster Entertainment are expanding in many other markets outside of North America. The dramatic changes in Europe and the need to rebuild the economies of the former Soviet republics may provide other opportunities. Variations of the permanent international career are also possible—for example, some companies may alternate pe-riods of work at "headquarters" with "field" assignments in foreign countries. Finally, a domestic international career—working for a foreign-owned company with an office in Canada—may be appealing.

Applicants for international positions should first develop a skill that can be applied in an international setting. In addition, however, internationally competent employees will need language and cultural skills. A Conference Board description illustrates the point:

> The successful managers of the future will probably be those who speak both Japanese and English, who have a strong base in Brussels and contacts in the Pacific Rim, and who know the cafes and bars of Singapore.

Further, in many organizations, international experience has become a necessity for promotion and career advancement.[11]

THE JOB SEARCH PROCESS

Activities you should consider during your job search process include assessing your-self, identifying job opportunities, preparing your résumé and related correspondence, and going on job interviews.

Assessing Yourself

You must know your product—you—so that you can market yourself effectively to prospective employers. Consequently, a critical first step in your job search is con-ducting a self-analysis, which involves critically examining yourself on the follow-ing dimensions: interests, abilities, education, experience, personality, desired job

INTERESTS

How do I like to spend my time?
Do I enjoy being with people?
Do I like working with mechanical things?
Do I enjoy working with numbers?
Am I a member of many organizations?
Do I enjoy physical activities?
Do I like to read?

ABILITIES

Am I adept at working with numbers?
Am I adept at working with mechanical things?
Do I have good verbal and written communication skills?
What special talents do I have?
At which abilities do I wish I were more adept?

EDUCATION

How have my courses and extracurricular activities prepared me for a specific job?
Which were my best subjects? My worst? The most fun? The least?
Is my GPA an accurate picture of my academic ability? Why?
Do I aspire to a graduate degree? Before beginning my job?
Why did I choose my major?

EXPERIENCE

What previous jobs have I held? What were my responsibilities in each?
Were any of my jobs applicable to positions I may be seeking? How?
What did I like the most about my previous jobs? Like the least?
Why did I work in the jobs I did?
If I had it to do it over again, would I work in these jobs? Why?

PERSONALITY

What are my good and bad traits?
Am I competitive?
Do I work well with others?
Am I outspoken?
Am I a leader or a follower?
Do I work well under pressure?
Do I work quickly, or am I methodical?
Do I get along well with others?
Am I ambitious?
Do I work well independently of others?

DESIRED JOB ENVIRONMENT

Am I willing to relocate? Why?
Do I have a geographical preference? Why?
Would I mind travelling in my job?
Do I have to work for a large, nationally known firm to be satisfied?
Must the job I assume offer rapid promotion opportunities?
If I could design my own job, what characteristics would it have?
How important is high initial salary to me?

PERSONAL GOALS

What are my short-term and long-term goals? Why?
Am I career-oriented, or do I have broader interests?
What are my career goals?
What jobs are likely to help me achieve my goals?
What do I hope to be doing in 5 years? In 10 years?
What do I want out of life?

FIGURE C-3

QUESTIONS TO ASK IN YOUR SELF-ANALYSIS

environment, and personal goals.[12] The importance of performing this assessment was stressed by a management consultant:[13]

> Many graduates enter the world of work without even understanding the fact that they are specific somebodies, much less knowing the kinds of competencies and motivations with which they have been endowed. . . . The tragedy of not knowing is awesome. Ignorant of who they are, most graduates are doomed to spend too much of their lives in work for which they are poorly suited. . . . Self-knowledge is critical to effectively managing your career.

Asking key questions   A self-analysis, in part, entails asking yourself some very important and difficult questions (Figure C-3). It is critical that you respond to the questions honestly, because your answers ultimately will be used as a guide in your job selection.[14] A less-than-candid appraisal of yourself might result in a job mismatch.

Identifying strengths and weaknesses   After you have addressed the questions posed in Figure C-3, you are ready to identify your strengths and weaknesses. To do so, draw a vertical line down the middle of a sheet of paper and label one side of the paper "strengths" and the other side "weaknesses." Based on your answers to the questions, record your strong and weak points in their respective column. Ideally

FIGURE C-4

HYPOTHETICAL LIST OF JOB
CANDIDATE'S STRENGTHS AND
WEAKNESSES

STRENGTHS	WEAKNESSES
Enjoy being with people	Am not adept at working with computers
Am an avid reader	Have minimal work experience
Have good communication skills	Have a mediocre GPA
Am involved in many extracurricular activities	Am sometimes impatient
Work well with others	Resent close supervision
Work well independently	Work methodically (slowly)
Am honest and dependable	Will not relocate
Am willing to travel in the job	Anger easily sometimes
Am a good problem solver	Lack of customer orientation
Have a good sense of humour	
Am a self-starter, have drive	

this cataloguing should be done over a few days to give you adequate time to reflect on your attributes. In addition, you might seek input from others who know you well (such as parents, close relatives, friends, professors, or employers) and can offer more objective views. They might even evaluate you on the questions in Figure C-3, and you can compare the results with your own evaluation. A hypothetical list of strengths and weaknesses is shown in Figure C-4.

Additional information about yourself can be obtained by developing a list of the five experiences or activities you most enjoy and analyzing what they have in common. Don't be surprised if the common characteristics are related to your strengths and weaknesses!

Taking job-related tests   Personality and vocational interest tests, provided by many colleges and universities, can give you other ideas about yourself. After tests have been administered and scored, test takers meet with testing service counsellors to discuss the results. Test results generally suggest jobs for which students have an inclination. The most common tests at the university level are the Strong Interest Inventory and the Campbell Interest and Skill Survey. Some counselling centres also administer the Myers-Briggs Type Indicator—a personality measure that helps identify professions you may enjoy.[15] If you have not already done so, you may wish to see whether your school offers such testing services.

Identifying Your Job Opportunities

To identify and analyze the job market, you must conduct some marketing research to determine what industries *and* companies offer promising job opportunities that relate to the results of your self-analysis. Several sources that can help in your search are discussed below.

College placement office   Your college placement office is an excellent source of job information. Personnel in that office can (1) inform you about which companies will be recruiting on campus, (2) alert you to unexpected job openings, (3) advise you about short-term and long-term career prospects, (4) offer advice on résumé construction, (5) assess your interviewing strengths and weaknesses, and (6) help you evaluate a job offer. In addition, the office usually contains a variety of written materials focusing on different industries and companies and tips on job hunting.

On-line career and employment services   Many companies no longer make frequent on-campus visits. Instead, they may use the many on-line services available to advertise an employment opportunity or to search for candidate information. Human Resources Development Canada also has a special employment web site. The Electronic Labour Exchange matches work to people and people to work faster than traditional methods. You can use this service to search for job opportunities all across Canada (www.ele-spe.org). If you are not on-line, often your college placement office has a computer available to access this web site.

Library   The public or college library can provide you with reference material that, among other things, describes successful firms and their operations, defines the content of various jobs, and forecasts job opportunities. For example, *The Financial Post* magazine publishes a report on the 500 largest Canadian companies and their respective sales and profits; Dun & Bradstreet also publishes directories of companies in Canada. A librarian can indicate reference materials that will be most pertinent to your job search.

Advertisements   Help-wanted advertisements provide an overview of what is happening in the job market. Local (particularly Sunday editions) and school newspapers, trade press (such as *Marketing*), and business magazines contain classified advertisement sections that generally have job opening announcements, often for entry-level positions. Reviewing the want ads can help you identify what kinds of positions are available and their requirements and job titles, which firms offer certain kinds of jobs, and levels of compensation.

Employment agencies   An employment agency can make you aware of several job opportunities very quickly because of its large number of job listings available through computer databases. Many agencies specialize in a particular field (such as sales and marketing). The advantages of using an agency include that it (1) reduces the cost of a job search by bringing applicants and employers together, (2) often has exclusive job listings available only by working through the agency, (3) performs much of the job search for you, and (4) tries to find a job that is compatible with your qualifications and interests. Employment agencies are much maligned because some engage in questionable business practices, so check with the Better Business Bureau or your business contacts to determine the quality of the various agencies.

Personal contacts   An important source of job information that students often overlook is their personal contacts. People you know often may know of job opportunities, so you should advise them that you're looking for a job. Relatives and friends might aid your job search. Instructors you know well and business contacts can provide a wealth of information about potential jobs and even help arrange an interview with a prospective employer. They may also help arrange "informational interviews" with employers who do not have immediate openings. These interviews allow you to collect information about an industry or an employer and give you an advantage if a position does become available. It is a good idea to leave your résumé with all your personal contacts so they can pass it along to those who might be in need of your services. Student organizations (such as the student chapter of the American Marketing Association) may be sources of job opportunities, particularly if they are involved with the business community. Local chapters of professional business organizations (such as the American Marketing Association) also can provide job information; contacting their chapter president is a first step in seeking assistance from these organizations. In the past decade, small employers have provided the greatest growth in employment, and their most common source of new employees is through personal referrals.[16]

Direct contact   Another means of obtaining job information is direct contact—personally communicating to prospective employers (either by mail or in person) that you would be interested in pursuing job opportunities with them. Often you may not even know whether jobs are available in these firms. If you correspond with the companies in writing, a letter of introduction and an attached résumé should serve as your initial form of communication. Your major goal in direct contact is ultimately to arrange a job interview.

Writing Your Résumé

A résumé is a document that communicates to prospective employers who you are. An employer reading a résumé focuses on two key questions: (1) What is the candidate like? and (2) What can the candidate do for me? It is imperative that you design a résumé that addresses these two questions and presents you in a favourable light. Personnel in your campus placement office can provide assistance in designing résumés.

The résumé itself   A well-constructed résumé generally contains up to nine major sections: (1) identification (name, address, and telephone number), (2) job or career objective, (3) educational background, (4) extracurricular activities, (5) work experience or history, (6) skills or capabilities (that pertain to a particular kind of job for which you may be interviewing), (7) accomplishments or achievements, (8) personal interests, and (9) personal references. There is no universally accepted format for a résumé, but three are more frequently used: chronological, functional, and targeted. A *chronological* format presents your work experience and education according to the time sequence in which they occurred (i.e., in chronological order). If you have had several jobs or attended several schools, this approach is useful to highlight what you have done. With a *functional* format, you group your experience into skill categories that emphasize your strengths. This option is particularly appropriate if you have no experience or only minimal experience related to your chosen field. A *targeted* format focuses on the capabilities you have for a specific job. This alternative is desirable if you know what job you want and are qualified for it. In any of the formats, if possible, you should include quantitative information about your accomplishments and experience, such as "increased sales revenue by 20 percent" for the year you managed a retail clothing store. A résumé that illustrates the chronological format is shown in Figure C-5.[17]

Technology is creating a need for a new type of résumé—the electronic résumé. While traditional versions of résumés may be easily delivered through fax machines, today most career experts suggest that a second electronic version be available. The reason? Computers read differently than people. To fully utilize on-line opportunities, an electronic résumé with a popular font and relatively large font size—and without italic text, graphics, shading, underlining or vertical lines—must be available. In addition, because on-line recruiting starts with a key-word search, it is important to include key words and avoid abbreviations.[18]

Letter accompanying a résumé   The letter accompanying a résumé, or cover letter, serves as the job candidate's introduction. As a result, it must gain the attention and interest of the reader or it will fail to give the incentive to examine the résumé carefully. In designing a letter to accompany your résumé, address the following issues:[19]

- Address the letter to a specific person.
- Identify the position for which you are applying and how you heard of it.
- Indicate why you are applying for the position.
- Summarize your most significant credentials and qualifications.
- Refer the reader to the enclosed résumé.
- Request a personal interview, and advise the reader when and where you can be reached.

A sample letter comprising these six factors is presented in Figure C-6. Some students have tried creative approaches to making their letter stand out—sending a gift with their letter or using creative packaging, for example. Although these tactics may gain a recruiter's attention, most hiring managers say that a frivolous approach makes for a frivolous employee. As a general rule, nothing works better than an impressive cover letter and good academic credentials.[20]

FIGURE C-5

CHRONOLOGICAL RESUME

SALLY WINTER

Campus address (until 6/1/97):
Elm Street Apartments #2B
College Town, ON M1B 0A7
Phone: (416) 555-1648

Home address:
123 Front Street
Vancouver, BC V6C M1B
Phone: (613) 555-4995

Education
B.S. in Business Administration, Omega University, 1998, 3.3 overall
GPA—3.6 GPA in major

Work Experience
Paid for 70 percent of my college expenses through the following part-time and summer jobs:
Legal Secretary, Smith, Lee & Jones, Law Firm, Burnaby, BC—summer 1996
• Took dictation and transcribed tapes of legal proceedings
• Typed contracts and other legal documents
• Reorganized client files for easier access
• Answered the phone and screened calls for the partners
Salesclerk, College Varsity Shop, College Town, 1995–1997 academic years
• Helped customers with buying decisions
• Arranged stock and helped with window displays
• Assisted in year-end inventories
• Took over responsibilities of store manager when she was on vacation or ill
Assistant Manager, Treasure Place Gift Shop, Vancouver—summers and Christmas vacations—1993–1995
• Supervised two salesclerks
• Helped select merchandise at trade shows
• Handled daily accounting
• Worked comfortably under pressure during busy seasons

Campus Activities
• Elected captain of the women's varsity tennis team for two years
• Worked as a reporter and night editor on campus newspaper for two years

Personal Interests
• Collecting antique clocks, listening to jazz, swimming

References Available on Request

Interviewing for Your Job

The job interview is a conversation between a prospective employer and a job candidate that focuses on determining whether the employer's needs can be satisfied by the candidate's qualifications. The interview is a "make or break" situation: if the interview goes well, you have increased your chances of receiving a job offer; if it goes poorly, you probably will be eliminated from further consideration.

Preparing for a job interview   To be successful in a job interview, you must prepare for it so you can exhibit professionalism and indicate to a prospective employer that you are serious about the job. When preparing for the interview, several critical activities need to be performed.

Before the interview, gather facts about the industry, the prospective employer, and the job. Relevant information might include the general description for the occupation; the firm's products or services; the firm's size, number of employees, and financial and competitive position; the requirements of the position; and the name and personality of the

FIGURE C-6

SAMPLE LETTER ACCOMPANYING

A RÉSUMÉ

Sally Winter
Elm Street Apartments #2B
College Town, Ontario M1B 0A7
January 31, 1998

Mr. J. B. Jones
Sales Manager
Hilltop Manufacturing Company
Markham, Ontario L1N 9B6

Dear Mr. Jones:

Dr. William Johnson, Professor of Business Administration at Omega University, recently suggested that I write to you concerning your opening and my interest in a sales position. With a B.S. degree in business administration and courses in personal selling and sales management, I am confident that I could make a positive contribution to your firm.

During the past four years I have been a salesclerk in a clothing store and an assistant manager in a gift shop. These two positions required my performing a variety of duties including selling, purchasing, stocking, and supervising. As a result, I have developed an appreciation for the viewpoints of the customer, salesperson, and management. Given my background and high energy level, I feel that I am particularly well qualified to assume a sales position in your company.

My enclosed résumé better highlights my education and experience. My extracurricular activities should strengthen and support my abilities to serve as a sales representative.

I am eager to talk with you because I feel I can demonstrate to you why I am a strong candidate for the position. I have friends in Markham with whom I could stay on weekends, so Fridays or Mondays would be ideal for an appointment. I will call you in a week to see if we can arrange a mutually convenient time for a meeting. I am hopeful that your schedule will allow this.

Thank you for your kind consideration. If you would like some additional information, please feel free to contact me. I look forward to talking with you.

Sincerely,

Sally Winter

enclosure

interviewer.[21] Obtaining this information will provide you with additional insight into the firm and help you formulate questions to ask the interviewer. This information might be gleaned, for example, from corporate annual reports, *The Globe and Mail, The Financial Post,* or trade publications. If information is not readily available, you could call the company and indicate that you wish to obtain some information about the firm before your interview.

Preparation for the job interview should also involve role playing, or pretending that you are in the "hot seat" being interviewed. Before role playing, anticipate questions interviewers may pose and how you might address them (Figure C-7). Do not memorize your answers, though, because you want to appear spontaneous, yet logical and intelligent. Nonetheless, it is helpful to practice how you might respond to the questions. In addition, develop questions you might ask the interviewer that are important and of concern to you (Figure C-8).

When role playing, you and someone with whom you feel comfortable should engage in a mock interview. Afterward, ask the stand-in interviewer to candidly appraise

INTERVIEWER QUESTIONS

1 What can you tell me about yourself?
2 What are your strengths? Weaknesses?
3 What do you consider to be your most significant accomplishment to date?
4 What do you see yourself doing in 5 years? In 10 years?
5 Are you a leader? Explain?
6 What do you really want out of life?
7 How would you describe yourself?
8 Why did you choose your university major?
9 In which extracurricular activities did you participate? Why?
10 What jobs have you enjoyed the most? The least? Why?
11 How has your previous work experience prepared you for a job?
12 Why do you want to work for our company?
13 What qualifications do you think a person needs to be successful in a company like ours?
14 What do you know about our company?
15 What criteria are you using to evaluate the company for which you hope to work?
16 In what kind of city would you prefer to live?
17 What can I tell you about our company?
18 Are you willing to relocate?
19 Are you willing to spend at least six months as a trainee? Why?
20 Why should we hire you?

INTERVIEWEE QUESTIONS

1 Why would a job candidate want to work for your firm?
2 What makes your firm different from its competitors?
3 What is the company's promotion policy?
4 Describe the typical first-year assignment for this job.
5 How is an employee evaluated?
6 What are the opportunities for personal growth?
7 Do you have a training program?
8 What are the company's plans for future growth?
9 What is the retention rate of people in the position for which I am interviewing?
10 How can you use my skills?
11 Does the company have development programs?
12 What kind of image does the firm have in the community?
13 Why do you enjoy working for your firm?
14 How much responsibility would I have in this job?
15 What is the corporate culture in your firm?

your interview content and style. You may wish to videotape the mock interview; ask the personnel in your campus placement office where videotaping equipment can be obtained for this purpose.

Before the job interview you should attend to several details. Know the exact time and place of the interview; write them down—do not rely on your memory. Get the full company name straight. Find out what the interviewer's name is and how to pronounce it. Bring a notepad and pen along on the interview, in case you need to record anything.

Make certain that your appearance is clean, neat, professional, and conservative. And be punctual; arriving tardy to a job interview gives you an appearance of being unreliable.

Succeeding in your job interview   You have done your homework, and at last the moment arrives and it is time for the interview. Although you may experience some apprehension, view the interview as a conversation between the prospective employer and you. Both of you are in the interview to look over the other party, to see whether there might be a good match. You know your subject matter (you); furthermore, because you did not have a job with the firm when you walked into the interview, you really have nothing to lose if you don't get it—so relax.

When you meet the interviewer, greet him or her by name, be cheerful, smile, and maintain good eye contact. Take your lead from the interviewer at the outset. Sit down after the interviewer has offered you a seat. Do not smoke. Sit up straight in your chair, and look alert and interested at all times. Appear relaxed, not tense. Be enthusiastic.

During the interview, be yourself. If you try to behave in a manner that is different from the "real" you, your attempt may be transparent to the interviewer or you may ultimately get the job but discover that you aren't suited for it. In addition to assessing how well your skills match those of the job, the interviewer will probably try to assess your long-term interest in the firm.

As the interview comes to a close, leave it on a positive note. Thank the interviewer for his or her time and the opportunity to discuss employment opportunities. If you are still interested in the job, express this to the interviewer. The interviewer will normally tell you what the employer's next step is. Rarely will a job offer be made at the end of the initial interview. If it is and you want the job, accept the offer; if there is any doubt in your mind about the job, however, ask for time to consider the offer.

Following up on your job interview   After your interview, send a thank-you note to the interviewer and indicate whether you are still interested in the job. If you want to continue pursuing the job, "polite persistence" may help you get it. You *can* have an impact on the interviewer *after* the interview is over.

The thank-you note is a gesture of appreciation and a way of maintaining visibility with the interviewer. (Remember the adage, "Out of sight, out of mind.") Even if the interview did not go well, the thank-you note may impress the interviewer so much that his or her opinion of you changes. After you have sent your thank-you note, you may wish to call the prospective employer to determine the status of the hiring decision. If the interviewer told you when you would hear from the employer, make your telephone call *after* this date (assuming, of course, that you have not yet heard from the employer); if the interviewer did not tell you when you would be contacted, make your telephone call a week or so after you have sent your thank-you note.

As you conduct your follow-up, be persistent but polite. If you are too eager, one of two things could happen to prevent you from getting the job: the employer might feel that you are a nuisance and would exhibit such behaviour on the job, or the employer may perceive that you are desperate for the job and thus are not a viable candidate.

Handling rejection   You have put your best efforts into your job search. You developed a well-designed résumé and prepared carefully for the job interview. Even the interview appears to have gone well. Nevertheless, a prospective employer may send you a rejection letter. ("We are sorry that our needs and your superb qualifications don't match.") Although you will probably be disappointed, not all interviews lead to a job offer because there normally are more candidates than there are positions available.

If you receive a rejection letter, you should think back through the interview. What appeared to go right? What went wrong? Perhaps personnel from your campus placement office can shed light on the problem, particularly if they are in the custom of having interviewers rate each interviewee. Try to learn lessons to apply in future interviews. Keep interviewing and gaining interview experience; your persistence will eventually pay off.

SELECTED SOURCES OF MARKETING CAREER INFORMATION

The following is a selected list of marketing information sources that you should find useful during your academic studies and professional career.

Business and Marketing Reference Publications

Peter D. Bennett, ed., *Dictionary of Marketing Terms,* 2nd ed. (Chicago: NTC Business Books, 1995). This dictionary contains definitions of more than 3000 marketing terms.

Victor P. Buell, ed., *Handbook of Modern Marketing,* 2nd ed. (New York: McGraw-Hill, 1986). This handbook was designed to provide a single authoritative source of information on marketing and marketing-related subjects. Sections and chapters contain conceptual background material to aid the reader in overall understanding, followed by "how-to" information.

Canadian Business Index. This is available on-line (CAN/OLE) and covers 200 business periodicals.

Jill Cousins and Lesley Robinson, eds., *The Online Manual,* 2nd ed. (Cambridge, Mass.: Blackwell Publishers, 1993). This manual is a practical tool to help both the experienced and inexperienced information user select from the thousands of databases now available on-line.

Jeffrey Heilbrunn, ed., *Marketing Encyclopedia* (Chicago: NTC Business Books, 1995). This book provides a collection of essays by professional and academic marketing experts on issues and trends shaping the future of marketing.

Jerry M. Rosenberg, *Dictionary of Business and Management,* 3rd ed. (New York: John Wiley & Sons, 1992). This dictionary contains more than 10 000 concise definitions of business and management terms.

Career Planning Publications

Richard N. Bolles, *What Color Is Your Parachute? A Practical Manual for Job Hunters and Career Changers* (Berkeley, Calif.: Ten Speed Press, 1995).

Karmen Crowther, *Researching Your Way to a Good Job* (New York: John Wiley, 1993).

Ronald W. Fry, ed., *Advertising Career Directory* (Detroit, Mich.: Visible Ink Press, 1992).

Fred E. Jardt and Mary B. Nemnich, *Using the Internet in Your Job Search* (Indianapolis, Ind.: JIST Works, 1995).

Joyce Lain Kennedy and Thomas J. Morrow, *Electronic Job Search Revolution* (New York: John Wiley & Sons, 1994).

Tom Jackson, *The Perfect Résumé* (New York: Doubleday, 1990).

Ronald L. Krannich and Caryl R. Krannich, *The Complete Guide to International Jobs and Careers,* 2nd ed. (Woodbridge, Va.: Impact Publications, 1992).

Dorothy Leeds, *Marketing Yourself* (New York: HarperCollins, 1991).

Adele Lewis, *How to Write Better Résumés,* 4th ed. (Hauppauge, N.Y.: Barron's Educational Services, 1993).

David W. Rosenthal and Michael A. Powell, *Careers in Marketing* (Englewood Cliffs, N.J.: Prentice Hall, 1984).

Selected Periodicals

Advertising Age, Crain Communications, Inc. (semiweekly).
Business Horizons, Indiana University (bimonthly).
Business Week, McGraw-Hill (weekly).
Fortune, Time, Inc. (biweekly).
Harvard Business Review, Harvard University (bimonthly).
Industrial Marketing Management, Elsevier Science Publishing Co., Inc. (quarterly).
Journal of Advertising Research, Advertising Research Foundation (bimonthly).
Journal of Business and Industrial Marketing, MCB University Press (quarterly).
Journal of Consumer Research, Journal of Consumer Research, Inc. (quarterly).
Journal of Health Care Marketing, American Marketing Association (quarterly).
Journal of Marketing, American Marketing Association (quarterly).
Journal of Marketing Research, American Marketing Association (quarterly).
Journal of Retailing, Institute of Retail Management (quarterly).
Marketing, McLean Hunter (weekly).
Marketing News, American Marketing Association (biweekly).
Sales and Marketing Management, Bill Communications, Inc. (16 per year).

Professional and Trade Associations

American Marketing Association
250 South Wacker Drive
Chicago, IL 60606-5819
(312) 648-0536
Website: www.ama.org
Toronto Chapter
100 University Avenue
Toronto, Ontario M5W 1V8
(416) 367-3573

Canadian Advertising Foundation
350 Bloor St. E. #402
Toronto, Ontario M4W 1H5
(416) 961-6311

Canadian Advertising Research Foundation
175 Bloor St. E. South Tower #307
Toronto, Ontario M4W 3R8
(416) 964-3832

Canadian Association of Broadcasters
350 Sparks Street #306
P.O. Box 627 Stn. B
Ottawa, Ontario K1P 5S2
(613) 233-4035
e-mail: CAB-ACR.ca

Canadian Direct Marketing Association
1 Concorde Gate #607
Don Mills, Ontario M3C 3N6
(416) 391-2362

Canadian Federation of Business and
　　Professional Women's Clubs
56 Sparks Street #308
Ottawa, Ontario K1P 5A9
(613) 234-7619

Canadian Federation of Independent Business
4141 Yonge Street #401
Willowdale, Ontario M2P 2A6
(416) 222-8022

Canadian Institute of Marketing
41 Capital Drive
Nepean, Ontario K2G 0E7
(613) 727-0954

Conference Board of Canada
255 Smyth Road
Ottawa, Ontario K1H 8M7
(613) 526-3280
Website: www.Conference Board.ca

Institute of Canadian Advertising
Yonge-Eglinton Centre
2300 Yonge St.
Box 2350—Suite 500
Toronto, Ontario M4P 1E4
Website: www.goodmedia.com/ica/

Purchasing Management Association of Canada
2 Carlton Street #1414
Toronto, Ontario M5B 1J3
(416) 977-7111

Professional Marketing Research Society
2323 Yonge Street #806
Toronto, Ontario M4P 2C9
(416) 493-4080

Retail Council of Canada
121 Bloor St. E #1210
Toronto, Ontario M4W 3M5
(416) 922-6678

Retail Merchants Association of Canada
1780 Birchmount Road
Scarborough, Ontario M1P 2H8
(416) 291-7903

Alternate Cases

CASE 1   Windows 95 (A)

It would be hard to have missed the introduction of Microsoft Corporation's Windows 95 (www.windows95.com). Windows 95 is probably the biggest marketing story of the decade. Although Windows 95 was years in the making, the marketing war for personal computer (PC) operating systems was virtually over before Microsoft (www.microsoft.com) formally launched the product in August 1995.

THE PRODUCT

A computer's operating system controls exactly how the computer hardware interacts with other software and directs the basic functions of the computer. For years, the PC industry—defined here as IBM-compatible personal computers—was dominated by DOS (for Disk Operating System). However, the old DOS was user-unfriendly and required PC users often to learn and use cryptic codes to interact with the computer. Microsoft observed how successful Macintosh computers were in enabling computer users to interact easily with their computers using a graphical interface, and consequently, it developed MS (Microsoft) Windows, a user-friendly interface to DOS. MS Windows was the precursor, or first generation, which would ultimately be replaced by Windows 3.1, and then—two generations later—by Windows 95. Windows 95 acts as both an interface and an operating system, completely replacing DOS.

Even somewhat recently, computers were the exclusive domain of computer specialists, and complex, unfriendly operating systems abounded. The systems were also designed for early, relatively slow, computers. Declining prices, rapidly improving technology, and the widespread acceptance of computers among the general population were the driving forces behind the development of a new PC operating system. To contend with these factors, Microsoft was determined to provide an advanced, stable operating system that would be more "user-oriented" than existing systems. Microsoft spent several years and millions of dollars testing its new Windows 95 operating system. This 32-bit operating system was designed to take advantage of the full power of today's 32-bit chips, look prettier on the screen than Windows 3.1, allow more than one application program to run simultaneously, and generally make life easier for PC owners.

THE INDUSTRY

The highly competitive PC operating system market is driven by two important factors. First, modern high-performance PCs have been criticized as being unable to perform to their full potential because the common DOS operating system was developed for much more primitive computers. New 32-bit operating systems (such as Windows 95) can unleash the full power of the 486 and Pentium processors to take advantage of demanding software. Second, there is little doubt that the company with the most widely adopted operating system will have a competitive advantage in terms of developing other system-compatible software. For example, consumers may perceive that other Microsoft software would run faster and more reliably on a Microsoft operating system. Operating system dominance is particularly important given the rapidly growing PC industry. Industry growth rates are around 30 percent annually.

There have also been rapid changes in consumer attitudes toward computers. The purchase of a computer for the home is no longer for an elite segment of the population. As acceptance of PCs expands, operating system dominance may lead to industry dominance.

THE COMPETITION

Microsoft's largest competitor in the PC operating system market was IBM's OS/2 Warp. OS/2 Warp had the advantage of being released earlier than Microsoft's highly touted Windows 95 system. In fact, Warp beat Windows 95 to the market by almost a year. OS/2 Warp was released to the market with mixed reviews, however. While *PC Week* was unimpressed with the product, another trade journal, *InfoWorld,* claimed Warp was superior to a prerelease version of Windows 95.

IBM also took a big gamble by announcing that OS/2 Warp would not provide any way for users to run programs designed for Windows 95. This would force OS/2 to stand on its own in the market. If software developers were persuaded to create special OS/2 versions of their programs, it could give OS/2 a boost. If the move failed to encourage software manufacturers to develop OS/2 programs, it could kill OS/2 completely.

IBM also faced other obstacles. OS/2 had a hard time gaining an inroad to the market because most PC manufacturers were selling their PCs preloaded with the Windows 3.1 operating system simply because they had paid for it. Microsoft had a practice of charging computer makers a licensing fee on each machine sold, regardless of whether it contained MS-DOS or Windows. Microsoft got away with this because computer manufacturers lived "in fear of retribution from Microsoft," according to Lee Reiswig, IBM's personal software chief.

THE ISSUES

Both OS/2 Warp and Windows 95 entered the market priced at about $90. Windows entered the market at this price despite the fact that millions of dollars had gone into extensively testing the software; further millions went into promoting the package. In fact, Microsoft practically gave away more than 500 000 copies of Windows 95 to test the system on a variety of PCs and in a variety of conditions, and worldwide promotional expenditures for the Windows 95 launch was estimated at $700 million. Microsoft wanted to ensure that its operating system would be priced within reach of the average PC owner.

To ensure widespread acceptance of its operating system, Microsoft depended on PC user input during the "beta-testing" phase. Beta testing is taking a new product to lead users for input and feedback prior to full-scale product introduction. At Microsoft headquarters, software developers carefully studied exactly how users interacted with the operating system and what confused them. They then made modifications to the product to try

and make sure that computer users could focus on the tasks they wanted their computers to do and not on how to navigate a complicated operating system.

Microsoft also spared no expense in promoting the "product of the decade." Millions of dollars were spent on advertising and special promotions. Great pains were taken to ensure that sufficient quantities of Windows 95 were shipped to stores worldwide so that no store faced shortages of the product when the customers came for the product. Windows 95 was available at computer stores, electronic stores selling computers, and mass merchandisers. After the product was launched, Microsoft also made sure that there were adequate support staff personnel available at the end of a toll-free support line to answer any questions new users had or solve any early problems.

By early August 1995, industry speculation was that IBM had given up on the home PC market. OS/2 Warp was relatively strong in the corporate market but was facing strong competition from yet another Microsoft operating system—Windows NT. IBM's chairman claimed that the consumer and stand-alone desktop markets were always secondary to the company and that IBM intended to continue its long-standing focus for OS/2 on the corporate market. Despite having almost a year advantage on Microsoft in getting to the market, it appeared by early 1996 that Microsoft's Windows 95 would win the desktop operating system war.[1]

Questions

1. What are the various environmental factors influencing the potential success of Windows 95 and OS/2 in the marketplace?
2. If you were in charge of launching Windows 95 in late 1995, what would be your marketing mix decisions (4Ps) for the product, and why?
3. What role did customer needs play in Microsoft's Windows 95 development and launch? How did Microsoft's marketing mix add customer value?

CASE 2 Kingpin Snowboarding

What looks like a slalom water ski, feels like surfing, but takes place on snowy downhill ski slopes? The answer is snowboarding—one of the fastest growing sports.

THE COMPANY

In 1992 Doran Nurmi and Roger Walsberg started Kingpin Manufacturing with an initial investment of $2400. In the first year, the partners sold 15 of the 30 snowboards pro-

duced. Production increased to 300 boards the second year, 1500 boards the third year, and 2900 in 1995. With firm orders already received for more than 6500 boards, Kingpin estimates total sales of more than 9500 boards in 1996. Initially, more than 70 percent of the snowboards produced by Kingpin were custom orders. Now, however, a majority of the snowboards manufactured by Kingpin are "private labels" manufactured for other companies. Also, as the popularity of their snowboards rapidly rose, Kingpin moved away from custom orders and now offers 10 different models as standard products.

PHOTO BY MIKE COUSINO.

The Idea

Snowboarding is a wintertime sport that resembles surfing on a ski hill. The modern snowboard industry began around 20 years ago. Currently, snowboarding is considered the hottest sport around, with an annual growth rate of 20 percent. The number of snowboarders is expected to exceed the number of skiers by 2010.

There are about 20 manufacturers producing snowboards in North America. Barriers to entry are relatively low, so new entrants can be expected. Industry giants such as Burton, Nitro, Sims, and Santa Cruz account for about 60 percent to 65 percent of the market and offer entire lines of boards that range in price from $300 to $800.

The Japanese Market

Snowboarding is also achieving worldwide attention and acceptance. The International Olympic Committee and the International Ski Federation accepted snowboarding as a medal sport in the 1998 Winter Olympics held in Nagano, Japan. In fact, the Japanese market is an important one for Kingpin. Kingpin has been selling boards in Japan since 1993. Nurmi finds some interesting differences between the North American and Japanese markets. The Japanese market is much more "fashion conscious" than the North American market. In North America, snowboarding has been around long enough that it has become a fairly well-established sport. It is still very much a fashion trend in Japan. Wants are strongly dictated by what is seen in snowboarding magazines. As a result, the number one attribute sought in snowboards by the Japanese consumer is the appearance of the board, followed by quality. Performance is probably at the bottom of the list. In contrast, Nurmi finds that performance is the number one buying criterion for consumers selecting snowboards in the North American market.

Snowboards in Japan are smaller in size than the boards sold in North America and styled a little differently. The Japanese in general have a smaller average foot size than their North American counterparts. The size and style are also different because of differences in snowboarding style. The Japanese ride differently—freestyle snowboarding is much more common in Japan. Interestingly, this ties into the influence of snowboarding magazines. Despite the fact that more than half of the snowboarders in North America are either "free riders" or "all-mountain riders," they get little publicity in the popular snowboarding magazines. Since freestyle gets a lot more space in magazines, Japanese desire snowboards styled for freestyle riding. Free riders or mountain riders tend to ride on steeper terrain, in deep powder, and at the better resorts. These riders tend to be more expert than freestyle riders, who use different maneuvers on easier runs. Accordingly, Kingpin manufactures four snowboard models designed exclusively for the Japanese market.

The ski industry environment is also different. Snowboarding is not as widely accepted on Japanese slopes. Apparently many Japanese ski slope managers still see snowboarding as a fad that will die soon and, consequently, provide only limited ski slope access to snowboarders.

Kingpin's business dealings with the Japanese market also differ. According to Nurmi, the biggest difference is that all communications are via fax because of the time zone difference and the language barrier. Nurmi finds it inconvenient doing business this way since he is more comfortable dealing one-on-one with customers, and he finds it difficult to judge "tone" when reading faxes.

Kingpin sells to the Japanese market through a distributor. This eliminates extensive dealings with individual Japanese retailers. While Kingpin also utilizes an indirect channel of distribution in North America, the channel is longer in Japan. Kingpin generally sells directly to North American retailers in order to reach the consumer. An additional intermediary is used for the Japanese market. According to Nurmi, this indirect exporting market entry strategy is more appropriate than any direct market entry strategy for two important reasons. First, the Japanese consumers do not want to buy Japanese-made boards. As mentioned earlier, the image associated with American snowboards is important to the Japanese consumers. Second, manufacturing snowboards in Japan would be difficult since the most important component of the snowboard is the wood core. Given Japan's limited natural resources, the wood would probably have to be imported into Japan anyway. It is easier to export the completed snowboard rather than components for assembly in Japan.

Wholesalers, such as Kingpin's Japanese distributor, are offered a special wholesale price. In addition, there are quantity discounts to encourage large orders.

THE ISSUES

What does the future hold? Doran Nurmi thinks that the inclusion of snowboarding in the 1998 Olympics will significantly influence future demand in Japan. He is certain that it will change the Japanese market. In addition to expanding the market in Japan, he feels it will change how the Japanese view snowboarding: not only will snowboarding be taken more seriously, but the market will shift from a focus on appearance to performance.[2]

Questions

1. What are the pros and cons of a global versus a multidomestic approach to marketing snowboards in Japan? Which approach do you feel would have more merit, and why?
2. What are some of the significant environmental factors that could have a *major* impact on the marketing of snowboards internationally? Describe each factor and what the nature of the impact would be. For example, one of the social/cultural factors that could have an impact is whether there is a tradition, an interest level, critical mass of skiers and snowboarders, and an interest in snowboarding in a given country or area.
3. What marketing mix recommendations would you have suggested for Kingpin for the 1998 Olympics in Japan and beyond?
4. Kingpin currently uses indirect exporting. What are the advantages and disadvantages of indirect exporting versus other methods of global marketing such as direct exporting, licensing, joint venture, or direct ownership?

CASE 3   Honeywell, Inc.: Optoelectronics Division

After several years of developing fiber-optic technology for Department of Defence projects, executives in the Optoelectronics Division of Honeywell, Inc. (www.honeywell.com) decided to pursue commercial applications for their products and technology. The task would not be easy because fiber optics was a new technology that many firms would find unfamiliar. Fiber optics is the technology of transmitting light through long, thin, flexible fibers of glass, plastic, or other transparent materials. When it is used in a commercial application, a light source emits infrared light flashes corresponding to data. Millions of light flashes per second send streams through a transparent fiber. A light sensor at the other end of the fiber "reads" the data transmitted. It is estimated that sales of fiber-optic technology could exceed $3 billion in 1995. Almost half the dollar sales volume would come from telecommunications, about 25 percent from government or military purchases, and about 25 percent from commercial applications in computers, robotics, cable TV, and other products.

Interest in adapting fiber-optic technology and products for commercial applications had prompted Honeywell executives to carefully review buying behaviour associated with the adoption of a new technology. The buying process appeared to contain at least six phases: (1) need recognition, (2) identification of available products, (3) comparison with existing technology, (4) vendor or seller evaluation, (5) the decision itself, and (6) follow-up on technology performance. Moreover, there appeared to be several people within the buying organization who would play a role in the adoption of a new technology. For example, top management (such as the president and executive vice presidents) would certainly be involved. Engineering and operations management (e.g., vice presidents of engineering and manufacturing) and design engineers (e.g., persons who develop specifications for new products) would also play a major role. Purchasing personnel would have a say in such a decision and particularly in the vendor-evaluation process. The role played by each person in the buying organization was still unclear to Honeywell. It seemed that engineering management personnel could slow the adoption of fiber optics if they did not feel it was appropriate for the products made by the company. Design engineers, who would actually apply fiber optics in product design, might be favourably or unfavourably disposed to the technology depending on whether they knew how to use it. Top management personnel would participate in any final decisions to use fiber optics and could generate interest in the technology if stimulated to do so.

This review of buying behaviour led to questions about how to penetrate a company's buying organization and have fiber optics used in the company's products. Although Honeywell was a large, well-known company with annual sales exceeding $5 billion, its fiber-optic technology capability was much less familiar. Therefore the executives thought it was necessary to establish Honeywell's credibility in fiber optics. This was done, in part, through an advertising image campaign that featured Honeywell Optoelectronics as a leader in fiber optics.[3]

Questions

1. What type of buying situation is involved in the purchase of fiber optics, and what will be important buying criteria used by companies considering using fiber optics in their products?

2. Describe the purchase decision process for adopting fiber optics, and state how members in the buying centre for this technology might play a part in this process.

3. What effect will perceived risk have on a company's decision of whether to use fiber optics in its products?

4. What role does the image advertising campaign play in Honeywell Optoelectronics' efforts to market fiber optics?

CASE 4   Windows 95 (B)

It's been variously described as "marketing history," "a defining moment," and "a global sensation." Combined international marketing expenditures for Microsoft's (www.microsoft.com) personal computer (PC) operating system Windows 95 (www.windows95.com) promotional campaign were estimated at $700 million. Beyond just an intensive advertising campaign, Microsoft used every element of the promotional mix to ensure that only the remotest corners of the globe remained unaware of Microsoft's new product.

THE PRODUCT

Microsoft's Windows 95 is an operating system for IBM-compatible personal computers. A computer's operating system controls exactly how the computer hardware interacts with other software and directs the basic functions of the computer. The Windows 95 interface enables computer users to easily interact with their computers with a graphical interface, inspired by Apple Computer's icon-friendly interface and operating system. In addition to providing a more user-friendly operating system, Windows 95 was designed to take full advantage of the power of today's 32-bit chips.

THE PROMOTIONAL LAUNCH

In promoting Windows 95, Microsoft made effective use of integrated marketing communications to get the best return on its promotional investment. It was essential that all of Microsoft's promotional and marketing activities were integrated to promote a consistent image to consumers. In the case of the Windows 95 launch, Microsoft was communicating with its consumers with a variety of media. Each event added to the message that Windows 95 was not simply a slightly modified version of Windows 3.1 but rather a major replacement for Windows 3.1. Microsoft used the Windows 95 logo prominently in all its advertising and promotional efforts. The company provided retailers with point-of-purchase displays that were bathed in the logo and prominently displayed the "START" button to demonstrate the easy interface Windows 95 used to launch programs within Windows 95. Product packaging, advertising, and everything at the Windows 95 launch site—signs, cups, the polo shirt worn by Bill Gates—all carried the Windows 95 design elements: the "START" button and the blue-sky-and-clouds motif. To help reinforce this unified theme, Microsoft is rumoured to have spent more than $10 million simply to gain the rights to use the Rolling Stones song "Start Me Up" in their promotional campaign. To communicate the dominance of Microsoft in the PC industry to consumers, Microsoft even required marketers demonstrating the software to use Microsoft brand keyboards and computer mice.

In New York City, the Empire State Building was bathed in the colours of the Windows 95 logo. In Toronto, a massive banner announcing the arrival of Windows 95 graced the CN Tower—the world's largest free-standing structure. In the United Kingdom, *The Times* was distributed free, courtesy of Microsoft. Of course, the free issue contained a prominent Windows 95 advertising supplement. To ensure that travellers in between two UK destinations didn't miss out on the event, entire fields were painted with the Windows 95 logo so that it was visible from the air. In the land down under, Australian residents on the country's eastern coast witnessed an unusual sight—a four-story-high Windows 95 box sailed into Sydney Harbor on a barge. At Microsoft headquarters in Redmond, Washington, a large event was planned that people around the globe could attend—virtually. Microsoft set up a World Wide Web (WWW) site that anyone could connect to if they wanted to participate "live" in the events on launch day.

Combined with these spectacular events, Microsoft benefited from a great deal of publicity spurred on by the grand scale of the launch. According to an analysis by MediaLink Public Relations Research, in the week preceding the launch, Windows 95 was the topic of 345 television news stories compared with 432 for the war in Bosnia during the same period. The publicity machine was also churned by Bill Gates's designation as the wealthiest human being in the solar system.

Microsoft spent years testing and, one could argue, even sampling the product. Windows 95 has been hailed as the most tested software program in history. Lead users could download beta versions of the program from the Internet for trial and testing at several stages of product development.

The Windows 95 launch was not simply Microsoft's show. Several manufacturers of computer hardware and software jumped on the bandwagon, eager to take advantage of this strategic window. Software manufacturers readied their Windows 95 products for shelves to try to take advantage of the enormous traffic the Windows 95 launch was expected to generate. PC hardware managers were optimistic—of the 200 million PCs now in use globally, only 39 percent have the horsepower necessary to run Windows 95.

Computer retailers planned their own events around the launch date. Some planned to stay open 95 minutes past midnight into August 24 so that consumers could get their hands on the software as soon as Windows 95 was available for sale. Since PC owners of a whole range of PCs were expected to feel the urge to buy into the Windows 95 hype, most also prominently displayed hardware upgrades in terms of larger disk drives, more memory, and faster video cards that consumers could snatch up along with their copies of Windows 95.

THE COMPETITION

Interestingly, IBM did virtually no promotion for their OS/2 Warp operating system, considered the primary direct competition for Windows 95, during the Windows 95 launch or subsequently. While it could be argued that doing any promotion during this launch period would have been counterproductive, IBM has been surprisingly quiet since the Windows 95 launch, seemingly conceding the battle for PC operating system dominance to Microsoft. Only Apple made a play for media attention during the Windows 95 hoopla, poking fun at Microsoft's attempt to mimic the user-friendly format of Apple computer systems. To remind consumers that Windows 95 developed from the IBM PC operating system was still more complex than Apple's operating system ever was, Apple took out a full page ad in *The Wall Street Journal* on the day of the launch which simply said, in bold letters "C:\ONGRTLNS.W95" followed by the Apple logo.[4]

Questions

1. What are the primary promotional objectives for Microsoft's launch of Windows 95?
2. How did Microsoft use integrated marketing communication to launch Windows 95? What are the strengths and weaknesses of each element of the promotional mix, and how do they correspond to Microsoft's promotional objectives for Windows 95?
3. The promotional tactics described in the case appear to be part of a pull promotional strategy. Discuss whether you feel a push strategy is necessary to support this pull promotional strategy. How could Microsoft utilize a push strategy (what types of tactics for the trade would be effective)?

CASE 5   Timex

"Takes a licking and keeps on ticking." For years this is the image that has been associated with Timex watches—dependable, reliable, almost indestructible. Timex's (www.timex.com) advertising was closely associated with the Timex image. The advertising campaign featured different attempts to destroy Timex watches that failed to stop the Timex from ticking. One memorable ad showed a Timex watch strapped to the propeller of a motor boat before being driven across the lake. The dripping watch was proudly displayed as the second hand swept past the face of the watch.

THE COMPANY

Timex has been the industry leader since 1960. In fact, Timex's share of the Canadian and US watch market was 50 percent by the late 1960s, and as much as 20 percent worldwide. However, Timex missed several important environmental trends that changed the industry. For one thing, Timex stuck to analog technology, losing money and market share to competitors that adopted digital technology in the 1970s. By the time Timex caught on to the importance of the electronic watch, competitors had already developed and marketed far-superior products. Timex employees dubbed the first Timex electronic watches "quarter pounders" because of their clumsy, clunky appearance. In 1982, a Swiss company approached Timex and asked it to do the worldwide marketing for a new product. Timex turned down the offer, believing the garish plastic watches would be a flop. It was a major blunder for Timex. Swatches became a fashion success around the globe. By 1983, domestic market share for Timex had fallen to about 17 percent, with operating losses approaching $100 million.

THE MARKET

Times changed and so did consumer needs and wants for watches. C. Michael Jacobi, Timex president since 1992, says that Timex's biggest mistake was failing to keep up with the watch's evolution from a functional object to a fashion accessory. Your watch tells the world who you are or what you want to be. Coordinating watches with clothing, changing watch bands for different occasions, and wearing designer watches that convey status and prestige is increasingly important to consumers. According to research, the average consumer today owns five watches compared with 1½ 30 years ago. Timex was left behind as the rest of the industry moved from watches as a functional tool to watches as fashion statements.

THE PRODUCT

Timex appears to have learned from its mistakes. Fashion consultants now visit twice a year from New York and Paris to provide insight to Timex on trends and interests that can translate into new watch styles. Jacobi and other executives travel to retailers and other trade shows to spot fashion trends.

Timex took advantage of consumer interest in sport watches to develop the Indiglo watch. Indiglo patented technology uses energy from the watch battery to excite electrons in the watch face. Unlike other watches that require exposure to the sun or lamp, the Timex Indiglo does not need to be "charged" to emit light.

Timex was also very successful advertising the Indiglo watches when the technology was introduced in 1992. Its introductory commercial effectively conveyed the simple message about the glowing watch face while hinting at the "takes a licking and keeps on ticking" theme. In the background, Sinatra sings "strangers in the night . . . " as a smitten firefly hovers over the glowing watch dial. Smack! A huge hand suddenly swats at the infatuated firefly but misses, hitting the watch. *Time* magazine called this campaign "the best television campaign of 1992." The 1992 Gallup Watch Brand Survey found that 98 percent of consumers knew the Timex brand, followed by Seiko (87 percent).

Recognizing that simply introducing a unique product with a patented technology is insufficient to gain market share, Timex boosted its 1993 ad budget by more than 50 percent. Timex also faced increasing competition from major competitors. Hearing that Seiko, Armitron, and Citizen planned to add watches to their lines with a lighting technology similar to Indiglo, Timex spent a record $10 million on advertising—just in the fourth quarter of 1993. Additionally, Timex made a major change in its advertising strategy. Watch companies traditionally focused their advertising campaigns in the spring and fall. In what industry executives called a first, Timex began advertising continuously throughout the year. As a result, in 1993 Timex unit sales rose about 30 percent, with more than half the increase attributed to Indiglo.

Given its success, it is not surprising that Timex continued to put almost its entire advertising budget into campaigns for Indiglo in 1994. And the Indiglo is *HOT*. Timex was fortunate enough to get some impressive testimonials from customers that rolled in along with sales. These stories provided some fascinating material for potential ad campaigns. Consider the following:

- A man led a group of people down 34 unlit flights of stairs in the bombed World Trade Center in New York City by the light of an Indiglo.
- A Los Angeles couple lit their way to safety after an earthquake with an Indiglo watch.
- Four people clung to a capsized fishing boat overnight, comforted by the reassuring blue beam of a Timex Indiglo.

The Indiglo technology is "making ho-hum Timex kind of hip." In fact, earlier attempts to upscale the product line and develop more fashionable products were hampered by perceptions that the products have "got a $12.95 name on them."

Currently Timex has 20 to 30 watch styles with the Indiglo technology, part of a product line that includes 1500 styles, up from 300 in 1970. Indiglo models accounted for 40 percent to 50 percent of all Timex sales. And Timex has some dramatic stories to tell, rivalling those of the old "takes a licking and keeps on ticking" ads.

THE COMPETITION

Competitors are taking two positions with respect to the popularity of the Timex Indiglo. Some are attempting to imitate the technology. For example, Seiko's LumiBrite watch has dials coated with a nonradioactive compound that absorbs light during the day and re-emits it for up to five hours in the dark. Others suggest that the light-up dial is a novelty that will not appeal to the masses. Bulova's marketing vice president, Philip Shaw, does not feel that night-lighting technology will become a watch standard, unlike water resistance. Shaw states, "People buy our watches for style."

THE ISSUES

Industry observers expect the next big technological trend in watches to be two-way voice communication timepieces—Dick Tracy style. Prototypes have been too large, they don't easily fit on the wrist. However, early test models of the Indiglo were too large as well.

Timex also scored a critical hit with its high-tech Data-Link watch. Coupled with Microsoft personal computer (PC) software, the watch allowed users to download a variety of information from their PCs, such as phone numbers, appointments, and birthdays, to their Timex watches simply by pointing the face of their watches to a flashing PC screen.[5]

Questions

1. What advertising objectives should Timex have for the Indiglo? How do objectives for the Indiglo affect advertising objectives for other Timex products?

2. Discuss what sort of promotional message should be emphasized in Timex ads. (Emphasize the technology, the styling, competitive advantages.)

3. What type of advertisements, media, and scheduling would you recommend?

4. Should the Indiglo advertising program be part of a comprehensive advertising program for all Timex products?

CASE 6   Field Furniture Enterprises

Edward Meadows, president of Field Furniture Enterprises, met with representatives of Kelly, Astor, & Peters Advertising (KAP) and Andrew Reed, Field's vice president of marketing and sales, to discuss the company's advertising program for 1997. The KAP representatives recommended that Field Furniture increase its advertising in shelter magazines (such as *Good Housekeeping* and *Better Homes and Gardens,* which feature home improvement ideas and new ideas in home decorating) by $250 000 and maintain the expenditures for other promotional efforts at a constant level during 1997. The rationale given for the increase in advertising was that Field Furniture had low name recognition among prospective buyers of furniture and it intended to introduce new styles of living and dining room furniture. Reed, however, had a different opinion as to how Field Furniture should spend the $250 000. He thought it was necessary to (1) hire additional salespeople to call on the 30 new retail stores to be added by the company in 1997, (2) increase the funds devoted to cooperative advertising, and (3) improve the selling aids given to retail stores and salespeople.

THE COMPANY

Field Furniture is a medium-sized manufacturer of medium- to high-priced living and dining room furniture. Sales in 1996 were $50 million. The company sells its furniture through 1000 furniture specialty stores nationwide, but not all stores carry the company's entire line. This fact bothered Meadows because, in his words, "If they ain't got it, they can't sell it!" The company employs 10 full-time salespeople, who receive a $40 000 base salary annually and a small commission on sales. A company salesforce is atypical in the furniture industry since most furniture manufacturers use selling agents or manufacturer's representatives who carry a wide assortment of noncompeting furniture lines and receive a commission on sales. "Having our own sales group is a policy my father established 30 years ago," noted Meadows, "and we've been quite successful having people who are committed to our company. Our people don't just take furniture orders. They are expected to motivate retail salespeople to sell our line, assist in setting up displays in stores, coordinate cooperative advertising plans, and give advice on a variety of matters to our retailers and their salespeople."

In 1996, Field spent $2.45 million for total promotional expenditures, excluding the salary of the vice president of marketing and sales. Promotional expenditures were categorized into four groups: (1) sales expense and administration, (2) cooperative advertising programs with retailers, (3) trade promotions, and (4) consumer advertising. Cooperative advertising allowances are usually spent on newspaper advertising in a retailer's city and are matched by the retailer's funds on a dollar-for-dollar basis. Trade promotion is directed toward retailers and takes the form of catalogues, trade magazine advertisements, booklets for consumers, and point-of-purchase materials such as displays for use in retail stores. Also included in this category is the expense of trade shows. Field Furniture is represented at two trade shows a year. Consumer advertising is directed to potential consumers through shelter magazines. The typical format used in consumer advertising is to highlight new furniture and different living and dining room arrangements. Dollar allocation for each program in 1996 was as follows:

PROMOTIONAL PROGRAM	EXPENDITURE
Sales expense and administration	$ 612 500
Cooperative advertising	1 102 500
Trade advertising	306 250
Consumer advertising	428 750
TOTAL	$2 450 000

THE INDUSTRY

The household wooden furniture industry is composed of hundreds of firms, but no one firm captured more than 3 percent of the total household wooden furniture market.

The buying and selling of furniture to retail outlets centres around manufacturers' expositions at selected times and places around the country. At these marts, as they are called in the furniture industry, retail buyers view manufacturers' lines and often make buying commitments for their stores. However, Field's experience has shown that sales efforts in the retail store by company representatives account for as much as half the company's sales in a given year. The major manufacturer expositions are held in October and April. Regional expositions are also scheduled in June through August.

Company research on consumer furniture-buying behaviour indicated that people visit several stores when shopping for furniture, and the final decision is made jointly by a husband and wife in about 90 percent of furniture purchases. Other noteworthy findings are as follows:

- Eighty-four percent of buyers believe "the higher the price, the higher the quality" when buying home furnishings.
- Seventy-two percent of buyers browse or window shop in furniture stores even if they don't need furniture.
- Eighty-five percent read furniture ads before they actually need furniture.
- Ninety-nine percent agreed with the statement, "When shopping for furniture and home furnishings, I like the salesperson to show me what alternatives are available, answer my questions, and let me alone so I can think about it and maybe browse around."
- Ninety-five percent get redecorating ideas from shelter magazines.
- Forty-one percent have written off for a manufacturer's booklet.
- Sixty-three percent feel they need decorating advice for "putting it all together."

BUDGETARY ISSUES

After the KAP Advertising representatives made their presentation, Reed again emphasized that the incremental $250 000 should not be spent for consumer advertising. He noted that Field Furniture had set as an objective that each salesperson would make six calls per year at each store and spend at least four hours at each store on every call. "Given that our salespeople work a 40-hour week, 48 weeks per year, and devote only 80 percent of their time to selling due to travel time between stores, we already aren't doing the sales job," Reed added. Meadows agreed but reminded Reed that the $250 000 increment in the promotional budget was a maximum the company could spend, given other cost increases.[6]

Questions

1. How might you describe furniture buying using the purchase decision process described in Chapter 6?
2. How might each of the elements of the promotional program influence each stage in the purchase decision process?
3. What should Field's promotional objectives be?
4. How many salespeople does Field need to adequately service its accounts?
5. Should Field Furniture emphasize a push or pull promotional strategy? Why?

CASE 7   Hasbro, Inc.

How does a toy company become a leader in an industry marked by fads? Just ask the executives at Hasbro, Inc. (www.hasbro. com), a market leader with worldwide sales exceeding $1.4 billion. Recognizing that toy companies must replace 60 percent of their toy volume each year with new products and that 80 percent of new toys introduced each year are failures, Hasbro executives know that the secret lies in deft product development and marketing.

HASBRO PRODUCT DEVELOPMENT AND MARKETING

Hasbro, Inc. looks for three qualities in new products: (1) lasting play value, (2) the ability to be shared with other children, and (3) the ability to stimulate a child's imagination. In addition, the company provides different toys for the various stages of a child's development. Beginning with items for infants and preschool children, it also has toys and games for preadolescents of both sexes, and some adults (e.g., the game Scruples).

For example, preschool toys include Glo Worm and Teach Me Reader, young boys' toys include action figures like Transformers and G.I. Joe, and young girls have items such as My Little Pony. In addition, Hasbro markets stuffed toys such as Yakity Yaks and Watchimals and games and puzzles including Candyland and Bed Bugs. An element of the company's marketing strategy includes reaching mothers at the time of the child's birth, for infant toys. As the child develops, toys such as G.I. Joe are promoted through Saturday morning cartoon shows where complementary toys (aircraft carriers) are advertised.

However, even Hasbro had found it difficult to compete against Mattel, Inc.'s Barbie doll for young girls. Two entries, Jem and Maxie, were both dropped after disappointing sales. Similarly, Hasbro's investment of $20 million in its Nemo videogame, designed to compete against Nintendo in the late 1980s, proved to be a failure.

TOY INDUSTRY

The toy industry produces more than $16 billion in sales annually. This figure has remained largely unchanged in recent years. A percentage breakdown of volume by toy category, excluding videogames and children's books, is shown here:

CATEGORY	PERCENTAGE OF MARKET
Dolls and action figures	31.6
Games and puzzles	11.6
Preschool and infant toys	10.1
Activity toys	9.5
Toy vehicles	9.0
Riding toys	8.6
Stuffed toys	7.6
Arts and crafts	4.2
Other	7.8
	100.0

According to the editor of *Toy & Hobby World,* a trade publication, the toy industry is a "hit-driven business." Some hits include Cabbage Patch Kids by Coleco, which produced estimated sales of $600 million in 1985 but fell to an estimated $115 million in 1987. Teddy Ruxpin, made by Worlds of Wonder, Inc. was the hit of 1986 and 1987; but sales declined rapidly by 1990. Creating a hit in the children's toy industry also involves making large marketing expenditures. It is estimated that a full-scale introduction of a major toy requires $5 million to $10 million in advertising, plus $12 million to $15 million to produce a cartoon show featuring the toy or character.

In recent years, some toy companies have focused on specific children. For example, some firms have recently produced Black, Hispanic, and Asian dolls and action figures to reach previously untapped buyers. Other firms have produced dolls for disabled children. Mattel, for example, markets the Hal's Pals line, which includes a girl with leg braces and a cane and a boy in a wheelchair. The company donates the proceeds from Hal's Pals sales to disabled-children groups.[7]

Questions

1. How do toy marketers, including Hasbro, apply concepts from consumer behaviour in the marketing of toys?
2. What variables might be used to segment the toy market?
3. What might a product-market grid for Hasbro look like, and where are new product-market opportunities for the company?
4. What are your thoughts on the subject of marketing ethnic dolls, action figures, and dolls of disabled children?

CASE 8   Second Harvest

Second Harvest is a charitable, nonprofit organization that began in Toronto in 1985. Its mission: to locate and collect surplus perishable food and deliver it to social services agencies and community organizations in Metro Toronto that feed the hungry. Second Harvest is not a food bank; it handles perishable food only and it does not warehouse food. It serves as a link between surplus food—food which would otherwise go to waste—and organizations that provide food to people in need. Many social service agencies and community organizations have difficulty keeping up with the demand for emergency food assistance. In Toronto it is estimated that over 154 000 people depend on emergency food programs each month. Most of those people are single women and children. Ironically, while people are going hungry, more than 20 percent of all food produced in North America is wasted.

Second Harvest's basic day-to-day operation are conducted out of a small office under the direction of an executive director, working with a small staff, and primarily a core group of volunteers. Using a small fleet of trucks, donated by good corporate citizens, Second Harvest retrieves surplus food from any industry, group, or individual who regularly or occasionally has excess food, including food producers, farmers, retailers, wholesalers, restaurants, hospitals, production houses, and organizers of special events. It then delivers this food to a variety of agencies or organizations including drop-ins or soup kitchens, food pantries or food banks, residences or shelters, and subsidized housing developments. In 1997 Second Harvest picked up and delivered more than 1 million pounds of food. This food consisted of bread, baked goods, dairy products, produce, beverages, meat, snack foods, and prepared foods.

Second Harvest has also been involved with several self-help initiatives, including the publication of a cookbook which contains inexpensive, easy-to-prepare recipes designed to help those on fixed incomes who need to stretch their food dollars. Second Harvest also plays a role as an advocate for change in public policy as it pertains to hunger and poverty.

In order to achieve its objectives, Second Harvest attempts to create awareness of the organization and its efforts through public relations activities, including PSAs, news releases, newsletters, and special events. One of its major events is an annual fund raiser called Toronto Taste, where attendees pay to sample the food dishes created by Toronto chefs. Second Harvest also participates in hospitality industry trade shows where it hopes to create greater awareness of its activities, and to increase its food donor base. It also has a public relations firm that donates its time and talent in order to help heighten Second Harvest's profile in the community.[8]

Questions

1. How can Second Harvest motivate more individuals and organizations to donate to their cause?
2. What specific marketing communication tools would you recommend that Second Harvest use to reach those prospective donors?
3. What are some unique sources of surplus food that Second Harvest could tap into?

CASE 9   National Community Tree Foundation

In the 1990 Green Plan, the Government of Canada made clear its commitment to providing a safe and healthy environment for present and future generations. A key part of the Green Plan is a program called Tree Plan Canada. It recognizes the fundamental importance of our rural and urban forests in addressing the problem of global warming and improving the quality of life for all Canadians. The National Community Tree Foundation (NCTF) was formed as a nonprofit (nongovernmental) organization to manage the Tree Plan Canada program and to ensure that its objectives became realities. The fundamental purpose of the NCTF is "to foster and encourage the planting and care of trees in and around more than 5000 cities, towns, and villages by 1998."

Tree planting is certainly not a new idea in this country. The forestry sector plants millions of trees each year. But virtually all of these trees are planted to compensate for the effects of timber harvesting or forest fires. So the first hurdle facing the foundation was to educate Canadians that they too had an important role to play in planting new trees in urban and rural areas. If NCTF's objectives were to be achieved within the time-frame specified, then average Canadians would have to be motivated to plant trees in and around their communities. But Canadians would only plant trees if they understood the benefits of trees as an integral part of the ecosystem. The public's affinity for trees and forests was a good starting point, with the aesthetic appreciation and a belief in the "goodness of green."

What was still needed was crystal-clear communication of the solid science that makes trees vital to human survival. Canadians needed to know, or be reminded, that trees are the lungs of the earth, filtering the air we breathe and removing pollutants. NCTF wanted Canadians to appreciate that a mature tree keeps on cleaning and cleaning, at no charge, for many decades. But if the message was only seen as a lesson, NCTF would lose its audience—just providing boring facts about an issue that people believed they already understand simply would not work. The chal-

lenge would be to create broad awareness, if not change a mindset, with regard to the value and benefits of trees, and, in doing so, prompt Canadians to take action in planting our urban and rural forests. NCTF allocated an initial $420 000 for promotional activities designed to accomplish these objectives.[9]

Questions

1. Given the challenges facing NCTF, what promotion techniques would you recommend the foundation use?
2. Besides the initial target audience of "average adult Canadians," who else should NCTF target for involvement in the program?
3. What type of creative theme would prompt Canadians to action?

CASE 10 Metro Toronto Works Department

In recent years there has been a pronounced increase in the public's awareness of environmental issues. Yet the perceived magnitude of some of the problems was so overwhelming that many people weren't modifying their behaviour, thinking that one person could hardly make a difference. Moreover, in Metro Toronto, there was both ignorance and uncertainty as to the range of environmental or waste management services offered by the Metro Toronto Works Department. While the Blue Box Recycling program had high visibility (a walk through the neighbourhood on collection days would show many blue containers by the curbside), other initiatives of the Works Department were less well known.

Metro Toronto Works Department wanted Metro residents to become part of the solution. This meant continuous education about what was and what wasn't recyclable through the Blue Box program, and raising awareness of other less familiar programs. But increased participation in waste management programs would only happen if residents perceived them to be simple and convenient rather than time-consuming and complex.

The department determined an advertising and public relations campaign would be necessary to generate awareness and encourage increased household participation in the

waste management programs. The campaign would focus on all waste management programs including the Blue Box Recycling, Backyard Composting, Water Efficiency, and Household Hazardous Waste Disposal. Seasonal projects (such as summer lawn watering reduction, and Christmas tree recycling) and special events (such as Environmental Days and Waste Reduction Week) also had to be highlighted. The department decided no scare tactics would be used. The campaign would be a positive one. Citizens would be encouraged to participate and shown that their co-operation was necessary, easy, and meaningful. The thrust of the campaign would rest on the premise that, although the magnitude of environmental waste was huge, every single one of us, every single day, could make small contributions that, when added together, became significant.[10]

Questions

1. Given the campaign's objective, what would you recommend as the primary advertising media choice for Metro Works?
2. What would be the basic message appeal you would recommend to encourage residents to participate?
3. What public relations activities would you recommend for Environmental Days and Waste Reduction Week?

GLOSSARY

80/20 rule The principle that 80 percent of sales (and costs) are generated by 20 percent of the items or customers.

above-, at-, or below-market pricing Pricing based on what the market price is.

accelerated development The second stage of the retail life cycle, characterized by rapid increases in market share and profitability.

account management policies Policies that specify whom sales people should contact, what kinds of selling and customer service activities should be engaged in, and how these activities should be carried out; in advertising agency, refers to policies used by an account executive in dealing with clients.

action item list An aid to implementing a market plan, consisting of three columns: (1) the task, (2) the name of the person responsible for completing the task, and (3) the date by which the task is to be finished.

adaptive selling A need-satisfaction sales presentation involving adjusting the presentation to fit the selling situation.

advertising Any paid form of nonpersonal communication about an organization, good, service, or idea by an identified sponsor.

advocacy advertisements Institutional advertisements that state the position of a company on an issue.

all you can afford budgeting Allocating funds to advertising only after all other budget items are covered.

anchor stores Well-known national or regional stores that are located in regional shopping centres.

approach stage In the personal selling process, the initial meeting between the salesperson and prospect where the objectives are to gain the prospect's attention, stimulate interest, and build the foundation for the sales presentation.

atmosphere A store's ambience or setting.

attitudes Learned predispositions to respond to an object or class of objects in a consistent manner.

average revenue The average amount of money received for selling one unit of a product.

baby boomlet The generation of children born in 1977 and later.

baby boomers The generation of children born between 1946 and 1964.

back translation The practice of retranslating a word or phrase into the original language by a different interpreter to catch errors.

bait-and-switch advertising An advertising practice in which a company shows a product that it has no intention of selling to lure the customer into the store and sell him a higher-priced item.

balance of trade The difference between the monetary value of a nation's exports and imports.

barriers to entry Business practices or conditions that make it difficult for a new firm to enter the market.

barter The practice of exchanging goods and services for other goods and services rather than for money.

basing-point pricing Selecting one or more geographic locations (basing point) from which the list price for products plus freight expenses are charged to buyers.

beliefs A consumer's subjective perception of how well a product or brand performs on different attributes; these are based on personal experience, advertising, and discussions with other people.

benchmarking Discovering how other organizations do something better than yours so your firm can imitate or leapfrog competition.

bidder's list A list of firms believed to be qualified to supply a given item.

blended family Two families from prior marriages merged into a single household as spouses remarry.

brand equity The added value a given brand name provides a product.

brand extension The practice of using a current brand name to enter a completely different product class.

brand loyalty A favourable attitude toward and consistent purchase of a single brand over time.

brand manager (*see* product manager)

brand name Any word or device (design, shape, sound, or colour) that is used to distinguish one company's products from a competitor's.

branding Activity in which an organization uses a name, phrase, design, or symbol, or a combination of these, to identify its products and distinguish them from those of a competitor.

breadth of product line The variety of different items a store or wholesaler carries.

break-even analysis An analysis of the relationship between total revenue and total cost to determine profitability at various levels of output.

break-even chart A graphic presentation of a break-even analysis.

break-even point (BEP) Quantity at which total revenue and total cost are equal and beyond which profit occurs.

brokers Channel intermediaries that do not take title to merchandise and make their profits from commissions and fees by negotiating contracts or deals between buyers and sellers.

buildup forecast Summing the sales forecasts of each of the components to arrive at a total forecast.

bundle pricing The marketing of two or more products in a single "package" price.

business analysis Involves specifying the features of the product and the marketing strategy needed to commercialize it and making necessary financial projections.

business analysis stage Step 4 of the new-product process, which involves specifying the product features and marketing strategy and making necessary financial projections to commercialize a product.

business culture Comprises the effective rules of the game, the boundaries between competitive and unethical behaviour, and the codes of conduct in business dealings.

business firm   A privately owned organization that serves its customers in order to earn a profit.

business marketing   The marketing of goods and services to commercial enterprises, governments, and other profit and nonprofit organizations for use in the creation of goods and services that they then produce and market to other business customers as well as individuals and ultimate consumers.

business plan   A roadmap for the entire organization for a specific future period of time, such as one year or five years.

business portfolio analysis   Analysis of a firm's strategic business units (SBUs) as though they were a collection of separate investments.

business unit   Element of a firm that markets a set of related products to a clearly defined group of customers.

business unit competencies   Special capabilities resulting from the business unit's personnel, resources, or functional units.

business unit goal   A performance target the business unit seeks to reach to achieve its mission.

business unit level   Level at which business unit managers set directions for their products and markets.

business unit mission   A statement specifying the markets and product lines in which a business unit will compete.

buy classes   Groups of three specific buying situations organizations face: new buy, straight rebuy, and modified rebuy.

buyer turnover   The frequency with which new buyers enter the market to buy a product.

buying centre   The group of persons within an organization who participate in the buying process and share common goals, risks, and knowledge important to that process.

buying criteria   The factors buying organizations use when evaluating a potential supplier and what it wants to sell.

capacity management   Managing the demand for a service so that it is available to consumers.

case allowance   A trade-oriented sales promotion in which retailers receive a discount on each case ordered during a specific time period.

cash and carry wholesaler   A limited-service merchant wholesaler that takes title to merchandise but sells only to buyers who call on it and pay cash for and transport their own merchandise.

category killers   Specialty discount outlets that focus on one product category such as electronics or business supplies at very competitive prices

cause-related marketing   Tying the charitable contributions of a firm directly to the customer revenues produced through the promotion of one of its products.

caveat emptor   A Latin term that means "let the buyer beware."

census metropolitan area   Geographic labour market areas having a population of 100 000 persons or more.

central business district   The oldest retail setting; the community's downtown area.

channel captain   A marketing channel member that coordinates, directs, and supports other channel members; may be a manufacturer, wholesaler, or retailer.

channel of communication   The means (e.g., a salesperson, advertising media, or public relations tools) of conveying a message to a receiver.

channel partnering   Agreements and procedures among channel members for ordering and physically distributing a producer's product through the channel to the ultimate consumer.

closed-end question   (*see* fixed alternative question)

closing stage   The stage in the personal selling process that involves getting a purchase commitment from a prospect.

co-branding   The pairing of two brand names of two manufacturers for joint marketing purposes.

code of ethics   A formal statement of ethical principles and rules of conduct.

cognitive dissonance   The feeling of postpurchase psychological tension or anxiety a consumer often experiences.

combination compensation plan   A compensation plan whereby a salesperson is paid a specified salary plus a commission based on sales or profit.

commercialization   The final phase of the new-product process in which the product is positioned and launched into full-scale production and sale.

communication   The process of conveying a message to others. Six elements—a source, a message, a channel of communication, a receiver, and the processes of encoding and decoding—are required for communication to occur.

community shopping centre   A retail location that typically has one primary store (usually a department store branch) and 20 to 40 smaller outlets and serves a population base of about 100 000.

company forecast   (*see* sales forecast)

comparative advertisements   Advertisements that show one brand's strengths relative to those of competitors.

competition   The set of alternative firms that could provide a product to satisfy a specific market's needs.

Competition Act   Key legislation designed to protect competition and consumers in Canada.

competitive advantage   A unique strength relative to competitors, often based on quality, time, cost, innovation, or customer intimacy.

competitive advertisements   Advertisements that promote a specific brand's features and benefits.

competitive institutional advertisements   Institutional advertisements that promote the advantages of one product class over another and are used in markets where different product classes compete for the same buyer.

competitive parity budgeting   Matching the competitors' absolute level of spending or the proportion per point of market share.

computer-assisted retailing   A retailing method whereby customers order products over computer linkups from their home after viewing items on the TV or on their computer monitor.

concept tests   External evaluations of a product idea that consist of preliminary testing of the new product idea (rather than the actual product) with consumers.

conference selling   A form of team selling where a salesperson and other company resource people meet with buyers to discuss problems and opportunities.

consultative selling   A need-satisfaction sales presentation where the salesperson focuses on problem definition and serves as an expert on problem recognition.

consumer behaviour   Actions of a person to purchase and use products and services, including the mental and social processes that precede and follow these actions.

consumer ethnocentrism   The tendency to believe that it is inappropriate, indeed immoral, to purchase foreign-made products.

consumer goods   Products purchased by the ultimate consumer.

consumer socialization   The process by which people acquire the skills, knowledge, and attitudes necessary to function as consumers.

consumer-oriented sales promotion   Sales tools used to support a company's advertising and personal selling efforts directed to ultimate consumers; examples include coupons, sweepstakes, and trading stamps.

consumerism   A movement to increase the influence, power, and rights of consumers in dealing with institutions.

contest   A sales promotion in which consumers apply their analytical or creative thinking to win a prize.

continuity programs   Sales promotions used to encourage and reward repeat purchases by acknowledging each purchase made by a consumer and offering a premium as purchases accumulate.

continuous innovations   New products that require no new learning to use.

contracting   A strategy used during the decline stage of the product life cycle in which a company contracts the manufacturing or marketing of a product to another firm.

contractual vertical marketing system   A channel arrangement whereby independent production and distribution firms integrate their efforts on a contractual basis to obtain greater economies and marketing impact.

convenience goods   Items that the consumer purchases frequently and with a minimum of shopping effort.

cooperative advertising   Advertising programs in which a manufacturer pays a percentage of the retailer's local advertising expense for advertising the manufacturer's products.

corporate chain   A type of retail ownership in which a single firm owns multiple outlets.

corporate culture   The shared values, beliefs, and purpose of employees that affect individuals and group behaviour.

corporate culture   A system of shared attitudes and behaviours held by the employees that distinguish an organization from others.

corporate goals   Strategic performance targets that the entire organization must reach to pursue its vision.

corporate level   Level at which top management directs overall strategy for the entire organization.

corporate philosophy   The values and "rules of conduct" for running an organization.

corporate takeover   The purchase of a firm by outsiders.

corporate vertical marketing system   A channel arrangement whereby successive stages of production and distribution are combined under a single owner.

corporate vision   A clear word picture of the organization's future, often with an inspirational theme.

cost of goods sold   Total value of the products sold during a specified time period.

cost focus strategy   Involves controlling expenses and, in turn, lowering prices, in a narrow range of market segments.

cost leadership strategy   Using a serious commitment to reducing expenses that, in turn, lowers the price of the items sold in a wide range of market segments.

cost per thousand (CPM)   The cost of reaching 1000 individuals or households with an advertising message in a given medium. (*M* is the Roman numeral for 1000.)

cost plus fixed-fee pricing   A pricing method where a supplier is reimbursed for all costs, regardless of what they may be, plus a fixed percentage of the production or construction costs.

cost plus percentage-of-cost pricing   Setting the price of a product or service by adding a fixed percentage to the production or construction costs.

cost-plus pricing   The practice of summing the total unit cost of providing a product or service and adding a specific amount to the cost to arrive at a price.

countertrade   Using barter rather than money in making global sales.

coupons   Printed certificates that give the bearer a saving or a stated price reduction when they purchase a specific product.

cross-cultural analysis   The study of similarities and differences between consumers in two or more nations or societies.

cross-functional teams   A small number of people from different departments in an organization who are mutually accountable to a common set of performance goals.

cross-tabulation   Method of presenting and relating data on two or more variables to display summary data and discover relationships in the data.

cue   A stimulus or symbol perceived by the consumer.

cultural ethnocentricity   The belief that aspects of one's culture are superior to another's.

cultural symbols   Things that represent ideas and concepts.

culture   The sets of values, ideas, and attitudes of a homogeneous group of people that are transmitted from one generation to the next.

cumulative quantity discounts   The discount given to a buyer based on the accumulation of purchases of a product over a given time period, typically a year.

customary pricing   A method of pricing based on a product's tradition, standardized channel of distribution, or other competitive factors.

customer contact audit   A flow chart of the points of interaction between a consumer and a service provider.

customer service   The ability of a logistics system to satisfy users in terms of time, dependability, communications, and convenience.

customer value   The unique combination of benefits received by targeted buyers that includes quality, price, convenience, on-time delivery, and both before-sale and after-sale service.

customs   Norms and expectations about the way people do things in a specific country.

database marketing   An organization's effort to collect demographic, media, and consumption profiles of customers in order to target them more effectively.

deal   A sales promotion that offers a short-term price reduction.

deceptive pricing   A practice by which prices are artificially inflated and then marked down under the guise of a sale.

decision making   The act of consciously choosing from alternatives.

decline stage   The fourth and last stage of the product life cycle when sales and profitability decline.

decoding   The process of having the receiver take a set of symbols, the message, and transform them back to an abstract idea.

deletion   A strategy of dropping a product from the product line, usually in the decline stage of the product life cycle.

delivered pricing   Practice of refusing a customer delivery of an article on the same terms as other customers in the same location.

Delphi forecast   Polling people knowledgeable about the forecast topic to obtain a sequence of anonymous estimates.

demand curve   The summation of points representing the maximum quantity of a product consumers will buy at different price levels.

demand factors   Factors that determine the strength of consumers' willingness and ability to pay for goods and services.

demand-backward pricing   Setting a price by estimating the price consumers would be willing to pay for goods and services.

demographics   The study of the characteristics of the population.

depth interviews   Detailed individual interviews with people relevant to the research project.

depth of product line   The assortment of each item a store or wholesaler carries.

derived demand   Sales of a product (typically industrial) that result from the sales of another item (often consumer).

desk jobber   (*see* drop shipper)

development   Phase of the new product process in which the idea on paper is turned into a prototype; includes manufacturing and laboratory and consumer tests.

dichotomous question   A fixed alternative question that allows only a "yes" or "no" response.

differentiation focus strategy   Using significant points of difference in the firm's offerings to reach one or only a few market segments.

differentiation positioning   avoiding direct (head-to-head) competition by stressing unique aspects of the product.

differentiation strategy   Using innovation and significant points of difference in product offerings, higher quality, advanced technology, or superior service in a wide range of market segments.

diffusion of innovation   The process by which people receive new information and accept new ideas and products.

direct channel   A marketing channel where a producer and ultimate consumer interact directly with each other.

direct exporting   A firm selling its domestically produced goods in a foreign country without intermediaries.

direct forecast   An estimate of the value to be forecast without the use of intervening steps.

direct investment   In global marketing, a domestic firm actually investing in and owning a foreign subsidiary or division.

direct marketing   Selling products by having consumers interact with various advertising media without a face-to-face meeting with a salesperson.

direct ownership   In international trade, a domestic firm actually investing in and owning a foreign subsidiary or division.

discontinuous innovations   New products that require totally new consumption patterns.

discounts   Reductions from list price that a seller gives a buyer as a reward for some buyer activity favourable to the seller.

discretionary income   The money that remains after taxes and necessities have been paid for.

disposable income   The money a consumer has left after taxes to use for food, shelter, and clothing.

diversification   A strategy of developing new products and selling them in new markets.

downsizing   The practice of reducing the content of package without changing package size and maintaining or increasing the package price.

drive   A stimulus that moves an individual to action.

drop shipper   A merchant wholesaler that owns the merchandise it sells but does not physically handle, stock, or deliver; also called a desk jobber.

dual distribution   An arrangement by which a firm reaches buyers by employing two or more different types of channels for the same basic product.

dumping   When a firm sells a product in a foreign country below its domestic price.

durable good   An item that lasts over an extended number of uses.

dynamically continuous innovations   Products that disrupt the consumer's normal routine but do not require learning totally new behaviours.

early adopters   The 13.5 percent of the population who are leaders in their social setting and act as an information source on new products for other people.

early growth   The first stage of the retail life cycle, when a new outlet emerges as a sharp departure from competitive forms.

early majority   The 34 percent of the population who are deliberate and rely on personal sources for information on new products.

ecology   The relationship of physical resources in the environment.

economic infrastructure   A country's communication, transportation, financial, and distribution systems.

economy   The income, expenditures, and resources that affect the cost of running a business and household.

elastic demand   A situation where a percentage decrease in price produces a larger percentage increase in quantity demanded, thereby actually increasing sales revenue.

electronic data interchange (EDI)   Computers linked in two different firms to transmit documents such as purchase orders, bills of lading, and invoices.

elements of the marketing mix   (*see* marketing mix)

encoding   The process of having the sender transform an abstract idea into a set of symbols.

environmental factors   The uncontrollable factors involving social, economic, technological, competitive, and regulatory forces.

environmental scanning   Acquiring information on events occurring outside the company and interpreting potential trends.

ethics   The moral principles and values that govern the actions and decisions of an individual or group.

euro-branding   The strategy of using the same brand name for the same product across all countries in the European Community.

evaluative criteria   Both the objective and subjective attributes of a brand important to consumers when evaluating different brands or products.

everyday low pricing   The practice of replacing promotional allowances given to retailers with lower manufacturer list prices.

evoked set   The group of brands a consumer would consider acceptable out of the set of brands in the product class of which he or she is aware.

exchange   The trade of things of value between buyer and seller so that each is better off after the trade.

exclusive dealing   An arrangement a manufacturer makes with a reseller to handle only its products and not those of competitors.

exclusive distribution   A distribution strategy whereby a producer sells its products or services in only one retail outlet in a specific geographical area.

exclusive territorial distributorship   A manufacturer grants a reseller sole rights to sell a product in a specific geographic area.

experience curve pricing   A method of pricing where price often falls following the reduction of costs associated with the firm's experience in producing or selling a product.

experiment   Manipulation of an independent variable (cause) and measuring its effect on the dependent variable (effect) under controlled conditions.

exporting   Producing goods in one country and selling them in another country.

express warranties   Written statements of a manufacturer's liabilities for product deficiencies.

facilitators   Intermediaries that assist in the physical distribution channel by moving, storing, financing, or insuring products.

fad   A product whose life cycle has two stages consisting of rapid introduction and equally quick decline.

failure fees   A penalty payment made to retailers by manufacturers if a new product does not reach predetermined sales levels.

family branding   (*see* multiproduct branding)

family life cycle   The concept that each family progresses through a number of distinct phases, each of which is associated with identifiable purchasing behaviours.

fashion product   A product whose life cycle curve may decline, then return through another life cycle.

feedback   The communication flow from receiver back to sender; indicates whether the message was decoded and understood as intended.

field experiment   A test of marketing variables in actual store or buying settings.

field of experience   A person's understanding and knowledge; to communicate effectively, a sender and a receiver must have a mutually shared field of experience.

finance allowance   A trade-oriented sales promotion in which retailers are paid for financing costs or financial losses associated with consumer sales promotions.

fixed alternative question   A question in which the respondent merely checks an answer from predetermined choices.

fixed cost   An expense of the firm that is stable and does not change with the quantity of product that is produced and sold.

flexible-price policy   Offering the same product and quantities to similar customers, but at different prices.

flighting schedule   A scheduling approach in which periods of advertising are scheduled between periods of no advertising to reflect seasonal demand.

FOB (free on board)   Refers to the point at which the seller stops paying transportation costs.

FOB origin pricing   A method of pricing where the title of goods passes to the buyer at the point of loading.

FOB with freight-allowed pricing   A method of pricing that allows the buyer to deduct freight expenses from the list price of the product sold; also called freight absorption pricing.

focus groups   Informal interview sessions of 6 to 10 persons relevant to the research project, brought together in a room with a moderator to discuss topics surrounding the marketing research problem.

follow-up stage   The phase of the personal selling process that entails making certain that the customer's purchase has been properly delivered and installed and that any difficulties in using the product are promptly and satisfactorily addressed.

forced distribution markets   (*see* selected controlled markets)

forgetting rate   The speed with which buyers forget a brand if advertising is not seen.

form of ownership   Who owns a retail outlet. Alternatives are independent, corporate chain, cooperative, or franchise.

form utility   The value to consumers that comes from production or alteration of a good or service.

formula selling presentation   The selling format that consists of providing information in an accurate, thorough, and step-by-step manner to persuade the prospect to buy.

forward buying   A response to discounts offered by manufacturers in which supermarkets purchase more merchandise than they plan to sell during the promotion. The remaining stock is sold at regular price later, or diverted to another store.

four I's of service   Four unique elements to services: intangibility, inconsistency, inseparability, and inventory.

four P's   (*see* marketing mix)

franchising   The contractual agreement between a parent company and an individual or firm that allows the franchisee to operate a certain type of business under an established name and according to specific rules.

freight consolidators   (*see* freight forwarders)

freight forwarders   Firms that accumulate small shipments into larger lots and then hire a carrier to move them, usually at reduced rates.

frequency   The average number of times a person in the target audience is exposed to a message or advertisement.

full warranty   A statement of liability by a manufacturer that has no limits of noncoverage.

full-service agency   An advertising agency providing a complete range of services, including market research, media selection, copy development, artwork, and production.

full-service retailer   A retailer that provides a complete list of services to cater to its customers.

functional groupings   Organizational groupings in which a unit is subdivided according to the different business activities within a firm, such as manufacturing, marketing, and finance.

functional level   Level at which groups of specialists create value for the organization.

gap analysis   An evaluation tool that compares expectations about a particular service to the actual experience a consumer has with the service.

General Agreement on Tariffs and Trade (GATT)   An international treaty intended to limit trade barriers and promote world trade through the reduction of tariffs.

general merchandise stores   General merchandise stores carry a broad product line with limited depth.

general merchandise wholesaler   A full-service merchant wholesaler that carries a broad assortment of merchandise and performs all channel functions.

Generation X   The generation of children born between 1965 and 1976.

generic brand   A branding strategy that lists no product name, only a description of contents.

generic business strategy   Strategy that can be adapted by any firm, regardless of the product or industry involved, to achieve a competitive advantage.

geographical groupings   Organization groupings in which a unit is subdivided according to geographical location.

global competition   A competitive situation that exists when firms originate, produce, and market their products and services worldwide.

global consumers   Customer groups living in many countries or regions of the world who have similar needs or seek similar features and benefits from products and services.

global marketing strategy   The practice of standardizing marketing activities where there are cultural similarities and adapting them when cultures differ.

goal   A targeted level of performance set in advance of work.

government units   The federal, provincial, and local agencies that buy goods and services for the constituents they serve.

grey market   A situation in which products are sold through unauthorized channels of distribution; also called parallel importing.

green marketing   Marketing efforts to produce, promote, and reclaim environmentally sensitive products.

gross domestic product   The monetary value of all goods and services produced in a country during one year.

gross income   The total amount of money earned in one year by a person, family, or household.

gross margin   Net sales minus cost of goods sold.

gross rating points (GRPs)   A reference number for advertisers, created by multiplying reach (expressed as a percentage) by frequency.

growth stage   The second stage of the product life cycle characterized by rapid increases in sales and by the appearance of competitors.

harvesting   A strategy used during the decline stage of the product life cycle in which a company continues to offer a product but reduces support costs.

head-to-head positioning   Competing directly with competitors on similar product attributes in the same target market.

hierarchy of effects   The sequence of stages a prospective buyer goes through from initial awareness of a product to eventual action (either trial or adoption of the product). The stages include awareness, interest, evaluation, trial, and adoption.

high learning product   A product that has a long introductory phase to its life cycle because significant education is required for consumers to use the item or appreciate its benefits.

horizontal conflict   Disagreements between intermediaries at the same level in a marketing channel.

horizontal price fixing   The practice whereby two or more competitors explicitly or implicitly collaborate to set prices.

hypermarket   A large store (over 200 000 square feet) offering a mix of food products and general merchandise.

idea generation   A phase of the new product process, in which a firm develops a pool of concepts as candidates for new products.

idle production capacity   A situation where a service provider is available but there is no demand.

implied warranties   Warranties assigning responsibility for product deficiencies to a manufacturer even though the item was sold by a retailer.

inbound telemarketing   The use of toll-free telephone numbers that customers can call to obtain information about products or services and make purchases.

inconsistency   A unique element of services; variation in service quality because services are delivered by people with varying capabilities.

independent retailer   A retail outlet for which there is an individual owner.

indirect channel   A marketing channel where intermediaries are situated between the producer and consumers.

indirect exporting   A firm selling its domestically produced goods in a foreign country through an intermediary.

industrial distributor   A specific type of intermediary between producers and consumers that generally sells, stocks, and delivers a full product assortment.

industrial espionage   The clandestine collection of trade secrets or proprietary information about a company's competitors.

industrial firms   Organizational buyers that in some way reprocess a good or service it buys before selling it again.

industrial goods   Products used in the production of other items for ultimate consumers.

industry   A group of firms offering products that are close substitutes for each other.

industry potential   (*see* market potential)

inelastic demand   A situation where a small percentage decrease in price produces a smaller percentage increase in quantity demanded.

information technology   Involves designing and managing computer and communication systems to satisfy an organization's requirements for information processing and access.

infomercials   Program length advertisements, often 30 minutes long, that take an educational approach to communicating with potential customers.

in-house agency   A company's own advertising staff which may provide full services or a limited range of services.

innovators   The 2.5 percent of the population who are venturesome and highly educated, use multiple information sources, and are the first to adopt a new product.

inseparability   A unique element of services; the fact that a service cannot be separated from the deliverer of the service or the setting in which the service occurs.

institutional advertisement   Advertisements designed to build goodwill or an image for an organization, rather than promote a specific good or service.

intangibility   A unique element of services; the fact that services cannot be held, touched, or seen before the purchase decision.

integrated marketing communications   The concept of designing marketing communications programs that coordinate all promotional activities—advertising, personal selling, sales promotion, and public relations—to provide a consistent message across all audiences and to maximize the promotional budget.

intensive distribution   A distribution strategy whereby a producer sells products or services in as many outlets as possible in a geographic area.

intermodel transportation   Combining different transportation modes in order to get the best features of each.

internal marketing   The notion that a service organization must focus on its employees, or internal market, before successful programs can be directed at customers.

intertype competition   Competition between dissimilar types of retail outlets brought about by scrambled merchandising.

introductory phase   The first stage of the product life cycle in which sales grow slowly and profit is low.

inventory   (1) Physical material purchased from suppliers, which may or may not be reworked and is available for sale to customers. (2) A unique element of services; the need for and cost of having a service provider available.

involvement   The personal, social, and economic significance of the purchase to the consumer.

ISO 9000   International standards for registration and certification of a manufacturer's quality management and quality assurance system.

job analysis   A written description of what a salesperson is expected to do.

job description   Written document that describes job relationships and requirements that characterize each sales position.

joint venture   An arrangement in which a foreign company and a local firm invest together to create a local business.

jury of executive opinion forecast Asking knowledgeable executives inside the firm about likely sales during a coming period.

jury test A pretest in which a panel of customers is shown an advertisement and asked to rate its attractiveness, how much they like it, and how much it draws their attention.

just-in-time (JIT) concept An inventory supply system that operates with very low inventories and requires fast, on-time delivery.

laboratory experiment A simulation of marketing-related activity in a highly controlled setting.

laggards The 16 percent of the market who have fear of debt, use friends for information sources, and accept ideas and products only after they have been long established in the market.

late majority The 34 percent of the population who are skeptical, below average in social status, and rely less on advertising and personal selling for information than do innovators or early adopters.

laws Society's values and standards that are enforceable in the courts.

lead time Lag from ordering an item until it is received and ready for use.

learning Those behaviours that result from (1) repeated experience and (2) thinking.

level of service The degree of service provided to the customer by the retailer: self, limited, or full.

licensing A contractual agreement whereby a company allows another firm to use its brand name, patent, trade secret, or other property for a royalty or fee.

lifestyle A mode of living that is identified by how people spend their time and resources (activities), what they consider important in their environment (interests), and what they think of themselves and the world around them (opinions).

Likert scale A fixed alternative question in which the respondent indicates the extent to which he agrees or disagrees with a statement.

limited-coverage warranty A manufacturer's statement indicating the bounds of coverage and noncoverage for any product deficiencies.

limited-line store A retail outlet, such as a sporting goods store, that offers considerable assortment, or depth, of a related line of items.

limited-service agency An agency that specializes in one aspect of the advertising process such as providing creative services to develop the advertising copy or buying previously unpurchased media space.

limited-service retailer A retailer that provides selected services such as credit or merchandise return to customers.

line extension The practice of using a current brand name to enter a new market segment in its product class.

line positions People in line positions, such as group marketing managers, have the authority and responsibility to issue orders to the people who report to them, such as marketing managers.

local approach (*see* customized approach)

logistics management Organizing the cost-effective flow of raw materials, in-process inventory, finished goods, and related information from point of origin to point of consumption to satisfy customer requirements.

loss-leader pricing Deliberately pricing a product below its customary price to attract attention to it.

lost-horse forecast Starting with the last known value of the item being forecast, listing the factors that could affect the forecast, assessing whether they have a positive or negative impact, and making the final forecast.

low-learning product A product that has an immediate gain in sales in the introductory phase because the benefits are easily observed by consumers and little education is required to use it.

macromarketing The study of the aggregate flow of a nation's goods and services to benefit society.

mail-order retailer A retailing operation in which merchandise is offered to customers by mail.

maintained markup The difference between the final selling price and retailer cost; also called gross margin.

major account management The practice of using team selling to focus on important customers to build mutually beneficial long-term, cooperative relationships.

make-buy decision An evaluation of whether a product or its parts will be purchased from outside suppliers or built by the firm.

management by exception A tool used by a marketing manager that involves identifying results that deviate from plans, diagnosing their cause, making appropriate new plans, and taking new actions.

manufacturer branding A branding strategy in which the brand name for a product is designated by the producer, using either a multiproduct or multibranding approach.

manufacturer's agents Individuals or firms that work for several producers and carry noncompetitive, complementary merchandise in an exclusive territory; also called manufacturer's representatives.

manufacturer's branch office A wholly owned extension of a producer that performs channel functions, including carrying inventory, generally performed by a full-service merchant wholesaler.

marginal analysis Principle of allocating resources that balances incremental revenues of an action against incremental costs.

marginal cost The change in total cost that results from producing and marketing one additional unit.

marginal revenue The change in total revenue obtained by selling one additional unit.

markdown Reduction in retail price usually expressed as a percentage equal to the amount reduced, divided by the original price and multiplied by 100.

market People with the desire and ability to buy a specific product.

market-based groupings Organizational groupings that assign responsibility for a specific type of customer to a unit.

market development Selling existing products to new markets.

market growth rate The annual rate of growth of the specific market or industry in which a firm or SBU is competing; often used as the vertical axis in business portfolio analysis.

market modification Attempts to increase product usage by creating new-use situations or finding new customers.

market orientation Focusing organizational efforts on (1) continuously collecting information about customers' needs and competitors' capabilities, (2) sharing this information across departments, and (3) using the information to create customer value.

market penetration A strategy of increasing sales of present products in their existing markets.

market potential   Maximum total sales of a product by all firms to a segment under specified environmental conditions and marketing efforts of the firms (also called industry potential).

market segmentation   Aggregating prospective buyers into groups, or segments, that (1) have common needs and (2) will respond similarly to a marketing action.

market segments   The groups that result from the process of market segmentation; a relatively homogeneous collection of prospective buyers.

market share   The ratio of sales revenue of the firm to the total sales revenue of all firms in the industry, including the firm itself.

market testing   A phase of the new product process, in which prospective consumers are exposed to actual products under realistic purchase conditions to see if they will buy.

market-product grid   Framework for relating market segments to products offered or potential marketing actions by a firm.

marketing   The process of planning and executing the conception, pricing, promotion, and distribution of ideas, goods, and services to create exchanges that satisfy individual and organizational objectives.

marketing audit   A comprehensive, unbiased, periodic review of the strategic marketing process of a firm or a strategic business unit (SBU).

marketing channel   People and firms involved in the process of making a product or service available for use or consumption by consumers or industrial users.

marketing concept   The idea that an organization should (1) strive to satisfy the needs of consumers (2) while also trying to achieve the organization's goals.

marketing decision support system (MDSS)   A computerized method of providing timely, accurate information to improve marketing decisions.

marketing mix   The marketing manager's controllable factors of product, price, promotion, and place he or she can take to solve a marketing problem.

marketing orientation   When an organization focuses its efforts on (1) continuously collecting information about customers' needs and competitors' capabilities, (2) sharing this information across departments, and (3) using the information to create customer value.

marketing plan   A roadmap for the marketing activities of an organization for a specified future period of time, such as one year or five years.

marketing program   A plan that integrates the marketing mix to provide a good, service, or idea to prospective consumers.

marketing research   The process of defining a marketing problem and opportunity, systematically collecting and analyzing information, and recommending actions to improve an organization's marketing activities.

marketing strategy   The means by which a marketing goal is to be achieved, characterized by (1) a specified target market and (2) a marketing program to reach it.

marketing tactics   The detailed day-to-day operational decisions essential to the overall success of marketing strategies.

markup   The amount added to the cost of goods sold to arrive at a selling price, expressed in dollar or percentage terms.

materials handling   Moving goods over short distances into, within, and out of warehouses and manufacturing plants.

mature market   Market consisting of people over age 50.

maturity phase   The third stage of the product or retail life cycle in which market share levels off and profitability declines.

merchandise allowance   A trade-oriented sales promotion in which a retailer is reimbursed for extra in-store support or special featuring of the brand.

merchandise line   The number of different types of products and the assortment a store carries.

message   The information sent by a source to a receiver in the communication process.

micromarketing   How an organization directs its marketing activities and allocates its resources to benefit its customers.

missionary salespeople   Sales support personnel who do not directly solicit orders but rather concentrate on performing promotional activities and introducing new products.

mixed branding   A branding strategy in which the company may market products under their own name and that of a reseller.

modified rebuy   A buying situation in which the users, influencers, or deciders change the product specifications, price, delivery schedule, or supplier.

monopolistic competition   A competitive setting in which a large number of sellers offer unique but substitutable products.

monopoly   A competitive setting in which there is a single seller of a good or service.

moral idealism   A personal moral philosophy that considers certain individual rights or duties as universal regardless of the outcome.

motivation   Motivation is the energizing force that causes behaviour that satisfies a need.

multibranding   A manufacturer's branding strategy in which a distinct name is given to each of its products.

multidomestic marketing strategy   A firm's worldwide marketing strategy that offers as many different product variations, brand names, and advertising programs as countries in which it does business.

multiple-zone pricing   Pricing products the same when delivered within one of several specified zones or geographical areas, but with different prices for each zone depending on demand, competition, and distance: also called zone-delivered pricing.

multiproduct branding   A branding strategy in which a company uses one name for all products; also called blanket or family branding.

national character   A distinct set of personality characteristics common among people of a country or society.

need   That which occurs when a person feels deprived of food, clothing, or shelter.

need-satisfaction presentation   A selling format that emphasizes probing and listening by the salesperson to identify needs and interests of perspective buyers.

new buy   The first-time purchase of a product or service, characterized by greater potential risk.

new-product concept   A tentative description of a product or service a firm might offer for sale.

new-product process   The sequence of activities a firm uses to identify business opportunities and convert them to a saleable good or service. There are seven steps: new-product strategy, idea generation, screening and evaluation, business analysis, development, testing, and commercialization.

new-product strategy development   The phase of the new-product process in which a firm defines the role of new products in terms of overall corporate objectives.

news conference   A publicity tool consisting of an informational meeting with representatives of the media who received advanced materials on the meeting content.

news release A publicity tool consisting of an announcement regarding changes in the company or product line.

noise Extraneous factors that work against effective communication by distorting a message or the feedback received.

noncumulative quantity discounts Price reductions based on the size of an individual purchase order.

nondurable good An item consumed in one or a few uses.

nonprobability sampling Using arbitrary judgments to select the sample so that the chance of selecting a particular element may be unknown or zero.

nonprofit organization A nongovernmental organization that serves its customers but does not have profit as an organizational goal.

nonrepetitive decisions Those decisions unique to a particular time and situation.

North American Industry Classification System (NAICS) A system for classifying organizations on the basis of major activity or the major good or service provided used by the three NAFTA countries—Canada, Mexico, and the United States.

objective and task budgeting A budgeting approach whereby the company (1) determines its advertising objectives, (2) outlines the tasks to accomplish the objectives, and (3) determines the advertising cost of performing these tasks.

objectives Specific, measurable performance targets and deadlines.

observation Watching, either mechanically or in person, how people actually behave.

odd-even pricing Setting prices a few dollars or cents under an even number, such as $19.95.

off-peak pricing Charging different prices during different times of the day or days of the week to reflect variations in demand for the service.

off-price retailing Selling brand name merchandise at lower than regular prices.

oligopoly A competitive setting in which a few large companies control a large amount of an industry's sales.

one-price policy Setting the same price for similar customers who buy the same product and quantities under the same conditions.

one-price stores A form of off-price retailing in which all items in a store are sold at one low price.

open-end question A question that a respondent can answer in his or her own words.

opinion leaders Individuals who exert direct or indirect social influence over others.

order cycle time (*see* lead time)

order getter A salesperson who sells in a conventional sense and engages in identifying prospective customers, providing customers with information, persuading customers to buy, closing sales, and following on customer experience with product or service.

order taker A salesperson who processes routine orders and reorders for products that have already been sold by the company.

organizational buyers Units such as manufacturers, retailers, or government agencies that buy goods and services for their own use or for resale.

organizational buying behaviour The decision-making process that organizations use to establish the need for products and identify, evaluate, and choose among alternative brands and suppliers.

organizational buying criteria The objective attributes of the supplier's products and services and the capabilities of the supplier itself.

organizational goals Specific objectives a business or nonprofit unit seeks to achieve and by which it can measure its performance.

original markup The difference between retailer cost and initial selling price.

outbound telemarketing Use of the telephone rather than personal visits to contact customers.

outsourcing Contracting work that formerly was done in-house by employees such as those in marketing research, advertising, and public relations departments to small, outside firms.

Pacific Rim The area of the world consisting of countries in Asia and Australia.

packaging The container in which a product is offered for sale and on which information is communicated.

panel A sample of consumers or stores from which researchers take a series of measurements.

parallel development An approach to new product development that involves the simultaneous development of the product and production process.

penetration pricing Pricing a product low in order to discourage competition from entering the market.

perceived risk The anxieties felt because the consumer cannot anticipate the outcome but sees that there might be negative consequences.

percent of sales budgeting Allocating funds to advertising as a percentage of past or anticipated sales, in terms of either dollars or units sold.

perception The process by which an individual selects, organizes, and interprets information to create a meaningful picture of the world.

perceptual map A graph displaying consumers' perceptions of product attributes across two dimensions.

personal selling The two-way flow of communication between a buyer and seller, often in a face-to-face encounter, designed to influence a person's or group's purchase decision.

personal selling process Sales activities occurring before and after the sale itself, consisting of six stages: (1) prospecting, (2) preapproach, (3) approach, (4) presentation, (5) close, and (6) follow-up.

personality A person's consistent behaviours or responses to recurring situations.

physical distribution management Organizing the movement and storage of finished product to the customer.

piggyback franchising A variation of franchising in which stores operated by one chain sell the products or services of another franchised firm.

pioneering advertisements Advertisements that tell what a product is, what it can do, and where it can be found.

pioneering institutional advertisements Institutional advertisements about what a company is or can do or where it is located.

place-based media Advertising media alternative that places messages in locations that attract a specific target audience such as airports, doctor's offices, and health clubs.

place utility The value to consumers of having a good or service available where needed.

point-of-purchase displays Displays located in high-traffic areas in retail stores, often next to checkout counters.

points of difference Those characteristics of a product that make it superior to competitive substitutes.

portfolio test A pretest in which a test ad is placed in a portfolio with other ads and consumers are questioned on their impressions of the ads.

possession utility The value of making an item easy to purchase through the provision of credit cards or financial arrangements.

posttests Tests conducted after an advertisement has been shown to the target audience to determine whether it has accomplished its intended purpose.

power centre Large strip malls with multiple anchor (or national stores), a convenient location, and a supermarket.

preapproach stage The stage of the personal selling process that involves obtaining further information about a prospect and deciding on the best method of approach.

premium A sales promotion that consists of offering merchandise free or at significant savings over retail.

presentation stage The core of the personal selling process in which the salesperson tries to convert the prospect into a customer by creating a desire for the product or service.

prestige pricing Setting a high price so that status-conscious consumers will be attracted to the product.

pretests Tests conducted before an advertisement is placed to determine whether it communicates the intended message or to select between alternative versions of an advertisement.

price The money or other considerations exchanged for the purchase or use of the product, idea, or service.

price discrimination The practice of charging different prices to different buyers for goods of like trade and quality.

price elasticity of demand The percentage change in quantity demanded relative to a percentage change in price.

price fixing A conspiracy among firms to set prices for a product.

price lining Setting the price of a line of products at a number of different specific pricing points.

pricing constraints Factors that limit a firm's latitude in the price it may set.

pricing objectives Goals that specify the role of price in an organization's marketing and strategic plans.

primary data Data gathered and assembled specifically for the project at hand.

primary demand Desire for a product class rather than for a specific brand.

private branding When a company manufactures products that are sold under the name of a wholesaler or retailer.

proactive strategies New product strategies that involve an aggressive allocation of resources to identify opportunities for product development.

probability sampling Using precise rules to select the sample such that each element of the population has a specific known chance of being selected.

product A good, service, or idea consisting of a bundle of tangible and intangible attributes that satisfies consumers and is received in exchange for money or other unit of value.

product advertisements Advertisements that focus on selling a good or service and take three forms: (1) pioneering (or informational), (2) competitive (or persuasive), and (3) reminder.

product (program) champion A person who is able and willing to cut red tape and move a product or program forward.

product class An entire product category or industry.

product counterfeiting Low cost copies of a popular brand, not manufactured by the original producer.

product development A strategy of selling a new product to existing markets.

product differentiation A strategy having different but related meanings; it involves a firm's using different marketing mix activities, such as product featuring and advertising, to help consumers perceive the product as being different and better than other products.

product form Variations of a product within a product class.

product item A specific product noted by a unique brand, size, and price.

product life cycle The life of a product over four stages: introduction, growth, maturity, and decline.

product line A group of products closely related because they satisfy a class of needs, are used together, are sold to the same customer group, are distributed through the same outlets, or fall within a given price range.

product line groupings Organizational groupings in which a unit is responsible for specific product offerings.

product line pricing The setting of prices for all items in a product line.

product manager A person who plans, implements, and controls the annual and long-range plans for the products for which he or she is responsible.

product mix The number of product lines offered by a company.

product modifications Strategies of altering a product characteristic, such as quality, performance, or appearance.

product placement Advertising media alternative in which the manufacturer pays for the privilege of having a brand name product used in a movie.

product positioning The place an offering occupies in consumers' minds on important attributes relative to competitive offerings.

product repositioning Changing the place an offering occupies in a consumer's mind relative to competitive products.

production goods Products used in the manufacturing of other items that become part of the final product.

profit A business firm's reward for the risk it undertakes in offering a product for sale; the money left over after a firm's total expenses are subtracted from its total revenues.

profit equation Profit = Total revenue − Total cost.

profit responsibility The view that companies have a single obligation, which is to maximize profits for its owners or shareholders.

profitability analysis A means of measuring the profitability of the firm's products, customer groups, sales territories, channels of distribution, and order sizes.

program schedule A formal time-line chart showing the relationships through time of the various program tasks.

promotional allowance The cash payment or extra amount of "free goods" awarded sellers in the channel of distribution for undertaking certain advertising or selling activities to promote a product.

promotional mix The combination of one or more of the promotional elements a firm uses to communicate with consumers. The promotional elements include: advertising, personal selling, sales promotion, and public relations.

prospecting stage In the personal selling process, the search for and qualification of potential customers.

protectionism The practice of shielding one or more sectors of a country's economy from foreign competition through the use of tariffs, or quotas.

protocol In the new product development process, an early statement that identifies a well-defined target market; specifies customers' needs, wants, and preferences; and states what the product will be and do.

psychographics Characteristics represented by personality and lifestyle traits (activities, interests, and opinions).

public relations A form of communication management that seeks to influence the feelings, opinions, or beliefs held by customers, shareholders, suppliers, employees, and other publics about a company and its products or services.

public service announcement (PSA) A publicity tool that uses free space or time donated by the media.

publicity A nonpersonal, indirectly paid presentation of an organization, good, or service.

publicity tools Methods of obtaining nonpersonal presentation of an organization, good, or service without direct cost. Examples include news releases, news conferences, and public service announcements.

pull strategy Directing the promotional mix at ultimate consumers to encourage them to ask the retailer for the product.

pulse schedule The combination of a steady schedule and a flighting schedule because of increases in demand, heavy periods of promotion, or introduction of a new product.

purchase decision process Steps or stages a buyer passes through in making choices about which products to buy.

purchase frequency The frequency of purchase of a specific product.

pure competition A competitive setting in which a large number of sellers compete with similar products.

push strategy Directing the promotional mix to channel members or intermediaries to gain their cooperation in ordering and stocking a product.

quality Those features and characteristics of a product that influence its ability to satisfy customer needs.

quantity discounts Reductions in unit costs for a larger order quantity.

questionnaire data Facts and figures obtained by asking people about their attitudes, awareness, intentions, and behaviours.

quota A restriction placed on the amount of a product allowed to enter or leave a country.

rack jobber A merchant wholesaler that furnishes racks or shelves to display merchandise in retail stores, performs all channel functions, and sells on consignment.

rating (TV or radio) The percentage of households in a market that are tuned to a particular TV show or radio station.

reach The number of different people or households exposed to an advertisement.

reactive strategies New product strategies are defensive approaches in response to competitors' new items by developing new products.

rebate A sales promotion in which money is returned to the consumer based on proof of purchase.

receivers The consumers who read, hear, or see the message sent by a source in the communication process.

reciprocity An industrial buying practice in which two organizations agree to purchase products from each other.

reference group People to whom a person turns as a standard of self-appraisal or source of personal standards.

regional marketing A form of geographical segmentation that develops marketing plans to reflect specific area differences in taste preferences, perceived needs, or interests.

regional rollouts Introducing a new product sequentially into geographical areas to allow production levels and marketing activities to build up gradually.

regional shopping centres Suburban malls with up to 100 stores that typically draw customers from a 8 to 16-km radius, usually containing one or two anchor stores.

regulation The laws placed on business with regard to the conduct of its activities.

reinforcement A reward that tends to strengthen a response.

relationship marketing An organization's effort to develop a long-term cost-effective link with individual customers for mutual benefit.

relationship selling The practice of building ties to customers based on a salesperson's attention and commitment to customer needs over time.

relative market share The sales of a firm or SBU divided by the sales of the largest firm in the industry; often used as a horizontal axis in business portfolio analysis.

reminder advertisements Advertisements used to reinforce previous knowledge of a product.

reminder institutional advertisements Institutional advertisements that bring a company's name to the attention of the target market.

repeat purchasers People who tried the product, were satisfied, and buy again.

repetitive decisions Decisions repeated at standard intervals during the work year.

replenishment time (see lead time)

repositioning Changing the place an offering occupies in a consumer's mind relative to competitive offerings.

requirements contract A contract that requires a buyer to meet all or part of its needs for a product from one seller for a period of time.

reseller A wholesaler or retailer that buys physical products and resells them again without any processing.

restructuring (reengineering or streamlining) Striving for more efficient corporations that can compete globally by reducing duplicate efforts in multiple company locations, closing or changing unprofitable plants and offices, and laying off employees.

retail life cycle A concept that describes a retail operation over four stages: early growth, accelerated development, maturity, and decline.

retailer-sponsored cooperative chain A contractual system involving independently owned stores that bind together to act like a chain.

retailing All the activities that are involved in selling, renting, and providing goods and services to ultimate consumers for personal, family, or household use.

retailing mix The strategic components that a retailer manages, including goods and services, physical distribution, and communication tactics.

retailing positioning matrix A framework for positioning retail outlets in terms of breadth of product line and value-added.

return on investment (ROI) The ratio of after-tax net profit to the investment used to earn that profit.

returns Refunds or credit granted a customer for an item returned to the seller.

reverse marketing The effort by organizational buyers to build relationships that shape suppliers' products, services, and capabilities to fit a buyer's needs and those of its customers.

sales analysis A tool for controlling marketing programs where sales records are used to compare actual results with sales goals and to identify strengths and weaknesses.

sales component analysis A tool for controlling marketing programs that traces sales revenues to their sources such as specific products, sales territories, or customers.

sales engineer A salesperson who specializes in identifying, analyzing, and solving customer problems and who brings technological expertise to the selling situations, but does not actually sell goods and services.

salesforce automation The use of technology designed to make the sales function more effective and efficient.

salesforce survey forecast   Asking the firm's salespeople to estimate sales during a coming period.

sales forecast   What one firm expects to sell under specified conditions for the uncontrollable and controllable factors that affect the forecast.

sales management   Planning, implementing, and controlling the personal selling effort of the firm.

sales plan   A statement describing what is to be achieved and where and how the selling effort of salespeople is to be deployed.

sales promotion   A short-term inducement of value offered to arouse interest in buying a good or service.

sales response function   The relationship between the expense of marketing effort and the marketing results obtained. Measures of marketing results include sales revenue, profit, units sold, and level of awareness.

samples   A sales promotion consisting of offering a product free or at a greatly reduced price.

sampling   The process of gathering data from a proportion of the total population rather than from all members of that particular population.

scrambled merchandising   Offering several unrelated product lines in a single retail store.

screening and evaluation   The phase of the new product process in which a firm uses internal and external evaluations to eliminate ideas that warrant no further development effort.

seasonal discounts   Price reductions granted buyers for purchasing products and stocking them at a time when they are not wanted by customers.

secondary data   Data previously collected and assembled for some project other than the project at hand.

selected controlled markets   These sites also referred to as forced distribution markets are where a market test for a new product is conducted by an outside agency and retailers are paid to display the new product.

selective demand   Demand for a specific brand within a product class.

selective distribution   A distribution strategy whereby a producer sells its products in a few retail outlets in a specific geographical area.

self-concept   The way people see themselves and the way they believe others see them.

self-liquidating premium   A sales promotion offering merchandise at a significant cost savings to the customer, its price covering the cost of the premium for the company.

self-regulation   An industry policing itself rather than relying on government controls.

selling agent   A person or firm that represents a single producer and is responsible for all marketing functions of that producer.

semantic differential scale   A seven-point scale in which the opposite ends have one- or two-word adjectives with opposite meanings.

seminar selling   A form of team selling where a company team conducts an educational program for a customer's technical staff describing state-of-the-art developments.

semiotics   The field of study that examines the correspondence between symbols and their role in the assignment of meaning for people.

sensitivity analysis   Asking "What if . . . " questions to determine how changes in a factor like pricing or advertising affect marketing results like sales revenues or profits.

service continuum   A range from the tangible to the intangible or good-dominant to service-dominant offerings available in the marketplace.

services   Activities, deeds, or other basic intangibles offered for sale to consumers in exchange for money or something else of value.

share points   Percentage points of market share; often used as the common basis of comparison to allocate marketing resources effectively.

shelf life   The time a product can be stored before it spoils.

shopping goods   Products for which the consumer will compare several alternatives on various criteria.

shrinkage   A term used by retailers to describe theft of merchandise by customers and employees.

single-line store   A store that offers tremendous depth in one primary line of merchandise; for example, a running shoe store.

single-source data   Information provided by a single firm on household demographics and lifestyle, purchases, TV viewing behaviour, and responses to promotions like coupons and free samples.

single-zone pricing   Pricing policy in which all buyers pay the same delivered product price, regardless of their distance from the seller; also known as uniform delivered pricing or postage stamp pricing.

situation analysis   Taking stock of where the firm or product has been recently, where it is now, and where it is headed in terms of the organization's plans and the external factors and trends affecting it.

situational influences   A situation's effect on the nature and scope of the decision process. These include (1) the purchase task, (2) social surroundings, (3) physical surroundings, (4) temporal effects, and (5) antecedent states.

skimming pricing   A high initial price attached to a product to help a company recover the cost of development.

slotting fees   Payment by a manufacturer to place a new product on retailer's shelf.

social audit   A systematic assessment of a firm's objectives, strategies, and performance in the domain of social responsibility.

social classes   The relatively permanent and homogeneous divisions in a society of people or families sharing similar values, interests, and behaviour.

social forces   The characteristics of the population, its values, and its behaviour in a particular environment.

social responsibility   The idea that organizations are part of a larger society and are accountable to society for their actions.

societal marketing concept   The view that an organization should discover and satisfy the needs of its customers in a way that also provides for society's well-being.

societal responsibility   The view that firms have obligations to preserve the ecological environment and benefit the general public.

solution   The best alternative that has been identified to solve the problem.

source   A company or person who has information to convey.

special merchandise wholesaler   A full-service merchant wholesaler that offers a relatively narrow range of products but has an extensive assortment within the products carried.

specialty outlet   Retailers that offer large selections in a narrow range of products.

specialty goods   Products that a consumer will make a special effort to search out and buy.

splitting 30s   Reducing the length of a standard commercial from 30 seconds to 15 seconds.

staff positions   People in staff positions have the authority and responsibility to advise people in the line positions but cannot issue direct orders to them.

stakeholder responsibility   The view that an organization has an obligation only to those constituencies that can affect achievement of its objectives.

standard markets   Sites where companies test market a product through normal distribution channels and monitor the results.

standard markup pricing   Setting prices by adding a fixed percentage to the cost of all items in a specific product class.

Starch test   A posttest that assesses the extent of consumers' recognition of an advertisement appearing in a magazine they have read.

statistical inference   Drawing conclusions about a population from a sample taken from that population.

steady schedule   A scheduling approach in which advertising is run at a steady schedule throughout the year; sometimes called "drip" scheduling.

stimulus discrimination   The ability to perceive differences in stimuli.

stimulus generalization   When a response elicited by one stimulus (cue) is generalized to another stimulus.

stimulus-response presentation   A selling format that assumes the prospect will buy if given the appropriate stimulus by a salesperson.

stock keeping unit (SKU)   A distinct ordering number to identify a product item.

store audits   Measurements of the sales of the product in stores and the number of cases ordered by a store from the wholesaler.

straight commission compensation plan   A compensation plan where the salesperson's earnings are directly tied to his sales or profit generated.

straight rebuy   The reordering of an existing product or service from the list of acceptable suppliers, generally without checking with the various users or influencers.

straight salary compensation plan   A compensation plan where the salesperson is paid a fixed amount per week, month, or year.

strategic alliances   Agreements between two or more independent firms to cooperate for the purpose of achieving common goals.

strategic business unit (SBU)   A decentralized profit centre of a large firm that is treated as though it were a separate, independent business.

strategic channel alliances   A practice whereby one firm's marketing channel is used to sell another firm's products.

strategic marketing process   The activities whereby an organization allocates its marketing mix resources to reach its target markets.

strip location   A cluster of stores that serves people who live within a 5- to 10-minute drive in a population base of under 30 000.

subcultures   Subgroups within the larger or national culture with unique values, ideas, and attitudes.

subliminal perception   Means that a person sees or hears messages without being aware of them.

supply partnerships   A relationship between an organizational buyer and its supplier created to adopt mutually beneficial efforts to lower the cost and/or increase value delivered to the ultimate consumer.

support goods   Items used to assist in the production of other goods.

survey   A research technique used to generate data by asking people questions and recording their responses on a questionnaire.

survey of buyers' intentions forecast   A method of forecasting sales that involves asking prospective customers whether they are likely to buy the product or service during some future time period.

survey of experts forecast   Asking experts on a topic to make a judgment about some future event.

sustainable competitive advantage   A strength, relative to competitors, in the markets served and the products offered.

sweepstakes   Sales promotions consisting of a game of chance requiring no analytical or creative effort to win a prize.

SWOT analysis   An acronym describing an organization's appraisal of its internal strengths and weaknesses and its external opportunities and threats.

synergy   The increased customer value achieved through performing organizational functions more efficiently.

target market   One or more specific groups of potential consumers toward which an organization directs its marketing program.

target profit pricing   Setting a price based on an annual specific dollar target volume of profit.

target return-on-investment pricing   Setting a price to achieve a return-on-investment target.

target return-on-sales pricing   Setting a price to achieve a profit that is a specified percentage of the sales volume.

tariff   A government tax on goods or services entering a country.

team selling   Using a group of professionals in selling to and servicing major customers.

technological forecast   Estimating when scientific breakthroughs will occur.

technology   An environmental force that includes inventions or innovations from applied science or engineering research.

telemarketing   Involves the use of the telephone to interact with and sell directly to consumers.

test marketing   The process of offering a product for sale on a limited basis in a defined area to gain consumer reaction to the actual product and to examine its commercial viability and the marketing program.

theatre test   A pretest in which consumers view test ads in new television shows or movies and report their feelings on electronic recording devices or questionnaires.

time utility   The value to consumers of having a good or service available when needed.

timing   The issue of deciding when to discount the price of merchandise.

top-down forecast   Subdividing an aggregate forecast into its principal components.

total cost   The total expense a firm incurs in producing and marketing a product, which includes fixed cost and variable cost; in physical distribution decisions, the sum of all applicable costs for logistical activities.

total logistics cost   Expenses associated with transportation, materials handling and warehousing, inventory, stockouts, and order processing.

total revenue   The total amount of money received from the sale of a product.

trade (functional) discounts   Price reductions granted to wholesalers or retailers on the basis of future marketing functions they will perform for the manufacturer.

trade feedback effect   A country's imports affect its exports and exports affect imports.

trade name   The commercial, legal name under which a company does business.

trade-oriented sales promotions   Sales tools used to support a company's advertising and personal selling efforts directed to wholesalers, distributors, or retailers. Three common approaches are allowances, cooperative advertising, and salesforce training.

trademark   Legal identification of a company's exclusive rights to use a brand name or trade name.

trading down   Reducing the number of features, quality, or price of a product.

trading up   Adding value to a product by including more features or higher-quality materials.

trend extrapolation   Extending a pattern observed in past data into the future.

trial   The initial purchase of a product by the consumer.

truck jobber   Small merchant wholesalers that usually handle limited assortments of fast-moving or perishable items that are sold directly from trucks for cash.

ultimate consumers   People who use the goods and services purchased for a household; sometimes also called ultimate users.

uncontrollable factors   (see environmental factors)

uniform delivered pricing   A geographical pricing practice where the price the seller quotes includes all transportation costs.

unit train   A train that is dedicated to one commodity, is loaded and unloaded with sophisticated equipment, and runs from origin to destination at high speed.

unit variable cost   Variable cost expressed on a per unit basis.

unitary demand elasticity   A situation where the percentage change in price is identical to the percentage change in quantity demanded.

universal product code (UPC)   A number assigned to identify each product, represented by a series of bars of varying widths for scanning by optical readers.

unsought goods   Products that the consumer does not know about or knows about and does not initially want.

usage rate   Refers to quantity consumed or patronage during a specific period, and varies significantly among different customer groups.

utilitarianism   A personal moral philosophy that focuses on the "greatest good for the greatest number" by assessing the costs and benefits of the consequences of ethical behaviour.

utility   The benefits or customer value received by users of the product.

Valdez Principles   Guidelines that encourage firms to focus attention on environmental concerns and corporate responsibility.

value   Specifically, value can be defined as the ratio of perceived quality to price (Value = Perceived benefits/Price).

value added   In retail strategy decisions, a dimension of the retail positioning matrix that refers to the service level and method of operation of the retailer.

value analysis   A systematic appraisal of the design, quality, and performance requirements of a product to reduce purchasing costs.

value consciousness   Consumer concern for obtaining the best quality, features, and performance of a product or service for a given price.

value pricing   The practice of simultaneously increasing service and product benefits and maintaining or decreasing price.

values   Personally or socially preferable modes of conduct or states of existence that are enduring.

variable cost   An expense of the firm that varies directly with the quantity of product produced and sold.

vending machines   A retailing operation in which products are stored in and sold from machines.

venture teams   Multidisciplinary groups of marketing, manufacturing, and R&D personnel who stay with a new product from conception to production.

vertical conflict   Disagreement between different levels in a marketing channel.

vertical marketing systems   Professionally managed and centrally coordinated marketing channels designed to achieve channel economies and maximum marketing impact.

vertical price fixing   The practice whereby sellers are required to not sell products below a minimum retail price, sometimes called resale price maintenance.

want   A need that is shaped by a person's knowledge, culture, and individual characteristics.

warehouse   A location, often decentralized, that a firm uses to store, consolidate, age, or mix stock; house product-recall programs; or ease tax burdens.

warehouse clubs   Large retail stores (over 100 000 square feet) that require a yearly fee to shop at the store.

warranty   A statement indicating the liability of the manufacturer for product deficiencies.

wasted coverage   People outside a company's target audience who see, hear, or read the company's advertisement.

wheel of retailing   A concept that describes how new retail outlets enter the market as low-status, low-margin stores and change gradually in terms of status and margin.

whistleblowers   Employees who report unethical or illegal actions of their employers.

wholesaler-sponsored voluntary chain   A contractual system involving independently owned wholesalers who band together to act like a chain.

word of mouth   People influencing each other during their face-to-face conversations.

workload method   A formula-based method for determining the size of a salesforce that integrates the number of customers served, call frequency, call length, and available time to arrive at a salesforce size.

World Trade Organization   An institution that sets rules governing trade among its members through a panel of experts.

CHAPTER NOTES

CHAPTER 1

1. Chad Rubel, "Advertisers Go to Extremes to Target Young Athletes," *Marketing News* (August 28, 1995), pp. 26, 29; and Lisa Feinberg Densmore, "Taking Extreme Mainstream," *Inline* (November 1995), pp. 30–37, 62.
2. Joshua Rosenbaum, "Wheeler Dealers," *Continental Profiles* (February 1991), pp. 22–42.
3. Mary Horwath, "Rollerblade: Creation of an American Original," a talk in Rome, Italy, November 1992.
4. Steven A. Meyerowitz, "Surviving Assaults on Trademarks," *Marketing Management* (1994, no. 1), pp. 44–46; and Carrie Goerne, "Rollerblade Reminds Everyone That Its Success Is Not Generic," *Marketing News* (March 2, 1992), pp. 1–2.
5. Peter D. Bennett, *Dictionary of Marketing Terms,* 2nd ed. (Lincolnwood, IL: NTC Publishing Group, 1995), p. 166.
6. J. Stanco, *Utilizing The Strategic Marketing Organization* (New York: The Haworth Press Inc., 1996).
7. Richard P. Bagozzi, "Marketing as Exchange," *Journal of Marketing* (October 1975), pp. 32–39; and Gregory T. Gundlach and Patrick E. Murphy, "Ethical and Legal Foundations of Relational Marketing Exchanges," *Journal of Marketing* (October 1993), pp. 35–46.
8. Patricia Sellers, "So You Fail. Now Bounce Back!" *Fortune* (May 1, 1995), pp. 48–66; and Christopher Power, Kathleen Kerwin, Ronald Grover, Keith Alexander, and Robert Hof, "Flops," *Business Week* (August 16, 1993), pp. 76–82.
9. E. Jerome McCarthy, *Basic Marketing: A Managerial Approach* (Homewood, IL.: Richard D. Irwin, 1960); and Walter van Waterschoot and Christophe Van den Bulte, "The 4P Classification of the Marketing Mix Revisited," *Journal of Marketing* (October 1992), pp. 83–93.
10. Carl P. Zeithaml and Valarie A. Zeithaml, "Environmental Management: Revising the Marketing Perspective," *Journal of Marketing* (Spring 1984), pp. 46–53; and P. Rajan Varadarajan, Terry Clark, and William M. Pride, "Controlling the Uncontrollable: Managing Your Market Environment," *Sloan Management Review* (Winter 1992), pp. 39–47.
11. Michael Treacy and Fred D. Wiersema, *The Discipline of Market Leaders* (Reading, MA: Addison-Wesley, 1995); Michael Treacy and Fred Wiersema, "How Market Leaders Keep Their Edge," *Fortune* (February 6, 1995), pp. 88–98; and Michael Treacy, "You Need a Value Discipline—But Which One?" *Fortune* (April 17, 1995), p. 195.
12. Michael Hammer and James Champy, *Reengineering the Corporation: A Manifesto for Business Revolution* (New York, NY: HarperCollins Publishers Inc., 1993); and Thomas O. Jones and W. Earl Sasser, Jr., "Why Satisfied Customers Defect," *Harvard Business Review* (November–December 1995), pp. 88–99; and William Winston, "Vale Marketing: The Marketing Tool for the Year 2000," *Journal of Customer Service in Marketing & Management,* vol. 1, no. 1 (1995), pp. 2–8.
13. Horwath, "Rollerblade."
14. Ibid.
15. Lee Schafer, "It's Not a Fad," *Corporate Report Minnesota* (April 1992), pp. 31–39.
16. "The Best of 1994," *Business Week* (January 9, 1995), p. 119.
17. Justin Martin, "Minor Diversions Draw Sports Fans," *Fortune* (September 18, 1995), p. 24; and Jeff Jensen, "NHL's Icebreaker," *Advertising Age* (April 17, 1995), p. 35.
18. For a contrary view, see Ronald A. Fullerton, "How Modern Is Modern Marketing? Marketing's Evolution and the Myth of the 'Production Era'," *Journal of Marketing* (January 1988), pp. 108–25.
19. Robert F. Keith, "The Marketing Revolution," *Journal of Marketing* (January 1960), pp. 35–38.
20. *1952 Annual Report* (New York: General Electric Company, 1952), p. 21.
21. Stanley F. Slater and John C. Narver, "Market Orientation and the Learning Organization," *Journal of Marketing* (July 1995), pp. 63–74; Stanley F. Slater and John C. Narver, "Market Orientation, Customer Value, and Superior Performance," *Business Horizons* (March–April 1994), pp. 22–28; George S. Day, "The Capabilities of Market-Driven Organizations," *Journal of Marketing* (October 1994), pp. 37–52; and Robert Monagham, "Customer Management Teams Are Here to Stay," *Marketing News* (November 6, 1995), p. 4.
22. N. Craig Smith, "Marketing Strategies for the Ethics Era," *Sloan Management Review* (Summer 1995), pp. 85–97; Oswald A. J. Mascarenhas, "Exonerating Unethical Marketing Executive Behaviors: A Diagnostic Framework," *Journal of Marketing* (April 1995), pp. 43–57; and Russell Mitchell and Michael Oneal, "Managing by Values," *Business Week* (August 1, 1994), pp. 46–52.
23. Donald P. Robin and R. Eric Reidenbach, "Social Responsibility, Ethics, and Marketing Strategy: Closing the Gap between Concept and Application," *Journal of Marketing* (Summer 1982), pp. 9–26.
24. Minette E. Drumwright, "Socially Responsible Organizational Buying: Environmental Concern as a Noneconomic Buying Criterion," *Journal of Marketing* (July 1994), pp. 1–19; Michael E. Porter and Claas van der Linde, "Green and Competitive: Ending the Stalemate," *Harvard Business Review* (September–October 1995), pp. 120–34; Jacquelyn Ottman, "Edison Winners Show Smart Environmental Marketing," *Marketing News* (July 17, 1995), pp. 16, 19; and Jacquelyn Ottman, "Mandate for the '90s: Green Corporate Image," *Marketing News* (September 11, 1995), p. 8.
25. Shelby D. Hunt and John J. Burnett, "The Macromarketing/Micromarketing Dichotomy: A Taxonomical Model," *Journal of Marketing* (Summer 1982), pp. 9–26.
26. Philip Kotler and Sidney J. Levy, "Broadening the Concept of Marketing," *Journal of Marketing* (January 1969), pp. 10–15.
27. Horwath, "Rollerblade."

Rollerblade, Inc.: This case was written by Linda Rochford and William Rudelius.

CHAPTER 2

1. Information supplied by Gulf Canada, 1997; and George Koch, "He Ain't No Oilman," *The Financial Post Magazine* (March 1996), pp. 14–20.
2. Ibid.
3. Roger A. Kerin, Vijay Mahajan, and P. Rajan Varadarajan, *Contemporary Perspectives on Strategic Marketing Planning* (Boston, MA: Allyn & Bacon, 1990), Chapter 1; and Orville C. Walker, Jr., Harper W. Boyd, Jr., and Jean-Claude Larreche, *Marketing Strategy* (Homewood, IL: Richard D. Irwin, 1992), Chapters 1 and 2.
4. Gary Hamel and C. K. Prahalad, "Strategic Intent," *Harvard Business Review,* (May–June 1989), pp. 63–76.
5. "Coca-Cola Co. Restructures Itself into Units Covering Globe," *Star Tribune* (January 13, 1996), p. D2.
6. John M. Ivancevich, Peter Lorenzi, Steven J. Skinner, with Philip B. Crosby, *Management: Quality and Competitiveness* (Burr Ridge, IL: Richard D. Irwin, 1996), p. 621.
7. Lesley Dow, "Pillsbury Turnover," *Marketing* (July 14, 1997)—www.marketingmag.ca, July 17, 1997.
8. Jeffrey Abrahams, *The Mission Statement Book* (Berkeley, CA: Ten Speed Press, 1995), p. 41.
9. Mark Fawcett, "Getting with the Program," *The Financial Post Magazine* (March 1996), pp. 48–49, and p. 58; and "Ford's Marketing Maven," *Marketing* (June 30, 1997)—www.marketingmag.ca, July 17, 1997.
10. Robert S. Kaplan and David P. Norton. "The Balanced Scoreboard Measures That Drive Performance," *Harvard Business Review* (January–February 1992), pp. 71–79.

11. Fawcett, "Getting with the Program."
12. Adapted from "The Experience Curve Reviewed, IV. The Growth Share Matrix of the Product Portfolio" (Boston, MA: The Boston Consulting Group, 1973).
13. Kerin, Mahajan, and Vardarajan, *Contemporary Perspectives*, p. 52.
14. Strengths and weaknesses of the BCG technique are based largely on Derek F. Abell and John S. Hammond, *Strategic Market Planning: Problem and Analytic Approaches* (Englewood Cliffs, NJ; Prentice Hall, 1979); and Yoram Wind, Vijay Mahajan, and Donald Swire, "An Empirical Comparison of Standardized Portfolio Models," *Journal of Marketing* (Spring 1983), pp. 89–99.
15. Rich Brown, "Making the Product Portfolio a Basis for Action," *Long Range Planning* (February 1991), pp. 102–10.
16. J. Scott Armstrong and Roderick J. Brodie, "Effects of Portfolio Planning Methods on Decision Making: Experimental Results," *International Journal of Research in Marketing* (Winter 1994), pp. 73–84.
17. George Stalk, Phillip Evans, and Lawrence E. Shulman, "Competing on Capabilities: The New Rules of Corporate Strategy," *Harvard Business Review* (March–April 1992), pp. 57–69.
18. Roger A. Kerin and Robert A. Peterson, *Strategic Marketing Problems: Cases and Comments,* 7th ed. (Englewood Cliffs, NJ: Prentice-Hall, 1995), pp. 2–3; and Derek F. Abell, *Defining the Business* (Englewood Cliffs, NJ: Prentice Hall, 1980), p. 18. Also see Doug McCuain and Christopher Holt, "Getting Intimate with Customers," *Marketing* (July 14, 1997)—www.marketingmag.ca, July 17, 1997.
19. Christopher Meyer, *East Cycle Time* (New York: Free Press, 1993); and Michael E. Porter, *Competitive Advantage* (New York: Free Press, 1985).
20. *1994 Hewlett-Packard Annual Report* (Palo Alto, CA.: Hewlett-Packard, 1995).
21. Thomas C. Powell, "Total Quality Management as Competitive Advantage: A Review and Empirical Study," *Strategic Management Journal*, vol. 16 (1995), pp. 15–37.
22. Loyd Eskildson, "TQM's Role in Corporate Success: Analyzing the Evidence," *National Productivity Review* (Autumn 1995), pp. 25–38; and Keith Naughton, "This Taurus Sure Won't Blend into the Crowd," *Business Week* (October 30, 1995), pp. 168–70.
23. Mark Maremont, "Kodak's New Focus," *Business Week* (January 30, 1995), p. 63–68.
24. Mark Maremont, "The Times of Your Life—As Many Times As You Want," *Business Week* (January 30, 1995), p. 68.
25. Wendy Bounds, "Kodak Under Fisher: Upheaval in Slow Motion," *The Wall Street Journal* (December 22, 1994), pp. B1, B4; and Wendy Bounds, "Fuji, Accused by Kodak of Hogging Markets, Spits Back: 'You Too' " *The Wall Street Journal* (July 31, 1995), pp. A1, A4.
26. Mark Maremont, "The New Flash at Kodak," *Business Week* (May 16, 1994), p. 32.
27. Stephen H. Wildstrom, "Not Yet Picture Perfect," *Business Week* (November 20, 1995), p. 30.

Specialized Bicycle Components, Inc.: This case was written by Giana Eckardt.

APPENDIX A

1. Personal interview with Arthur R. Kydd, St. Croix Venture Partners.
2. Examples of guides to writing marketing plans include: William A. Cohen, *The Marketing Plan* (New York: John Wiley & Sons, Inc., 1995); Mark Nolan, *The Instant Marketing Plan* (Santa Maria, CA: Puma Publishing Company, 1995); and Roman G. Hiebing, Jr. and Scott W. Cooper, *The Successful Marketing Plan* (Lincolnwood, IL: NTC Business Books, 1990 with 1995 printing).
3. Examples of guides to writing business plans include: Rhonda M. Abrahms, *The Successful Business Plan: Secrets & Strategies,* 2nd ed. (Grants Pass, OR: The Oasis Press/PSI Research, 1993); Michael O'Donnell, *Writing Business Plans That Get Results: A Step-by-Step Guide* (Chicago, IL: Contemporary Books, Inc., 1991); W. Keith Schilit, *The Entrepreneur's Guide to Preparing a Winning Business Plan and Raising Venture Capital* (Englewood Cliffs, NJ: Prentice Hall, 1990); and Joseph A. Covello and Brian J. Hazelgren, *The Complete Book of Business Plans* (Naperville, IL: Sourcebooks, Inc., 1994).
4. Abrahms, *The Successful Business Plan,* p. 30.
5. Some of these points are adapted from Abrahms, pp. 30–38; others are adapted from William Rudelius, *Guidelines for Technical Report Writing* (Minneapolis, MN: University of Minnesota, undated).
6. The authors are indebted to Randall F. Peters for being allowed to adapt elements of a business plan for Paradise Kitchens, Inc. for the sample marketing plan and for his help and suggestions.

7. Lesley Dow, "Pillsbury Turnover," *Marketing* (July 14, 1997)—www.marketingmag.ca, July 17, 1997.

CHAPTER 3

1. J. Duncan Herrington, Albert Smith, and Michael J. Cotter, "Using TV to Reach Generation X: Some Implications for Media Planning and Selection," *Journal of Promotion Management,* vol. 3, no. 1/2 (1996), pp. 107–120; "Making Generational Marketing Come of Age," *Fortune* (June 26, 1995), pp. 110–14; Randall Lane, "Computers Are Our Friends," *Forbes* (May 8, 1995), pp. 102–108; Kemba Johnson, "Generation X Finds a Voice for Advertising," *Advertising Age* (September 18, 1995), p. 12; and "What Xers Cross Out," *Marketing* (April 17, 1995), p. 30.
2. Shannon Dortch, "Coffee at Home," *American Demographics* (August 1995), pp. 4–6; and Marcia Mogelonsky, "Instant's Last Drop," *American Demographics* (August 1995), p. 10.
3. Statistics Canada, CANSIM matrices 6367, 6379, on-line, July 18, 1997.
4. Statistics Canada, CANSIM matrix 6900, on-line, July 18, 1997.
5. Ibid.
6. Patricia Braus, "The Baby Boom at Mid-Decade," *American Demographics* (April 1995), pp. 40–45; and Cheryl Russell, "On the Baby-Boom Bandwagon," *American Demographics* (May 1991), pp. 24–31.
7. Marcy Magiera and Pat Sloan, "Levis, Lee Loosen Up for Baby Boomers," *Advertising Age* (August 3, 1992), p. 9.
8. Diane Crispell, "Generations to 2025," *American Demographics* (January 1995), p. 4; and Scott Donaton, "The Media Wakes Up to Generation X," *Advertising Age* (February 1, 1993), pp. 16–17.
9. Susan Mitchell, "The Next Baby Boom," *American Demographics* (October 1995), pp. 22–31.
10. Statistics Canada, *Market Research Handbook,* cat. 63-224 (Ottawa, 1997).
11. Jim McElgunn, "TV Must Get Serious Says Angus Reid," *Marketing* (November 4, 1991), p. 29.
12. Douglas Bell, "Immigration Trends Shape Demand," *Marketing* (May 21, 1993), p. 29.
13. "Grizzlies Capitalize on Asian Fan Interest in NBA," *Marketing* (August 5, 1996), p. 2.
14. Chad Rubel, "Parents Magazines Make Room for Daddy," *Marketing News* (February 27, 1995), pp. 1, 5, 14.
15. Donalee Moulton, "Sobeys Takes Low Road in Food Pricing," *Marketing* (August 5, 1996), p. 2.
16. "Banks Poach Credit Card Business with Lower Rates," *Marketing* (August 5, 1996), p. 4.
17. Statistics Canada, *Income Distribution by Size in Canada,* cat. 13-207 (Ottawa, 1997).
18. "The Future of Spending," *American Demographics* (January 1995), pp. 12–19.
19. Robert Lenzner, "The Reluctant Entrepreneur," *Forbes* (September 11, 1995), pp. 162–68; Joshua Quittner, "A Mighty Morphing," *Time* (January 16, 1995), p. 56; Amy Cortese, John Verity, Russell Mitchell, and Richard Brandt, "Cyberspace," *Business Week* (February 27, 1995), pp. 78–86; Rebecca Piirto, "Cable TV," *American Demographics* (June 1995), pp. 40–43; and David Woodruff, Larry Armstrong, and John Carey, "Electric Cars," *Business Week* (May 30, 1994), pp. 104–14.
20. Neil Gross, Peter Coy, and Otis Post, "The Technology Paradox," *Business Week* (March 6, 1995), pp. 76–84.
21. Leon Jaroff, "Smart's the Word in Detroit," *Time* (February 6, 1995), pp. 50–52.
22. Mark Campbell, "Dial a Bank," *Canadian Banker* (September/October, 1996), pp. 18–23.
23. Mike Hewitt, "Hobby Horse," *Marketing* (November 21, 1996), p. 20; and Dawn Iacobucci, "The Quality Improvement Customers Didn't Want," *Harvard Business Review* (Jan./Feb. 1996), pp. 28–29.
24. Jacquelyn Ottman, "Mandate for the '90s: Green Corporate Image," *Marketing News* (September 11, 1995), p. 8.
25. Jacquelyn Ottman, "New and Improved Won't Do," *Marketing News* (January 30, 1995), p. 9: and Maxine Wilkie, "Asking Americans to Use Less Stuff," *American Demographics* (December 1994), pp. 11–12.
26. "Rural Phone Firm Takes Aim at Giant Rival," *The Chronicle Herald* (July 15, 1997), p. C3.
27. Michael Porter, *Competitive Advantage* (New York: Free Press, 1985); and Michael Porter, *Competitive Strategy* (New York: Free Press, 1980).
28. James B. Treece, Kathleen Kerwin, and Heidi Dawley, "Ford," *Business Week* (April 3, 1995), pp. 94–104; Keith Hammonds, Kevin Kelly, and

Karen Thurston, "The New World of Work," *Business Week* (October 17, 1994), pp. 76–87.

29. "McCain's Ore-Ida Buy Excludes Brand Equity," *Marketing* (March 24, 1997)—www.marketingmag.ca. July 17, 1997.

30. Michael Mandel, Christopher Farrell, and Catherine Yang, "Land of the Giants." *Business Week* (September 11, 1995), pp. 34–35; and Howard Chua-Eoan, "Too Big or Not Too Big?" *Time* (October 2, 1995), pp. 32–33.

31. Department of Consumer and Corporate Affairs Canada. *Competition Policy in Canada* (Ottawa, 1989), pp. 4–5.

Imagination Pilots Entertainment: This case was prepared by Steven W. Hartley.

CHAPTER 4

1. Information supplied by Molson Breweries, Public Affairs Department, Toronto, 1997.

2. For a discussion of the definition of ethics, see Eugene R. Lazniak and Patrick E. Murphy, *Ethical Marketing Decisions: The Higher Road* (Boston, MA: Allyn & Bacon, 1993), Chapter 1.

3. Verne E. Henderson, "The Ethical Side of Enterprise," *Sloan Management Review* (Spring 1982), pp. 37–47.

4. M. Bommer, C. Gratto, J. Grauander, and M. Tuttle, "A Behavioral Model of Ethical and Unethical Decision Making," *Journal of Business Ethics,* vol. 6 (1987), pp. 265–80.

5. F. G. Crane, "What's Ethical and What's Not with Canadian Business Students," Working Paper, 1997.

6. "The Bottom Line on Ethics," *U.S. News & World Report* (March 20, 1995), pp. 61–66; "Business Week/Harris Poll: Is an Antibusiness Business Backlash Building?" *Business Week* (July 20, 1987), p. 71.

7. "Who's Trusted, Who's Not?" *American Demographics* (June 1995), p. 55.

8. N. Craig Smith, "Marketing Strategies for the Ethics Era," *Sloan Management Review* (Summer 1995), pp. 85–97; Kenneth Labich, "The New Crisis in Business Ethics," *Fortune* (April 20, 1992), pp. 167ff.

9. For a comprehensive review on marketing ethics, see Gregory T. Gunlach and Patrick E. Murphy, "Ethical and Legal Foundations in Relational Marketing Exchanges," *Journal of Marketing* (October 1993), pp. 35–46; and John Tsalikis and David J. Fritzche, "Business Ethics: A Literature Review with a Focus on Marketing Ethics," *Journal of Business Ethics,* vol. 8 (1989), pp. 695–743.

10. William Beaver, "Levi's Is Leaving China," *Business Horizons* (March–April 1995), pp. 35–40.

11. "It's All in the Cards," *Time* (November 7, 1988), p. 101.

12. Russell Watson, "A Little Fight Music," *Newsweek* (February 13, 1995), pp. 38–39; and Damon Darlin, "Where Trademarks Are Up for Grabs," *The Wall Street Journal* (December 5, 1989), pp. B1, B4.

13. "Nabbing the Pirates of Cyberspace," *Time* (June 13, 1995), pp. 62–63; "A Little Fight Music," *Newsweek* (February 13, 1995), pp. 38–39; "What Information Costs," *Fortune* (July 10, 1995), pp. 119–21; see also Moshe Givon, Vijay Mahajan, and Eitan Muller, "Software Piracy: Estimation of Lost Sales and the Impact of Software Diffusion," *Journal of Marketing* (January 1995), pp. 29–37.

14. Vern Terpstra and Kenneth David, *The Cultural Environment of International Business,* 3rd ed. (Cincinnati, OH: South-Western Publishing Co., 1991), p. 12.

15. For an extended treatment of ethics in the exchange process, see Gregory T. Gundlach and Patrick E. Murphy, "Ethical and Legal Foundations in Relational Marketing Exchanges."

16. Malcolm Gladwell, "Group Challenges Parts of Dalkon Shield Pact," *The Washington Post* (August 25, 1989), p. C2; "Some Dalkon Shield Claimants Attack Trust's Settlement Policies," *The Wall Street Journal* (March 12, 1992), p. B4.

17. Lois Therrion, "Want Shelf Space at Supermarkets? Ante Up," *Business Week* (August 7, 1989), pp. 60–61.

18. Robert Johnson and Edward T. Pound, "Hot on the Trail of Trade-Secret Thieves, Private Eyes Fight All Manner of Snakes," *The Wall Street Journal* (August 12, 1992), pp. B1, B4. See also "Companies on the Lookout for Spies," *USA Today* (February 24, 1995), p. 48.

19. "P&B Expected to Get about $120 Million in Settlement of Chewy-Cookie Lawsuit," *The Wall Street Journal* (September 11, 1989), p. B10.

20. "Hard Graft in Asia," *The Economist* (May 27, 1995), p. 61.

21. "Good Grief," *The Economist* (April 8, 1995), p. 57; and "Odds and Ends," *The Wall Street Journal* (February 25, 1992), p. B1.

22. "Ismael P. Akaah and Daulatram Lund,"The Influence of Personal Values and Organizational Values on Marketing Professionals' Ethical Behavior," *Journal of Business Ethics,* vol. 13 (1994), pp. 417–30.

23. "The Uncommon Good," *The Economist* (August 19, 1995), pp. 55–56; "Workers Who Blow the Whistle on Bosses Often Pay a High Price," *The Wall Street Journal* (July 18, 1995), p. B1.

24. For an extensive discussion on these moral philosophies, see R. Eric Reidenbach and Donald P. Robin, *Ethics and Profits* (Englewood Cliffs, NJ: Prentice-Hall, 1989); and Shelby D. Hunt and Scott Vitell, "A General Theory of Marketing Ethics," *Journal of Macromarketing* (Spring 1986), pp. 5–16.

25. James Q. Wilson, "Adam Smith on Business Ethics," *California Management Review* (Fall 1989), pp. 59–72; and Edward W. Coker, "Smith's Concept of the Social System," *Journal of Business Ethics,* vol. 9 (1990), pp. 139–42.

26. George M. Zinkhan, Michael Bisesi, and Mary Jane Saxton, "MBAs: Changing Attitudes toward Marketing Dilemmas," *Journal of Business Ethics,* vol. 8 (1989), pp. 963–74.

27. Alix M. Freedman, "Bad Reaction: Nestlé's Bid to Crash Baby-Formula Market in the U.S. Stirs a Row," *The Wall Street Journal* (February 16, 1989), pp. A1, A6; and Alix Freedman, "Nestlé to Drop Claim on Label of Its Formula," *The Wall Street Journal* (March 13, 1989), p. B5.

28. Milton Friedman, "A Friedman Doctrine: The Social Responsibility of Business Is to Increase Profits," *New York Times Magazine* (September 13, 1970), p. 126.

29. "Beating the Odds in Biotech," *Newsweek* (October 12, 1992), p. 63.

30. "Can Perrier Purify Its Reputation?" *Business Week* (February 26, 1990), p. 45; and "Perrier Expands North American Recall to Rest of Globe," *The Wall Street Journal* (February 15, 1990), pp. B1, B4.

31. Mark Stevenson, "Waste Not," *Canadian Business* (January 1994), pp. 20–26; "Downy Refill Makes a Splash on Shelves," *Advertising Age* (July 1991), p. 16; "Levi's Esprit Spin New Cotton into Eco-friendly Clothes," *Marketing News* (April 24, 1992), p. 11; and Rosemary Frei, "Green Floyd," *The Financial Post Magazine* (March 1996), p. 10.

32. For an extended discussion on this topic, see P. Rajan Varadarajan and Avil Menon, "Cause-Related Marketing: A Coalignment of Marketing Strategy and Corporate Philanthropy," *Journal of Marketing* (July 1988), pp. 58–74. The examples given are found in this article and "McD's Ties to World Cup," *Advertising Age* (April 13, 1992), p. 17; Scott M. Smith and David S. Alcorn, "Cause Marketing: A New Direction in the Marketing of Corporate Responsibility," *The Journal of Consumer Marketing* (Summer 1991), pp. 19–35; and "Are Good Causes Good Marketing?" *Business Week* (March 21, 1994), pp. 64–65.

33. These steps are adapted from J. J. Carson and G. A. Steiner, *Measuring Business Social Performance: The Corporate Social Audit* (New York: Committee for Economic Development, 1974). See also E. M. Epstein, "The Corporate Social Policy Process: Beyond Business Ethics, Corporate Social Responsibility, and Corporate Social Responsiveness," *California Management Review* (Spring 1987), pp. 99–114.

34. *Research Report: The Only Environment We Have: How Can We Save It?* (New York: Council on Economic Priorities, November 1989); and Rajib N. Sanyal and Joao S. Neves, "The Valdez Principles: Implications for Corporate Social Responsibility," *Journal of Business Ethics,* vol. 10 (1991), pp. 883–90.

35. "The Drought Is Over at 3M," *Business Week* (November 7, 1994), pp. 140–41; and "How to Make Lots of Money, and Save the Planet Too," *The Economist* (June 3, 1995), pp. 57–58.

36. For a listing of unethical consumer practices, see Robert E. Wilkes, "Fraudulent Behavior by Consumers," *Journal of Marketing* (October 1978), pp. 67–75. See also Catherine A. Cole, "Research Note: Determinants and Consumer Fraud,"*Journal of Retailing* (Spring 1989), pp. 107–20.

37. "Coupon Scams Are Clipping Companies," *Business Week* (June 15, 1992), pp. 110–11; "Video Vice: 1 in 10 Copy Videotapes Illegally," *USA Weekend* (February 9–11, 1990), p. 18; and "Trade Tripwires," *The Economist* (August 27, 1994), p. 61.

38. "Consumers Keen on Green But Marketers Don't Deliver," *Advertising Age* (June 29, 1992), pp. S-2, S-4.

39. "Green Campaigns Don't Always Pay Off, Survey Finds," *The Wall Street Journal* (April 11, 1994) p. 88; "Green Product Sales Seem to Be Wilting," *The Wall Street Journal* (May 18, 1992), p. B1.

40. Dicter Bradbury, "Green Forest Products Gain Marketing Niche," *Maine Sunday Telegram* (May 11, 1997), p. B1, p. B14.

Pricing in the Pharmaceutical Industry: This case was prepared by Roger A. Kerin. Sources: "How Many Times Must a Patient Pay?" *Business Week* (February 1, 1993), pp. 30–31; "What's Up Doc?" *U.S. News & World Report* (April 12, 1993), pp. 26–29; Richard A. Spinello, "Ethics, Pricing, and the Pharmaceutical Industry," *Journal of Business Ethics* (August 1992), pp. 617–26; "The Big Pill," *The Economist* (March 6, 1993), p. 67; and

Shawn Tully, "Why Drug Prices Will Go Lower," *Fortune* (May 3, 1993), pp. 56–66.

CHAPTER 5

1. James Pollock, "The Taste of Success," *Marketing* (January 23, 1995), pp. 11, 13.
2. These estimates are based on statistics reported in *International Financial Statistics Yearbook* (New York: International Monetary Fund, 1995) and trend projections by the authors.
3. "Regionalism in World Trade: The End of an Era?" *The Economist* (March 25, 1995), p. 66.
4. Nathaniel Gilbert, "A Case for Countertrade," *Across the Board* (May 1992), pp. 43–45; and E. Amann and D. Marin, "Risk-Sharing in International Trade: An Analysis of Countertrade," *The Journal of Industrial Economics* (March 1993), pp. 63–77.
5. Statistics Canada, CANSIM matrix 6627; and cat. 65-001 (Ottawa, 1997).
6. Michael E. Porter, *The Competitive Advantage of Nations* (New York: The Free Press, 1990), pp. 577–615; and Michael E. Porter, "Why Nations Triumph," *Fortune* (March 12, 1990), pp. 94–108.
7. "Japan's Price of Protection," *Fortune* (March 6, 1995), p. 48.
8. "A Survey of Multinationals," *The Economist,* Special Report (June 24, 1995).
9. For a concise overview of the WTO, see Philip R. Cateora, *International Marketing,* 9th ed. (Chicago, IL: Richard D. Irwin, 1996), pp. 51–53.
10. "The EU Goes Cold on Enlargement," *The Economist* (October 28, 1995), pp. 57–58.
11. For a comprehensive report on strategy for the European Union, see Colin Egan and Peter McKiernan, *Inside Fortress Europe: Strategies for the Single Market* (Reading, MA: Addison-Wesley, 1994).
12. "Asia, Par for the Course," *The Economist* (December 16, 1995), pp. 31–32.
13. "Kimberly-Clark and P&G Face Global Warfare," *The Wall Street Journal* (July 18, 1995), pp. B1, B6; and "Coca-Cola Still in India Despite Fight from Pepsi," *Advertising Age* (July 18, 1994), pp. I-1, I-4.
14. "Spoon-to-Spoon Combat Overseas," *The New York Times* (January 1, 1995), p. 17.
15. For an overview of different types of global companies and marketing strategies, see Warren J. Keegan, *Global Marketing Management,* 5th ed. (Englewood Cliffs, NJ: Prentice Hall, 1995), pp. 43–54.
16. "The Avon Lady of the Amazon," *Business Week* (October 24, 1994), pp. 93–94.
17. E. S. Browning, "In Pursuit of the Elusive Euroconsumer," *The Wall Street Journal* (April 23, 1992), pp. B1, B3; and "Global Campaigns Don't Work; Multinationals Do," *Advertising Age* (April 18, 1994), p. 23.
18. "Ford: Alex Trotman's Daring Global Strategy," *Business Week* (April 3, 1995), pp. 94–104.
19. For an extensive discussion on identifying global consumers, see Jean-Pierre Jeannet and H. David Hennessey, *Global Marketing Strategies,* 3rd ed. (Boston, MA: Houghton Mifflin Company, 1995), pp. 236–39.
20. Chip Walker, "The Global Middle Class," *American Demographics* (September 1995), pp. 40–47; William Echikson, "Luxury Steals Back," *Fortune* (January 16, 1995), pp. 112–19; Ricardo Sookdeo, "The New Global Consumer," *Fortune* (Autumn–Winter 1993), pp. 68–72.
21. Chip Walker, "Can TV Save the Planet?" *American Demographics* (May 1996), pp. 42–49; "Teens Seen as the First Truly Global Consumers," *Marketing News* (March 27, 1995), p. 9; John Greenwald, "No Passage to India," *Time* (September 18, 1995), pp. 91–92; "Rock Around the World," *Newsweek* (April 24, 1995), p. 65.
22. For an extended discussion on cross-cultural analysis, see Vern Terpstra and Kenneth David, *The Cultural Environment of International Business,* 3rd ed. (Cincinnati, OH: South-Western Publishing, 1991).
23. These examples are adapted from Terpstra and David; "In India, Beef-Free Mickey D.", *Business Week* (April 17, 1995), p. 52; and "After Early Stumbles, P&G Is Making Inroads Overseas," *The Wall Street Journal* (February 6, 1989), p. B1.
24. Louis Kraar, "Meet 25 People You Ought to Know," *Fortune,* Pacific Rim Special Issue (Fall 1989), p. 108; and Susan Feyder, "In 3M's Eyes, All the World's a Market," *Minneapolis Star Tribune* (April 16, 1990), pp. 1D, 7D.
25. See Terpstra and David, "Beef Free Mickey D."; and "Valentine's Day in Japan: Ladies Don't Expect a Gift," *The Christian Science Monitor* (February 13, 1989), p. 6.
26. Roger E. Axtell, *Do's and Taboos Around the World,* compiled by the Packer Penn Company (New York: John Wiley and Sons, 1985).
27. "Greeks Protest Coke's Use of Parthenon," *Dallas Morning News* (August 17, 1992), p. D4.
28. For a comprehensive review of research on country-of-origin effects, see Saeed Samiee, "Customer Evaluation of Products in a Global Market," *Journal of International Business Studies,* third quarter, 1994, pp. 579–604.
29. These examples are adapted from Terpstra and David, "Beef Free Mickey D.", p. 21; David A. Ricks, "Products that Crashed into the Language Barrier," *Business and Society Review* (Spring 1983), pp. 46–50.
30. "Global Thinking Paces Computer Biz," *Advertising Age* (March 6, 1995), p. 10.
31. Terrence A. Shimp and Subhash Sharma, "Consumer Ethnocentrism: Construction and Validation of the CETSCALE," *Journal of Marketing Research* (August 1987), pp. 280–89.
32. Nancy Giges, "Europeans Buy Outside Goods, But Like Local Ads," *Advertising Age* (April 27, 1992), pp. I-1, I-26.
33. This example is based on Shawn Tully, "Nestlé Shows How to Gobble Markets," *Fortune* (January 16, 1989), pp. 74–78; "Global Coffee Market Share Comparisons," *Advertising Age* (December 10, 1995), p. 47; and Carla Rapoport, "Nestlé's Brand Building Machine," *Fortune* (September 19, 1995), pp. 147–56.
34. "Finding the Next Japan," *Sales & Marketing Management* (August 19, 1995), p. 83.
35. "Selling in Russia: The March on Moscow," *The Economist* (March 18, 1995), pp. 65–66.
36. Carole Howard, "*Reader's Digest* Meets Eastern Europe," *Express Magazine* (Summer 1992), pp. 28–31.
37. "Selling in Russia: The March on Moscow."
38. This discussion is based on "Multinationals in Vietnam," *The Economist* (December 9, 1995), pp. 63–64; Bill Saporito, "Where the Global Action Is," *Fortune* (Autumn/Winter 1993), pp. 63–65; and Walker, "The Global Middle Class."
39. Cateora, *International Marketing,* p. 560.
40. This discussion is based on "Why Japanese Deregulation Won't Much Help America," *Business Week* (April 3, 1995), p. 72; "EC Vote May Threaten Ads Aimed at Kids," *Advertising Age* (December 11, 1995), p. 4; "Japan's Big Problem: Freeing Its Economy from Over-Regulation," *The Wall Street Journal* (April 25, 1995), pp. A1, A6; and "Euro Telemarketing in Trouble," *Advertising Age* (November 27, 1995), p. 4.
41. For an extensive discussion on ISO 9000, see H. Michael Hayes, "ISO 9000: The New Strategic Consideration," *Business Horizons* (May–June 1994), pp. 52–60.
42. For an extensive examination of these market entry options, see Cateora, *International Marketing,* pp. 340–345; Keegan, *Global Marketing Management,* pp. 351–59; and Jeannet and Hennessey, *Global Marketing Strategies,* pp. 296–316. See also Krishna M. Erramilli and C. P. Rao, "Service Firms' International Entry-Mode Choice: A Modified Transaction-Cost Analysis," *Journal of Marketing* (July 1993), pp. 19–38; and Franklin R. Root, *Entry Strategies for International Markets* (Lexington, MA: D. C. Heath, 1994).
43. Martin Knelman, "Mickey on the Road to Avonlea," *The Financial Post Magazine* (March 1996), pp. 22–28.
44. Andrew E. Serwer, "McDonald's Conquers the World," *Fortune* (October 17, 1994), pp. 103–16.
45. Cateora, *International Marketing,* p. 480.
46. "From Cookies to Appliances, Pan-Euro Efforts Build," *Advertising Age* (June 22, 1992), pp. I-1, I-29. See also, "Can the Queen of Cosmetics Keep Her Crown?" *Business Week* (January 17, 1994), pp. 90–91.
47. This discussion is based on John Fahy and Fuyuki Taguchi, "Reassessing the Japanese Distribution System," *Sloan Management Review* (Winter 1995), pp. 49–61.
48. For an excellent treatment on global pricing, see S. Tamer Cavugil, "Unraveling the Mystique of Export Pricing," in Sidney J. Levy et al., eds., *Marketing Manager's Handbook,* 3rd ed. (New York: The Dartnell Corporation, 1994), pp. 1356–74.
49. Cateora, *International Marketing,* pp. 552–55.

The Coca-Cola Company: Japan: This case was prepared by Roger A. Kerin. Sources: The Coca-Cola Company 1994 *Annual Report,* p. 29; "We Got the Achtung Baby," *Brandweek* (January 18, 1993), pp. 23–26; and "Cola War Bubbles in Japan," *Advertising Age* (March 23, 1992), p. 4.

CHAPTER 6

1. Warren Brown, "Meet the Beetle," *Maine Sunday Telegram* (June 22, 1997), pp. F1–F2; "Automotive Marketing," *Advertising Age* (April 3, 1995), p. S2; and "Auto Update," *Better Homes and Gardens* (May 1995), p. 230.

2. James F. Engel, Roger D. Blackwell, and Paul Miniard, *Consumer Behavior,* 8th ed. (Fort Worth, TX: Dryden Press, 1995), p. 176. See also Gordon C. Bruner III and Richard J. Pomazal, "Problem Recognition: The Crucial First Stage of the Consumer Decision Process," *Journal of Consumer Marketing* (Winter 1988), pp. 53–63.

3. For thorough descriptions of consumer experience and expertise, see Stephen J. Hoch and John Deighton, "Managing What Consumers Learn from Experience," *Journal of Marketing* (April 1989), pp. 1–20; and Joseph W. Alba and J. Wesley Hutchinson, "Dimensions of Consumer Expertise," *Journal of Consumer Research* (March 1987), pp. 411–54.

4. Julie L. Ozanne, Merrie Brucks, and Druv Grewal, "A Study of Information Search Behavior during the Categorization of New Products," *Journal of Consumer Research* (March 1992), pp. 452–63.

5. "CD Players," *Consumer Reports* (March 1995), p. 204.

6. F. G. Crane and T. K. Clarke, *Consumer Behaviour in Canada: Theory and Practice,* 2nd ed. (Toronto: Dryden, 1994), pp. 26–28.

7. For an extended discussion on why consumers postpone decisions, see Eric A. Greenleaf and Donald R. Lehman, "Reasons for Substantial Delay in Consumer Decision Making," *Journal of Consumer Research* (September 1995), pp. 186–99.

8. Ruth N. Bolton and James H. Drew, "A Multistage Model of Customers' Assessments of Service Quality and Value," *Journal of Consumer Research* (March 1991), pp. 376–84.

9. See Chip Walker, "Word of Mouth," *American Demographics* (July 1995), pp. 38–45.

10. Rahul Jacob, "The Struggle to Create an Organization for the 21st Century," *Fortune* (April 3, 1995); and John E. G. Bateson, *Managing Services Marketing* (Fort Worth, TX: Dryden, 1995).

11. Steven E. Prokesch, "Competing on Customer Service: An Interview with British Airways' Sir Colin Marshall," *Harvard Business Review* (November–December 1995).

12. For a discussion on customer retention strategies see John E. G. Bateson, *Managing Services Marketing;* and Janis L. Miller, Larry Fredendall, and J. Wayne Patterson, "A Markov Analysis of Customer Retention and Recruitment," *Journal of Customer Service in Marketing and Management,* vol. 3, no. 2 (1997), pp. 35–53.

13. Many different definitions and perspectives on involvement exist. See, for example, Judith Lynne Zaichkosky, "The Personal Involvement Inventory: Reduction, Revision, and Applications to Advertising," *Journal of Advertising Research* (December 1994), pp. 59–70; and Crane and Clarke, *Consumer Behaviour in Canada,* pp. 375–401.

14. J. Paul Peter and Jerry C. Olson, *Consumer Behavior: Marketing Strategy Perspectives,* 4th ed. (Homewood, IL: Richard D. Irwin, 1996), p. 101; Del Hawkins, Roger J. Best, and Kenneth J. Coney, *Consumer Behavior: Implications for Marketing Strategy,* 6th ed. (Homewood, IL: Richard D. Irwin, 1995), pp. 423–26; and Engel, Blackwell, and Miniard, *Consumer Behavior,* pp. 164–66.

15. Russell Belk, "Situational Variables and Consumer Behavior," *Journal of Consumer Research* (December 1975); and Crane and Clarke, *Consumer Behaviour in Canada,* pp. 403–423.

16. K. H. Chung, *Motivational Theories and Practices* (Columbus, OH: Grid, 1977). See also A. H. Maslow, *Motivation and Personality* (New York: Harper & Row, 1970).

17. Arthur Koponen, "The Personality Characteristics of Purchases," *Journal of Advertising Research* (September 1960), pp. 89–92; Joel B. Cohen, "An Interpersonal Orientation to the Study of Consumer Behavior," *Journal of Marketing Research* (August 1967), pp. 270–78; and Rena Bartos, *Marketing to Women Around the World* (Cambridge, MA: Harvard Business School, 1989).

18. Terry Clark, "International Marketing and National Character: A Review and Proposal for an Integrative Theory," *Journal of Marketing* (October 1990), pp. 66–79. For a discussion on Canadians' reputation for being mild-mannered see Michael MacDonald, "Canadian Managers Lack Aggressiveness, Survey of CEOs Says," *The Chronicle Herald* (July 15, 1997), p. C6.

19. J. Neher, "Toro Cutting a Wide Swath in Outdoor Appliances Marketing," *Advertising Age* (February 25, 1979), p. 21.

20. For further reading on subliminal perception, see Dennis L. Rosen and Surendra N. Singh, "An Investigation of Subliminal Embed Effect on Multiple Measures of Advertising Effectiveness," *Psychology & Marketing* (March/April 1992), pp. 157–73; and Kathryn T. Theus, "Subliminal Advertising and the Psychology of Processing Unconscious Stimuli: A Review of Research," *Psychology & Marketing* (May/June 1994), pp. 271–90.

21. "Dr. Feelgood Goes Subliminal," *Business Week* (November 6, 1995), p. 6; and Michael R. Soloman, *Consumer Behavior,* 3rd ed. (Englewood Cliffs, NJ: Prentice Hall, 1996), pp. 68–72.

22. Ronald Alsop, "Brand Loyalty Is Rarely Blind Loyalty," *The Wall Street Journal* (October 19, 1989), p. B1; and *Brand-Driven Marketers Are Beating Themselves in the War Against Price-Based and Private Label Competition* (New York: Bates USA, 1994); and Jo Marney, "Building Splurchases," *Marketing* (January 27, 1997)—www.marketingmag.ca, July 18, 1997.

23. Gordon Allport, "Attitudes," in Martin Fishbein, ed., *Readings in Attitude Theory and Measurement* (New York: John Wiley & Sons, 1968), p. 3.

24. Hawkins, Best, and Coney, *Consumer Behavior,* pp. 364–65; See also Richard J. Lutz, "Changing Brand Attitudes through Modification of Cognitive Structure," *Journal of Consumer Research,* vol. 2 (1975), pp. 49–59.

25. "Pepsi's Gamble Hits Freshness Dating Jackpot," *Advertising Age* (September 19, 1994), p. 50.

26. For an extended discussion of self-concept, see M. Joseph Sirgy, "Self-Concept in Consumer Behavior: A Critical Review," *Journal of Consumer Research* (December 1982), pp. 287–300. For a broader perspective, see Russell Belk, "Possessions and the Extended Self," *Journal of Consumer Research* (September 1988), pp. 139–68.

27. This description of the VALS Program is based on Judith Waldrop, "Markets with Attitude," *American Demographics* (July 1994), pp. 22–32; *The VALS 2 Segmentation System* (Menlo Park, CA: SRI International, 1989); Martha Richie, "Psychographics for the 1990s," *American Demographics* (July 1989), pp. 25–31, 53; and "SRI's New Psychographic Typology Reasserts Old Stereotypes of Aging," *Maturity Market Perspective* (September/October 1989), pp. 1, 6.

28. Adapted from *The Goldfarb Segments: A Marketing Tool* (Toronto: Goldfarb Consultants, March 1992).

29. See, for example, Lawrence F. Feick and Linda Price, "The Market Maven: A Diffuser of Marketplace Information," *Journal of Marketing* 51 (January 1987), pp. 83–97; and Peter H. Block, "The Product Enthusiast: Implications for Marketing Strategy," *Journal of Consumer Marketing* 3 (Summer 1986), pp. 51–61.

30. "Maximizing the Market with Influentials," *American Demographics* (July 1995), p. 42.

31. "Put People Behind the Wheel," *Advertising Age* (March 22, 1993), p. S-28.

32. F. G. Crane and T. K. Clarke, "The Identification of Evaluative Criteria and Cues Used in Selecting Services," *Journal of Services Marketing* (Spring 1988), pp. 53–59.

33. Representative work on positive and negative word of mouth can be found in Jacqueline Brown and Peter H. Reingen, "Social Ties and Word-of-Mouth Referral Behavior," *Journal of Consumer Research* (December 1987), pp. 350–62; and Marc Weinberger and Jean B. Romeo, "The Impact of Negative Product News," *Business Horizons* (January–February 1989), pp. 44–50.

34. "Pork Rumors Vex Indonesia," *Advertising Age* (February 16, 1989), p. 36.

35. John C. Mowen, *Consumer Behavior,* 2nd ed. (New York: MacMillan, 1990), pp. 464–65.

36. William O. Beardon and Michael G. Etzel, "Reference Group Influence on Product and Brand Choice," *Journal of Consumer Research* (September 1982), pp. 183–94; and Terry L. Childers and Akshay R. Rao, "The Influence of Familial and Peer-based Reference Groups on Consumer Decisions," *Journal of Consumer Research* (September 1992), pp. 198–211.

37. "Honda Revs Up a Hip Cycle Campaign," *The Wall Street Journal* (July 31, 1989), p. B1.

38. For an extended discussion on consumer socialization, see George P. Moschis, *Consumer Socialization* (Lexington, MA: Lexington Books, 1987). See also Laura A. Peracchio, "How Do Young Children Learn to Be Consumers? A Script-Processing Approach," *Journal of Consumer Research* (March 1992), pp. 425–40.

39. "How Children Decide on Gifts They Want, and Plot to Get Them," *The Wall Street Journal* (December 23, 1993), pp. A1, A5.

40. This discussion is based on Robert E. Wilkes, "Household Life-Cycle Stages, Transitions, and Product Expenditures," *Journal of Consumer Research* (June 1995), pp. 27–42; and Patrick E. Murphy and William A. Staples, "A Modernized Family Life Cycle," *Journal of Consumer Research* (June 1979), pp. 12–22.

41. "What's Good for the Goose May Gag the Gander," *American Demographics* (May 1994), pp. 15–16; and Diane Crispell, "Dual-Earner Diversity," *American Demographics* (July 1995), pp. 32–36.

42. For a discussion of social class in Canada see Crane and Clarke, pp. 127–49.

43. Milton Yinger, "Ethnicity," *Annual Review of Sociology* (1985), pp. 151–80.

44. Francois Vary, "Quebec Consumer Has Unique Buying Habits," *Marketing* (March 23, 1992), p. 28; Louise Gagnon, "Metro Plays to Decline in Impulse Purchases," *Marketing* (May 12, 1997)—www.marketingmag.ca, July 20, 1997; Louise Gagnon, "Eaton's Quebec Ads Target Hip Shoppers," *Marketing* (June 16, 1997)—www.marketingmag.ca, July 18, 1997; Louise Gagnon, "Price Cuts Escalate Beer Battle," *Marketing* (June 30, 1997)—www.marketingmag.ca, July 17, 1997.

45. Louise Gagnon, "Same Butter, Different Sell," *Marketing* (June 30, 1997)—www.marketingmag.ca, July 17, 1997.

46. Ann Boden, "Aiming at the Right Target," *Marketing* (January 28, 1991), p. 6.

Three Sisters Cafe: This case was prepared by Frederick G. Crane.

CHAPTER 7

1. Interview courtesy of Steve Whitacer, Honeywell, MICRO SWITCH Division.

2. Peter LaPlaca, "From the Editor," *Journal of Business and Industrial Marketing* (Summer 1992), p. 3.

3. Peter LaPlaca, "From the Editor," *Journal of Business and Industrial Marketing* (Winter 1988), p. 3.

4. "FAA Announces Contract for New Workstations," *Dallas Morning News* (April 30, 1995), p. 16H.

5. This discussion is based on *The Federal Register,* "Economic Classification Policy Committee: Standard Industrial Classification Replacement—The North American Industry Classification System Proposed Industry Classification Structure" (Washington, DC: Office of Management and Budget, July 26, 1995).

6. An argument that consumer buying and organizational buying do not have important differences is found in Edward F. Fern and James R. Brown, "The Industrial/Consumer Marketing Dichotomy: A Case of Insufficient Justification," *Journal of Marketing* (Spring 1984), pp. 68–77. However, most writers on the subject do draw distinctions between the two types of buying. See, for example, Michael D. Hutt and Thomas W. Speh, *Business Marketing Management,* 5th ed. (Ft. Worth, TX: The Dryden Press, 1995); and V. Kasturi Rangun, Benson P. Shapiro, and Rowland T. Moriarity, Jr., *Business Marketing Strategy* (Chicago, IL: Richard D. Irwin, 1995).

7. This discussion is based on Robert E. Reeder, Edward G. Brierty, and Betty Reeder, *Industrial Marketing,* 2nd ed. (Englewood Cliffs, NJ: Prentice Hall, 1991); Robert W. Eckles, *Business Marketing Management* (Englewood Cliffs, NJ: Prentice Hall, 1990); Frank G. Bingham, Jr., and Barney T. Raffield III, *Business to Business Marketing Management* (Homewood, IL: Richard D. Irwin, 1990); and Robert W. Haas, *Business Marketing Management* (Boston: PWS-Kent Publishing Company, 1992).

8. Based on "The I-Way Will Be Paved with Silicon," *Business Week* (January 9, 1995), p. 77; and *1995 U.S. Industrial Outlook* (Washington, DC: US Department of Commerce, January 1995).

9. For a study of buying criteria used by industrial firms, see Daniel H. McQuiston and Rockney G. Walters, "The Evaluative Criteria of Industrial Buyers: Implications for Sales Training," *Journal of Business & Industrial Marketing* (Summer/Fall 1989), pp. 65–75. See also "What Buyers Look For," *Sales & Marketing Management* (August 1995), p. 31.

10. David L. Blenkhorn and Peter M. Banting, "How Reverse Marketing Changes Buyer-Seller Roles," *Industrial Marketing Management* (August 1991), pp. 185–90; and Michael R. Leenders and David L. Blenkhorn, *Reverse Marketing: The New Buyer-Supplier Relationship* (New York: The Free Press, 1988).

11. David Woodruff and Karen Lowry Miller, "Chrysler's Neon," *Business Week* (May 3, 1993), p. 119.

12. Richard N. Cardozo, Shannon H. Shipp, and Kenneth Roering, "Proactive Strategic Partnerships: A New Business Markets Strategy," *Journal of Business & Industrial Marketing* (Winter 1992), pp. 51–63.

13. For a discussion of JIT, see Gary L. Frazier, Robert E. Spekman, and Charles R. O'Neal, "Just-in-Time Exchange Relationships in Industrial Markets," *Journal of Marketing* (October 1988), pp. 52–67; Paul A. Dion, Peter M. Banting, and Loretta M. Hasey, "The Impact of JIT on Industrial Marketers," *Industrial Marketing Management* (February 1990), pp. 41–46; and Steve McDaniel, Joseph G. Ormsby, and Alicia Gresham, "The Effect of JIT on Distributors," *Industrial Marketing Management* (May 1992), pp. 145–49.

14. Shirley Cayer, "Welcome to Caterpillar's Quality Institute," *Purchasing* (August 16, 1990), pp. 81–84.

15. *The Financial Post Magazine* (March 1996), p. 60.

16. Mary C. LaForge and Louis H. Stone, "An Analysis of the Industrial Buying Process by Means of Buying Center Communications," *Journal of Business & Industrial Marketing* (Winter/Spring 1989), pp. 29–36.

17. "$35 Million Machine: Wires not Included," *Newsweek* (April 15, 1995), p. 25.

18. Bingham and Raffield III, p. 11.

19. This discussion is based on N. Craig Smith and John A. Quelch, *Ethics in Marketing* (Homewood, IL: Richard D. Irwin, 1993), p. 796; Nathaniel Gilbert, "The Case for Countertrade," *Across the Board* (May 1992), pp. 43–45; Alan J. Dubinsky, Marvin A. Jolson, Masaaki Kotobe, and Chae Un Lim," A Cross-National Investigation of Industrial Salespeople's Ethical Perceptions," *Journal of International Business Studies* (Fourth Quarter 1991), pp. 651–70; and Jacob Schlesinger, "Fenced Out," *The Wall Street Journal* (June 10, 1993), pp. A1, A9.

20. Pratibha A. Dabholkar, Wesley J. Johnston, and Amy S. Cathey, "The Dynamics of Long-Term Business-to-Business Exchange Relationships," *Journal of the Academy of Marketing Science,* vol. 22, (1994), pp. 130–45.

21. "Boeing Receives a Key Order for Airliners," *The Wall Street Journal* (March 15, 1995), pp. A3, A10.

22. This discussion is based on Robert D. Buzzell and Gwen Ortmeyer, "Channel Partnerships Streamline Distribution," *Sloan Management Review* (Spring 1995), pp. 85–96; James C. Anderson and James A. Narus, "Partnering as a Focused Market Strategy," in *Marketing Manager's Handbook,* 3rd ed. Sidney J. Levy, George R. Frerichs, and Howard L. Gordon, eds. (Chicago: The Dartnell Corporation, 1994); Paul A. Herbig and Bradley S. O'Hara, "The Future of Original Equipment Manufacturers," *Journal of Business and Industrial Marketing,* vol. 9, (1994), pp. 38–43; and Donald G. Norris, "Intel Inside," *Journal of Business & Industrial Marketing,* vol. 8, (1993), pp. 14–24.

23. Thomas V. Bonoma, "Major Sales: Who Really Does the Buying?" *Harvard Business Review* (May–June 1982), pp. 111–19. For recent work on buying groups, see Ajay Kohli, "Determinants of Influence in Organizational Buying: A Contingency Approach," *Journal of Marketing* (July 1989), pp. 50–65; and John R. Ronchetto, Jr., Michael D. Hutt, and Peter H. Reingen, "Embedded Influence Patterns in Organizational Buying Systems," *Journal of Marketing* (October 1989), pp. 51–62.

24. Carl R. Ruthstrom and Ken Matejka, "The Meaning of 'Yes' in the Far East," *Industrial Marketing Management,* vol. 19 (1990), pp. 191–92; John L. Graham and Yoshihiro Sano, "Across the Negotiating Table from the Japanese," *International Marketing Review* (Autumn 1986), pp. 58–71; and Peter Banting, Jozsef Beracs, and Andrew Gross, "The Industrial Buying Process in Capitalist and Socialist Countries," *Industrial Marketing Management* (May 1991), pp. 105–13.

25. Julia M. Bristor, "Influence Strategies in Organizational Buying: The Importance of Connections to the Right People in the Right Places," *Journal of Business-to-Business Marketing,* vol. 1 (1993), pp. 63–98; and Herbert E. Brown and Roger W. Brucker, "Charting the Industrial Buying Stream," *Industrial Marketing Management* (February 1990), pp. 55–61.

26. Based on an interview with Steve Whitacer, Honeywell, MICRO SWITCH Division.

27. These definitions are adapted from Frederick E. Webster, Jr., and Yoram Wind, *Organizational Buying Behavior* (Englewood Cliffs, NJ: Prentice Hall, 1972), p. 6.

28. For an extensive description of 18 industrial purchases, see Arch G. Woodside and Nyren Vyas, *Industrial Purchasing Strategies: Recommendations for Purchasing and Marketing Managers* (Lexington, Mass.: Lexington Books, 1987); see also Joseph A. Bellizzi, "Business-to-Business Selling and the Organizational Buying Process," in *Marketing Manager's Handbook,* 3rd ed., Sidney J. Levy, George R. Frerichs, and Howard L. Gordon, eds. (Chicago, IL: The Dartnell Corporation, 1994).

29. For insights into buying industrial services, see James R. Stock and Paul H. Zinszer, "The Industrial Purchase Decision for Professional Services," *Journal of Business Research* (February 1987), pp. 1–16; and Ralph W. Jackson, Lester A. Neidell, and Dale A. Lunsford, "An Empirical Investigation of Differences in Goods and Services as Perceived by Organizational Buyers," *Industrial Marketing Management,* vol. 24 (1995), pp. 99–108.

30. Patrick J. Robinson, Charles W. Faris, and Yoram Wind, *Industrial Buying and Creative Marketing* (Boston, MA: Allyn & Bacon, 1967).

31. Recent studies on the buy-class framework that document its usefulness include Erin Anderson, Wujin Chu, and Barton Weitz, "Industrial Purchasing: An Empirical Exploration of the Buy-Class Framework,"

Journal of Marketing (July 1987), pp. 71–86; Morry Ghingold, "Testing the 'Buy-Grid' Buying Process Model," *Journal of Purchasing and Materials Management* (Winter 1986), pp. 30–36; P. Matthyssens and W. Faes, "OEM Buying Process for New Components: Purchasing and Marketing Implications," *Industrial Marketing Management* (August 1985), pp. 145–57; and Thomas W. Leigh and Arno J. Rethans, "A Script-Theoretic Analysis of Industrial Purchasing Behavior," *Journal of Marketing* (Fall 1984), pp. 22–32. Studies not supporting the buy-class framework include Joseph A. Bellizi and Philip McVey, "How Valid Is the Buy-Grid Model?" *Industrial Marketing Management* (February 1983), pp. 57–62; and Donald W. Jackson, Janet E. Keith, and Richard K. Burdick, "Purchasing Agents' Perceptions of Industrial Buying Center Influences: A Situational Approach," *Journal of Marketing* (Fall 1984), pp. 75–83.

32. See, for example, R. Venkatesh, Ajay Kohli, and Gerald Zaltman, "Influence Strategies in Buying Centers," *Journal of Marketing* (October 1995), pp. 61–72; Gary L. Lilien and Anthony Wong, "An Exploratory Investigation of the Structure of the Buying Center in the Metal Working Industry," *Journal of Marketing Research* (February 1984), pp. 1–11; and Wesley J. Johnston and Thomas V. Bonoma, "The Buying Center: Structure and Interaction Patterns," *Journal of Marketing* (Summer 1981), pp. 143–56. See also Christopher P. Puto, Wesley E. Patton III, and Ronald H. King, "Risk Handling Strategies in Industrial Vendor Selection Decisions," *Journal of Marketing* (Winter 1985), pp. 89–98.

Energy Performance Systems, Inc.: This case was written by William Rudelius. Sources: Personal interviews with L. David Ostlie, Tom Kroll, and Paul Helgeson.

CHAPTER 8

1. Brent Schlender, "Steve Jobs' Amazing Movie Adventure," *Fortune* (September 18, 1995), pp. 155–72; and Ronald Grover, "This Movie Winds Up Old Favorites," *Time* (November 20, 1995), p. 8.
2. Ivor Davis, "Costner Braces for Opening of Notorious 'Waterworld'," *Star Tribune* (July 23, 1995), p. F3.
3. Thomas R. King, "How Big Will Disney's 'Pocahontas' Be?" *The Wall Street Journal* (May 15, 1995), pp. B1, B8.
4. Richard Turner and John R. Emshwiller, "Movie-Research Czar Is Said by Some to Sell Manipulated Findings," *The Wall Street Journal* (December 17, 1993), p. A1.
5. Helene Diamond, "Lights, Camera . . . Research!" *Marketing News* (September 11, 1989), pp. 10–11; and "Killer!" *Time* (November 16, 1987), pp. 72–79.
6. Thomas R. King, "Sad Endings: How Sure-Fire Films Flopped," *The Wall Street Journal* (February 15, 1995), pp. B1, B8.
7. "New Marketing Research Definition Approved," *Marketing News* (January 2, 1987), pp. 72–79; for a discussion of the marketing research process see Robert E. Stevens, Bruce Wrenn, Morris E. Ruddick, and Philip K. Sherwood, *The Marketing Research Guide* (New York: The Haworth Press Inc., 1997).
8. Joseph Pereira, "Unknown Fruit Takes on Unfamiliar Markets," *The Wall Street Journal* (September 9, 1995), pp. B1, B5.
9. Cyndee Miller, "Kiddi Just Fine in the U.K., But Here It's Binky," *Marketing News* (August 28, 1995), p. 8.
10. Scott B. Dacko, "Data Collection Should not Be Manual Labor," *Marketing News* (August 28, 1995), p. 31.
11. Dale Burger, "Pushing Creativity to the Limit," *Computing Canada* (May 24, 1995), p. 37.
12. Ken Riddell, "Shoppers Adds Life to Pop Market," *Marketing* (July 26, 1993), p. 2.
13. Kenneth Wylie, "Special Report: Eager Marketers Driving New Globalism," *Advertising Age* (October 30, 1995), pp. 28–29.
14. Patrick E. Murphy and Gene R. Laczniak, "Emerging Ethical Issues Facing Marketing Researchers," *Marketing Research* (June 1992), pp. 6–11.
15. Adapted from Donald S. Tull and Del I. Hawkins, *Marketing Research: Measurement and Method*, 5th ed. (New York: Macmillan Publishing Company, 1990), Chap. 23.
16. Larry Percy, *Marketing Research That Pays Off* (New York: The Haworth Press Inc., 1997).
17. Lesley Dow, "Success Insurance," *Marketing* (July 17, 1997)—www.marketingmag.ca, July 17, 1997.

Bookworms, Inc.: This case was prepared by James E. Nelson.

CHAPTER 9

1. Kenneth Labich, "Nike vs. Reebok: A Battle for Hearts, Minds, and Feet," *Fortune* (September 18, 1995), p. 90–106.
2. Labich, "Nike vs. Reebok," pp. 90–106; and Geoffrey Smith, "Sneakers That Jump into the Past," *Business Week* (March 13, 1995), p. 71.
3. Dennis J. Cahill, *Strategic Segmentation and Target Marketing* (New York: The Haworth Press Inc., 1997).
4. Example supplied by Allison Scoleri, Goldfarb Consultants, Toronto, March 10, 1992.
5. James Pollock, "Ault Whips Up the Dairy Industry with PurFiltre," *Marketing* (March 13, 1995), p. 2.
6. For a discussion of the business travel segment see Sanjay S. Mehta and Gurinderjit B. Mehta, "Development and Growth of the Business Class: Strategic Marketing Implications for the Airline Industry," *Journal of Customer Service in Marketing and Management*, vol. 3, no. 1 (1997), pp. 59–78.
7. Doug McCuaig and Christopher Holt, "Getting Intimate with Customers," *Marketing* (July 14, 1997)—www.marketingmag.ca, July 17, 1997.
8. Jim Carlton, "Apple's Choice: Preserve Profits or Cut Prices," *The Wall Street Journal* (February 22, 1995), pp. B1, B4.
9. Kathy Rebello, "Apple's Assault," *Business Week* (June 12, 1995), pp. 98–99.
10. Peter Burows and Kathy Rebello, "Is Spindler a Survivor?" *Business Week* (October 2, 1995), p. 62.
11. Jim Carlton, "What's Eating Apple? Computer Maker Hits Some Serious Snags," *The Wall Street Journal* (September 21, 1995), pp. A1, A8; Julie Pitta, "Apple Braces for Windows 95," *Star Tribune* (September 17, 1995), p. 5D; and Jim Carlton, "Apple's Net Fell 48% in 4th Quarter as Computer Shortages Hurt Results," *The Wall Street Journal* (October 19, 1995), p. B10.
12. Jim Carlton, "Apple Is Facing Widespread Shortages of Its Products," *The Wall Street Journal* (August 11, 1995), p. B8.
13. Pitta, "Apple Braces for Windows 95," p. 5D.
14. Rebello, "Apple's Assault," p. 98.
15. Bart Ziegler, "PC Makers Big Push into the Home Market Comes at Risky Time," *The Wall Street Journal* (November 1, 1995), pp. A1, A13.
16. Advantages and disadvantages of cross tabulations are adapted from Roseann Maguire and Terry C. Wilson, "Banners or Cross Tabs? Before Deciding, Weigh Data-Format, Pros, Cons," *Marketing News* (May 13, 1983), pp. 10–11.
17. Andrew Purris, "Cheaper Can Be Better," *Time* (March 18, 1991), p. 70.
18. Alex Taylor III, "GM's $11,000,000,000 Turnaround," *Fortune* (October 17, 1994), pp. 54–74; David Woodruff and Mark Maremont, "GM Learns to Love an Outsider," *Business Week* (July 3, 1995), p. 32; Alex Taylor III, "GM: Some Gain, Much Pain," *Fortune* (May 29, 1995), pp. 78–84; Jesse Snyder, "4 GM Car Divisions Are Repositioned in an Effort to Help Sales," *Automotive News* (September 15, 1986), pp. 1, 49; and Joseph B. White, "GM Puts Low Price on Saturn to Sell in Small-Car Field," *The Wall Street Journal* (October 5, 1990), pp. B1, B6.
19. Gabriella Stern, "As Old Cadillac Buyers Age, the GM Division Fights to Halt Slippage," *The Wall Street Journal* (August 24, 1995), pp. A1, A9.

Cantel: This case was prepared by Frederick G. Crane.

CHAPTER 10

1. Raymond Serafin and Julie Ralston, "Jeep Sets Up Camp to Help Build Stronger Bonds with Owners," *Advertising Age* (June 26, 1995), p. 40; Don Peppers and Martha Rogers, "Ask the Marketing Doctors," *Inc.* (October 1995), pp. 68–70; Jonathan Berry, John Verity, Kathleen Kerwin, and Gail DeGeorge, "A Potent New Tool for Selling: Database Marketing," *Business Week* (September 5, 1994).
2. Adapted from David Shani and Sujana Chalasani, "Exploiting Niches Using Relationship Marketing," *Journal of Consumer Marketing* (Summer 1992), pp. 33–42.
3. Jeffrey F. Rayport and John J. Sviokla, "Exploiting the Virtual Value Chain," *Harvard Business Review* (November–December 1995), pp. 75–85; Robert Benjamin and Rolf Wigand, "Electronic Markets and Virtual Value Chains on the Information Superhighway," *Sloan Management Review* (Winter 1995), pp. 62–72; and Jeffrey F. Rayport and John J. Sviokla, "Managing in the Marketspace," *Harvard Business Review* (November–December 1994), pp. 141–50.
4. Bill Gates, *The Road Ahead* (New York: Viking, 1995); Gary McWilliams, "Small Fry Go Online," *Business Week* (November 20, 1995), pp. 158–64; and Rayport and Sviokla, "Exploiting the Virtual Value Chain."

5. Antonio Kovacevic and Nicolas Majluf, "Six Stages of IT Strategic Management," *Sloan Management Review* (Summer 1993), pp. 77–87.

6. This example is from *Canadian Advertising Success Stories* (Toronto: Canadian Congress of Advertising, 1995), p. 64.

7. Stan Sutter, "Winds of Change Blowing," *Marketing* (February 8, 1993), p. 14; and *Marketing* (June 28, 1993), p. 8.

8. Don Peppers and Martha Rogers, *The One to One Future: Building Relationships One Customer at a Time* (New York: Doubleday, 1993); and Frederick Newell, *The New Rules of Marketing* (Homewood, IL: Irwin/McGraw-Hill, 1997).

9. Mark Gleason, "Time to Perform or Perish," *Advertising Age* (October 2, 1995), p. 32; and Bradley Johnson, "Behind All the Hype Lies a Hidden, Crucial Asset," *Advertising Age* (October 2, 1995), pp. 30, 32.

10. Shelby D. Hunt and Robert M. Morgan, "Relationship Marketing in the Era of Network Competition," *Marketing Management* no. 1 (1994), pp. 19–27.

11. Faye Rice, "How to Deal with Tougher Customers," *Fortune* (December 3, 1990), pp. 39–48.

12. Mark Fawcett, "Getting with the Program," *The Financial Post Magazine* (March 1996), pp. 48–49, and p. 58.

13. Gary Levin, "Media Ads Blasted for Loss of Impact," *Advertising Age* (November 2, 1992), p. 14.

14. Frank V. Cespedes and H. Jeff Smith, "Database Marketing: New Rules for Policy and Practice," *Sloan Management Review* (Summer 1993), pp. 7–22.

15. Chad Rubel, "CD-ROM Takes a Back Seat to Other Tools," *Marketing News* (January 15, 1996), p. 10.

16. W. Steven Perkins and Ram C. Rao, "The Role of Experience in Information Use and Decision Making by Marketing Managers," *Journal of Marketing Research* (February 1990), pp. 1–10.

17. Regis McKenna, *Relationship Marketing* (Reading, MA: Addison-Wesley, 1991).

18. Richard S. Teitelbaum, "Reader's Digest: Are Times Tough? Here's an Answer," *Fortune* (December 2, 1991), pp. 101–02.

19. William Keenan, Jr., "Numbers Racket," *Sales and Marketing Management* (May 1995), pp. 64–76.

20. Statistics Canada, CANSIM matrices, 6367, 6379, on-line, December 4, 1997; and Retail Council of Canada, Toronto, 1997.

21. Doug McCuaig and Christopher Holt, "Getting Intimate with Customers," *Marketing* (July 14, 1997)—www.marketingmag.ca, July 17, 1997.

UPS: This case was prepared by Linda Rochford. Sources: Laurie M. Grossman, "Federal Express, UPS Face Off on Computers," *The Wall Street Journal* (September 17, 1993), pp. B1, B6; "UPS Awarded $1 Billion JC Penney Contract: Extends Partnership into Year 2000," UPS Home Page.

CHAPTER 11

1. Information supplied by Clearly Canadian Beverages (July 7, 1997).

2. Al Urbanski, "Floating a New Idea," *Food and Beverage Marketing* (June 1996), p. 25.

3. Information supplied by Clearly Canadian Beverages (July 7, 1997).

4. Definitions within this section are from Committee on Definitions, *Marketing Definitions: A Glossary of Marketing Terms* (Chicago: American Marketing Association, 1960).

5. Brenton R. Schlender, "How Sony Keeps the Magic Growing," *Fortune* (February 24, 1992), pp. 76–84.

6. Robert G. Cooper, *Winning at New Products,* 2nd ed. (Reading, MA: Addison-Wesley Publishing, 1993), pp. 49–66.

7. Atefeh Sadri McCampbell, "Strategy for New Product Development: How to Avoid Failures," *Journal of Customer Service in Marketing and Management,* vol. 3, no. 1 (1997), pp. 39–58.

8. Lesley Dow, "Pillsbury Turnover," *Marketing* (July 14, 1997)—www.marketingmag.ca, July 17, 1997.

9. Clare Ansberry, "Eastman Kodak Is Pulling Plug in Its UltraLife," *The Wall Street Journal* (April 10, 1990), p. B1, B2.

10. John Gilbert, "To Sell Cars in Japan, U.S. Needs to Offer More Right-Drive Models," *Star Tribune* (May 27, 1995), p. M1.

11. John Helyar, "Licensed Sports Gear Takes a Hit from Alienated Fans," *The Wall Street Journal* (February 23, 1995), pp. B1, B10.

12. James Walsh, "New Products Elbow for Space on Grocery Shelf," *Star Tribune* (June 7, 1995), p. T1.

13. Mikala Folb, "Black's Develops Net Photofinishing Offering," *Marketing* (June 16, 1997)—www.marketingmag.ca, July 17, 1997.

14. "They're Still Talkin' about 'Team Talk'," *3M Stemwinder* (May 17, 1995), pp. 1, 4.

15. Thomas M. Burton, "Drug Company Looks to 'Witch Doctors' to Conjure Products," *The Wall Street Journal* (July 7, 1994), pp. A1, A4; and letter from Professor Goran Hellekant, University of Wisconsin-Madison dated January 9, 1995.

16. William M. Bulkeley, "Scientists Try to Make Broccoli 'Fun'," *The Wall Street Journal* (July 17, 1995), pp. B1, B3.

17. Steve Alexander, "New Product Machine," *Star Tribune* (June 5, 1995), pp. 1D, 4D.

18. Don Clark, "Amid Hype and Fear, Microsoft Windows 95 Gets Ready to Roll," *The Wall Street Journal* (July 14, 1995), pp. A1, A4.

19. Stephanie Simon, "Imposter Merchandise," *Star Tribune* (July 7, 1995), p. 1D; and Anne O'Connor, "Investigators Wrinkle Plans of Clothing Counterfeiters," *Star Tribune* (August 4, 1995), p. 3B.

20. William M. Carley, "Engine Troubles Put GE Behind in Race to Power New 777s," *The Wall Street Journal* (July 12, 1995), pp. A1, A6.

21. Gabriella Stern, "GM Puts off Launch of Some Models," *The Wall Street Journal* (August 4, 1995), pp. A4, A12.

22. Atefeh Sadri McCampbell, "Strategy for New Product Development."

Orbitz: This case was prepared by Frederick G. Crane based on information supplied by Clearly Canadian Beverages.

CHAPTER 12

1. Bob Phillips, "When Alternative Becomes Mainstream," *Beverage Aisle* (July 1996), pp. 50–51; and Clearly Canadian Beverage Corporation's web site (www.orbitz.com, August 4, 1997).

2. For an extended discussion of the generalized product life cycle curve, see David M. Gardner, "Product Life Cycle: A Critical Look at the Literature," in Michael Houston, ed., *1987 Review of Marketing* (Chicago: American Marketing Association, 1987), pp. 162–94.

3. "The SunChip Also Rises," *Advertising Age* (April 27, 1992), p. S2, S6; "Gillette to Launch Women's Sensor," *Advertising Age* (February 10, 1992), p. 36.

4. Orville C. Walker, Jr., Harper W. Boyd, Jr., and Jean-Claude Larréché, *Marketing Strategy,* 2nd ed. (Chicago, IL: Richard D. Irwin, 1996), p. 215.

5. Portions of the discussion on the fax machine industry are based on "U.S. SemiCon Corporation: Facsimile Technology Program," in Roger A. Kerin and Robert A. Peterson, *Strategic Marketing Problems: Cases and Comments,* 7th ed. (New York: Prentice-Hall, Inc., 1995), pp. 454–67; "The Fax Gets a Face-Lift," *Business Week* (November 7, 1994), p. 15; and "Fax-on-Demand Grows," *ComputerWorld* (January 17, 1995), p. 59.

6. "Shocker at GM: People Like the Impact," *Business Week* (January 23, 1995), p. 47; Alex Taylor III, "Why Electric Cars Make No Sense," *Fortune* (July 26, 1993), pp. 126–27; "Saturn May Market GM's Electric Vehicles," *Automotive News* (March 13, 1995), p. 6; "French EVs Hinted for Calif.," *Automotive News* (March 14, 1994), pp. 1, 47; and "Ford Electric Truck Set for California," *The New York Times* (June 14, 1995), p. D19.

7. Lawrence P. Feldman and Albert L. Page, "Harvesting: The Misunderstood Market Exit Strategy," *Journal of Business Strategy* (Spring 1985), pp. 79–85.

8. Mikala Folb, "Tamagotchi Hits North American Market," *Marketing* (May 12, 1997)—www.marketingmag.ca, July 20, 1997.

9. Based on "Sega Leaps Ahead by Shipping New Player Early," *The Wall Street Journal* (May 11, 1995), pp. B1, B4; "The Christmas Videogame Massacre," *The Economist* (November 19, 1994), p. 71; and "Sega!" *Business Week* (February 21, 1994), pp. 66–74.

10. Everett M. Rogers, *Diffusion of Innovations,* 3rd ed. (New York: The Free Press, 1983).

11. S. Ram and Jagdish N. Sheth, "Consumer Resistance to Innovation: The Marketing Problem and Its Solution," *Journal of Consumer Marketing* (Spring 1989), pp. 5–14.

12. Lesley Dow, "Dual Purpose Products Share in Soap Category," *Marketing* (June 9, 1997)—www.marketingmag.ca, July 18, 1997.

13. For a historical perspective on the product/brand manager system, see George S. Low and Ronald A. Fullerton, "Brands, Brand Management, and the Brand Manager System: A Critical-Historical Evaluation," *Journal of Marketing Research* (May 1994), pp. 173–90.

14. "Haggar, Farah, Levi's Iron Out the Wrinkles," *Advertising Age* (March 6, 1995), p. 12; and Nancy Boomer, "Frozen Iced Tea Heats Up Summer Drink Category," *Marketing* (June 2, 1997)—www.marketingmag.ca, July 18, 1997.

15. "Brand Scorecard: Premium Products Lather Up Sales," *Advertising Age* (July 24, 1995), p. 24; and "Vitamin Shampoo Brings Shine to P&G Profits," *The Wall Street Journal* (October 21, 1993), pp. B1, B7.

16. "P&G Plans Big New Ivory Push," *Advertising Age* (November 23, 1992), p. 12; and "P&G's Soap Opera: New Ivory Bar Hits the Bottom of a Tub," *The Wall Street Journal* (October 23, 1992), p. B11.

17. Bob Geiger, "Liquid Yogurts Pour in the U.S.," *Advertising Age* (June 1, 1987), pp. 3, 62.

18. Cyndee Miller, "Food Producers Appeal to Fat-Free Crowd," *Marketing News* (August 14, 1995), p. 3.

19. "Et tu, Brut?" *Consumer Reports* (March 1992), p. 205.

20. "Marketers Try to Ease Sting of Price Increases," *Marketing News* (October 9, 1995), pp. 5–6; "It's the Pits," *Consumer Reports* (February 1992), p. 203; and John B. Hinge, "Critics Call Cuts in Package Size Deceptive Move," *The Wall Street Journal* (February 5, 1991), pp. B1, B8.

21. For an extended treatment of brand equity, see David Aaker, *Managing Brand Equity* (New York: The Free Press, 1991); also see, Betsy Morris, "The Brand's the Thing," *Fortune* (March 4, 1996), pp. 72–86.

22. Donalee Moulton, "Egg Co-op Hatches Eden Valley Brand," *Marketing* (July 7, 1997)—www.marketingmag.ca, July 17, 1997.

23. "Corporations Latch onto Licensing," *Advertising Age* (August 14, 1995), p. 28.

24. "Ruffles Makes Waves in Israel," *Advertising Age* (November 23, 1992), p. J-12.

25. Daniel L. Doden, "Selecting a Brand Name that Aids Marketing Objectives," *Advertising Age* (November 5, 1990), p. 34.

26. "A Survey of Multinationals," *The Economist* (June 24, 1995), p. 8.

27. For a review of brand extensions, see David A. Aaker and Kevin Lane Keller, "Consumer Evaluations of Brand Extension," *Journal of Marketing* (January 1990), pp. 27–41.

28. "Missteps Mar Church & Dwight's Plans," *The Wall Street Journal* (April 28, 1995), p. B5.

29. Lara Mills, "Companies Conclude That Two Big Brands Can Market Better Than One," *Marketing* (December 23/30, 1996)—www.marketingmag.ca, July 18, 1997.

30. www.rogers.com/RCI, November 13, 1996.

31. "Kodak Pursues a Greater Market Share in Japan with New Private-Label Film," *The Wall Street Journal* (March 7, 1995), p. B11.

32. *These Prices Are Killing Us: What Brand-Driven Marketers Must Do to Combat Price-Based Competition* (New York: Bates Advertising USA, Inc., 1994).

33. "The National Peztime," *The Dallas Morning News* (October 9, 1995), pp. 1C, 2C; and David Welch, *Collecting Pez* (Murphysboro, IL: Bubba Scrubba Publications, 1995).

34. "Molson Takes Two New Marketing Tacks," *Marketing* (March 24, 1997)—www.marketingmag.ca, July 17, 1997.

35. "Coca-Cola Finds Success Trading New for the Old," *The Wall Street Journal* (March 24, 1995), p. B5.

36. Carl McDaniel and R. C. Baker, "Convenience Food Packaging and the Perception of Product Quality," *Journal of Marketing* (October 1977), pp. 57–58.

37. "Which Hue Is Best? Test Your Color I.Q.," *Advertising Age* (September 14, 1987), pp. 18, 20.

38. "Supreme Court to Rule on Colors as Trademarks," *Marketing News* (January 2, 1995), p. 28.

39. This discussion is based, in part, on Barry N. Rosen and George B. Sloane III, "Environmental Product Standards, Trade and European Consumer Goods Marketing," *Columbia Journal of World Business* (Spring 1995), pp. 74–86; "Life Ever After," *The Economist* (October 9, 1993), p. 77; and "How to Make Lots of Money, and Save the Planet Too," *The Economist* (June 3, 1995), pp. 57–58.

40. This example is based on John A. Quelch, "The Procter & Gamble Company: The Lenor Refill Package," Harvard Business School case N9-592-016; and "Procter and Gamble, Inc.: Downy Enviro-Pak," University of Western Ontario Case 9-90-A006.

41. Paula Mergenbagen, "Product Liability: Who Sues?" *American Demographics* (June 1995), pp. 48–54; "Bottled Up," *The Economist* (December 17, 1994), p. 69.

42. Sonia L. Nazario, "Microwave Packages that Add Crunch to Lunch May also Pose Chemical Risks," *The Wall Street Journal* (March 1, 1990), pp. B1, B6.

Polaroid Canada: This case was prepared by Frederick G. Crane. Adapted from *Canadian Advertising Success Stories* (Toronto: Canadian Congress of Advertising, 1995).

CHAPTER 13

1. John E. G. Bateson, *Managing Services Marketing* (Fort Worth: Dryden, 1995).

2. Herbert G. Grubel and Michael A. Walker, *Service Industry Growth* (Vancouver: The Fraser Institute, 1989).

3. Valarie A. Zeithaml, "How Consumer Evaluation Processes Differ Between Goods and Services," in James H. Donnelly and William R. George, eds., *Marketing of Services* (Chicago, IL: American Marketing Association, 1981).

4. Keith B. Murray, "A Test of Services Marketing Theory: Consumer Information Acquisition Activities," *Journal of Marketing* (January 1991), pp. 10–25; and F. G. Crane, *Professional Services Marketing: Strategy and Tactics* (New York: The Haworth Press, Inc., 1993).

5. Murray, "A Test of Services Marketing Theory."

6. John Ozment and Edward Morash, "The Augmented Service Offering for Perceived and Actual Service Quality," *Journal of the Academy of Marketing Science* (Fall 1994), pp. 352–63.

7. A. Parasuraman, Valarie A. Zeithaml, and Leonard L. Berry, "Reassessment of Expectations as a Comparison Standard in Measuring Service Quality: Implications for Further Research," *Journal of Marketing* (January 1994), pp. 111–24; and Leonard L. Berry, *On Great Service* (New York: Free Press, 1995).

8. A. Parasuraman, Valarie A. Zeithaml, and Leonard L. Berry, "Reassessment of Expectations as a Comparison Standard in Measuring Service Quality."

9. Amy Ostrom and Dawn Iacobucci, "Consumer Trade-Offs and the Evaluation of Services," *Journal of Marketing* (January 1995), pp. 17–28; and J. Joseph Cronin, Jr., and Steven A. Taylor, "Measuring Service Quality: A Reexamination and Extension," *Journal of Marketing* (July 1992), pp. 55–68; A. H. Kizilbash, Nessim Y. Hanna, and John S. Wagle, "Is Gap Analysis a Useful Aid for Measuring Service Quality in Industrial Product Sales Organizations?" *Journal of Customer Service in Marketing and Management*, vol. 3, no. 4 (1997), pp. 75–80; Alain Genestre and Paul Herbig, "Service Quality: An Examination of Demographic Differences," *Journal of Customer Service in Marketing and Management*, vol. 3, no. 3 (1997), pp. 65–83; and Jack Dart, "Professional Service Quality: The Practice or the Professional?," *Journal of Customer Service in Marketing and Management*, vol. 3, no. 2 (1997), pp. 7–21.

10. Thomas S. Gruca, "Defending Service Markets," *Marketing Management* (1994 No. 1), pp. 31–38; and Leonard L. Berry, Jeffrey S. Conant, and A. Parasuraman, "A Framework for Conducting a Services Marketing Audit," *Journal of the Academy of Marketing Science* (Summer 1991), pp. 255–68.

11. Patriya Tansuhaj, Donna Randall, and Jim McCullough, "A Services Marketing Management Model: Integrating Internal and External Marketing Functions," *Journal of Services Marketing* (Winter 1988), pp. 31–38.

12. Christian Gronroos, "Internal Marketing Theory and Practice," in Tim Bloch, G. D. Upah, and V. A. Zeithaml, eds., *Services Marketing in a Changing Environment* (Chicago, IL: American Marketing Association, 1984); and Dennis J. Cahill, *Internal Marketing* (New York: The Haworth Press Inc., 1996).

13. Ibid.

14. Hong Lee and Robert Boissoneau, "Empowering People in Modern Organizations for Improved Customer Service," *Journal of Customer Service in Marketing and Management*, vol. 3, no. 2 (1997), pp. 55–69; and Scott W. Kelly, "Developing Customer Orientation among Service Employees," *Journal of the Academy of Marketing Science* (Winter 1992), pp. 27–36.

15. Sundar G. Bharedwaj, P. Rajan Varadarajan and John Fahy, "Sustainable Competitive Advantage in Services Industries: A Conceptual Model and Research Propositions," *Journal of Marketing* (October 1993), pp. 83–99.

16. Frederick H. deB. Harris and Peter Peacock, "Hold My Place, Please," *Marketing Management* (Fall 1995), pp. 34–46.

17. Christopher Lovelock, *Services Marketing*, 3rd ed. (Upper Saddle River, NJ: Prentice Hall, 1996), pp. 204–23.

18. F. G. Crane, "The Relative Effect of Price and Personal Referral Cues on Consumers' Perceptions of Dental Services," *Health Marketing Quarterly*, vol. 13, no. 4 (1996), pp. 91–105.

19. Christopher Lovelock, *Services Marketing*.

20. Robert E. Hite, Cynthia Fraser, and Joseph A. Bellizzi, "Professional Service Advertising: The Effects of Price Inclusion, Justification, and Level of Risk," *Journal of Advertising Research* 30 (August/September 1990), pp. 23–31; and F. G. Crane, *Professional Services Marketing: Strategy and Tactics*.

21. F. G. Crane, *Professional Services Marketing: Strategy and Tactics*.

22. Thomas A. Stewart, "A New 500 for the New Economy," *Fortune* (May 15, 1995), pp. 166–78; Philip Elmer-Dewitt, "Mine, All Mine," *Time* (June 5, 1995), pp. 46–54; and James Brian Quinn and Penny C. Paquette, "Technology in Services: Creating Organizational Revolutions," *Sloan Management Review* (Winter 1990), pp. 67–78.

23. Daniel Pedersen, "Dissing Customers," *Newsweek* (June 23, 1997), pp. 56–57; and Dennis J. Cahill, "What's Wrong with Service Providers? A Customer-Service Perspective," *Journal of Customer Service in Marketing and Management,* vol. 3, no. 2 (1997), pp. 71–79.

24. Ibid; Leonard L. Berry, A. Parasuraman, and Valarie A. Zeithaml, "Improving Service Quality in America: Lessons Learned," *Academy of Management Executive,* vol. 8, no. 2 (1994), pp. 32–52.

National Hockey League: This case was prepared by Frederick G. Crane. Source: National Hockey League.

CHAPTER 14

1. *Boeing 1995 Annual Report* (Seattle, WA: The Boeing Company, 1996); and *Boeing 1994 Annual Report* (Seattle, WA: The Boeing Company, 1995).

2. Valerie Reitman and Jathon Sapsford, "To See Issues Vexing Japanese Business Now, Consider JAL Flight 176," *The Wall Street Journal* (August 9, 1994), pp. A1, A6.

3. Jeff Cole, "Boeing Is Offering Cuts in Prices of New Jets, Rattling the Industry," *The Wall Street Journal* (April 24, 1995), pp. A1, A8.

4. Alex Taylor III, "Boeing: Sleepy in Seattle," *Fortune* (August 7, 1995), pp. 92–98.

5. This box is based on Boeing 1995 Annual Report; Boeing 1994 Annual Report; Cole; Taylor; and Alison L. Sprout, "How to Sit Pretty in the Boeing 777," *Fortune* (August 7, 1995), p. 29.

6. Sprout, "How to Sit Pretty."

7. Raymond Sarafin, "Even Lamborghini Must Think Marketing," *Advertising Age* (May 1, 1995), p. 32.

8. Adapted from Kent B. Monroe, *Pricing: Making Profitable Decisions,* 2nd ed. (New York: McGraw-Hill, 1990), chapter 4. See also David J. Curry, "Measuring Price and Quality Competition," *Journal of Marketing* (Spring 1985), pp. 106–17.

9. Numerous studies have examined the price-quality-value relationship. See, for example, William B. Dodds, Kent B. Monroe, and Dhruv Grewal, "Effects of Price, Brand, and Store Information on Buyers' Product Evaluations," *Journal of Marketing Research* (August 1991), pp. 307–19; and Roger A. Kerin, Ambuj Jain, and Daniel J. Howard, "Store Shopping Experience and Consumer Price-Quality-Value Perceptions," *Journal of Retailing* (Winter 1992), pp. 235–45. For a thorough review of the price-quality-value relationship, see Valarie A. Zeithaml, "Consumer Perceptions of Price, Quality, and Value," *Journal of Marketing* (July 1988), pp. 2–22. Also see Jerry Wind, "Getting a Read on Market-Defined 'Value,' " *Journal of Pricing Management* (Winter 1990), pp. 5–14.

10. These examples are from Roger A. Kerin and Robert A. Peterson, "Morgantown Furniture, Inc. (A)," *Strategic Marketing Problems: Cases and Comments,* 7th ed. (Englewood Cliffs, NJ: Prentice Hall, 1995), pp. 282–91; and F. G. Crane, "The Relative Effect of Price and Personal Referral Cues on Consumers' Perceptions of Dental Services," *Health Marketing Quarterly,* vol. 13, no. 4 (1996), pp. 91–105.

11. N. Craig Smith and John A. Quelch, *Ethics in Marketing* (Homewood, IL: Richard D. Irwin, 1993); and F. G. Crane, "What's Ethical and What's Not with Canadian Business Students," *Working Paper,* 1997.

12. David Wessel, "The Price Is Wrong, and Economists Are in an Uproar," *The Wall Street Journal* (January 2, 1991), pp. B1, B6.

13. Jeff Lobb, "The Right (Pepsi) Stuff," *Marketing* (July 8, 1996), p. 15.

14. "Price War Is Raging in Europe," *Business Week* (July 6, 1992), pp. 44–45.

15. Michael Garry, "Dollar Strength: Publishers Confront the New Economic Realities," *Folio: The Magazine for Magazine Management* (February 1989), pp. 88–93; Cara S. Trager, "Right Price Reflects a Magazine's Health Goals," *Advertising Age* (March 9, 1987), pp. 5–8ff; and Frank Bruni, "Price of Newsweek? It Depends," *Dallas Times Herald* (August 14, 1986), pp. S1, S20.

16. For an overview of price elasticity studies, see Ruth N. Bolton, "The Robustness of Retail-Level Elasticity Estimates," *Journal of Retailing* (Summer 1989), pp. 193–219; and Gerald J. Tellis, "The Price Elasticity of Selective Demand: A Meta-Analysis of Econometric Models of Sales," *Journal of Marketing Research* (November 1988), pp. 331–41.

17. Kent B. Monroe, *Pricing: Making Profitable Decisions,* 2nd ed. (New York: McGraw-Hill, 1990), pp. 24–26.

18. W. Nylen, *Marketing Decision-Making Handbook* (Englewood Cliffs, NJ: Prentice Hall, 1990), pp. G237–G239.

Washburn International, Inc.: This case was prepared by William Rudelius.

CHAPTER 15

1. "Picture-Phone Marketers Target the Home PC," *The Wall Street Journal* (February 27, 1996), p. B1, B6; "The Difficult Art of Videophone Conversation," *New Scientist* (January 14, 1995), p. 20; "Voyeurs vs. Exhibitionists," *Forbes* (May 23, 1994), p. 210; and "An Eye on Phones," *U.S. News and World Report* (June 22, 1992), pp. 78–82.

2. Kim Heinrich, "On the Cutting Edge," *The Financial Post Magazine* (March 1996), p. 11.

3. "Sony Prices Its Advanced Game Player at $299, Near Low End of Expectations," *The Wall Street Journal* (May 12, 1995), p. B4; and Jeffrey A. Trachtenberg, "Sony Sells 100,000 Video-Game Units on First Weekend," *The Wall Street Journal* (September 12, 1995), p. A12.

4. "Nintendo Plans to Release New Game Player in Fall," *The Wall Street Journal* (May 16, 1996), p. B17.

5. Thomas T. Nagle and Reed K. Holden, *The Strategy and Tactics of Pricing,* 2nd ed. (Englewood Cliffs, NJ: Prentice Hall, 1995).

6. "PC Prices Cut in Japan," *The Wall Street Journal* (October 21, 1992), p. B7.

7. Jeffrey H. Birnbaum, "Pricing of Products Is Still an Art, Often Having Little Link to Costs," *The Wall Street Journal* (November 25, 1981), p. 25.

8. "Luxury Steals Back," *Fortune* (January 16, 1995), pp. 112–19.

9. See, for example, V. Kumar and Robert P. Leone, "Measuring the Effect of Retail Store Promotions on Brand and Store Substitution," *Journal of Marketing Research* (May 1988), pp. 178–85.

10. Robert C. Blattberg and Scott A. Neslin, *Sales Promotion Concepts, Methods and Strategies* (Englewood Cliffs, NJ: Prentice Hall, 1990); and Kent B. Monroe, *Pricing: Making Profitable Decisions,* 2nd ed. (New York: McGraw-Hill, 1990).

11. "PCs: The Battle for the Home Front," *Business Week* (September 25, 1995), pp. 110–14; and David Kirkpatrick, "The Revolution at Compaq Computer," *Fortune* (December 14, 1992), pp. 80–82ff.

12. Nagle and Holden.

13. Rogers Cantel Inc., web site—www.cantel.com, November 6, 1996.

14. "Lawyers Start to Stop the Clock," *Business Week* (August 17, 1992), p. 108.

15. George E. Belch and Michael A. Belch, *Introduction to Advertising and Promotion,* 3rd ed. (Homewood, IL: Richard D. Irwin, 1996).

16. For a comprehensive discussion on the experience curve, see Roger A. Kerin, Vijay Mahajan, and P. Rajan Varadarajan, *Contemporary Perspectives on Strategic Market Planning* (Boston, MA: Allyn and Bacon, 1990).

17. Based on information provided by Amber, Bergen and Drecker Associates; "Digital Daze," *The Economist* (October 3, 1992), p. 65; and Andrew Kupfer, "Phones That Will Work Anywhere," *Fortune* (August 24, 1992), pp. 100–12.

18. William Taylor, "Message and Muscle: An Interview with Swatch Titan Nicolas Hayek," *Harvard Business Review* (March–April 1993), pp. 98–110.

19. Jim Carlton, "Hewlett-Packard Cuts Office-PC Prices in Wake of Moves by Compaq and IBM," *The Wall Street Journal* (August 22, 1995), p. B11.

20. Trachtenberg, "Sony Sells 100,000 Video-Game Units."

21. Monroe, *Pricing.*

22. "Store-Brand Pricing Has to Be Just Right," *The Wall Street Journal* (February 14, 1992), p. B1.

23. "Price Cuts and Lesbians," *Marketing* (July 7, 1997)—www.marketing mag.ca, July 17, 1997.

24. For a review of quantity discounts, see George S. Day and Adrian B. Ryans, "Using Price Discounts for a Competitive Advantage," *Industrial Marketing Management* (February 1988), pp. 1–14; and James B. Wilcox, Roy D. Howell, Paul Kuzdrall, and Robert Britney, "Price Quantity Discounts: Some Implications for Buyers and Sellers," *Journal of Marketing* (July 1987), pp. 60–70.

25. "Burger King, in Big Blow to Pepsi, Is Switching to Coke," *The Wall Street Journal* (May 2, 1990), pp. B1, B6.

26. Judy Myrden, "MacLellan Tables Own Sable Offer," *The Chronicle Herald* (July 15, 1997), pp. A1, A2.

27. "Automobile Marketing," *Advertising Age* (April 3, 1995), pp. S1, S32.

My Own Meals: This case was prepared by William Rudelius. Sources: Personal interview with Mary Anne Jackson; Lisa R. Van Wagner, "Kids Meals: The Market Grows Up," *Food Business* (May 20, 1991); Mary Ellen Kuhn, "Women to Watch in the 90's," *Food Business* (September 10, 1990).

CHAPTER 16

1. Christie Brown, "Pooper-scooper dooper," *Forbes* (February 13, 1995), pp. 78–79; "Reigning Cats and Dogs," *American Demographics* (April 1995), p. 10; "Deluxe Brands, Pet Supers Wag the Market," *Advertising Age* (September 27, 1995), p. 22; "Why True Love Is Like Puppy Chow," *American Demographics* (January 1996), pp. 14–15; and "Sick Pets: A Healthy Pharmaceutical Market," *The Wall Street Journal* (January 3, 1996), pp. B1, B6.
2. See Peter D. Bennett, ed., *Dictionary of Marketing Terms,* 2nd ed. (Chicago: American Marketing Association, 1995).
3. Based on Frederick E. Webster, Jr., *Industrial Marketing Strategy,* 2nd ed. (New York: John Wiley & Sons, 1988).
4. "Pepsi, Concerned about Market Share in France, Will Break with Local Bottler," *The Wall Street Journal* (November 7, 1989), p. A12.
5. This discussion is based on John A. Quelch, "Why Not Exploit Dual Marketing?" *Business Horizons* (January–February 1987), pp. 52–60; *PepsiCo, Inc. 1994 Annual Report;* "GM Says Sales Arm Plans to Distribute Saab Cars in Canada," *The Wall Street Journal* (May 10, 1990), p. B2; and Rustan Kosenko and Don Rathz, "The Japanese Channels of Distribution: Difficult but Not Insurmountable," *AMA Educator's Proceedings* (Chicago: American Marketing Association, 1988), pp. 233–36.
6. For a recent discussion on strategic channel alliances, see P. Rajan Varadarajan and Margaret H. Cunningham, "Strategic Alliances: A Synthesis of Conceptual Foundations," *Journal of the Academy of Marketing Science* (Fall 1995), pp. 282–96; and Johny K. Johansson, "International Alliances: Why Now?" *Journal of the Academy of Marketing Science* (Fall 1995), pp. 301–04.
7. "Spoon-to-Spoon Combat Overseas," *New York Times* (January 1, 1995), p. 17; "Cafe au Lait, a Croissant and Trix," *Business Week* (August 24, 1992), pp. 50–51; and "Cereal Partners Gains in European Market," *Advertising Age* (May 17, 1993), p. I-10.
8. For an extended treatment of direct marketing, see Mary Lou Roberts and Paul D. Berger, *Direct Marketing Management* (Englewood Cliffs, NJ: Prentice Hall, 1989); and Herbert Katzenstein and William S. Sachs, *Direct Marketing* (Columbus, OH: Merrill, 1986).
9. "Telemarketing Cited as Chief Form of Direct Marketing," *Advertising Age* (January 1, 1996), p. 9.
10. Adapted from Louis W. Stern, Adel I. El-Ansary, and James R. Brown, *Management in Marketing Channels* (Englewood Cliffs, NJ: Prentice Hall, 1989), pp. 99–108; Kenneth G. Hardy and Allan J. McGrath, *Marketing Channel Management* (Glenview, IL: Scott, Foresman, 1988), pp. 3–5, 310–34; and Bert Rosenbloom, *Marketing Channels,* 3rd ed. (Hinsdale, IL: Dryden Press, 1987), pp. 44–47.
11. *Health o meter Products, Inc. 1994 Annual Report;* and Interview with Mr. James Yurak, executive vice president, Mr. Coffee, June 1, 1990.
12. Louis W. Stern and Adel I. El-ansary, *Marketing Channels,* 4th ed. (Englewood Cliffs, NJ: Prentice Hall, 1991).
13. Statistics provided by the International Franchise Association.
14. For a review of channel partnering, see Robert D. Buzzell and Gwen Ortmeyer, "Channel Partnerships Streamline Distribution," *Sloan Management Review* (Spring 1995), pp. 85–96.
15. Edwin R. Rigsbee, *The Art of Partnering* (Dubuque, IA: Kendall/Hunt Publishing, 1994), pp. 82–83.
16. Interview with Flowers On-line July 20, 1997.
17. "Distributors: No Endangered Species," *Industry Week* (January 24, 1983), pp. 47–52.
18. This exhibit is based on "PCs: The Battle for the Home Front," *Business Week* (September 15, 1995), pp. 110–14; "The Computer Is in the Mail (Really)," *Business Week* (January 23, 1995), pp. 76–77; "Mass Market Transforms PC Retailing," *The Wall Street Journal* (December 18, 1990), p. B1; "More Computer Marketers Taking the Direct Approach," *Marketing News* (October 26, 1992), p. 6; and "A Surprise Lift for Computer Retailers," *Business Week* (October 4, 1992), pp. 63–64.
19. "Revolution in Japanese Retailing," *Fortune* (February 7, 1994), pp. 143–46.
20. "Japanese Retailing: The Emporia Strike Back," *The Economist* (October 29, 1994), pp. 83–84.
21. "Gillette Tries to Nick Schick in Japan," *The Wall Street Journal* (February 4, 1991), pp. B3, B4.
22. This discussion is based on John Fahy and Fuyuki Taguchi, "Reassessing the Japanese Distribution System," *Sloan Management Review* (Winter 1995), pp. 49–61; and Michael R. Czinkota and Jon Woronoff, *Unlocking Japanese Markets* (Chicago, IL: Probus Publishing, 1991), pp. 92–97.

23. Allan J. Magrath and Kenneth G. Hardy, "Avoiding the Pitfalls in Managing Distributor Channels," *Business Horizons* (Sept.–Oct. 1987), pp. 29–33.
24. "Distributors' Links to Producers Grow More Fragile," *The Wall Street Journal* (October 28, 1992), p. B2; and "Wal-Mart Draws Fire," *Advertising Age* (January 13, 1992), p. 3.
25. "Bloody, Bowed, Back Together," *Business Week* (March 19, 1990), pp. 42–43.
26. "Heinz Struggles to Stay at the Top of the Stack," *Business Week* (March 11, 1985), p. 49.
27. "Black Pearls Recast for Spring," *Advertising Age* (November 13, 1995), p. 49.
28. Studies that explore the dimensions and use of power and influence in marketing channels include the following: Gul Butaney and Lawrence H. Wortzel, "Distributor Power versus Manufacturer Power: The Customer Role," *Journal of Marketing* (January 1988), pp. 52–63; Kenneth A. Hunt, John T. Mentzer, and Jeffrey E. Danes, "The Effect of Power Sources on Compliance in a Channel of Distribution: A Causal Model," *Journal of Business Research* (October 1987), pp. 377–98; and F. Robert Dwyer and Jule Gassenheimer, "Relational Roles and Triangle Dramas: Effects on Power Play and Sentiments in Industrial Channels," *Marketing Letters,* vol. 3 (1992), pp. 187–200.
29. Based on Gene R. Laznick and Patrick E. Murphy, *Ethical Marketing Decisions: The Higher Road* (Boston, MA: Allyn & Bacon, 1993), pp. 117–18; and N. Craig Smith and John A. Quelch, *Ethics in Marketing* (Chicago, IL: Richard D. Irwin, 1993), pp. 478–79.

Creston Vineyards: This case was prepared by Steven W. Hartley.

CHAPTER 17

1. Ronald Henkoff, "Delivering the Goods," *Fortune* (November 28, 1994), p. 64.
2. Henkoff, "Delivering the Goods," pp. 64–78.
3. Definition provided by the Council of Logistics Management, Chicago, 1986. Emphasis added.
4. Elizabeth Edwardson, "Workers at L. L. Bean Busy as Santa's Elves Filling Christmas Orders," *Minneapolis Star Tribune* (December 23, 1992), p. 5D.
5. Bernard Wysocki, Jr., "Improved Distribution, Not Better Production, Is Key Goal in Mergers," *The Wall Street Journal* (August 29, 1995), pp. A1, A2; Laura Landro, "Giants Talk Synergy but Few Make It Work," *The Wall Street Journal* (September 25, 1995), pp. B1, B2; and Henkoff, "Delivering the Goods," pp. 64–78.
6. Henkoff, "Delivering the Goods," p. 64.
7. John Holusha, "P&G Downy Bottles Use Recycled Plastic," *The New York Times* (January 14, 1993), p. C5; and Bruce VanVoorst, "The Recycling Bottleneck," *Time* (September 14, 1992), p. 52.
8. Lee Smith, "The Customer with Clout," *Fortune* (October 2, 1995), p. 100.
9. Jon Bigness, "In Today's Economy, There Is Big Money to Be Made in Logistics," *The Wall Street Journal* (September 6, 1995), pp. A1, A9.
10. Joseph Pereira, "In Reebok-Nike War, Big Woolworth Chain Is a Major Battlefield," *The Wall Street Journal* (September 22, 1995), pp. A1, A5; and Kenneth Labich, "Nike vs. Reebok: A Battle for Hearts, Minds and Feet," *Fortune* (September 18, 1995), pp. 90–106.
11. Michael Saul, "Penney-UPS Deal Valued at $1 Billion," *The Dallas Morning News* (July 11, 1995), p. 4D; and Scott McCartney, "Dell to Outsource All Its Shipping to Roadway Unit," *The Wall Street Journal* (February 15, 1995), p. B8.
12. James Pollock, "Breaking Away," *Marketing* (June 28, 1993), p. 3.
13. Henkoff, "Delivering the Goods," pp. 66–74; and Philip Evers and F. J. Beier, "The Portfolio Effect and Multiple Consolidation Points: A Critical Assessment of the Square Root Law," *Journal of Business Logistics* (Fall 1993), pp. 117–126.
14. "Europeans Think Alike When It Comes to Customer Service," *International Ambassador* (August 1990), p. 25; and "The European Customer Service Survey: Results," *Europa* (September 1990), p. 1.
15. John J. Coyle, Edward J. Bardi, and C. John Langley, Jr., *The Management of Business Logistics,* 5th ed. (St. Paul, MN: West Publishing, 1992), pp. 85–90.
16. Bigness, "In Today's Economy." p. A1.
17. David Greising, "Watch Out for Flying Packages," *Business Week* (November 14, 1995), p. 40.
18. Christina Duff and Bob Ortega, "How Wal-Mart Outdid a Once-Touted Kmart in Discount-Store Race," *The Wall Street Journal* (March 24, 1995), pp. A1, A4; and Thomas J. Winninger, "Price Wars," *Minnesota Ventures* (September/October 1994), pp. 31–34.
19. Henkoff, "Delivering the Goods," pp. 64–78.

Navistar International: This case was prepared by Steven W. Hartley.

CHAPTER 18

1. Richard C. Leventhal, "The Information Superhighway: Will This Change the Way That Customers Are Being Served?" *Journal of Customer Service in Marketing and Management,* vol. 3, no. 1 (1997), pp. 79–89; Stratford Sherman, "Will the Information Superhighway Be the Death of Retailing?" *Fortune* (April 18, 1994), pp. 98–110; and Allyson L. Stewart, "Future of Shopping: Shop as You Flop," *Marketing News* (November 21, 1994), p. 15.

2. www.marketingmag.ca, July 21, 1997. Suzanne Oliver, "Virtual Retailers," *Forbes* (April 24, 1995), pp. 126–27; and Susan Chandler, "The Grocery Cart in Your PC," *Business Week* (September 11, 1995), pp. 63–64.

3. Robert Lenzner and Philippe Mao, "Banking Pops Up in the Strangest Places," *Forbes* (April 10, 1995), pp. 72–76; Faye Rice, "One Writer's Hunt for the Perfect Jeans," *Fortune* (April 17, 1995), p. 30; and Cyndee Miller, "Gaze into the Crystal Ball for '95 and Beyond," *Marketing News* (January 30, 1995), pp. 1, 10.

4. Statistics Canada, *Market Research Handbook,* cat. 63-224 (Ottawa, 1997).

5. "World's Top Stores," *Marketing* (March 1, 1993), p. 18.

6. Carla Rapoport and Justin Martin, "Retailers Go Global," *Fortune* (February 20, 1995), pp. 102–8; William Symonds, "Invasion of the Retail Snatchers," *Business Week* (May 9, 1994), pp. 72–73; and Eugene Fram and Riad Ajami, "Globalization of Markets and Shopping Stress: Cross-Country Comparisons," *Business Horizons* (January–February 1994), pp. 17–23.

7. Gene Koretz, "Those Plucky Corner Stores," *Business Week* (December 5, 1994), p. 26.

8. Christopher Palmeri, "Who's Afraid of Wal-Mart?" *Forbes* (July 31, 1995), p. 81.

9. Richard C. Hoffman and John F. Preble, "Franchising into the Twenty-First Century," *Business Horizons* (November–December 1993), pp. 35–43.

10. Allen Whitehead, "Trouble in Franchise Nation," *Fortune* (March 6, 1995), pp. 115–29; and Jennifer S. Stack and Joseph E. McKendrick, "Franchise Market Expands as Rest of Economy Slumps," *Marketing News* (July 6, 1992), p. 11.

11. Robert E. Bond and Christopher E. Bond, *The Source Book of Franchising Opportunities* (Homewood, IL: Dow Jones-Irwin, 1991).

12. Tara Parker-Pope, "New Devices Add Up Bill, Measure Shoppers' Honesty," *The Wall Street Journal* (June 6, 1995), pp. B1, 13.

13. Bill Merrilees and Dale Miller, "The Nexus Between Human Resource Expectations and Competitive Advantage in Retail Personal Service," *Journal of Customer Service in Marketing and Management,* vol. 3, no. 1 (1997), pp. 19–29.

14. Joseph Pereira, "Toys 'Я' Us Grows Up," *The Wall Street Journal* (March 20, 1995), p. B4.

15. Lesley Dow, "Maxi Advances onto Loblaws' Home Turf," *Marketing* (July 14, 1997)—www.marketingmag.ca, August 4, 1997.

16. Peter D. Bennett, ed., *Dictionary of Marketing Terms* (American Marketing Association, 1995).

17. Susan Chandler and Therese Palmer, "Can Spiegel Pull Out of the Spiral?" *Business Week* (August 28, 1995), p. 80; and Gary McWilliams, Susan Chandler, and Julie Tilsner, "Strategies for the New Mail Order," *Business Week* (December 19, 1994), pp. 82–85.

18. Lenzner with Mao; Dyan Machan, "Sharing Victoria's Secrets," *Forbes* (June 5, 1995), pp. 132–33; and Charles Waltner, "Interactive Catalogs a Tough Sell," *Advertising Age* (March 6, 1995), p. 19.

19. Donna Bursey, "Targeting Small Businesses for Telemarketing and Mail Order Sales," *Direct Marketing* (September 1995), pp. 18–20.

20. Laura Loro, "Downside for Public Is Privacy Issue," *Advertising Age* (October 2, 1995), p. 32; Cyndee Miller, "Concern Raised over Privacy on Infohighway," *Marketing News* (January 2, 1995), pp. 1, 7; "Telemarketing Rules OK'd," *Marketing News* (September 11, 1995), p. 1.

21. Gail DeGeorge and Lori Bongiorno, "Polishing Up the Cubic Zirconia," *Business Week* (July 31, 1995), pp. 83–84; and Leventhal, "The Information Superhighway." Chad Rubel, "Home Shopping Network Targets Young Audience," *Marketing News* (July 17, 1995), pp. 13, 26.

22. www.merl.shop.ibm.com, July 18, 1997.

23. Robert Benjamin and Rolf Wigand, "Electronic Markets and Virtual Value Chains on the Information Superhighway," *Sloan Management Review* (Winter 1995), pp. 62–72; "Malling the Net," *Adweek* (September 25, 1995), pp. 32–37; Paul Judge, "Mr. Smith Goes to Cyberspace," *Business Week* (October 30, 1995), pp. 72–73; Scott Danaton and Dagmar Musey "Online's Next Battlefront: Europe," *Advertising Age* (March 6, 1995), p. 18; and Philip Elmer-Dewitt, "Battle for the Internet," *Time* (July 25, 1995), pp. 50–56.

24. Mathew Schifrin, "Okay, Big Mouth," *Forbes* (October 9, 1995), pp. 47–48; Veronica Byrd and Wendy Zellner, "The Avon Lady of the Amazon," *Business Week* (October 24, 1994), pp. 93–96; and Ann Marsh "Avon Is Calling on Eastern Europe," *Advertising Age* (June 20, 1994), p. I-16.

25. "Vending Machine Software," *Marketing News* (May 8, 1995), p. 1; and "Coke Machine Modems Send Distress Signals," *Marketing News* (October 9, 1995), p. 2.

26. The following discussion is adapted from William T. Gregor and Eileen M. Friars, *Money Merchandising: Retail Revolution in Consumer Financial Services* (Cambridge, MA: Management Analysis Center, Inc., 1982).

27. William Lazer and Eugene J. Kelley, "The Retailing Mix: Planning and Management," *Journal of Retailing* (Spring 1961), pp. 34–41.

28. "Annual Report on Discount Retailing," *Discount Store News,* (July 3, 1995), p. 23.

29. Stephanie Anderson Forest, "I Can Get It for You Retail," *Business Week* (September 18, 1995), pp. 84–88; and Adrienne Ward, "New Breed of Mall Knows: Everybody Loves a Bargain," *Advertising Age* (January 27, 1992), p. 55.

30. Barry Brown, "Edmonton Makes Size Pay Off in Down Market," *Advertising Age* (January 27, 1992), pp. 4–5.

31. "Shoppers Returning," *The Cape Breton Post* (July 18, 1997), p. 19.

32. Pierre Martineau, "The Personality of the Retail Store," *Harvard Business Review* (January–February 1958), p. 47.

33. Julie Baker, Dhruv Grewal, and A. Parasuraman, "The Influence of Store Environment on Quality Inferences and Store Image," *Journal of the Academy of Marketing Science* (Fall 1994), pp. 328–39.

34. Jo Marney, "Building Splurchases," *Marketing* (January 27, 1997)—www.marketingmag.ca, July 18, 1997. Mary Jo Bitner, "Servicescapes: The Impact of Physical Surroundings on Customers and Employees," *Journal of Marketing* (April 1992), pp. 57–71.

35. The wheel of retailing theory was originally proposed by Malcolm P. McNair, "Significant Trends and Development in the Postwar Period," in A. B. Smith, ed., *Competitive Distribution in a Free, High-Level Economy and Its Implications for the University* (Pittsburgh: University of Pittsburgh Press, 1958), pp. 1–25; see also Stephen Brown, "The Wheel of Retailing—Past and Future," *Journal of Retailing* (Summer 1990), pp. 143–49; and Malcolm P. McNair and Eleanor May, "The Next Revolution of the Retailing Wheel," *Harvard Business Review* (September–October 1978), pp. 81–91.

36. William R. Davidson, Albert D. Bates, and Stephen J. Bass, "Retail Life Cycle," *Harvard Business Review* (November–December 1976), pp. 89–96.

37. Russell Mitchell, "The Smart Money Is on Smart Cards," *Business Week* (August 14, 1995), p. 68.

38. Roger Taylor, "Halifax's First Big-Box Car Dealer," *The Chronicle Herald* (July 17, 1997), p. D16; and *Hardware Industry Report: Home Improvement Retailing in Canada*—hardline @ terraport.net, July 21, 1997.

39. Mary Kuntz, "These Ads Have Windows and Walls," *Business Week* (February 27, 1995), p. 74; Richard Corliss, "What's Hot, Doc? Retail! *Time* (May 9, 1994), pp. 64–66.

40. Lara Mills, "Sears Planning to Think Like a Brand," *Marketing* (June 30, 1997)—www.marketingmag.ca, July 18, 1997.

IKEA: This case was prepared by Frederick G. Crane.

CHAPTER 19

1. Blair R. Fischer, "Making Your Product the Star Attraction," *Promo* (January 1996), pp. 42–47, 88; Damon Darlin, "Junior Mints, I'm Going to Make You a Star," *Forbes* (November 6, 1995), pp. 90–94; Lisa Bannon, "Will Natty 007 Charm the Grunge Generation?" *The Wall Street Journal* (November 7, 1995), pp. B1, B11; and Fara Warner, "Why It's Getting Harder to Tell the Shows from the Ads," *The Wall Street Journal* (June 15, 1995), pp. B1, B10.

2. Wilbur Schramm, "How Communication Works," in Wilbur Schramm, ed., *The Process and Effects of Mass Communication* (Urbana, IL: University of Illinois Press, 1955), pp. 3–26.

3. F. G. Crane and T. K. Clarke, *Consumer Behaviour in Canada: Theory and Practice,* 2nd ed. (Toronto: Dryden, 1994), pp. 287–98.

4. David A. Ricks, Jeffrey S. Arpan, and Marilyn Y. Fu, "Pitfalls in Advertising Overseas," *Journal of Advertising Research,* vol. 14 (December 1974), pp. 47–51.

5. Adapted from *Dictionary of Marketing Terms,* 2nd ed., Peter D. Bennett, ed. (Chicago: American Marketing Association, 1995), p. 231.

6. Scott Markham, "Company/Product Image Studies and Other Considerations of Fortune 500 Public Relations Departments," *Journal of Promotion Management,* vol. 3, no. 1/2 (1996), pp. 15–29.

7. F. G. Crane and T. K. Clarke, pp. 237–38, and 346.

8. Ken Riddell, "Advertising Sees Share of Pie Dwindling," *Marketing* (January 7, 1994), p. 2.

9. Joseph Weber, "Drug Ads: A Prescription for Controversy," *Business Week* (January 18, 1993), pp. 58–60.

10. Tom Duncan, "Is Your Marketing Communications Integrated?" *Advertising Age* (January 24, 1994), p. 26.

11. Kim Cleland, "Few Wed Marketing, Communications," *Advertising Age* (February 27, 1995), p. 10.

12. Don Schultz, "Objectives Drive Tactics in IMC Approach," *Marketing News* (May 9, 1994), pp. 14, 18; and Neil Brown, "Redefine Integrated Marketing Communications," *Marketing News* (March 29, 1993), pp. 4–5.

13. Andrea Mandel Campbell, "Honduras Drink Up Aggressive Pepsi Promo Push," *Marketing* (August 5, 1995), p. 6.

14. Keith McIntyre, "Sometimes Smaller is Better," *Marketing* (November 28, 1994), p. 14.

15. Magid M. Abraham and Leonard M. Lodish, "Getting the Most Out of Advertising and Promotion," *Harvard Business Review* (May–June 1990), pp. 50–60; Steven W. Hartley and James Cross, "How Sales Promotion Can Work for and Against You," *Journal of Consumer Marketing* (Summer 1988), pp. 35–42; Robert D. Buzzell, John A. Quelch, and Walter J. Salmon, "The Costly Bargain of Trade Promotion," *Harvard Business Review* (March–April 1990), pp. 141–49; and Mary L. Nicastro, "Break-Even Analysis Determines Success of Sales Promotions," *Marketing News* (March 5, 1990), p. 11.

16. *The 1996 Review of Couponing Trends* (Markham: Ontario: NCH Promotional Services, January 1997).

17. Kapil Bawa and Robert W. Shoemaker, "Analyzing Incremental Sales from a Direct-Mail Coupon Promotion," *Journal of Marketing* (July 1989), pp. 66–78.

18. Roger A. Strang, "Sales Promotion—Fast Growth, Faulty Management," *Harvard Business Review,* vol. 54 (July–August 1976), pp. 115–24; and Ronald W. Ward and James E. Davis, "Coupon Redemption," *Journal of Advertising Research,* vol. 18 (August 1978), pp. 51–58.

19. Larry Armstrong, "Coupon Clippers, Save Your Scissors," *Business Week* (June 20, 1994), pp. 164–66.

20. Gail Chiasson, "Men's Fragrance Market Gets A Couple of New Players," *Marketing* (March 27, 1995), p. 4.

21. James Pollock, "The Poop on Ultra Diapers," *Marketing* (November 22, 1993), p. 4.

22. Jeff Lobb, "The Right (Pepsi) Stuff," *Marketing* (July 8, 1996), p. 15.

23. Kathleen Deveny, "Displays Pay Off for Grocery Marketers," *The Wall Street Journal* (October 15, 1992), pp. B1, B5; "VideOcart Is Rolling Again," *Promo* (August 1991), pp. 1, 36; and Bradley Johnson, "Retailers Check Out In-Store," *Advertising Age* (December 16, 1991), p. 23.

24. "Marketers Trumpet 'Swan Princess,' " *Promo* (June 1995), p. 1.

25. Marvin A. Jolson, Joshua L. Wiener, and Richard B. Rosecky, "Correlates of Rebate Proneness," *Journal of Advertising Research* (February–March 1987), pp. 33–43.

26. Darlin, "Junior Mints," pp. 90–94.

27. George E. Belch and Michael A. Belch, *Introduction to Advertising and Promotion,* 2nd ed. (Burr Ridge, IL: Richard D. Irwin, 1993), pp. 613–18.

28. Ibid, p. 613.

29. G. A. Marken, "Firms Can Maintain Control over Creative Co-op Programs," *Marketing News* (September 28, 1992), pp. 7, 9.

30. Leon Reinstein, "Intel's Pentium: A Study in Flawed Public Relations," *Business Week* (January 23, 1995), p. 13; and David Kirkpatrick, "Intel's Tainted Tylenol?" *Fortune* (December 26, 1994), pp. 23–24.

31. Scott Hue, "Free 'Plugs' Supply Ad Power," *Advertising Age* (January 29, 1990), p. 6.

32. Marc Weinberger, Jean Romeo, and Azhar Piracha, "Negative Product Safety News: Coverage, Responses, and Effects," *Business Horizons* (May–June 1991), pp. 23–31.

33. "AT&T Saddles Up with Stampede," *Marketing* (July 14, 1997)—www.marketingmag.ca, July 17, 1997; "News in Brief," *Marketing* (July 7, 1997)—www.marketingmag.ca, July 17, 1997; "Marketers Warming to the Caribana Festival," *Marketing* (June 30, 1997)—www.marketingmag.ca, July 17, 1997.

34. Michael McCullough, "Salmon Farmers Aim to Remake Their Image," *Marketing* (August 5, 1996), p. 2.

35. Michael Treacy and Fred Wiersema, "Customer Intimacy and Other Value Disciplines," *Harvard Business Review* (January–February 1993), pp. 84–93.

36. Scott Hume and Ricardo Davis, "Successful Promos Stress Value-Added," *Advertising Age* (September 21, 1992), p. 35; Zachary Schiller, "Not Everyone Loves a Supermarket Deal," *Business Week* (February 17, 1992), pp. 64–68; and Patricia Sellers, "The Dumbest Marketing Ploy," *Fortune* (October 5, 1992), pp. 88–94.

37. Herbert J. Rotfeld, Avery M. Abernathy, and Patrick R. Parsons, "Self-Regulation and Television Advertising," *Journal of Advertising,* 19, no. 4 (1990), pp. 18–26.

Vitality Health Food Store: This case was prepared by Frederick G. Crane.

CHAPTER 20

1. Debra Aho Williamson, "Marketers Link Up to the Tune of $54.7 Mil," *Advertising Age* (January 22, 1996), p. 28.

2. David Farwell, "What's Cooking on the Web," *Marketing* (July 7, 1997)—www.marketingmag.ca, July 17, 1997.

3. Ibid; and Julian Dibbell, "Nielsen Rates the Net," *Time* (November 13, 1995), p. 121.

4. David A. Aaker and Donald Norris, "Characteristics of TV Commercials Perceived as Informative," *Journal of Advertising Research,* vol. 22, no. 2 (April–May 1982), pp. 61–70.

5. William Wilkie and Paul W. Farris, "Comparison Advertising: Problems and Potentials," *Journal of Marketing,* vol. 39, no. 4 (October 1975), pp. 7–15.

6. Jennifer Lawrence "P&G Ads Get Competitive," *Advertising Age* (February 1, 1993), p. 14; Jerry Gotlieb and Dan Sorel, "The Influence of Type of Advertisement, Price, and Source Credibility on Perceived Quality," *Journal of the Academy of Marketing Science* (Summer 1992), pp. 253–60; and Cornelia Pechman and David Stewart, "The Effects of Comparative Advertising on Attention, Memory, and Purchase Intentions," *Journal of Consumer Research* (September 1990), pp. 180–92.

7. Bruce Buchanan and Doron Goldman, "Us vs. Them: The Minefield of Comparative Ads," *Harvard Business Review* (May–June 1989), pp. 38–50; Dorothy Cohen, "The FTC's Advertising Substantiation Program," *Journal of Marketing* (Winter 1980), pp. 26–35; and Michael Etger and Stephen A. Goodwin, "Planning for Comparative Advertising Requires Special Attention," *Journal of Advertising,* vol. 8, no. 1 (Winter 1979), pp. 26–32.

8. Lewis C. Winters, "Does It Pay to Advertise to Hostile Audiences with Corporate Advertising?" *Journal of Advertising Research* (June/July 1988), pp. 11–18; and Robert Selwitz, "The Selling of an Image," *Madison Avenue* (February 1985), pp. 61–69.

9. Robert J. Lavidge and Gary A. Steiner, "A Model for Predictive Measurement of Advertising Effectiveness," *Journal of Marketing* (October 1961), p. 61.

10. Brian Wansink and Michael Ray, "Advertising Strategies to Increase Usage Frequency," *Journal of Marketing* (January 1996), pp. 31–46.

11. "Global Ad Spending Growing," *Marketing* (June 30, 1997)—www.marketingmag.ca, July 17, 1997.

12. J. Enrique Bigne, "Advertising Budgeting Practices: A Review," *Journal of Current Issues and Research in Advertising* (Fall 1995), pp. 17–31.

13. John Philip Jones, "Ad Spending: Maintaining Market Share," *Harvard Business Review* (January–February 1990), pp. 38–42; and Charles H. Patti and Vincent Blanko, "Budgeting Practices of Big Advertisers," *Journal of Advertising Research,* vol. 21 (December 1981), pp. 23–30.

14. James A. Schroer, "Ad Spending: Growing Market Share," *Harvard Business Review* (January–February 1990), pp. 44–48.

15. Jeffrey A. Lowenhar and John L. Stanton, "Forecasting Competitive Advertising Expenditures," *Journal of Advertising Research,* vol. 16, no. 2 (April 1976), pp. 37–44.

16. Daniel Seligman, "How Much for Advertising?" *Fortune* (December 1956), p. 123.

17. James E. Lynch and Graham J. Hooley, "Increasing Sophistication in Advertising Budget Setting," *Journal of Advertising Research,* 30 (February/March 1990), pp. 67–75.

18. Jimmy D. Barnes, Brenda J. Muscove, and Javad Rassouli, "An Objective and Task Media Selection Decision Model and Advertising Cost Formula to Determine International Advertising Budgets," *Journal of Advertising,* vol. 11, no. 4 (1982), pp. 68–75.

19. Bob Garfield, "Allstate Ads Bring Home Point about Mortgage Insurance," *Advertising Age* (September 11, 1989), p. 120; and Judann Dagnoli, " 'Buy or Die' Mentality Toned Down in Ads," *Advertising Age* (May 7, 1990), p. S–12.

20. Jeffery D. Zbar, "Fear!" *Advertising Age* (November 14, 1994), pp. 18–19; John F. Tanner, Jr., James B. Hunt, and David R. Eppright, "The Protection Motivation Model: A Normative Model of Fear Appeals," *Journal of Marketing* (July 1991), pp. 36–45; Michael S. LaTour and Shaker A Zahra, "Fear Appeals as Advertising Strategy: Should They Be Used?" *The Journal of Consumer Marketing* (Spring 1989), pp. 61–70; and Joshua Levine, "Don't Fry Your Brain," *Forbes* (February 4, 1991), pp. 116–17.

21. "Price Cuts and Lesbians," *Marketing* (July 7, 1997)—www.marketing mag.ca, July 17, 1997; and "Regulator Holds up Molson's Lesbian Kiss," *Marketing* (June 16, 1997)—www.marketingmag.ca, July 18, 1997.

22. Dana L. Alden, Wayne D. Hoyer, and Chol Lee, "Identifying Global and Culture-Specific Dimensions of Humor in Advertising: A Multinational Analysis," *Journal of Marketing* (April 1993), pp. 64–75; and Johny K. Johansson, "The Sense of 'Nonsense': Japanese TV Advertising," *Journal of Advertising* (March 1994), pp. 17–26.

23. Iris Cohen Selinger, "DDB Needham Turns a Clever Phrase," *Advertising Age* (April 10, 1995), pp. S-4, 34.

24. Alan R. Miciak and William L. Shanklin, "Choosing Celebrity Endorsers," *Marketing Management,* vol. 3, no. 3 (1995), pp. 51–59; and Kevin Goldman, "Candice Bergen Leads the List of Top Celebrity Endorsers," *The Wall Street Journal* (September 17, 1993), pp. B1, 10.

25. Kim Cleland, "More Advertisers Put Informercials into Their Plans," *Advertising Age* (September 18, 1995), p. 50; and John Pfeiffer, "Six Months and a Half a Million Dollars, All for 15 Seconds," *Smithsonian* (October 1987), pp. 134–35.

26. Giles D'Souza and Ram C. Rao, "Can Repeating an Advertisement More Frequently than the Competition Affect Brand Preference in a Mature Market?" *Journal of Marketing* (April 1995), pp. 32–42.

27. *Media Digest* (Toronto: Canadian Media Directors' Council, 1996–97).

28. Ibid.

29. Surendra N. Singh, Denise Linville, and Ajay Sukhdial, "Enhancing the Efficacy of Split Thirty-Second Television Commercials: An Encoding Variability Application," *Journal of Advertising* (Fall 1995), pp. 13–23.

30. Joe Mandese, "In New Growth Phase, Cable Feeding on Itself," *Advertising Age* (March 27, 1995), pp. S-1, 2, 10.

31. Jacqueline M. Graves, "The Fortune 500 Opt for Infomercials," *Fortune* (March 6, 1995), p. 20; and William McCall, "Infomercial Pioneer Becomes Industry Leader," *Marketing News* (June 19, 1995), p. 14.

32. *Media Digest*

33. Ibid.

34. Arch G. Woodside, "Outdoor Advertising as Experiments," *Journal of the Academy of Marketing Science,* 18 (Summer 1990), pp. 229–37.

35. "News," *Marketing* (June 23, 1997)—www.marketingmag.ca, July 18, 1997.

36. Mikala Folb, "E-mail Marketers Avoid Serving Spam," *Marketing* (July 7, 1997)—www.marketingmag.ca, July 17, 1997.

37. Sehoon Park and Minhi Hahn, "Pulsing in a Discrete Model of Advertising Competition," *Journal of Marketing Research* (November 1991), pp. 397–405.

38. Rob Norton, "How Uninformative Advertising Tells Consumers Quite a Bit," *Fortune* (December 26, 1994), p. 37; and "Professor Claims Corporations Waste Billions on Advertising," *Marketing News* (July 6, 1992), p. 5.

39. Mary Kuntz, "Now Mad Ave Really has to Sing for Its Supper," *Business Week* (December 18, 1995), p. 43.

40. The discussion of posttesting is based on William F. Arens, *Contemporary Advertising,* 6th ed. (Burr Ridge, IL: Richard D. Irwin, 1996), pp. 181–182.

41. David A. Aaker and Douglas M. Stayman, "Measuring Audience Perceptions of Commercials and Relating Them to Ad Impact," *Journal of Advertising Research,* 30 (August/September 1990), pp. 7–17; and Ernest Dichter, "A Psychological View of Advertising Effectiveness," *Marketing Management,* vol. 1, no. 3 (1992), pp. 60–62.

42. Dave Kruegel, "Television Advertising Effectiveness and Research Innovation," *Journal of Consumer Marketing* (Summer 1988), pp. 43–51; and Laurence N. Gold, "The Evolution of Television Advertising-Sales Measurement: Past, Present, and Future," *Journal of Advertising Research* (June/July 1988), pp. 19–24.

43. Roland T. Rust and Richard W. Oliver, "The Death of Advertising," *Journal of Advertising* (December 1994), pp. 71–77; Richard J. Fox and Gary L. Geissler, "Crisis in Advertising?" *Journal of Advertising* (December 1994), pp. 79–84; and Zachary Schiller and Ron Grover, "And Now, a Show from Your Sponsor," *Business Week* (May 22, 1995), pp. 100–2.

44. Ronald B. Lieber, "Here Comes the TV Commercial No Remote Control Can Zap," *Fortune* (October 16, 1995), p. 31.

45. Jeffery D. Zbar, "Blurring the Ad-Editorial Line," *Advertising Age* (November 13, 1995), p. 14; Keith J. Kelly, " 'Time,' 'Newsweek' Say Hi to Tech Titles," *Advertising Age* (July 31, 1995), p. 7.

Lysol: This case was prepared by Frederick G. Crane based on information supplied by the Television Bureau of Canada (TVB).

CHAPTER 21

1. Peter Serenyi, "The Pink Revolution," *The Dallas Morning News* (September 25, 1995), pp. 1C, 11C.

2. "Tying the Knot," *The Economist* (May 14, 1994), p. 3.

3. Statistics Canada, *Canada Year Book,* cat. 11-402E (Ottawa, 1997).

4. Paul S. Busch and Michael J. Houston, *Marketing: Strategic Foundations* (Homewood, IL: Richard D. Irwin, 1985), p. 706.

5. Jaclyn Fierman, "The Death and Rebirth of the Salesman," *Fortune* (July 25, 1994), pp. 80–91; "Teaming Up," *Sales & Marketing Management* (October 1993), pp. 98–104; "Getting Hot Ideas from Customers," *Business Week* (May 18, 1992), pp. 86–87; and Brian Tracy, "Stop Talking and Start Asking Questions," *Sales & Marketing Management* (February 1995), pp. 79–87.

6. For different perspectives on relationship selling, see Catherine Romano, "Death of a Salesman," *Management Review* (September 1994), pp. 10–15; Lawrence A. Crosby, Kenneth R. Evans, and Deborah Cowles, "Relationship Quality in Services Selling: An Interpersonal Influence Perspective," *Journal of Marketing* (July 1990), pp. 68–81; Barry J. Farber and Joyce Wycoff, "Relationships: Six Steps to Success," *Sales & Marketing Management* (April 1992), pp. 50–56; and Gerrard Macintosh, Kenneth A. Anglin, David M. Szymanski, and James W. Gentry, "Relationship Development in Selling: A Cognitive Analysis," *Journal of Personal Selling and Sales Management* (Fall 1992), pp. 23–34.

7. David W. Cravens, "The Changing Role of the Sales Force," *Marketing Management* (Fall 1995), pp. 49–57; and Charles E. Pettijohn, Linda S. Pettijohn, and R. Stephen Parker, "An Exploratory Analysis of the Impact of Salesperson Customer-Orientation on Sales Force Productivity," *Journal of Customer Service in Marketing and Management,* vol. 3, no. 4 (1997), pp. 5–24.

8. For a perspective on types of selling, see Thomas R. Wotruba, "The Evolution of Personal Selling," *Journal of Personal Selling & Sales Management* (Summer 1991), pp. 1–12.

9. For up-to-date information on selling costs, see *Sales & Marketing Management* magazine's yearly June issue.

10. "Despite Hangups, Telemarketing a Success," *Marketing News* (March 27, 1995), p. 19.

11. For recent research on team selling, see Dawn R. Deeter-Schmelz and Rosemary Ramsey, "A Conceptualization of the Functions and Roles of Formalized Selling and Buying Teams," *Journal of Personal Selling & Sales Management* (Spring 1995), pp. 47–60.

12. "The Selling Game," *The Wall Street Journal* (March 29, 1994), p. A1; "Smart Selling," *Business Week* (August 3, 1992), pp. 46–50; and Susan Caminti, "Finding New Ways to Sell More," *Fortune* (July 27, 1992), pp. 100–103.

13. For further reading, see Marvin A. Jolson and Thomas R. Wotruba, "Prospecting: A New Look at This Old Challenge," *Journal of Personal Selling & Sales Management* (Fall 1992), pp. 59–66. See also Bob Donath et al., "When Your Prospect Calls," *Marketing Management,* vol. 3, no. 2 (1994), pp. 26–37.

14. Carol J. Loomis, "Have You Been Cold-Called?" *Fortune* (December 16, 1991), pp. 109–15.

15. "Corporate Cultures: Clearing Customs," *SKY Magazine* (July 1995), pp. 35–40.

16. See Irma Zandl and Richard Leonard, *Targeting the Trendsetting Consumer* (Homewood, IL: Business One Irwin, 1992), p. 141.

17. James Pollock, "In Pursuit of Privacy," *Marketing* (June 4, 1993), pp. 1, 4.

18. Ronald B. Marks, *Personal Selling: An Integrative Approach,* 3rd ed. (Boston, MA: Allyn & Bacon, 1988), p. 239.

19. "Doing Business in Chili," *American Way Magazine* (July 15, 1995), p. 40.

20. "Corporate Cultures: Clearing Customs."

21. For a variation on the "canned presentation," see Marvin A. Jolson, "Canned Adaptiveness: A New Direction for Modern Salesmanship," *Business Horizons* (January–February 1989), pp. 7–12.

22. Thomas Blackshear and Richard E. Plank, "The Impact of Adaptive Selling on Sales Effectiveness within the Pharmaceutical Industry," *Journal of Marketing Theory and Practice* (Summer 1994), pp. 106–25.

23. Based on David Mercer, *High-Level Selling* (Houston, TX: Golf Publishing, 1990), pp. 130–31; and Ronald D. Balsley and E. Patricia Birsner, *Selling: Marketing Personified* (Hinsdale, IL: Dryden Press, 1987), pp. 261–63.

24. Philip R. Cateora, *International Marketing,* 9th ed. (Chicago: Richard D. Irwin, 1996), pp. 126–27; Carl R. Ruthstrom and Ken Matejka, "The Meanings of 'Yes' in the Far East," *Industrial Marketing Management,* 19 (1990), pp. 191–92. See also Terri Morrison, Wayne A. Conaway, and George A. Borden, *Kiss, Bow, or Shake Hands* (Newton Square, PA: Adam Media Group, 1994).

25. Theodore Levitt, *The Marketing Imagination* (New York: Free Press, 1983), p. 111.

26. Janis L. Miller, Larry Fredendall, and J. Wayne Patterson, "A Markov Analysis of Customer Retention and Recruitment," *Journal of Customer Service in Marketing and Management,* vol. 3, no. 2 (1997), pp. 35–53; and "Leading Edge," *Sales and Marketing Management* (July 1995), p. 13.

27. *Management Briefing: Marketing* (New York: The Conference Board, October 1986), pp. 3–4.

28. Based on Barton A. Weitz, Stephen B. Castleberry, and John F. Tanner, Jr., *Selling: Building Partnerships* (Homewood, IL: Richard D. Irwin, 1992), pp. 7–8; Alan J. Dubinsky, Marvin A. Jolson, Ronald E. Michaels, Masaaki Kotobe, and Chae Un Lim, "Ethical Perceptions of Field Sales Personnel: An Empirical Assessment," *Journal of Personal Selling & Sales Management* (Fall 1992), pp. 9–21; and Alan J. Dubinsky, Marvin A. Jolson, Masaaki Kotobe, and Chae Un Lim, "A Cross-National Investigation of Industrial Salespeople's Ethical Perceptions," *Journal of International Business Studies* (Fourth Quarter 1991), pp. 651–70.

29. Benson Shapiro, *Sales Program Management: Formulation and Implementation* (New York: McGraw-Hill, 1977), pp. 250–55.

30. Several variations of the account management policy grid exist. See, for example, Gilbert A. Churchill, Jr., Neil M. Ford, and Orville C. Walker, Jr., *Sales Force Management: Planning, Implementation, and Control,* 5th ed. (Chicago, IL: Richard D. Irwin, 1997), p. 249; and David W. Cravens, Thomas N. Ingram, and Raymond W. LaForge, "Evaluating Multiple Channel Strategies," *The Journal of Business & Industrial Marketing* (Fall 1991), pp. 37–48.

31. Churchill, Ford, and Walker, *Sales Force Management.*

32. This discussion is based on Douglas J. Dalrymple and William L. Cron, *Sales Management,* 5th ed. (New York: John Wiley & Sons, Inc., 1995), pp. 421–24.

33. "What Buyers Look For," *Sales & Marketing Management* (August 1995), p. 31.

34. Neil M. Ford, Orville C. Walker, Jr., Gilbert A. Churchill, Jr., and Steven W. Hartley, "Selecting Successful Salespeople: A Meta-Analysis of Biographical and Psychological Selection Criteria," in Michael J. Houston, ed., *Review of Marketing 1987* (Chicago: American Marketing Association, 1988), pp. 90–131.

35. "Is There a Payoff?" *Sales & Marketing Management* (June 1995), pp. 64–71.

36. Earl D. Honeycutt, Jr., Clyde E. Harris, Jr., and Stephen B. Castleberry, "Sales Training: A Status Report," *Training and Development Journal* (May 1987), pp. 42–47.

37. Dalrymple and Cron, *Sales Management;* Joseph P. Vaccaro, *Managing Sales Professionals* (New York: The Haworth Press Inc., 1995).

38. Harry A. Harmon, "Customer Satisfaction: The Sales Manager's Role in Reducing the Communication Gap," *Journal of Customer Service in Marketing and Management,* vol. 3, no. 3 (1997), pp. 35–52; William L. Cron, Alan J. Dubinsky, and Ronald E. Michaels, "The Influence of Career Stages on Components of Salesperson Motivation," *Journal of Marketing* (January 1988), pp. 78–92; and Walter Kiechel III, "How to Manage Salespeople," *Fortune* (March 14, 1988), pp. 179–80.

39. For statistics and research on salesperson turnover, see "Turnover Rates by Industry Group," *Sales & Marketing Management* (June 22, 1992); René Y. Darmon, "Identifying Sources of Turnover Costs: A Segmental Approach," *Journal of Marketing* (April 1990), pp. 46–56; and Thomas R. Wotruba and Pradeep K. Tyagi, "Met Expectations and Turnover in Direct Selling," *Journal of Marketing* (July 1991), pp. 24–35.

40. Mark Fawcett, "Getting with the Program," *The Financial Post Magazine* (March 1996), pp. 48–49, and 58; and David E. Bowen and Edward E. Lawler III, "Contemporary Service Employees," *Sloan Management Review* (Summer 1995), pp. 73–84.

41. George W. Colombo, *Sales Force Automation* (New York: McGraw-Hill, 1994).

42. Robert L. Lindstrom, "Training Hits the Road," *Sales & Marketing Management,* part 2 (June 1995), pp. 10–14.

43. Cravens, "Evaluating Multiple Channel Strategies."

44. "The Office That Never Closes," *Forbes* (May 23, 1994), pp. 212–13.

Contemporary Developments in Selling Today: This case was prepared by Linda Rochford.

CHAPTER 22

1. Greg Burns, "A Fruit Loop by Any Other Name . . ." *Business Week* (June 26, 1995), pp. 72–76.

2. *General Mills 1995 Midyear Report* (Minneapolis, MN: General Mills, Inc., 1995); and Richard Gibson, "General Mills to Spin Off Restaurants in Effort to Focus on Its Core Business," *The Wall Street Journal* (December 15, 1994), pp. A3, A9.

3. Kevin Goldman, "General Mills to Launch Frosted Cheerios," *The Wall Street Journal* (July 25, 1995), p. B3; Terry Fledler, "Soul of a New Cheerios," *Star Tribune* (January 28, 1996), pp. D1, D4; and Tony Kennedy, "New Cheerios about to Sweeten Cereal Market," *Star Tribune* (July 25, 1995), pp. 1D, 2D.

4. Pankaj Ghemawat, "Sustainable Advantage," *Harvard Business Review* (September–October 1986), pp. 53–58.

5. Clare L. Comm, "The Use of Scheduling and Inflight Customer Service Quality as Competitive Marketing Tools in the Asian Airline Industry," *Journal of Customer Service in Marketing and Management,* vol. 3, no. 3 (1997), pp. 101–108; and Roger A. Kerin, P. Rajan Varadarajan, and Robert A. Peterson, "First-Mover Advantage: A Synthesis, Conceptual Framework, and Research Propositions," *Journal of Marketing* (October 1992), pp. 33–52.

6. Murali K. Mantrala, Prabhakant Sirha, and Andris A. Zoltners, "Impact of Resource Allocation Rules on Marketing Investment-Level Decisions and Profitability," *Journal of Marketing Research* (May 1992), pp. 162–75.

7. Leah Rickard, "General Mills Gathers Rewards of Change," *Advertising Age* (July 10, 1995), p. 4.

8. This discussion and Figure 22-3 are adapted from Stanley F. Stasch and Patricia Longtree, "Can Your Marketing Planning Procedures Be Improved?" *Journal of Marketing* (Summer 1980), p. 82; by permission of the American Marketing Association.

9. Fledler, "Soul of a New Cheerios."

10. Ibid.

11. Adapted with permission of The Free Press, a Division of Macmillan, Inc., from *Competitive Advantage: Creating and Sustaining Superior Performance* by Michael E. Porter. Copyright 1985 by Michael E. Porter.

12. William B. Wertner, Jr. and Jeffrey L. Kerr, "The Shifting Sands of Competitive Advantage," *Business Horizons* (May–June, 1995), pp. 11–17.

13. Michael Treacy and Fred Wiersma, "How Market Leaders Keep Their Edge," *Fortune* (February 6, 1995), pp. 88–89; and Comm, "The Use of Scheduling."

14. J. Martin Fraering and Michael S. Minor, "The Industry-Specific Basis of the Market Share-Profitability Relationship," *Journal of Consumer Marketing,* vol. 11, no. 1 (1994), pp. 27–37.

15. Michael Oneal, " 'God, Family, and Domino's—That's It,' " *Business Week* (January 30, 1995), pp. 57–60.

16. Stratford Sherman, "How Intel Makes Spending Pay Off," *Fortune* (February 22, 1993), pp. 57–61.

17. Lee Ginsburg and Neil Miller, "Value-Driven Management," *Business Horizons* (May–June 1992), pp. 23–27; Richard L. Osborn, "Core Value Statements: The Corporate Compass," *Business Horizons* (September–October 1991), pp. 28–34; and Charles E. Watson, "Managing with Integrity: Social Responsibilities of Business as Seen by America's CEOs," *Business Horizons* (July–August 1991), pp. 99–109.

18. Reprinted by permission of the *Harvard Business Review.* An exhibit from "Making Your Marketing Strategy Work" by Thomas V. Bonoma (March/April 1984). Copyright © 1984 by the President and Fellows of Harvard College; all rights reserved.

19. Larry Hirschhorn and Thomas Gilmore, "The New Boundaries of the 'Boundaryless' Company," *Harvard Business Review* (May–June 1992), pp. 104–15.

20. Stephen J. Tvorik and Robet Boissoneau, "Developing Effective Teams in Marketing Organizations for Service and Quality Enhancements," *Journal of Customer Service in Marketing and Management,* vol. 3, no. 3 (1997), pp. 19–34; John Byrne, Richard Brandt, and Otis Port, "The Virtual Corporation," *Business Week* (February 8, 1993), pp. 98–103; Hans Hinterhuber and Wolfgang Popp, "Are You a Strategist or Just a Manager?" *Harvard Business Review* (January–February 1992), pp. 105–13; Thomas Steward, "The Search for the Organization of Tomorrow," *Fortune* (May 18, 1992), pp. 92–98; George Stalf, Philip Evans, and Lawrence Shulman, "Competing on Capabilities: The New Rules of Corporate Strategy," *Harvard Business Review* (March–April 1992), pp. 57–69; and Jon Katzenbach and Douglas Smith, *The Wisdom of Teams* (Boston, MA: Harvard Business School Press, 1992).

21. Don Frey, "Learning the Ropes: My Life as a Product Champion," *Harvard Business Review* (September–October 1991), pp. 46–56.

22. Thomas J. Peters and Robert H. Waterman, Jr., *In Search of Excellence: Lessons from America's Best-Run Companies* (New York: Harper & Row, 1982).

23. Tim Falconer, "A Classic Comes of Age," *Marketing* (September 13, 1993), pp. 1, 3.

24. The scheduling example is adapted from William Rudelius and W. Bruce Erickson, *An Introduction to Contemporary Business,* 4th ed. (New York: Harcourt Brace Jovanovich, 1985), pp. 94–95.

25. Robert W. Ruekert and Orville W. Walker, Jr., "Marketing's Interaction with Other Functional Units: A Conceptual Framework and Empirical Evidence," *Journal of Consumer Marketing* (Spring 1987), pp. 1–19; and Steven Lysonski, Alan Singer, and David Wilemone, "Coping with Environmental Uncertainty and Boundary Spanning in the Product Manager's Role," *Journal of Consumer Marketing* (Spring 1989), pp. 33–43.

26. Doug McCuaig and Christopher Holt, "Getting Intimate with Customers," *Marketing* (July 14, 1997)—www.marketingmag.ca, July 17, 1997.

Clearly Canadian: This case was prepared by Frederick G. Crane based on information supplied by Clearly Canadian Beverage Corporation.

APPENDIX C

1. Denny E. McCorkle, Joe F. Alexander, and Memo F. Diriker, "Developing Self-Marketing Skills for Student Career Success," *Journal of Marketing Education* (Spring 1992), pp. 57–67.

2. "Jobs, jobs, jobs," *Marketing* (June 30, 1997)—www.marketingmag.ca, July 17, 1997.

3. Linda M. Gorchels, "Traditional Product Management Evolves," *Marketing News* (January 30, 1995), p. 4.

4. David Kirkpatrick, "Is Your Career on Track?" *Fortune* (July 2, 1990), pp. 38–48.

5. Robin T. Peterson, "Wholesaling: A Neglected Job Opportunity for Marketing Majors," *Marketing News* (January 15, 1996), p. 4.

6. "The Climb to the Top," *Careers in Retailing* (January 1995), p. 18.

7. Michael R. Wukitsch, "Should Researchers Know More about Marketing?" *Marketing Research* (Winter 1993), p. 50.

8. "Market Research Analyst," in Les Krantz, ed., *Jobs Rated Almanac,* 3rd ed. (New York: John Wiley & Sons, 1995).

9. Cyndee Miller, "Marketing Research Salaries Up a Bit, But Layoffs Take Toll," *Marketing News* (June 19, 1995), pp. 1, 3.

10. Joby John and Mark Needel, "Entry-Level Marketing Research Recruits: What Do Recruiters Need?" *Journal of Marketing Education* (Spring 1989), pp. 68–73.

11. Kathryn Petras and Ross Petras, *Jobs 95* (New York: Fireside, 1994), pp. 100–18.

12. "Your Job Search Starts with You," *Job Choices: 1996,* 39th ed. (Bethlehem, PA: National Association of Colleges and Employers, 1995), pp. 6–9.

13. Arthur F. Miller, "Discover Your Design," in *CPC Annual,* vol. 1 (Bethlehem, PA: College Placement Council, Inc., 1984), p. 2.

14. Robin T. Peterson and J. Stuart Devlin, "Perspectives on Entry-Level Positions by Graduating Marketing Seniors," *Marketing Education Review* (Summer 1994), pp. 2–5.

15. Diane Goldner, "Fill in the Blank," *The Wall Street Journal* (February 27, 1995), pp. R5, R11.

16. Constance J. Pritchard, "Small Employers—How, When & Who They Hire," *Job Choices: 1996,* 39th ed. (Bethlehem, PA: National Association of Colleges and Employers, 1995), pp. 66–69.

17. Adapted from C. Randall Powell, "Secrets of Selling a Résumé," in Peggy Schmidt, ed., *The Honda How to Get a Job Guide* (New York: McGraw-Hill, 1985), pp. 4–9.

18. Joyce Lain Kennedy and Thomas J. Morrow, *Electronic Résumé Revolution* (New York: John Wiley & Sons, 1994).

19. Arthur G. Sharp, "The Art of the Cover Letter," *Career Futures,* vol. 4, no. 1 (1992), pp. 50–51.

20. Perri Capell, "Unconventional Job Search Tactics," *Managing Your Career* (Spring 1991), pp. 31, 35.

21. Julie Griffin Levitt, *Your Career: How to Make It Happen* (Cincinnati, OH: South-Western Publishing Co., 1985).

APPENDIX D

1. This case was prepared by Rajiv Vaidyanathan and Linda Rochford from the following sources: Amy Cortese, "Windows of Opportunity for Big Blue?" *Business Week* (October 17, 1994), p. 184; Laurie Flynn, "IBM Software Chief Sees an Opening for OS/2," *New York Times* (July 24, 1994), p. 7; Craig Stedman, "What's Ahead for OS/2?" *Computerworld,* vol. 29 (August 7, 1995), p. 4; Bart Ziegler, "Glitch Halts IBM Software Production," *The Wall Street Journal* (October 27, 1994), p. B8; Bart Ziegler, "IBM Won't Provide Way for Programs for Windows 95 to Run on OS/2 System," *The Wall Street Journal* (June 20, 1995), p. B6; and Laurence Zuckerman, "IBM Chief Concedes OS/2 Has Lost Desktop War," *New York Times* (August 1, 1995), p. D4.

2. This case was prepared by Linda Rochford and Rajiv Vaidyanathan from the following sources: Interview with Doran Normi, Kingpin Manufacturing; and the National Sporting Goods Association, "1993 Sports Participation Study."

3. This case was prepared by Roger A. Kerin.

4. This case was prepared by Rajiv Vaidyanathan and Linda Rochford from the following sources: "Heights and Depths of Hype," *Advertising Age* (August 28, 1995), pp. 1, 33; Matt Carmichael, "Web Sites Showcase Win 95," *Advertising Age* (August 28, 1995), p. 33; Alice Z. Cuneo, "Apple Gets Gnarly Over Introduction," *Advertising Age* (August 28, 1995); Michael Himowitz "Windows 95: Do You Need the Most Overhyped Product of the Decade?" *Fortune* (September 18, 1995), pp. 191–96; Bradley Johnson "D-Day Countdown for Win 95, Microsoft Net," *Advertising Age* (August 7, 1995), p. 3; and Bradley Johnson, "Windows 95 Opens with Omnimedia Blast," *Advertising Age* (August 28, 1995), pp. 1, 32.

5. This case was prepared by Linda Rochford and Rajiv Vaidyanathan from the following sources: "Image-conscious Consumers Wear Social Ambitions on Wrist," *Duluth News Tribune* (August 2, 1995), p. 6; "Timex Plans $10M Push in 4th Quarter," *Advertising Age* (September 6, 1993), p. 23; "Timex, Swatch Campaigns Set for Battle," *The Wall Street Journal* (May 31, 1995), p. B9; "The Best Advertising of 1992," *Time* (January 4, 1993), p. 70; Riccardo A. Davis, "More Ads to Watch," *Advertising Age* (February 7, 1994), p. 50; Elaine Underwood, "Indiglo Watch Lights Up, Better Times for Timex," *Brandweek* (April 25, 1994), pp. 30–32; Neal McGrath, "Timex, After a Licking, They're Back Ticking," *Asian Business* (December 1994), pp. 18–20; and Chris Roush, "At Timex, They're Positively Glowing," *Business Week* (July 12, 1993), p. 141.

6. This case was prepared by Roger A. Kerin.

7. This case was prepared by Roger A. Kerin from the following sources: "Hasbro's Hopes for Maxie Model Come to an End," *The Wall Street Journal* (February 12, 1990), p. B4; "For Video Games, Now It's a Battle of Bits," *The Wall Street Journal* (January 9, 1990), pp. B1, B4; "Barbie Is on the Front Line for Marketing Ethnic Dolls," *Dallas Times Herald* (August 30, 1990), pp. D1, D4; "It's Kid Brother's Turn to Keep Hasbro Hot," *Business Week* (June 26, 1989), pp. 152–53; "Toyland Turnaround," *Forbes* (January 9, 1989), pp. 168–69; Andrea Stone, "Toy Fair No Picnic for Toy Industry," *USA Today* (February 8, 1988), pp. B1–B2; and "Mattel Takes Page from Hasbro Playbook," *The Wall Street Journal* (January 30, 1996), p. B7.

8. This case was prepared by Frederick G. Crane. Source: Second Harvest.

9. This case was prepared by Frederick G. Crane based on information contained in *Canadian Advertising Success Stories* (Toronto: Canadian Congress of Advertising, 1995). Used with permission.

10. Ibid.

NAME INDEX

COMPANY/PRODUCTS INDEX

NutraSweet, 338, 340
Nutro Pet Food, 387

O

Ocean Spray, 196, 197, 199, 205
Office Depot, 431
Oil of Olay, 268, 298
O'Keefe 6.2, 162
Oldsmobile, 82, 235
Olestra, 340
Olympics, 18
Olympus cameras, 138
OmmiLogic, 175
Oneida Factory Store, 441
1-2-3 Dollar Store, 531
Onkyo CD player, 145
Online Photo Centre, 275
Ontario Hydro, 339
Opel Omega, 236
Oppenheimer & Co., 533
Orbitz, 264, 265–266, 292, 550, 551
    case, 288–289
Ore-Ida Foods Inc., 86
Osborne Computers, 24
Oscar Mayer Low-Fat Lunchables, 300
Owens-Corning insulation, 310
Oxfam Canada, 245

P

Pampers, 123, 301, 404
Panasonic Plain Paper Laser Fax, 225
Pantene shampoo, 299
Paradise Kitchens, Inc., 39, 41
    marketing plan, 43-44, 55–69
Parents Magazine, 78
Parlour Signature ice cream, 272
PCjr, 11–12, 304
PC Week, 567
Pennisula Farms, 31
Pentium processors; *see* Intel
PepsiCo, 116, 389–390
PepsiCo Foods International, 303, 304
Pepsi-Cola, 76, 123, 125, 138, 155, 263, 284, 341, 369, 393, 399, 461, 462, 463, 466
Perrier mineral water, 104–105
Personal communications services (PCS), 238
Personal Pair jeans, 430
PertPlus shampoo, 306
Pert shampoo, 128
Petco, 387, 402
Pet Food Warehouse, 387
PetsMart, 387, 402
Pez Candy, 308
Pfizer Inc., 340
Pharmacia and Upjohn, Inc., 86, 300
Philips CD player, 145, 146, 147
Photo CD System, 46, 49
Picturephone, 355
Pillsbury, 19–20, 253, 543–544, 545
Pillsbury Canada, 32, 267, 273, 298, 466, 552
Pillsbury's Toaster Strudel, 271
Pitney Bowes, Inc., 502
Pizza Hut Canada, 76, 161

Planta Dei Plant Medicines Inc., 78
Play Station video game, 297, 357, 366
Plunkett Communications Research Services, 210
Plymouth Neon, 174, 175
Pocahontas (film), 192
Polaroid, 11–12, 159, 267
    case, 314
Polavision, 8, 11
Polo/Ralph Lauren, 397
Pontiac, 235
Pontiac Grand Prix, 234
Pontiac models, 236
Pontiac Sunfire, 286
Popov brand of vodka, 358
Porsche, 234
Portable Personal Shopper, 434
Power Macs, 230, 231
PowerShip, 260
Pratt & Whitney, 169
Price Club, 433, 441
Price/Costco, 15
Prima Salsa Tomato Sauce, 284
PROBE, THE, 120
Problade, 26
Procter & Gamble, 21, 100, 105, 123, 125, 138, 176, 206, 301, 306, 340, 411
    advertising and promotion, 126, 128, 298, 470, 476–477, 480, 492
    careers in marketing, 552, 553, 554
    marketing channels, 399, 404
    market penetration strategy, 532
    new product development, 278, 282
    packaging, 310, 311, 414
    pricing, 371
    product modification or repositioning, 299, 300
    sales force, 502, 510, 512
Prodigy, 159, 393
Professional Marketing Research Society of Canada (PMRS), 210
Prolife, 110
Provigo Inc., 435
Publisher's Clearing House, 465
Purina Puppy Chow, 458

Q

Quaker Oats, 172, 177
Quaker State, 309
Quenchers, 292, 550
Quest software, 92
QVC, 429, 436

R

Radio Shack, 307
Ragu Extra Thick & Zesty, 284
Ralph Lauren, 397, 404
Ralston Purina Company, 21
Random House Webster's College Dictionary, 9
Reader's Digest, 130, 251–252, 465
Red Lobster restaurants, 523
Reebok Insta-Pump, 125
Reebok International, 78, 415
    market segments, 215–219
Reebok Step Trainer, 217

Remington Products, 498
Retin-A, 101
Retrovir, 110
Revlon, 157, 158, 364, 486
Ricoh Company, 400
Ritz Carlton hotels, 515
Road to Avonlea series, 134
Rockhopper bicycle, 51
Rogaine Topical Solution, 300
Rold Gold Pretzels, 452, 482, 483
Rolex, 401
Rollerblade, Inc., 3, 5–8, 12, 16–19, 41–42, 289
    case, 26–27
Roller Hockey International, 19
Rolling Stone magazine, 289
Rolls-Royce, 126, 293, 358
Ronald McDonald Houses, 106
Royal Bank, 163, 318, 325, 430, 480, 552
Royal Bank Visa, 241, 325
Royal Canadian Mint, 169
Rubbermaid, 414
Ruffles potato chips, 147, 303
Runner's World magazine, 487, 492
Ryder System, 425

S

S.O.S. pads, 22, 107
Saab, 393
Sable Gas, 372
Safeway, 177, 360, 391, 398
St. Croix Venture Partners, 53
Saks Fifth Avenue, 431
Sales and Marketing Management magazine, 253
Sam's Club, 441
Samsung, 117
Sanyo, 307
SAP Canada, 175
Saturn game, 297
Saturn Motors, 38, 235, 365, 372, 425, 541
    consumer utilities, 430
Scandinavian Airlines System, 176, 334
Schick razors, 403
Schwan's Sales Enterprises, 391
Schweppes Tonic Water, 128
Scope, 536
Scotch Archive Tape, 219
Scotch-Brite floor cleaner, 127
Scotch Brite Never Rust Wool Soap Pads, 22, 107
Scotch Collections Tape, 219
Scotch Just for Kids Tape, 219
Scotch Re-Taping Tape, 219
Scotch Tape, 9
Scotch videotapes, 219
Scott Paper, 86
Sears Canada, 76, 92, 177, 244–245, 301, 302, 307, 312, 339, 358, 364, 388, 391, 393, 442, 446
    "soft side" promotional program, 39, 491
Second Cup, 306
Second Harvest, 245
    case, 577
Sega Enterprises, Ltd., 125, 126, 297
Sega Saturn game, 297

SUBJECT INDEX

CREDITS

MN/Advertising agency: Seitsema, Engel and Partners, Minneapolis, MN; p. 272, Courtesy of American Harvest, Inc.; p. 273, Courtesy of Cadbury; "Many Predictions from the Past Missed Mark Badly," p. 2D, Reprinted from Bob Schwabach's column ON COMPUTERS, January 12, 1995, © 1995 Universal Press Syndicate, reprinted by permission; p. 275, Photograph by Sharon Hoogstraten, p. 278, Photograph by Caroline Parsons; p. 280, Courtesy of Frito-Lay, Inc.; p. 281, Photograph by AP/Wide World Photos; p. 282, Photograph by Jose Azel/AURORA; p. 283, Photograph by John Madere/The Stock Market; p. 284, Courtesy of Campbell Soup Company; p. 285, Photo courtesy of Hewlett-Packard Company.

CHAPTER 12

p. 290, Courtesy of Clearly Canadian Beverage Corporation; p. 299, Courtesy of Mars, Incorporated; p. 300, Courtesy of Oscar Mayer Foods. Oscar Mayer, Lunchables, the Oscar Mayer rhomboid, Will Snore No More are trademarks of Oscar Mayer Foods, Madison, Wisconsin; p. 304, Courtesy of Elite Foods Inc.; p. 306, Courtesy of Black & Decker (U.S.), Inc.; p. 306, Courtesy of DeWalt Industrial Tool Company; p. 307, Courtesy of Eastman Kodak Company; p. 308, Courtesy of Pez Candy, Inc.; p. 309, Photograph by Sharon Hoogstraten; p. 310, Courtesy of The Coca-Cola Company; p. 310, Courtesy of Owens-Corning; p. 311, Courtesy of McDonald's Corporation.

CHAPTER 13

p. 316, Photograph by Lori Adamski Peek/Tony Stone Images; p. 319, Courtesy of Canadian Pacific Hotels and Harrod & Mirlin; p. 320, Courtesy of Oxford Properties; p. 325, Logos Courtesy of McDonald's Corporation, Courtesy of Sprint, and Courtesy of Canadian Red Cross; p. 327, Courtesy of Deloitte & Touche; p. 328, Courtesy of Toronto Dominion Bank.

CHAPTER 14

p. 332, Photograph by Kevin Horan/Tony Stone Images; p. 334, © Kohler Company; p. 336, Photograph by Robbie McClaran; p. 338, Courtesy of Sony Electronics Inc.; p. 340, Photograph by Sharon Hoogstraten; p. 341, Courtesy of H.J. Heinz Company; p. 342, Courtesy of Fiat USA Inc.; p. 342, Photograph by Sharon Hoogstraten.

CHAPTER 15

p. 354, Photograph by Pascale de Laubier; p. 359, Courtesy of Compaq Computer Corporation; p. 366, Photograph by Sharon Hoogstraten; p. 369, Courtesy of The Toro Company.

CHAPTER 16

p. 386, Photograph © Amy Etra; p. 388, "Dictionary of Marketing Terms," Reprinted by permission of the publisher from *Dictionary of Marketing Terms,* Peter D. Bennett, Editor, © 1996 by The American Marketing Association; p. 394, Courtesy of General Mills, Inc.; p. 397, Photograph by Voyles; p. 402, Courtesy of Q Lube Inc.

CHAPTER 17

p. 408, Photograph by Robert Ziebell; p. 413, Courtesy of United Parcel Service; p. 413, Photograph by Sharon Hoogstraten; p. 420, Courtesy of Canadian National Railways; p. 421, Canadian Airlines, Canadian Air Cargo; p. 422, Courtesy of Federal Express Corporation; p. 423, Courtesy of Supervalu Inc.; p. 424, Courtesy of Rapistan Demag Corp.

CHAPTER 18

p. 428, The Galileo Group Inc.; p. 431, Photograph by The Bettmann Archive; p. 433, Courtesy of Midas International Corporation; p. 438, Photograph by Paul Chesley/Tony Stone Images; p. 441, Courtesy of West Edmonton Mall; p. 444, Courtesy of Taco Bell.

CHAPTER 19

p. 450, James Bond and car courtesy of MGM/UA; p. 453, Courtesy of Lexus, agency: Team One Advertising, photographers: © Rick Rusing and © 1996 Kathleen Norris Cook; p. 455, Courtesy of Eastpak; p. 459, Courtesy of IBM, agency: Ogilvy & Mather/New York; p. 464, Courtesy of Friday's; p. 466, Photograph by Ray Marklin.

CHAPTER 20

p. 474, Courtesy of TSN; p. 476, Courtesy of AT&T, agency: NW Ayer & Partners, photographer: ©Hunter Freeman Studio; p. 476, Courtesy of Corel Corporation; p. 476, Courtesy of Godiva Chocolatier; p. 477, Courtesy of DDB Needham Worldwide and The Dial Corporation; p. 478, Courtesy of Molson Breweries; p. 483, Courtesy of Frito-Lay, Inc., agency: DDB Needham, Chicago; p. 486, Courtesy of Ford Motor Company; p. 487, Courtesy

of McCann-Erickson Italiana S.P.A. and Levi Strauss International; p. 488, Federation des producteurs d'oeufs de consommation du Quebec; p. 491, Courtesy of Roper Starch Worldwide Inc.

CHAPTER 21

p. 496, Photograph by Peter Serenyi, Special to *The Dallas Morning News;* p. 499, Courtesy of Remington Products Company; p. 501, Courtesy of Xerox Corporation; p. 504, Photograph by C/B Productions/The Stock Market; p. 514, Courtesy of Mary Kay, Inc.; p. 516, Courtesy of Toshiba America Medical Systems and Interactive Media; p. 516, Photograph by SUPERSTOCK; p. 517, Courtesy of MO-V.

CHAPTER 22

p. 520, Photograph by Michael Hruby; pp. 522 and 529, Courtesy General Mills; p. 530, "Competitive Advantage: Creating and Sustaining Superior Performance," Reprinted with permission of The Free Press, a division of Simon & Schuster from COMPETITIVE ADVANTAGE: Creating and Sustaining Superior Performance by Michael E. Porter, copyright © 1985 by Michael E. Porter; p. 536, Courtesy of Domino's Pizza International; p. 538, "Making Your Marketing Strategy Work," Reprinted by permission of *Harvard Business Review,* an exhibit from "Making Your Marketing Strategy Work," by Thomas V. Bonoma, March-April 1984, copyright © 1984 by the President and Fellows of Harvard College, all rights reserved; p. 539, © 1996 Swatch/A division of SMH (U.S.) Inc.; p. 541, © 1995 Saturn Corp. All rights reserved; p. 542, figure from *An Introduction to Contemporary Business,* Fourth Edition by William Rudelius and W. Bruce Erickson, copyright © 1985 by Harcourt Brace & Company, reproduced by permission of the publisher; p. 543, figure from *An Introduction to Contemporary Business,* Fourth Edition by William Rudelius and W. Bruce Erickson, copyright © 1985 by Harcourt Brace & Company, reproduced by permission of the publisher; p. 544, Photograph by Sharon Hoogstraten.

APPENDIX C

p. 564, Thatch cartoon by Jeff Shesol/Reprinted with permission of Vintage Books.

APPENDIX D

Kingpin Snowboarding, Courtesy of Kingpin Snowboarding.